VOLUME IV

URBAN DEVELOPMENT IN SOUTHERN EUROPE: ITALY AND GREECE

HT
111
.G8
V.4

E. A. GUTKIND

THE FREE PRESS
A Division of Macmillan Publishing Co., Inc.
NEW YORK

Collier Macmillan Publishers
LONDON

Copyright© 1969 by The Free Press
A Division of Macmillan Publishing Co., Inc.

The Free Press
A Division of Macmillan Publishing Co., Inc.
866 Third Avenue, New York, N.Y. 10022

Collier Macmillan Canada, Ltd.

Library of Congress Catalog Card Number: 64:13231

Printed in the United States of America

printing number
    2 3 4 5 6 7 8 9 10

A S THE SERIES title implies, the *International History of City Development* is an attempt to present a worldwide survey of the origin and growth of urban civilization. Throughout history, cities have been the power stations of new ideas and the seismographs on which the impact and the transformation of these ideas can be read.

The *International History of City Development* endeavors to describe and analyze this continually renewed interplay of adaptation and readaptation, of challenge and response, which has made cities in all parts of the world the most significant agents of renewal and decline, of expansion and contraction.

With a few exceptions, all the important countries are represented. Those few that are missing had to be excluded because no cooperation (or only insufficient information) from their governments or local administrations was forthcoming, in spite of sustained efforts and repeated approaches to the heads of state. Without this assistance, the standards aimed at in this work could not have been maintained. It is to be hoped that these shortcomings can be eliminated in a later edition.

The "City Survey" sections contained in the present volume are selective rather than encyclopedic presentations of restricted numbers of cities and towns. They should be viewed in their entirety as a mosaic in which each small piece is part of the whole; only all together can they give a complete picture. The periods covered in the City Survey sections and the length of descriptions of individual cities differ considerably according to the importance of the historical evolution and the significance of the relevant data for the *History* in general, apart from the desirability of avoiding repetition where the origin and development of several cities were in many respects similar.

Certain basic problems, such as the changing ideas of space and scale, have been discussed in Volume I. This discussion should be consulted, if possible, whenever relevant questions are mentioned.

The number of footnotes has been kept to a minimum. Complete acknowledgment of references to sources is, in any case, impossible in a work of this kind, nor am I convinced that innumerable footnotes are a proof of scholarly competence.

The bibliography for each country is fairly comprehensive, although by no means complete. Completeness would have been not only unattainable but also undesirable, especially since many of the books mentioned in the bibliographies contain full lists of works on the general history of the respective countries and on the local history of individual cities.

In a history of city planning, old plans, maps, drawings, and engravings of general and detailed aspects of cities are the most

Preface

v

valuable primary source. The documentation therefore includes a considerable number of reproductions of this type of material, apart from ground and aerial photographs of historically important views. As far as possible, no city, town, or even village has been described in the text without relevant visual documentation. Where documentation is missing—and such cases are rare—it is because difficulties in procuring the material were insuperable.

I cannot emphasize too strongly that the scholarly value of a work of this kind does not primarily and exclusively depend on recorded historical evidence. In dealing with the historical development of city planning, especially with the physical growth of cities, one is in the fortunate position of having available a considerable quantity of visual documentation, very often of outstanding quality. I maintain that this visual documentation is more important for scholarly research in this field than most of the available written evidence and that its wise interpretation is more enlightening than the usual old records and other similar sources. This is not to say that written evidence should not be used but merely to stress the point that in many cases it tells us only something about so-called facts, about symptoms, and rarely anything about causes. Moreover, the value of this evidence is often dubious, since it was frequently written by people who lacked objectivity and for opportunist reasons glossed over or tampered with the "how it really was." But even if we accept the recorded evidence at its face value, a definite interpretation is more often than not difficult, as the squabbles of learned men prove only too well. This overestimation of written evidence has led to a "scholarly" distrust of visual documentation. But these doubters should be reminded that, for instance, air photography has produced, in many cases, results that written records could never have revealed. It is the same with old maps, drawings, and other contemporary representations. Consequently, ample use has been made of this sort of material *in addition* to old written records in those cases that could furnish incontestable interpretation.

Readers should keep these considerations in mind and should regard the volumes of the *International History of City Development* not as picture books, but as works diagnosing the intricate problems of urban development by what we can still see *and* by what we can still read about them.

Moreover, it is essential to remember that this work is a history of city development, not of architecture or of the general unfolding of historical evolution. This explains why some cities, famous for individual architectural achievements, may not have been mentioned while others, without claim to architectural excellence, have been included in the City Surveys, their layout, growth, and origin being of particular interest as characteristic stages of urban development.

As in all other volumes the urban development in Italy has been surveyed only up to the middle of the 19th century. It is intended to devote a supplementary volume to the more recent period during which urbanization in all parts of the world has resulted in a general decrease of the individuality of cities on an international scale. As to Greece, the description of cities of post-antiquity has been reserved for a later volume.

An initial grant was made by the Rockefeller Foundation in 1956 on the recommendation of Mr. Edward F. D'Arms, now at the Ford Foundation, to whom must go my most cordial thanks for his interest in the work and his understanding of its importance.

The Mary Reynolds Babcock Foundation has generously supported the project by several grants to the University of Pennsylvania, which enabled us not only to proceed with the *History* as originally planned but to accelerate the research and preparation of the volumes for publication. My particular thanks go to Dr. A. Hollis Edens, Executive Director of the Mary Reynolds Babcock Foundation, whose understanding of the problems and of the importance of the work as a whole cannot be praised too highly.

I owe a special debt, which I am particularly glad to acknowledge, to my colleagues, Professor G. Holmes Perkins, Dean of the Graduate School of Fine Arts, and Professor Robert B. Mitchell. I have not only enjoyed their assistance, but, above all, have had the benefit of their great administrative experience, which they placed unhesitatingly at the disposal of the work and which piloted it through financial and organizational difficulties. It is not only this assistance but also the freedom of research compatible with the highest standards of academic independence that I have valued most highly.

Finally, I owe more than I can express to my daughter, Gabriele M. E. Gutkind, now acting as research associate, for the unflagging patience with which she has sorted out the sometimes chaotic mass of material and has gone over the manuscripts again and again. Her considerable knowledge of the subject and her conscientious persistence in weeding out mistakes and improving the text cannot be valued too highly. Her work deserves public thanks.

I take this welcome opportunity to express appreciation to the governments, government agencies, public and private institutions, and, especially, the mayors of numerous towns and cities who have supplied comprehensive documentation consisting of local histories, photographs, old plans, maps, and books. Without their ever-ready willingness to respond to my repeated requests and without their assistance, which I hope not to have taxed unduly, the *History* could never have been written.

My thanks go to numerous individual persons and experts who have given valuable assistance to this work. I cannot mention all these helpers by name, but I wish to express in a general though no less sincere manner my great obligation to them, as well as to all those writers whose contributions to the literature of city development have been of inestimable value for the completion of this *History*.

The *International History of City Development* has been sponsored by and produced and published under the auspices of the Institute for Environmental Studies. But the responsibility for its scope and character, for possible mistakes, and for sometimes very personal opinions is exclusively my own.

E. A. G.

May, 1967
University of Pennsylvania

May, 1967

Contents

ANCIENT GREECE

xii

List of Illustrations

XV

ITALY

THE GREATEST LENGTH of Italy in a straight line from the western end of the Alps to the Strait of Otranto is about 700 miles. The breadth of the northern part from the Alps in the west to the mouth of the Po in the east is about 270 miles and more, measured from Mont Cenis to Fiume. The breadth of the Peninsula varies considerably from 150 to about 100 miles. The Apennines extend from the Maritime Alps east of Genoa to the Adriatic and thence southward through Central and Southern Italy. They constitute a clearly marked division between the northern part and the rest of the Peninsula.

Four main regions may be distinguished: Northern Italy, Central Italy, Southern Italy, and Insular Italy.[1]

1. **Northern Italy.** The North Italian Plain, situated between the Alps and the Apennines, was an arm of the Adriatic in Pliocene times, connected with the Ligurian Sea by several straits. This depression was filled up by the deposits which the Po and its tributaries brought down from the Alps. The glaciers, moving from most of the Alpine valleys to the Plain, created a series of morainic arcs that dammed up the rivers and formed lakes. The rivers have cut through the zone of glacial outwash, gravel, and sand and are separated from each other by raised terraces. The bed of the Po is steadily rising, owing to the great amount of sediment it carries down from the mountains. Its lower course flows on a higher level than that of the surrounding country. This difference in level makes irrigation easy but necessitates the building of dikes to prevent flooding; as a consequence only a few towns are located on its banks. The left-bank tributaries of the Po are more important than those that join it on the right bank. The Ticino drains Lake Maggiore; the Adda, Lake Como; and the Mincio, Lake Garda. These are narrow and long mountain lakes which have been formed by the damming up of the valleys at their lower end by morainic material. The large lagoons that together with the marshy tracts form the delta of the Po are separated from the Adriatic by strips of sand interrupted by openings through which the sea flows in and out. Venice has been built in one of these lagoons. Other cities which were formerly seaports, like Ravenna, now lie inland owing to the eastward extension of the Plain. It has been calculated that this alluviation proceeds at the rate of about three miles in a thousand years.

The westernmost part of Northern Italy is the Plain of Piedmont and the plateau of Monferrato, the latter specializing in viticulture. Irrigation is widespread; textile, small metalworking, and agricultural-processing industries have been characteristic of this region for a long time. The lack of coal and the unavoidable import of fuel have favored decentralization of settlement and

The Land

1. R. H. Barrow. *The Romans.* 1951.
W. G. East. *An Historical Geography of Europe.* 1956.
E. C. Semple. *The Geography of the Mediterranean Region.* 1932.
D. S. Walker. *A Geography of Italy.* 1958.

the significance of railway centers. Hydroelectric power, introduced at the beginning of this century, furthered the trend. Turin is the principal city, with large-scale industry and important railway connections with France, Switzerland, and the rest of Italy. The other Piedmontese towns have been left behind by the rapid development of Turin. They stand either on the Plain (for instance, Vercelli, Novara, and Allessandria) or are situated in the zone where the mountains and the plain meet (as Biella, Ivrea, Cunco, and others).

The agriculture of the Plain of Lombardy varies in accordance with the quality of the soil. The low hills, which constitute the zone of morainic arcs, are not fertile by nature. The soil is too porous and the hills were previously covered with heath.[2] But in spite of these disadvantages most of the land is under cultivation. Vines, cereals, and mulberries are grown in the drier parts and dairy cattle are raised on the wetter portions. More to the south—where the soil is porous—maize, rye, and soft wheat are the principal crops. The fine deposits and an abundance of water supply in the next zone permit an almost horticultural cultivation of the country with soft wheat, maize, potatoes, beet, flax, and hemp. The fourth zone is less varied. Here, near the Po and the lower courses of its tributaries, rice, water meadows, and dairy cattle are the characteristic features of the landscape. Milan owes its importance to its strategic position at the focal point of the routes over the Alpine passes and later of the railway lines through the Simplon and St. Gotthard tunnels. It is the leading industrial city of Italy and the second largest of the country. Most of the other towns lie at the entrances to the valleys leading to the Alpine passes, or at the foot of the Apennines or in the lower parts of the Plain.

The Venetian Plain is a predominantly agricultural region. Its physical zones are similar to those of Lombardy, but irrigation and water supply in general do not reach the high standards of the central part of the Plain. Verona is situated on both sides of the Adige where it enters the Plain and where the north-south and east-west routes meet. Padua is the center of a rich agricultural district in the gap between the lagoons and the range of the Euganei Hills. It is one of the oldest and once most famous university towns of Europe. Venice, the lagoon island, stands at the point where the Mediterranean penetrates most deeply into the Continent. The Plain of Emilia and Romagna stretches from the *Via Aemilia* in the south to the Po in the north and to the coast in the east, with lagoons at the mouth of the Po. It is roughly triangular, with its apex at Piacenza. The main crops are wheat and maize, sugar beet, and vines. Emilia-Romagna is a region of large farms. More towns are situated along the *Via*

2. D. S. Walker, *op. cit.*, p. 129. Also for the following.

Aemilia and on the routes over the Apennines. Bologna, Cremona, Piacenza, Ravenna, Ferrara are some of the more important cities. Liguria extends as a narrow strip for about 200 miles between the Ligurian Alps and the Apennines in the north and the Mediterranean in the south from the French frontier to the Gulf of Spezia. The mountains fall abruptly into the sea at some points and slope gently down toward the Po in the north. Liguria is an industrial region of greatest importance to Italy and Genoa, which stands at the northernmost point of this coast— the leading port of the country and the principal outlet for the Northern Plain. An ancient coastal road, the *Via Francigena,* connected Genoa with the Provence and Tuscany.

2. **Central Italy.** The main geographical factor of Central Italy is the mountain mass of the Apennines. They traverse the peninsula from north-northeast to south-southwest and run almost parallel to the Adriatic coast from Rimini to Pescara. In the west they recede from the coast while in the east the coastal areas are narrow and sometimes absent, with the exception of Apulia. Throughout historical times the west coast, which has several good harbors and valleys connecting it with the interior, has been more important than the east coast with its lack of good harbors—except Brindisi and Ancona—and with only a few good routes leading inland. Tuscany is a hilly country with the exception of the regions near the coast and around Lucca, Arezzo, and Florence, where prehistoric lakes have formed plains. The valley of the Arno is the most fertile part of this region. Tuscany was the cradle of Italian civilization. Southern Etruria, which developed earlier and comprised the more important towns, is a volcanic and alluvial land belonging to the hill and lake system of Latium. Northern Etruria spreads over the foothills of the Apennines and has a rich vegetation, being traversed by rivers. Mt. Albano separates the middle from the lower basin of the Arno Valley. Pistoia and Prato in the northern foothills on the margin of the Plain control the passes over the Apennines. Florence, on both banks of the Arno, owes much of its importance to its location on the direct route between Milan and Rome and as the center of the fertile basin of the Arno, which carries an abundant water supply after it is joined by the Sieve and Ombrone headwaters above the city. The surrounding hills provide excellent pastures for sheep and were thus an indispensable prerequisite for the local textile industry.

The coastal plain of the Maremma derived its origin from the large amount of silt which the rivers carried down from the mountains and hills and deposited behind sand bars. This area was avoided by settlers because malaria was rampant and

5

led to a depopulation of the country. It was only recently that an efficient drainage system was installed and the land reclaimed for cultivation. Siena, San Gimignano, Pisa, and many other small towns have made outstanding contributions toward city planning, as have the cities of Umbria. This is a hilly region and almost all Umbrian towns are hilltop settlements. The *Via Flaminia* ran through Umbria linking Rome with the Northern Plain. The Abruzzi Highlands include the central part of the Apennines. There are no towns of any significance and the local industries are small, comprising, for example, arms, cutlery, and majolica manufacture. Latium (Lazio) was the ancient name given to the country around Rome, including Campania. In its center rise the Alban Hills. Several of the old Latin towns stood on this terracelike surface or on the slopes of the Volscian Mountains. The plain is broad and undulating with many depressions. The highest point of the hills on the right bank of the Tiber is Monte Mario. The isolated hills and ridges, which were to form the city of Rome, possessed natural advantages over the other early settlements of this region: they rose fairly steeply from the plain and were partly surrounded by marshes. The volcanic materials of the neighborhood provided an excellent building material.

Between the sea and the volcanic tract of the Campagna there is a sandy and barren plain. The ancient coastline is now marked by a belt of sand hills about half a mile or more inland extending for about 30 miles from the mouth of the Tiber to the promontory of Antium. The Pontine Marshes occupy almost the whole area between the sand belt on the seashore and the Volscian Mountains. Rome is the center of this basically agricultural area which never supplied enough food to the capital. She had to rely on imports from the provinces. As a matter of fact, the region surrounding the capital was never of great interest to its imperial or later rulers. But before Roman times the Campagna was well drained and irrigated. Underground tunnels, *cuniculi,* provided an efficient system of drainage and irrigation, and the country was well cultivated and populated. At the beginning of her history Rome was a frontier town between Etruria and Latium and routes from Etruria and Campania met at the ford which Rome controlled.

3. **Southern Italy.** The main regions of Southern Italy are Campania, Apulia, Basilicata, and Calabria. Campania was an ancient sea gulf which was raised and filled in with volcanic tufa and surrounded by broken hills. Its soil was fertile consisting of decomposed tufa. The coastline provided since early times excellent harbors and easily defensible hillsites such as Naples,

Paestum, and Cumae. The northern coastal plain, the Plain of Campania, is separated from the southern plain, the Plain of Paestum, by the Sorrento Peninsula with an outlying range of the central mountains. The volcanic cone of Vesuvius is separated from the other mountains by a narrow plain. Naples is situated at the foot and on the slopes of volcanic hills. A transverse ridge running south ends in the promontory of Pizzofalcone and divides the city into two natural semicircles. The relative isolation of Apulia from the rest of Italy opened it to non-Roman influences, particularly in Antiquity to Greek colonization. The long promontory which runs toward the east to Brindisi and Otranto continues to the low-lying parts of Apulia.

The hills, the Murge of Gravina and Altamura, merge gradually with those between Brindisi and Taranto, stretching down to the southeastern tip of Italy, the Cape of S. Maria di Leuca. Apulia is an agricultural region and practically all towns are agricultural in character and function. Even Bari and Taranto base their industries mainly on the processing and export of agricultural goods. Basilicata (Lucania) is a mountainous province with the Lucanian Apennines, the Vulture volcanic region and a low and dissected plateau. A belt of marsh extending along the Gulf of Taranto has been built up by the great amount of silt which the rivers carry down from the plateau. The small towns are situated on the interfluves, not in the valleys. It is an almost purely agricultural region with only small and local industries. From the area of Potenza in Basilicata the Apennines run southward toward the Gulf of Policastro on the west coast and to Mt. Pollino. Thence they continue to the "toe" of Italy but after the Plain of Sibari the great mass of granite mountains begins. Calabria is a region of great variety, of coastal areas with a luxurious vegetation, alluvial flats, and wooded tablelands. It was one of the most important outlets for Greek colonization. The lowlands of the coast are densely populated and intensively cultivated. As in the entire Mediterranean region, the agricultural population lives in small, compactly built towns. Reggio stands on the Strait of Messina formed by an exceptionally deep fracture in the crust of the earth which caused severe earthquakes such as that of 1908, when Reggio and Messina were entirely destroyed.

4. **Insular Italy.** By far the most important islands are Sicily and Sardinia. The successive layers of civilization which the Phoenicians, Greeks, Romans, Arabs, Normans, French, Spaniards, and Italians spread over Sicily have made it the most fascinating region of Italy. Nowhere else can the interaction of different cultures and their creative genius be felt with greater

intensity than in this historically almost overburdened island. It is situated in a strategic position, dividing the Mediterranean into two basins. In general the north coast is steep and has many good harbors, with Palermo as the most important city. The hills are lower and more distant from the sea on the west, south, and the southern part of the east, where the coast is mostly flat and more regular, the northern part of the east coast being rocky and steep, except for the Plain of Catania which slowly rises toward the highest point of the island—the volcano of Etna, with its majestic and beautiful silhouette.

The interior of Sicily consists of hills and valleys with little level land. The numerous rocky and steep hills offered excellent sites for settlements that could easily be defended. By far the greatest portion of the population is engaged in agriculture, which comprises areas of intensive and extensive cultivation. The former is carried on mainly on the north and east coasts and on the small coastal flats of the west. Extensive cultivation is on the whole restricted to the interior and the south, where latifundia have existed since Roman times.

Palermo, Catania, and Messina are the largest cities. All the other towns are small and predominantly agricultural. In contrast to Sicily, the history of Sardinia has hardly been shaped by outside influences. Its strategic value was negligible and its coasts did not offer good harbors or fertile lands. The interior is mountainous and wooded, consisting to a considerable degree of granite rock with plateaus in the east and a volcanic character in the west. This geographical structure explains why there are no sedimentary coastal areas between the sea and the highland. Fertile volcanic soil can be found only in the Cagliari Valley of the southwest. Cagliari and Sassari are the principal towns.

CHAPTER 2

THE EARLIEST HISTORY of Italy is obscure and our knowledge of the Etruscan civilization is still fragmentary despite diligent research and a large amount of archeological evidence. We do know, however, that the region, which stretches roughly from Florence to Rome, was inhabited long before the Etruscans began to emerge as a distinct people. The finds, exhibited in the prehistoric museum at Perugia, span a period from palaeolithic to historical times. No traces of imposing buildings have been discovered as in Egypt or in early Greece and Crete; nothing justifies the assumption that permanent settlements occupied the same sites for a long time. No evidence has been found that anything like a Troy or Babylon existed in the millennia that preceded the foundation of Rome or of the Etruscan cities. It is likely that temporary groups of simple huts formed the earliest settlements. These huts may have resembled the urns in which the dead were buried: round, with heavy conical roofs of straw or reed, possibly similar to the shepherds' huts one sometimes sees today in the more remote parts of the country.

The earliest Italian settlements known to us and dating back to the second millennium B.C. were self-contained and, therefore, self-supporting agricultural communities. Passo di Corvo, 8 miles northeast of Foggia in northern Apulia, was one of these neolithic villages discovered and partially excavated only recently. It occupied a level site and may have been a tribal center.[1] The irregular oval enclosure of about 800 by 500 yards, with two (and at one side with three) ditches, surrounded the village proper. The latter was situated at one end of a large enclave, protected by a ditch. Professor Ward Perkins suggests that this may have been the "home farm." The village consisted of almost a hundred units, approximately circular and enclosed by a ditch, interrupted by the entrance to the interior, a level area of about 60 by 50 feet. The houses, of which no remains have been found, were, in all likelihood, only very flimsily built. Regardless of the shortcomings, it is safe to conclude that the site had been continuously occupied. Another neolithic settlement that should be mentioned in this connection has been identified at Lucera in Apulia. These villages are but two examples of the large number of similar discoveries that have been made through air reconnaissance. They all have in common a loose and casual layout. So far no traces of any regular plan have been found.

The early settlements of Bronze-Age people around Modena, Reggio nell' Emilia, and Parma in the north of Italy have been subsumed under the name of the *terremare,* a term derived from *terra marna,* meaning marshy soil—that is, the dark earth mixed

Antiquity

Historical Notes

1. J. Bradford. *Ancient Landscapes.* 1957. p. 101-102.
J. B. Ward Perkins. "Early Roman Towns in Italy," *Town Planning Review,* Vol. XXXVI, No. 3, 1955. p. 127-28.

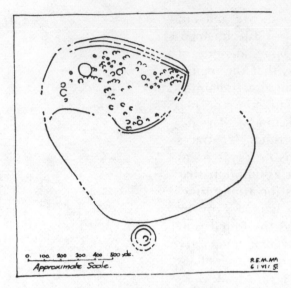

1. Passo di Corvo, Apulia. An enclosed Neolithic farmstead.

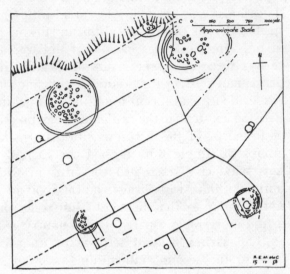

2. Lucera, Neolithic settlements and two adjacent systems of centuriation.

with decomposed organic remains and used locally as fertilizer. About the interior layout of these places we have no reliable data. The assumptions of earlier archeologists—for instance, Pigorini, who partially excavated Castellazzo di Fontanellato in the Province of Parma—that these settlements were regularly and systematically planned cannot be maintained. They rested on a purely speculative basis without confirmation by archeological facts.

The beginnings of Etruscan civilization—that is, the authentic history of Etruria—date back to the ninth and eighth centuries B.C. It reached its height in the sixth century and came to an end in the last pre-Christian century when it was finally absorbed into the cultural orbit of Rome. Etruscan civilization thus covered about the same period as Greek history from the invasion of northern tribes to the Hellenistic era. The original homeland of the Etruscans stretched from the Arno to the Tiber and bordered the Tyrrhenian Sea. Within this territory lay the twelve cities which formed the Etruscan nation and which were organized in a loose federation.[2] These small regional states passed from monarchical to republican societies and were more or less independent political units. Our knowledge of this period is mainly derived from the contacts which developed between Etruria and Carthage, Greece, and Rome as recorded in Greek and Roman sources. Some of these cities, in particular Caere,

2. M. Pallottino. *The Etruscans*. 1955. Pp. 85 ff. Also for the following.

Tarquinii, and Vulci, seem to have surpassed their rivals in importance and splendor during the seventh and sixth centuries. Then at the end of the sixth century Clusium became the most influential city when the coastal towns declined.

The Etruscans extended their domain to the north and the south. In the north they spread over the Apennines and the lower valley of the Po, and in the south over Latium and Campania, thus establishing their influence from the Alps around Trento to the Gulf of Salerno. On their southward march they encountered the Greeks. Chalcis had founded Cumae and the early colonists of the eighth century had established outposts on the coast of Campania. In response to what they regarded as a challenge to their expansion and authority, the Etruscans built Capua farther inland. In the end they embarked upon and succeeded in a large-scale colonization of Campania, in the course of which they founded, apart from Capua, a remarkable number of cities such as Nola, Acerrae, and Nuceria. Like Etruria proper, the Campanian territory was divided into twelve small city-states—very likely with Capua as the leading city.

Etruscan hegemony over Latium was broken by an alliance between the Latins and the Greeks from Cumae. Probably in connection with this defeat Rome was liberated and the Tarquin kings were expelled. Campania was separated from Etruria proper and was finally conquered by Italic Samnites at about 430 B.C. The penetration of the north began later than the expansion to the south. It started from the interior of Etruria. A legendary chief set out from Perugia to conquer the valley of the Po. He was credited with the foundation of Felsina (Bologna) and Mantua. This was, however, an undeserved credit, at least so far as Bologna is concerned, which existed before the Etruscans visited it and was probably an important market for the trade between the South and Northern Europe. But on or near the Adriatic they founded or occupied the cities of Caesena (Cesena), Ravenna, Ariminum (Rimini), and Spina, the latter developing into an emporium for the trade with Greece. Farther inland they made some contribution to the origins of Parma, Placentia (Piacenza), Mutina (Modena), and Melpum near Milan. Traces of prehistoric and Etruscan pile dwellings have been found near Parma, but these remains do not prove that the Etruscans were the actual founders of the original city. By far the most interesting site has been discovered near the village of Marzabotto in the vicinity of Bologna. It is one of the earliest cities with a gridiron layout. Etruscan influence in Northern Italy was short-lived. After about one century—at the end of the fifth and the beginning of the fourth century B.C.—the Gaulish invasion pressed the Etrurians back to their homeland.

It is probable that the composition of the Etruscan League changed in the course of time: the original member states are not known. It is possible, for instance, that Veii, which the Romans occupied and destroyed in 396 B.C., was replaced by another city. It seems that toward the end of Etruria's independence the following twelve cities formed the League: Arezzo (Arretium); Caere (Cerveteri); Chiusi (Clusium); Cortona; Perugia (Perusia); Populonia (Populonium); Rusellae; Tarquinia (Tarquinii); Vetulonia; Volterra (Volaterrae); Vulci; Orvieto (Volsinii). The cities of southern Etruria developed earlier and in particular those on the coast relatively near to one another. To this group belonged Veii, Caere, Tarquinii, and Vulci. The cities of inland northern Etruria were at greater distances from one another and grew up more slowly, reaching the highest point of their development toward the end of the Etrurian civilization and under the Romans. These cities included Clusium, Cortona, Perusia, Arretium, Faesulae, and Volaterrae.

The two zones were separated by the rivers Fiora and Paglia, the former flowing into the Tyrrhenian Sea and the latter into the Tiber. This line corresponds mainly to the present frontier between Tuscany and Latium. The southern zone is volcanic and alluvial as part of the hilly and lake region of Latium; the northern zone stretches over the foothills of the Apennines. In general, the cities were situated on the natural traffic arteries of the Etruscan territory, inland in the valleys of the Arno, Tiber, and Chiana rivers and on the north-south route along the coast.

3. Map of Etruscan tumuli at Banditaccia (Cerveteri).

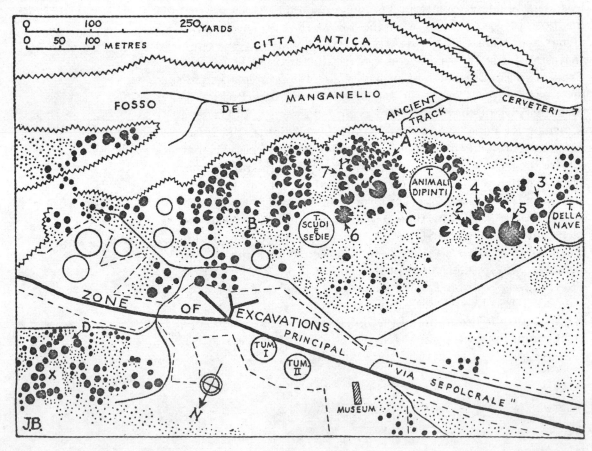

The distribution of the Etruscan cities in time and space suggests a colonization of the coastal strip by successive groups of emigrants from the Tyrrhenian area, who settled on the most inviting points, then spread their occupation and influence gradually inland over the whole of the Italian peninsula from the Po to the southern Tyrrhenian. Their only serious rivals were the Greek colonies of Southern Italy and Sicily.

In all other peripheral regions the people lived in primitive villages. It was the genius of the Etruscans that transformed this rudimentary civilization into an urban society and laid the foundation for the unifying rule of Rome. It is certain that twelve was a sacred number and that the Etruscan League consisting of twelve cities had a precedent in the League of the twelve cities of Ionia.[3] There were "consultative meetings held by the Etruscan states and their heads (principes) at the Fanum Voltumnae." To understand the religious significance of the number twelve and of the "annual pan-Etruscan festivals and games at the sanctuary of Voltumna (similar to the Panhellenic games at Ephesus, Olympia, Delphi, and Corinth)," it is essential to realize that the real importance of each individual city was derived, not from its size or economic prominence, but from its sacred uniqueness which distinguished it from the rest of the world and related it to the cosmic order. The foundation of an Etruscan city was a religious act of the greatest significance.[4]

That the number of twelve cities was not an arbitrary but a deliberate choice is obvious, for in the course of the sixth century two other Leagues were formed—one in the north, with the principal city of Mantua dedicated to Mantus, the God of the dead, and the other in the south comprising Campania to the valley of the Sele River which flows into the Gulf of Salerno with Capua as the capital city—each League consisting of twelve cities.[5] The political and social structure of these small urban units may have been similar to that of the early Greek *poleis*. It may be assumed that the more powerful cities gradually extended their territory and in this process incorporated their weaker rivals. As in Greece, these central cities represented state and city at the same time, and *populus*, corresponding to the Greek *demos*, meant in some of its connotations *urbs* as *demos* denoted *polis*. And also, as in Greece, the Etruscan colonies may have preserved some sort of relationship with the mother city. But, in general, autonomy and independence were the main political characteristics of those city-states.

The early Etrurian city-states were ruled by kings who were military and religious leaders. This primitive monarchy was followed, in the sixth and fifth centuries, by an oligarchic government with some resemblance to a republican regime. The

3. M. Pallottino, *op. cit.*, p. 132.
4. The ritual of the foundation is described later.
5. O. W. von Vacano. *Die Etrusker in der Welt der Antike*. 1957. P. 168.

13

ruling minority exerted its power through collegiate magistracies elected for restricted periods, a principle which had as its basic aim "to parcel out power, to decrease it and to place it under constant reciprocal control, so as to prevent the rise of a tyrant."[6] The social organization was based on gentilitial lines. But

if a society of freemen, subdivided into numerous small family units, can be reconciled with a monarchical constitution of an archaic type (like the one dominant in Etruria up to the end of the sixth century B.C.), the same cannot be said for the later oligarchic state. . . . Certain *gentes* may have gradually predominated over others belonging to the same original social system, and formed the new oligarchy.

It is difficult to clarify the position of the lower or plebeian *gentes*

within the framework of the oligarchic state, and the characteristic features of the proletarian and serving classes. . . . A social and political rising of the lower classes took place in Arretium and Volsinii during the third century B.C.: as historical tradition tells us, it took the form of an actual proletarian revolution with the seizure of power and the temporary abolition of caste differentiations between the lower and the aristocratic classes.

Religion and ritual pervaded the life of the Etruscans and made them feel insignificant before their gods much more so than the Greeks or Romans did before their divinities. Although our knowledge of Etruscan religion is far from complete, there can be no doubt that Etruscan society was deeply embedded in nature, and that nature was the visible manifestation of the divine. Superficially, this may appear as not too dissimilar from the Greek or Roman attitude. In reality, it was something entirely different. Behind the religious mood of the Greeks there was at work the unresolved conflict between the animistic nature of the world kept in motion by unseen divine or semidivine beings and the urge to understand and explain it through intellectual speculation even when they felt powerless before Fate. The Romans, less given to mystical irrationality and abstract speculation, applied their pragmatic and rational faculties to the relationship of man and god and tended to adapt religion to the practical demands of life. For both Greeks and Romans, man remained the measure of all things. Not so for the Etruscans: the conception of the nothingness of man before the gods was accepted as the essence of existence. This did not prevent them from seeing their gods in human shape and thus assembling a galaxy of deities similar to those of Greece. The religious ritual through which the divine will was questioned and revealed to mortal men, guiding their actions and thoughts, was the inescapable manifestation around which life revolved.

6. M. Pallottino, *op. cit.*, pp. 146, 149-50.

4. Etruscan bronze of Mercury Psychopompos who, in his capacity as messenger, guided the souls of the departed to the underworld, placing them before the throne of the deities below.

These rules were contained in the so-called *Disciplina Etrusca* that governed the religious fabric of existence and the relationship of the Etruscan people to their gods. The medium through which the gods spoke was the interpretation of the entrails of animals and of lightning. The ritual ceremonies and the conception of the universe and of space and time were all intimately connected with the foundation and layout of Etruscan cities, and through them probably with the cities of the Romans. The Etruscans believed that, just as man was moving from year to year to his final death, the peoples of the world had a beginning and an end and a predetermined sequence of growing, flowering, and decaying. Thus eight (or according to another tradition, ten) *saecula* were accorded to the *nomen Etruscum*. It was the end rather than the beginning that occupied the Etruscan mind: not the beginning of a new era, or a new year, but the end of a *saeculum* or a year was celebrated. A *saeculum* was not a definitely fixed number of years: it lasted from the end of the

5. Etruscan bronze liver of the third century B.C. used in divination rituals.

preceding *saeculum* to the moment when the last man died who had been alive at its beginning.[7] Censorinus, the Roman grammarian and writer, published in A.D. 238 his *De Die Natali* in which he said (17.6) that each of the first four *saecula* had lasted one hundred years; the fifth, one hundred and twenty-three; the sixth and seventh, one hundred and nineteen each; the eighth was still going on; a ninth and tenth were still to come; and when these had run their course, the end of the Etruscan name was sealed. This proves that time meant to the Etruscans something entirely different from our present-day concept. Time was variable and not dependent on its practical usefulness; realistic events of everyday life were less significant than the divine manifestations inherent in conspicuous natural phenomena. And just as time was the expression of the will of the gods, space and its orientation and division were shaped and determined by the omnipresence and the infinite wisdom of the deities.

Heaven and earth were thought to be divided into four parts by two axes crossing each other at right angles. The space thus subdivided was considered sacred. It was called *templum* in Latin, whether it was the sky or a consecrated area on earth such as a shrine or a city or even a much smaller object—for example, the liver of an animal used in divination—provided that orientation and division of the area corresponded to that of the celestial model. The two main intersecting lines were orientated toward the four cardinal points. The north-south line was called

7. O. W. von Vacano, *op. cit.*, p. 19 and *passim*.

16

6. Subdivision of the sacred space.

PARS N POSTICA

cardo and the east-west line *decumanus*. The space to the north of the *decumanus* was the *pars postica*, and the part to the south *pars antica*—meaning posterior and anterior part respectively, assuming that an observer stood in the center with his back to the north. The part to the left of the *cardo*, the eastern sector, was called *pars sinistra* or *familiaris* and was of good augury; the part to the right, the western sector, was the *pars dextra* or *hostilis* and symbolized ill fortune. By a further subdivision the sky was partitioned into sixteen smaller parts, each housing another deity. This arrangement guided the priests in their interpretation of divine messages as indicated by the flight of birds, the direction of lightning, and the appearance of a sacrificial animal's liver, the *haruspex* interpreting the entrails of animals and the *fulguriator* the lightning.

It seems that in general the great and favorable deities occupied the northeastern sector of the sky; the chthonic gods the south; and the inexorable and dangerous gods the west, especially the northwest. Thus the northeast was the most favorable sector; the northwest the most unfavorable; the east-south less favorable and the west-south less unfavorable. The main principles of the division of the sky were applied to the layout of sacred enclosures, cities, and the partition of fields.

A city conceived and laid out according to these sacred rules was not an ordinary place where men built their homes, worked, and congregated. It was a sacred space in a universe created and maintained by the gods. In Etruria and later in the Roman Empire, no city was built without the dedicated observations of these sacred principles.[8] The nucleus of Rome, the *urbs quadrata*, is said to have been laid out according to Etruscan rules,

8. This does not necessarily mean that Roman town planning with its regular layout developed directly and exclusively from Etruscan prototypes. Our knowledge of Etruscan towns is still too incomplete to draw definite conclusions about Roman planning as a continuation and derivation of Etruscan planning. Many other factors may have been operative, such as Hippodamian influences and the general principle of layout of colonial cities on a gridiron system.

although this is merely legend. Rome had never been planned. It just grew spontaneously. Etruscan and Roman cities were conceived as a whole from the very beginning, as limited entities organized in clearly delimited quarters through the intersecting streets of the *cardo* and *decumanus*. They were limited and partitioned in imitation of the universe; they could not grow beyond the enclosing walls, which were fixed once and for all—just as the gates and consequently the main streets were marked in the founding ceremony. Plutarch (*Romulus.* 10) has described the foundation of Rome in detail:

Romulus, having buried his brother Remus, together with his two foster-fathers, on the mount Remonia, set to building his city; and sent for men out of Tuscany, who directed him by sacred usages and written rules in all the ceremonies to be observed, as in a religious rite. First, they dug a round trench about that which is now the Comitium, or Court of Assembly, and into it solemnly threw the first-fruits of all things either good by custom or necessary by nature; lastly, every man taking a small piece of earth of the country from whence he came, they all threw them in promiscuously together. This trench they call, as they do the heavens, Mundus; making which their centre, they described the city in a circle round it. Then the founder fitted to a plough a brazen ploughshare, and, yoking together a bull and a cow, drove himself a deep line or furrow round the bounds; while the business of those that followed after was to see that whatever earth was thrown up should be turned all inwards towards the city, and not to let any clod lie outside. With this line they described the wall, and called it, by a contraction, Pomoerium, that is, *post murum,* after or beside the wall; and where they designed to make a gate, there they took out the share, carried the plough over, and left a space; for which reason they consider the whole wall as holy, except where the gates are; for had they adjudged them also sacred, they could not, without offence to religion, have given free ingress and egress for the necessaries of human life, some of which are in themselves unclean.

Numerous though dispersed references to the original ceremony have been preserved. They describe how the founder and his followers should be dressed and how they should wear their robes; how the plow which cut the furrow that marked the course of the wall should be driven anticlockwise around the city area, how the turned-up clods should be thrown inward; how the plow should be drawn by a white cow on the inner and by a white bull on the outer side.

The central intersection where the *cardo* and the *decumanus* crossed each other was called *mundus.* It was a shaft leading to the underworld and closed with a large stone, the *lapis manalis,* the stone of the dead souls, which was removed three times a

7. Ceremony of the tracing of city walls.

year on the days which were dedicated to the gods of the underworld. On these days the spirits of the dead, the *manes,* would
rise to the surface through this "gate of the sorrowful and nether
gods." Such a city with its regular sacrifices to the dead and the
deities of fertility offered at the *mundus,* with its sacred walls
and gates, separated from the rest of the world by the barrier
of the water-filled *fossi* and beyond by the vast cemeteries with
their innumerable *tumuli*—such a city never let the inhabitants
forget that their earthly life was deeply embedded in the cosmic
order and was a preparation for the hereafter. To them death
meant passing through a gate into another world, a conviction
which they symbolized by the picture of a gate on their rock
tombs and the tombstones; and like other peoples of antiquity
the Etruscans provided their dead with all the numerous objects which they would need in their afterlife. They believed
that the dead could be transformed into immortal gods, and that
this metamorphosis could be accomplished by the sacrifice of the
blood of certain animals and religious rituals.

The will of the gods was paramount and, although their
character and identity were often vague and open to the not
always selfless interpretation of the priests, their will had to be
obeyed. This unquestioning attitude, this extreme and abject
humility before the divine power, confined life within a narrow
circle, but within these limits it must have been of an extraordinary intensity and fullness, pervaded by the conviction that
the idea—that is, the meaning of an event—brings this event
about. Seneca explains this mentality, the diametrically opposite of the Greek mind, in his *Quaestiones Naturales* (II. 32. 2)
written about A.D. 63:

The difference between the Graeco-Roman way of thinking and the
Etruscans' . . . is the following: whereas we believe lightning to be

19

released as a result of the collision of clouds, they believe that clouds collide so as to release lightning (for as they attribute all to the deity, they are led to believe not that things have a meaning in so far as they occur, but rather that they occur because they must have a meaning.)

However incompatible with our "scientific" mind these ideas may appear, they were the essence of existence around which the thinking of the Etruscans revolved. They determined the form of worship and explain the significance attached to the orientation of buildings and cities, and the similarity between domestic and religious architecture. The buildings within the sacred enclosure, the *templum*, generally faced the south—for example, on the *acropolis* of Marzabotto. Sepulchral urns often had the form of a temple or a hut. The cupola and the arc seem to have been sacred forms filled with a meaning that transcends their practical usefulness. In general, the architectural form of the houses of the living and the abodes of the dead were the same.

The economic organization of Etruria was probably similar to that of the early Greek cities in Asia Minor. The Etruscan aristocracy lived in the cities. This class consisted of the owners of large estates and workshops, and of wholesale merchants who derived their income from the labor of the slaves who tilled their land and worked in their workshops. It is doubtful whether a more advanced cultivation existed in Etruria outside the suburban estates of the ruling class. In any case, the murals in the tombs, depicting scenes of daily life, do not show any change, at least from the fifth to the third century B.C., and in general it cannot be proved from the archeological evidence available that the archaic conditions existing at the time of the conquest had undergone a far-reaching change during the six centuries of the existence of the League. It was a life of elegant leisure for the rich and of drudgery for the poor. Etruria remained what she always had been—a land of big estates and large-scale slave labor.[9]

The main agricultural districts were Caere, Rusellae, Clusium, Perusia, Arretium, and Volaterrae. Populonia seems to have been an ironworking center and Arretium an industrial city. The mining areas lay within the territories of Vetulonia and Populonia, including the island of Elba. It has rightly been stressed that the extraction of metals was an activity of the greatest importance to the history and life of the Etruscans, inasmuch as the Etruscan mines were the only ones of any importance in the Central Mediterranean.[10] It has been established that

As regards the manufacture of bronze and iron articles, the most important cities were Perugia (for tripods and other objects in wrought

9. M. I. Rostovtzeff. *The Social and Economic History of the Roman Empire.* 1926. Chapter 1.
10. M. Pallottino, *op. cit.*, pp. 219-20.

8. Sepulchral urn in the form of a temple from Chiusi.

iron) whence its products spread towards Umbria (the famous bronze chariot found at Monteleone di Spoleto, now at the Metropolitan Museum in New York, was probably made at Perugia); Visentium (Bisenzio) with its manufactured articles, especially during the archaic period; Vulci with its tripods, candelabra, weapons, etc.; Arezzo too. . . . Etruscan iron and bronze were also worked in Campania, and it is probably from here that both the crude metal and the finished products reached the Greek world. . . . Nor must other aspects of Etruscan industrial production be overlooked, such as the textile industry, the leather industry, with especial reference to footwear renowned throughout the Mediterranean world . . . And only an advanced hydraulic technique . . . can explain the conquest of the marshy lands of the lower Po valley wrested inch by inch from the river and its stagnant pools, and where cities such as Ravenna had still to be built on piles. Nor could such intensely active life on the marshy areas of the Maremma or of the lower Po be explained had malarial infection already been common during the golden age of Etruscan civilization.

The ascendancy of the Etruscan nation seems to throw back the prehistoric civilizations, which preceded the meteoric rise of these city-building adventurers, into the shadows of an unhistorical dreamland and to disrupt the continuity between the pre- and post-Etruscan history of the Italian peninsula. The splendor of the Etruscan culture reduces these primitive peasant civilizations to an almost unreal existence although they upheld their essential characteristics and their way of life under the direct rule of the Etruscans until late in the sixth century. Spiritually and socially the chasm between the two civilizations was so wide that this alone gave the Etruscans an advantage and a superiority that enabled them to extend their sway—apparently without any serious opposition and within the short span of two and three generations—not only over Latium and Campania but also over the Plain of the Po to the Alps. Within this short period a small group of piratical and hardy adventurers established their power over the indigenous peoples and became the ruling feudal aristocracy of a vast territory.

This success is one of very few similar events in history, comparable perhaps only to the conquest of America by Columbus and his successors with their handful of soldiers—or the conquest of India whereby a small group of Englishmen not only subjugated a vast territory in a short time and with a minimum of effort but made this victory the beginning of an historical mission. The Etruscan conquerors settled the "Greek question" before Rome as a nation existed; they stemmed the Greek advance northward and drew a line across the peninsula which the Greeks never crossed—not even after the fall of the Etruscan empire. On her own soil Rome never had to fight against the Greeks. This task was accomplished for Rome by the Etruscans. It was Etruria from which Rome inherited her first culture, her religion, and her art of city building; what had penetrated from Greece reached Rome, in the first stages, through Etruscan hands and minds.

Our knowledge of the layout of Etruscan cities is without exception negligible. The cities of the dead have revealed more secrets than the cities of the living which still await the spade of diligent excavators. The choice of sites permits certain general conclusions as to their size and fortifications, and those together with the *tumuli* of the *necropoleis* surrounding the cities have enabled Etruscan scholars to estimate the approximate number of inhabitants, although it should be added that all these calculations are very vague. As to the origin of the great Etruscan cities, it may be assumed that they were formed by the union of a number of prehistoric villages built on high and naturally protected ground.[11] And as to the actual layout of the early cities there is no evidence whatsoever that they were built according to an orderly plan. They were "the product of spontaneous growth rather than of orderly planning."[12] This assumption is probably not too wide of the mark, for the shape

11. *Art et Civilisation des Etrusques.* Catalogue of the Etruscan Exhibition at the Musée du Louvre. 1955. P. 91.
12. J. Ward Perkins. "The Early Development of Roman Town-Planning." *Proceedings of the Second International Congress of Classical Studies, Copenhagen, 1954.* Vol. IV, p. 113.

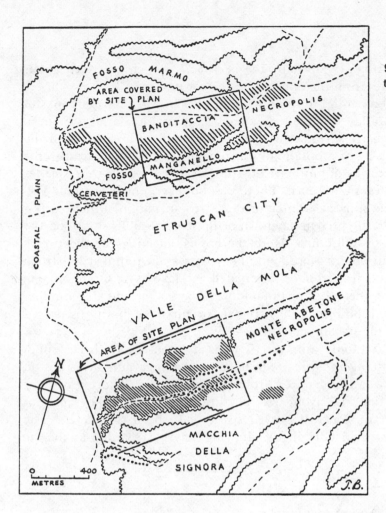

9. Map of the site of Etruscan Cerveteri with the cemeteries.

of the cities and their internal layout were mostly dependent
on the configuration of the terrain.

Of the Etruscan period of Rome, the *Ruma* of the Etruscans,
very little has survived. Only a few sacred sites have been excavated from which no evidence as to the layout can be derived.
It is similar at Veii, which stood on the right bank of the Tiber
a few miles from Rome at the confluence of the two branches of
the Cremera.[13] Caere (Cerveteri), situated between the Lake of
Bracciano and the Sea, was also one of the great *metropoleis*
of Etruria. It stood on a flat-topped hill with steep slopes and
covered an area of about 375 acres. The cemeteries surrounding
the city on all sides occupied more than 1,000 acres.[14] Caere was
an important coastal town and although a few miles inland, had
three harbors. It reached its greatest prosperity in the seventh and
sixth centuries B.C. Tarquinii, like the other Etruscan towns, consisted of a zone of the dead and a zone of the living. Here these
two "cities" faced one another across a valley. The situation of
Tarquinii favored its role as a city-state that held sway over the
land and sea connections in its neighborhood. The ancient city
stood on the plateau called *Piano di Civita,* parallel to which ran

13. G. Dennis. *Cities and cemeteries of Etruria.* 1883. Also for the following.
14. J. Bradford. *Ancient Landscapes.* 1957. P. 116.

23

a long ridge occupied by the *necropolis,* which extended about two miles from the outskirts of the town.

Twelve miles to the northwest of Tarquinii on the banks of the Fiora lay Vulci, another important city of southern Etruria. Its ruins are spread over a large uninhabited area between the two villages of Montalto di Castro and Canino. In contrast to the coastal towns of southern Etruria, the inland towns were smaller and of less significance. There was, however, one exception: Volsinii, the spiritual center of the Etruscan nation, which corresponds to the present-day town of Bolsena. Near its site stood the temple of Voltumna. Here the annual meetings of the twelve Etruscan *populi* were held. The city was surrounded by strong walls and its *acropolis* dominated the lake.[15] At Orvieto, commanding the valley of the middle Tiber, a considerable number of sacred buildings of Etruscan origin have been discovered within the urban enclosure.

At Vetulonia ruins of city walls and houses have been found. The vast *necropolis* attests to its importance and the scale on which it was inhabited from the beginning. The excavations reveal that its layout was conditioned by the topography of the terrain. Parts of curved streets have been discovered. The street marked G-H in the drawing may be regarded as the *via decumana.*[16]

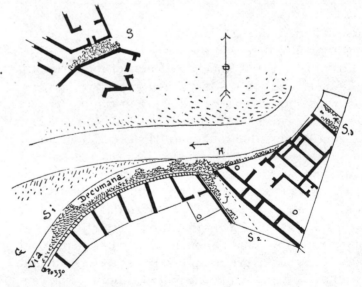

10. **Group of houses in Vetulonia.**

Populonia to the north of Vetulonia was the only Etruscan city situated on the very shore of the Tyrrhenian Sea. It stood on a hill which rose above the surrounding marsh. Populonia was one of the important iron centers of antiquity, a fact still evi-

15. M. Pallottino, *op. cit.,* p. 118.
16. J. Falchi. *Notizie degli Scavi di Antichità.* 1896. Pp. 272 ff.

dent from the large fields of iron slag that surround it—the result of the smelting of iron ores from the island of Elba extracted during Etruscan and Roman times.[17]

Of the inland cities Clusium (Chiusi) may be mentioned whose greatest prosperity coincided with the beginning of the decline of the coastal cities. The smaller towns in the region of Clusium were culturally similar to the metropolis and practically dependent on it. Perusia (Perugia) experienced its most splendid period from the third to the first century B.C.—that is, during the final stage of the Etruscan civilization. Parts of the early walls and gateways have been preserved. Volaterrae (Volterra) stood on a hill above the valley of the Cerina. Capua was the center of the Etruscan dominion in Campania. It was later one of the most important cities of the Italic and Roman period.

The foregoing survey of Etruscan cities is hardly more than a very generalized enumeration of some of the more famous places. It is of necessity insufficient in terms of city planning as such. But it may convey a picture, however unsatisfactory, of the strong urbanizing tendencies so characteristic of Etruscan civilization as the forerunner of Roman urbanization—the instrument through which Rome conquered and consolidated her empire. Although we know virtually nothing of the detailed layout of these cities, we may assume that they grew up spontaneously without an orderly plan.

The only exception was Marzabotto, 15 miles south of Bologna, in the valley of the upper Rena at the foothills of the Apennines. Founded about 500 B.C., it was destroyed less than a century later by the Gauls and never reoccupied. The *acropolis* was situated on a hill crowned with a temple and other sacred buildings. The city itself stood on level ground, laid out on a gridiron plan of wide major streets intersecting at right angles, with secondary streets dividing the urban area into unequal *insulae*. The excavations have revealed a defensive wall and a street running parallel to it on the inside. This street was about 60 feet wide and was probably the equivalent of the inner *pomerium,* the space originally along the inner and outer side of the city wall left empty and regarded as holy by the Romans. Cemeteries began immediately outside the gates.

The streets were oriented to the four cardinal points and paved with a fairly elaborate drainage system. The *insulae* were 495 feet long and varied in width from 120 to 180 feet. The two main streets, the *decumanus* and *cardo,* were each 45 feet wide, of which 15 feet were reserved for traffic and 15 feet on either side for pedestrians. At certain intervals large stones were set

17. M. Pallottino, *op. cit.,* p. 121.

above the surface of the road so that in bad weather pedestrians could cross without wetting their feet.[18]

Marzabotto was a perfect example of Etruscan theory of city planning in the fifth century, and as such is the oldest known city on Italian soil laid out on a regular plan in accordance with the strict application of Etruscan rituals. This raises the question whether the evolving Roman practice of the regular layout of cities owes more to Etruscan than to Greek prototypes. In the light of our present knowledge, a final answer cannot yet be given. However, certain features seem to suggest that it was Etrurian rather than Greek tradition that exerted a lasting influence on Roman city planning. The plan of Marzabotto is more flexible than the typical Greek gridiron plan with its equal *insulae.* Above all, Marzabotto was most likely conceived and laid out as a whole from the very beginning, a procedure that was contrary to the usual concept of Greek cities. Moreover, as Ward Perkins correctly remarks, the relationship in Greece between the plan of a city's streets, houses, and walls was mostly very casual. Ward Perkins cites in this respect Dura Europos, where despite its military character the residential area and the fortifications are more or less two independent entities.

At Marzabotto, just as in later Roman foundations, the inhabited area and the walls were organically interdependent. In contrast to the Greek cities which had less need for it, the Italian cities had a road immediately at the inside of the ramparts—definite proof of the organic relationship of the interior layout and the fortifications. Moreover, Marzabotto was a military foundation in a territory newly conquered by the Etruscans. Like all such colonies it was laid out on a regular plan, with defense considerations given first priority. In this respect it was also the true predecessor of numerous later Roman settlements.

On the other hand, the possibility cannot be ruled out that Etruscan city planning developed entirely independently of Greek practice. Etruscans and Greeks had established contacts in Campania and other regions, and it would have been strange if a cross-fertilization of ideas had not taken place. Roman city planning had to find a concrete solution for its problems when the early military colonies were founded in the fifth and fourth centuries B.C. At this time, Rome's contacts were stronger with Etruria than with Southern Italy. More intimate and continuous intercourse between Rome and *Magna Graecia* developed only late in the fourth century. Taking these admittedly rather vague considerations into account, it would appear that Etruria rather than Greece supplied the principles on which the early Roman colonies were founded.

18. J. Ward Perkins, *op. cit.,* pp. 113-14.
 E. Brizio. *Una Pompeii etrusca a Marzabotto nel Bolognese.* 1928.
 P. E. Arias. "Considerazioni sulla città etrusca a Pian di Misano (Marzabotto)." In *Atti e Memorie della Deputazione di Storia Patria per le Provincie di Romagna.* Nuova Serie, Vol. IV, Part III. 1953.

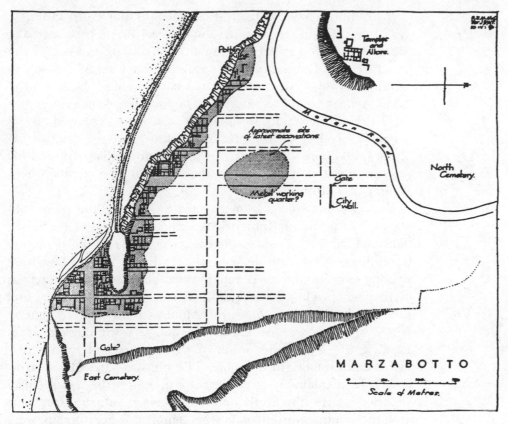

11. Map of Marzabotto.

At Marzabotto, the foundations of a residential district have been excavated. The conviction that life after death was a continuation of earthly existence explains the fact that urns imitated the architecture of the houses, and the interior of tombs the layout and the various types of arrangement of rooms. The original houses consisted of a single room and were rectangular, covered by a double-sloped roof. This simple structure grew more complex at a very early stage. Porticoes were added and the number of rooms increased. As early as the sixth century something like a standard type came into existence. This may be considered as the prototype of the Italic or "Pompeian" house. It had an open entrance hall, a central room, and possibly a small courtyard with two open lateral rooms. At the back there was a transverse passage and a number of other rooms. The three-roomed type was most common. The *atrium*—the term seems to be of Etruscan origin—was the invention of the Etruscans, though in a less developed form than the Roman houses adopted it. The introvert type of the houses gave the Etruscan cities their characteristic atmosphere. Only the *tabernae*, the shops, and workshops, opened onto the streets which—with this exception and the interruption of the entrance gates—were lined by the plain walls of the buildings.

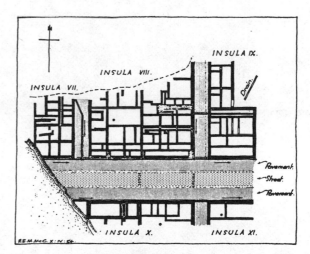

12. Streets and drainage system at Marzabotto.

27

Rome   Alba Longa was probably the oldest of the Latin cities. It was situated about twelve miles southeast of Rome between Lake Albanus and Mount Albanus—or more likely on the site of the present Castel Gandolfo. It was called Alba Longa because, according to Livy, it stretched across a narrow ridge. Ascanius, the son of Aeneas, is said to have been the founder of the city. It was the head of the Latin League but was soon destroyed by its daughter city Rome. Romulus and Remus were the descendants of Ascanius. It is likely that the neighboring villages united for defense, trade, and worship at the shrine of the common god, Jupiter of Latium.

Later, tribes moved down from the hills to the plain and settled on the site of Rome where compact villages of the Sabellians and Sabines occupied the higher ground, the Palatine, the Capitoline, the Esquiline, and the Quirinal hills. They were pastoral peoples and their religion was adapted to the interests of shepherds. They offered milk, not wine, to their gods, and their wealth consisted of cattle. Money—or in a more general sense "wealth"—was in Latin *pecunia,* a word derived from *pecus,* cattle. From the union of these tribes and their settlements dates the origin of Rome. The site was particularly favorable. This explains its great attraction: it was the most central situation of the Peninsula and was likewise valuable for trade and the administration of a great empire. The Romans were aware of these advantages; Livy remarked on them in detail (v.54):

Not without cause did gods and men select this place for establishing our City—with its healthful hills; its convenient river, by which crops may be floated down from the midland regions and foreign commodities brought up; its sea, near enough for use, yet not exposing us, by too great propinquity, to peril from foreign fleets; a situation in the heart of Italy—a spot, in short, of a nature uniquely adapted for the expansion of a city.

The commons of a city were organized in ten wards, *curiae.* The fact that Rome had thirty *curiae* seems to imply that it consisted of three settlements which already had developed a certain political organization. The early tribes had apparently settled as village communities on hills which offered good protection and a sufficient water supply. It is not improbable that the surrounding land was allotted to private owners and correspondingly partitioned, and that each village had common pastures. A portion of the land was reserved for religious purposes connected with the tribal cult. At an early period, more and more of these small, undefended, and isolated villages were abandoned in favor of better sites. Here, cities gradually developed and undermined

28

the tribal coherence. Protection and trade were the principal agents of this movement. Thus about six city-states came into being in Latium, each replacing a number of previously inhabited villages. This migration to the cities had several important results. A better administration was needed, a more efficient army had to be organized, and the cities had to be fortified by walls or earthen enclosures.

The traditional date of the foundation of Rome is 753 B.C.; that of the expulsion of the Etruscans, 509 B.C. Between these years Rome was governed by kings of whom the first three were Latins and the last three Etruscans. Under the Etruscan rulers a stone wall was built which enclosed all the then-existing hill settlements; the *forum* was drained and its area used as a marketplace. The population of Rome and Latium toward the end of the regal period must have been relatively large, although it may not have reached the number of 200,000 in Rome and the same size in the rural districts as has been repeatedly suggested. However, as Rome grew the building activity in the city increased: houses had to be built for the mounting influx of people, as well as temples to various gods. These works demanded a large labor force of skilled and unskilled workers and artisans.

Trade in general and the more refined needs of the Court were, as everywhere, urbanizing factors of primary importance, swelling the population and accentuating the stratification of society. The expulsion of the kings was followed by the institution of a republican government which, in reality, meant the oligarchy of a few families. These patricians arrogated to themselves the important offices of state and the exclusive right to interpret and ratify the laws.

The two centuries following this change of *régime* were a turbulent period for the small city-state. It was attacked by external enemies and split by internal discord—the latter mainly provoked by the fight of the *plebs* for equal social, political, and religious status with the patricians. By the end of the fourth century, the power of the plebeian citizens was a recognized fact although, as so often happened in history, the aristocratic minority managed through greater skill, experience, and leadership qualities to maintain a considerable influence in all political, economic, and social spheres.

The tribunes of the people were plebeian officers who were sacrosanct and who, in the course of time, became popular leaders, widening their political power and imposing the will of the people upon the administration by their right of veto. But the Twelve Tables—the earliest civil laws of Rome, posted in the *forum* after 450 B.C.—still recognized the patricians as a privileged caste; it was not until 445 B.C. that marriages between plebeians and patricians were legalized, and not until 367 that the office of the supreme magistracy—the consulate—was thrown open to the plebeian citizens. After this success the other offices of state followed rapidly and in 300 B.C. the religious colleges of the pontiffs and augurs finally had to admit plebeians.

Economic changes accompanied the class struggle. In the early years of the republic the prosperity, which Rome had enjoyed under the kings, disappeared. Overseas commerce and inland trade, especially with Etruria, came to an end, bringing in their train poverty, unemployment, and a steadily rising demand for a more just distribution of the land. The latter was of vital importance to the state, for the political and military power of Rome rested firmly on the soil. Citizens were farmer-soldiers who could be stirred to action in defense of their land and who would apply the skill, patience, and endurance they had learned the hard way—by working in the fields and waiting through the cycle of nature to harvest her fruits—to the practical tasks of building roads, camps, fortifications, houses, and laying out their fields. Agrarian reforms were one of the main demands which throughout Roman history created violent social and political tensions especially because, among the wealthier patricians and plebeians, it became an ever-growing habit to acquire large estates in conquered countries, thus robbing the less fortunate citizens of a just share in the distribution of the new land.

Rome's expansion proceeded in three stages: the conquest of Italy, the rivalry with Carthage and her sovereignty over the western Mediterranean, and her supremacy over the East. The first period, lasting from the middle of the fifth century to about 270 B.C., saw such important events as the capture of Veii and the conquest of southern Etruria; the sack of Rome by the Gauls in 390; the end of the Latin League; the contact with the Greek cities on the coast of Campánia; the struggle with the Samnites (343-290) which established Rome's rule over the lands to the north of the Apennines and eastward to the Adriatic; and the fight with Pyrrhus, King of Epirus, whose ambition was to rival Alexander's conquests by carving out an empire for himself in the West. His inability to check the Roman advance southward and his retreat to Greece left the field free for the Romans. Tarentum was occupied between 273 and 263 B.C. New colonies were founded at Paestum, Beneventum, and Aesernia (Isernia) and on the Adriatic coast, to guard against invasions, at Ariminum (Rimini), Firmum (Fermo), and Castrum Novum (to the south of Firmum); and on the Tyrrhenian Sea at Cosa. The Roman dominium then stretched roughly southward from a line between the mouth of the Arnus in the west to the mouth of the Aesis in the east, covering about one third of the Peninsula. This territory was held together by the establishment of colonies in a decreasing scale of importance and municipal self-government, and by military roads radiating from Rome.

The *Via Appia,* leading to the coast, was the earliest road begun in 312 B.C. by the *censor* Appius Claudius; it was later continued to Apulia and Brundisium (Brindisi). The *Via Latina* connected Rome with Capua and further inland. The *Via Flaminia* crossed the Apennines to Ariminum (Rimini) and later ran to Placentia (Piacenza) as the *Via Aemilia.* In the second century, Rome was connected with Spain by the *Via Domitia* and with Thessalonica (Salonika) and the Hellespont via the Balkan peninsula by the *Via Egnatia.*

The *coloniae civium Romanorum* stood at the head of the colonial stratification; then followed the *municipia* with the full Roman franchise; and finally the *civitates sine suffragio* having civil but no political rights. There were further Roman settlers installed on state-owned lands and the inhabitants of village communities in the mountainous districts of Central Italy which had been enfranchised. The Roman colonies were not independent like the colonial city-states of the Greeks. They were camps of the farmer-soldiers who had to keep the conquered territories subjected to Rome.

The main events of the second period, lasting from 265 to 146 B.C., were the wars between Rome and Carthage and the expansion of Roman rule over the western and southern Mediterranean. The first Punic War added Sicily, Corsica, and Sardinia to the Roman dominion; the second war ended with the conquest of Spain and the surrender of Carthage; after the third war Carthage was razed to the ground and its territory incorporated into the Roman state as the Province of Africa. The existing Greek and Carthaginian cities were later, in the imperial period, remodeled on the usual Roman layout and adorned with numerous buildings, while the African village-towns grew up haphazardly and were peopled with veterans and natives from the countryside. In Italy the region north of the Po was opened to Roman settlers and the Celtic tribes, which had assisted Hannibal or had been sympathetic to his cause, were romanized. In 181 B.C. the colony of Aquileia was founded in the extreme northeast as bulwark against the Celts and Istrians, and in 180 B.C. the colony of Luna (Luni) in the northwest, on the coast to the north of Pisa, was established against the Ligurians whose territory was intensively settled in 173 B.C. with Roman citizens and Latins. In the south the Greek cities declined in population and trade and new colonies, such as Brundusium (Brindisi) and Puteoli (Pozzuoli), were founded.

The third period saw the expansion of the Roman state and

influence in the East. Within the almost unbelievably short time of ten years Macedonia and the Seleucid Empire were conquered and reduced to Roman dependencies. Beyond the eastern provinces stretched a zone of principalities such as Syria, the remnant of the Seleucid Empire, Egypt, and Numidia in Africa, and numerous petty states all governed by indirect rule but dependent on Rome, especially in foreign policy. Her task in the West was fundamentally different from the problems she faced in the East. To the peoples of the West she came as the great civilizing power, bringing a higher culture and law and order to barbaric or semibarbaric tribes. In the East she encountered civilizations with a long history and cultural achievements superior to her own. The East remained fundamentally Greek; Roman civilization spread over this part of the empire only as a thin veneer. It never penetrated to the deeper layers of Eastern thought and habits, but left on this alien soil a monumental display of ostentatious and, to oriental and Greek feeling, vulgar achievements of Roman power and organization.

In the last period, before the fall of the Republic, conditions developed which made inevitable the decay of the city-state and rendered it ripe for transformation into an empire. It was a time of internal and external unrest and bloodshed, of superficial adaptation of the intellectual and spiritual heritage of ancient civilizations, of an ever-widening expansion and the painful shaping of new methods of government and administration. In name and in law Rome was a democracy, but in fact and in spirit this democracy was ruled by an oligarchy. This was not unusual, as we know from our own experience. The Senate was the governing body, not the representatives who made up the assembly. The people were rarely consulted. The Senate and the magistracies were filled by a privileged class which, without a firm constitutional basis, had assumed the status and acquired the influence of a dominant minority. The centralization of power in the hands of an *élite* and the expansion of the state were like communicating pipes; they were interdependent. It was a small power *élite* of military, political, and economic groups that made the vital decisions, and the more the state expanded the more these organs became centralized and bureaucratized, the more communities—and with them personal and direct relations—disappeared and gave way to an impersonal, cold organization and the deadening influence of the machinery of the state. The wealth that flowed into Rome from the exploitation of the East and the West; the rise of a plutocratic minority which spread its political and economic tentacles from Rome over the provinces; the growing luxury and speculation; the large estates; the decline of the class of small farmers; and the increase of an economy based on an extensive use of slave labor—all these trends undermined the very nature of the old Roman city-states and prepared Rome for the role as mistress of the world, the most powerful nation in terms of military strength, political and administrative organization, and enforced peace backed by military bases in faraway lands. These bases were to contain her enemies and, euphemistically, were said to provide "protection" of her voluntary and involuntary allies against external aggression.

But Rome could not offer a creative culture nor could she impose her way of life on unwilling peoples. It was a clash of civilizations in which Rome often enough played the role of the unwelcome and despised parvenu. The intellectual and cultural *élite,* the poets and writers, the architects and sculptors, the philosophers and scientists who transformed the legacy of Greece into the Roman language of form and reshaped her ideas, were a class apart. Their influence on the masses was virtually nil; but all the same, just because it was subtle and an influx of ideas rather than of material advantages, the fabric of traditional values slowly disintegrated. The spiritual and ideal expansion of Greece was a match for the material and administrative expansion of Rome, and Greece, as Horace put it (Epistles II. 1. 156), "took captive her rude conqueror"—though, we may add, only by similarities of the surface and the adoption of tenets not fully understood.

This inability to penetrate deeply into the very essence of the Greek spirit is not astonishing. Fundamentally Greek and Roman cultures were mutually exclusive. This fact should be borne in mind if we are to understand the true nature of Roman cities—which, in their conception and physical appearance, were worlds apart from their Greek predecessors. What the Romans took over from Greece was not the classical ideal of the sixth, the fifth, and fourth centuries, not the ideas of the great writers and philosophers of the Golden Age of Athens, but elements of the Hellenistic civilization which, whatever its merit, was a descent from the summit reached by classical Greece. The Romans, the representatives of the New World, found a storehouse of Old World art, literature, and philosophy thrown open to them. But they were unable to distinguish between what was first- or second-rate, original or secondhand. And the Greeks, whom the Romans met, were far removed from the Athenians of the fifth century. These men were for the Romans *Graeculi,* small men whom they despised because they did not live up to their idealized images of the greatness of ancient Greece.

The Romans had no use for the theoretical speculations of the Greeks. They were, above all, practical people whose pragmatism prevented them from searching for the formative ideas behind the artistic genius of their new wards. Thus they used the skill and the knowledge of these second-rate transmitters of a secondhand civilization; what emerged from this intercultural contact was a mass of undigested ideas and a crude, indiscriminate choice of Greek prototypes. True, this contact gave an immense stimulus to the Roman civilization but it remained a stimulus of form, not of substance. The fundamental difference between the principles of Greek and Roman thinking and the association of ideas arising from their distinctive ways of reasoning and feeling is evident in their attitudes toward the environment in general and Nature in particular. To the Greeks, Nature remained something to be admired, conquered, used, and speculated about. But the Greeks never entered into a deeply felt communion with the Greek soul as an indispensable part of their longings, despite the unsurpassed beauty of some Greek verses or even despite the anthropomorphic character which the Greeks attributed to Nature. To the Romans, especially the Roman poets, the love of Nature was a part of their inner being, an intimate relationship. Those Romans who could afford it and those poets who yearned to be surrounded by Nature—and they were numerous—abandoned the city for the country. They were the discoverers of country life. They rejuvenated their creative genius through their intercourse with Nature. They were "the first to appreciate a country home and to create a resort for time and leisure among the mountains or by the sea. So Catullus quitted Rome for his villa on the Lake of Garda, Horace for his Sabine farm, Virgil for the Bay of Naples. It was the same with the man of business and the lawyer, when, as in Horace's famous simile, he shook off the burden of public affairs and retired to 'the fields of Venafrum or Lacedaemonian Tarentum.' "[19] But "the Greek lived in and for the city, and, if he traveled abroad, it was to see the cities of men; his estates were a source of revenue, not a chosen retreat."

The revolutionary period which closed the republican era and which was filled with internal strife and social unrest saw a determined attack upon the Senate. The protagonists of this movement were Tiberius and Gaius Gracchus. Both were killed in civil riots. Their agrarian reforms met with the violent opposition of the Senate. Tiberius Gracchus, tribune in 133 B.C., tried to introduce measures to arrest the decline of agriculture and the depopulation of the countryside following the Hannibalic War. The small farmers who carried the main burden of military service had, apart from these exertions, to compete with overseas imports of corn and with the slave labor introduced by the wealthy landowners. The small farmers, feeling that theirs was a life of drudgery and missed opportunities, sought their fortune in the provinces or cities—if they did not prefer to join the army.

19. W. G. De Burgh. *The Legacy of the Ancient World.* 1953. Vol. I, p. 255. Horace. *Odes.* III. 5.

They left their farms which remained untilled or were absorbed into the large estates of the wealthy owners. The situation became so serious that between 200 and 160 B.C. the government tried repeatedly to remedy the situation. Twenty colonies were founded; veterans frequently received land grants; 40,000 Ligurians were resettled on land left vacant by a Samnite tribe; and the Pontine Marshes were drained to make them available for cultivation. These efforts, however, were of no avail except in a few cases such as the new colonies in *Gallia Cisalpina,* Northern Italy north of Liguria and Umbria, and south of the Alps, and Picenum, the province in Eastern Italy on the Adriatic with the main cities of Ancona and Asculum Picenum. The veterans were apparently not fitted or inclined to be farmers, for many left the land and returned to the banner of the eagles. After 160 B.C. no new attempts to improve the agrarian situation were made till Tiberius Gracchus was elected to the tribunate. He suggested the resumption by the government of all "common land" occupied by unauthorized persons contrary to the existing laws, and a redistribution of this newly available land. These proposals evoked the opposition of the Senate as partisan of the wealthy landowners—or rather occupiers.

After the death of Tiberius his brother Gaius continued the fight. He too was unsuccessful and had to pay for his democratic idealism with his death. But a few of his measures were at least not outstanding failures. Two of his colonies, at Tarentum and Scylacium in Southern Italy, survived because they were peopled with well-selected men. Six thousand experienced farmers were settled in the province of Africa. But the Senate nullified the colonial charter although it did not revoke the allotments. The last attempt made by Gaius Gracchus led to his final defeat and his death. When he tried to put democracy on a firm and truly popular basis by extending the franchise to the Latins, he met the opposition of the urban populace, who in their selfish shortsightedness feared losing their privileges and control of the Assembly. As so often happens, the uneducated masses, not understanding the real intentions of reformers and possibly misled by their inveterate enemies, played directly into the hands of those whose advantages were diametrically opposed to their own. It was a tragic example of urban versus rural interests, a clash between the unthinking many and the determined and knowing few, in which the cities were the victors.

The time immediately before the end of the Republic was an age of strong individuals who sought to change the course of history in their own favor. Their fights culminated in the assassination of Caesar and were ended by the battle of Actium in 31 B.C. with the victory of Octavianus over Marcus Antonius. The state was ripe for the imperial power of one man. The Empire was established by Augustus in 27 B.C. The Republic died through its internal weakness. Its body politic was exhausted, its social organism rotten, its economic structure decaying, and the chasm between the plutocratic minority and the poor masses unbridgable. Agriculture had declined and slaves worked the soil that free men had conquered and tilled. Self-interest was the professed motivation of the ruling circles, the financial magnates, and the city proletariat—which accepted *panem et circenses* for their political rights. The old republican virtues had ceased to be standards of morality. How could such a state maintain its hold over its own citizens and its dependent peoples? It had lost command of the armies, which had become the tools of ambitious generals.

All these conditions worked together to seal the fate of the Republic and to close the era of the city-state. A city cannot govern an empire. A new spirit, a new administration, a new conception, and a new scale of action were needed which demanded the utmost centralization of power in the person of one man, the emperor—another empty dream of mankind, for it did not and could not change human nature, nor could it make men happier or alter their station in life. Rome, the Imperial City, became more and more a parasite blinded by her greatness and glory yet slowly moving toward her decline and fall—toward the time when the veil of the Dark Ages would exclude her from active participation in history before setting out again on the ascent toward the Middle Ages and the Renaissance. The imperial era was an important interlude in the history of city development not only in Italy but in the whole Empire. It was a sunset, majestic in its colorful beauty—but a sunset withal. And it was an interlude, for no new ideas were formed and no new types of cities were built.

The great task confronting Augustus was the consolidation of the authority of Rome over the lands that Caesar and the republican generals had conquered and the establishment of the *Pax Romana* in the vast area of the Empire, which now extended from the African deserts to the Atlantic Ocean, in the north to Britannia and thence along the Rhine and Danube to the Pontus Euxinus and the Euphrates, including Armenia as an "independent" ally. Augustus was successful: The frontiers were secured and his imperial administration became an efficient instrument of his power and policy. He wisely restricted a further expansion of the Empire, wishing "to keep it within bounds." The principal role of the army was to guard the frontiers, and its generals received their orders directly from the emperor as supreme commander. It ceased to be the unruly instrument of ambitious and greedy provincial governors. Under Augustus, Hellenistic influence receded and Roman ideas and ideals, Roman art and literature—encouraged by the personal initiative of the emperor—surged up in an outburst of intense activities which rejuvenated the spirit and energy of the nation. But despite this regeneration and notwithstanding the peace and prosperity which the emperor had bestowed on the nation (or perhaps just because of the easy and secure life) he had to confess at the end of his reign that he had failed, and that the spreading moral corruption had proved stronger than his intentions and deeds.

However, his great achievements should not blind us to the fact that Augustus was a clever politician and that he succeeded in presenting his monarchy as a principate based on and surrounded by republican forms, a masterpiece of political camouflage and almost ironic deception. "I transfer the republic from my own authority to the control of the Roman Senate and people." These words were inscribed on tablets set up in various cities of the Empire and were contained in the record of the deeds of Augustus, the *index rerum a se gestarum*.[20] Needless to remark, the Senate was a servile instrument of the emperor, a decorative and powerless House of Lords; and the popular assemblies were a meaningless concession to the proletariat. The emperor was supreme and his will was the sole source from which the Empire derived its idea, strength, and leadership.

"And it came to pass in those days, that there went out a decree from Caesar Augustus that all the world should be taxed." This meant that a general census was to be made for the whole Empire as one of the major steps in the reorganization of the administrative machinery. But by far the most effective and important instrument of the administrative, social, and economic consolidation of the Empire was urbanization. The same methods toward the same ends had been applied by the Chinese emperors. The numerous cities in their vast domain were the nodal points of the imperial administration represented by the mandarins who resided in the midst of the citizens. As with the Chinese, city life to the Romans meant civilization and pacification. Rome had ceased to be a peasant state ruled by an oligarchy of owners of large estates. A new class of wealthy merchants, a prosperous bourgeoisie, grew up and dominated the life of the cities yet without taking an active part in the political life of the state. They were too preoccupied with their own narrow economic pursuits and the development of their cities. Moreover, they were in agreement with the official policy which was in accordance with their personal interests. The Romans were city builders *par excellence* less by what they did in detail or how they laid out their cities—this side of their work was not inspired by

20. Found in a temple at Ancyra (Angora, Ankara) in Asia Minor and called *Monumentum Ancyranum*.

imagination and sensitivity—than by the sheer number of new cities they founded and the numerous hamlets, villages, and small towns they elevated to cities.

This development, so assiduously fostered by the emperors, was dictated by political and social considerations: The inhabitants of the cities, the civilized class of the Empire, were the cornerstone of the imperial power, and the provincials were attracted to the better and more varied life which the cities offered. The granting of full Roman citizenship would have been a simpler way to win and to retain the support of the urban masses, but too liberal use of this expedient would have alienated the Roman citizens of Italy who were jealous of their privilege. These considerations explain why Augustus and his immediate successors were reluctant to grant Roman citizenship to the provincials, and preferred the foundation of new towns with a gradually growing number of townsmen. The emperors knew that these citizens, once they had enjoyed the cultural advantages of the cities, would be the best pillars of their *régime* which guaranteed them peace and order and a status superior to the country people. For the beginning, however, the cities which were not Roman or Latin colonies generally received municipal rights of a secondary category as "allied" or "dependent" cities.[21] Thus cities came into existence in all parts of the Roman world. Their civilizing influence penetrated their hinterland and was the cement that held the Empire together. Where cities already existed, they were often enlarged and replanned. They vied with each other in the erection of public buildings but less so in the provision of housing for the masses. New cities were founded in regions such as Germany, Britain, Roumania, and Austria that had never seen anything resembling a city.

The actual organization of the Empire rested, above all, on innumerable small urban units originally founded either as purely military colonies from which the natives were excluded, or as civilian and military settlements, as in Spain and Africa. Military conquest and economic penetration were the means and the ends of this expansionist policy. Both were concentrated in and represented by the cities, from which they spread their influence over the provinces and allied states. The expansion of the Greek city-states proceeded as overseas colonization restricted to the immediate hinterland of the new colonies. Its principal aim was the settlement of a surplus population and trade. The expansion of Rome was, at least in the beginning, based on a tribal and defensive organization which had led, about 300 B.C., to the annexation of the lands south of the Apennines as allied or subject city-states or as Roman colonies with dispersed Roman farms and estates.

21. M. I. Rostovtzeff. *The Social and Economic History of the Roman Empire.* 1926. *Passim.*

After the golden century of the Antonines, the catastrophic decline of the third century unveiled the forces of destruction which hitherto had been hidden by the surface splendor of the age. Their eroding power, gaining an ever-increasing momentum, undermined the thin veneer of the political experience and success that had held the Empire together. According to Rostovtzeff, there were two trends instrumental in this process which reached their culmination under the Antonines: urbanization and the rise of an urban bourgeoisie. The conquest of the Hellenistic East had taught the Romans how the Greek city-states were administered and had organized their social and economic structure. Under Augustus, Rome became a Hellenistic city and gradually the Roman emperors assumed more and more of the trappings of a Hellenistic monarchy. This Hellenization spread from Rome to the provincial cities. The economic power was decentralized. The instrument of this process was urbanization, and in its wake a self-satisfied and saturated urban citizenry developed.

But the prosperity of the cities and the citizens did not wholly rest on the same type of commercial enterprise as the Middle Ages experienced in their trade with the countryside and distant regions. It was not a free-enterprise economy; the state was in many cases the main customer, the army the main consumer. The cities on the Rhine frontier were prosperous because they supplied the armies stationed along the Rhine. Those of Britain lived on the armies of this distant province; those of the East, on the Black Sea and beyond, supplied the armies stationed in these regions. Thus the cities were irrevocably drawn into the power politics of the Empire. The urban aristocracy, the leading minority, were the main promoters and beneficiaries of this lucrative but unholy alliance between state and wealth, between power and profit. They enjoyed their privileged position and expressed their pride and affluence by ostentatious gifts to their cities, by the erection of public buildings, and by their readiness to assume offices that sometimes entailed excessive expenses which would, they believed and hoped, immortalize their names for generations to come.

But these expectations were shattered. When they concentrated on the improvement of their cities, they had left out of account the countryside. It was the eternal antagonism between city and country, the shortsighted preoccupation of the dominant urban-born and urban-bred minorities that had excluded the peasants from the progress and the amenities of the cities. Rostovtzeff sees in this development one of the main reasons for the decline and fall of the Roman Empire. It was a dissolution from within, a failure of political understanding, an overestimation of the power of the state and of the influence of the cities as focal points of the imperial administration. The peasants hated the cities, regarding them as alien to their way of life, as the seats of their oppressors who enjoyed the comfortable and cultured life of the romanized urban communities. The country people, who had retained their identity as natives of the region where they had been born and lived their whole life, were for the Romans barbarians.

And barbarians they were; oppressed, uncultured, unromanized; speaking a foreign tongue unintelligible to the Greek or Roman townspeople, eking out a miserable existence which excluded them from everything the cities stood for. They were "cannon fodder" for the Roman armies. They had to defend an empire which meant nothing to them and which they despised. But they were the same people who had to be armed. When in the third century the prosperity of the cities and their strength began to decline, the time was ripe for a terrible vengeance. The peasants, the exploited and suppressed rural masses, rose to destroy the rule of the urban bourgeoisie. But they had no positive program and in the end they gained nothing. In merely changing their masters they helped bring down the Roman civilization and usher in the final period of the Empire. Ironically, the excessive urbanization of the Empire—which had degenerated into a vast federation of cities surrounded by hostile natives who were not absorbed into the social and economic structure—opened the way not only to the destructive influences of the internal but also of the external proletariat, to the ruralization of the Empire and to "the triumph of barbarism and religion," to borrow a phrase from Gibbon's *The Decline and Fall of the Roman Empire.*

Roman Pragmatism

The rise of the Roman cities to the pre-eminent position in the Empire and their physical structure cannot be understood without an appreciation of the Roman character. The Romans were, above all, practical people and as such they were intensely proud of their material achievements. They were organizers *par excellence*, yet they failed to create a sound economy and to lay the foundations for a modest scientific development. They covered their shortcomings by grandiloquent self-praise of their visible success. However, this behavior was not unusual as we know from our own era. But they had possibly less qualms and were less conscious of their hypocrisy than other peoples. The superpatriotic outburst of Pliny that deserves to be mentioned as an example of supreme hypocrisy is characteristic of this self-glorification. It reveals a deplorable lack of insight into the deeper causes of the fate of nations and an even more dangerous overestimation of outward appearances:

Rome the capital of the world, Italy the land which is at once the foster-child and parent of all lands; chosen by the providence of the Gods to render heaven itself more glorious, to unite the scattered empires of the earth, to bestow a polish on men's manners, to unite the discordant and uncouth dialects of many different nations by the powerful ties of a common language, to confer the enjoyments of discourse and of civilization upon mankind, and to become in short the mother-country of all nations of the earth.[22]

The Romans were more interested in acquiring existing knowledge and spreading it than in exploring new fields of learning. They borrowed and vulgarized Greek culture until it fitted their daily needs. They simplified Greek philosophy and adapted it to the aspirations of the common man. They took over elements of Greek architecture which they used—or misused—for their monumental buildings. But at the same time they were the first to span the great areas of their baths and basilicas with large vaults. The Pantheon is the most memorable exponent of this important achievement. Their amphitheaters, *thermae,* aqueducts, their roads and bridges were their genuine contribution to civilization—above all to city life. It was the Romans who used Greek geometry for the layout of the land, and for the supply of water; they turned Greek medicine to practical use by building hospitals and organizing medical services for the army. They enjoyed the management of their estates and made deserts habitable. But they were bad economists. The prosperity of the Empire, as long as it lasted, rested not on its own inner strength but on its expansion and the wealth plundered from the newly added provinces. It was a parasitic capitalism of a very primitive nature without new techniques and inventions. In spite of their materialistic tendencies, the ruling class shunned the very economic activities which were the origin of their wealth. The leading minorities of the provinces invested their money in property rather than in business or industry, for property was more compatible with the aristocratic status to which they aspired.

As usual, we know little about the urban masses and the peasants, whereas slightly more information is available on the slaves attached to the wealthier families. The great number of available slaves depressed the status and opportunities of rural and urban workers, and of free peasants—who drifted to the cities if they did not become *coloni* on the *latifundia* of the big landowners. An abundance of cheap labor has always been detrimental to industrial progress and progressive agriculture. It never helped

22. *Historia Naturalis,* III. 6.

to increase the inner market, because cheap labor perpetuated the poverty of the great masses as consumers. The practical Romans, possibly aware of this inconsistency, were obviously disinterested and unable to remedy this situation. True, they had their ideals, the ideal of *humanitas,* of order and law, of religion and political stability. But these ideals were almost invariably put into cold storage when and if the realities of life demanded it—and this happened quite often. In any case the urban proletariat and the peasants were kept in ignorance and excluded from the benefits that a more humane empire might have bestowed upon them. Instead of receiving tangible advantages, they were fed on and diverted by bread and circuses, the eternal offerings of the few to the many, and the equivalent of today's high standard of living and cinema and sports. Where the Greeks had been active participants in great athletic festivals and the cult of the body, the Romans remained passive spectators of organized brutality and cruelty.

But what else had the Roman masses to turn to for recreation? They were helpless victims of a system that made their life miserable and dejected. They lived in large tenements erected by unscrupulous profiteers—structures so flimsily built that they sometimes collapsed and buried the inhabitants in the ruins. And yet posterity still admires the huge amphitheaters and *stadia* of the Roman world where these inhuman atrocities were committed. The Romans remained true to their role as organizers: These games, which were part and parcel of urban existence, were organized on a huge scale as opiates for the masses and as stepping stones to the realization of political ambitions by men who as individuals would have been shocked by this glorification of brutality.

The breakdown of human decency on so colossal a scale explains the sterility of Roman city planning. The soul of a civilization that was capable of these monstrosities was blind to the imponderable values of a creative art which would grow out of the spontaneous and sublime unison of the spiritual aspirations. It is most instructive to compare the Roman and National Socialist attitudes in this respect: both indulged in the organization of unheard-of brutalities and both murdered not only human beings but also the arts and architecture. Both reveled in grandiose monumentality, in superorganization, convinced that their empires would endure forever. But both failed. Their cities remained empty demonstrations and their art sterile and secondhand. Creative city planning needs something more than mere pragmatism—even without the organized cruelty of the Romans. City planning is more than organization and the solution of practical problems. It is the creative translation of man's most cherished aspirations as a social being into the language of form as expressed in the dynamic unity of the many diverse elements comprising our environment. In this fundamental respect the all too pragmatic Romans failed quite dismally. The grandiose public buildings, the *fora* and temples, the colonnaded streets, the roads and aqueducts should not deceive us. They were nothing more than practical solutions of practical problems. When the end came most of these monuments fell into ruin and oblivion. The way was free for a new beginning and for an art of organic city planning that was the opposite of the organized pseudoculture of the Roman cities.

"Ubicumque vicit Romanus, habitat." Where the Roman has conquered, he settles. These words of Seneca (*Dialogi.* XII. 7) explain succinctly the miraculous growth of the Roman Empire. Conquest and settlement were almost synonymous. The Empire expanded too rapidly to absorb fully and organically this principle, the observance of which could have made the Roman world the prototype of a humane and integrated commonwealth of nations. The stigma of violent conquest could not be erased from the minds of the vanquished, nor could it help the conquerors to forget they had come as undesirable intruders to impose their will and ideas upon the inhabitants of the newly acquired provinces. But the fact remained that this expansion of Roman civilization was based on a sound principle—the understanding that military conquest alone was not enough if the incorporation of the new territories into the Roman Empire was to last and create a merging—or at least a certain mutual accommodation—of different cultures. The Roman attitude to this problem was not too dissimilar from the policy of the English when they followed their conquest of North America with a deliberate settlement policy. Just as great parts of Europe fell under the lasting spell of Roman ideas and institutions, so the North American continent became part and parcel of the Anglo-Saxon civilization. The French failed. They came merely as conquerors and traders but not as settlers except in Quebec, where they retained their influence and individuality.

It would be an error to assume that the familiar type of the regular Roman schemes of city planning dates back to prehistoric times. The whole of Italy had been thickly covered with settlements ever since the Neolithic period. But these settlements were self-contained, self-supporting villages with a purely agricultural economy. Towns did not, even in rudimentary form, begin to appear before the first millennium had far advanced. A considerable number of prehistoric villages have been discovered by air-archeology in Apulia and some other parts of Italy. Most of these

Structure of Settlement

Apulian villages lay on low ground in positions which had little or no defensive advantages and were often at a distance from water.[23] Others were situated near the edges of the low escarpments and spurs, but only in a few cases did the contours of the escarpment act as protection of one of the sides of the settlement. Every village was surrounded by one or more—sometimes up to eight—roughly circular ditches which were placed concentrically. The smaller settlements (possibly for single families) were usually enclosed by one ditch or two, whereas the larger sites had several ditches. The smaller units had a simple entrance—visible in the air photographs as a small bulge protruding outward from the line of the ditch. At the larger sites with several ditches, the entrances were of an inturned form; where the ditch has been left unexcavated, both arms turn inward and form a narrow funnellike approach. Inside these settlements numerous smaller enclosures with ditches were discovered. These compounds varied in size from 40 to 150 feet in diameter. So far no definite evidence as to the function of these compounds is available, although it is probably safe to assume that they were individual homesteads. Analogous groupings are known from parts of Africa, where comparable topographical and tribal conditions produced similar results. One of the largest villages at Passo di Corvo, eight miles northeast of Foggia, has already been mentioned. This may have been a tribal center. It covered an area of 800 by 500 yards with more than one hundred compounds, the whole surrounded by several wide ditches. Although defense played a not insignificant part in the siting of these settlements, there is no evidence that the layout was conceived as the result of clearly formulated ideas. Topography and the needs of the individual site determined the shape of the whole and the arrangement of the compounds. The origin of the typical Roman city plan cannot be found in these neolithic settlements. It was derived from the Etruscan ritual and partly influenced later by Greek contacts emanating from Southern Italy.

As previously observed, the instrument of Roman expansion was settlement. And just as this expansion proceeded simultaneously on the civil and military level, so the structure and shape of the settlement in general and the settlement units in detail were a mixture of civic and military planning. The early colonies, established by Rome to consolidate her conquest in Italy, were pertinent examples of this mutual adaptation of civil and military requirements. Cosa may serve as perhaps the most instructive illustration. It was an early colony of Rome about 85 miles northwest of its mother city. It was founded as a military colony in 273 B.C. between the sea and the coastal road, later the *Via Aurelia*, on a coastal headland near Orbetello.[24] The lime-

23. J. Bradford. *Ancient Landscapes*, *op. cit.*, pp. 93ff.
24. J. Bradford, *op. cit.*, pp. 227 ff.
F. E. Brown. "Cosa I, History and Topography." In: *Memoirs of the American Academy in Rome*, XX. 1951. *Passim.*
J. Ward Perkins. "Early Roman Towns in Italy," *Town Planning Review*, Vol. XXXVI, No. 3, 1955. *Passim.*

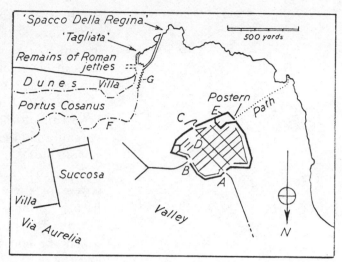

13. The Roman colony of Cosa founded in 273 B.C. A B C gates; D Forum; E Arx; F small temple; G cliff face, artificially scarped.

stone hill rises about 370 feet above sea level. The site was easily defensible yet not too difficult to approach—a choice typical of the earlier hilltop settlements in the Mediterranean world. Cosa may have housed about 2,500 to 4,000 families, or between 7,500 to 12,000 settlers.

Like the foundation of Paestum in the same year, its position on the coast reflects the importance that Rome attached to the development of her sea power. The strong walls enclosed an area of about 34 acres and their course followed the defensive contours of the terrain. Roads descended the slopes from the three gates. A street followed the circumference on the inside. The special interest of the layout of Cosa consists in the combination of the irregular circuit with its three gates and the gridiron plan of the streets which were also adapted to the natural contours running northeast to southwest and northwest to southeast. Their layout was related to the gates, the position of which was determined by the topographical conditions and by the situation of the *forum* and the *arx* (D and E in the sketch plan). Here at Cosa military considerations followed the usual principles of selecting a site that was easily defensible by its natural configuration. However, this changed during the next centuries.

As an illustration of this transformation, Ward Perkins compares Cosa with Augusta Praetoria (Aosta) in Piedmont, founded about 24 B.C. as a Roman military post by Augustus. It occupied an area of roughly 2,170 by 1,700 feet with twenty square towers, subdivided by a rectangular grid of streets. Such a town and the typical camp resembled each other so closely that one may be inclined to assume that a Roman town was merely a civil version of the military *castrum* from which it took over the basic principles of the layout. However, this is not correct; rather it was the reverse procedure. Such was apparently also the opinion of

45

Polybius when he said that the plan of the *castrum* imitated that of the town: "thus the whole camp forms a square, and the way in which it is divided up by streets and the general internal disposition give it a layout like that of a city" (VI. 31. 10). In any case, the basic principles on which city and camp were planned date back, as Ward Perkins points out, to a period long before the Roman army had evolved even the rudiments of a system of field engineering. If we may believe Frontinus (*Strategematicon* IV. 1.14), "It was the capture of the camp of Pyrrhus, in 275, that first inspired the Romans to develop an orderly system of their own." In the light of this evidence "we can hardly doubt that, in the first instance, it was the camp that borrowed from the town, rather than the town from the camp."

In the course of time field engineering made rapid strides and the establishment of a camp became standard practice. It is obvious that in the later periods of Roman expansion this could not fail to influence the planning of the towns. But the basic principle of Roman city planning "had been established *independently* long before (at least as early as the fourth century B.C.)."

Most of the earlier colonies which were founded by Rome were situated on hilltops in good defensive positions and may often have occupied the sites of the native settlements preceding them. But the more Rome's influence increased and her domain grew, the more the need for military roads became obvious. Strategic points on these roads had to be guarded by military installations. Thus the choice of site was restricted and it was impossible, in many cases, to rely primarily on naturally well-protected sites. As examples in this connection, Ward Perkins cites Interamna Lirenas, founded in 312 B.C. in the plain of the river Liris near Cassino, and the *castrum* at Ostia.

The real test on a large scale came when Roman expansion reached Northern Italy and the Po Valley. Here the country was flat, and good protective sites were rare. Moreover, the experience of the army was of considerable advantage—its camps could easily be pitched quite independently of the nature of the terrain. The city planners who had to build the later colonies followed the example of the army. They adopted the military principles of layout, a procedure that did not demand any ingenuity or particular mental effort. But as Ward Perkins remarks,

The surprising thing is, not that Roman architects were ready to adopt so logical and convenient a pattern, but that, once it had been adopted, they should have been so ready to depart from it, often seemingly for the most trivial reasons. Roman towns that were completely rectangular in plan, like Aosta or Torino, were by no means common.

When a new colony was founded, a large territory was added and subdivided among the settlers according to a definite scale of allotment. This *ager centuriatus* or *limitatus* was assigned to *coloniae* and sometimes also to *municipia* and even *fora* (local centers of commerce and jurisdiction; country towns). The assignment of land to new foundations was not unusual; it has very often happened in most countries and at all times. Nor was it uncommon for the land to be subdivided among the settlers according to a certain scale. But where the medieval division of land was adapted, so far as possible, to the varying quality of the soil in order to guarantee an equal share to every settler in the productive capacity of the land, the Romans adhered to a rigid system which they superimposed on the natural landscape without regard to the quality of the units. This difference between the Roman and the medieval procedures reflects the eternal contrast between organization and organism, between drawing-board planning and functional adaptation to the environment.

The Roman grid system was disingenuously applied to town and country alike. The division of the land assigned to a new colony was part of the founding of the town itself. The medieval system was like the layout of the towns—functional and individualistic, irregular and seemingly unsystematic. However, both were proof that town and country were conceived as a unit and that neither could live without the other. This partition of land, the Roman centuriation, was applied in its origin to newly conquered territories and imposed with ruthless logic upon the natural landscape.[25]

The more common unit of the grid system was a square, the *centuria quadrata* with a side of 20 *actus* (776 yards) and an area of 200 *jugera*.[26] The regular division of the land by *limites* intersecting at right angles continued into the towns. In both cases these demarcation lines were called *cardo* and *decumanus*, and so far as possible both were similarly oriented, the *cardo* from north to south and the *decumanus* from east to west. As width of the two primary roads, the *Cardo Maximus* and the *Decumanus Maximus*, 20 and 40 Roman feet were recommended. Hyginus, surnamed Gromaticus (from *groma*, a surveyor's measuring rod), a writer on land surveying who lived under Trajan (c. A.D. 103), mentions in a treatise that the two principal roads should, so far as possible, originate within the town or at least as near to the urban area as possible.

The foundations of the second century tended to be situated on level terrain in contrast to the older towns such as Cosa and Alba Fucens, where the gridiron plan was imposed upon a hillside. But this type—the town in the plain on level ground—presupposed safety and peace. It became so much the expression of

25. J. Bradford, *op. cit.*, pp. 145-78.
26. A *jugerum* corresponded to an area that could be plowed by a man with two oxen in one day. It equaled about 5/8 acre.

the *Pax Romana* that it was introduced in the provinces not only for the *coloniae* but also, during the imperial period, for the *civitates,* the main centers of the provincial tribal societies. Finally, in the first century the type of the "level town" was generally accepted as the most suitable solution. The settlements laid out on the military roads in the preceding epochs were mostly *fora,* market towns—provisioning stations where the inhabitants of the neighboring mountain villages sold their produce to the Roman traders for the armies marching through their region.[27]

After the final pacification of Italy the need for the founding of military colonies ended. A genuine resettlement policy began which was to heal the devastations of the wars with the now subjugated tribes. But it took a certain time for the state to shed its militaristic-political mentality and to develop an efficient state-guided settlement policy. Thus, in the earlier stages the "squatters"—those who came first—could not be prevented from occupying the *ager publicus,* nor could delays in the payment of taxes and other fees be avoided. But gradually the State asserted its rights and duties, and the application of centuriation became increasingly common as a convenient and administratively simple instrument of the official agrarian policy. It is obvious that only the State could create and apply such a system sanctioned by religion and custom, whose ritual lived on long after its original meaning had begun to fade.

Urbanization was the instrument of the expansion of the Roman Empire, and the intimate interdependence of city and country was the foundation on which the structure of settlement rested and grew. Of the innumerable cities which were founded by Rome a vast number survived the decline and fall of the Empire and became once more focal points of civilization during the early Middle Ages when the great migrations spread over Europe from West to East. We can still follow the organic growth of numerous frontier camps into villages, towns, and cities and in some cases the development of an urban hierarchy: a big city would administer not only the surrounding country but also a number of townships. The apex of this pyramid was the city of Rome, "the loveliest sight on earth," if we believe Horace's enthusiastic description or the eulogy of Aristides. According to him the Empire is a realm of cities and the Roman world a universal festival. The earth has been transformed into a vast pleasure garden. But we have to ask: for whom? Certainly not for the urban masses and the slaves or for the rural population. The two nations, the rich and the poor, faced each other over an ever-widening abyss. The pleasure garden was reserved for the rich; the poor had to be content with the annual vote at

27. E. Kirsten. "Römische Raumordnung in der Geschichte Italiens." In: *Historische Raumforschung II,* Forschungsberichte der Akademie für Raumforschung und Landesplanung. 1958. P. 56. *Passim.*

the elections, and with bread and circuses. Outwardly the cities had a full life but they were by no means independent units of the imperial organization. They were, as in China, the nodal points of the imperial administration and as such never really free as the Free Cities of the Middle Ages had been. Their great contribution was their role as the protagonists of the spread of Roman settlement but not of freedom and free thinking. They were not the seats of creative rebellion so characteristic of the rising burgher class of the medieval cities. And yet without them the periods following the fall of the Roman Empire and the Dark Ages would never have attained the cultural and material eminence on which our own achievements are founded.

Roman city planning was so intimately connected with the political and military expansion and organization of the Empire that this fact alone explains the paucity of ideas and the sterility of spatial conception that dominated almost all Roman cities. The men responsible for the foundation of new cities were hard-boiled realists—politicians, administrators, and soldiers. They were far-sighted and intelligent according to their lights, yet not

The City

14. Roman soldiers constructing a camp. Relief from the Column of Trajan.

inspired dreamers who would search for new solutions to a problem that (as they believed) had found its rational and final formulation. Theirs was basically a utilitarian attitude. Once a workable principle had been established they stuck to it, adapting it in detail to different conditions but retaining it in general. This was the exact opposite of the Greek response to the challenge of their historical mission with their unsurpassed gift for spontaneous and individual solutions. Roman cities were constituent parts of a rigidly organized empire; the main task was to represent the grandeur and power of Rome. Greek cities were independent entities competing with each other in political, cultural, and artistic achievements. Their symbolic significance was freedom of action and independence and an ever-renewed readiness to adapt the urban space to changing topographical realities. The symbolic importance of Roman cities was their role as outposts of Rome, and their stereotyped ground plans were true expressions of the military spirit that had made Rome mistress of the world.

The *castrum* or military camp was the principal and perhaps the only contribution of Rome to the art of city planning. Its general layout and internal arrangement were repeated *ad infinitum* with a few variations that did not alter the essence of this rigid conception. This strict adherence to the same principle is understandable, for the foundation of new towns in conquered lands was above all a military task. The *castrum* was a solution common to all colonial foundations at all times and in all countries. Its regular layout was the best and simplest device under conditions demanding a combination of safety and convenience.

The ideal form of the *castrum* was a square whose sides were oriented toward the four cardinal points of the compass. In the middle of each side was a gate connected with the others by the principal streets. These streets met in the center of the camp. Since the west, the direction of sunset, was regarded as fraught with danger, the west gate was often missing. At the intersection of the two principal streets the *forum* was situated with the main buildings, the *praetorium*, the headquarters of the camp; the *augurale,* the altar of the camp; the *tribunal,* a bank of earth on which the commander took his stand when he addressed the troops or administered justice; and the *quaestorium,* the quarters of the paymasters.[28] The camp was fortified with a rampart and a ditch the construction of which always began before the tent of the general was pitched. Inside a road, the *pomerium,* about 30 feet wide, ran parallel to the line of the ramparts. The walls were sacred and no one was allowed to touch or repair them without permission from the pontiffs.[29]

In the course of time this system underwent many changes in

28. For further details, see pp. 16-19.
29. N. D. Fustel de Coulanges. *The Ancient City.* 1956. P. 138 and *passim.*

15. Roman soldiers loading boats on the Danube with a Roman fortress in the background. Relief from the Column of Trajan.

detail but the principle always remained the same whether it was a *castrum aestivum* (summer camp) or a *castrum stativum* (permanent camp). A circular form was ruled out because this would make it easier for the enemy to invest the camp; a square or a rectangle would force him to spread his troops and disperse them over a longer perimeter. Settlements of traders, craftsmen, and camp followers grew up outside the walls along the roads. These places, called *canabae*—shops or booths—often developed into permanent settlements—*vici*—or towns. Their main function was that of a market but in many cases they were also used for the accommodation of the families of the soldiers.

The foundation of a town proceeded in conformity with a religious ritual.[30] This consisted of four stages. The first duty of the founder was to select the site. This task, called the *inauguratio,* was determined by consulting the will of the gods through

30. See pp. 18-19.

the *augures* who interpreted the omens given by birds. It was a procedure not too dissimilar from the geomancy of the Chinese, which was also applied for the foundation of a town. Then followed the *limitatio,* the fixing of the boundaries of the town, accomplished by sacrifices and the lighting of a sacred fire of brushwood through which each of the companions of the founder had to leap as a symbol of purification. The next stage was the *orientatio,* which determined the *decumanus* running from west to east. The final rite, the *consecratio,* placed the town under the protection of the gods. This elaborate ritual, always observed when a new town was founded, was an additional reason why the original principle of the layout was not changed—at least not fundamentally. The Greeks also consulted the gods—that is, the Oracle of Delphi—when they had to choose a site for a new town. But such consultation was regarded as sufficient. Greek city builders did not adhere to a rigid formula that might stifle spontaneity or originality in the layout of a new town. The Romans, on the other hand, clung to a sacred formula that restricted their freedom and forced them to an endless repetition of the same plan. They preferred standardization to spontaneity and change. The sacred formula became for them the rule; it was a guarantee against arbitrariness and therefore against mistakes. Both military considerations and religious orthodoxy aimed at unifying principles. Both were, therefore, responsible for the paucity of new ideas and the preservation of the original principle of the layout of Roman towns during centuries.

As to the internal structure of Roman towns certain features were derived from Greece. The *forum* is a direct successor of the *agora,* if for no other reason than that a public meeting place was an indispensable need for every town. Hellenistic elements, especially the arcaded streets, comprised another contribution that had migrated from the East to Italy, just as the Greek language of form was adopted though modified to a more-or-less formalistic or decorative treatment of outer and inner surfaces of the buildings.

The genuinely great and independent innovation of the Romans was the discovery of space. This element was most evident in their large public buildings, in the *Thermae* of Caracalla, the *Basilica* of Maxentius, and the Pantheon. A new dimension was added to the small scale and "spaceless" Greek conception. But this change did not extend to city planning, which lagged behind this development. Possibly only the sequence of the *fora* and the arcaded streets in their more elaborate version show a faint awareness of this new attitude. However, unified and large-scale compositions which reveal a new sense and new idea of space were missing. The private dwelling houses were introvert built around an inner courtyard, the *atrium*; the later tenements, erected in Rome and a few large cities, were the same nondescript anomalies we still see all too often in our cities today. Four types of building blocks may be distinguished: those with low *atrium* houses, with and without shops, *tabernae,* opening on to the streets; blocks only with *tabernae*; and blocks with multistoried buildings.

It is characteristic and understandable after what has been explained about the limitation of Roman towns that the extension of a town remained to the Romans a sealed book. The city proper would have been laid out on the usual regular pattern, but the suburbs would grow haphazardly without any orientation or limitation. The problem of an organic growth and inclusion of the outlying parts did not exist for Roman city planners. They were exclusively concerned with the preservation of the original town plan, made sacrosanct by religious tradition.

The other great achievements of Rome were the sheer quantity of her new town foundations and the monumental scale of most of the public buildings. Both were tangible symbols of the grandeur of Rome, of her purposeful energy and undeviating faith in her destiny. Qualitatively the results were less impressive, and there is no reason to regret the disappearance of innumerable towns and buildings. The new monumentality was paid for by an‘equally monumental neglect of the quarters for the urban proletariat and the quality of the public buildings themselves. They were crude, mass-produced showpieces appealing to the parochial pride while deluding the people into a superficial contentment with their lot—a life circumscribed by slums. The theatrical monumentality of Rome stood in striking contrast to the intimate human scale of Greek architecture and city planning. It was the contrast between imperialist ostentation and democratic common sense and awareness of human values. Roman city planning, rigid in spirit and form, was unable to cope with the tremendous changes brought about by the social and economic urban structure. Its limitation and its failure to adapt itself to changing conditions were its curse. It stagnated and finally disappeared when more youthful peoples overwhelmed the Roman Empire.

However, all this should not lead us to believe that all Roman towns were built on a regular ground plan. Rome itself is the most representative example of this other type. It was never planned. It simply grew. The story of *Roma quadrata* is a legend, nothing else. It never existed in reality. Apart from Rome there were numerous other towns—tribal and market centers, harbor towns and posting stations and small settlements at the intersection of roads—which had never been planned but had grown in accordance with local and contemporary needs. Were these towns the forgotten outsiders untouched directly by the Roman advance? Many of them were older than the Roman colonies and as such retained their original structure. But others were so located that a stereotyped rigid layout could not be used. In any case they were not typical Roman towns so far as their ground plan was concerned. They remained outside the main stream of Roman city planning.

Roman pragmatism was not favorable to theoretical speculations about the physical and social structure of cities. The only treatise containing references to city planning is Vitruvius' *De Architectura Libri Decem*. As the title implies, this work is primarily concerned with architecture. His remarks on the layout of cities are disingenuous and cannot be regarded as an indispensable contribution to the art of city building. His town plan is hardly more than a diagram dominated by an undue preoccupation with the directions of the prevailing winds. This concern resulted in a radial arrangement of the main streets and a demand that the market square be in the center of an inland town and in a seaport near the harbor. Walls with towers enclosed this town. Circular walls were regarded as preferable because the defenders were in a better position to see the attackers: towns with projecting corners were, according to Vitruvius, "difficult to defend because a corner protects the enemy more than the citizens." (I. 5.) Vitruvius' Ideal City is far from being Ideal; if it proves anything at all it is his lack of social awareness and responsibility and his dry and rigid approach to a problem of such overwhelming complexity as an urban community. His scheme completely neglects a discussion of the life of the common people. He is almost exclusively concerned with the provision and arrangement of the houses for the upper classes and with formalistic and very general suggestions on the building program which should be organized in three groups—sacred, public, and private buildings.

Streets and Houses. The Roman street system was based on the cross formed by the *decumanus* and the *cardo*. The streets crossed each other at right angles and the gridiron plan was, so far as possible, the basic principle of the layout. Exceptions did exist —for instance, in Pompei and Ostia and above all in Rome—but even in these cases the rectangular street net was used within the individual quarters. The average width of the main streets, of the *decumanus* and *cardo*, was about 36 and 18 feet respectively. But in general there were no hard-and-fast rules; the sidewalks, if there were any, differed in width according to whether or not

Elements of City Planning

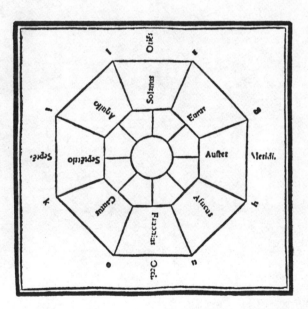

16. **Town plan by Vitruvius.**

54

they had arcades, apart from the open footpaths. At Roman Corinth, for example, the main street was 80 feet wide, consisting of the roadway with 24 feet, the two footpaths each with 10 feet, and the two arcades each with 18 feet. The footpaths rose about a foot and a half above the roadway. Flagstones of the same height permitted crossing from one side to the other. The Laws of the Twelve Tables (451-450 B.C.), *Duodecim Tabulae,* distinguished three categories of roads: the *via* for vehicles with a minimum width of 8 feet; the *actus* for animals—4 feet; and the *iter* for pedestrians—2 feet. In most cities traffic was subject to regulations. The use of private carriages in the center of cities was prohibited or permitted only during certain hours. Caesar decreed that no vehicles were to be used in the streets of Rome during the first ten hours of the day. Delivery vans, except those for public services, were excluded from the center of Rome between sunrise and sunset. Goods were unloaded during the night. Members of the nobility and wealthy people were carried in litters by their slaves.

Colonnades were first used in the Hellenistic period in Asia Minor and Syria to line processional streets. When this custom spread throughout the Roman Empire it was increasingly applied to other streets as a convenient protection against sun and rain and as a welcome opportunity for cheap ostentation and embellishment. Artistically the quality of the colonnades was mediocre but a new and important architecural element was introduced, changing the character of the streets from a mere ribbon of traffic to two clearly separated vehicular and pedestrian movements. This functional distinction satisfied the needs of the growing traffic in the main streets and permitted the pedestrians to linger on under the colonnades without being disturbed by the moving vehicles. The advantages of this system were obvious. It spread to the Byzantine world and from there to the towns and cities of the Middle Ages, to Central Europe, Spain, and other parts of Europe.

As in our modern cities there were two main types of houses in Rome and in some, by no means in all, provincial towns: the *domus,* the one-storied house built around the *atrium,* and the *insula,* the tenement house, with several stories. The first category was "an aristocratic minority compared with the *immensus numerus insularum* (to speak with Suetonius, *Nero* 38)."[31] The origin of the *domus* can be traced back to the Etruscans while the tenement house developed from a row of *tabernae*—that is, shops each with a door toward the street or a courtyard. These *tabernae,* with their workshops and living rooms often in a mezzanine, were dwellings for the urban proletariat and petty

31. A. Boëthius. "Urbanism in Italy." *Proceedings of the Second International Congress of Classical Studies, Copenhagen, 1954.* Vol. IV, p. 90.
   The meaning of the term *insula* is controversial. According to the dictionaries it is defined as either apartment house or apartment—not as building blocks, which were called *vici.* However, this latter term is also not quite clear. Its original meaning was a house and later a collection of houses, a street or a section of a town.

tradesmen. According to Boëthius these tenement towns with their combinations of shops, workshops, and flats were a local Roman creation which distributed production and trade all over the towns. It was a social and economic system fundamentally different from the separation of residential and bazaar quarters in the Orient and in a more rudimentary form in Greece and the Hellenistic world. Boëthius suggests four types of planning of these standardized tenement houses:

1. One row of *tabernae* with upper stories.
2. Two rows of *tabernae* built back to back with upper stories.
3. Rows of *tabernae* around an inner courtyard or establishment such as *horrea,* storerooms, or *thermae.*
4. Great houseblocks combining *tabernae* toward the streets and inner courts with peristyles in two or three stories.

Apart from these types there were *atrium*-houses with *tabernae* —for instance, at Pompei and Herculaneum—and also tenement houses with *tabernae,* staircases to the upper stories and a passage from the street to the *atrium* or peristyle in the inner part of the dwellings.

In imperial times the larger Roman *insulae* were often the joint property of several owners. These *partes insulae* were always divided into vertical sections. This arrangement—that is, the joint ownership—was not too dissimilar to the present-day cooperative ownership of apartment houses. Boëthius draws attention to the fact that

the Roman tenement houses were parts of a collective system, where most of the social life, entertainments and baths, and a good deal of the food and personal comfort were provided outdoors, by the town-community. They cannot be understood without those appendages, which as a matter of fact covered a remarkably large part of the essential needs of domestic life.

The technical quality of the tenement houses was bad. As we have seen, they were structurally unsound and often collapsed, but they were a lucrative source of profit for the speculators and jerry builders. Their height was restricted by Augustus to 70 Roman feet and reduced by Trajan to 60 feet. Numerous regulations and bylaws tried to curb the excesses of private enterprise with their disregard for safety and even the minimum standards of domestic amenities. There were laws to reduce the danger of fires; to prevent the deterioration of buildings through the removal of decorative parts to other towns; and to further the restoration of dilapidated houses. After the great fire of Rome in A.D. 64 the *Lex Neronis de modo aedificiorum* was promulgated. It demanded the following:

1. Renewed and strict adherence to the *Lex Julia,* according to which the maximal height of houses should not exceed 70 feet.
2. Isolation of newly built houses and the abolition of common party walls.
3. Increase of the *ambitus,* the space between two adjoining buildings, to 10 feet.
4. Preservation of an open area on every *insula.*
5. A veranda at the façade of a building from whose flat roof the upper stories could easily be reached in case of fire.

Vespasian issued a decree according to which any citizen could appropriate a building site if its owner failed to rebuild his dilapidated and destroyed house after a certain time, provided that the new owner assumed the responsibility of rebuilding it.

However, despite all these attempts to regulate the building activities, especially in the metropolis, the bad quality of the tenement houses and the disregard of the needs of the masses persisted. The pressure of the overflowing population and the scarcity of space proved stronger than the best intentions of the emperors—the more so as these very tangible factors were reinforced by the profit motive and lack of social awareness and responsibility. All in all, the living conditions of the urban masses of the ancient world under the rule of Rome were similar to those of today in numerous big cities in all parts of the world. And just as today the real quality of city life cannot be judged by a few showpieces, by imposing city halls, commercial centers and large squares, so the cities of antiquity should not be evaluated by their public buildings, their palaces, *fora,* basilicas, and triumphal arches. This proposition may at first appear to be self-evident. But unfortunately it is not always self-evident to city planners or laymen. To them the history of ancient city planning, and for that matter of city planning in general, is sometimes nothing more than a survey of monumental buildings, streets, and squares. Fortunately this mistaken attitude is changing slowly. There may even be a modicum of truth in it because public buildings and other works were constructed more solidly and therefore had a better chance to survive. But the common people were, and always will be, the most formative factor of city life and of the physical appearance of an urban community, even if their abodes have a shorter lifetime than the ostentatious edifices erected by emperors, feudal lords—or bank presidents.

Ideally the *forum* should be situated in the center of a town, at the intersection of the *decumanus* and the *cardo.* This principle was observed in many cases, though not in all. According to Vitruvius (V. 1) the shape of the *forum* should be oblong, its best proportion being 2:3, and two-storied arcades should surround it. It should not be so small that people would have to jostle each other, yet not so large that they would feel lost. In this demand something of the Greek preoccupation with the preservation of the human scale was still reverberating, of Aristotle's dictum that the *polis* should house "the largest number which suffices for the purpose of life and can be taken in at a single view." But this ideal conception was soon swept aside by the irrepressible passion of the Romans for monumentality and bigness. There were *fora civilia,* civic centers for assemblies and religious rituals with public buildings, temples, and administrative establishments; and the *fora venalia,* the market squares for trade and commerce where all sorts of goods were sold and bought. As in the Middle Ages, a certain specialization developed. There was a *forum olitorium* for vegetables; a *forum boarium* for cattle; a *forum suarium* for pigs; a *forum piscarium* for fish; a *forum macellum* for meat; a *forum pistorium* for grain and bread; and a *forum nundinarium,* the weekly market. However, in most towns the number of markets was small and sometimes a special market square did not exist at all—for instance, in the eastern part of the Empire, at Antiochia, where selling and buying was carried on all over the town; or at Damascus where the main street served as market. The colonnades of the Eastern cities were the ideal place for the merchants and traders who, like their medieval successors, used them as offices or for exhibiting their goods.

In the cities of Italy [reports Vitruvius (V. 1)], it was an old custom to arrange gladiatorial combats in the *fora.* It was, therefore, necessary to increase the intervals between the columns [the *intercolumnia*] to add rooms for money-changers under the colonnades [*argentariae tabernae*] and on the upper story balconies [*maeniana*] so that everything was well prepared for the convenience of the public as well as for the receipt of the payment of the rents [for the *tabernae* and *maeniana*].

The function of the *forum* as a place for public spectacles, which the spectators could follow from the colonnades and the balconies, belonged to a period prior to the building of amphitheaters erected for this particular purpose. But as long as a *forum* was used for these performances its whole area was kept free. There were no statues, no altars, and no temples within the precincts proper. The *forum* was then something similar to the *plaza mayor* in the larger cities of Spain which were also empty and where the spectators could look down from the galleries and enjoy either a civic spectacle or the sight of heretics burning at the stake.

In contrast to Greece where streets touched the *agora* almost always tangentially—for example, at Miletus and Priene—Roman *fora* were often surrounded on all four sides by principal streets or approached by streets penetrating them at the middle of the long or short sides, sometimes through a triumphal arch. Here was an entirely different concept of the relationship of square and streets. It originated in the location of the *forum* at the intersection of the *decumanus* and *cardo*—the *tetrapylon* was another reminder of this origin—and in general in the fundamentally different Roman attitude towards city planning: The ground pattern of streets crossing each other at right angles was the primary factor and the building blocks were a mere residue whose shape and size were determined by the rigid layout of the street ribbons. Consequently, streets and squares formed an organic unity and a coherent and integrated pattern of communication.

But the primary importance of the streets as an element of city planning had more than purely practical consequences. It led to the discovery of the axis as an aesthetic factor which would enhance the monumentality of the architectural composition, as well as to the introduction of the perspective view. This was a natural by-product of the regularly laid out city plans which demanded a clear and preconceived conception of the city as a whole, and therefore a certain amount of planning. It was always inherent and implicitly accepted wherever the street pattern was the primary concern of city builders, although they may not even have been aware of these implications. The essence of a straight street is movement and an uninterrupted view which intrinsically contains the basic elements of a perspective: In appearance the horizontal lines made by rows of houses seem to converge with increasing distance while the houses themselves become smaller.

From these elementary, inherent, and spontaneous perspective effects to the deliberate creation of a vista with a definite *point de vue* at the end is but a step. The Romans with their innate sense for organization, systematic layout, and monumental ostentation understood these possibilities and responded to the challenge raised by their regular street pattern. Their sense of order, their passion for public magnificence however shallow and theatrical, their deep-rooted conviction that it was their mission to spread the idea and the power of the Roman Empire to all parts of their realm and to symbolize its grandeur through imposing architectural feats including the erection of triumphal arches, pompous public buildings, and grandiose avenues—all these character traits produced the preconditions for monumental perspectives. But these perspectives were static, arrested, limited, without tensions. It was still a far cry from the passionate excitement of the vistas of the Baroque with their search for infinity. And yet what a contrast to the more egalitarian, spontaneous, and unpretentious city planning of the Greeks, for whom this sort of monumentality would have been anathema!

Nothing is perhaps more symptomatic of the diametrically opposed Greek and Roman attitudes to the relationship of streets and buildings than the tangential approach of streets toward public buildings and squares in Greece and the axial approach of the Romans. From tangent to axis—this antithesis of two basic architectural conceptions says more about the contrasting mentality of these two civilizations than all learned treatises on stylistic differences. The symbol of Rome was the triumphal avenue leading through a triumphal arch to a monumental edifice. The symbol of Greece was the processional way winding between religious shrines and altars up to the *acropolis* with its temples or through the sacred precincts seemingly without any system or rigidity to a public square which it entered almost casually. Or going further back in history we may refer to the long, stately axes of the Egyptian temples with their symmetrical repetition of similar elements. Through the alley of Sphinxes, through gates, over ramps at every entrance, through forecourts, and through a forest of columns in the great halls, through rooms growing darker, lower, and narrower, the way leads eventually to the Holy of Holies, accompanied throughout by an endless sequence of reliefs and paintings. It was like a gradual withdrawal from the surrounding world. What a difference between this axial conception—this telescopic narrowing—and the monumental axes of the Romans with their worldly realism and their crude and boastful emphasis on material achievements!

The Pantheon is the most perfectly balanced building in the history of architecture. Its height is equal to its diameter and the central opening in the dome sheds an evenly distributed light over all parts of the interior. There is no fundamental difference between this solution and a beehive hut by an African tribe. The Pantheon is really a gigantic cave, and the space enclosed by the exterior shell is not static but stagnant. It is a space without tension; as such it is a symbol of the Roman attitude to the problem of space. Space as an activated "building material" did not exist for the Romans. They were not aware of space as a sensation, as an all-pervading element of architectural composition. The space of the Pantheon—and for that matter of Roman buildings in general, and of city planning—was "a perceptual space at the sensorimotor level"; it was a topological experience without a consciousness of space. "Even a temple can be built as an imposing mass and express no awareness of a contained space.[32] Yet the difference between the Pantheon and a Greek temple is extraordinary. The Greek temple was a sculpture and the *cella* merely a utilitarian room for the statue of the god. It was dark and received light only through the door. The Pantheon represents the next stage of development. It was not a sculpture in

32. H. Read. *Icon and Idea*. 1955. P. 60.

space, but a "building composed as an interior"[33] where the spatial element as a creative function of architecture was not recognized.

It was the same with the streets and the siting of public buildings in a Roman town. Public buildings provided accents in the architectural composition. But there was no deliberate creation of space and space relations which would have released a sensation of space. This should be clear if we want to understand the particular type of Roman city planning, its architectural composition, and the emphasis on axial components in the general plan. Then we will realize how intimately even the later imposing vistas reflected the early principles of the *castrum* layout, focused on the center and in a perfect yet not dynamic equilibrium. Perhaps the most representative illustration of these tendencies were the imperial *fora* at Rome. Here we have a sequence of units, one following the other without any attempt at dynamic unification. It remains a side-by-side arrangement, an accretion. Compare this with the *fora*like group of squares at Nancy with their unsurpassed unity full of movement and tension, and the Roman contribution is revealed as what it is—a stale demonstration of monumentality.

The character of the origin of Roman city planning, its rigidity hallowed by religion and tradition, sowed the seeds of its failure to cope with the intricate problems raised by the growth of cities and by the change in their social and economic structure. There was no flexibility, no impulse to adapt the original layout to new conditions. Above all, there was no understanding of the possibilities of developing a new framework, a fresh yet organic continuity out of the existing and limited conception of the city. Roman art has been called soldier's art. Indeed it was often nothing more than a "trooping of the colors," the parading of the grandeur of the Empire which could not be successfully accomplished by spontaneous or improvised demonstrations. Such demonstrations, whether through architecture, city planning, or masses of human beings, had to be organized, had to be orderly, and had to function according to plan, like the movements of troops on the parade ground. Roman art was therefore eminently dedicated to the creation of a representative image of the Roman State, of its will to power and its consciousness of this power. This explains why Rome's artistic achievements were most original (though not particularly noble) in the field of public architecture and—above all—in the magnificent portrait busts of emperors, consuls, and other persons of public importance.

Roman art and city planning had a definitely masculine char-

33. C. R. Morey, *Medieval Art.* 1942. P. 260.

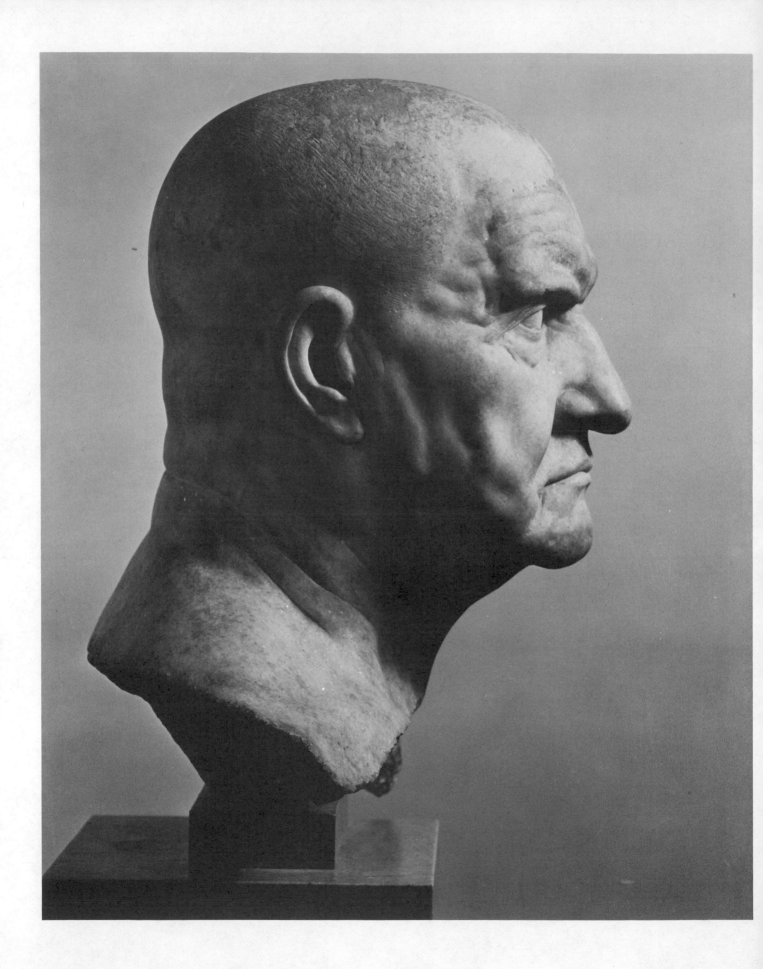

acter, lacking in sensuous adaptability and suppleness. Its sphere of influence reached no further than the outermost limits of the realm which the legions of Rome had conquered. This was in striking contrast to Greek art, with its polarity of male and female components remaining open to other civilizations and merging in a sonorous accord in Hellenistic times with the art of the Middle East and India. The paintings and sculptures of Gandhara are the outposts of this mutual adaptation. Greek art and the spirit of their *poleis* spread beyond the frontiers of Greek power. It was voluntarily accepted; and it accepted external influences voluntarily. Greek art was like a wonderful dew that sank softly down over other civilizations while Rome imposed her language of form and military city planners upon subject peoples. There was no mutual adaptation, only a deterioration to a second-rate and secondhand colonial art comparable to the Spanish art exported to the Americas.

Roman art did not experience, through its contact with other civilizations, a rebirth in a modified form as Greek art—for example in Pergamon, especially in the sculptures of the Pergamon altar. It was an either-or, an imposition of superficial forms. It remained at all times a form of propaganda directed by the State and a cult of bigness under the guise of cultural greatness and superiority. But this self-confidence, this all too unquestioning assurance, was nevertheless disintegrating from within. When the splendor of Imperial Rome was still at its zenith, when the palaces on the Palatine and the temples of the *forum Romanum* were still proclaiming the grandeur of the Empire, the catacombs of the Christians began spreading their underground passages and modest chapels in the very center of Roman power, undermining the visible symbols of this power and captivating the religious spirit of the people. A new era was beginning. When this new world, after many turbulent and insurgent centuries, was emerging, the Roman cities had disappeared and entirely new cities were coming into existence. A new urban culture had to be created out of the raw materials of human experience and aspirations.

17. *Opposite:* Roman portrait bust from the first century B.C.

CHAPTER 3

The General Setting

From the Middle Ages to the Baroque

IN THE YEAR 476 Romulus Augustulus, the last Roman emperor of the West, was deposed. In the following centuries Italy became more and more engulfed in the chaotic struggle of contending invaders. The cities of Northern Italy became the prey of ruthless conquerors hostile to urban civilization and contemptuous of the vanquished population. Gothic rulers were followed by Lombard and Frankish conquerors. In contrast to the Goths, the Lombards intervened actively and tyranically in the structural conditions of the subjugated regions. Italy was divided into three separate areas: the Kingdom of the Lombards, Ravenna, and Rome. When the Lombards had settled down they discovered that the cities and the fortified *castra* were excellent instruments for consolidating their rule over their new subjects and, at the same time, the best defense against external enemies. Thus one of the primary functions of the city as an offensive and defensive stronghold was recognized and used by the conquerors, a proof that certain elementary characteristics of urban settlement survived the centuries and continued to fulfill their original function independent of the particular demands of the time. King Rothari expressed this awareness not only in the *Edictus Langobardorum* which he promulgated at a diet held at Pavia in 643 but also by his actions. Several cities in Liguria which had opposed him, such as Genoa, were punished by degrading them to *vici* and destroying their walls: *"Muros earum usque ad fundamentum destruens, vicos has civitates nominari praecepit."* ("And destroying their walls down to the very foundation, he decreed that the cities be called villages.")[1]

The same punishment had been inflicted by the Spartans upon conquered city-states. Like the Lombards, the Spartans were primitive and ruthless warriors who knew only too well how to humiliate their enemies most painfully and to deprive them of their most cherished ideals. This attitude of the Lombards was a clear indication of the distinction between unprotected *vici* and walled-in *civitates* which enjoyed among other privileges a special truce. In this conception the ancient Roman idea of the sanctity of the walls was revived, and the Lombards who have been described as "the most savage of the savage barbarians used to living in dispersed small groups" acknowledged the city as a place with a special jurisdiction despite or perhaps because of their own antagonism to urban life and civilization. The continuity of development was maintained because the Italian cities and the urban population had survived the holocaust of the Great Migrations to a much greater degree than those north of the Alps. It is characteristic that the Germanic nobility continued to live in Italy in the countryside while the cities remained the refuge of the Italian population. Urban life was a long-established

---

1. E. Ennen. *Frühgeschichte der Europäischen Stadt.* 1953. P. 224. Also for the preceding and following remarks.
The Fourth Book of the Chronicle of Fredegar. Cap. 71.

custom in the Mediterranean region, and the cities remained an essential part of the medieval structure of settlement just as they had been in antiquity.

It is of the utmost importance to realize that in Northern Europe the cities had to be created *ab ovo,* as new focal points of the great west-east migrations, while in the South they did exist and survived the turmoil of the invasions in the face of considerable drawbacks. When after the Dark Ages Charlemagne established his empire it was a realm without cities, without roads, and without administrative institutions. He was an itinerant ruler and his castles remained temporary residences similar to the manor houses of the Germanic nobility, though on a grander scale. They were not fortified, or at best were situated near a simple walled-in *Burg.* Charlemagne did not interfere too much with the internal policy of the Italian kingdom. But by breaking up the larger fiefs of the Lombards he prevented the growth of feudalism or at least reduced it to a lesser role, thus indirectly conferring upon the cities certain advantages which they would have lost under a fully developed feudal system.

After the death of Charlemagne, Italy fell a prey to invasions from the north by Magyars and Huns and in the south by Greeks and Saracens. Anarchy, depression, and misery spread over the peninsula. The cities were pillaged and ravaged. Bishops and counts rivaled in usurping authority, at least within the precincts of their towns. The nobles withdrew from the urban communities and, following their old custom, built fortified castles in favorable positions in the neighborhood. This state of affairs lasted until Otto I, King of Germany, entered Italy and was crowned emperor in 962. He deprived the counts of the jurisdiction within the chief burghs and furthered municipal independence. The bishops and the citizens were freed from the rule of the counts and became directly dependent on the emperor. The fiefs were redivisioned and thus the power of the feudal lords was once more reduced.

The urban and rural population began to increase after the great decline during the Dark Ages. It has been estimated that the population of Italy was less than four million in the middle of the fourth century. At about 400, St. Ambrose described Bologna, Modena, Reggio, and other places in Aemilia as "corpses of half-ruined cities," and toward the end of the fifth century, Pope Gelasius called Aemilia and Tuscany almost uninhabited.[2] The decline of the population was evident in the smaller area enclosed by the city walls—for example, at Florence: the earlier wall had enclosed 32.1 acres, whereas the new one included only 22.2 acres. This decline may, however, have been attributable less to a general reduction of population than to a

2. J. C. Russell. *Late Ancient and Medieval Population.* Transactions of the American Philosophical Society. 1958. P. 73. *Passim.* Also for the following.

Dates of New Walls, Medieval Italy

City	Century				
	10	11	12	13	14
Bologna				1203	
Brescia			(2)		
Florence			1172		(1)
Lucca				1200	
Mantua				1242	
Parma				1250	
Pavia	(2)		(3)		
Piacenza			1139		
Pisa		1000	1156		
Pistoia			(2)		
Siena					(1)

The number within parentheses is the number of walls or large additions to walls built in the city in that century. The walls of Brescia and Pistoia were all built in the second half of the twelfth century.

Pre-Plague Population of Italy
(late thirteenth century)

Place	Population
Corsica, Sardinia	173,746
Sicily, 1240–1250	600,000
Naples, 1275	2,000,000
Papal States	1,447,846
Tuscany	730,160
Po Duchies	641,540
Genoa	300,000
Milan, etc.	1,000,000
Venice, etc.	1,500,000
Total	8,393,292

migration to the new hill towns. The plague of the sixth century probably reduced the population to less than three million by the year 600.

Toward the end of the eighth century and at the beginning of the ninth, an economic revival set in which seems to have been especially marked in the south. However, all population estimates for this period are vague and can give only an approximate idea of the demographic conditions. But, in general, it is safe to assume that Italy took part in the great increase in Western Europe between the middle of the tenth century and the middle of the fourteenth. The decline in population after the fall of the Roman Empire had reduced the size of the cities. It took a considerable time before the population increase "filled up the cities again and created suburbs outside of the Roman walls."[3] The table shows that new walls were built mostly between 1150 and 1250.

By the year 1200, the number of inhabitants of Italy had surpassed the population of Roman Italy, estimated at about seven million. It may have been over eight million at the end of the 13th century. The estimated distribution of the population according to regions can be seen from the second table.

The feuds between the emperors and the popes which filled the first centuries of the Middle Ages benefited the cities. It strengthened their self-reliance and their autonomy. Their administration was headed by consuls whose original task was to protect the lower classes. Gradually these magistrates gained in importance with the growing political maturity of the communes and at the same time became representatives of the urban districts, the *portae*. They were the leaders of the urban militia and of the fleet, and the chief negotiators in all matters concerning neighboring cities. In the course of time they grew in stature and influence. Popes and emperors had to turn to them when they wanted to enlist support of a city in their favor. The consuls were assisted by a deliberative assembly, the *credenza*, consisting of members of the most privileged families, and by a *gran consiglio* of the burghers as well as by a large assembly, the *parlamento*, which included all adult inhabitants.

The discord between popes and emperors made Italy a house divided against itself. The cities were forced to take sides and party warfare was carried on within the city boundaries. This internecine struggle went on under Frederick Barbarossa and his successors. A permanent peace was concluded at Constance in 1183 between the Lombard League composed of many cities of Northern Italy and the imperialist faction. It confirmed the right of self-government of the communes by consuls and the right of

3. J. C. Russell, *op. cit.*, p. 109-10. Also for the tables.

warfare. These privileges were extended to the cities of Tuscany.

The next stage in ascendancy of the cities was marked by their fight against the nobility. It ended with the defeat of the nobles, who were absorbed into the urban community—although it did not eliminate their mutual feuds and their antagonism to the communes. The feudal lords had retained a substantial part of their power in spite of their growing weakness. Now they were gradually forced to leave their rural strongholds and to take up residence in the cities. They mortgaged their country seats and lands to wealthy citizens, entered the service of the communes as *condottieri,* and became military leaders in the fight of one city against another. But this change produced a new struggle, for it had not destroyed the bellicose spirit of the nobles. The clash between the warring factions was now carried on within the walls of the cities. The municipal government had to be strengthened. Instead of consuls, *podestà* were appointed with power over life and death and the command of the armed forces. It was a dictatorship with limitations: the *podestà* were elected only for a year, and were in all cases foreigners. The most brilliant figure of this period was the emperor Frederick II (1194-1250). His fight with the pope and his external wars exerted a strong influence upon the cities. He was at least a century ahead of his times—a man of the Renaissance weighed down by the realities of the Middle Ages. As patron of the arts and literature, a founder of universities, and a lawgiver he contributed greatly to Italian culture. As the cities were the seat of all cultural activities, they were the principal gainers of the rule of this enlightened monarch.

But the internal wars went on, though they decreased in violence at the beginning of the 14th century. Petty tyrants were followed by grand despots and the armies of the burghers were gradually superseded by levies of mercenaries. Diplomacy, cunning, and opportunism gained the upper hand over the more primitive (but possibly more honest) simple brutality and individual audacity of preceding periods. The great city-states of Milan, Florence, Venice, and Genoa and numerous smaller republics continued to assert their ascendancy not only in the political field but, above all, as agents of cultural dissemination. They emulated each other by employing the best artists of their time, by erecting churches and public buildings in accordance with the spirit of the epoch, and by opening the narrow gates which, during the Middle Ages, had obscured the vision of a new world slowly and painfully emerging from the unfathomed depths of man's spirit. Politically this period was the nadir of Italy as a state, but culturally it was a prelude to the Renaissance, a prologue to the undercurrent of change that was to usher in the modern age.

Thus the Creator spake to Adam: "Thou, constrained by no limits, in accordance with thine own free will, in whose hand We have placed thee, shalt ordain for thyself the limits of thy nature. We have set thee at the world's centre that thou mayest from thence more easily observe whatever is in the world. We have made thee neither of heaven nor of earth, neither mortal nor immortal, so that with freedom of choice and with honor, as though the maker and molder of thyself, thou mayest fashion thyself in whatever shape thou shalt prefer. Thou shalt have the power to degenerate into the lower forms of life, which are brutish. Thou shalt have the power, out of thy soul's judgment, to be reborn into higher forms which are divine."

These words are contained in the *Oration on the Dignity of Man* by Pico della Mirandola written probably in 1486 but printed only after his death, owing to his conflict with the Church. Pico attacked the traditional idea that man is distinguished from other creatures by his central place in the scheme of things or by his role as a microcosm of universal happenings. He held that the uniqueness of man is most creatively expressed in his universality, in his freedom from all fixed qualities, and in his power to participate in the essence of all other beings in accordance with his own free will. What is original and typically Renaissance about Pico's thought is not that he reiterated the praise of man as a universal being, but that he emphasized man's liberty, his independence of Nature and his reliance on his own majesty and creative vision. The words of Pico reveal an urge to understand human existence in a new spirit, to widen man's outlook and to break through the shell of medieval thought. For the leading spirits of the time the hallowed tradition of the past centuries was like a prison. Never before had they felt so lonely; never before had they sensed so strongly the excitement of the fresh air that surrounded their exalted position. These men, listening to their spiritual ancestors, accepted the heritage of antiquity as *studia Humanitatis*. As humanists and as intellectuals they were the harbingers of individualism and individual freedom. Their need was the prerogative of the few before it began to influence the thinking and feeling of the many. The period as a whole remained the awakening of a small minority, not yet of the people. But their zeal and sincerity laid bare for the first time in the history of the Occident the roots from which developed the lonely individual relying on his own conscience, dependent on himself despite the limitations and bonds still powerfully linked with the age of unquestioning belief.

The Italians of the early Renaissance had much in common with their contemporaries in other parts of Europe. Yet at the same time they differed fundamentally. These men who grew up in the Italian city-states with their emerging capitalistic *élan vital* were the direct heirs of antiquity—of its urbanity, enlightenment, and art. They lived in the same environment, within the same walls where the drama of ancient life had been enacted. They still sensed the impact of the innumerable forces that in the past had converged upon their old country, and were receptive to the rational and calculating legacy of the ancient world. It was the *Quattrocento* that eventually created the conditions for an awakening on a wider front and for the possibility of a collective experience of antiquity. The language of form in all its artistic manifestations was not a mere imitation but an independent continuation and reinterpretation of Graeco-Roman art. The new *poleis* competed with one another for the best architects, painters, sculptors, and artisans. These artists were rebels and experimentalists. They were both theoreticians and pragmatists. They developed a new science of space, a new technique of perspective, and new building methods.

But this artistic ascendancy was not accompanied by a corresponding political movement. On the contrary, although humanistic influences had fostered trends toward a common culture, language, and nationality, the country was headed for ruin. The sophisticated despotism of the princes so creative in the cultural field was politically a heavy liability. Its parochialism, ambitious immorality, and basic weakness were powerless toward the impact of external forces. Italy became the pawn of power politics in Spain, France, Germany, and Austria. The last remnants of independence were lost. Her destiny was in the hands of foreign monarchs. She changed masters repeatedly, and her people were traded like cattle without the slightest influence on or even knowledge of what was in store for them.

Only a few were aware of the real forces that rendered their country impotent and prevented a political consolidation. Men like Macchiavelli—who was not a mere theorist but a politician actively participating in the ups and downs of politics in his native Florence—finally came to the conclusion after some hesitation that the only salvation for Italy was to mobilize the same forces that had given rise to the new powerful national states of Western and Northern Europe. Only large political units ruled by absolute monarchs would be able to master the complexity of the disintegrating influences and lead to national unity and national freedom. In the *Principe* he therefore exhorts Lorenzo di Medici to use the opportunity offered "to a prudent and capable man to introduce a new system that would do honour to himself and good to the mass of people." And he continues: "It seems to me that so many things concur to favour a new ruler that I do not know of any time more fitting for such an enterprise" . . .

69

for "in order that the might of an Italian genius might be recognised, it was necessary that Italy should be reduced to her present condition. . . . This opportunity must not, therefore, be allowed to pass, so that Italy may at length find her liberator." The *Principe* remained, at least for the time being, an unpublished manuscript, a theoretical document of frustrated nationalism. It was published only five years after Macchiavelli's death in 1532. But it was symptomatic of the spirit of the time. It glorified the strong individual personality and expressed the need for an all-embracing understanding of the new scale of events, superseding the parochial attitude of the people and the rulers.

Macchiavelli's ideas were the typical product of the period. They were rational and realistic, concentrating on the essential. To this extent they were in accord with the artistic development of the time, which also concentrated on essential factors—essential in the sense of harmonic articulation of architectural grandeur and realistic representation of space. The scientific perspective with its vanishing points ushered in a new concept of space in which man recognized the reality of social space surrounding him. This space was as real as the painted figures with which artists like Masaccio filled it. It created an illusion of reality and of the physical interaction of man and environment. It is obvious that this new sense and this new idea of space, first elaborated and perfected in painting, soon spread to sculpture, architecture, and city planning—beginning in unrelated rivulets but finally swelling to a mighty stream that engulfed all the arts.

It is wrong to say that the Renaissance gave birth to modern individualism. In reality it merely created certain conditions favorable to the rise of a number of outstanding personalities. The man in the street remained untouched by the new trends that stirred the small minority of the cultural leaders. He still remained "bounded in a nutshell," deeply embedded in the narrow world of his city-state, restricted by his period and retarded by the demands of his religious outlook. What happened was more like the beginning of a revolt against the growing sterility and limitations of old institutions than a conscious embracing of a new mode of thinking and living. The really revolutionary deed of the High Renaissance was the cult of genius, the exalting of the extraordinary in human beings, and the awareness dimly felt by the masses that new rebellious forces were at work that would in time reshape the world.

The Baroque continued and intensified these trends. The daring *condottieri* and bellicose princes gave way to more domesticated politicians, connoisseurs and promoters of the arts. Ostentation and personal pride were the motive powers. The ideal of the medieval knight was to be rediscovered in the newly

70

forming aristocracy. Its members were, above all, courtiers who had lost the vitality of their predecessors. Jealously guarded privileges, rigid codes of customs, habits, and a wide gulf of morals and education separated the social classes. Popes and kings, clergy and the rich displayed their social standing and quality by the erection of buildings and by various schemes for the rebuilding of their cities. Yet not even the mightiest efforts and the most impressive splendor of the papal court and of the higher dignitaries of the Church could compete with the mass hysteria of the Middle Ages—the devout communal sacrifices and enthusiasm that drove whole populations, rich and poor, to work together on the building of a great cathedral as a testament of their passionate faith. Baroque art is torn between two irreconcilable aspirations—the urge to restore the intensity of the religious feeling of the past and the tendency to accept the worldly pretentiousness of the present.

The tensions called forth by this insoluble dilemma were aggravated by the decline of the Church and the ascendancy of the secular powers. The social classes drifted further apart, and the arts of architecture and city building became almost the exclusive privilege of the secular and ecclesiastical aristocracy. But beyond these social tensions far more important forces were at work. The finite concept of the universe had lost its meaning. The simple limitations of the Renaissance were disintegrating and the great adventure into spatial infinity began. The *maniera grande* of the Baroque had a far-reaching effect on the structure and appearance of the towns. The restful balance of Renaissance squares and streets gave way to movement and expansion, and the circle and square to the oval and rectangle. Practically every square became a forecourt, a preparation for one building dominating the configuration of all buildings surrounding it. The Baroque abhors space at rest, space as a complete and limited unity. Movement, diversity, coalescence, and development in depth were the media of expression.

The Baroque was the last period of great architecture and of great city planning. In an era of political impotence, confusion, political intrigues, rivalries, and ambitions the arts were almost the only gainers of the insurgent ideas that were undermining the legacy of the past. But however brilliant their achievements were it was a sunset though a sunset of an unsurpassed beauty. What came afterward was a decline, a gradual descent which eventually led to the artistic nadir of the 19th century. The forces that were to usher in the modern world and were to burst out in the Scientific Revolution of the 17th century absorbed gradually more and more of the creative potentialities of mankind. Italy at first took a leading part, but after this early eruption of scientific intuition began to fall behind. It is against this background, against the tremendous changes in all spheres of life from the Middle Ages to the beginning of the modern era, that the development of the cities of Italy has to be viewed and interpreted. Their social and economic structure, their physical appearance in general and in detail, and above all their spirit are like a seismographic chart on which the whole sequence of the transformation of urban life can be read.

Town and Country

As in other lands, town and country in Italy belonged together. During the Dark Ages the countryside was the main attraction for the invading barbarians. The towns were hostile, obstacles which had to be overcome. It was the quest for new living space that had driven the invaders from their old homes, not the search for a new, more civilized environment. The barbarians were unable to understand the idea of urban life. For them the towns were merely more densely settled parts of their new domain. Consequently the towns declined—especially in Northern Italy, which bore the brunt of the first and most furious phase of the invasion. But it was a decline that proceeded in steps: in quieter times the towns recovered when the countryside was left in peace and could supply the needed raw materials, or when the roads converging on them were free of enemies. However, when Italy had finally reached its nadir in the middle of the sixth century a general desolation spread over town and countryside alike. Their hatred and misunderstanding of the function of towns frequently prevented the barbarians from appreciating even their military value. Outside the walls that were still standing they built their watchtowers, the *gardinghi*, from which they dominated the country. Centuries later, the fortified castles of the Ghibellines fulfilled the same purpose, and the terms "lord of the castle" and "Lombard" were synonymous. Government from the countryside and fortified castles was consonant with Germanic ideas and customs which were directed toward the ruralization of the towns.

But under the surface the old Roman tradition of urban life persisted, and finally emerged again as soon as conditions became more favorable for the towns. The Middle Ages revived the Roman definition of a town: *civitas nihil aliud est quam hominum multitudo societatis vinculo adunata*[4]—the town is a community of men joined together by social bonds. And even more: a genuine *civitas* demands political independence and internal liberty in contrast to the unfortified villages and the fortified *castelli*.

4. Augustinus. *Civitas Dei*, 8.

Community life is a conception which we also know only in the monastic sphere. . . . For the Middle Ages, town and monastery were analogous attempts to counteract the misery of the time and the dangers of the century by an organized communal life. Both reflect heavenly orders, the monastery the paradise, the town the celestial city and the eternal Jerusalem.[5]

The more the development of the towns progressed the closer grew the bonds between the towns and their hinterland, the *contado*. Emperors and feudals tried for a long time to restrict the rights of the towns and to arrogate to themselves jurisdiction over the surrounding country, or to use force to achieve this end. The response of the towns to this challenge consisted in establishing small, carefully fortified places in remote districts in which the peasantry was concentrated and, at the same time, compelling the feudals to reside within the towns. In the statutes of Siena of 1262 it was decreed that every year one hundred families of the *contado* had to build houses in the town. For especially influential families, palaces were erected at the expense of the community, or a subsidy was granted for the building of a town house. In other cases at least one member of the family had to live one month each year in the town—a similar method was applied in Japan where the unruly nobles had to live for a certain time in the capital—which granted exemption from taxation but demanded military service.[6] However, those who moved to the towns did not lose the claim to their land according to civil law. The result was that the landed property was to a considerable degree in the hands of families who lived in the towns. Even the lower classes, the craftsmen and artisans, owned a field outside the walls.

In the course of time the urban communities almost appeared as a synoicism of landed nobles and at least at the beginning seemed to repeat the early formation of Roman towns. But the final result was different. The urbanized nobility of medieval Italy did not exclusively live on the income from its landed property, but very soon turned to commercial activities—especially to overseas trade. Thus the nobility merged with the *nouveaux riches* and the economic function of the towns gained preponderance, whereas in antiquity the religious, political, and administrative functions had been predominant. The absorption of these nobles into the economic and social life of the towns influenced the structure of agricultural production, which had become fairly well adapted by this time to the demands of the market, while from the 10th century on taxes formerly paid in kind were gradually being replaced by payments in cash. The assimilation of the Italian nobles to the merchants and their

5. W. Braunfels. *Mittelalterliche Stadtbaukunst in der Toskana.* 1953. Pp. 22 ff. Ample use has been made of this excellent study in the present chapter.
6. After W. Braunfels, *op. cit.,* p. 24.

political and economic participation in the urban life was one of the main factors distinguishing the southern from the northern and northwestern towns of Europe, where the urban patricians formed a class separated from the landed gentry by social barriers, by their urban way of life, and by their economic activities.[7]

The fortified hilltop villages—or "townlets" as they have been called—dating back to antiquity or the Middle Ages were known as *castello* or *borgo,* the former generally more strongly fortified than the latter. The great period of *castello* building lasted from the eighth century to the twelfth.[8] The procedure of the foundation was not too dissimilar from that in other countries. The *bastides* of Southern France come easily to mind, to mention one example. A feudal lord would attract the peasants of a district and promise some concessions to them in return for building a *castello.* Their houses and small plots were exempt from taxation and alienation. The size of these *castelli* differed considerably. In the neighborhood of Rome the average population was about 500. Matelica, in the Marches west of Ancona, had around the year 1300 roughly 8,000 inhabitants, together with those of the surrounding district. A *castello* such as Villafranca near Verona had 179 families at its foundation in 1185. The average *castello* in the hills near Bologna was very much smaller: It had ten to twenty houses. The residence of the lord with its tower—a veritable fortress in itself—called a *rocca,* was the dominating architectural feature, often accompanied by the tower of the commune. The *castelli* were protected by a wall and moat with one or two gates, in addition to the natural protection which the hilltop site afforded.

Villages without fortifications were always small, whereas agricultural towns often had more than 10,000 inhabitants. Isolated, dispersed farms were rare. They did not offer sufficient security in the turbulent time of the Middle Ages. From the 13th century onward residential fortified castles increased in Tuscany and in the neighborhood of Bologna. In many cases the lord of the *castello* removed the inhabitants by force or by cash settlement and turned the whole structure into a single *cassaro* for his own exclusive use. The inhabitants then built a new suburb, a *borgo,* outside the castle—for instance, at Passignano on Lake Frasimeno—or emigrated to another place. In the course of this process a certain concentration of population developed in or around existing towns. Apart from the policy of the feudal lords just described, this was the result of the usual movement to the towns, which were safer than the *castelli*, offered more attractions, a better life, and above all more freedom. This migration to the towns led to a considerable increase of the urban population in general and to the extension of the fortified town area.[9]

7. E. Ennen, *op. cit.,* pp. 262-67 and *passim.*
8. G. Mickwith. "Medieval Agrarian Society in its Prime." In: *The Cambridge Economic History of Europe.* Vol. 1. 1941. Pp. 323-43 and *passim.*
9. See tables, p. 66.

18. Hilltop village of Calcata, Latium.

The migration of peasants to the towns, however, should not be overestimated. In any case it should not be compared to the corresponding and far more widespread trend north of the Alps. Several reasons operated in Italy against a mass movement to the towns. First there was the reluctance of most towns to grant citizenship to immigrants before they had been members of the community for ten years.

Immigrants were not so much runaway "villeins" as the richer farmers and those free landless labourers whose movements are so hard to follow. On the whole, in fact, the disappearance of unfreedom was a process of secondary importance in Italian agrarian history. It did not increase the mobility of labour, for the free cultivator was, economically if not legally, as much bound to the soil as the unfree. Much more important was the fact that in this same period long leasehold changed from a contractual into a possessory institution, and so became alienable.[10]

Then there was the Mediterranean habit of living in a town or village-town and only very seldom in the fields. As in other parts of Europe, the rural economy of Italy was a mixture of market and home economy. The peasant would buy from the townsmen what he could not produce himself. It is improbable that rural

10. G. Mickwith, *op. cit.*, p. 328.

75

trades flourished on anything like a larger scale in the country-side, at least not in the earlier period. Consequently the social composition of the village population was simple: there were, apart from the full-time agriculturists, smiths—the ubiquitous craftsmen in almost all villages in all countries—possibly shoe-makers, bakers, and similar providers of daily needs. But there were numerous craftsmen in the *castelli* and village-towns. And as everywhere else during the Middle Ages and later, the economy of the countryside was practically dictated by the economic policy of the towns, which used either their economic and political superiority or pressure to enforce what appeared to be in their own best interest. But in general the interdependence of town and country was much closer in Italy than in Central Europe in the Middle Ages—if for no other reason than that many inhabitants, especially of the smaller towns, derived a major part of their income from agriculture.

To sum up: During the long process of retrogression in the Dark Ages, the Roman towns were gradually losing their char-acter as indispensable centers of trade and commerce and of the formation of capital. Already in the late Empire they had been "sitting like leeches in the interest of the public revenue over the Empire."[11] With the fall of the Empire even this function had ended. The Gothic wars and the Lombard invasions sealed their fate. What was left became the seats of an agricultural population who settled in the ruins as best they could. This held good not only for Northern Italy but also for the *castelli* of the Exarchate of Ravenna, and may have been similar on the Venetian coast where refugees, retreating before the Huns, had settled on the islands of the Adriatic lagoons, gradually building the twelve townships that developed into the city of Venice.

The countryside itself was very thinly settled. Vast tracts of wasteland extended between the few villages and hamlets. Irriga-tion and drainage installations had fallen into ruin, leaving barren fields and marshes where once had been fertile land. *"Nunc . . . desolata ab hominibus praedia atque ab omni culture destituta, in solotudine vacat terra: nullus hanc possessor inhabi-tat."* ("The countryside, uncultivated, became a wilderness. The land was no longer occupied by its owners.")[12] During the Middle Ages and the Renaissance certain efforts were made to reclaim at least part of the area lost through neglect in the preceding centuries. This was especially attempted in the Po Basin through small-scale drainage and clearance by individual landowners, and on a larger scale by the religious orders, espe-cially the Cistercians—and also by a number of municipalities. Ef-forts were also made in other parts of Italy—for example, around Lucca, Arezzo, and in the Pontine Marshes. Early clearings of the

11. M. Weber. *Römische Agargeschichte in Ihrer Bedeutung für das Staats- und Privatrecht.* 1891. P. 267.

12. "Gregorii Magni Dialogi. III. 38." In: *Scriptores rerum langobardicarum et italicarum saec. VI-IX.* 1878.

woodlands seem to have been mainly the work of agricultural pioneers who were offered favorable terms by landowners either in the form of low rents or as outright grants. The first moves in this direction dated back to the beginning of the sixth century, when the authorities promised to anyone who would reclaim wasteland not only full property rights but also tax exemption. Later towns and lay and ecclesiastical lords rivaled one another in encouraging immigrant families to settle in hitherto uninhabited areas where they would found new communities. The names of these new foundations indicate their origin: Villanuova, Villafranca, Castelfranco, Castelnuovo, Borghetto, and others.[13]

These conditions should be borne in mind if we are to understand the slow and hesitant steps in reviving urban life in Italy and the intimate interaction of town and country. It was a new beginning for many people in a new world, and a monumental effort to change the face of the land on which they wanted to live. A desolate country had to be reconquered, to be remade into a hospitable and fertile environment.

In the late Roman period Italy was a land of towns. This does not mean that the majority of the population lived in urban communities behind the protection of walls. Rather it should be understood as the concentration of the whole administrative organization in the towns as centers of the surrounding regions greatly different in size and character and as the all-powerful organs determining the economic and social structure of the area under their jurisdiction. After the disintegration of the Roman Empire the towns declined and the distinction between town and country became less marked. Under Charlemagne and his successors the counts and their feudal adherents distributed the land they had conquered—for the possession of land was regarded as payment of the warriors. The continuous wars made it imperative for every feudatory to fortify his residence, if only to demonstrate and uphold his allegiance to his lord. Thus the countryside, hitherto undefended and open, was now covered with the castles of the higher and lower nobility. This development gained momentum in the ninth century.

At the same time towns began to rebuild their walls. This work was no longer opposed by the barbarian kings, since they themselves were constantly threatened by rivals and foreign invaders. They could not possibly deny the townspeople the right to protect their homes and the life of their families by strengthening the defenses of their town, or forbid them to manufacture and buy arms. Rebuilding and strengthening of their fortifications heralded the turning point in the long decline of the towns. The burghers were now in a position to reassert themselves, to

Rebirth of Urban Communities

13. G. G. Coulton. *Medieval Village, Manor and Monastery.* 1960. P. 218.

demand more respect from the feudals, and to repulse aggressors. They began to revive their industrial activities, however modest the first fruits may have been. But now they worked for their own profit, defending their own property and wealth. From this time on the power and influence of towns increased, and with their growing prestige and greater safety the number of their citizens rose. It was a mutually interdependent evolution: The urban communities knew that their strength depended on the number of their citizens, and that the better their defenses the greater the influx of newcomers would be. The smaller towns followed suit and even the villages were influenced by this trend: the majority had a castle or at least a strong tower where the population could take refuge in case of sudden attack.

Where the circle of the same wall formed a common interest, the spirit of association was developed. Courage grew with liberty; and the Italians, no longer oppressed, found at last in themselves their own defence.[14]

But defense was not the only attraction of towns nor the sole characteristic that distinguished them from the countryside. Another great drawing power was the market, which was held regularly within the town's walls but was a rare event indeed in the countryside. Since the ninth century—that is, since the slowly developing revitalization of trade and commerce—the towns became the centers of industrial activities which separated them economically from the countryside yet at the same time welded both together in a new union based on mutual interests and exchange of production. Seaports like Genoa, Pisa, and Venice were the main beneficiaries of the growing commerce, whereas inland trade developed much more slowly. Only Milan was an exception. The revival of its economic importance gave it an early lead over other inland towns. It was favored by its position as the dominant city of the Po Basin with which it was connected not only by the natural waterway of the Lambro but also (in the later Middle Ages) by the artificial *naviglio grande,* by its control of the southern exits of several Alpine passes, and by its central situation in an extremely fertile area. Relatively early Milan began to fill out again its ancient walls, especially since the navigation on the middle Po and its tributaries had revived; apart from luxury goods, valuable commodities like salt and grain, arms, and textiles could now be shipped. Soon Milan surpassed the older Pavia and Verona at the southern end of the Brenner Pass.[15]

Cremona, Piacenza, Ferrara, and Bologna shared in the increasing commerce, though to a lesser degree. The industrial

14. J. C. L. Simonde de Sismondi. *A History of the Republics, being a View of the Origin, Progress and Fall of Italian Freedom.* Everyman's Library. 1907. P. 27.
15. A. Doren. *Italienische Wirtschaftsgeschichte.* 1934. Pp. 119-20.

and commercial life of Florence did not fully develop before 1100. Prior to that time Florence was second to Lucca, which had made the most of its situation at the exit of the La Cisa Pass over Monte Bardone—important for the imperial armies and the emperors on their way to Central and Southern Italy and, above all, for the pilgrimage to Rome. Rome herself had remained essentially a city of consumers with numerous small traders, middlemen, and money changers who were indispensable for the innumerable pilgrims and clerics from all over the world.[16]

The more the towns changed into centers of commercial and diversified industrial activities the more the division of labor between town and country proceeded; the more a few leading communities were able to hold annual fairs and to develop their long-distance and overseas trade, the more favorable grew conditions for the development of a merchant class. The daily market and the numerous workshops and booths of craftsmen and artisans made the towns, as it were, one vast market distributed over the entire urban area. Simultaneously a concentration of supply and demand in space and time had set in which benefited, above all, those places that were in a particularly favorable position or still had a tradition as commercial centers. Fairs came into existence, as elsewhere in the then known world, as adjuncts to much frequented church festivals, but more particularly at the intersection of several important routes, or where a main road crossed a river—in short, wherever traffic conditions were especially suitable for the exchange or sale of merchandise. There were the fairs at Piacenza, Pavia, Milan, and Ferrara which grew in prominence until the fairs of Champagne surpassed and finally paralyzed them.

Apart from the central markets and fairs there existed innumerable market places for local trade with the more immediate hinterland where the rural population exchanged their products for those made by the urban craftsmen or imported from other countries. Sismondi's description of this period and of the great change that had taken place since the internecine wars of the feudals is worth quoting at some length. In Chapters 3 and 5 of the History he writes:

The more the social tie was weakened in the kingdom of Lombardy, the more eager the nobles became to be admitted into the cities. Their wealth and military education soon led them, by the suffrages of their fellow-citizens, to the magistracy in this their new country. But if they displayed more talent for war and politics, they evinced much less subordination or submission to the laws. Their aversions were more virulent, and they gloried in cherishing them as a family inheritance. Accustomed in their castles to decide every question by the sword, they brought the same habits to the towns. Retaining,

16. A. Doren, *op. cit.*, p. 121.

when they became inhabitants of cities, the wild independence of their ancient fastnesses, their houses were fortresses; thick walls, high and narrow windows, a massive door of oak, secured with iron bars, promised to resist more than one attack; and if they were at last forced, a high square tower still served for refuge. From these palaces of the nobles bands of assassins were often seen issuing, to rob or murder citizens, who were treated as enemies: chains were prepared to be thrown across the streets, and in an instant form barricades; behind which were seen ranged several hundred warriors. . . . The power of the consuls seemed insufficient to repress these fiery passions. All the towns saw the necessity of adopting the institution of the *podestà*.

And of the end of the 13th century Sismondi remarks that

It is right to give a sketch of the general aspect of the country, particularly as the violent commotions which it experienced might give a false idea of its real state. This aspect was one of a prodigious prosperity which contrasted so much the more with the rest of Europe that nothing but poverty and barbarism were to be found elsewhere. The open country, designated by the name of *contado,* appertaining to each city, was cultivated by an active and industrious race of peasants, enriched by their labour, and not fearing to display their wealth in their dress, their cattle, and their instruments of husbandry. The proprietors, inhabitants of towns, advanced them capital, shared the harvests, and alone paid the land-tax: they undertook the immense labour which has given so much fertility to the Italian soil,—that of making dikes to preserve the plains from the inundation of the rivers, and of deriving from those rivers innumerable canals of irrigation. . . . The cities, surrounded with thick walls, terraced, and guarded by towers, were, for the most part, paved with broad flagstones; while the inhabitants of Paris could not stir out of their houses without plunging into the mud. Stone bridges of an elegant and bold architecture were thrown over rivers; aqueducts carried pure water to the fountains. The palace of the podestàs and *signorie* united strength with majesty. . . . The prodigies of this first-born of the fine arts multiplied in Italy: a pure taste, boldness, and grandeur struck the eye in all the public monuments, and finally reached even private dwellings. . . . The arts of necessity and of luxury had been cultivated with no less success than the fine arts: in every street, warehouses and shops displayed the wealth that Italy and Flanders only knew how to produce.[17]

By the middle of the 16th century the population of Italy had reached about 8,850,000.[18] Farms, hamlets, and villages grew, and the influx into the towns increased—nourished mainly from the countryside and in particular as the result of the disintegration of the manor economy and of feudalism. This trend continued even when the need to seek safety behind the urban walls

17. J. C. L. Simonde de Sismondi. *A History of the Republics, being a View of the Origin, Progress and Fall of Italian Freedom.* 1907. Pp. 52-53, 98-99.
Quoted by permission of E. P. Dutton & Co. Inc., Everyman's Library.
18. J. C. Russell, *op. cit.,* p. 126.

had lost much of its earlier urgency. However, the founding of new towns was still a rare event and hardly any of the fortified castles, built as refuges for the countrypeople, developed into an urban community. But the inner structure of the existing towns underwent far-reaching modifications: Only now, during the later Middle Ages, did they fully regain their ancient place as centers of industrial and commercial life. The visible outward symbols of this reawakening of urban life were the extensions of numerous towns[19] and the formation of *suburbia*.

Within the walls the building density increased and houses grew in height when there was not enough space in width. Stone began to replace wood as building material. New churches were erected and those built in earlier centuries were enlarged or enriched. Guilds developed, modeling their internal organization essentially on the prototype of the communal administration. The result was an efficient mixture of self-government by laymen and administration by technically trained officials. For the individual guild members it meant a wholesome practical education in matters of public interest which taught them to look beyond the narrow sphere of their own economic advantage and to balance the needs of their private and small enterprises with those of the community[20] and the demands of interstate and international policies. Weekly and annual markets and fairs served as centers of distribution and contributed to the growth of the towns and the diversity of their industrial structure. When in the 15th century the Italian economy was going downhill and the other states began to protect their own production against inundation by Italian goods, an attempt was made to bolster the domestic commerce by establishing new fairs as a counterweight against the shrinking of the export trade. However, the general economic situation of the country was not favorable enough to derive more permanent advantages from these minor remedies.[21]

On these foundations, laid in the Middle Ages and the preceding centuries, the towns of Italy continued their rise to greatness until in the Renaissance they reached the zenith of their creative faculties. Out of the ruins of the Roman Empire they saved, after a perilous atrophy, enough energy and imagination to rally anew the forces of civilization and self-confidence. In a long and painful development they again forged the cultural fabric that had made them the standard-bearers of the arts, city building, and social life—and, unhappily, the leaders in the use of force and bribery. When the traditional structure of society and with it the age of unquestioning faith began to fade away, medievalism also receded into the shadows of the past. A new philosophy of life was emerging slowly and imperceptibly, not

19. See pp. 65-66.

20. A. Doren. *Italienische Wirtschaftsgeschichte. Op. cit.* Pp. 260 ff.
H. Pirenne. *Economic and Social History of Medieval Europe.* 1937. *Passim.* Also *Medieval Cities.* 1925. *Passim.*

C. W. Previté-Orton. "The Italian Cities." In: *The Cambridge Medieval History.* Vol. V. 1926. Pp. 208-41.

21. A. Doren, *op. cit.,* p. 417.

yet shared by the people as a whole although enthusiastically and imaginatively embraced by the few. Worldliness began to pervade the Church till it reached its full impact under the pagan popes, and earthly wealth dethroned the charisma of aristocratic birth as a qualification for leadership. Traditional symbols and forms were drained of their spiritual meaning and became hollow and confining until finally thrown overboard and the stage was set for a new beginning. The outlook widened; new energies were harnessed; new visions filled the horizon; a new way of thinking spread its invisible net over the Italian people. The age of expansion was dawning, expansion in every sphere of life, in learning and understanding, in the arts and sciences; and above all in the souls of men. Subconscious forces were released and a new picture of the world and the universe began to take shape.

The Renaissance was an age both of awakening and of transition. And like every age of a transitional nature it created not only something new but also a bewildering uncertainty in face of the tremendous onslaught of hitherto unknown potentialities impatiently awaited, anxiously explored, yet not fully understood. Just as medieval man was torn between the spiritual demands of the future life and the realistic demands of the present, so Renaissance man was overwhelmed by the growing chasm between faith and search for knowledge, between Church and State, between the conflicting ideas of an earth-centered and a sun-centered universe. From this time onward man set out on his long march toward individual self-expression and individual responsibility in a world that grew more and more impersonal, that seemed to escape him, destroying old bonds and old ideas until he finally had lost wholeness and had become a lonely individual in a depersonalized environment.

The towns of Italy experienced this turmoil of ideas that came to represent the vanguard and rallying point of the great transformation in society. Their physical appearance, however, changed but slowly: the ballast of existing buildings and of the ancient ground plans prevented, as always, a rapid and revolutionary change. Painting and sculpture and the erection of individual buildings took the lead. But when the practical obstacles gradually disappeared through the obsolescence of buildings, streets, squares, or districts, the new ideas were eagerly put into practice. A more rational approach, a more deliberate and systematic conception began to influence city planning. And with it the sense and idea of space and scale underwent a profound transformation. The multiplicity of viewpoints which had dominated the appearance of medieval towns gave way to a unified layout and to perspective views.[22] The Baroque continued this development to its ultimate perfection. This was the climax, the

22. See Vol. I, pp. 173-83.

beginning of the end of great architecture and great city planning. The more the creative energies of the time shifted to the exploration of the scientific frontiers of human knowledge, the more the springs of artistic inspiration dried up. City planning degenerated into empty ostentation before finally disappearing as a matter of public concern and becoming a *quantité négligeable*.

It was the awareness of the unique value of urban life and the consciousness of the creative strength of concerted action that exerted the greatest influence upon the rebirth of the towns of Italy. The imponderable aspirations of the people—vaguely felt yet powerfully operating in the deep recesses of the human soul—and their eternal longing for a better and dignified existence were the major factors that induced the population to congregate in the ruins of the Roman towns, and to set out on the long march that lay before them. The emotional urges were stronger than the utilitarian impulses, however cogent their demands may have been in reality. They were inextricably interwoven with the primordial needs for shelter and safety, for cooperative action, and individual self-expression. But they remained the fountainhead in the struggle for survival. "For," as Tolstoy expressed it in the Epilogue to *War and Peace*, "if we allow that life is always guided by reason, we destroy the premise that life is possible at all."

The urban communities which slowly and with difficulty arose from the wreckage of the ancient towns were symbols of an ideal and civilized life, of the coordination of the external form and the internal pattern of existence, of the promise of physical security and social coherence, and above all of the victory of man over nature. Broadly speaking, the towns of Italy followed the same line of development as those in other parts of Europe. But in one important respect they differed: almost all of the larger towns of Italy were already existing at the beginning of the Middle Ages. Not one was a new foundation or had to be completed as a regularly planned enterprise. Not one of the smaller towns that were built according to a preconceived regular plan was successful: they either soon became extinct, or stagnated, or were later totally transformed. Everywhere in Italy town development was a continuation of existing urban elements. There was no ideal plan—at least not at the beginning—that could have served as a starting point. The actual task was to introduce order into a confused assembly of buildings and to adapt the progress of this enterprise to ever-changing ideas.[23] The guiding principle was to harmonize the new with the old and to embody in the physical structure and appearance of the town the idea and the ideal of the spiritual values and communal

The Town as
a Work of Art
in the Middle Ages

23. W. Braunfels, *op. cit.*, p. 12.

83

aspirations held to be valid according to prevailing conditions. Much more than today, each step was subordinated to its effect upon and its relation to the whole.

For in whatever way a town has developed *de facto* as a work of the centuries, it was viewed at every moment as a towering edifice conceived and built in a spirit of harmony whose systematic composition expressed a high and ideal vision. Such a vision—it was never the same—determined successively the building activities of the bishops, the free communes, the later tyrants and the princes. . . . We know this ideal picture of the *civitas* from literature. The Latin Middle Ages have given much thought to the essential nature of a town. One was convinced that it should provide the framework and the stage for a life pleasing to God and ordered significantly.[24]

Numerous municipal statutes prove that at least since the middle of the 13th century local authorities paid great attention to every detail of public and private buildings. These bylaws reflect not only the constant efforts of the administration to establish a better order for improving the architectural quality but also the change in thinking that took place in the course of the centuries. Three periods are clearly distinguishable. In the first period, until the end of the 12th century, the bishops and the consuls were the agents and patrons of town planning. Under their guidance, the municipal authorities were mainly interested in buildings that served both the spiritual needs and the safety of the town—churches, monasteries, and protecting walls. During the second period, from the 13th century onward, the urban area as a whole and as the social *Lebensraum* of the inhabitants was the concern of the administration. Streets and squares, public fountains, bridges, and town palaces were subject to regulations. The personal rights of the feudal lords, who had built fortified castles and even private churches within the walls, were placed under public supervision, and the monasteries were absorbed as integral parts into the urban structure. All building activities were dependent on the permission of the town council, and a serious attempt was made to reconcile the clerical and public with the private interests. The emphasis shifted from preoccupation with the safety and defense of the community to the establishment of order and coherence. In the third period, at the beginning of the 15th century, the private element came again to the fore: Instead of the erection of churches and town halls as monumental accents in the architectural concept of the towns, individual castles and palaces became the showpieces of the community.

Broadly speaking, these three periods corresponded to the Romanesque, the Gothic, and the Renaissance. Braunfels remarks

24. W. Braunfels, *op. cit.*, pp. 12-13. Also for the following.

with full justification that the Romanesque churches were in fact and in spirit like fortified castles; that in the Gothic period they were experienced as a symbol of the celestial and ideal order; and in the Renaissance and Baroque as festival halls in honor of God, even as *theatrum sacrum*. And the town can also be understood as a fortified castle or *theatrum*—as it was indeed called in this period. However, it would be a mistake to believe that these three stages in the development of town planning can be rigidly separated. All the trends outlined above overlapped. What distinguished the towns of Italy from those in other European countries was that they were revived and developed in the shadow of the past and that from the 11th to the 16th century a later period rarely or completely disrupted the continuity of artistic expression or refused to recognize the achievements of the past.

North of the Alps this was different. Here we find new foundations of towns that were built totally independent of the past on virgin soil in the course of the great colonial movement from West to East. But what the urban communities of the South and the North had in common was that they reached their greatest prosperity and highest artistic achievements when the individual and collective wills were in unison, despite all strife and diversity, and when what may appear as restrictions imposed by the authorities were readily accepted and understood as in the common interest.

The vision of urban life as the ideal form of society was ever present. All the numerous and petty regulations could not extinguish this concept as a whole. Such rules or ordinances were the expression of a sense of order and organic integration; they were received, often with considerable hesitation and grumbling, as the inevitable by-product of the complexity of medieval life but in the end adopted as necessary for the unity of the community in fact and in spirit. The town as a work of art was the goal for which a unifying expression had to be found. For the Middle Ages this meant unity in diversity, not unity through repetition or regularity. The town within its walls, the densely built-up urban area girdled by this circumvallation was not only a realistic creation, it was a symbol offered to God or to a patron saint. In the mystical experience of medieval man the town, like the cathedral, combined the earthly, the finite, and the heavenly infinite. During the Middle Ages the painters represented the town as a single, uniformly shaped building which the patron saints or the founder held in outstretched hands as an offering to the Supreme Being.

The walls were the most expressive symbol of the town. They were more often than not synonymous with the urban community. "*Murus autem ipsius civitatis inexpugnabilem fidei, cari-*

19. Symbolic representation of a city from the *Utrechtpsalter.*

20. Symbolic representation of a city from the *Codex Egberti.*

tatis speique firmitatem significat" ("Moreover, the wall of this city stands for the impregnable fortress of faith, and the strength of charity and hope") wrote Hrabanus Maurus, archbishop of Mainz (c. 776-865) in *De Universo* (XIV).[25] The walls signified the town as a shelter of law, safety, and order in contrast to the open country with its dangers and lawlessness. Towns were represented on medieval maps by a ring of walls. For the Italians perhaps more than for other peoples the walls were a promise of a haven where they had little or nothing to fear from invading hordes, robber barons, or mercenaries during the centuries of unrest and strife. It was a time that in many respects may be compared with the Urban Revolution more than three thousand years earlier, for it not only offered safety but also created anew out of the raw materials of what had survived the cataclysm of the ancient world a space *sui generis* in opposition to Nature "with its own rights against her," as Ortega y Gasset says in *The Revolt of the Masses.*

Within it man, cut loose from every solidarity with plant and animal, creates a realm of his own restricted to itself. . . . The town is the super-house, it is superseding the house and the subhuman nest. . . . It is the *res publica,* the *politeia,* made up not by men and women but by citizens. A new dimension irreducible to any dimension of Nature, always so much nearer to the animal, is thrown open to human life; and for it these new citizens will give the utmost of their powers. Thus the city originates from its very beginning as a state.

25. In: J. P. Migne. *Patrologiae Latina.* Vol. 111, Lib. XIV. P. 384.

These words describe accurately the re-emergence of the Italian towns and the rebellious spirit of their citizens—rebellious in their opposition to the natural environment and to all its dangers and primordial atavism.

The ideal form of a town was circular like the celestial city or the eternal Jerusalem, which were symbolized in the circular *coronae lucis* suspended from the vaults of the churches and decorated with towers or *aediculae*. The usual twelve towers or gates corresponded to the twelve apostles. This symbolism was often transferred to town walls. Milan, for instance, has been described as a city with twelve powerful gate-towers, and smaller towns were sometimes divided into twelve equal districts in order to manifest the higher significance of the community.[26] For medieval man the imperfect reality of daily life was deeply embedded in the vision of an ideal city. But this ideal city was not the result of theoretical and ingenious schemes worked out on the drawing board. It was the product of an intense empathy, of the projection of man's whole personality into the mystic experience of the spiritual world. Every detail was *pars pro toto*, instinctively coordinated and intimately felt as such. For medieval men the final appearance of their town was a symbol of eternity and of holy oneness, and only as such can its multiplicity be understood.

26. W. Braunfels, *op. cit.*, p. 50.

21. Scene of the nativity set within the safety of city walls with gates and towers symbolizing the peace surrounding this event. Ivory carving of the 12th century.

87

The Italian Middle Ages have produced no design for an Ideal City that could serve as an archetype of the emotional, intellectual, and social urges of the era and eventually be embodied in terrestrial architecture. The only Ideal City that existed for medieval man was the celestial Jerusalem, and this heavenly city was reproduced symbolically in the medieval cathedral. Hence the first and principal church is the ideal and realistic center of the city, the *imago mundi*. The symbolism of the center was gradually extended to all churches, to any place where the minds of men were in need of it for their spiritual salvation. Thus the city as a whole was conceived as a composition of churches which were, in the early Middle Ages, the sole, dominating, focal points giving unity and structural coherence to the urban community. Their location and their interrelationship were elements of "planning" in the Middle Ages.

The symbolic meaning of the city as a sanctuary, as the destination of pilgrimages, and as a shelter of holy places erected over the relics of martyrs and in honor of saints, was most cogently expressed in the way to and between the churches within the urban area. This higher meaning was embodied in the sequence of sacred buildings as the primary experience of pilgrims and inhabitants alike. The ritual orientation of the churches and their distribution and interconnection were the elements of symbolical planning, adding homogeneity and accentuation to the medieval community. This was not an over-all planning but an instinctive coordination guided by a unity of vision and symbolic significance. Thus the elements which held the medieval town together architecturally and socially were the walls, the realistic and at the same time ritual protection against hostile forces, and the churches—the focal points of the internal composition.

But gradually the reality of daily life began to assert its rights and to enfeeble the intensity of the vision. New focal points appeared—town halls, guildhalls, and market squares. The dichotomy of the Middle Ages, the complementary antagonism in the soul of medieval man, grew stronger as the image of the celestial city faded into the background. The open spaces of the towns were built up and the activities of daily life began to compete on a level with the demands of religion. But it was still a half-awakening—not a breaking loose from the fetters of medieval belief—that was reflected in the slow transformation of the towns. As Jacob Burckhardt describes it in his *Civilization of the Renaissance,*

In the Middle Ages both sides of human consciousness—that which was turned within as that which was turned without—lay dreaming or half awake beneath a common veil. The veil was woven of faith, illusion, and childish prepossession, through which the world and history were seen clad in strong hues. Man was conscious of himself only as a member of a race, people, party, family, or corporation—only through some general category.[27]

The ascendancy of the earthly demands and the awareness of the importance of bringing order into the physical structure of the towns found its expression in the growing concern of the municipal councils for the need to regulate the building activity through bylaws and statutes. At the same time the erection and completion of churches and the layout of their surroundings remained a prominent task of the citizens and their representatives. Both streams were flowing in the same direction and finally met to make the medieval towns places of functional unity and rare beauty.

That the location of the churches within the urban area, their number and their distance from one another were the noblest and most tangible criteria of the dignity of a town in the early Middle Ages is obvious from numerous chronicles of the time. Everything else was irrelevant when a town had to be represented or described. Only the churches and the walls and the route which the pilgrims followed determined the picture or the description.[28] This preoccupation with what was regarded as the essential features of the town contained the germ of a trend toward order and systematization, goals which were always part of man's desire to transform his environment in accordance with his needs and aspirations. One of the major misinterpretations of medieval towns was the assumption, so widespread in the 19th century, that a sense and an idea of order and functional clarity was missing and that their seemingly unsystematic "picturesque" appearance was the main contribution of the Middle Ages to the art of city building. This is, of course, a childish idea but it was characteristic of a period that had reached the nadir of city planning and failed to understand that irregularity was not necessarily tantamount to a lack of clear vision. But

Wherever towns were founded or extended according to a preconceived plan in the Middle Ages, the streets were regular, straight, and relatively wide. . . . Where, in freely developing settlements—be it within the Roman walls, be it on virgin soil—the lively picture of an irregular settlement had taken shape out of the combination of houses, churches, monasteries, and feudal castles, the authorities were no less anxious, at least since the beginning of the thirteenth century, to see their laws and regulations respected in this chaos. The more irregular the town, the more detailed and comprehensive the rules. Siena, situated on its three hills, defied every formalism

27. 1945 edition, p. 81.
28. W. Braunfels, *op. cit.*, pp. 131-73. *Passim.*

and produced the most exact bylaws for the building of the streets. This did not make it less regular. But the ideal of a town homogeneous in all its parts is nevertheless reflected in its streets. . . . The medieval town planners had, like all their successors, to begin with improvements of their town, if they wanted to remain on the level of realistic necessities.[29]

Braunfels cites a great number of municipal regulations which are of considerable interest but cannot be discussed in this connection. These statutes and bylaws dealt with individual infringements and, at the same time, with general improvements. To the former category belonged bylaws concerning oriels, arcades, and external stairs and façades of individual buildings. To the latter belonged the general supervision of streets and squares. As early as the 12th century the administration of Florence distinguished three categories of streets: *viae publicae*, public main streets; *viae vicinales*, streets of the parishes and neighborhood units; and *viae privatae*, private streets. Four streets in Florence were paved before paving of streets became general. These streets corresponded to the two main axes of the Roman period and were protected by special regulations. Monasteries and feudals owned whole districts where either private laws or complete lawlessness reigned. Braunfels gives a description of one of these "towns within the town with its own churches, own walls, the palace and the houses of the bondsmen." The following description is so illustrative of the conditions in some of the Italian towns that it is appropriate to quote it.

Here everyone is allowed to build as he pleases. Nobody troubles about street cleaning, paving, drainage and lighting. The private streets are veritable public cesspools. They are closed up by projecting structures and oriels, the so-called *sporti*. Under the protection of the fortified towers of the feudal families they turn into private fortresses, and even whole fortress-systems. Streets make war upon streets. Irregular and arbitrary buildings block the passage and often separate the streets completely from the outer world. Craftsmen use them as workshops. One lives in these streets and squares but one does not walk through them. Here the women are spinning and carding wool. Dyers and tanners hang up fabrics and hides to dry. Oxen are slaughtered and processed; pigs feed on refuse in front of the houses. The streets serve as yards for timber and stones.

Numerous enforcement officers were employed by the town councils whose main job was to supervise the street system and to reconcile the habits and private interests of the inhabitants with those of the community as a whole. Apart from the regulation of existing streets, new roads were built and whole districts laid out, measures that became necessary because of the increase

29. W. Braunfels, *op. cit.*, pp. 86-87 ff.

in urban population of Northern Italy, and also of other parts of the country. Moreover, in Tuscany, for instance, it was not unusual for whole towns to be resettled: the victorious communities would force the inhabitants of the conquered places to settle within their walls. In general, in the 13th and 14th centuries, the policy of the urban administration was to increase their population. But most of the new roads were built to improve the communications not only within the urban area but also within the surrounding country. The widening and regulating of existing streets was undertaken for practical and aesthetic reasons—the latter especially when it would result in a unitary vision, less because an individual building would gain from this improvement. The concern of the authorities was not only with the course of a street, its paving, drainage, and cleaning but also with its appearance as a homogeneous space. The houses lining both sides of the street had to be of equal size, serve the same purpose, and stand close together—if possible without an open space between. In this respect the cities of Italy and of the whole Mediterranean region are fundamentally different from those of Northern Europe, where each building preserved its own identity and was, in most cases, a separate unit.

This building together of the houses in Italian cities was the precursor of the continuous block front of the Baroque in the whole of Europe when regimentation and rigidity (but also the understanding of contrasting values—between the monumental and public buildings and the modest houses of the burghers) became recognized means of town planning. The Italian communities led the way in this direction. In general, since the last third of the 13th century, every new building activity, especially in Northern Italy, was subjected to carefully elaborated laws. As far as possible, similarity of the façades, of the building materials and their colors, of the size and shape of windows and doors was the aim of many of these regulations.

Just as the external appearance of the buildings was to be identical, so their interior purpose had to correspond to this outward similarity. Bylaws which tried to further this tendency are known from Florence, Siena, and other towns. The sense of purpose and order demanded that the same trades should occupy the same streets. In other words, the population should be grouped according to their professions, that is, members of the same guild should live together. A petition of the *ufficiali sopra l'ornata* in Siena of the year 1398 complains that it is a disgrace to the city that individual guilds are not grouped together but dispersed all over the urban area.

A regulation should be issued such as exists in every good city for its protection and its perfection. You have your *piazza del Campo* which is the most beautiful that can be found; you have this jewel of a *strada di Banchi* beginning at the *piazza Tolomei* and leading to the *porta Solaria* and no city in this country, neither Venice nor Florence, has a more beautiful one. Now it is spoiled because shoemakers and tailors live there. Our mayor should decree that a committee of four citizens is to be elected. This body should preserve the beauty of the street by concentrating the bankers in one part, the drapers in the next one, the goldsmiths, the furriers and the armourer in the following part so that each trade is allowed to establish itself only in one section of the street.[30]

The idea behind this separation of the trades was not dictated only by practical reasons of convenience—although the idea itself was not new. It had been common in the whole Orient, and when used in the cities of Europe it was merely a visible expression of the solidarity of the guild members. But in the Italian cities with their outspoken inclination for functional and aesthetic order it meant more. The external unity of the buildings, the similarity of the building material, the size of windows and other details, all were to be harmonized with this purpose. The interior would determine the exterior or else the discrepancy between appearance and purpose would destroy the very sense of organic order. The aim was to create unity in diversity, to make the city one homogeneous work of art, not through repetition and uniformity, but through the combination of order in general and diversity in detail. The grouping of the trades in clearly separated sections was, therefore, more than a pragmatic expediency. It was a strongly felt necessity and an expression of the unfailing instinct of the Middle Ages for functional clarity—a conviction that every part could fulfil its purpose only if it was in itself purposeful and placed in the right relation to the whole. The medieval cathedrals are the most telling examples of this attitude. The Italian mentality, so much nearer to the artistic empathy of Greek antiquity and to the Roman preoccupation with organization, differed considerably from the thinking of Northern Europe. It was more extrovert, more given to the deliberate elaboration of monumental effects and to an ideal of beauty that sought and found its fulfilment less in dynamic contrasts than in balanced coordinations and synoptic views.

It has been explained before that the representative symbols of the towns in the early Middle Ages were the walls and the churches, and that these symbols remained during this period the major and almost sole concern of the municipal councils. It was not until the 13th century that secular buildings began to occupy the active interest of the administration. Only then was the erection of town halls contemplated and a new, now secular element added to the symbolic and physical characteristic of the

30. Municipal Archives in Siena. Concistoro 2111. Quoted after W. Braunfels, *op. cit.*, p. 122.

towns. At the beginning a private house was rented for the *podestà*. In Florence he often resided in the palace of the bishop. The legislative assemblies of the citizens met in the churches. Only slowly, the town councils began to build town halls where the *podestà* and the administration were housed.

Before palaces became important features of the towns the *casa torre,* the residential tower, was the most typical of the more conspicuous private buildings. They were private fortresses belonging to an age of violence and personal prowess. These *torri gentilizie* were sometimes so numerous that a contemporary described Siena as a town where there were *tante torri che la città pareva un canetto.* The rooms were arranged one above the other and were reached by a ladder which was then drawn up so that the entrance to the tower was inaccessible, a precaution urgently needed as protection against surprise assaults. These towers were equally useful for defense and attack. They had embrasures and often vaulted corridors connecting them with the lower dwellings as emergency exits in case of danger.

Because not every family was wealthy enough to build its own tower, related or friendly families which lived closely together united in "tower associations" that would erect and maintain these private fortresses. These groups had their own statutes with special regulations which forbade intermarriages with hostile families, a measure that often led to tragic conflicts and complications. Lucca possessed the greatest number of towers; it is said to have had seven hundred. The reason may have been that numerous feudal families whose origin dated back to Lombard times had moved their residences from the country to the town. Bologna had about 250 towers, and even smaller places such as S. Gimignano had a considerable number. Since the late 12th century, the height of the towers was restricted in the interest of public safety, although their number, size, and strength were regarded as the expression of a town's grandeur. In the early period the tower of a church, the *campanile,* and the tower of the town were identical. It was the same bell that summoned the people to the church, the military service, and later to the assembly.

Church towers were fortified watchtowers. As late as 1329, it was demanded in Pistoia that the *campanile communis* which was called the *fortezza del campanile della chiesa maggiore* should be strengthened.[31] The habit of building free-standing church towers may be attributed to this early identification of the secular towers of the community and the sacred towers of the churches. It is difficult to decide whether the most famous tower, Giotto's *campanile* at Florence, is a profane or a religious building. It is not even relevant to consider this alternative; it was both. It was

31. After W. Braunfels, *op. cit.,* p. 180.

a monument to the glory of Florence, to her noble cultural achievements in all spheres of life. And this monument should be freely visible from all sides in its greatness. It should have a life of its own and not be merely part of another building where it would have been subordinated to other considerations.

The Ideal City of the Middle Ages was never fully brought to perfection. But, as in other ages, it clearly existed in man's mind, and in its innumerable details and even in some larger parts of the urban scenery the religious social and artistic aspirations of the time found their ideal expression. The lure of Utopia was the ultimate driving force behind the unison of the individual and the collective will, as in all periods which produced great architecture and great cities (which is not the same as big buildings and big cities). The towns of medieval Italy, with their striving for balanced correlations, their plain and homogeneous houses closely built together, their fountains and bridges, their harmonious squares and street widenings, were the physical embodiment of a group consciousness, a religious and social spirit that transcended individual interests however strong these may have been. It was this interaction of individual liberty and communal responsibility that made the towns of medieval Italy what they are—great works of art and great Ideal Cities irrespective of their imperfections. They reconciled the all-embracing idea with the language of form and enthusiasm for details. They were a vital interlude between antiquity and the Renaissance. To regard them as the preliminary stage of the latter, as has often been done, is a fundamental misunderstanding of their mission and of their nature.

However, reality demands its rights. Nothing would be further from the truth than to overlook the negative side of Italian city life and to forget that the ideal found its representative expression more or less exclusively, in a few showpieces such as the principal squares, streets and public buildings. This was not unusual, being characteristic of all ages including our own. The streets of the towns of medieval Italy were gloomy. They were paved with bricks, if paved at all, and so narrow that pedestrians often had to take refuge in the entrance of a house to let vehicles pass. On the other hand, the narrowness of the street was an important factor in the frequent street fighting. Heavy chains were drawn across the roads and whole districts could easily be barricaded.

The scarce sunlight that filtered down between the houses was still further reduced by numerous balconies projecting so far into the streets that the monks who accompanied a funeral had to lower their crosses to avoid striking them. The windows had panes of a kind of parchment made of the skin of goats or covered with linen curtains soaked in oil. Doors and windows were small, thus better suited for defense and protection. Most houses had no cellar. Water and garbage were thrown into the street, and larger quantities of refuse and sweepings were carried to public dumping places which were a source of epidemics and all forms of illnesses. The open spaces along the water and in other parts of the town served the same purpose; even outside churches, heaps of refuse were a common view. The not unimportant role of official street cleaners was entrusted to the pigs, which were allowed to roam through the town, devouring the garbage thrown out of windows. It was a valuable privilege when the *podestà* permitted the feeding of the pigs in the streets. In 1296, a sow with four young pigs was officially employed in Siena to clean the *campo* after every market; in 1382, six pigs *di Sant' Antonio,* their patron saint, had the official duty of loitering about the town. These "employees" of the sanitation department were extremely effective. In Venice and Florence they were raised especially for scavenging, and in Bologna the *ospitalieri di Sant' Antonio* had the privilege of feeding one hundred pigs in the streets. The duty of these porcine clean-up squads was to scour the city streets; each animal had to wear a small bell with the coat of arms of the *podestà* and have its right ear clipped to indicate that it belonged to the fraternity. A pleasant example of the cooperation of public and free enterprise!

Water for the household was supplied from public fountains, which were fairly clean. The barbers, for instance, were not allowed to establish their shops near the fountains lest the wind carry hair clippings into the water—a strange though laudable inconsistency when compared with the dirty conditions of the streets in general. Public safety was at a low level. Street lighting as such did not exist; here and there a small lamp before the statue of a saint might provide a dim light. People who had to go abroad after sunset were accompanied by servants or, if they were less well off, went armed. Murder, robbery, brawls, and trickery were the order of the day. Manners were rude and the example from the upper classes mostly unedifying. Flats or apartments were primitively furnished. Two or three persons often slept together in the same bed, mostly without clothing. But with the growing prosperity this changed and toward the end of the 15th century the furniture of the houses of the well-to-do grew more and more elaborate and luxurious. Yet carriages were extremely rare. The main roads were in bad condition and, for the most part, could only be used by beasts of burden. The trunk roads between Siena and Pisa, Florence and Rome were, therefore, crowded by caravans of mules with numerous drivers and helpers. In Pisa, Siena, Florence, and other towns the houses of the wealthy merchants and the depots of the trading companies were surrounded by whole quarters of storehouses, sheds, and stables enclosed by walls. Fires were a frequent occurrence. The *podestà* of Siena employed special inspectors whose task it was to prohibit the storage of fuel in houses or workshops.

Inns were a common feature at the main roads, and taverns played an important role in the life of the urban population. They were the meeting places of rich and poor, of troubadours, jugglers, and other itinerant people. The town councils meddled with everything, and the liberation of the individual from medieval narrowness and tutelage proceeded only slowly and painfully. Men who did not carry on a trade in the town or in the neighborhood either personally or through employees were excluded from public offices, with the exception of knights, doctors, notaries, students, and clerics. The clock of the town hall regulated the life of the community. Nobody was allowed to leave his house before the first stroke of the clock, and all doors had to be closed by the last stroke of this impersonal supervisor. There were statutes that decreed the color of the dress and quality of the fabrics, the number of dishes at weddings and other feasts, and even how many rings the bride was to receive as presents. Similar restrictions are known from Greek antiquity, which proves that people living in too close proximity within a narrow area are exposed to the misuse of power by half-enlightened authorities, and that human nature remains the same, similar conditions producing similar social and intellectual attitudes.

Open and Closed Squares

The *Piazza del Duomo* at Pisa, the *Piazza della Signoria* at Florence, and the *Piazza del Campo* at Siena represent three different types of squares which are characteristically medieval in their composition and yet follow fundamentally different principles of layout and spatial concepts. The square at Pisa is an example of the loose grouping of a number of monumental buildings as isolated units, seemingly without any correlations, standing in a wide-open area. The second square, at Florence, is a composition of several spatial elements, the main square and its extension along the side of Palazzo Vecchio; it is irregular and surrounded by buildings which, as an old engraving by J. Zocchi shows, are homogeneous in spirit though not in size and height. They do not form a continuous wall but are interrupted by streets of different width and by the narrow connection with the Uffizi that is strongly accentuated by the Loggia dei Lanzi. The third square, at Siena, is completely closed by buildings. The streets which enter it are irrelevant to the composition as a whole. In Pisa the religious monuments stand alone. There are no private or other buildings. It is a composition created by a divine unity, by a vision directed to a life to come. In Florence and Siena the squares are secular manifestations of the civic spirit and surrounded by private and public buildings.

Let us now examine each of the three squares in detail. The *Piazza del Duomo* at Pisa is occupied by the cathedral, the *campanile*, the baptistery, the *campo santo*, and a small fountain. This group of religious buildings, though situated at the periphery of the old town outside the residential area, is nevertheless its spiritual center. Pisa, like Venice and Ravenna, was a lagoon town which grew when and where the sea receded. The eccentric location of the cathedral buildings near the walls can be traced back to the fact that here the lagoon had formed a strip of land sufficiently protected from the sea. The church was built in memory of the victory over the Saracens and the conquest of Palermo in 1063. The selection of this site was influenced by its former use as a cemetery. This tradition together with the availability of dry land was for the early Middle Ages a sufficient justification for concentrating the most important buildings of the community in this area. The choir of the church faces the town. Its west façade opens its portals to the baptistery. The main entrance to the church, which is still used today, is at the transept next to the apse, the part of the whole complex which the visitor coming from the town sees and reaches first.

The intimate interrelationship of the group is not produced by external means such as connecting structures, arcades, and passages or other buildings and walls bordering the square. The visual and emotionally experienced unity rests, above all, on the inseparable correlation of the functions which each building has

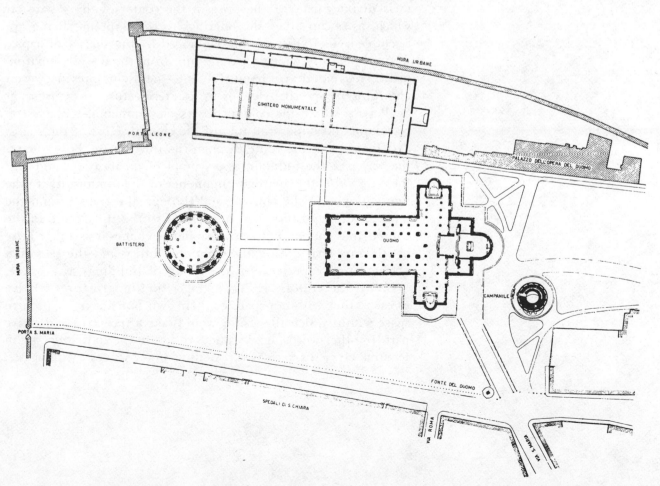

**23. Contrasting harmony of the Baptis-
ery, the Cathedral, and the Campanile,
at Pisa.**

to fulfill. Unlike most other architectural compositions the
church, baptistery, and *campanile* are not elements that limit
or enclose the square. They create it through the emanation of
their divine mission. They rise in the center of the square on
which, as on an altar, the offerings to the Supreme Being are
assembled. The visitor is not embraced by the shelter of a protecting enclosure which separates him from the worldly environment. He is not drawn irresistibly into the divine presence by an
absorbing perspective view or by an architectural overture as at
St. Peter's, where the colonnades like monumental tentacles receive him and impel him toward the church. Here at the *Piazza
del Duomo* it is the route through the town to the holy square,
the way past the fountain as a symbol of purification, and past
the *campanile*, the guardian-summoner of the community, to the
side entrance of the church; and through the transept and the
nave to the baptistery, which responds to the full accord of the
church like the choir in an antiphonal chant—it is this course
or itinerary that creates the emotional unity and the sensation
of the actual experience of the group of buildings as a whole.

What the visitor sees is a juxtaposition of structures relative
to each other within a space of their own but not in relation to
space within which the visitor would take a receptive and active
part. In other words, he does not synthesize the individual architectural elements by clear reasoning but by sensory processes,

98

"for, the sense, too, is a kind of reason as is every cognitive power," as Thomas Aquinas put it.[32] To quote Panofsky,

Small wonder, then, that a mentality which deemed it necessary to make faith "clearer" by an appeal to imagination, also felt bound to make imagination "clearer" by an appeal to the senses. . . . Pre-scholasticism had insulated faith from reason by an impervious barrier much as a Romanesque structure conveys the impression of a space determinate and impenetrable, whether we find ourselves inside or outside the edifice.[33]

This is precisely the sort of sensation the visitor feels in the *Piazza del Duomo* with its Romanesque buildings. His faith and senses experience the distance he has traveled to the sanctuaries and the achievement of his goal where consolation and beatitude raises him above the temptations of daily life. The group of the church, the baptistery, and the *campanile* is a composition of sculptures in space. In this respect they resemble Greek temples, which also stood in the landscape like sculptures without creating an architectural space.

The *Piazza della Signoria* at Florence was the civic center of the town, the *Piazza del Duomo* the religious and the *Mercato Vecchio* the commercial center. The Palazzo Vecchio or Palazzo della Signoria was built between 1299 and 1314. A small square was laid out before 1306. During the whole of the 14th century efforts were made to enlarge it, which can hardly have been the intention of the architect Arnolfo di Cambio. Originally the low houses of the neighborhood closely surrounded the *palazzo* and gave scale and relief to its plain and massive architecture. Moreover, large open spaces around public buildings were not generally in keeping with the architectural ideas of the Middle Ages. However, there were obviously certain tendencies that favored a freer view and therefore a larger square. Braunfels reports a story from Florence which may shed some light on this problem, although it concerns the *duomo*.[34] A lively controversy developed as to whether the dome of the cathedral should be raised by a tambour so that it would be visible at a greater distance, or whether the interior effect was to be decisive. Two parties opposed one another. The masters of the *opera del duomo* held the view that the exterior was beautiful and significant only as the expression of the interior and that, therefore, the dome should not be raised, the less so as, in their opinion, the tambour would contradict all static principles which hitherto had been applied to the vaulting of larger space units. The other party, consisting of representatives of the painters, sculptors, and goldsmiths, maintained that the outward appearance of the cathedral was more

32. *Summa Theologica*. I. Q. Art. 4, Ad. I.
33. E. Panofsky. *Gothic Architecture and Scholasticism*. 1958. P. 38 and p. 43 for the following.
34. W. Braunfels, *op. cit.*, p. 173.

important. The decisive meeting took place in October 1367. All distinguished citizens were invited and the two models were presented. The assembly agreed with the painters who thought first of the external impression of the church. Civic pride demanded a monument that would dominate the city and be visible from afar. Could similar considerations have been at work when the extension of the square around Palazzo Vecchio was decided?

However this may have been, the palace was built first and the square grew around it in successive stages. The palace and the tower, to quote Nietzsche, were the visible form of "man's pride, man's triumph over gravitation, man's will to power . . . a sort of oratory of power by means of forms." But the more the square was enlarged the more the palace lost its original and almost brutal grandeur, and the majestic scale of the tower which pointed to heaven like a threatening fist was reduced to a neutral landmark. The palace occupies the southeast of the square which surrounds it on two sides in the shape of an L. The square was never fully completed, although Michelangelo—whom Cosimo I had especially asked to advise him in this respect —suggested enclosing the whole square with arcades as a continuation of the Loggia dei Lanzi. But despite the lack of a unifying motif the appearance of the square is relatively coherent. The streets, which enter it without being hidden by connecting structures, do not disturb its closed character but open interesting vistas on the palace and the *Loggia*. The present fairly regular shape of the square and its size are due to the acquisition of the necessary land and the demolition of houses, especially in 1319 and 1355. There was no over-all plan for the layout of the square except the desire to enlarge it as much as possible. It grew gradually by improvisation, not by deliberate planning.

The Florentine square occupies an intermediary position between the *Piazza del Duomo* at Pisa and the *Piazza del Campo* at Siena. It is surrounded by buildings which are coordinated more in spirit than by their architectural structure, and it developed only slowly after the palace had been built. It was the civic center of the town in contrast to the *Piazza del Duomo*, the religious center of Pisa, and as such was the expression of the great change that had taken place being a manifestation of the greatness of the urban community, a secular demonstration of civic pride and power, rather than a religious symbol. Public life became more ostentatious, more extrovert. However, when plans were ventilated in 1356 for the erection of "a beautiful and stately Loggia," the citizenry objected and the administration was blamed because it had too hastily demolished "the noble palace and the watch-tower of the mint." A *loggia*, it was felt, was fitting for a tyrant but not for a free people. This realization was not unjustified,

24. Plan of the Piazza della Signoria in Florence.

for when the Loggia dei Lanzi (named after Cosimo I's *Landsknechte*) had been built, it was used by these mercenaries to intimidate the burghers. A *loggia* was not uncommon as part of the palaces of the noble families. It was usually situated on the ground level, separated from the palace by a street, and opened on a square.

The Loggia dei Lanzi, planned in 1356, possibly after a design by Orcagna but built only in the years 1376-82, was originally called *Loggia della Signoria* and was used for major political functions and public events. Its location diagonally opposite the Palazzo Vecchio resembled the situation of the *logge* of the private palaces. The Loggia dei Lanzi embodied the power of the rising republic and was intended for official manifestations of the state and their display in full view of the citizens, in the same way that the noble families had paraded their private wealth and pretensions before the populace in an earlier period. Life had become more worldly and the idea of the state as a work of art gained in importance. For this new attitude, a visible and impressive symbol had to be found. This symbol of an emerging era was found in the Loggia dei Lanzi, although its functions were not to remain unadulterated. Its original ideal significance was soon lost; a few years after its completion it began to serve a double and strangely contradictory purpose. It became the stage for swaggering mercenaries and, at the same time, an exhibition hall for sculptures. The three great arches and deep shadows of the *Loggia* contrasted sharply with the massive surface of the Palazzo Vecchio. They added an element of arrested movement, of a semiopenness to the continuous rows of plain houses which closed the other sides of the square and were a marvelous preparatory transition for the monumental entrance to the square through the long passage of the Uffizi.

That the administration was aware of the value of architectural contrasts is obvious from the strict supervision of the private building activity. It was recognized that the palace and the *loggia* would gain considerably if the eye were not distracted by too great a variety of details. Although this intention was not completely successful, it is interesting to follow the measures that were planned and at least partly put into practice. As already mentioned, the first layout of the square, the unfortunate location and shape of the palace, and the high building density of the whole area made any improvement difficult. Two churches had to be rebuilt on another site further back. The via Calzaiuoli was partly widened. Many houses were expropriated, though with compensation, and the building material of the demolished dwellings was sold to the *opera del Duomo*. The families wanting to acquire a new site at the square were under obligation to erect houses uniform in design, and as "embellishment of the square" to use ashlar stones for the lower part of the façade. The architects of the *duomo* who had to supervise the work interfered directly with the design. A document of March 29, 1390 repeated the demands in detail.[35] The design (*ornamentum*), size (*forma*), and method (*exemplum*) were clearly defined. Similarity was to be enforced. "The architects shall endeavor to build the houses on both sides of the street in such a way that their beautiful and noble appearance exactly resembles the house of the Guelphs that is situated in the same street." It was expressly stated that the new buildings were erected as "an adornment of the whole town." An unusual and interesting structure completed these efforts: a long wall apparently as high as the ashlar work of the façades— that is, about seven yards—was built in front of the low houses on the west side of the square. It was said to be constructed by Pisan prisoners and therefore called *la mura dei Pisani*. This wall blocked the access to the square for the inhabitants of these houses but helped to increase the impression of the square as a closed and homogeneous composition.

The history of the *Piazza della Signoria*, though long, confused, and full of contradictions, is an instructive example of the pressure of antagonistic tendencies which in this case were coordinated only with difficulty by two unifying principles: the desire to enlarge the area of the square, and to give it a coherent and closed appearance.

The *Piazza del Campo* at Siena occupies the depression between three hills which were covered by settlements that gradually grew together and formed the city of Siena.[36] The Palazzo Pubblico rises at the lowest point of the square, which like a shallow amphitheater uses the natural configuration of the terrain. Here, where the three hills converged, arose the civic center of Siena in the middle of the urban area. Originally it was the site of two older and smaller squares which were combined to fulfill the function of the market square for the whole community. No records are extant which would explain why the Palazzo Pubblico stands at the lowest point of the *piazza*, an almost unique situation in the history of city planning. The reason may have been that the *palazzo* could not possibly have been built with its back to the *duomo* and the street leading to it. Although the civic and religious centers were each a self-contained architectural unit, they were nevertheless interrelated in spirit and in fact. In the 13th century, the route from the *piazza* to the *duomo* was long and tortuous. It led through the main streets of the town, the present via di Città and the via del Capitano. But it is likely that the shorter way through the via dei Pellegrini (street of the pilgrims) was more frequently used, ending immediately at

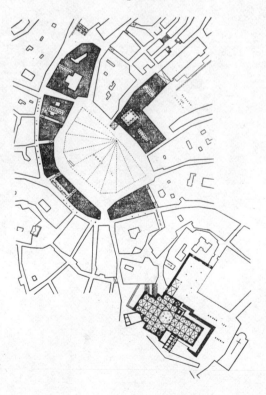

25. Plan of the cathedral square and Piazza del Campo in Siena.

35. W. Braunfels, *op. cit.*, p. 119.
36. *Ibid.*, pp. 193-98. *Passim*.

26. Palazzo Comunale in Siena.

the later baptistery. For the pilgrims and visitors who followed this route, the baptistery was situated in front of the *duomo*, the usual arrangement inasmuch as the baptistery had to be reached first. In this way the organic connection between the two centers was restored.

The building history of the *duomo* and the baptistery is not very clear, but it may safely be assumed that the interrelations between the secular and religious centers played an important role in the decision to erect the Palazzo Pubblico with its front facing the direction to the *duomo;* since there was no other choice, the lowest part of the *piazza* was selected for this purpose. The extraordinary height of the tower of the *palazzo,* the *torre del Mangia,* called after the first summoner, who with the stroke of a hammer against the bell tolled the hours, was another consequence of this situation: the difference between the low location of the *palazzo* and the *duomo* on the highest point of the town had to be neutralized in order to restore a visible and symbolic balance between the two centers. Thus the *torre del Mangia,* with its slender and long shaft, vied with the *campanile* in height and significance. Both were landmarks of equal importance, rising high above the houses of the burghers and proclaiming the pride and power of the worldly and religious life of the city.

The *Piazza del Campo* was conceived from the beginning as a uniform square. Special regulations were issued stipulating that all windows in the *piazza* should be of the same shape: *che in Ciascuna casa, la quale si facesse di nuovo d'intorno al Campo del mercato, tutte le finestre si facciano a colonelli* (May 10, 1297).[37] The whole square was to be surrounded by a continuous and completely uniform front of buildings. All projecting structures had to be removed: *di non fare ballatoia d'intorno al campo del mercato* (1309-10). Not the individual building but the continuous façades were the basis and object of the architectural conception. The houses, plain and reserved, were excellently adapted to this task. They formed a simple background for the events that took place in the arena of the square, for the ordered life of a genuine community, for *senza ordine non si fa alcuna cosa buona.* (From a speech in the town council of Siena in 1357.)[38] It was an open-air interior perfectly enclosed and removed from the less stately other parts of the town. The arenalike shape of the square was accentuated by a pavement consisting of concentric travertine slabs. The importance of the *palazzo* as the principal building was emphasized by white dividing lines in the pavement converging on the *palazzo.* Although continuous block fronts of uniform inconspicuous houses contrasting with more monumental buildings and monuments were not unusual in Italy, the *Piazza del Campo* is unique in its grand simplicity,

37. Quoted after W. Braunfels, *op. cit.,* p. 250. Regulation contained in the Statutes No. 20 of 1309/10.

38. Quoted after W. Braunfels, *ibid.,* p. 253. Document in the State Archives of Siena. Consiglio Generale, Deliberationi, Vol. 160, C. 37.

homogeneity, and determined consistency. It shares this uniqueness perhaps only with the *plaza mayor* at Salamanca. Both are open-air interiors of such perfect beauty that they are ranked among the masterpieces of great city planning. The idea of a uniform composition of the *Piazza del Campo* was ever present in the deliberations of the town council. At the beginning of the 16th century, the possibility was discussed of surrounding the whole square with arcades. Whether this would have been an improvement may be doubted. In any case this plan was abandoned.

The *Piazza del Campo* has often been called *un bel teatro*. This description is fully justified. The houses surround the square like tiers of boxes in a theater. The broad circular passage, interposed between the houses and the concave area, the Greek dancing place (*orchestra*), with the altar (*thymele*), encloses the central part like the circles the stalls. The whole is a perfectly contained space with a clear structure and articulation. It is a space at rest, a daily life space far from the transcendental space of the Gothic cathedrals. But it represents a stage for which an awareness of place rather than an awareness of space was the creative factor. This place had to be limited, solidity enclosed by the plain walls of the houses without distracting accents, and the manner in which this place was actually experienced arose not from a structural idea or consciousness of spatial relations but from a topographical sense of contiguous unity. This contiguity was not disturbed by the streets which entered the square radially centered on the *palazzo*—a movement continued by the pattern of the pavement and the white dividing lines converging on the lowest point. The symmetry of the square was accentuated by the *Fonte Gaia,* the Fountain of Cheerfulness, by Jacopo della Quercia. Its shape follows the gentle incline of the concave terrain. It owes its name to the enthusiastic reaction of the population when the first fountain was installed.

The *piazza,* the *palazzo,* the *torre del Mangia,* and the *Fonte Gaia* were symbols of the wealth and the permanence of a city deeply rooted in the imagination of the Sienese citizens. Generation after generation worked on the completion of this architectural composition and made it a harmonious whole. The passage of time has had no disintegrating influence. The *palazzo* was begun after 1298. The *torre del Mangia* was erected in the years 1338-49. The fountain was added between 1409 and 1419. Eight architects were employed on the tower. When the first design was presented to the government the councillors refused to believe that such a daring structure could last. Not until the architects had pledged themselves on their word of honor that the building would not collapse—*che non cade*—was the design approved. They pledged their word, and the tower still stands.

CHAPTER 4

The Renaissance

The Geometric Spider

THE DAWN of the Renaissance did not materially affect the cities and the towns of Italy. The transition proceeded in an almost imperceptible manner. The old tenets began to fade away. The principles of city planning, valid for centuries, disintegrated only slowly. It took a long time before new ideas and a new language of form were embodied in the architectural principles which influenced the reshaping of urban communities. There was nothing exceptional in this. Apart from the slow and hesitant dissemination of new ideas generally, city planning always lags behind the more rapid changes in painting and sculpture. The solid obstacles are greater, more difficult to overcome, which alone explains the more sedate pace of physical transformation in cities and towns. None of the cities existing before this transitional period ever absorbed all the fundamental characteristics of Renaissance city planning. New individual buildings were erected, new squares and streets were laid out—but the town, as a whole, retained its old appearance for a long while. What did change, slowly and gradually, was the spirit, the atmosphere, the tenor and rhythm of life, and, above all, the situation of man in the general scheme of things and his attitude to his environment.

These new trends were seeping down into the collective soul of the population, very tardily and incompletely. Only a few individuals were the inspired agents of this adventure into the vast realm of hitherto unexplored potentialities. But these few—many-sided men as Burckhardt called them—were the catalysts who molded the general opinion, however imperceptibly, by their example. They were the leaders in the break-up of the established structure of society which had motivated communal life for generations. They were the prime movers who emptied the traditional forms of their spiritual significance and opened the way to expansion and reason. As Burckhardt remarked, "At the close of the thirteenth century Italy began to swarm with individuality; the ban laid upon human personality was dissolved; and a thousand figures meet us each in its own special shape and dress." The age of faith was melting away; the old symbolism and spiritual appeal were losing their intensity and finally their meaning, discarded as narrow and rigid limitations standing in the way of a rejuvenation of existence. Life became increasingly secularized, and a scientific outlook devoid of spiritual purpose began to dissolve the image of man in his wholeness as an immortal being inescapably ensnared in the web of his spiritual loyalties. The alchemical and pseudoscientific trend of the medieval search for unveiling Nature's secrets stimulated and guided more by a playful curiosity and intuition than by a serious urge and systematic procedure, turned into the deliberate and irresistible impulse to analyze through scientific investigation the *modus operandi* of natural phenomena. Scientific research was conducted for its own sake; along with other branches of mathematics, geometry became the guiding spirit of architecture and city planning.

It was in this atmosphere heavily charged with geometry and theoretical exercises—sometimes not much more than an all-too-sophisticated and purely intellectual playing with external forms and their various combinations—that the revolution in city planning began to take shape. It was a revolution of extraordinary complexity. Old trends which had lingered on from antiquity were revived, new trends were followed up, and these conflicting tendencies were absorbed into a new consciousness of an external objective world. The change was most obvious in painting. Compare a work of Giotto, with its relieflike figures standing against a flat background, and a painting by Masaccio in which human forms move as corporeal entities, like animated sculptures within a realistic space from which the spectator is no longer excluded. This effect was accomplished by the introduction of perspective, of an awareness of volume, and a consequent integration of the hitherto more-or-less independent elements of the composition. The discovery of the third dimension as an artistic means of realistic representation through the illusion of perspective—through the sensation of spatial relations that hold the individual elements together and relate them to the space within which the spectator himself moves—this discovery, which by its very nature was one of the essential media of architecture, exerted the greatest influence on city planning. The third dimension, the conscious creation of space in depth as an architectural device, had been unknown to antiquity. It was simply "there," and the buildings were arranged like sculptures within the existing space. There had been, of course, a sense of space, yet not a clearly conceived idea of space. Now this changed with the discovery of perspective. A new element was added to the art of city planning.

The dimensions of the perspective views were modest—at least at the beginning. Moreover, use of perspective layouts on a larger scale was still rare, owing to the great difficulty and expense involved in securing the necessary space. But the conception of perspective was nevertheless revolutionary. The multiple and coordinated viewpoints of the Middle Ages were reduced to one that gave meaning and coherence to the composition. In contrast to the Middle Ages, with the almost stationary space relations of their squares and streets, the perspective layout engendered a degree of motion and exerted a certain attraction to the point on which the perspective was focused. It was still a far cry to the violent movement of the Baroque. It was an arrested, a balanced motion. Renaissance space was still at rest but it

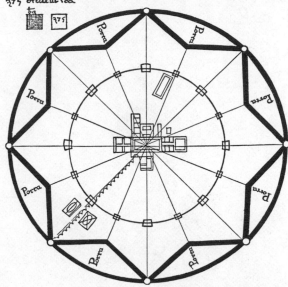

27. **Design for the Ideal City of Sforzinda by Filarete, from** *Codex Magliabecchianus.*

made those who moved into it active participants of the architectural composition, just as the viewer of a Renaissance painting is drawn into the orbit of events represented in the painting. The space of the Middle Ages was outspokenly nonperspective in painting and in city planning. The typical space of the Renaissance, most clearly expressed in the design of an Ideal City, was decidedly perspective in theory and reality.

Let us return to the complex character of the revolution in city planning. Old and new trends combined to create an atmosphere in which the existing physical structure of a city was eventually changed beyond recognition, giving rise to a very different language of form. Renaissance city planning was more than the mere reshaping of a tradition, as it has sometimes been described. There were, of course, influences that like intermittent streams continued to flow under the surface, only to reappear again when and where conditions were favorable. To this group belong, as a legacy of Roman antiquity, the emphasis laid on symmetry, regularity, and organized composition. These trends were never wholly absent from medieval city planning in Italy, much less so than in Northern Europe.

In Italy the architects and even the man in the street still experienced the ancient buildings as *their* buildings, the old Roman towns as *their* towns, and the old monuments as *their* monuments. They sensed behind the ruins of the *fora* and the town walls the great achievements of their forebears in architectural discipline and competence. Living tradition was never completely broken, however casual and faint this experience may have been. These old tendencies had to be reconciled with the new ideas which were most potently expressed in the upsurge of mathematics and geometry and in the study of optics, leading to the architectural device of perspective and a rationally organized layout of new cities. Thus the reconciliation was effected. Spontaneous empathy so characteristic of medieval city planning gave way to a careful and objective assessment of the intended purpose, and how this purpose could best be expressed in the spirit of the times and as an architectural design commensurate with the new ideas. The basic conception of a town was changed: the medieval town, with the exception of those laid out by the will of one person as deliberately limited entities from the beginning, developed gradually by increasing the originally small nucleus through the inclusion of suburbs, whereas the Ideal City of the Renaissance was conceived from the start as one unit that was not supposed to grow beyond its intended size. But this new theory and rationalism led to a certain formalism and finally to a drawing-board routine that lost all contact with reality.

The Roman gridiron plan and the geometric spider plan

28. The Copernican system of the universe, from an old Atlas of Astronomy.

of the Renaissance are interrelated by an elective affinity, not merely by the factual survival of Roman street patterns in cities like Turin, Florence, and Lucca. The architects of the Renaissance rediscovered the spirit of these layouts as congenial expressions of their own ideas, which they expressed not by a slavish imitation or external adoption of what was handed on to them but by the awareness of what their own time had in common with antiquity, of the same mental attitude that demanded order and discipline, limitation, and rationality. They studied the Roman legacy but this side of their efforts remained theoretical. They did not copy the still extant Roman town plans but tried to understand the thoughts of their predecessors as the formative forces behind their practical work.

Limitations must have had a special appeal for the Renaissance architects. Their idea of the universe was dominated by the Aristotelian concept. The Copernican revolution did not change this outlook. It still conceived the world as limited, bounded by the sphere of the fixed stars. It replaced the geocentric by the heliocentric system and to that extent made the old system meaningless. Man moved like the earth from the center, looked at the world from a peripheral standpoint; but his world was as yet not infinite. It was still pervaded by Aristotle's dictum: "Evil is a form of the unlimited, and good of the limited." This peripheral view led inevitably to the introduction of perspective and the pre-eminence of streets as means of implementing perspective principles. Thus two important elements of Renaissance city planning were reconciled—limitation and perspective—in other words, the Roman plan with its organized restriction, nonperspective in essence, and the Renaissance layout with its emphasis on the periphery and vistas. The architects of the early Renaissance were unable to conceive an architectural composition as open and infinite, as a symbolic expression of infinite space. They were convinced that clarity of form was identical with limitation of form. Within these limits they created a certain loosening, a greater variety, and arrested movement. They were sensitive rationalists who had discarded the tenets of the Age of Faith and relied on reason. The illusion of religious-symbolic significance was lost. The illusion of reality—of a world that could be understood, not merely believed in—was in ascendancy and exerted its powerful influence upon man and all his works.

Another trend is of interest. An affinity similar to that between the Roman and Renaissance town plans existed between the tenement houses of Imperial Rome and those of the Middle Ages and the Renaissance. Here again it was the analogy of ideas and purpose that created an almost unbroken living tradition. Neither the Middle Ages nor the Renaissance imitated the many-storied tenement houses of Imperial Rome but they revived certain features and, above all, retained the old Mediterranean habit still evident today of building dwelling houses close together with shops along the streets, staircases leading directly to the upper floors, and garrets above the shops. It is interesting to observe that these features were not transplanted to England, France, or Asia Minor. This fact would confirm the assumption that a connection existed between the dwelling houses of Imperial Rome and those of the Italian Middle Ages and the Renaissance. It also tends to show that certain functional needs—for instance, the rows of shops along the streets—once they had found a satisfactory solution, survived even under greatly changed conditions and more by their own utilitarian suitability than by direct imitation. For it is most unlikely that rows of ancient Roman shops still existed in the Middle Ages or in the Renaissance.

Utopia and theory were as closely interrelated in the Renaissance as in other periods. Utopias tried to find solutions for a society in transition; city planning and architectural theories attempted to give these new ideas concrete form and expression. The utopias based their arguments on two principles whose interactions would create, as their originators believed, the ideal society consisting of ideal individuals. The first principle was that human happiness and perfection rest on moral criteria; the second principle claimed that, given a proper physical environment, human beings living in this improved setting will also improve. Both postulates are correct but the problem remains, who shall begin—the moralists or the environmentalists? The assumption obviously was that both should act in unison, gradually and simultaneously lifting inner and outer life to a higher level. This duality was clearly expressed by St. Thomas Aquinas in *De Regimine Principum*:

For an individual to lead a good life two things are required. The first and most important is to act in a virtuous manner, for virtue is that by which one lives well; the second, which is secondary and as it were instrumental, is a sufficiency of those bodily goods whose use is necessary to an act of virtue.

These words were written as early as the 13th century but expressed clearly the thoughts that also ran through all later utopias. However, these general and laudable ideas were buttressed by more detailed arguments in which Thomas Aquinas discussed the interdependence of city and country:

Now there are two ways in which an abundance of food stuffs can be supplied to a city. The first is when the soil is so fertile that it nobly provides for all the necessities of human life. The second is by trade, through which the necessities of life are brought to the town from different places. But it is quite clear that the first means is better. For the higher a thing is the more self-sufficient it is; since whatever needs another's help is by that very fact proven inferior.

He was aware of the disintegrating effect of trade upon the social structure of a city:

If the citizens themselves devote their lives to matters of trade, the way will be opened to many vices. For since the object of trading leads especially to the making of money, greed is awakened in the hearts of citizens through the pursuit of trade . . . each will work only for his own profit, despising the public good.[1]

1. Translated by G. P. Phelan. 1938. Quoted by permission of the Pontifical Institute of Mediaeval Studies, Toronto, Canada.

Utopia and Theory

All utopias of the Renaissance laid special emphasis on manual labor as an honorable occupation. This was in striking contrast to the Greek idea that work was merely an unavoidable by-product of life that should be left to slaves or professional craftsmen who, as a class, were excluded from the conduct of the affairs of state. But since the medieval towns were sufficient proof that a community almost exclusively composed of producers (that is, workers who in one way or the other toiled with their hands) could efficiently govern itself, this demand simply set the seal upon the accomplishment of a past period. However, the real and momentous significance of this sanction by men, who belonged to the intellectual *élite* and the *avant-garde* of the age, was that they not only made work an honorable duty but also established the right to work as a justified claim of everybody. With this step they anticipated one of the most fundamental doctrines of capitalism and the development of one of the explosive trends which were to disintegrate the social and physical structure of cities and towns. But the right to work, the cornerstone of individualization, was, at the same time, the beginning of the end of the integrated communities that were economically and socially well balanced and physically limited within a small circumference. The sprawling cities of today have their origin in the attitude toward work as an honored right. This trend is not to be regretted. It was inevitable. What is regrettable is merely the misuse of a morally justified idea and the inability of later generations to cope with the problems initiated in the Renaissance.

The utopianists of the Renaissance were aware, as St. Thomas Aquinas before them, that a durable society must accommodate the interests of town and country, with craftsmen and peasants on the same level of importance. They demanded, therefore, that agricultural workers should enjoy equal rights with those of the townsmen. In this respect they were influenced by the example of the monastic orders, from which they also took over other features, incorporating them into the social and administrative structure of their Ideal Cities. This preoccupation with the integration of society was, at least partly, a reaction against the intense individualism of the Renaissance, which they regarded with full justification as a socially disintegrating force. They did not and possibly could not understand that the nature of man cannot be constructed to order, that man is more than the sum total of numerous individual character traits, and that efforts to dam the assertion of man's individuality were doomed to failure. The dawn of the Age of Reason was a fact. They did not recognize that the growth of knowledge and questioning criticism were moving in the same direction as the awakened individualism.

This movement which was represented by a few "many-sided men" was, as Burckhardt said, "antipopular," and "through it Europe became for the first time sharply divided into cultivated and uncultivated classes." Although this statement should be taken with some reservation—there had always been cultivated and uncultivated classes—it contains a certain truth, inasmuch as the strength of the new *élite* was based on knowledge and learning and not exclusively on mere power and affluence. What is especially interesting is that the utopian writers of the Renaissance, in spite of their prophetic vision of a better future and their progressive ideas, denied the very ideals which the new age had kindled and cherished most. Their ideal was not the many-sided, individualistic man but the "normal" or community man. Admittedly these writers were pre-eminently concerned with man as a member of a community. They did not want to reduce him to a standard type. But what makes the modern reader suspicious is that the utopianists suggested an environment which was, to say the least, dull, uniform, and regimented, with identical houses, identical clothes, and a rigid discipline of work. If one takes all the various trends together which the utopianists of the Renaissance embodied in their writings, it is only too obvious that they were the representatives of a transitional period and that, more often than not, they were not fully aware of what they were advocating. But do we moderns, who pride ourselves on our down-to-earth realism, really know what *we* want? It is clearly more human, more modest to view the utopian writer of the Renaissance and of other times as an initiator of new ideas who groped his way forward to new adventures of the mind and who was like every other

> Man, proud man,
> Drest in a little brief authority,
> Most ignorant of what he's most assured.

Yet the great positive value of the utopias is that they made people aware of the fact—almost inaccessibly buried under mountans of frustration and an all too human preoccupation with the things of daily life—that man alone could change the conception and appearance of urban communities. That the hopes of the utopias failed is obvious. Nevertheless they were of great importance, for they reflected in unambiguous terms the spirit of the times, their aspirations and ideals, and as such were the indispensable counterpart to the theories on city planning which the Renaissance produced in abundance.

All utopias have in common the assumption that the Ideal City and the Ideal State which they describe are architecturally unimaginative. Their layout is a repetition of similar elements grouped in different geometrical patterns. Concentric rings or squares and radial streets had obviously a spatial appeal for the amateur utopian city planners. The old symbolism of the Heavenly Jerusalem was still alive, but now greatly diluted by the rationalism and regimentation of the Renaissance. Tommaso Campanella's *Civitas Solis* (City of the Sun), first published in 1623, is a fairly representative example.

On a vast plain rises a hill on which the greater part of the city is built, but its circles extend for some distance beyond the base of the hill, which is of such a size that the diameter of the city is two miles or more and its circumference about seven. But being built on a slope the city has more houses than if it were built on a plain. The city is divided into very great circles named after the seven planets, and one passes from one to the other through four streets and four gates which look towards the four corners of the earth. It is so arranged that if the first circle were stormed, it would require more effort to storm the second, and still more for the others. . . . Entering then through the Northern Gate, which is covered with iron and which can be raised and lowered thanks to an ingenious device, one sees a level space fifty paces wide between the first and second walls. . . . And so one enters the second circle . . . and sees the second walls with ravelins and galleries for promenading. . . . The ground is always level except when one goes through the doors which are double because of the interior and exterior walls, and going from one to the other one mounts some steps which are scarcely noticeable, as they proceed in a slanting direction and their height is hardly perceptible. On the top of the hill there is a great flat space on which a temple has been built with wondrous art.

The study of sciences and manual labor occupy an important place. Agriculture is carried on scientifically and all citizens work in the fields. Sexual relationships are regulated with the aim to breed a healthy race. Men and women "go to bed by order of the magistrate and the matron." Before this "they slept in separate cells until the hour in which they must mate has come and then the matron goes and opens the doors of both cells." Then they are let out and, like the bull in a bull ring, storm into battle. In this apparently all too Ideal City slave labor was abolished. There was no need for it since individual freedom did not exist and everybody had to do what he or she was told to do. Everybody was a slave except, of course, the "leaders."

The details of this ideal scheme are less important than the spirit in which it was conceived. It had all the characteristics of the designs for the Ideal City of the Renaissance: playing with superficial symbolism and geometrical forms; regimentation and rigidity; theoretical speculations and subordination of content to institutional devices; pseudoscientific trimmings and a pseudo-many-sidedness. "Everyone is taught all the arts" and "he who has studied most arts and knows how to practice them is considered most noble." The affinity in spirit and execution between the utopias and the Ideal Cities is obvious. Both are the products of an age that had just begun to discover the unimaginable potentialities of intellectual freedom but was not yet fully ripe for the venture. Hence the preoccupation with unrealistic formalism, with lifeless patterns of layout, and with regimentation finally leading to sterility.

It is one of the ironies of history that the new many-sided men, seeing the world opening up before their eyes, imposed the straitjacket of rigid geometrical form upon their designs for Ideal Cities that were to embody novel ideas of a rejuvenated society. Their newly won intellectual freedom was still too immature, too groping to imbue them with the spirit of sovereign mastery of the manifold realities of life, with the supreme disregard of the Baroque for limitation, rigidity, and symmetry. They believed that the all too perfect patterns of their neatly worked out drawing-board schemes could encompass the fullness of life-centered communities. This belief was rooted in the idea that life on earth for every citizen was guided by the movements of the heavenly bodies in which the infallibility of the teachings of Christ is most manifest.

This combination of astrology and Christianity could not fail to lead to the adoption of the Copernican picture of the world in which men like Campanella believed. His plan for the City of the Sun was the reflection of this system on earth: the seven concentric rings surrounding the sun were repeated in his design. There can hardly be any doubt that Campanella was strongly influenced by the heliocentric system of Copernicus. The name of his city points directly to this source. However, despite these symbolic connections with the Creator and the unquestioning conviction that the majesty of His infinite power and wisdom would lift the inhabitants of the Ideal Cities to a higher level of existence, these many-sided men were bound to fail. Yet with all their shortcomings they were true representatives of the age of insurgence that had already begun.

Spontaneity was taboo, premeditation the order of the day in the numerous designs of Ideal Cities. The radial and concentric schemes of this period have exerted a questionable influence upon city planners up to the present day. They contributed to the growing sterility and hollowness of city planning and retarded the liberation from old ideas and old habits. The long

29. Medallion of Leone Battista Alberti attributed to Matteo di Andrea de' Pasti.

115

line of the Italian theoreticians of city planning begins with Leone Battista Alberti (1404-72). In his work, he combined trends of medieval and Renaissance planning. *Commoditas* and *Voluptas* were the poles between which his ideas moved—*Commoditas* meaning the functional adaptation to a definite purpose, the legacy of the Middle Ages, and *Voluptas* standing for sensuous beauty, visual enjoyment, the demands of the new age. He maintained that

A city is not built wholly for the sake of shelter, but ought to be so contrived, that besides more civil conveniences there may be handsome spaces left for squares, courses for chariots, gardens, places to take the air in, for swimming, and the like, both for amusement and recreation.

Alberti did not leave a design for an Ideal City but his treatise *De re aedificatoria* contains important contributions to the principles of city planning which was for him more than dry theory. He coined the phrase *tutta quella musica*—this whole music—to express the integrity and emotional appeal of architecture and city building. But he was also aware of the social and practical implications. He understood that the rise of capitalism would create a structure of urban society quite different from that of the Middle Ages, and that this would fundamentally alter the physical layout of cities and towns. He recognized the need for selecting a suitable site. Once this had been done, everything else would follow as a matter of course: layout and shape of the city, whether circular or square, could easily be adapted to the site. In all his suggestions the two aspects of *Commoditas* and *Voluptas*— of the practical and the ideal—are visible. The city area should be clearly zoned and the obnoxious and smelly trades of the tanners, fullers, and the like should be located in the outer and less frequented districts. There should be different markets for butchers, goldsmiths, timber merchants, and the like. Residential districts for the wealthy burghers should be separated from those of the poorer classes. Alberti's demand that larger open spaces should be included in the urban area (IV. 3) was a typically medieval notion: *hanc malim quae adauctum civium numerum percommode possit accipere.*[2]

All this was hardly new; it was the general practice of the Middle Ages. But it justified the separation of the trades in different streets not solely for utilitarian reasons but also on aesthetic grounds, because the ever-changing picture of the various professional activities would enhance the liveliness and beauty of the city and create unity in diversity. Streets should not be straight, but "like a river turning gently first to one side then to the other in many round about ways," which would make

2. "I would prefer a city which could hold comfortably a greater number of citizens."

the city appear larger and more magnificent. Moreover, Alberti asserts, this irregularity would produce an ever-changing appearance of the buildings and of the course of the streets. "This winding of the streets will make the passenger at every step discover a new structure, and the front and door of any house will directly face the middle of the street." Finally, he uses the old argument that winding streets are better for defense. Yet at the same time he defended the straight streets, where all houses are arranged in a straight line and have the same height. These seemingly contradictory suggestions are not mutually exclusive. On the contrary, they are proof of the open-mindedness of a great personality that rose beyond the limitations of pure theory and abstraction, endeavoring to combine what appeared to him valuable in the traditional layout of cities with the new, more rationalistic attitude which was by no means identical with the functionalism of the Middle Ages.

Alberti's views were still, in many important respects, formed by medieval ideas. He was more concerned with the individual elements of the city than with the relationships between them. For him the city was above all a utilitarian product which should be "beautiful," if this was possible. Here we have strong undertones of medieval functionalism, although it is unlikely that he was aware of this affinity. On the other hand, it never occurred to him that the city of the Middle Ages was conceived and experienced as a spiritual entity. His theories were a halfway house between the Age of Faith and the Age of Rationalism. He was aware of the complexity of the human personality and of the unavoidable shallowness that would result from a dissociation from sensibility and a split between intellect and emotion. In this respect Alberti differed from all other Renaissance theoreticians who tried to install Reason as the Supreme Being, believing that a superficial involvement with the magic of numbers and geometry was sufficient concession to emotional aspirations.

The aim of the Italian theoreticians was the development of the city in its totality as an integrated work of art. As Vincenzo Scamozzi said, the relationship of the whole city to its parts is like that of the human body to its members, and the streets are its arteries. Antonio Averulino, better known as Filarete (c. 1400-69), was the first artist—it seems he was originally not an architect but a sculptor, for he was commissioned in 1433 by Pope Eugenius IV to execute in bronze the main door of St. Peter's—who designed an entire Ideal City. In *Il trattato d'architettura,* published between 1451 and 1464, he described (Books VI and VIII) the city of Sforzinda, named after his patron Francesco Sforza. The city was conceived as part of the surrounding country, not just as an isolated and artificial product without relationship to the natural setting. In this respect Filarete was an exception, although he did not elaborate this aspect of the design. Nevertheless he was aware of the fact that no city, not even an Ideal City, can exist in isolation.

Before we proceed to a detailed description of Sforzinda, a few general remarks may be pertinent. The Ideal Cities of the Renaissance, not only in Italy but also in other countries, were programmatic statements expressing the new ideas that developed following the disintegration of medieval mentality. Insofar as they expressed the new attitude in a new language of form they were of decisive importance. But it would be a serious mistake to regard them as the first and only attempts at conceiving a city from the very beginning as a self-contained unit limited in size and structure. In the Middle Ages many cities were built which were limited in scope and character and conceived in their layout as unalterable entities. The *bastides* of France or the regular and limited cities of Spain are obvious examples which incorporated the same principles. This fact is mostly overlooked when medieval cities are considered. True, most cities of the Middle Ages grew gradually. But this does not mean that all cities did the same. What is essential to understand is that both growth and planning existed side by side and that a gradual development happened to be more frequent and perhaps more congenial to the generally more spontaneous character of medieval city planning. However, if certain conditions demanded a design of limited scope and form, the Middle Ages did exactly that, but—and here is the fundamental difference—they did not look at these regular and limited cities as programmatic statements of new ideas. In this respect the cities of China come more closely to the Ideal Cities of the Renaissance—in spirit, intention, and execution.

On the other hand, colonial cities in all countries and at all times were limited entities regularly laid out and stereotyped. The Royal Ordinances included in the *Leyes de Indias* concerning the laying out of the new towns issued by Philip II in 1573 expressed these tendencies quite definitely. They may stand as an example for numerous other occasions when the same principles were applied. It was stipulated, among many other details to be observed, that "in order that entries of these assignments be better made, a plan of the town is always to be made in advance," and that "settlers are to endeavor as far as possible to make all structures uniform, for the sake of the beauty of the town."

Roman cities more closely resembled those of China in that their limitation and regularity were conditioned by religious considerations. The Ideal Cities of the Renaissance occupy a special place in the history of city planning because they were the results of cold, conscious reasoning and pure theory without any links to religious or emotional causes. They were secular and formalistic manifestations intended as arguments in the great debate of how the exigencies of a new life could be met and expressed in a new language of form. Practical considerations, of course, played a considerable role: a complicated system of defense was needed which should withstand more efficiently the new technique of far-ranging firearms.

But these utilitarian and other principles, however important they had been, were overshadowed by one development which sowed the seeds for a radical break with the past. The rigid formalism of all schemes for Ideal Cities subordinated content to form and the unforeseeable multiformity of the human drama to regimentation and equalization, until in the end a dull and deadening sterility dissolved the last vestiges of creative imagination and audacity. The role of the Ideal Cities was, therefore, of twofold significance: they were representative interpretations of a new spirit in city design and as such stood at a turning point of human development; at the same time they were the beginning of the end, the first designs to abandon the principle of a sound functional balance between houses and streets. It is characteristic that not a single plan of an Ideal City contains even the slightest indication of the arrangement of the houses. Only streets, squares, and walls are shown. In spite of all the magnificent performances of the architects and city planners of the following century, the designers of the Ideal Cities of the early Renaissance had the doubtful privilege of being the unintentional originators of the Cult of the Street, which finally led to the empty plans of drawing-board architects and vista mongers.

To return to Filarete's design for Sforzinda: The layout of the city is perfectly symmetrical, its outer walls forming a polygon of sixteen sides with salient and re-entrant angles, a figure formed by two superimposed squares. The eight salient angles are occupied by towers and the eight re-entrant angles by the gates. The eight towers are connected with the center by canals and the eight gates by roads. The eight salient angles with the towers are linked by a circle. This line has been interpreted by several scholars as a road. It is, however, more likely that it was a moat into which the water of the canals was directed, for without it the canals would have had no outlet. Moreover, it would be incomprehensible why a road outside the fortifications, not even connected with the gates, should surround the city. If this were so, it would have been merely an advantage for an attacking enemy.

Each of the eight canals and the eight streets passed through a square. Of these sixteen squares those situated on the canals leading to the towers are reserved for churches and those leading to the gates for specialized markets such as wood, straw, grain, and wine to make easier the uninterrupted flow of traffic to and from the latter. All sixteen squares were interconnected by a circular road. In Filarete's own words:

In the center [of the inner city] the *piazza* is situated extending from east to west, 150 *braccia* wide and 300 *braccia* long. [A *braccio* equals about 28 inches.] Each small square of the plan corresponds to one square *stadio*. [A *stadio* is about 220 yards.] At the eastern end of the *piazza* stands the Chiesa Maggiore and opposite, at the western end, the Palace of the Prince. On the north the *piazza* is adjoined by the Piazza de' Mercatanti (93¾ by 187½ *braccia*) and on the south by the great food market (125 by 250 *braccia*). To the west of the latter I will erect the palace of the captain of the police which, in this way, is separated from the palace only by one street. To the south there will be the baths and brothels, and to the east taverns and inns. Butchers' shops and stalls for the sale of fish and fowl will be established later. At the west of the Piazza de' Mercatanti stands the Town Hall with the prison, and on the north the Palace of the Mayor. And further west the mint and the customs office . . . From all the eight gates at the obtuse angles as well as from the eight round towers at the rectangular corners of the fortifications main streets lead to the *piazza*. Each one of these sixteen streets is intersected approximately in the middle of its course by a square of 80 by 160 *braccia*. At each of the eight squares, situated at the streets leading to the towers, there will be a parish church owned by different religious orders. The other eight squares serve as markets. In the two western and eastern [markets] straw and timber will be sold, in the two northern oil and similar commodities, and in the two southern corn and wine. Around the markets craftsmen will be settled and one or two butchers' shops will be set up. All streets slope down from the *piazza* toward the periphery so that water will run quickly out of the city. The principal streets are lined on both sides with colonnades, 8 to 10 *braccia* wide, rising 1 to 2 *braccia* above the street level. The main streets will be 40 and the secondary streets 20 *braccia* wide. The great volume of water provided by the Indo and Auerlo rivers enables us to distribute the water to all parts of the city. In order to reduce the noise from vehicular traffic and for the greater convenience of the inhabitants we will surround the *piazza* and the other markets with navigable canals and will make every second principal street a waterway lined by colonnades. Vehicles and horsemen will be restricted therefore to the other well-paved streets. In the *piazza* there will be a large water basin from which, through the opening of valves, all streets and squares can be flooded and flushed. Numerous bridges over the canals will provide convenient connections.[3]

Filarete's plan for Sforzinda was not merely a geometrical exercise. In his own opinion at least, it had a deep symbolical

3. W. von Oettingen. "Antonio Averlino Filarete's Tractat über die Baukunst." Book VI, Folio 42 v.–43 v. In: *Quellenschriften für Kunstgeschichte und Kunsttechnik des Mittelalters und der Neuzeit*. N.F., Vol. III. 1890.

meaning. But it is difficult if not impossible to take this symbolism too seriously. It had nothing in common with the genuine spiritual symbolism of the Middle Ages—for example, at Pisa. Filarete's symbolism is in essence a symbolism of the surface, a forced similarity of forms. It remains hollow and meaningless. In the first book of his *Treatise* Filarete expresses the conviction that the stars and the planets exert a direct influence on the behavior of men. In Book XV describing the garden of the prince we are informed that it was laid out like a map of the earth, with high mounds from which the water in the canals flowed and to which it returned. The latter might be a justification for assuming that the outer circle around the city was not a moat after all; but then what was it? The circulation of the water may have been an allusion to the circulation of the blood, the canals being the arteries and veins. The superimposed squares resemble an ancient magic symbol. It is possible and indeed likely that Filarete knew this and used it intentionally for his design. There is still another possibility: he may have had in mind the Wheel of Fortune when he designed the spokelike layout of the streets and canals.

The predilection of the period for symbolism is well attested, not only in Italy but also in other countries. For instance, in Holland the number of bastions of several cities was seven—in itself an ancient symbolic number, but for the Dutch it was also the symbol of the seven United Provinces. The magic of numbers was part of the general spell which the preoccupation with geometry had cast over the architects and city builders. Rationalism and magic symbolism—this strange combination of antagonistic trends influenced the many-sided men of the Renaissance. However, it had the sanction of Alberti, who had reminded the architects that every number had its own significance and that "the ancients had connected with every number a definite meaning."

At about the same time as Filarete's treatise, Francesco di Giorgio Martini (1439-1502) published his *Trattato di architettura civile e militare*. Martini laid special emphasis on the need to adapt the street pattern to the site. If a city is built on a hill, the streets should rise in spirals to the center or as diagonals or rectilinear connections; if a level site is chosen, a checkerboard layout is the ideal solution; and if the architect is completely free in the choice of the plan, a radial-concentric street system should be preferred. Abstract formalistic speculations without any regard to the particular function of the city or the daily life of its citizens! It seems that Martini was the first architect to use a checkerboard scheme for the internal layout of his Ideal City. However, like Filarete's plan his octagonal scheme was certainly influenced by Vitruvius and consequently by Filarete himself. It was based on sixteen sectors transversed by eight streets of which

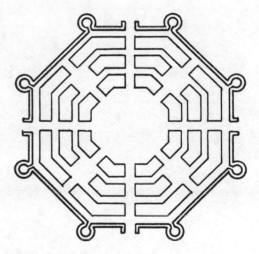

30. **Design for a fortress town by Giorgio Martini.**

four led to four gates from a central octagonal square. The combination of the checkerboard layout with a polygonal circumference reappeared later in the designs of other architects, possibly because the radial plan encountered too many difficulties or because a combination of the two types offered a greater variety.

Giorgio Martini was one of the first originators of the theory and technique of modern fortifications which from this time on exerted an ever-growing influence on the internal layout of cities. The fortifications of the medieval towns, consisting of simple walls, towers, and gates, had hardly affected the town plan as such. After the introduction of firearms the walls were strengthened and semicircular bastions were added where cannons could be installed. But this was insufficient, for from these emplacements the guns could not open a flanking fire to protect the walls between the bastions. Since the second half of the 15th century the technique of firearms greatly improved and armies were more and more equipped with cannons. The need for improvements was drastically demonstrated to the Italians when Charles VIII of France, after the crossing of the Alps in 1495, advanced to the extreme south of Italy almost without resistance. Niccolò Machiavelli expressed the general bewilderment when he wrote his *Arte della guerra* in 1520.

The contemporaries described in eloquent words the revolution that was taking place. The old cannons were heavy, difficult to move, and fired slowly at long intervals. "The French armies brought along lighter pieces which almost always could keep abreast with the army, could be mounted with incredible speed, and accomplished in a few hours what formerly had taken days. They used this devilish rather than human instrument just as much in the field as for a siege." This revolutionary change made new methods of defense imperative. The old walls were insufficient and the urban area could no longer be extended without considerable difficulties. The fortifications assumed a permanent character which modified the layout of the town as a whole. The military engineer then came upon the stage. For these experts the city was a unit whose layout was determined by the needs of defense, by the fortifications. Their starting point was the *enceinte*. The whole organization of the town and its details had to be subordinated to this rigid framework. The periphery became more important and the central square, which in former times served civic functions, was now fundamentally a mere meeting or juncture of a number of streets running to important points of the circumvallation. The *piazza d'armi*, the rallying place for defense, became the town's center, and military necessities pushed back the peaceful functions which for centuries had dominated the inner structure of the towns.

An interesting modification of an Ideal City built around a central focal point has survived in a design attributed to Fra Giocondo, *"d'après un maître inconnu italien,"*[4] although no definite proof is offered for this suggestion.. The original sketch was copied by the Frenchman Jacques Androuet du Cerceau in the 16th century. The city is surrounded by two walls. Against the outer wall a continuous row of gabled houses is built. Both walls are fortified by towers and gates. Radial streets lead to a central templelike building with a cupola. The usual *piazza d'armi* has been abandoned and the military functions of the central square have disappeared. The gabled houses, only one block deep, are a distinctly un-Italian motif, while the architecture of the central edifice and of the gates are conspicuously Italian in design. The whole is a strange mixture of different styles but it may be adduced as proof that such schemes aroused considerable interest at this time. These ideas were in the air, and there is no need to assume that this design was directly influenced by Filarete or any other architect. It may have been different with the Ideal City designed by Girolamo Maggi. His plan was certainly modeled on Filarete's city. It was published in 1564 in Venice in the treatise *Della Fortificatione delle Città* and showed a similar outline, a similar street system, and an octagonal central square from whose corners eight streets lead outward. But in general Maggi's scheme is more elaborate and if anything more playful in detail and in its artificial combination of different forms. On the other hand, Maggi left a design which reduced the idea of an Ideal City to its essential principles: a square ground plan with bastions at the four corners and gates in the middle of each wall. Eight streets converge on the central square. Here we have the bare minimum of an ideal layout, an abstract statement enunciating the rigidity and disingenuity of all similar schemes in undiluted purity.

About 1490, Milan and its environs suffered a plague which killed almost half the population. Leonardo da Vinci (1452-1519) may have been influenced by this event when he made proposals for the reconstruction of Milan. He suggested that a more hygienic city should be rebuilt by grouping the population in ten smaller towns each of 5,000 inhabitants. Possibly in this connection he also evolved a scheme for an Ideal City which would be situated on a beautiful river, free from sediments, gravel, or boulders, which would not flood the surrounding country or dry up. The river with its canals would be of great advantage because it would carry away all the dirt and refuse of the city. The width of the streets should be equal to the average height of the houses. There were to be two categories of streets, the upper ones with gutters in the middle and the lower ones flushed by the

31. **Ideal City by Jacques Androuet du Cerceau.**

32. **Ideal City by Girolamo Maggi (1564).**

4. A. E. Brinckmann. *Platz und Monument.* 1923. P. 43.
H. von Geymüller. *Les Du Cerceau. Leur Vie et Leur Oeuvre.* 1887.

33. Design for an Ideal City by Scamozzi.

regulated water from the river. Stairways connect the upper and lower level. The upper streets were reserved for the gentry—the *gentili nomini*—and for strolling; those on the lower level for service vehicles and other wheeled traffic, and in general for the use and convenience of the people. The lower parts of the houses and the underground roads were to receive light only indirectly through openings in the top-level streets. The houses were to be built back to back, leaving the space between them for the lower streets.

L'Idea della Architettura Universale, published in 1615 at Venice, was the title of a treatise by Vincenzo Scamozzi (1522-1616). *Architettura Universale*—this grandiose claim makes no mystery of the true pretensions of the protagonists of the Ideal Cities. It shows more clearly than any design their conviction that what they had to offer was of supreme and all-embracing significance. They did not realize that playing with abstract and empty forms was leading them astray, and that their theories were in the last resort hollow and uncreative. Scamozzi's plan tries to combine all the features then *en vogue*: the starlike fortifications, the polygonal circumference, the gridiron layout, squares of different shape and size, and a canal leading through the city and connecting two waterways which were partly incorporated in the fortifications. This hodgepodge of details inorganically thrown together produced most incongruous solutions in the layout of the streets—especially when they touched the polygonal outline of the city—and in the arrangements of the squares. The principal square is occupied by the ducal palace, the administration buildings, and the cathedral. The other five squares are reserved for commercial activities and the general and specialized markets.

Scamozzi gives certain directives concerning the width of the streets, which should depend on their length and importance and measure 30 to 60 feet—but under no conditions more than the height of the houses. Streets that are too wide needed too much terrain and were difficult to defend, while streets that are too narrow make a city ugly and melancholic, prevent the access of air and light, and impede traffic. Especially in a hot climate the streets should be wide and long so that the prevailing winds can have a cooling effect. This was, of course, the old formula of Vitruvius which Scamozzi, like other architects, thoughtlessly took over without even considering the possible advantage of narrow streets in a hot climate in providing protection from the sun and excessive heat. The principal streets should be straight and lined by houses of the same height. Such a city would be beautiful and worthwhile to look at: the visitor would get a panoramic view of it at fairly close quarters, while the approach of festive processions would be visible from afar. Yet it remains an unimaginative scheme without any original ideas.

Similar to Scamozzi's plan was the earlier design by Pietro Cataneo (?-1569) published in 1554 at Venice. Cataneo produced a sort of pattern book with standard plans for towns on square to decagonal ground plans. It is most likely that Scamozzi knew of these schemes. If he did, his own ideas were even less original than they appear to be, and are possibly pure plagiarism. However, it is not improbable that he designed Palma Nova, although there is no definite proof of his authorship. But even in this case he would not have been an original innovator. The plan of Palma Nova was certainly influenced by Filarete's Sforzinda and was not a new or independent contribution to the design of Ideal Cities.[5] He was a compiler, not a creator.

Vasari il Giovanni (1511-71) had designed an Ideal City which was published in 1598 and therefore preceded Scamozzi's plan. The octagonal area is subdivided by concentric and radial streets repeating the outline of the central square or leading from its corners and sides to the gates. Secondary rectangular and circular squares interrupt these streets.

The formalism and the stereotyped rigidity of the Ideal City did not exclude certain illusory devices which were especially evident in the perspective views and *points de vue*. This sensation of space in depth based on a knowledge of the laws of optics or, so far as city planning was concerned, at least on the awareness that perspective space added coherence to the architectural composition—this sensation, which absorbed the spectator as an active participant into the perspective movement, was but one step removed from the make-believe of the stage. In the Teatro Olimpico at Vicenza by Andrea Palladio (built 1579-82) we have the sophisticated and detailed version of an ideal street in an Ideal City. The auditorium rises in thirteen rows as a semioval.

5. Palma Nova is described in the City Survey.

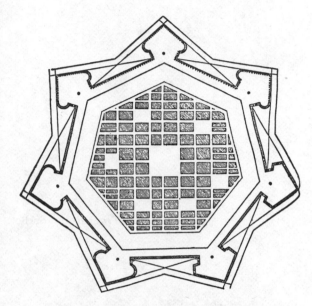

34. **Design for an Ideal City by Pietro Cataneo.**

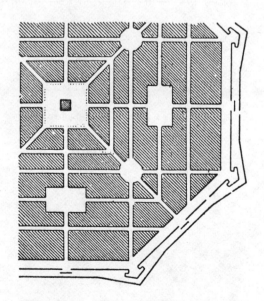

35. **Design for an Ideal City by Vasari.**

The scenery consists of a two-storied wall, richly decorated with figures and architectural detail. Streets are visible through one large and two small openings, creating the illusion of great length through their convergence and the repetition of detail. All the elements of a model perspective are used with the greatest skill. The result is a background that would have been the fulfillment of the most cherished dreams of every designer of an Ideal City. That Palladio was more aware than Alberti of the aesthetic attractiveness of vistas and the visual relationships of the elements of a city plan is evident from some remarks in the Fourth Book of his *Treatise on Architecture,* where he says that "these great and open places in a city besides the convenience of walking, discoursing, and contracting bargains, are very ornamental; as when there is a beautiful and spacious place of the

36. *La Scena Tragica* by Serlio.

head of a street, from whence you have the prospect of some curious edifice, and particularly of some church."

The theater-streets of Serlio (1475-1554) which he published in the second book of his *d'Architettura* belong to the same category, though more dramatized and more romanticized as was thought fitting for the theater. What is especially interesting is that *La Scena Tragica* is set in classical forms; *La Scena Comica* is a mixture of Gothic and Renaissance architecture, while the *Scena Satirica* has a rustic background. The newly discovered classical forms with their balanced and sedate rhythm obviously still had the aura of serenity, while the conglomerate of medieval

37. *La Scena Comica* by Serlio.

and more contemporary details, much less homogeneous in character and physical coherence, were supposed to produce an environment open to ridicule and an invitation to view it as a farcical and hollow anachronism. All three sceneries have in common a perspective setting, the Tragic Scenery being limited by a triumphal arch and the street lined by palaces with arcades and simpler houses. With its restricted vista through the narrow opening at one end, this is the kind of perspective that was so dear to the imagination of the Renaissance architects. The Comic

38. *La Scena Satirica* by Serlio.

Scenery is completely closed. Its perspective is broken with multiple points of view leading to the massive building of a church. In the Satiric Scene the trees enclosing a glade form a perspective view slightly curved toward the end and accentuated by some huts in the foreground.

The painters of the Renaissance followed the same principles. Architectural motifs as background had been used by their predecessors of the Middle Ages, but these remained essentially two-dimensional representations. The architecture which we now see on paintings by Perugino, Raphael, and others do not show Ideal Cities or ideal streets but they all have the elements of perspective compositions: the subordination of parts to a dominating center and strict symmetry. They were all systematically conceived in the same spirit that was the essence of Ideal Cities, and as such they contribute materially toward the true understanding of the ideas incorporated in the designs of the architects.

The Ideal Cities of the Renaissance marked a turning point in the art of city planning. Although it was more a change of direction than the beginning of an ascent to new heights, they expressed not only the *Zeitgeist* of the emerging era in general, but also the great change in the sphere of law and administration which created the framework for the practical execution of the new ideas on city planning. The confused political conditions and the weakness of most of the urban and territorial administrations led to the other extreme—a longing for a strong authority. A new rational philosophy of constitutional law developed during the 16th century. The aim was no longer, as in the Middle Ages, the casual elaboration of individual rights and privileges handed down by generations, but the formulation of a law based on *la nature des choses*. The authority of the state was acknowledged as "an intelligible unit of history," an entity whose authority was absolute in all spheres of life. The exercise of this absolute power found an especially favorable field in city planning. The new theories were a direct challenge to the government to interfere and seemed to be directly made for the use of the great powers which the new concept of the State had conferred upon them. Moreover, the princes of the 16th and following centuries favored all plans that would contribute to the improvement and adornment of their cities—and to their own glory. As Montesquieu said when he compared the monarchical and republican attitudes, "In a monarchy actions are not determined by morals, but by beauty; not by justice, but by pomp; not by reason, but by the extraordinary." This attitude was the driving power behind the fondness of the princes for expressing their aspirations through city-planning schemes and the erection of buildings that would demonstrate their social standing and prestige. Every building of every Ideal City was a promissory note on the future and a handsome gift to the present—not to be forgotten by generations to come, yet not to remain unnoticed by their contemporaries was the desire of these great and little potentates. The Ideal Cities of the early Renaissance were the forerunners of the absolutist period of city planning with its regimentation and shallow rigidity, with the *l'état c'est moi* spirit which undermined the vitality of the cities.

Having described the triumph of reason and dogmatic narrowness which finally ended in the admiration—or is it more appropriate to call it adoration?—of bigness, quantity and confusion, it is pertinent to devote the next chapter to city planning in practice and to some of the great achievements in detail.

Alberti defined the perfect form as something that cannot be altered, to which nothing can be added and from which nothing can be subtracted without destroying the harmony of the whole. Pure Renaissance space expresses this postulate with perfect consistency and undeviating clarity. Its accent is not on the illusion of fleeting appearances nor on a coalescence of forms as in the Baroque. Rather it works with a juxtaposition of forms—with surfaces, not with a development in depth; with the harmony by individual parts, not with cohesion through one unifying motif. It is a space at rest, not in motion.[6] In these contrasts we have the essential difference between the Renaissance and the Baroque, between the two opposite ways of looking at the surrounding world—as an assembly of concrete forms or as a panorama of changing appearances; vision at rest or vision in motion. It is therefore only natural that the Renaissance operates with proportions which are balanced and repeated so that the same proportions dominate the whole composition.

The *Piazza SS. Annunziata* at Florence is one of the most perfect examples of a space at rest. It is a rectangle measuring 240 by 150 feet and was completed only gradually in the course of time. Its two long sides are occupied by the Spedale degli Innocenti, the Foundling Hospital, built by Filippo Brunelleschi at the expense of the guild of the silk weavers, and by the Hall of the Confraternity Servi di Maria. The building of the Hospital was begun in 1419; from 1427 continued by Brunelleschi's successor Francesco della Luna, and finally finished in 1451. The Hall of the Confraternity by Antonio da Sangallo the elder and Baccio d'Agnolo, built in 1516-25, repeats exactly the façade of the Hospital, and the portico of the church of SS. Annunziata, added by Giovanni Caccini (1601-1604), continues the motif of the arcades. The height of the two buildings on the long sides of the square is about 60 feet from the ground level to the roof, of

Space at Rest

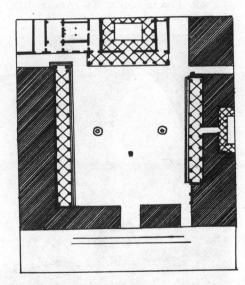

39. Plan of the Piazza della SS. Annunziata in Florence.

6. Cf. the chapter on Space and Scale in Vol. I, pp. 173-83.

which 24 feet are given to the arcades. The portico of the church rises directly without stairs from the pavement of the square, in contrast to the arcades of the other buildings. In order to eliminate this difference and to make all arcades equally high, the capitals of the portico are surmounted by a *coussinet*. Thus symmetry and horizontality are preserved.

Like other Renaissance squares the Piazza SS. Annunziata is essentially an enlarged palace courtyard. The proportions are perfectly balanced; they are at rest. The vertical columns and the horizontal lines of the entablature and cornices create a calming impression and spatial simplicity. Although the square is deeper than wide, the façade of the church does not appear to be pushed back. That this was deliberately avoided is evidenced by the equal height of all arcades—an artificial device that neutralized any distinction between the surrounding arcades and, at the same time, compensated for the minute decrease in size which the greater depth of the square might produce. The Piazza SS. Annunziata has not the character of a forecourt such as St. Peter's Square. It is an inner courtyard and a closed composition. An equestrian statue by Giovanni da Bologna, erected in 1608, stands in the main axis but not in the center of the square. It is moved back from the church toward the Via dei Servi which enters the square opposite the church. Two fountains by Pietro Tasca (1629) counterbalance the asymmetrical position of the

40. Piazza della SS. Annunziata at Florence.

statue, a further proof of the awareness that nothing should even slightly disturb the unity of the stable equilibrium of the square. The three streets near the church entering the square between the arcades are hardly visible and do not diminish the homogeneity and oneness of the composition.

The *Piazza San Marco* is in its present form the work of many generations. Its beauty, shape, and character cannot be understood unless one is constantly aware that both man and nature have had an equal share (perhaps more than in any other city) in the creation of this great festival hall—the religious, social, and architectural center of Venice. Like Amsterdam, the city has been wrested from the water and it is the water and its omnipresence that place the Piazza San Marco among the greatest achievements of man's cooperation with and conquest of nature. As Goethe wrote in his *Italian Journey,*

It was for no idle fancy that their colonists fled to these islands; it was no mere whim which impelled those who followed to combine with them; necessity taught them to look for security in a highly disadvantageous situation, which afterwards became most advantageous, enduing them with talent, when the whole of the northern world was immersed in gloom. Their increase and their wealth were the necessary consequence. New dwellings arose close against dwellings, rocks took the place of sand and marsh, houses sought the sky, being forced, like trees enclosed in a narrow compass, to seek in height what was denied to them in breadth. Being niggard of every inch of ground, as having been from the outset compressed into a narrow compass, they allowed no more room for the streets than was absolutely necessary for separating one row of houses from another, and affording a narrow way for passengers. Moreover, water was at once street, square, and promenade. The Venetian was forced to become a new creature; and Venice can only be compared with itself.

Yet even with this niggardliness "of every inch of ground," the inhabitants of the water-city did not hesitate to spare from this precious space a considerable large one for a square, because they regarded it as the symbol of their civic pride in the power and magnificence of their city.

The Piazza San Marco was originally the orchards of St. Mark's. In the 12th century it was a market square like the Piazzetta—that is to say, it was laid out in the typical medieval fashion for purely utilitarian reasons. The rebuilding of the church on the site of the ancient *basilica* (829-32) was begun in 1063 and consecrated in 1095. The first *campanile* was erected around 900 and rebuilt in 1148 and 1329. Its upper story was partly renovated in 1512 after an earthquake. It collapsed in 1902 and was re-erected in 1905. The Loggetta, *sotto il Campanile,* facing the Doge's Palace, the Palazzo Ducale, was built by Jacopo Sansovino in 1540 as meeting place for the Venetian nobles and was later used as the main guardhouse. It was rebuilt after the fall of the tower in 1902. The Ducal Palace, bordering with its 225-foot-long west side the Piazetta and with its 213-foot-long south side the *mòlo* and *laguna*, is said to have been founded as early as 814 as seat of the first *Doge*. It has been repeatedly renovated. Its southern part was rebuilt in the first half of the 14th century and its western wing between 1424 and 1442.

The Libreria Vecchia, facing the west side of the Ducal Palace, was built by Sansovino in 1536-54 and finished by Vincenzo Scamozzi in 1582.

The two three-storied palaces of the north and south side of the *Piazza* served originally as the residence of the nine procurators, the heads of the administration. The northern palace, the Procuratie Vecchie, was erected in 1480-1517 by Pietro Lombardo and the southern palace, the Procuratie Nuove, repeating the main motifs of the older building, was begun in 1584 by Scamozzi and finished in 1640 by Baldassare Longhena, while the building on the west side facing St. Mark's, the Fabbricca Nuova, toward which both palaces converge, was not completed until 1810. Two columns with the statue of St. Theodore, the patron saint of Venice, and the winged lion, the symbol of St. Mark, respectively accentuate the end of the Piazzetta proper and the beginning of the *mòlo*. Like an elegant portal they prepare the entrance to the Piazzetta with an almost unintentional lightness. This was for a long time the place of execution, and the Piazzetta was the meat market. Before Sansovino could begin the Libreria Vecchia, the view of the water was blocked by numerous stalls which had to be removed, together with many other temporary structures.

The *Piazza* has a length of 525 feet and a width of 270 feet near the church, which decreases to 174 feet at the other end. This convergence toward the Fabbricca Nuova creates an illusion that makes the square appear longer and the Fabbrica Nuova higher than they actually are. The architectural form of the *Piazza* has developed over many centuries. It took almost fifteen generations to complete it and to give it its present shape and character, but during this long time there was never any deviation from the visionary intention to create a civic and religious center that would express the greatness and the splendor of the city. At the beginning this division may have been inarticulate, deeply embedded in the unconscious longing for a representative symbol of the spirit, moving each generation anew to hand down to posterity a monumental conception that would guarantee a continuous development without destroying the unity of the composition as a whole. Not a single generation lost sight of this final goal. This may appear surprising and unbelievable to us of the 20th century, but let us not forget that the Renaissance and the Middle Ages were periods of an integrated culture and that art was a social activity. Culture was identical with life in its wholeness, not as today the pastime of a small minority. It was this all-embracing culture of the centuries during which the Piazza San Marco took shape that guided the artists as members of the community and endowed them with an unfailing instinct to do the right thing. It was this merging of individual artistic and social consciousness into group consciousness which produced the uninterrupted flow of empathy that made a break in the cultural tradition impossible.

The history of the Piazza San Marco is particularly instructive. It began with a loose and haphazard grouping of market places, orchards, lodging houses for pilgrims, and temporary structures such as market stalls, all serving utilitarian purposes. In the course of time social, religious, and political functions gained the upper hand and changed the form and character of the square. The L-shaped combination of the *Piazza* and the *Piazzetta* was by no means dictated by purely artistic considerations. It was far more the result of functional needs: the *Piazza,* which had no direct connection with the Canal Grande or any other waterway, was too isolated without a convenient access to the main traffic artery of the city. The best and nearest connection that would not destroy the coherence of the *Piazza* was to open it at the eastern end near the church. But a narrow passage would have been at variance with the character of the *Piazza.* Consequently, a smaller square, a forecourt, was added. The Piazzetta repeats the motif of the larger square. Both are open-air interiors, festival halls, separated from the bulk of the dwelling houses and the other buildings, from the inextricable mass of the innumerable lanes, streets, and canals. Each of the squares has a clearly defined individuality which enhances the unity of the whole because scale and space are homogeneous. It is a space at rest through which the visitor moves at ease, where he can linger without being forced along by the attraction of a *point de vue* at the end of a perspective vista. The proportions of both squares are about the same. The colonnades are like an uninterrupted girdle holding both squares together. The strong horizontal lines of the cornices and the repetition of identical elements create an atmosphere of repose and intimacy which is the more effective because it is not disturbed by traffic. Venice is the only city of the world where the pedestrian is supreme.

The *Piazza Pio II* at Pienza, Tuscany, some 30 miles south-southeast from Siena, is the center of this small town situated on the ridge of a steep and long hill. It was the birthplace of Aeneas Sylvio Piccolomini, afterward Pope Pius II. Its original name was Corsignano. But when the pope had decided to make it the see of a bishop, and to erect the group of buildings which surround the central square, and to enlarge the fortifications, its name was changed in honor of its most eminent citizen and became Pienza. The Pope commissioned the Florentine architect Bernardo Rossellino who created in the astonishingly short time of three years (1459-62) one of the most perfect and earliest masterpieces of Renaissance city planning.

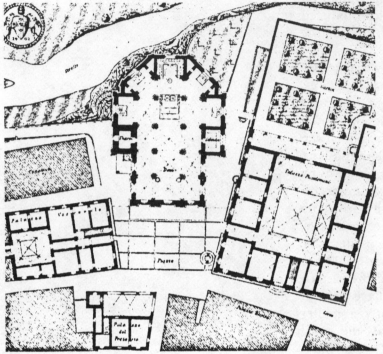

41. Plan of the Piazza, the Cathedral, and the Palazzo Piccolomini in Pienza.

Around a surprisingly small square he erected the church and four palaces. The narrow main street, which runs along the ridge of the hill from gate to gate, curves slightly opposite the church so that the buildings of the *Piazza* are already visible from a distance. The church occupies the south side of the square and is the center of the whole composition. Opposite rises the Palazzo Pubblico and on the left the Palazzo Vescovile, the Bishop's Palace. On the right stands the Palazzo Piccolomini. Its façade repeats Rossellino's own work at Florence, the Palazzo Rucellai, although its rustica-work and the general relief of the façade are more delicate and thus more appropriate for the very small square. The main entrance to the Palazzo Piccolomini is from the street, not from the square. This was especially desired by the Pope, who obviously wanted a vista through the portal, the arcaded courtyard, and the adjoining *loggia* to the garden and beyond over the open landscape. The setting of this marvel of early Renaissance architecture is unique. The *Piazza* is not rigidly separated from the natural scenery of the beautiful and insinuating landscape of Tuscany. The semiopenness of the square introduces a harmony between nature and man's works which cannot be found in any other square of the Renaissance period. The sensitive adaptation of the buildings to the terrain has the additional advantage that the lateral palaces diverge toward the church, thus leaving a gap through which the distant landscape can be overlooked as far as the chain of the Amiata Hills. One is re-

42. Cathedral and Palazzo Piccolomini in Pienza.

minded of Bath, which also opened a new chapter in city planning, where man utilized the natural features to highlight the effect of the buildings.

At Pienza, arcades do not play a significant role. Only the Palazzo Pubblico has a small portico. A charming and elegant fountain, also designed by Rossellino in 1462, stands at the corner of the Palazzo Piccolomini and the street. This small fountain, contrasting with the other buildings in scale and plasticity, enhances their monumentality and the effect of their restrained flat surfaces. The square itself remains free from any structures that would impair its small dimensions. It is obvious that the architect was aware that the area of the square proper had to remain an uninterrupted surface if the proportions of the whole composition were not to be marred: white lines on a dark ground divide it into a number of squares, giving it a definite individuality which does not tolerate anything that would disturb its unity and shape.

CHAPTER 5

The Baroque

Space in Motion

AFTER A PERIOD saturated with geometry, *la maniera grande* of the Baroque appears like the eruption of primeval forces that absorb man into the passionate movement of space and make him an active participant in the play of light, coalescing forms, and contrasting effects. The cosmology of Descartes is a typical product of the Baroque. He regards the universe as infinite, devoid of empty space, and matter as uniform though of endless variety in form and division. This universe is closely filled with matter without any vacuum. Consequently, the movement of any particle of matter entails the movement of all matter. This definition fits without any modification the nature of Baroque city planning and architecture: infinity through the continuous movement of matter—or in other words, through matter in motion; in a more realistic sense, through space in motion produced by the excitement, the restless and undulating plasticity of the projecting and receding volumes of the buildings that enclose it. The quiet balance of the Renaissance squares and streets gives way to movement and expansion; the circle to the oval; the square to the rectangle; and limitation to perspective views. Practically every square becomes a forecourt, a preparation for one building dominating the configuration of all buildings surrounding it. The value of a street is measured by its perspective effect.

The Baroque abhors space at rest, space as a complete and limited unity. Movement, diversity, coalescence, and development in depth are its media of expression. Every Baroque work—whether a sculpture, a painting, a building, or the layout of a city and its details—suggests innumerable possibilities for looking at it. It is never to be viewed in isolation and always devoid of functional clarity. This world, the Counter-Reformation of architecture and city planning, was born of a strange alliance—the longing for an unqualified expression of the subconsciously raging turmoil of emotions, and the abandonment to a welter of agitated forms sometimes combining almost mathematical precision with an irrational disregard of logical structure, a stilted ecstasy with a cold sobriety. This self-contradictory quality of the Baroque, especially strong in the later period, has been aptly described as a *complexio oppositorum,* meaning not merely a complicated and interwoven whole but, even more, a collection of repressed and subconscious ideas. Yet it would be a serious misapprehension of Baroque city planning and Baroque art in general if one were to assume that it is a style of capricious inconsequence. Irrespective of its multifarious nature, it possesses the faculty of organizing on a grand scale, of unifying innumerable details by a leading idea. The proof lies in the magnificent squares, in the coherent layout of whole towns, and in the great sweep of the palace gardens. To think and to act on a grand scale is the maxim of the Baroque. But this scale is too vast and the demand it makes on the average human being too exacting. It cannot be endured for long, and as soon as the social foundations are weakened it fades away into the embarrassing ostentation of an architectural revivalist like Napoleon.

How can the contrast be explained between the relative quiet and sedateness of the Renaissance and the excited atmosphere of the Baroque, charged with sensuality and irrationality? Or is it wrong to speak of a contrast? Is it not more fruitful to search for those trends that were already operative in the Renaissance, though still not fully visible and from which the spirit of the Baroque gradually developed? What may appear superficially as a break, a violent rupture, is in reality a continuous evolution nurtured by forces that had been present since the end of the Middle Ages, when group consciousness was fading, and the interaction of the general and the individual will was growing weaker, until in the Baroque it led to the supremacy of a small minority, and to the leveling down of the majority as an inarticulate mass of obedient subjects of the rising State.

We cannot understand the continuity of city planning and evaluate in true perspective the change from rest to motion, from limitation to infinity, and from plane surfaces to curvature and depth unless we isolate those trends and causes that have brought this about.

There was first the shift of artistic initiative from the group to a few individuals. The strong social, economic, and religious bonds that had enveloped and held together the small communities of the Middle Ages were broken, and in their place the abstract notion of the State threw its impersonal net over a confused population. The connoisseur, the maecenas, the promoter of the arts, appeared on the scene. Ostentation and personal pride were the motive powers. Baroque is the style of aristocrats, but it is not always an aristocratic style. This development had begun in the Renaissance. The Ideal Cities with their squares and streets were perfect playgrounds for propaganda, for parading magnificence, power, and wealth—in short, for the pageantry that is always connected with systematic preparation. The straight and wide streets, the large piazzas, the radial streets leading to a central square, the *coulisses* of continuous block fronts—all these features provided ideal starting points from which Baroque city planning could evolve an ever more pompous and alluring *crescendo* of sensuous excitement and impressive demonstration of the grandeur of the ruling minority. Yet even with the frantic efforts of the Counter-Reformation, the hold of the Church over the minds of the people was declining; the greatest splendor of the papal court and of the higher dignitaries of the Church could no longer compete with or restore the divine mass hysteria of the Middle Ages. Individual and not always selfless efforts to keep the power of the Church before the public eye had replaced the communal and devout sacrifices of small communities—the enthusiasm which, as Professor Coulton expressed it, "impelled whole populations, rich and poor, to labour together upon the town walls in time of danger, or upon some favoured church as a monument of livelier faith."[1]

Baroque art and city planning were torn between two irreconcilable aspirations: the urge to restore the intensity of the religious feeling of the past and the worldly pretension of the present. These trends had their origin in the Renaissance, in the growing secularization of life and art. One of the most characteristic symbols of this change was the altered function of the central square in the designs for Ideal Cities. In the past it was a civic center for peaceful purposes, mostly occupied by the main church around which the community had grown up. Now it is the *piazza d'armi* surrounded by secular buildings, while the church is mostly relegated to a secondary location.

The second trend, which also originated in the Renaissance, was the quest for infinity. This adventure into a world free of limitations and full of hitherto unimaginable possibilities was released by the Copernican revolution. It was the strongest and most potent reaction against medieval narrowness and an established order that had been regarded as eternal. The rationalism and humanism of the Renaissance destroyed the old limitations and traditional values. As John Donne described it in *An Anatomie of the World,*

> 'Tis all in peeces, all cohaerence gone;
> All just supply, and all Relation:
> Prince, Subject, Father, Sonne, are things forgot,
> For every man alone thinkes he hath got
> To be a Phoenix, and that then can bee
> None of that kinde, of which he is, but hee.

At first only a few dared to think freely and to experience the new freedom. Others fell in with the altered course more instinctively, and above all the artists, the discoverers, and inventors were seized with a fever of excitement. The architecture and the projects for the rebuilding of cities, whether they materialized or remained on paper, were like a reservoir into which all these streams discharged their precious gifts, sometimes hollow and paradoxical in detail and yet of a harmonious grandeur in their unity. In direct contrast to the ideas of the Middle Ages the Baroque strove to re-echo, to recapture in its earthly works the

1. G. G. Coulton. *Life in the Middle Ages.* 1928-30. Vol. II. P. 19.

infinity of the other world. A Gothic cathedral loses itself in the infinity of the beyond and leaves this world behind. The Renaissance had opened the way to the "architecture of humanism" through which existence in this world could be empirically experienced. Its balance, symmetry, harmonic division, and its conception of space at rest had restored the reality of daily life on earth, attempting to compensate for loss of faith by fulfilling the longing for sublimity so deeply ingrained in human nature. This sublimity and grandeur was offered by the architects and city planners of the Renaissance though in a still restrained form. It reached its climax in the Baroque when it assumed, unfortunately, something of the character of *panem et circenses,* an opiate for the people. The era of the masses was approaching. From now on the architects had to reckon with a new factor, an amorphous multitude of human beings without individuality. They had to adapt the scale, composition, and appeal of their work to these newcomers on the political scene who demanded to take part, at least as extras, in the pageants put on by the few, by the ruling minority, and by the State or municipality.

The third trend began with the voyages of Columbus. The awareness of the world as a limitless expanse was spreading, and this widening of scale and experience was projected into the consciousness of the individual being. The unity of the whole world ceased to be a dream and became a reality. Man's objectives widened in scope and character. They grew more complex and more closely related. This increasing complexity and size had to be mastered. Unification and synopsis were the obvious means of coping with the new problems. Isolation of the more or less self-contained space units of the Renaissance, for instance, a closed square such as the Piazza SS. Annunziata, from the other parts of the city had to be abandoned, and squares and streets had to be organically related to the entire urban area or at least to large districts. A continuous flow of spatial utilities was the ideal. This ideal was not always achieved but the closed, intimate, and restful square gave way to an open composition, to movement and multiformity. The result was unification on a large scale, a development that had begun in the Renaissance when streets, squares, and entire cities were conceived and built as coherent units.

Synopsis means, in this connection, optical synthesis. It is the by-product of unification. It tends to eliminate diverting details and to create conditions that permit viewing the composition as a whole or—and this is especially characteristic of Baroque city planning—to prepare by the shape and the particular character of the space relations for a sequence of space units, either of squares or streets. This subordination of numerous details to one unifying motif explains the importance of the façade and the frequent neglect of the sides of a building. This is especially evident in the layout of Italian squares in their relationship to the main building, and seems to contradict the suggestion that only many different views can do justice to the character of Baroque squares.

A Baroque building should not be appreciated in isolation. It is part of an integral composition consisting of street, square, and other buildings forming walls of the square. The inclusion of the side-façades as architecturally important elements would only distract the attention from the main motif—the interplay of the forecourt and the street with the front of the principal building. Hence the concave façade, or the projection of the front part of a building into the square or even the built-in façade. It is the composition as a whole which expresses the essence of Baroque planning, of its use of unification and synopsis.

Like so many other characteristics of Baroque art, unification and synopsis work with seemingly contradictory means: with simplification, that is, with a reduction to essentials, and, at the same time, with a complex array of individual and highly sophisticated elements. But this combination of sobriety and illusion, of a sense of reality and a sense of possibility, of directness and of the appeal to imaginative faculties, is an indispensable instrument of Baroque architecture and city planning.

This brings us to the fourth trend, the appeal to illusion as a legitimate means of creating space, giving it a particular shape and character—in other words, the use of theatrical effects. The essence of the theater is to produce the illusion of space and space sequences within a narrow area without any appreciable extension in depth or width, and to make the space appear greater than it actually is. This lure of largeness and wide vistas responded to the longing of the Baroque for grandeur and to the appeal to emotions rather than to reason; it glossed over the conviction that "the end justifies the means." The Baroque is the style of the "as if" *par excellence*. Appearance is more important than truthfulness. *La maniera grande* had to be kept up at all costs through illusion or through the exaggeration of scale and the turgidity of the architectural composition. The superhuman dimensions of the buildings and squares—St. Peter's Square, to name only one—diminish the stature of human beings and depreciate their individuality. In the search for infinity and in the urge to neutralize the limitations of the architectural space, the painters had the last word. They painted the sky on the vaults and cupolas of their buildings and continued solid architectural structure into their paintings as sham architecture.

Illusion and surprise, the occurrence of the unexpected, were the means which the architect-stage-designers of the Baroque un-

43. Painting on the ceiling in the Palazzo Barberini in Rome by Pietro da Cortona.

failingly used in order to achieve the desired effects. Their predecessors, a Serlio or a Palladio, had also employed similar devices in their theater designs, but with greater restraint and without surprise effects. The Jesuits were the leaders of this movement. One of the essential principles on which Ignatius of Loyola had built the system of his Spiritual Exercises was that the education of the intellect should always be supported by a parallel exhortation of the imaginative faculties. Every intellectually comprehended insight was to be immediately expressed in the form of an intelligible, figurative image. Only this simultaneous training of the intellect and the imagination would leave a permanent impression upon the consciousness of his disciples. These principles were applied with great success in the theater. The Jesuits recognized that they had to organize a "Counter-Reformation of the Theater," if they did not want to expose the fantasy of the masses to the dangerous appeal of worldly attractions—or even worse, to the influence of their Protestant adversaries—and in the end lose their allegiance altogether. It is extraordinarily interesting to observe the similarity between the ideas and motives which the Jesuits used in the theater and those used by architects and city planners. From the very beginning the Jesuits tried to fascinate the public through splendid scenery, impressive stage effects, and complicated technical tricks. By a clever arrangement of large curtains they divided the main stage into central, side, and back stages so that different scenes could be performed simultaneously. Perspective sceneries, trap doors, and props created effects that must have astonished the audience. Sometimes *coulisses* were mounted on triangular revolving bases, a sort of revolving stage *en miniature,* which were easily turned so that the scenery could be changed three times within a few moments. For certain effects the *laterna magica* was even used, especially in scenes depicting the evocation of visions and dreams. Performances with great masses of people were not at all unusual. Battle scenes, triumphal marches, and mass meetings sometimes employing more than a thousand actors and extras were not insurmountable obstacles to the ingenuity of the Jesuits.

It is characteristic that the Baroque excelled not only in theatrical performances but also in temporary buildings, in triumphal arches, in splendid decorations for festivals and processions, and in fireworks. The *theatrum sacrum* of the Jesuits was itself a mixture of reality and unreality, with only tenuous boundaries between the solemn architectural scenery and the sometimes gay and always alluring atmosphere of the performance. Famous architects, sculptors, and painters were the brains behind this pompous to-do. The family of Bibiena specialized in stage design, while others applied the effects of the temporary buildings and the theater to the permanent architecture of streets and squares, of churches, palaces, and gardens.

Andrea del Pozzo, the Jesuit painter-architect, contributed through his *Prospectiva Pingendi* perhaps more than any other artist to the spreading of the doctrine of perspective and sham architecture. He gave detailed instructions in the principles and methods of illusory effects, which were eagerly studied and used by numerous artists not only in Europe but even in China. He made his tricks popular by a clear formulation of practical directives, a procedure in keeping with his Jesuit training.

For Giovanni Lorenzo Bernini, the greatest of the many-sided artists of the High Baroque, the end justified every means. He, too, was in close contact with the Jesuits. He was a perfect stage manager. His methods applied equally to his theater designs and his city-planning designs. For him the problems and the requirements were the same, as indeed they were: the same pretentious *élan*, spaciousness, theatrical aplomb, propagandist allurement, and a desire to fly away into the unlimited sky—but there the urge ended. Bernini was a maker of illusion and grandeur, of a refined technique and vulgarity. He understood only too well the value of curved façades, of the curved line in general

44. Scene from the theatrical performance on the occasion of the wedding of the Prince Elector of Bavaria, by Giuseppe Galli Bibiena.

45. Palazzo and Piazza Farnese in Rome. Engraving by Vasi, 1754.

as a most potent medium to make space appear larger than it actually is. He tried to transfer from the stage the illusion of changing scenery by opening up ever-new vistas which induced a continual change in the field of vision of the beholder. Bernini's perspectives created compositions worthy of the most magnificent theater performances. The Piazza di S. Pietro is a splendid auditorium; the colonnades are the *couloirs;* the *Piazza retta* is the orchestra; and St. Peter's with the stairs is the stage. For Bernini there had to be a continuous flow of space sequences. These and other qualities he shared with his contemporary fellow artists. But Bernini was the greater technician, the greater and even more sincere and more passionate personality. This explains the secret of his all-pervading influence, of his power of persuasion, and paradoxically his sometimes unbearable banality.

Idea and Reality:
City Planning in Operation

How were the ideas described on the foregoing pages translated into brick and mortar? The guiding principles to which these ideas can be reduced are relatively few and simple. Each of the following examples illustrates one particular aspect of these principles although a certain overlapping cannot be avoided.

1. **Axis and Symmetry.** The Palazzo Farnese at Rome is the prototype of numerous palaces that were built in succeeding centuries. It took more than half a century to complete it. Antonio da Sangallo devoted sixteen years of his life to this work. Shortly before his death in 1546 Alessandro Farnese, who was elected to the papacy in 1534, arranged a competition in which Michel-

144

angelo among others took part. His design especially for the entablature was preferred by the pope and Michelangelo was commissioned to do the work. Street, square, palace, vestibule, inner courtyard, and garden form a continuous sequence of space units, following one another in a strictly axial and symmetrical arrangement. Vasari reports in his *Vita di Michelangelo* that it was intended to continue the axis through the garden and a second courtyard to the Tiber, and to build ramps and stairs leading down to the water. A bridge was to connect the palace gardens with the Villa Farnesina on the other bank, the river closing the long vista from the square. Two streets lead on either side of the palace from the square to the river one with a view to the Janiculus Hill and the other to a small church on the Lungo Tevere Tebaldi. Accordingly, not only is the façade of the palace exposed to the view, as was mostly the case in the Renaissance where the streets pass parallel to the front, but the building is perceived as a cube in its development in depth. Here was accomplished what Scamozzi had already recommended in his *L'Idea della Architettura Universale* (I. 3. XXII):

Le strade, che conducono à gli edifici Suburbani, & in Villa per far maggior conoscenza d'essi, deono incontrare l'aspetto, e la faccia loro principale, e tanto più quanto, che questa parte è sempre la più nobile, e magnifica, & anco la più ornata, e bella dell'altre. In capo di queste strade, e dinanzi a' Palazzi, ò fabriche importanti vi si richiede qualche Piazza ampia, e spaciosa; si perche rendi maestà....[2]

Two fountains by Vignola accentuate the symmetry of the square. The palace is a boxlike building with a strong horizontal articulation consisting of three stories of nearly equal height, of three rows of windows all of the same proportions, and the heavy entablature. It is a rare example of dignified grandeur and perfect harmony of proportion. Square and palace are supremely balanced in their relationship, and axial symmetry dominates the whole composition. It is a prelude to later Baroque city planning, still subdued and self-controlled without excitement and without coalescing space units, but of a determined and rational clarity.

2. **Movement and Volume.** Piazza S. Maria della Pace at Rome is the forecourt to the façade—one can hardly say to the church—which was added in 1656, together with the hexagonal square by the painter Pietro da Cortona. Nobody but a painter could have designed this ensemble. It could easily be the background of a typically Baroque painting frozen into architectonic corporeity. The projecting and receding volumes of the church and the broken outline of the walls of the square create an intensity of movement which cannot fail to leave the visitor un-

2. "For the sake of greater renown the buildings in the streets leading to the suburbs and *villae* should face them with their main façades, the more so because they are always not only the most noble and magnificent but also the most ornate and beautiful. The *palazzi* and other important buildings should front a large *piazza* into which the streets lead as this heightens their majestic appearance."

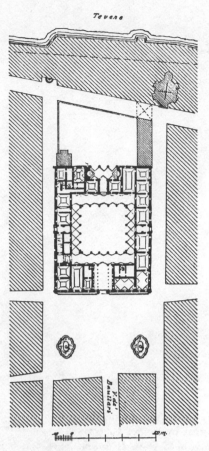

46. Plan of Palazzo and Piazza Farnese in Rome.

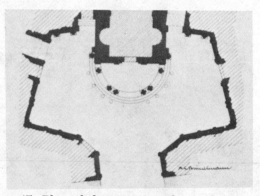

47. Plan of the square in front of S. Maria della Pace in Rome.

145

affected. The architect was faced with almost unsurmountable difficulties: to disentangle a maze of narrow streets and to create the impression of ample space in a setting without any actual space. This task was solved in a typically Baroque spirit, and only the Baroque could have achieved this theatrical masterpiece. One side of the hexagon is occupied by the church. A fairly broad street enters the square at the opposite side. The church closes the vista. Since the large carriages of the 17th century had great difficulty in turning, the re-entrant angles of the main street with the *Piazza* were suppressed, giving the impression, architecturally speaking, of being ground off by the movement which fills the whole square. A convex portico with double columns projects into the square. Deep shadows produce a *chiaroscuro*, heightening the agitation which permeates this secluded open-air interior. The upper part of the church is a convex semioval crowned by an elliptical and triangular pediment, which rests on pilasters and columns molded in strong relief, grouped on both sides of a large window ending in a semicircular arch. A profusion of shapes and volumes that can hardly be surpassed! The other sides of the square are more restrained. The effect of the whole composition is concentrated on the church, on its main and only façade. Side façades do not exist: the architecture of the portico continues on either side as low annexes of the main façade. The interplay of volumes and movement, of light and shadows, of vertical and horizontal and of straight and curved elements creates, within a very restricted space, an emotional appeal of great

48. S. Maria della Pace and Palazzo Gambirasi in Rome. Engraving by G. B. Falda from *Il nuovo teatro*, 1665.

strength. Forecourt and church are welded into an indissoluble unity. Nothing can be added or taken away without destroying the meaning, the beauty, and the wholeness of the design. One can well understand that the Piazza S. Maria della Pace must have made an extraordinary impression on contemporaries. On a plaque put up by Pope Alessandro VII the pontiff threatens with anathema anyone who would dare make any architectural alterations.

The interplay of volumes and movement is perhaps even more outspoken in the Piazza di S. Ignazio at Rome laid out about half a century after the completion of the church in 1675 by Filippo Raguzzini. The church occupies the south side of the *Piazza*, the shape of which has been developed from three ellipses—the larger one with its main axis parallel to the church and the two smaller ones with their main axes aslant the façade of the church. Two streets branch off the two smaller ellipses and join behind the church as one wide street. The whole composition is extremely agitated and a superb example of spatial coalescence. The small oval squares at the corners of the main *piazza* flow into the central space, forming a perfect unity out of great multiformity. The lessons of the interior of S. Ivo by Borromini (1660), built in honor of Urban VIII in the form of a bee which the papal family of Barberini bore in their coat of arms, were transferred to the open square of S. Ignazio, another and perhaps the most eloquent example of the identity of the conception of interior and exterior space and space relations.

3. **Unification and Perspective.** Piazza and Scala di Spagna and the Piazza del Popolo are magnificent examples of Baroque city planning, different in detail but similar in essence. The problem was the unification of previously unrelated individual parts. The solution was to create a regulated succession of contrasting and expanding space units focused on a prominent building or group of buildings. At the Piazza di Spagna the problem facing the architects was three-dimensional: unification in height, width, and depth within a narrow space. At the Piazza del Popolo it was two-dimensional on a grand scale. In the first case it was a suspended and complex perspective that had to be developed. In the second it was a simple and yet dynamic solution, very logical, very formalistic and yet a dignified welcome to the visitor who, following the ancient Roman *Via Flaminia*, entered the Eternal City from the north.

The Piazza and Scala di Spagna are the forecourt to SS. Trinità de Monti. The *Piazza*, the stepping stone from which the stairs rise to the church, surmounting the great natural difficulties of the site with dramatic *élan*, has not only the function of serving as the substructure of the Scala di Spagna; it is also a concourse

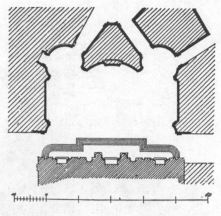

49. Plan of Piazza di S. Ignazio in Rome.

147

where several important arteries of the city meet—the Via del Babuino leading north in a straight line to the Piazza del Popolo (it is one of the three streets converging on the *Piazza*); the Via Condotti leading west, continuing the axis of the Scala di Spagna; and two diagonal streets leading south and beginning at the small Piazza Mignanelli at the southeastern end of the main *Piazza*. The Scala di Spagna is a fireworks of refined calculations with all the tricks of theater architecture. It is a polysynthesis of contrast-

50. Final design for the Scala di Spagna by Francesco de Sanctis, 1723.

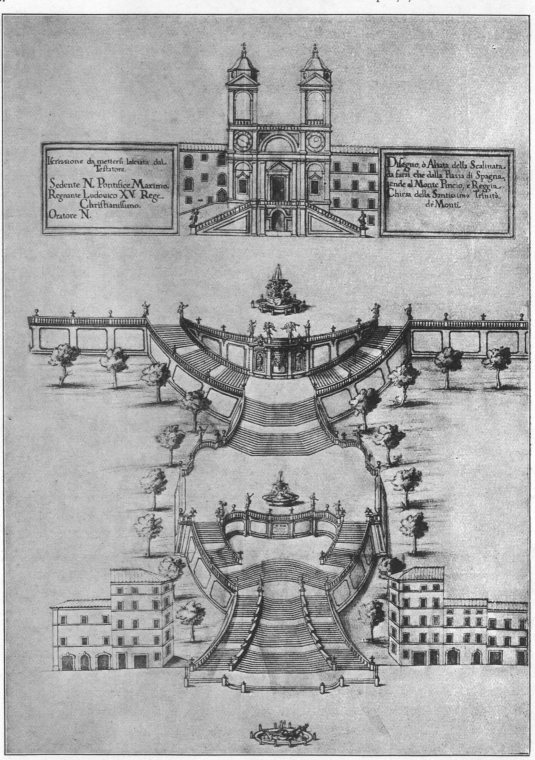

148

51. Air view of Scala di Spagna
and Trinità dei Monti in Rome.

ing horizontal lines of the private buildings and the vertical
towers of the church and the obelisk; of the dynamic flow of the
curves of the stairs and ramps; of preparation, suspension, and
resolution of the movement; of a closed composition focused on
the façade of the church; of an absorbing motion in depth and
height; of coalescence of forms, shades, and colors; and of a
cunning use of illusion by placing the obelisk not in the center
of the entrance to the church but slightly to the side, thus creating
the impression as if—in the Baroque it is always the "as if"—
street, stairs, and church are all strictly aligned on the same axis.
The Fontana della Barcaccia by Pietro Bernini, the father of
Lorenzo, in the form of a barge (hence its name), hardly rises
above the level of the pavement at the point where the axes of
the *Piazza* and the *Scala* meet. It was installed in 1629. It is therefore wrong to say, as several historians of city planning have done,

that its shape was cleverly adapted to the general picture and in particular to the Scala di Spagna. The flight of 137 steps was built not earlier than 1721-23 by Alessandro Specchi and Francesco de Sanctis, and the reason why the fountain was so deeply sunk into the pavement that it did not impair the free view toward the steps was purely technical: only a side branch of the Acqua Vergine with low pressure could be used, which did not permit installing the water pipes any higher.

The Piazza del Popolo, the forecourt to Rome, was laid out during the pontificate of Pius VII (1816-20) and was designed by Valadier, with its longer axis—like the Piazza di S. Pietro—at right angles to the main axis of the perspective. It is a typically Baroque solution of a typically Baroque problem. An obelisk, erected in 1596, stands in the exact center of three radial streets. This street system dates back in essence, though only in a rather rudimentary form, to antiquity. The Baroque regulated, completed, and unified it, adding the architectural "trimmings," the twin churches with the *campanili* at the central avenue and the oval-shaped outline of the *Piazza*. For those who entered Rome through the Porta del Popolo, it was a magnificent welcome, a *coup de théâtre* that foreshadowed the grand scale and the pomposity of the buildings, streets, and squares of the Eternal City. The central avenue, the *Corso,* leads in the direction of the Capitol; the Via del Babuino to the Quirinal; and the Via di Ripetta toward the Tiber. Thus a powerful system of axes and an organic articulation of large parts of the urban area were established. The actual perspective view is rather short: from the Porta del Popolo to the churches it is only about 400 to 450 feet; then it loses its precision and fades away into the vagueness of nondescript streets. The oval shape of the *Piazza* itself is merely delineated by the line of low semicircular walls. It is an open square, similar in this respect to the Place de la Concorde or any of the numerous traffic roundabouts with a monument—in this case the obelisk—as a stationary traffic policeman. The prototype of this starlike planning—three avenues radiating from one point—were the numerous schemes for Ideal Cities with their converging radial streets. What had been, at least at the beginning, a theoretical exercise appropriate to the preoccupation of the period with geometrical figures became in the course of time an even more shallow demonstration of formalistic rigidity and lack of inventiveness. The Piazza del Popolo, like Versailles, had a most unfortunate influence on city planning in the 18th and 19th centuries. This oversimplification which tried to impose a preconceived pattern on a living organism, a city, found its final consummation in Haussmann's plan for Paris, a monument of 19th-century ostentation and impotence.

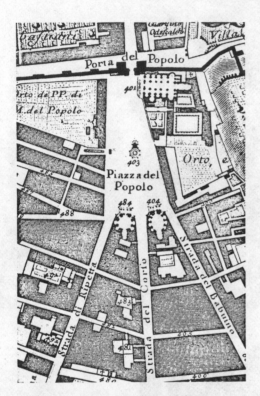

52. Piazza del Popolo. Detail from G. B. Nolli's Plan of Rome, 1748.

Unification through symmetry and concentration of radiating axes on a single point is the contribution of the Piazza del Popolo to city planning. Although the Porta del Popolo on the site of the ancient Porta Flaminia of the Aurelian Wall designed by Vignola—its inner side built by Bernini in 1655 on the occasion of the entry of Queen Christina of Sweden was the actual *raison d'être* of the whole scheme—it was reduced to a secondary role when the *Piazza* was laid out. It is removed from the vista through the side streets, which are focused on the obelisk. The two churches dominate the picture. One is tempted to ask, why two identical churches with the same cupolas and porticos? The only explanation is the mania for symmetry which had possessed the minds of all architects and city planners since the end of the Middle Ages. Symmetry at any price—an obviously unavoidable result of the all-pervading misuse and misunderstanding of the

53. Piazza del Popolo with the churches S. M. dei Miracoli and S. M. di Montesanto.

151

nature of geometrical logic and clarity! But it also expressed the conviction that repetition, the doubling of the same effect, would increase the unity of the design and the power of persuasion to which every work of the Baroque exposed the beholder. That this exhibitionist attitude—it is really nothing else—was deeply embedded in the mentality of the Baroque is evident. There are numerous designs which show the same duplication—for instance, the Piazza San Carlo at Turin designed by Vitozzi in 1620, to name only one Italian example; or the main square at Ludwigsburg in Württemberg; or Weinbrenner's design for Karlsruhe, both with two identical churches and other buildings. Repetition of similar architectural elements and symmetry were an inheritance of the Baroque from the Renaissance. But—and this is the fundamental difference—Renaissance architects used these means for the sole purpose of creating unity and balanced compositions. They never confused homogeneity with uniformity and regimented rigidity. However, this was exactly what Baroque architects were only too prone to do—an infallible sign of the decline of spontaneous creativeness, of imagination, and artistic originality.

4. **Animated Architecture.** The final response of Baroque city planning to the challenge of the ideas which pervaded every sphere of life, the response to the search for infinity and to the fascination of movement, was the lavish use of water. The fine spurts of fountains rising like obelisks, the vertical showers of cascades falling in terraces into large basins, the glimmering transluscence of reflected light and colors, the fleeting coalescence of brightness and shadows, the mist of scintillating spray scattered by the wind—all these created the illusion of unreality and infinity, of splendor and gaiety. It was the symbol of the very essence of Baroque architecture and city planning, and the logical and final consequence of the abhorrence of plane surfaces, of the immobility of solid matter and space at rest. Like mirrors so profusely used by the Baroque as wall decoration, water fulfilled this longing for visual and emotional excitement. The open-air mirrors of an artificial lake or a basin reflecting an entire building or a fountain are the perfect answer to the same problem: to break through the restricting boundaries of solid architecture. Fountains whether freestanding or built against a wall were, therefore, ideal instruments of city planning: they introduced movement, surprise, and excitement and, above all, the fleeting contours of ever-changing colors and shapes. But for the Baroque the gentle murmur of the thin flow of water, so characteristic of Renaissance fountains, was not sufficient. Carlo Fontana gives a vivid description of how *la maniera grande* had transformed the role of water as an essential part of Baroque planning. He is

54. Drawing of the architect Nicola Salvi, who for thirteen years was in charge of the work on the Fontana Trevi, by P. L. Ghezzi (1744).

exultant in his admiration of the force with which the two fountains in the Piazza di S. Pietro

. . . eject from their highest point a mighty volume of water that rises into the air and thunders down like rivers from the upper into the lower basin with such a din that it arouses the greatest delight. The vast quantity of water appears even more magnificent when strong winds drive it like spreading clouds beyond the basins and the sun fills them with iridescent colors, a spectacle that evokes the greatest admiration and surprise.[3]

A sufficient water supply was of vital necessity for the life of every city. In Rome hardly anything had survived of the ancient water system except parts of the Aqua Virgo. This aqueduct was restored and two others, the Acqua Felice and the Acqua Paola, were constructed. The Aqua Virgo, renamed Acqua Vergine, was built by Agrippa in 19 B.C. to carry the water from the Campagna, over a distance of more than 12 miles, to his baths. It was repeatedly restored, by Claudius in A.D. 46 and by the Popes Hadrian I and Nicolas V. In 1453 the latter commissioned Alberti to construct a wall fountain below the Quirinal. This was the Fontana di Trevi, whose name was a distortion of the ancient word *Trivio* referring to its three outlets. Originally it was a simple well used by washerwomen. The fountain we know today may be based on a design by Bernini submitted in 1640 but rejected by the pope. It was not before 1730 that interest in the project was revived when a competition was arranged. A second followed in 1732. However, Pope Clement XII gave the work not to the winner but to Nicola Salvi. After the death of Salvi, Giuseppe Pannini continued the work, completing it in 1762. The fountain, which has become one of the landmarks of Rome—why this has happened remains a mystery—has as a matter of fact nothing in common with the true spirit of the Baroque. It is a

3. Carlo Fontana. *Il. Tempio Vaticano e sua origine*. Roma. 1694. P. 199. Lib. IV, Cap. VI.

55. Fontana di Trevi before its reconstruction.

153

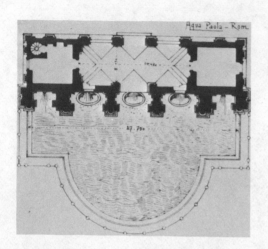

56. Plan of the Acqua Paola in Rome.

vulgar conglomeration of naturalistic features and architectural forms, lacking coherence and the grand sweep of genuine Baroque fountains. It is a telling example of the decadence of a style and as such has its dubious place in the history of city planning. It is akin to the artificial ruins which were *en vogue* in the 18th century. Its popularity is very likely the result of this "picturesque" confusion which appeals to the lower instincts—to sentimentality and triviality.

The other two aqueducts, the Acqua Felice and the Acqua Paola, supplied water to the Quirinal, Viminal, and Esquilin Hills and the Vatican and Trastevere quarters respectively. The former leading from the Alban Hills about 15 miles away owed its name to Felice Peretti, afterward Pope Sixtus V. It was built in 1585-87 by Domenico Fontana against the wall of the reservoir of the Acqua Felice. Water streams down from three openings into three basins. It is an insignificant and academic work, characteristic of the early period of the Baroque. The two fountainheads for the Acqua Paola on the Janiculus were designed and built in 1612 by Giovanni Fontana and Carlo Maderna for Paul V and were fed by the waters of Lake Bracciano, about 30 miles distant. The water flows in three cascades into a large and shallow pond. This is in striking contrast to the façade of the Acqua Felice, where the water falls, almost hidden from view, into separate basins.

In the Middle Ages fountains were utilitarian structures. This situation changed in the Renaissance, when they became an important element of city planning and their value as works of art was recognized. The Baroque not only continued this development but made the display of water an integral part of urban renewal. It is no exaggeration to say that Baroque city planning is unthinkable without fountains, without the fleeting architecture of cascades and ponds. The Baroque discovered a new ideal, a new vitality surrounded by the wonder of sensuous beauty and ever-changing harmony. Water, this restless agent, was the ideal instrument on which this music could be played. Architecture has been called frozen music. It is in this same sense that water, as used by the Baroque artists, may be called animated architecture. Two possibilities offered themselves: the fountain built against a wall, and the fountain standing as an isolated monument in a street or square. The Baroque used both methods with varying degrees of success. Wall fountains were the obvious solution for closing a vista with a conspicuous architectural work. Freestanding fountains were the ideal means of accentuating space relations and giving a distinctive character to a square or street. This development, which began with the subordination of the fountains to the spatial conception of the square, finally led in some cases to reverse effects: the square seems to exist for the fountains.

If a fountain was erected in a small square or at the widening of a street, it dominated the whole space. These fountains never stood in the center of the square, but mostly at its lowest point where the water would naturally collect. Here the Baroque evaded the tyranny of symmetry and proved its determination not to be diverted from its vision and its magnificent awareness of the value of asymmetrical groupings. Fountains were never set up in front of an important building. Instead of one fountain, and in order to keep the view unimpeded, two fountains were erected to the right and left of the facade if a display of water was deemed desirable. This was the case in front of Palazzo Farnese and in the Piazza di S. Pietro.

57. Fontana delle Tartarughe in Rome. This elegant and sprightly fountain stands in a small square against the plain façades of private houses. It is in almost every respect the opposite of the Acqua Paola with its severe architectural rigidity. The water flows down from a higher to a lower basin sunk in the pavement. It is a work by Taddeo Landini and Jacopo della Porta (1585).

155

58. A festival in the flooded Piazza Navona. Painting by G. P. Pannini in the Niedersächsische Landesgalerie, Hannover.

The Piazza Navona at Rome, originally a Roman circus, is one of the squares whose *raison d'être* are fountains. The buildings which surround it are to say the least indifferent, including the two churches and the Palazzo Pamfili. In the center the Fountain of the Four Rivers, by Bernini, was begun in 1647 and completed in 1651. In the middle of a circular basin rises a rock on which rests an obelisk. At the corners of the rock are seated four statues of rivers representing the four allegorical corners of the world—the Danube, the Nile, the Ganges, and the Rio de la Plata. Water cascades down into the basin. The fountain is slightly moved to the right so that it does not obstruct the view toward the façade of the church. The fountain at the south end of the square is surmounted by a Triton by Bernini; the other figures were made by his pupils. The fountain at the north end was erected in 1878 as a pendant to the other work at the opposite end. All three fountains are sunk into the pavement: they are level with the square, with the basins surrounded by a low rim. The surface of the water, the reflection of light and shadows, and the ripples caused by the gushing water help to emphasize the unity of the square and to enhance its otherwise indifferent character. The rocks and, above all, the running water are the essential elements. Everything else is mere decoration and of secondary importance. The Piazza Navona had a particularly strong attraction for the population, and the fountains certainly contributed to its popularity. The combination of lifeless rocks and flowing water fascinated all classes, strongly appealed to the play instinct, to *homo ludens*. How strong this fascination must have been is vividly illustrated by a painting of the 18th century: the *Piazza* was flooded and only narrow passages along the buildings were reserved for the spectators of this festival. Carriages in an uninterrupted stream circled the flooded area. A spectacle in *la maniera grande* by the wealthy few for the less fortunate many; an apotheosis of water and of the spirit of the Baroque!

59. Air view of the Piazza Navona in Rome.

5. **Monumental Synthesis.** Only a reconstruction of the original intentions can convey an idea of the great efforts made by the popes and their architects in the 17th and 18th centuries to give organic coherence to the chaotic character of the Eternal City. The actual results were fragmentary and are evident more in detail than in comprehensive replanning. However, the grand conception did exist and can be recalled to life by a study of the contemporary plans and projects. Consequently, two avenues are open: to investigate the development of city planning in general during this period, and to interpret this development in detail by an analysis of the two most representative examples—the Piazza del Campidoglio and the Piazza di S. Pietro. This double approach will crystallize the essence of the ideas which dominated the mind and action of the great master builders of the Baroque and led them to aspire to a synthesis on a monumental scale which would have made Rome a supreme manifestation of comprehensive city planning—as understood at this time.

(a) *The Framework.* The reigns of most popes are short, never lasting as long as the *régime* of a hereditary dynasty. This explains, apart from other factors such as shortage of funds or wars, why so many of the grandiose projects which one pope or another had planned or initiated existed only on paper or remained incomplete. However, it was not only the shortness of time of a pontificate but even more the unwillingness of the reigning pope to be merely the executor of schemes that his predecessors had begun. This attitude was basically not too dissimilar from that of the Pharaohs, who moved the capital at the beginning of their reign to a new site. For the popes of this period, self-glorification in this world was more important than being humble agents of a humanitarian and uninterrupted improvement of their city, which would have contributed to a steady civic development but less to their own secular pride. Ritual considerations—although these were not the only ones that had moved the Pharaohs to build a new capital where the spirit of their predecessors would not throw a spell over their short sojourns on earth—did not influence the decisions of the popes. Only a few were inclined to carry out a project, especially a city-planning scheme, that was not exclusively their own. This was one reason why Rome's chaotic growth was so difficult to reduce to order. But it was not the only reason. The far greater problem was to merge the past and the present, to reconcile the heritage of two millennia with the demands of the 17th and 18th centuries. In contrast to the preceding epochs, the Baroque was aware of this challenge, and its great contribution to city planning consists in just this awareness and in the readiness to respond to the challenge.

That the results were fragmentary and not wholly satisfactory does not diminish the essential value of the intentions or of the partial plans that were actually carried through. Taken together, the efforts of the Baroque left their imprint on Rome—as on other cities—and enable us to understand and evaluate the ideas and aspirations of an era full of contradictions yet inspired by a search for order, grandeur, and unification—and above all by the insight that life in its immense complexity is a drama in which the sense of reality and the sense of possibility are of equal importance. Hence the simultaneous use of abstract geometrical forms, the heritage of the ideal schemes of the Renaissance, and the emotional appeal to sensuous enjoyment and excitement— the secular version of the religious hysteria of the Middle Ages. It is in this sense that the city-planning schemes of the Baroque should be understood and the attempts at creating a "functional" unity out of the confusing and yet not wholly inorganic growth of the Eternal City should be appreciated.

But let it be repeated that the solutions proposed and the means employed were exactly those that ushered in the era of city planning from above, a travesty of what city planning should be and had been in the Middle Ages. Planning at the grass roots, from the bottom upward, was discarded. It did not even enter the minds of the architects and their patrons that such a possibility existed. Mass man appeared on the stage. City planning became an instrument of paternalistic tutelage used by the upper classes and the State (both virtually identical) to exclude the masses from an active participation of the rebuilding of their cities. The means to achieve these ends were ostentation and theatricality, imposing private and public buildings, luxurious spectacles, and grandiose avenues. An ingenuous propaganda by the few for the many, for the obedient subjects who had to be "conditioned" to their role as patient bystanders. The conviction that society is good enough as it is and rests quite naturally on the principle of "the two nations," the wealthy and the poor, was shamelessly expressed by Montesquieu when he said: *"Il faut bien qu'il y ait du luxe. Si les riches n'y dépensent pas beaucoup, les pauvres mourront de faim."* This principle had to be maintained.

The system of the grand avenues, which the Baroque cut through the amorphous mass of the congested quarters, has often been compared with Haussmann's work for Paris. The similarity is indeed striking in more than a mere architectural respect. Haussmann's wide, straight avenues were useful not only as traffic arteries but also as target lines, if it should ever be necessary to hold the masses in check with guns. It is not without interest to recall a story referring to similar considerations under the pontificate of Sixtus IV. When Ferdinand, King of Naples, visited the pope in 1475 he advised him to widen the streets and to remove all the turrets, balconies, and loggias because they were dangerous in case of an insurrection. "You will never be the master of Rome," he said, "as long as simple women can put to flight your best soldiers by throwing missiles down from these structures."[4] This story has been questioned, but only insofar as "the pope hardly needed the king of Naples to provide him with an argument which he had already found out for himself."

The Baroque reduced city planning to the layout of streets and squares and the erection of prominent buildings. Scant if any consideration was given to a systematic renewal of residential quarters or to other basic requirements of daily life. The Cult of the Street—the repeated use of this expression is unavoidable, if the true character of the attitude to these problems is to be correctly described—has dominated the thinking and acting of the whole era from the beginning of the Renaissance to the present day. As if a magic spell had been cast over the minds of those responsible for the rebuilding of Rome, the creation of a grand system of avenues was regarded as the only panacea for all the ills of the physical and social organization of the city.

We can study in detail the transformation of Rome from the small scale and unrelated fragmentation of the urban area in the Middle Ages to the large-scale and interrelated unification which the popes of the late Renaissance and the Baroque tried to carry through. Several old plans are available showing the subsequent stages of development from the beginning of the 16th century to the middle of the 18th century.[5] The most important of these are Leonardo Bufalini's plan of the year 1551 which shows Rome before the first schemes of the Baroque were begun. Then follows in 1555 Ugo Pinardo's *Pianta Prospettiva* and others, still mainly depicting the earlier medieval structure and numerous details, arcades on the ground floor and narrow and high houses. *Roma al Tempo di Clemente X, La Pianta di Roma di Giambattista Falda del 1676* is a large bird's-eye view that transports us into the period of the High Baroque. Many of the new avenues and other features are visible. Unification is proceeding and important squares such as the Piazza di S. Pietro are beginning to take shape. Then there is finally the *Nuova Pianta di Roma Data In Luce Da Giambattista Nolli 1748*. This is an exact ground plan, not a bird's-eye view. It gives a clear idea of the general layout and of the building blocks in detail, with the plans of the palaces, churches, squares, villas, and gardens.

As interesting as these and other extant plans are, they remain the cherished battleground of antiquarians and scholars

4. Quoted after P. Lavedan. *Histoire de l'Urbanisme. Renaissance et Temps Modernes.* 1941. P. 41 n.

5. In this connection it would be merely confusing to go into a detailed description of the growth of Rome. Many studies on this development have been published. A few are included in the Bibliography. Some are useful, others so much overloaded with details and irrelevant reforms that they do not convey a clear picture. See City Survey, Rome, pp. 414-441.

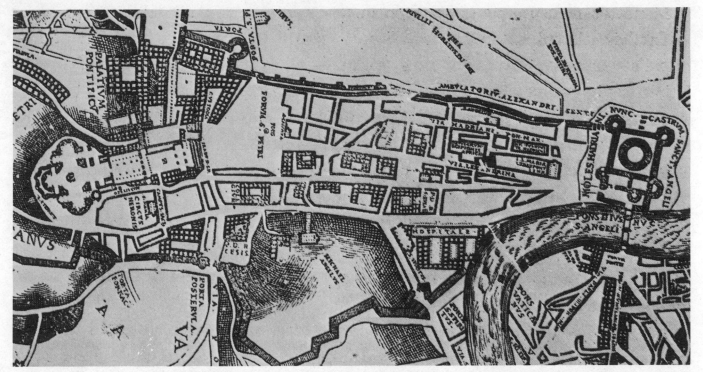

more eager to prove a point than to interpret principles and intentions. The popes and their architects had a fairly clear vision of what they wanted, but the results were fragmentary, as has been clearly pointed out. The guiding principle directing their efforts can be expressed in one word: unification. The means, especially in the earlier stages, were improvement, rectification, and widening of existing roads. This procedure in itself was not exceptional. What matters is how it was done. In contrast to the Renaissance, the Baroque conceived the Ideal Street as a preparation, a spatial and organic unit of a larger composition. It was a preparation for a *point de vue* which gave it meaning and direction. It was an organic spatial unit limited in scope and character insofar as it created a forward movement toward the building or monument which closed the view and thus produced a greater variety of visual impressions. This was indeed something new, quite different from the street merely lined by houses on either side and disappearing into nothingness in the distance.

The rebuilding of the Borgo Leonino is an excellent example of this changing attitude. The earlier project planned under Nicolas V around 1450 provided for three parallel streets leading to the Piazza di S. Pietro. The later project by Carlo Fontana abandoned this idea and concentrated the access to the *Piazza* and the view toward the Basilica into one fanlike "forecourt." Concentration on one point—a typical Baroque solution! The Piazza del Popolo is another example of the same principle and the re-

60. Plan of the Borgo Leonino and the Vatican from Bufalini's plan of 1551.

161

building of the streets at Santa Maria Maggiore by Domenico Fontana under Sixtus V (1585-90) illustrates a similar tendency.

Is there a contradiction between what has been termed the search for infinity and the perspective view focused on a building that closes the vista? On the face of it one possibility seems to exclude the other. However, it would be a misrepresentation of the spirit of the Baroque to equate infinity with unlimited architectural space. It is rather the feeling that Hamlet expresses when he says: "I could be bounded in a nutshell, and count myself a king of infinite space" that explains the seeming contradiction between infinity and limitation. Moreover, as has been explained on the foregoing pages, there were, as in all periods of history, many different aspects that shaped the artistic ideas of the Baroque. It was not only the search for infinity but also movement, symmetry, unification, the interplay of volume, space, and other factors that created the final synthesis of Baroque architecture and planning. The symbolism of the *Way*, of the processional route, was still alive in the Baroque, and it may be assumed that this too played a not insignificant role in the laying out of important thoroughfares. Hitherto these did not exist. It is symptomatic that as late as the first half of the 15th century it was still common to describe the progress of the papal processions through the city by referring to landmarks rather than streets, and to enumerate churches, towers, Roman ruins, porticos, and temples which the processions had to pass on their way.[6] In any case, all the main avenues and streets led to an important building and sometimes connected two buildings—for instance, the Palazzo del Laterano and the Colosseum.

Rome was, of course, a special case. As the principal city of Christendom she had to be hostess to enormous crowds of visitors

6. T. Magnuson, *Studies in Roman Quattrocento Architecture*, 1958.

61. Porta Pia and S. Maria degli Angeli. From E. Dupérac's *Plan of Rome* published in 1577.

at irregular intervals while at other times only the usual traffic had to be accommodated. This oscillation between maximum and minimum use of the roads created problems that were difficult to solve. The obvious answer was to develop a system of arteries commanding the main points which the organized processions or the unorganized crowds would pass. These arteries therefore had to fulfill a double task: they had to play both a purely functional, and a ceremonial and aesthetic role. These tasks were clearly recognized but their execution remained unfinished and fractional. We know, for instance, from Giannozzo Manetti, the biographer of Nicolas V, that the Pope had the intention of uniting all squares of Rome by porticos, a project never carried

62. View of the Via Pia. Fresco in the Lateran Palace, Rome.

out but one that gives an idea of the ambitions and motives of the papal patrons. This program was purely aesthetic and was to further the embellishment and glorification of Rome. As an example of functional improvement we may cite the restoration of the Ponte Sisto which was begun in 1473. In the Holy Year of 1475 a new route was planned to provide an approach to St. Peter's through Trastevere. This was regarded as essential after the great calamity of the Jubilee of 1450, when more than two hundred pilgrims were killed in a traffic jam on the Ponte Sant' Angelo. Many were trodden under foot or pushed into the Tiber. The opening of a new road and the restoration of the bridge were functional needs and as such part of a comprehensive road-building program.[7]

The Rome that the popes of the 15th century began to improve was still the medieval city with its maze of streets and houses, while the interiors of the blocks were often cultivated as gardens. The ancient Roman roads were still the principal lines of communication between Rome and other cities and towns of Italy. Within the Aurelian Wall they passed through the uninhabited hilly areas used as gardens and vineyards down to the populous quarters along the banks of the Tiber.

The restoration of Rome and the street system was dominated by the determination of the popes to make the principal religious centers the focal point of this enterprise. Three major schemes were undertaken, each opening up a particularly important district and all together creating a unified framework for the re-

63. View of Trastevere (left), Ponte S. Maria (center), the tower of the Palazzo Venezia above it, and the Capitoline Hill (right). From the late 15th-century *Codex Escurialensis.*

7. According to T. Magnuson, *op. cit.*, p. 29.

64. S. Maria Maggiore in the 16th century. Mural in the Library of the Vatican.

newal of the Eternal City. There was first of all the Vatican
Quarter; then the ancient Campus Martius between the Quirinal
and the Capitol to the east of the Tiber—uninhabited in the
earliest period, in the course of time more and more built up,
under Augustus laid out with magnificent parks, and most
densely settled in the Middle Ages and the following centuries;
then the regions on the south of the left bank of the Tiber with
the oldest churches, Santa Maria Maggiore, S. Giovanni in Laterano, and S. Croce in Gerusalemme. The rebuilding of the
Vatican Quarter will be described later in connection with the
Piazza di S. Pietro. Here it may be sufficient to refer to the detail
of Bufalini's plan of 1551, Figure 383. In this connection it is
important to mention the project executed under Julius II, possibly with the advice of Bramante. Two new access streets were
planned and laid out using partly existing roads. One street, the
Via del Lungara, led from Trastevere directly to the Vatican on
the same side of the Tiber; the other, the Via Giulia, on the opposite side of the river running parallel with La Lungara, was to
reach the Vatican over a bridge which was, however, not built.
These two principal axes were added focuses on the most important building complex of Rome. The northern quarters on the
Campus Martius were opened up by the three streets radiating

165

from the Piazza del Popolo connecting them with the central and the southeastern parts of the city. This system has been described above.

The third project was executed under Sixtus V. It connected the outlying districts in the southeast with the north, continuing the streets leading from the Piazza del Popolo to S. Maria Maggiore and beyond to S. Giovanni in Laterano and S. Croce in Gerusalemme respectively. The nucleus of this system is S. Maria Maggiore. Its relationship to the streets repeats in a less distinctive form the street pattern of the Piazza del Popolo: one street leads from the north to the apse of the church, and three streets (of which only two end in front of the façade of the church while the third one enters the middle street at a short distance before reaching the small square in front of the church) lead to the three outlying churches. These three projects provided a clear system of coordinates which greatly contributed toward the unification of the hitherto inarticulate structure of the city. Numerous other improvements were made but they were of minor importance and transformed only details not the structure as a whole.

(b) *Symbols of Monumental Synthesis*. The two spiritual centers of Rome are the Piazza del Campidoglio and the Piazza di S. Pietro with the Vatican. The secular and the religious symbol of the Eternal City—each representing one of the great creative periods of architecture, each resting on ancient foundations. As in innumerable other cities and towns in all parts of the world, city hall and church dominate the skyline but not the system of roads that divides the urban area and links important buildings,

65. Arterial street system of Rome. Mural in the Library of the Vatican.

squares, and districts. Both centers radiate an ubiquitous power and spirit over every section of the city. Both are independent self-contained architectural units yet exert an irresistible attraction on the whole urban region and beyond.

The Piazza del Campidoglio, the work of Michelangelo, lies in the depression between the two hillocks of the Capitoline Hill. It was here that Romulus, according to legend, founded his asylum and that the temple of Juno Moneta and the *arx,* the *acropolis,* were situated. On the southern height an area sacred to Jupiter was used by the last of the kings to erect an Etruscan temple to Jupiter Optimus Maximus which was dedicated in 509 B.C., the first year of the Republic. In the early Middle Ages the entire hill belonged to the monastery of S. Maria de Capitolio (S. Maria Aracoeli). The name of the southwestern height, Monte Caprino, Hill of the Goats, is evidence of the desolate condition at this time. In 1143, the municipal administration established its seat on the hill. The *Novum Palatium* for the assembly of the Senate is first mentioned in 1150. In 1348 the stairway to Aracoeli was built where a market square at this time was located.

Work on the *Piazza* began soon after 1538 when the equestrian statue of Marcus Aurelius was transferred from the Lateran to the Capitol and erected by Michelangelo in the center of the *Piazza.* After his death in 1564, other artists completed the work, but Michelangelo's design remained the groundwork for the square and the buildings. The square is a trapezium formed by the three palaces. A wide oval traced in the pavement surrounds the equestrian statue. The depth of the square is 237 feet, the width at the narrower end 126 feet, and at the Palazzo Senatorio,

66. Piazza del Campidoglio in the second half of the 16th century, before the replanning by Michelangelo.

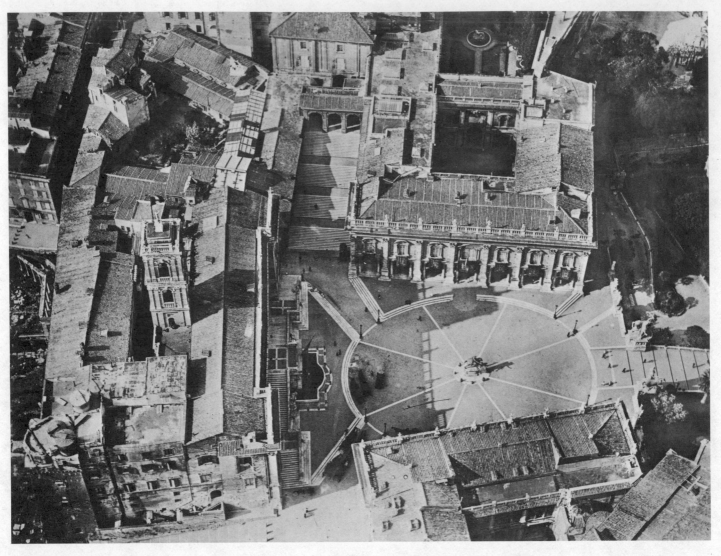

67. Air view of the Campidoglio in Rome.

the City Hall, 180 feet. The height of the lateral palaces is approximately 60 feet and that of the Palazzo Senatorio 81 feet.

In contrast to typical Renaissance squares, equally balanced in all directions and therefore without a distracting dominant orientation, the volumes of the buildings and the shape of the *Piazza* are symmetrically related to a central axis. Consequently the Palazzo Senatorio dominates the composition. It exerts an attraction in depth which is emphasized by the heavy principal cornice of the low and massive lateral palaces and again underlined by the strong moldings between the stories. The double flight of steps, the sculptures, the main portal, and the tower enhance the dominating power of the *Palazzo* and the development and depth of the square. This effect is heightened by the free view that opens between the palaces, extending far into the distance—a solution that resembles the beautiful grouping at Pienza. This semiopenness is of great importance for the whole composition and the interrelationship of the buildings: the movement in depth is not intercepted but spread out beyond the square at both sides.

The Piazza del Campidoglio is the last magnificent farewell performance of the Renaissance and the first gift of the dawn of the Baroque. Never in the whole history of architecture and city planning has the transition of two periods found a more characteristic, more perfect expression. In spite of the loose grouping of the buildings and the irregular form, the *Piazza* is a faultlessly closed composition because the functional and spatial elements operate with unmitigated clarity and logic.

The fourth side of the *Piazza* is open. Only a balustrade with a few statues indicates the edge of the hill. A stairway with shallow steps, the Cordonata, leads from the Piazza Aracoeli to the Capitol. A second stairway, beginning with an acute angle at the foot of the Cordonata, connects the Piazza Aracoeli with the church. A comparison of the Cordonata with the Scala di Spagna reveals the fundamental change between the two periods. At the Capitol a straight ascent of great composure never deviates from the shortest connection between the two levels. The Scala di Spagna is a fireworks of movement, of excitement, of contrasting effects, turning aside again and again from the straight and shortest way upward to the church. The weakest point of the Piazza del Campidoglio is perhaps the open side with the balustrade and the statues which turn their backs to the senatorial palace. It seems that this void was regarded as not wholly satisfactory and that a more conspicuous limitation would benefit the unity of the *Piazza*. This fact may explain why, on the occasion of a ceremonial reception after the election of Pope Paul V in 1605, a triumphal arch was erected on this side; later in 1670 two arches were built for Clement X, and in 1689 one for Alexander VIII.[8] However, it is irrelevant to criticize the architectural unity of the *Piazza*. It is there, and it is the greatest contribution to the arts of the transitional period between the Renaissance and the Baroque. It is a monumental synthesis of two eras in spirit and in material manifestation.

The Città del Vaticano, consisting of the Palazzo Vaticano, the Basilica, the Piazza di S. Pietro, the Borgo, and a small adjoining area, extends over 108 acres on the northwestern periphery of Rome. It is more an annex than an integral and organic part of the city with which it is but loosely connected through roads secondary in importance and appearance, although as the religious symbol of the Church of Rome it is the center of gravity toward which the life and even the physical structure of the city tend to move. This Versailles of the Popes occupies a position in relation to the urban area similar to that of the palaces of the

8. After A. E. Brinkmann. *Platz und Monument*. P. 60.

princes of the Baroque: it is a self-contained unit yet part of the city, to which it gives meaning and orientation. Like the palaces at Karlsruhe and Mannheim, the Vatican City is situated at the periphery. It dominates Rome from this peripheral situation. In the Residence Cities of the absolute princes it was the spirit of *l'état c'est moi* that was the fountainhead of the architectural conception. In the Città del Vaticano it was the identical claim of the *ecclesia triumphans* in all her glory and splendor. But there the similarity ends, for at Versailles, Karlsruhe, and Mannheim the whole structure, the entire system of streets, was oriented toward the palace of the ruler. At Rome nothing even faintly resembling this principle exists.

And yet the symbolic significance is perhaps even stronger than in the ostentatious demonstrations of the secular potentates. The Città del Vaticano—it is impossible to separate the constituent elements without destroying the idea and the structure of this complex entity—is more like the residence of a monarch than the seat of a humble servant of God. The *Città* as it presents itself today to the multitudes entering its precincts is a typically Baroque creation with all its pomp and solemnity, its demonstration of grandeur and persuasion. Not even with the utmost indulgence can it be said that this has been achieved exclusively through refined and aristocratic means. A strong element of coarseness and vulgarity disturbs the more sensitive visitor and adds an element of embarrassing uneasiness to the undiluted appreciation of this rough diamond. The Festival Hall in honor of God, the Basilica, and the Piazza di S. Pietro, its ceremonial forecourt; the Palace with its *cortili* and *logge*, with the Scala Regia, the great *stanze,* and the numerous other rooms, have so strong a secular character as almost to extinguish the beauty of holiness that should pervade this religious city and the church of St. Peter.

At the beginning of the 15th century Rome was a desolate and decaying city. This fact has to be kept in mind if one wants to appreciate the greatness of achievements of the architects and popes of the Baroque and their predecessors who took an active part in the rebuilding of the Vatican City. When Pope Martin V arrived in Rome in 1420, "he found it so dilapidated and deserted that it bore hardly any resemblence to a city. Houses had fallen into ruins, churches had collapsed, whole quarters were abandoned; and the town was neglected and oppressed by famine and poverty."[9] When after the Great Schism, the papacy was again permanently established in Rome, the way was open for the renewal of the Eternal City and a new age began. "Rome issued from her ruins in a new form, imparted to her by the popes, now become her masters. The Vatican, the fortress of the popes,

9. Quoted from T. Magnuson, *op. cit.,* p. 3, after *Platynae historici liber de Vita Christi ac omnium pontificum* RIS², III:1, 310.

arose, and its rival, the republican Capitol, degenerated into the monument of the liberty of the people and of a second past."[10]

The Borgo Leonino, the quarter between the Ponte S. Angelo, the only connection with the city and St. Peter's, had all the characteristics of a closely knit community with hardly any social, political, or economic relations to the rest of the city. In the ninth century it was surrounded by a wall and during the Middle Ages its original population had admitted a considerable number of foreigners. These newcomers established *scholae* where pilgrims and other travelers would be offered hospitality. In the 15th century the *Borgo,* the suburb of the fortified castle of the Vatican, was inhabited almost exclusively by people who were, in one way or another, connected with the Vatican either as clerics or administrators. Merchants and craftsmen were missing or constituted only a small fraction of the population. The task facing the popes and their architects in the 15th century was to reconstruct the fortifications, the two piazzas at either end of the Borgo, the connecting streets, and the buildings.

According to Manetti, the Vatican palace and the Basilica were to be part of the fortifications with the Castel Sant' Angelo as the most important point of the defense system. The *piazza* at the Castel Sant' Angelo had to be connected with the old *Platea Sancti Petri* in front of the Basilica. The plan was to build three streets, and it seems that these were to be laid out as strictly axial lines of communication and to terminate under colonnades opening onto the *piazza* at the Basilica. Manetti reports that the *Borgo,* which he calls characteristically *vicus curialis,* was to be the residential quarter of the *Curia,* providing offices and houses for its members, and that the canons, who were not directly associated with the *Curia,* should be accommodated in buildings to be erected south of the Basilica. Apart from these houses, Manetti mentions accommodation for merchants and craftsmen, indicating that the social structure of the reconstructed *Borgo* had changed and was not too dissimilar from that of the city itself.[11] It is possible that the admission of merchants and craftsmen as residents of the *Borgo* was at least partially influenced by the desire of the popes to make it a more modern and prosperous community, a goal unthinkable at that time without the inclusion of nonecclesiastical people. The different trades were to be accommodated as closed groups in a contiguous area. The money changers and drapers, the most esteemed members of the middle class, should occupy the central street, and the less important craftsmen the side streets, while living quarters over the porticos were reserved for minor officials including scholars.

The concentration of the Vatican community in an area relatively isolated from the city had various reasons: it made it easier

10. F. Gregorovius. *History of the City of Rome in the Middle Ages.* Vol. VI, Part 2, p. 670. 1898.
   11. T. Magnuson, *op. cit.,* pp. 82ff.

for the popes to exclude hostile influences, to keep all the members of the papal court under their own jurisdiction and, more importantly, to render the defense of the fortified *vicus* more efficient and more manageable. This latter consideration continued a medieval tradition that found its contemporary justification in Alberti's ideas laid down in his *De re aedificatoria*. It is not clear whether he was actually responsible for the project of rebuilding the *Borgo* or was merely the spiritual rector, whose teachings had influenced Manetti's report on the project. In any case we may assume that Alberti's influence played a role in the inception of the plan for the new *Borgo*.[12]

In the fifth book of *De re aedificatoria* Alberti suggests that a tyrant should build his fortified seat near or on the periphery and close to the city walls. To describe the popes as tyrants might be going too far, although it was not uncommon for them to defend themselves from the citizens of Rome and from a nobility often violently opposed to their temporal powers. However this may be, the Vatican was a strong fortress and its location fulfilled the demands which Alberti had made for the seat of a prince in an unruly city. But one consideration should not be lost sight of. The Basilica was erected over the tomb of Saint Peter who, according to legend, was crucified in the circus which Caligula had laid out on the site where now stands the church that bears the saint's name.

Since the tomb of the saint was the actual *raison d'être* of the Basilica, it is difficult to envisage any other place where it could have been built. That this site was at the periphery of the city, and as such corresponded to the requirements formulated by Alberti, was a mere coincidence which was most likely welcomed but could hardly have played any role in the choice of the site for the church. The building of the *Borgo* was one of the most important and interesting examples of city planning in the early 15th century, and whether Alberti was the architect or not is really irrelevant. Most probably he was one of several persons connected with the work whose original plan is not a perfect whole but shows contradicting influences, combining medieval and Renaissance features with other rather arbitrary characteristics.

The Vatican Palace was extended and rebuilt under Nicolas V. The medieval fortifications were strengthened and the whole complex with its courtyards, buildings, and gardens was to be enclosed by new walls within the circumvallation of the *Borgo*. This was still regarded as an essential precaution. Manetti reports that Nicolas V on his deathbed expressed the wish that the Palace should be fortified against external enemies as well as against popular uprisings within the city.[13] The Palace is, and

12. G. Dehio. "Die Bauprojecte Nikolaus V and L. B. Alberti," *Repertorium für Kunstwissenschaft,* 1880. Pp. 241-57. To be used with caution. Not wholly reliable and conclusive.
13. T. Magnuson, *op. cit.,* p. 144, footnote.

68. Self-portrait of Giovanni Lorenzo Bernini, about 1665. From the collection at Windsor Castle.

always has been, a vast conglomeration of numerous elements joined together without any apparent system. Expediency and the taste of the time dictated the additions of new parts and its growth in general. In this connection it is unnecessary to describe the history and the layout of the Palace in detail.[14] It is sufficient to treat it as a large group of buildings rising to the north of the Basilica and the *Piazza* and extending to the *Borgo*. This chaotic mass had to be screened off, at least in its lower parts, in order to create a symmetrical and harmonious approach to the Basilica. This result was magnificently achieved by the colonnades, which embrace the visitor like outstretched arms and concentrate his attention on the church. It is only in this negative aspect that the Palace has here to be mentioned: it had to be kept in the background if the architectural unity of the *Borgo,* the *Piazza,* and the Basilica was not to be spoiled.

The Piazza di S. Pietro—the monumental synthesis of the ideas and aspirations which had accumulated since the end of the Renaissance about a hundred years before Bernini began his

14. See the excellent chapter in Magnuson's book on The Project for the Vatican Palace, pp. 98-159.

work in 1656—is one of the two most perfect and commanding contributions to the art of Baroque city planning. Like the sequence of squares at Nancy, it is a rhythmic succession of spatial elements held together by one uniting conception, delicate in its simplicity yet monumental in its complex grandeur. Both are creations of the same absolutist will to power, the same spirit that only an absolute ruler, a prince or a pope, could command. The Piazza di S. Pietro, the Ninth Symphony of architecture, and the squares at Nancy, a chamber music of unsurpassable clarity and beauty, are compositions which represent the poles between which the great adaptability and dramatic variety of Baroque expressiveness could move.

The Piazza di S. Pietro consists of the trapezoid *Piazza retta* which widens toward the façade of the Basilica, and of the *Piazza obliqua* with the colonnades. The old Piazza Rusticucci has now disappeared, but while it existed it was a modest though a not entirely unimportant part of the general layout. Today a wide avenue, the Via della Conciliazone, leads to the *Piazza*. This bombastic monstrosity is lined by buildings five or six stories high in a modernistic insurance-company style and was begun under the *régime* of Mussolini. The motif of the obelisk has been degraded to lampposts with stable lanterns on top instead of the cross of Christ that crowns the original obelisk in the *Piazza*. This truly great demonstration of modern barbarism pretends to revive an old idea of Carlo Fontana. Unfortunately the main point of his scheme was overlooked. Fontana's plan provided for a low arcade connecting the two arms of the Piazza Rusticucci which would have retained the scale and the unity of the Piazza di S. Pietro, and which he had interposed *"per appagare la curiosità."* However, we should not be too squeamish about this misuse of an originally faultless conception. The original plan for the Basilica, as intended by Bramante and Michelangelo, has also been spoiled. Raphael conceived a plan in the form of a Greek cross and although Michelangelo returned to the original idea of a Latin cross, Carlo Maderna prolonged the nave toward the *Piazza* and built the present façade, which can hardly be called a masterpiece of Baroque architecture. In any case the dominating effect of the central dome was diminished and the unity of the interior and the exterior was destroyed. The façade itself is an independent showpiece without any artistic value, which cannot compete with the great sweep and the powerful simplicity of the colonnades.

The *Piazza* covers an area of 8.4 acres. Its lower point lies about 5 feet below, and the Basilica stands about 11 feet above the level of the colonnades—which consist of a quadruple covered passage formed by 284 columns and 88 piers and crowned with a

69. St. Peter's before the erection of the colonnades and part of the Vatican Palace. Painting by Jacob Isaacsz Swanenburgh in the Maximilian Museum, Augsburg.

balustrade with 140 statues of saints. The height of the columns is about 60 feet and the divergence of the two sides of the *Piazza retta* toward the Basilica is approximately 72 to 300 feet in depth. The *Piazza obliqua* is 588 feet wide and 426 feet deep. The height of the façade of the Basilica is over 130 feet—almost two and a half times greater than that of the colonnades. The extraordinary dimensions and the refined play of perspective effects let one forget the embarrassing and empty ostentatiousness of the façade of the Basilica. *La maniera grande* of the *Piazza* dominates everything. The shape of an ellipse and of a trapezium is an organic adaptation to the site and its limitations. It is far from being an artificial solution determined by perspective manipulations. Much has been written about the carefully considered optical effects, the different levels of the succession of squares, and the purposeful regulation of the scale of the individual parts in relation to the whole.

Many of these observations are true and helpful. But they tend to disregard or to minimize two factors of paramount importance: the natural condition of the site and the limitation which the proximity of the Palace demanded; and above all the spontaneity of an artist of the caliber of Bernini. What is mostly regarded as a predetermined calculation of certain effects was more likely a subsequent reaffirmation of his instinctive reactions to a complicated problem, a sort of controlling afterthought. Bernini himself as well as other architects submitted numerous projects either with a rectangular or a circular forecourt. All had

175

70. Air view of St. Peter's with the Castel S. Angelo and the Tiber.

in common a continuous enclosure of the *Piazza,* including the side opposite the Basilica.

But Bernini and his patrons would not have been men of the Baroque had they not finally fallen for an oval form and a succession of contrasting shapes, a dynamic sequence of movement in depth and width; and for the ever-changing vistas enhanced by light and shade, color and water that all these coalescing ele-

ments created out of the raw materials of the architectural composition. Carlo Fontana was aware of this when he wrote: "The beautiful view of the Piazza produces a marvelous and satisfactory impression. This would not be the case if the forecourt were rectangular as the designs of some architects have suggested and, in the words of Vitruvius, formed a peristyle."[15] The result was a monumental synthesis within a limited space of everything the

15. Carlo Fontana, *op. cit.*, pp. 183-84.

Baroque stood for, and as such the Piazza di S. Pietro is a more telling and more perfect manifestation than all the grandiose schemes for new avenues and streets which appeared more impressive on the drawing board than in reality.

This raises one of the most disturbing aspects of Baroque city planning. It was an art of a minority for a minority, not for the masses. Their needs were neglected or believed satisfied with the old promise of *panem et circenses*—in this case festivals, processions, and churches. Like ancient Rome the Eternal City of the Christian era was a place of splendid misery, of showpieces without social responsibility, lacking provisions of adequate housing for the bulk of the population. These considerations throw a dark shadow over even the most perfect architectural achievements. For the art historians, who so far have been almost the only interpreters of Baroque city planning, they did not even exist. It is one of the more urgent tasks of the social historian to investigate these aspects of life in the centuries since the Renaissance. Only then can our ideas of urban development be clarified and completed. Let us hope that a scholar with social responsibility will undertake this work.

At the beginning of this section, which traced the development of Italian cities from the early Middle Ages to the Baroque, an ivory carving of the 12th century was shown. It depicts the Holy Family surrounded by walls with gates and towers. The scene symbolizes the peace and the security within which the Holy Family lives and which only protecting walls can provide. For men of the Middle Ages walls were more than utilitarian structures. They were symbols of the Celestial Jerusalem and of peace on earth and of the shelter and security from the lawlessness of the open country. In medieval representations, walls signified the whole city. And even more, they indicated that the city was a space *sui generis* limited in extension and cut out from the surrounding country. The symbolic meaning of the city walls preserved the utilitarian function. It was ever present in the mind of the urban population even in later centuries when religion and symbolism were on the decline. The longing for shelter, for order, seclusion, and isolation from the hustle and bustle of daily life remained an integral part of human anxieties and hopes. In one form or another it was handed down from generation to generation and was expressed in architectural form.

In the colonnades, which enclose the Piazza di S. Pietro, this symbolism has survived. The colonnades were the walls which isolated the visitor from the outside world and sheltered him in the peace and security of the Holy City. It is the essential and original meaning of the two outstretched arms that receive him in a loving embrace. This symbolism was the primary though possibly subconscious motive of the popes and architects. It was more important than the practical function of the colonnades as solid limitations of the *Piazza* in a visible and intelligible form. To put it in other words: the idea of creating a preparation to the entrance into the Basilica, of emphasizing the end of a long pilgrimage preceded the architectural conception. This fact should always be present in our minds if we try to understand more than the external appearance of an architectural composition of the grandeur and significance of the Piazza di S. Pietro.

The continuity of the historical development in Italy is perhaps greater than that in other countries. There was never a sharp break between different periods. What we call Middle Ages, Renaissance, and Baroque are merely convenient historical labels which tend to hide the uninterrupted flow of tradition nourished by new ideas, diversified and enriched from century to century. The circle closes. It contains all the stages from the early primitive and powerful symbolism of the walled city as a place of peace and order to the refined and more latent expression of the same symbolic idea in the Piazza di S. Pietro.

CHAPTER 6

CITY SURVEY / ITALY

The selection of material for this City Survey has encountered formidable difficulties, not because there are too few but because there are too many cities and towns whose histories, spanning millennia, are still living realities. The environment that enfolds the modern Italian has been shaped and reshaped by past generations. The ever-present traditions, the monuments, the walls around the urban communities, the streets and squares—in short, the whole complexity of the *ambiente* and the inescapable impact of the all-pervading atmosphere saturated with the dreams and aspirations of times gone by—have left a legacy that is impossible to escape.

The abundance of cities and towns which should be represented in this City Survey is overwhelming. And yet a choice had to be made and the number restricted. As repeatedly expressed in preceding volumes, the series that constitutes *The International History of City Development* does not pretend to be a general history of the countries dealt with in this work. It is a history of urban development and, in particular, of the physical transformation through which cities and towns have passed. Its aim is not an encyclopedic but a selective description of representative examples, which are intended not so much individually as collectively to convey a complete picture of how urban communities originated, grew, stagnated, declined—and often revived. No doubt, different selections could have been made and cities may be missing that deserve to be mentioned, whereas others are named which in the opinion of some critics should have been left out. A certain subjectivity in this respect cannot be denied, but where does objectivity begin and where does it end?

Moreover, a not unimportant consideration was the availability of relevant documentation and, equally important, the time factor—the decision whether to wait unduly long for the arrival of requested material or to proceed without further delay. This is not to say that the cooperation of the Italian Government and of government agencies, municipal administrations, and individual persons has not been adequate. On the contrary, their assistance surpassed the greatest expectations. No other country has given more attention to and shown more understanding of what was needed than Italy. But a stop had to be made somewhere in the interest of the work.

It is not the purpose of the City Survey to provide comprehensive monographs of cities. The individual case studies should be regarded as specific illustrations of the problems discussed in the general text. To overburden the City Survey with a plethora of detailed descriptions of a limitless number of cities would have seriously impeded the quality of what had to be explained. The restriction imposed by external conditions was, therefore, a blessing in disguise. For the same reason the account of the historical development of individual cities had often to be more condensed than may have been desirable. On the other hand, the visual documentation assembled with the invaluable help of the local authorities more than makes up for this seeming shortcoming. It is, in fact, a very considerable stimulus to evaluate what can still be seen, experienced, and enjoyed. It adds weight to the contention that the value of written records alone should not be overestimated—a one-sided conviction of many historians who have been blinded to the reality of life by burying themselves in mountains of dusty documents without giving even a furtive glance to what the physical environment might have taught them. It is regrettable that virtually all historians who unearth material on, say, the social structure of urban communities, or the origin of cities—to mention but two of their subjects—neglect the wealth of information contained in visual documentation. Let us use our eyes! Let the past and the present speak through old views of cities, streets, squares, and buildings and through air views from which, if rightly interpreted, the whole history of a city can be read.

The illustrations and the captions presented in this volume should, therefore, be given maximum attention. This emphasis on illustrations may induce readers and those scholars who believe that an abundance of footnotes, references to old records, and petty arguments with colleagues are proof of scholarly qualifications to regard this work as something in the nature of a "picture book." Let it be absolutely clear that it is nothing of the kind. The illustrations are indispensable documentary evidence of the historical development, and their aesthetic appearance is a pleasant by-product of their historical value. They should be studied in connection with the general text preceding the City Survey and with the description of the individual cities. Both written and visible history together form an indissoluble entity, and neither can exist without the other.

For practical reasons the City Survey has been divided into two parts, Cities of Antiquity and Cities of the Christian Era. This is in contrast to the procedure applied in previous volumes in which the history of a city has been followed through from the beginning. While the same principle has been applied in this volume for quite a number of cases, there were certain considerations why this was not advisable for those cities whose history was more or less definitely circumscribed by their development in Roman times and the loss of their importance in the following periods. To include their early existence in an uninterrupted narrative from the very beginning to modern times would have not only reduced the clarity of their evolution but overburdened the later part of the City Survey.

With these criteria in mind only a relatively small number of cities have been selected for the first part of the Survey, each one more representing a special type than a link in the history of ancient Roman city planning. Moreover, this selection was obviously restricted by the results of archeological research—that is, by a fairly complete knowledge of the respective cities, ruling out those where speculation would have replaced factual evaluation owing to a lack of sufficient and reliable evidence in those cases where excavations are still in progress.

Thus, to mention but a few examples, Ostia represents a commercial city and port; Herculaneum a residential city; Pompei a mixture of residential and commercial center; cities like Verona, Torino, and Piacenza, provincial towns which, after the turbulent centuries following in the wake of the fall of the Roman Empire, revived, retaining from antiquity often no more than the original grid-iron layout.

Roman city planning was highly standardized notwithstanding certain individual characteristics of places outside the peninsula. To include too many cities would have resulted in monotonous repetition.

In many cases the break in continuity after the "triumph of barbarism and religion" has been almost complete, except that the original site of the ancient city remained the same on which during the Dark Ages (which were not as dark as they commonly appear to us) a new urban life began to take shape, evolving in a steady though slow stream for the next millennium and a half. Therefore the Christian era has been dealt with in the second part of the City Survey as an organic whole. But let us not forget that in spite of the reservations just mentioned the outburst of urbanization—possibly the greatest contribution of Rome to the civilization of Europe—had created the basic and lasting structure of settlement in many parts of the Continent. To that extent, continuity was never interrupted. It was the new language of form, the new atmosphere, the new men, and the new aspirations that built a new world out of the raw materials of antiquity.

Rome was, of course, an exception and as such it has been reserved for the end of the City Survey. In Rome all the innumerable branches of the wild and mighty river that the Roman genius for organization and rationality had released flowed together. Here the evolution can be followed from the serene primitive beginning sanctified by a meaningful religious ritual to the oligarchic puritanism of the Republic, to the vulgarity of imperial ostentation, to the degenerate and empty instability and loss of vision of a declining society—and, finally, to the revival through Christianity and the pompous papal face lifting of the Eternal City. In all these stages of development and decline the masses remained passive objects that had to be content with a minimum of comfort and care, living in miserable quarters at the mercy of the landowners. In these tenements mass man was born, and with him the foundations were laid for the unarticulated megalopolis of our own time.

In general the cities in the Survey are arranged geographically from north to south and as far as possible according to provinces.

Aosta. Aosta, in the valley of the Dora Baltea at the junction of the Great and Little St. Bernard Passes, was founded in 25 B.C. after the victory of Terentius Varro Murena over the Celtic tribe of the Salassi, the original inhabitants of this region. The prisoners were sold as slaves to Eporedia, the present Ivrea, which had been established as a *colonia* before 100 B.C. by the Romans as protection of the Alpine routes over the St. Bernard Passes and the valley. In 22 B.C. a strong fortified *castrum* was erected by Augustus which received the name of *Augusta Praetoria Salassorum*. It occupied the site of the destroyed settlement and was one of the last military stations installed in Italy proper.[1] It was settled with 3,000 soldiers, the *cohortes praetoriae,* with their families.

The plan of Aosta was, of course, dictated by military exigencies but, as Ward Perkins maintains, it would be wrong to assume that a Roman town such as Aosta was merely "a translation into civilian terms of a military camp." According to him just the opposite was true. As proof he cites Polybius (about 204-122 B.C.) who wrote: "thus the whole camp forms a square, and the way in which it is divided up by streets and the general internal disposition give it a layout like that of a city." This remark may mean nothing more than that the camp was laid out with streets and gates—not as an improvised or temporary, more-or-less unsystematic arrangement that might have been expected from a military camp but in an orderly fashion resembling the systematic and permanent plan of a city. However, a more convincing proof was the fact that "the basic pattern expressed by both camp and town goes back to a past long before we have any reason to believe that the Roman army had evolved even the rudiments of a system of field engineering." According to Sextus Julius Frontinus (about A.D. 40 to 103 or 104) "it was the capture of the camp of Pyrrhus, king of Epirus, in 275 B.C. that first struck the imagination of the Romans and led them to develop an

orderly system of their own." This argument is not totally convincing but it is mentioned if for no other reason than to draw attention to a controversial problem that still needs clarification.

It may be admitted that certain principles of Roman city planning, though by no means in definite form, had been developed independently as early as the fourth century B.C., and that once the layout of a Roman camp had become a standard operation this experience had a not negligible influence on the ground plan of the later Roman colonies. It is an established fact that virtually all colonial towns have been laid out, at all times and in all lands, as regularly planned entities—that is, as military outposts of the mother country. This fact can be observed all over the world, from China to Latin America, from Russia and the Scandinavian countries to Germany, France, Spain, and the Mediterranean region. The foundation of a colony in a foreign or endangered country was a military enterprise that had to be carefully prepared and carried through as quickly as possible. It is therefore not surprising that in all these cases military and civilian principles of city planning were almost identical. The relevant question is not what came first, the camp or the town, but how far the two principles have influenced each other.

These considerations are offered here because Aosta was in many respects a typical town and also because the great majority of Roman foundations were colonies established as outposts in foreign countries on strategically favorable sites protecting the military roads that held the Roman Empire together. In the early period naturally strong defensive positions on hilltops or in river bends, that had often been already used by the original inhabitants, fulfilled the desired purpose; but the more Rome expanded her influence the less were suitable sites available. Consequently, the missing natural advantages had to be compensated for by man-made works, which in turn account for the military character of the colonies and their camplike layout.

1. J. B. Ward Perkins. "Early Roman Towns in Italy," *Town Planning Review,* Vol. XXXVI, No. 3, 1955, p. 146.

Roman Aosta covered a rectangular area of about 100 acres, 620 yards long and 780 yards wide, surrounded by walls with twenty square towers. Six streets crossing each other at right angles divided the interior into sixteen large blocks which, in their turn, were subdivided into *insulae* of about 70 by 90 yards. The *decumanus maximus*, continuing the road from Rome to the frontier, ran through the middle of the town from southwest to northeast, entering at the *porta decumana* and leaving at the *porta praetoria*. The *cardo* crossed the urban area near the southwest end of the longer sides at the *porta principalis dextra* and the *porta principalis sinistra*. There were a theater and and amphitheater within the walls (not outside which was more usual); a temple, public baths, and a *forum*—near but not in the center of the town.

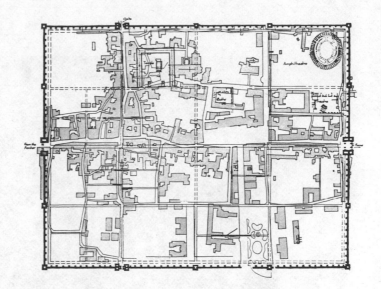

71. The Roman street plan of Aosta and the course of the walls have been preserved and can still be clearly distinguished in the modern town.

Pavia and **Piacenza.** Pavia and Piacenza may be mentioned in this connection, although they do not add greatly to our knowledge of Roman city planning.

Of *Pavia,* the ancient *Ticinum,* situated near the confluence of the *Ticinum* (Ticino) and the *Padus* (Po), we know that it was an important *municipium* in the second half of the first century B.C. on the extension of the *Via Aemilia* from *Ariminum* (Brindisi) to the *Padus*. The town covered a rectangular area down to the river and its *cardo maximus* led to a bridge over the *Padus*. It is possible that the internal gridiron layout dates also from the first century although it might be based on

an earlier street pattern.[2] The crossing of the two main roads in the center of the ancient town is still clearly visible.

Piacenza, at an important crossing of the *Padus*, was founded together with Cremona by the Romans in 218 B.C. as *Colonia Placentia* against Gallic tribes. In 187 B.C. it was connected with the south by the construction of the *Via Aemilia* and became an important road center. By 183, other *coloniae*, Bologna, Parma, and Modena, had been founded on the same road. In all these places additional numbers of veterans of the civil war were settled

2. J. Bradford. *Ancient Landscapes.* 1957. P. 263.

72. Reconstruction of Roman Pavia.

73. Air view of Piacenza, clearly showing the ancient Roman street system.

between 40 to 20 B.C.[3] It is not unlikely that the gridiron plan was readjusted during these later years. The square *insulae,* about 260 feet square, have survived the centuries. Their axial system was determined by the great overland routes, the *Via Aemilia,* the road across the *Padus* to *Mediolanum* (Milan), and the *Via Postumia.*

Placentia, like Cremona, was founded with a population of 6,000 families—a relatively large number that may have been justified by its location in hostile territory. It was conquered by Hannibal soon after its foundation and later (207 B.C.) besieged by Hasdrubal and Gallic tribes (200 B.C.), who burned large parts

of the town and reduced its population to about 2,000. Due to complaints to the Roman Senate about "the shortage of colonists, some having been taken off by the fortunes of war, some by disease, while others had left the colonies from reluctance to live with their Gallic neighbours," as Livy put it, 6,000 new families were sent to *Placentia* and Cremona. This together with the construction of the *Via Aemilia* initiated an upward turn in the history of *Placentia* and Cremona. It has been suggested that the commissioners, who had been appointed to supervise the enterprise, may have refounded the town about 15 miles east of its original site.[4]

3. *Ibid,* p. 261.

4. T. Frank. "Placentia and the Battle of the Trebia," *Journal of Roman Studies,* IX, 1919.

Verona. The earliest settlement on the site of the future Verona was a foundation by the Raetians and Euganeans of Northern Italy. Their *oppidum* stood, in all probability, on the hill on the east bank of the *Athesis* (Adige) on whose summit the Visconti built their castle of San Pietro.[5] The location of the *oppidum* was particularly important: It dominated a point where a bridge could best be constructed near Verona over the turbulent Adige and from which the old prehistoric route from the Brenner Pass in the north, and the west-east highway skirting the sub-Alpine foothills to Aquileia at the head of the Adriatic and further to the Balkans, could efficiently be dominated. A Latin colony was founded in 69 B.C. of which no trace has been discovered. We have to assume that this "earliest town was lost to sight under an Augustan standardization, like so many early foundations in Cisalpine Gaul." The town covered an alluvial plain within the river bend, which protected almost two thirds of its circumference. The rectangular layout with the *decumanus* and *cardo* consisted of eight blocks from north to south and nine from east to west, each forming a square of 260 feet and bounded by streets 20 feet wide—except the main streets, which were wider. Changes in the course of the Adige made certain modifications of the plan necessary although it may be assumed that the layout was completed as originally projected and that it was similar to that of Torino (28 B.C.) as regards the number of blocks and their dimensions. "The rebuilding of Verona is best connected with the preparation for the opening of the Brenner and the conquest of Raetia in 15 B.C. Thus the one plan may have inspired the other, and their resemblance is further evidence for the standardization of Augustan policy." There were an amphitheater and a circus outside the walls, a capitol occupying a block south of the *decumanus,* a theater on the east side of the river

built against the slopes of the hill, a convenient site for the rising tiers of the seats avoiding substructures and arcades; and two four-way arches. The Augustan walls were replaced in A.D. 265 by a new *enceinte* somewhat in advance of the older course but, in general, following the same outline except "at the south-west angle where it projected to include the amphitheatre like a great bastion."

74. Plan of Roman Verona.

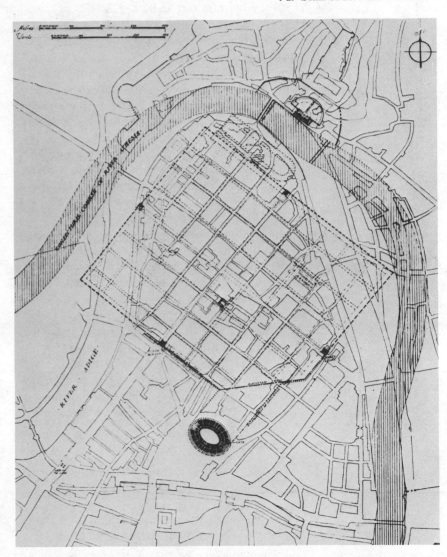

5. I. A. Richmond and W. G. Holford. "Roman Verona: The Archeology of its Town-Plan," *Papers of the British School at Rome,* XIII, 1935, pp. 69-76.
J. Bradford, *op. cit.,* pp. 256-61.

Ostia, Latium. Tradition has it that Ostia was founded by Ancus Marcius, the fourth king of Rome.[6] Whether this tradition is more than a legendary speculation cannot yet be decided with any degree of certainty. Archeological evidence is still missing although literary references by Quintus Ennius (239-170 B.C.), Iulius Florus (A.D. 117-138), and Livy (59 B.C.-A.D. 17) were persistent in repeating the old story of the founding of Ostia by Ancus Marcius. In any case, the last word has not yet been said about this question and "it is very, very possible," as Bradford remarks, "that field archeology will locate a settlement of this, or an earlier period, in the Ostia area." However this may be, negative evidence is still lacking that would refute the belief of the ancient writers that such an early settlement did not exist on or near the site of Ostia. According to these writers this would have been the oldest Roman colony planted—after the destruction of Ficana, the only town between Rome and the sea—by the king as protection of the mouth of the Tiber in a situation where the salt marshes in the surrounding region could be exploited.[7] What seems to be probable is that an unfortified village existed on or near the site of Ostia at a period about which we know little.

No remains have been discovered earlier than the walls of the *castrum,* probably built shortly before 330 B.C. to shield Rome from pirates. The rectangular area, enclosed by walls, covered about 5½ acres (636 by 412.2 feet) with a gate in the middle of each side. The camp stood in the angle between coast and river although at a small distance from both. From the river this was about 250 yards, and from the coast (which at this time was much nearer than today) perhaps several hundred yards. The unusual forklike continuation

of the *decumanus* west of the *castrum* may be explained as having been determined by the need to connect the interior street system with previously existing overland routes. The *decumanus,* as can be seen in the air view and the sketch, turned southwest instead of proceeding westward. At this point another street, the *Via della Foce,* branched off, running northwest to the mouth of the Tiber. Since the *castrum* was built near the crossing of two important pre-existing roads which had to be related to the main axes running through the town, it appears very likely that the unusual course of the chief thoroughfares was conditioned by these considerations. The route from Rome continued as the *decumanus* and the Laurentine track was diverted round the walls.[8] This early place may have been settled with about 300 colonists, judging from similar cases, whose main function was the defense of the coastline and who could grow their own food. At this time Rome was not yet a great naval power but her trade had increased and merchantmen began to visit the mouth of the Tiber in greater numbers.

As a naval base Ostia played an important role in the wars with Carthage and, from the end of the third century B.C., as a commercial port of entry for corn, timber, and many other goods. Its wealth and population increased and when the new *enceinte* was built about 80 B.C. it enclosed an area as large as Pompei.[9] The development as a naval base and commercial town was closely linked to the establishment of a shipbuilding industry. Since Italy was covered by forests in ancient times, a sufficient source of timber was available for this purpose. Like the flow in two interconnected pipes, the populations of Rome and Ostia grew apace, and with them the building activities increased. More food was needed for the capital and therefore more grain had to be imported. At first the supply was procured through private enterprise. Gaius Gracchus began this policy by stabilizing the price of grain and supplying it to the urban pro-

6. R. Meiggs. *Roman Ostia.* 1960. *Passim.*

J. Bradford, *op. cit.,* pp. 237-56.

G. Calza, G. Becatti, I. Gismondi, and others. *Scavi di Ostia.* Vol. I. 1953. In process of publication.

G. Calza and G. Becatti. *Ostia.* 1963. English edition.

H. Schaal. *Ostia. Der Welthafen Roms.* 1957.

F. H. Wilson. "Studies in the Social and Economic History of Ostia," *Papers of the British School at Rome,* XIII and XIV, 1935 and 1938.

7. F. H. Wilson, *op. cit.,* Vol. XIII, p. 42.

8. R. Meiggs, *op. cit.,* p. 121.

G. Calza, G. Becatti, I. Gismondi, and others, *op. cit.,* Vol. I, p. 93.

9. J. Bradford, *op. cit.,* p. 240.

letariat below cost. Gaius Marius followed this practice until finally the government stepped in and assumed the main responsibility by setting up a *cura annonae*, a center for food control.

At the end of the Republic Ostia was a busy commercial town with many shops lining the streets on the ground floors of dwellings; the modest quarters of the common people were interspersed with the more opulent homes of the upper classes. Temples and other public buildings had been erected, and trade flourished. Storage facilities were constructed, since the grain had to be transshipped from the sea-going vessels to river craft. Pozzuoli, the chief port for the import of grain from Alexandria, gradually lost its dominant position, whereas Ostia was on its way to becoming the emporium of Rome, absorbing a growing share of the food imports.

Under Augustus a considerable building activity developed. A theater was constructed and a large square, intended to serve as the focus of business, was laid out behind it. At the center of the *castrum* a *forum* was created —perhaps under Tiberius—and opposite the *capitolium* a marble temple to Rome and Augustus was erected. Agrippa was the patron to whose initiative the theater owed its exist-

ence. The square behind it, to the north, was surrounded by a double-colonnaded portico forming a coherent architectural composition with the theater. This had a very practical reason, for, as Vitruvius states (V. 9. 1), "behind the stage porticos should be built to provide a refuge for the audience when sudden showers interrupt the spectacle, and space for the setting up of the stage machinery." This square was remarkable in its scale and use.[10] It was 410 feet long and 262 feet wide. It had eight entrances. By the Severan period, the colonnades immediately behind the theater stage were occupied by traders, mainly from the provinces. At the beginning of the imperial period, water was supplied from wells and possibly from cisterns. An aqueduct was built, probably in the reign of Tiberius.

But in spite or because of the prosperity that Ostia enjoyed in the late Republic and early Empire, the river harbor proved insufficient. Consequently, an artificial harbor was built (A.D. 42-54) by Claudius and when this also was found unsatisfactory because too much exposed to the wind, a safer and improved harbor was constructed (A.D. 100-106) by Trajan, making Ostia the leading supply center for Rome and a valuable link in the east-west

10. R. Meiggs, *op. cit.*, p. 43.

75. Plan of Roman Ostia.

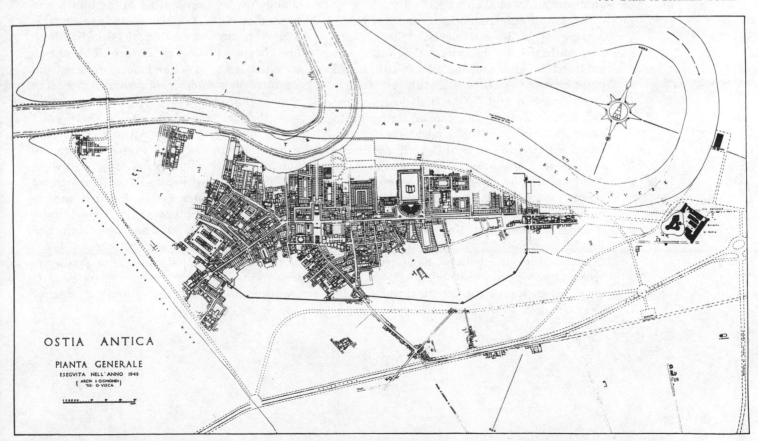

OSTIA ANTICA

PIANTA GENERALE
ESEGVITA NELL'ANNO 1949
(ARCH. I. GISMONDI)
DIS. O. VISCA

trade route. It was inevitable that this dominating role resulted in a great rebuilding in the first half of the second century. The population increased, prospered, and had to be housed. Private and public buildings were needed, drains had to be laid, and new shops built. The great fire at Rome in A.D. 64, which had created the opportunity of replanning large areas more systematically with wider streets and high apartments, no doubt had a certain influence on the urban renewal of Ostia. The new architecture reflected, as Meiggs correctly remarked, "the rise of a middle class growing rich on the profits of trade. . . . As the volume and distribution of trade increased Ostia became increasingly cosmopolitan"[11] and greater numbers of slaves who had been freed could now begin to "amass the fortune necessary to launch their families on a public career." Hand in hand with this social transformation went the growth in the number, size, and wealth of the guilds. As in the Middle Ages, an antagonistic distinction between the "capitalist" guilds of the corn merchants, shipowners, and builders—the men who controlled the trades—and the guilds of the craftsmen—the lower classes relying on their own handiwork—came into existence. The more influential guilds built guild houses and temples and took an active part in the administration of their city.

More public amenities were provided. Among other improvements at least eight new baths were constructed; the *forum* was enlarged by the addition of a *basilica* and *curia* on the western side and the *capitolium* at its northern end. The well-to-do employed painters, sculptors, and mosaic designers to decorate their houses and large blocks of apartments with shops—obviously a good investment for private entrepreneurs—and markets were constructed. The emperors took a personal interest. Under Hadrian so-called garden houses were built combining apartments, shops, and a small garden. But this building activity should not mislead us into believing that Ostia, despite its densely populated urban area and numerous public buildings, was more than a moderately-sized, middle-class town. Its

industries worked primarily for the local market and there were few spectacularly wealthy people. It remained a satellite town of Rome without a great and fertile territory of its own that would have served as a basis for an expanding economy. Its fate was intimately bound up with the fortunes of the capital. When in the third century the imperial administration was beset by internal disintegration, Ostia suffered acute difficulties. As a result of the shrinking trade prosperity declined and with it the population. There was apparently a surplus of supply over demand so that many houses and apartments remained unoccupied. Moreover, there was a definite shift of residential sites from the town to the harbor area.

Not much factual evidence for this shift is available except that of the cemeteries which developed from this area toward Ostia. But there cannot be any doubt that a small number of people lived near the Claudian harbor who guarded the warehouses and were employed to look after the maintenance of the installations. In the course of time this small settlement became a "self-contained" community, the *portus Augusti Ostiensis* or *portus Ostiensis*, or simply *Portus*, since the end of the second century. It had its own temples and guilds. When *Portus* was made an independent community by Constantine in the fourth century, this status marked a decisive change: The economic importance of Ostia had been lost, having shifted to *Portus*. The Ostian storehouses were more and more neglected and an increasing number of workers moved to the new town.[12]

At the end of Hadrian's reign Ostia was a "modern" city, possibly without, or almost without, slums, and in this respect superior to our present-day conglomerations. It had wide, straight streets with arcades, tall apartment blocks, a city center, public facilities such as latrines and water supply, a fairly good drainage system, clubs, taverns and inns, baths and temples, a theater and an amphitheater. What more could the inhabitants of a small, yet important commercial town demand as prerequisites of their great suburban society?

11. R. Meiggs, *op. cit.*, p. 70.

12. R. Meiggs, *op. cit.*, p. 88.

Whether this provision of the material blessings of a civilization that worshipped quantity more than quality—or perhaps it is more correct to say was ignorant of a more sophisticated culture—was matched by a corresponding supply of ideal goods, of a creative intellectual life, is open to doubt. Ostia was a small town for small folk devoted to the pursuit of commerce and trade. The businessman reigned supreme. The ferment of stimulating ideas, of philosophical speculations and experimental artistic achievements, was missing.

The urban environment in which this uninspiring conventional life flowed on was marvelously congenial to the matter-of-fact mentality of the people. The street pattern, which remained almost the same after Hadrian's death until the end of the Roman period, retained the characteristic gridiron system in the center of the town as it had been developed in the *castrum* of the fourth century, and east of the *forum* between the *decumanus* and the river. On the other side of the *decumanus* the uncontrolled development of the pre-Sullan period can still be seen in the the more irregular street plan as also near the *Via della Foce* where within the "fork" the "garden houses" were situated. In general, there was no clear distinction between residential and commercial districts, nor a sharp separation of poor and wealthy quarters—although there may have been certain social characteristics between different areas.[13] Rows of shops existed in almost all the streets, sometimes even in individual houses. The rents from the apartments and shops must often have been the source of considerable profit for the speculative builders.[14] In some cases it is obvious that rows of shops were built expressly for this purpose as, for instance, in the *Via delle Corporazioni*, where all the shops had been originally connected by doors so that they could be let to a large business; later the doors were blocked and the shops passed into the hands of individual traders. Even a "shopping center," the so-called *House of the Lararium*, has been discovered. It was situated south of the *Via della Foce*. A passage led through the front building into an open courtyard surrounded by shops on all sides.[15] There were premises for bakers for large-scale production, and for wholesale wine and oil merchants, the activities of the former concentrated in the *Forum Vinarium* and, of course, the *horrea* of grain importers and middlemen, sometimes hardly distinguishable from a shopping center in their layout.

13. R. Meiggs, *op. cit.*, p. 142.
14. F. H. Wilson, *op. cit.*, Vol. XIII, p. 55.
15. R. Meiggs, *op. cit.*, p. 274.

Pompei, Province of Napoli. The site, on which the earliest settlement of Pompei developed, had all the advantages that would attract pioneers venturing into unknown lands in an age of primitive defense needs. Not far from the Sarno River—whose mouth provided Greek and Phoenician sailors with a favorable landing place on the Campanian coast, almost at the foot of Vesuvius—the elevated site offered the natural defensive qualities which were one of the primary considerations for survival, security, and the establishment of at least rudimentary, satisfactory living conditions. For we may assume that agricultural peoples, living in the Sarno Valley, had settled on or near the site in the eighth century B.C. or even earlier.[16] Strabo tells us that old Pompei was founded by the Oscans and later occupied by the Etruscans. Its name (Oscan — "pompe" according to Maiuri) was purely Italian, not Greek as in the case of Cumae or

16. A. Boëthius. *The Golden House of Nero.* 1960.
J. Bradford. *Ancient Landscapes.* 1957.
M. Brion. *Pompeii and Herculaneum.* 1960. Only the photographs are of interest.
R. C. Carrington. *Pompeii.* 1936.
Cicero. *De republica.*
A. von Gerkan. *Der Stadtplan von Pompei.* 1940.
A. Maiuri. *Pompeii.* 1962.
A. Mau. *Pompeii. Its Life and Art.* 1908.
V. Spinazzola. *Pompei alla luce degli scavi nuovi.* 1953.
H. Tanzer. *The Common People of Pompeii.* 1939.
Vitruvius. *De Architectura, libri decem.* 1543.
Maps and Historical Atlases.

Neapolis. When the Greeks arrived in the sixth century B.C., they must have been aware of the strategic importance of the situation that together with Cumae, Diccarcheia (Puteoli), Neapolis, and Misenum could dominate the entire gulf down to Cape Athenéo on the Sorrentine peninsula, protected by the islands of Ischia and Capri which they soon occupied. This string of trading stations, the first outposts of Greek civilization in Italy, grew in a relatively short time into towns whose population increased the more their commerce flourished. Threatened by the Etruscans, Oscan Pompei entered into an alliance with the Greeks and Neapolis and Cumae. After the repulsion of the Etruscan attack in a naval battle off Cumae in 474 B.C., Pompei was finally absorbed into the political orbit of the Cumaean state. To this period belongs the archaic Doric temple, the *Triangular Forum*, originally dedicated to Hercules, the legendary founder of the town. It was probably on this site—a rocky spur formed by lava flowing down from Vesuvius in prehistoric times—that the

first occupants erected their huts and the later settlers formed the nucleus of the future Roman town. It also explains the resemblance of the oldest walls to the Greek rather than Italian type of fortifications.

At the end of the fifth century B.C. the Samnites conquered Campania, rebuilt Pompei, enlarged it, and imposed their religion, language, and customs upon the whole region. Many traces of this period have been found, such as remains of houses in the Samnite style and technique, using at first volcanic and later more tufa material. About 290 B.C., Rome established its rule over the region and Pompei, with all other towns, became a subject ally of the Republic. From this time onward until its sudden end in A.D. 79 the fate of Pompei was indissolubly bound up with the rise of Rome, the imperial mistress of the world.

As already mentioned, Pompei rose upon a ridge about 130 feet above sea level, produced by a large flow of lava from the flank or the center of Vesuvius in prehistoric times. This early layer was later covered and smoothed by

76. Vertical air view of Pompei.

strata of a tufaceous and volcanic nature mixed with lapilli and ashes.[17] The uneven terrain slopes down from north to south, to the sea and the mouth of the Sarno where the lava flow stopped, forming an almost inaccessible, clifflike structure as a natural bulwark toward the gulf. The only really level section of the town is the extreme western quarter, an advantage that was made use of in the layout of the *forum*. The main axial road, the *Via di Stabia,* runs along the steepest slope roughly from southeast to northwest. The walls follow the course of the lava flow partly along its crest. Their circumference of approximately two miles encloses an area of about 161 acres. Thus the external irregular shape of the town and the interior layout have been decisively influenced by the contours of the terrain. The *decumani* run more or less parallel to the larger extension, from east to west, and the *cardines* parallel to the shorter extension, from north to south of the enclosed urban area. These main roads were crossed at right angles by secondary streets, the *viae* or *itinera,* and were all flanked by raised, paved sidewalks and traversed at intervals by stepping stones for pedestrians.

In contrast to many other Roman towns the *forum* was not located in the center of Pompei but at the southwest end, on a large level site, near the walls and the *Porta Marina,* and, on a flat stretch of ground nearby stood the temple of Venus Pompeiana, the patron goddess of the city. Further south, on another level area, the Greek temple of the sixth century and the *Triangular Forum* were situated, connected with the theater on a lower level adjoining them. Finally at the extreme southwest a vast area was reserved for the amphitheater and the *palaestra.* It is obvious that the internal layout was adapted, to a high degree, to the natural configuration of the terrain. In any case it affected the selection of level sites for open spaces and the course of the walls, with the result that the residential areas formed a more or less compact unit without public buildings. The latter were mainly concentrated around the two *fora,* in the area of the amphitheater and at the crossing of the

17. A. Maiuri, *op. cit.,* p. 8.

77. General view of Pompei with one of the main streets.

Via di Stabia and the *Via di Nola* where, at the time of eruption, the new baths—the *thermae centrali*—were still under construction. All of this indicates a certain shift of the public amenities toward the east—that is, to the newer districts of the town.

In the last years before A.D. 79, Pompei had begun to spill over its walls into the open country. Most houses had two stories, and the population numbered about 20,000 inhabitants including, in addition to Roman patri-

78. General view of the *forum* in Pompei.

cian families and Samnite descendants, many merchants and craftsmen, and slaves and freedmen of Campanian, Greek, and Asian origin. This rather mixed assortment of people had been attracted by the growing commercial and industrial prosperity of the town under the Empire. This development induced the wealthy aristocracy to move out of the town to suburban *villae,* leaving the field free to other classes, especially to the merchants as effective organizers of the economic life of the town and to the craftsmen grouped in guilds and professional corporations.

The *forum* was the *centre d'animation* of Pompei. It was more than a religious or administrative or economic center individually or collectively. It was the hub of the *social* life of the town and as such the meaningful symbol, the focus of *social* coherence toward which the manifold personal and professional functions of the whole body of inhabitants gravitated. This fact may be fully understood only by comparing the role of the center in a small town such as Pompei with its densely knit social structure—as indeed in almost all towns of the past until the disintegrating effects of the Industrial Revolution—with the artificially puffed-up importance of the city centers of our own times. Today, these conglomerations of commerce and administration have lost their significance as agents of social coherence and as symbols of so-called decision making. The main justification of their still being regarded as "undisputed" centers is their central position within the urban area. More and more of their functions are taken over by decentralized institutions, and only diehard traditionalists and narrow-minded administrators and their inarticulate followers absorbed in their routine work and unable to break through the self-imposed thought barrier continue to cling to this fiction.[18] The *forum* of Pompei had a

18. E. A. Gutkind. *The Twilight of Cities.* 1962.

194

pre-eminently *social* function just as the *Plaza Mayor* of a Spanish town, to mention but one other example. Both were open-air interiors where personal and functional life merged into a collective identity.

It is in this respect that the Pompeian *forum* may be regarded as a representative expression of the desire for social intercourse and social identification, of "belonging to" as opposed to "contracting out" of society. In all other respects it is typical of the standardized layouts of innumerable other *fora*. Its architectural aspects are pleasant but not particularly impressive. The rectangular area, extending with its longer axis from north to south and measuring about 124 feet by 466 feet, was small enough to retain its intimacy. It was originally surrounded by a portico above which rose a gallery accessible by stairways. Behind this unifying screen there rose on the south, west, and east sides the façades of the adjoining

public buildings. Only at the northern end a single edifice, the Temple of Jupiter, flanked by two triumphal arches, was directly drawn into the architectural composition. The square was paved with travertine flagstones. Its uninterrupted plain surface, forming a forecourt to the temple—the dominating accent of the whole ensemble, and the portico enclosing it —created a spatial entity of festive repose. Space was at rest. Compare this with St. Peter's Square, with the enclosing arms of the two colonnades drawing the visitor irresistibly toward the stairs and the church. Here space is in motion. At Pompei it remained motionless, like a square of the early Renaissance—for instance, the Piazza dell' Annunziata at Florence. The *forum* was a perfect open-air interior within which people could move, chat, consort, or discuss business and yet feel at home, instinctively aware of the temple as the "centerpiece" and occasionally glancing at it but

79. Plan of the northwestern section of the residential area in Pompei.

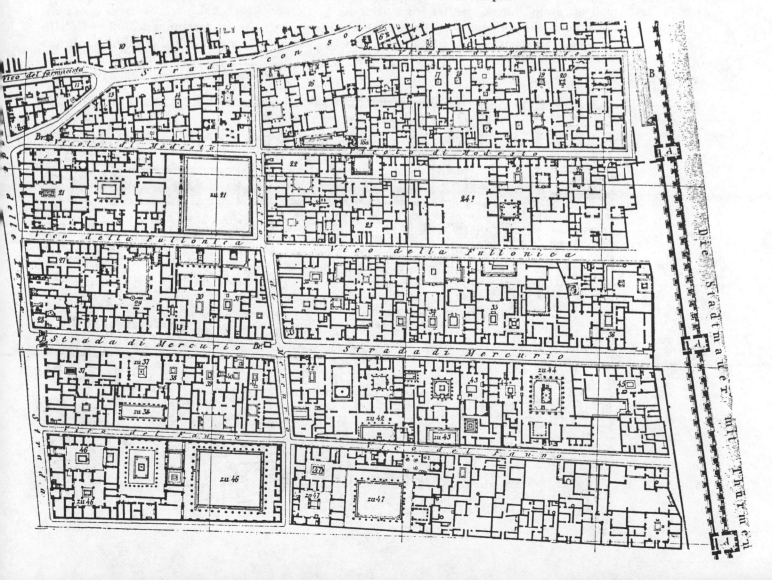

without being absorbed into any movement propelling them forward as in St. Peter's Square.

The atmosphere must have had something of an opulent drawing room with a large fireplace enhanced by a fine mantlepiece and crowned by reassuring ancestral portraits. The *forum* was indeed the drawing room—an expression derived from "withdrawing room"—of the urban "container" to which people could withdraw to enjoy the company of their fellow inhabitants. No vehicular traffic was allowed in or near it. It remained an area reserved exclusively for pedestrians. It is this function and the restfulness of the spatial composition that should be admired, rather than the architectural rendering in detail. There is no reason to be overawed by the Pompeian *forum* as "the most perfect and most grandiose example amongst all the *fora* of Roman or Italic cities known to us," as Maiuri claims. Architecturally it was certainly an attractive work with the usual panoply of recognized Roman attributes, but it was far from being a "grandiose" achievement as the uncritical admirers of everything old would have it. It is

very doubtful that the situation of the surrounding buildings behind the portico which cut off and screened the lower part of their façades was a particularly satisfactory solution. In this respect two antagonistic tendencies clashed: the desire to assemble as many public buildings as possible around the *forum*, and to do this in an architecturally perfect manner. Quantity and quality remained irreconcilable. Quantity appealed more to the Roman spirit of grandeur than aristocratic style, reticence, or quality.

Opposite the Temple of Jupiter, at the south end of the *forum*, were three large halls housing the municipal administration, the *curia*, the archives, the *tabularium*, and the offices of the *duumviri*. At the southeast corner stood the *comitium*, the assembly hall, where the municipal elections took place. Then followed, on the east side, the *eumachia*, a building erected by the priestess Eumachia, patroness of the *fullones*, the fullers, used by their corporation (which included also the cleaners, dyers, and clothmakers) as storehouse and salesroom, a forerunner of the cloth halls of the Middle Ages. Further to the north rose

80. **Forum and surrounding buildings at Pompei.**

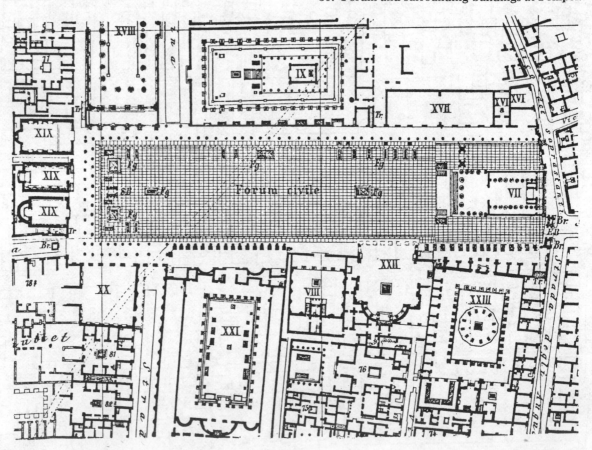

the Temple of Vespasian and the Temple of the Lares of the town; finally, at the northeast corner lay the *macellum,* or meat market, with a special section, equipped with gutters to drain off the water, for the sale of fish. It had shops facing the streets on the north and west side, and small *tabernae* on the interior south side. In the center of the square building stood a dodecagonal structure called *tholus,* from the shape of its roof, with a basin where the fishmongers washed their baskets and cleaned the fish. On the west side of the *forum,* next to the Temple of Jupiter, was the *horreum,* a storehouse for special agricultural produce, and in the extreme northwest corner a public latrine and two underground rooms, identified as the municipal treasury, have been discovered. In the middle of the west side rose the Temple of Apollo, its longer axis running parallel to the north-south axis of the *forum* in contrast to the other buildings whose fronts turned their gables to this side. The *mensa ponderaria* was installed in a recess of the outer wall of the Temple of Apollo. Here, as part of the market activities, all measures were controlled according to the fixed Roman standards. Between this and the *horreum* a passage that could be closed by a gate led to an area surrounded by stalls—possibly the *forum holitorium,* a corn and vegetable market. The southwest corner was occupied by the *basilica,* a large rectangular covered building repeating the basic architectural composition of the *forum* as in all Roman towns, with a *basilica* serving as the seat of the law courts and the center of the financial life of Pompei.

The *Triangular Forum,* the theaters, the *Little Palaestra,* and two small temples form another complex of public buildings at the south side of the town near the *Porta di Stabia.* The shape of the *Triangular Forum* is clearly determined by the natural configuration of the spur on which it was laid out. This small enclosure, with its Doric portico on the east and west sides, must have been an attractive place with unexpected seclusion and a view overlooking the marvelous scenery in the foreground. In spite of the rigid sequence of the columns of the portico and the impressive *propylaeum* there must have been something

casual and almost informal about it, especially when the original temple of Hercules (sixth century B.C.) had been reduced to a small shrine in the later Roman period. On the east side it was connected through a passage with the *palaestra* and the Great Theater. The Great Theater was built in the natural hollow of the hill and could hold about 5,000 spectators. In front of the orchestra platform there were basins where fountains played during intervals, and behind the stage was a *quadri-porticus,* or square—a sort of foyer for the public that was later used as the *ludo gladiatorio.* The Little Theater, the *odeon,* adjoining this complex immediately on the east side, was covered. Here concerts, lectures, mimes, and more refined performances took place before a small audience of less than a thousand spectators.

The third group of public buildings comprised the Amphitheater and the *Great Palaestra* at the extreme southeastern corner of the walled-in area. The Amphitheater could hold 20,000 spectators, almost the whole population of Pompei. Here, the vulgar brutality of Rome was paraded before crowds whose emotional outbursts frequently culminated in battles between partisans of the contesting gladiators. These bloodthirsty spectacles between men, and between animals and men, had to result in the death of one combatant else they would not fulfill the expectations of the public. Like Spanish bullfights, they had originated in religious rituals, in this case in connection with the funeral services intended to offer fresh blood to the deceased to sustain their vitality in the nether world. The surviving gladiators —forerunners of the film stars and champion boxers of today—were surrounded by an aura of adulation, enhanced by the fascination of impending death. Here we have the reverse side of Roman life, its primitive mass psychosis, its animal sensuality, and its emotional eccentricity. This crude emotionalism lay at the roots of the coarseness of Roman art, and of the unimaginative standardization of Roman cities. Compared with the Greeks, Romans could never shed their innate barbarism, their matter-of-fact aggressiveness.

For the Greeks the theater, the performance

of choral music, public recitals, and games were all inseparable from the political existence of the *polis*. Their games were indissolubly related to religion, the Olympian games in honor of Zeus, the Panathenaic games in honor of Athena, and the Pythian games in honor of Apollo. They were intended to show and to test the *aretê,* the efficiency, the perfection, the merit of the *whole* man, not merely of one particular skill. To the Greeks, the games were a contest, *agôn,* of body and soul, not brutalized mass spectacles. In these diametrically opposed attitudes we have the essence of the unbridgeable difference between Greek and Roman art, between Greek and Roman city planning despite the superficial similarity of the language of form and certain inherited qualities. On the one hand, we see a spontaneous empathy and identification of man with the totality of life. On the other, a pragmatic simplification, a fragmentation of the wholeness of existence into professional and practical qualifications with all the drawbacks resulting from commercialized entertainment—from religious degradation through the deification of emperors, from the *panem et circenses* opiate of the masses to the glorification of imperial conquest and all the hypocrisy that went with it.

But let us return to the reality of Pompeian life. The *Great Palaestra,* west of the amphitheater, was used for the gymnastic exercises and competition of the Pompeian youths. Its rectangular area of about 425 by 460 feet was enclosed by a wall with several entrances from the town and the amphitheater. Its interior was surrounded by porticoes. Around the swimming pool in the center, there was a double row of plane trees under whose shade athletes could rest during their exercises.

The *thermae,* the elegant and fashionable meeting places of Roman cities, were an important part of the public life. Pompei had three *thermae*—the *Stabian Thermae,* the *Forum Thermae,* and the *Central Thermae,* all with the usual different types of baths, separated for men and women. The *Stabian Thermae* were the oldest, largest, and most complete before the new *Central Thermae,* with only one bath for men, were built at the

intersection of the *Via di Stabia* and the *Via di Nola* occupying an entire *insula* and surrounded by shops opening to the outside along the west and north front.

Pompei was amply provided with public amenities, possibly more than many other provincial towns of a comparable size, a luxury that materially illustrated its wealth and prosperity and the munificence of its leading citizens. There were probably no excessively rich capitalists who could amass huge fortunes as in Ostia or Puteoli. But apparently there was a class that could afford to display its ambition by generous gifts to the community. There was the family of the Holconii who contributed to the rebuilding of the great theater; the priestess Eumachia, mentioned previously, who erected the cloth hall that bore her name; a M. Tullius whose gift was the site and the small temple of Fortuna Augusta. The amphitheater was built by two high officials, C. Quinctius Valgus and M. Porcius. But perhaps the most astonishing case was the erection of the Temple of Isis by a boy, six years of age who, in recognition of his generosity, was made a member of "the Splendid Order."[19]

In contrast to Ostia there were no higher apartment buildings in Pompei. The houses were low, usually one or two stories. The streets, lined with the plain walls of the buildings interrupted only by entrances and a few windows (except where shops, workshops, *tabernae,* and other similar establishments occupied the ground floor), were more like corridors lined with a sequence of rooms than independently conceived architectural elements—without any individuality of their own, or any outspoken physiognomy, as though they were mere interspaces left over between the solid mass of the houses. This was, of course, a typical feature common to the whole Mediterranean region, especially in antiquity; it is still evident today in numerous towns of Italy, Spain, and Greece, and in Islamic countries. The reasons are obvious. The houses were built around an inner courtyard, an *atrium,* or later a *patio.* Their introvert char-

19. S. Dill. *Roman Society from Nero to Marcus Aurelius.* 1956.

198

acter shunned outward ostentation turning it, as it were, inward and assigning to the streets only a subordinate role. In this connection, no detailed description of Pompeian homes is needed—our task is a history not of architecture but of city planning—the less so because possibly more has been published about them than about any other houses of antiquity. Our main concern is the relationship of buildings and streets, and for this aspect the immediately preceding short remarks and the general observations contained in the first part of this volume must be sufficient.

There were, however, a few exceptions from the simple layout of the introvert houses built on level ground. In region VIII, west of the *Triangular Forum* near the wall, the configuration of the terrain had resulted in a certain irregularity of the side streets and multistoried buildings. Here the land slopes downward and the whole of *insula* 2, one of the last expansions of the town in the first period of the Augustan era, occupied the area on the crest of the hill and its slopes formed by the lava flow. The houses on the southern margin on the flat part of the hill had their entrance, the *atrium* and the *tablinum*, a fairly large room opening off the *atrium* opposite the entrance, on the still-level brow of the hill; whereas the rest of the building projected outward down the hillside in several stories, with galleries and loggias supported by a substructure of terraces and buttresses from which the view of the valley and mountains could be enjoyed.[20]

Another interesting example, characteristic of the greater variety of building methods in the last period of Pompei's existence has been restored in the *Via dell'Abbondanza*, in the eastern part not far from the amphitheater in region IX. Here almost all houses had upper floors, balconies and galleries, and roofs projecting over the shops, elements at least partly explained, by the need to make the best use of the scarcity of space, more and more felt with the increase of population and by the

rising importance of the merchant class intent on sharing as much as possible, the way of life of the patricians.[21]

There were apparently no slums or seriously deteriorated quarters, judging from the three fifths of the urban area thus far excavated. The walls, which originally surrounded the whole town, were dismantled along the southern side toward the sea in the Augustan period to allow an extension of houses and other buildings in this direction. Suburbs existed on the road to Herculaneum, at the harbor, and at the saltworks—the *salinae*. Outside the *Porta Nocera,* on the south side, a necropolis has been excavated, and in the north, on the road to Herculaneum, the *Via dei Sepolcri* has been dug out as early as 1763 to 1838 with private *villae* and numerous tombs. This must have been a strange mixture, a solemn reminder of the transitory nature of earthly existence and the pleasures of the good life in this world. In any case, it was an approach that may still surprise a visitor from the New World more accustomed to seeing auto graveyards on the outskirts of his city than graveyards of deceased relatives.

There is no reason to believe that Pompei was extraordinary, an impression that has taken hold of the minds of many of its ad-

21. *Ibid.*, p. 67.

20. A. Maiuri, *op. cit.*, pp. 62-63.

81. Temple and statue of Apollo at Pompei.

mirers. It was nothing of the sort. It was "just a town" like many others in Roman Italy—pleasant, not too large, beautifully situated, and perhaps a bit more cultivated than others. The fact that we know more about it —about the customs of its inhabitants, their houses and furniture, their daily life, likes and dislikes, and their artistic taste has made Pompei the most famous town of antiquity. It has acquired this unique role, not because of its superior qualities, but exclusively because it had the dubious fortune to be buried under a thick layer of ashes and lava for centuries. Pompei is thus one of the most important sources of our knowledge of Roman life, an advantage that we can enjoy "just because it is there."

This small urban community was abruptly blotted out by the destructive force of the earthquake in A.D. 79. In letters to Tacitus, Pliny the Younger has left us a vivid and moving description of this event excerpts of which may conclude this section.

There had been for days before some shocks of an earthquake, which the less surprised us as they are extremely frequent in Campania; but they were so particularly violent that night, that they not only shook every thing about us, but seemed indeed to threaten total destruction. . . . Tho' it was now morning, the light was exceedingly faint and languid; the buildings all around us tottered, and tho' we stood upon open ground, yet as the place was narrow and confined, there was no remaining there without certain and great danger: we therefore resolved to quit the town. The people followed us in the utmost consternation, and (as to a mind distracted with terror, every suggestion seems more prudent than

its own) pressed in great crowds about us in our way out. Being got at a convenient distance from the houses, we stood still, in the midst of a most dangerous and dreadful scene. The chariots which we had ordered to be drawn out, were so agitated backwards and forwards, tho' upon the most level ground, that we could not keep them steady, even by supporting them with large stones. The sea seemed to roll back upon itself, and to be driven from its banks by the convulsive motion of the earth; it is certain at least the shore was considerably enlarged, and several sea-animals were left upon it. On the other side, a black and dreadful cloud bursting with an ingenious serpentine vapor, darted out a long train of fire, resembling flashes of lightening, but much larger. . . . Soon afterwards, the cloud seemed to descend, and cover the whole ocean; as indeed, it entirely hid the island of Caprea, and the promontory of Misenum. . . . The ashes now began to fall upon us, tho' in no great quantity. I turned my head, and observed behind us a thick smoke, which came rolling after us like a torrent. I proposed while we had yet any light, to turn out of the high road, lest she [his mother] should be pressed to death in the dark, by the crowd that followed us. We had scarce stepped out of the path, when darkness over-spread us, not like that of a cloudy night, or when there is no moon, but of a room when it is shut up, and all the lights extinct. Nothing then was to be heard but the shrieks of women, the screams of children, and the cries of men; some calling for their children, others for their parents, others for their husbands, and only distinguishing each other by their voices; one lamenting his own fate, another that of his family; some wishing to die, from the very fear of dying; some lifting their hands to the gods; but the greater part imagining that the last and eternal night was come, which was to destroy both the gods and the world together. Among these there

82. Strada dell' Abbondanza at Pompei.

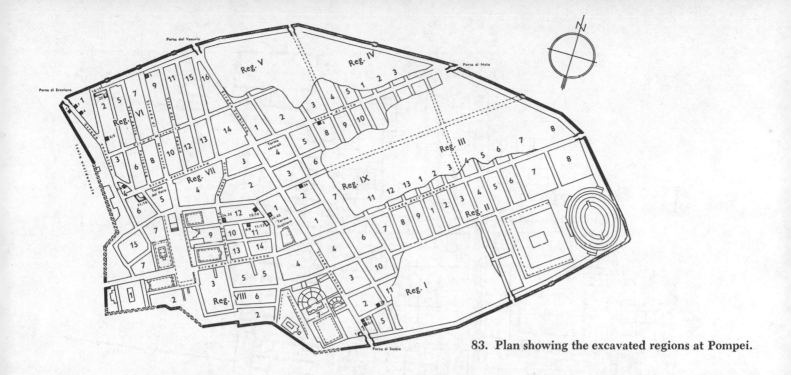

83. Plan showing the excavated regions at Pompei.

were some who augmented the real terrors by imaginary ones, and made the frightened multitude falsly believe that Misenum was actually in flames. At length a glimmering light appeared, which we imagined to be rather the forerunner of an approaching burst of flames (as in truth it was) than the return of day: however, the fire fell at a distance from us: then again we were immersed in thick darkness, and a heavy shower of ashes rained upon us, which we were obliged every now and then to shake off, otherwise we should have been crushed and buried in the heap. I might boast, that during all this scene of horror, not a sigh or expression of fear, escaped from me, had not my support been founded in that miserable, though strong consolation, that all mankind were involved in the same calamity, and that I imagined I was perishing with the world itself.

At last this dreadful darkness was dissipated by degrees, like a cloud or smoke; the real day returned, and even the sun appeared, tho' very faintly, and as when an eclipse is coming on. Every object that presented itself to our eyes (which were extremely weakened) seemed changed, being covered over with white ashes, as with a deep snow. We returned to Misenum, where we refreshed ourselves as well as we could, and passed an anxious night between hope and fear, tho' indeed, with a much larger share of the latter: for the earthquake still continued, while several enthusiastic people ran up and down heightening their own and their friends calamities by terrible predictions."[22]

22. *The Letters of Pliny.* Vol. I. Translated by William Melmoth. 1770.

Herculaneum, Province of Napoli. Herculaneum, one of the many cities claiming to have been founded by Hercules—it was first mentioned by Theophrastus (371-287 B.C.) as *Heracleion*—occupied a site on the lower slopes of Vesuvius between the deep beds of two torrents. It was a Greek trading post probably the successor of an Oscan settlement on the same spot. Cornelius Sisenna (120-67 B.C.) has referred to it as *oppidum tumulo in excelso loco propter mare, pravis moenibus, inter duos fluvios infra Vesuvium collocatum* (V. fr.

53).[23] It came under the hegemony of the Greek colonies of Neapolis and Cumae and later, toward the end of the fifth century, under that of the Samnites. It was conquered by Rome in 89 B.C. and afterward made a Roman *municipium.* Its regular ground plan and the orientation of the *decumani* and *cardines* had a striking resemblance to those of Neapolis, suggesting that its "real and proper urban de-

23. "A town on a high hilly terrain on account of the sea, between two rivers, below Vesuvius."

201

84. Map of Herculaneum.

SCALA 1:250

velopment was modelled on that of the great neighbouring Greek city."[24]

If the following hypothesis is correct, Herculaneum was destroyed by a torrent of mud, swept down from the crater where it had previously collected, that submerged everything

24. A. Maiuri. *Herculaneum*. 1956. P. 5 and *passim*. Also *I Nuovi Scavi di Ercolano. 1927-1958*. 2 vols. 1958.

in its path, first the villas above the town, and then the town itself. This stream of mud-lava penetrated into every hollow and after a time solidified into a compact crust varying from 36 to 60 feet in thickness. The hardness of this cover protected the town for many centuries but made the excavations extremely difficult. Although thus far only a small part of Herculaneum has been unearthed, three sides of the circumference are known, whereas the fourth side, occupied by the village of Resina, cannot yet be identified. From what has been excavated, however, certain conclusions as to the whole layout can be drawn. Five *cardines* and two *decumani,* crossing each other at right angles, have been brought to light. A third *decumanus* must, in all probability, have run to the north along eight other *insulae* bringing their total number to sixteen, apart from the more irregular blocks of the eastern and western quarters and buildings on the coast and suburban *villae.*

On this basis it has been estimated that the town covered an area of about 400 by 350 yards, that is approximately one third of that of Pompei, and that the inhabitants numbered four to five thousand persons, which would be less than one third of the Pompeian population. The *decumani* were running parallel to the coastline, from northwest to southeast, and the *cardines* from northeast to southwest at right angles to the coast, a street system more rigid than that of Pompei and, in this case, the more noteworthy because it was imposed upon a difficult site. However, this was not unusual: Priene's gridiron plan was also developed on a sloping terrain with considerable differences of its gradients. There, as in Herculaneum, this led to interesting solutions. The buildings rose on successive terraces and the irregularity of the terrain had to be adjusted to the building requirements by leveling of the ground and by artificial sub-

structures. The three *cardines* descended steeply down to the coast through archways, and the ground floor, in quite a number of houses, was on different levels in the same house.

We need not go into a detailed description of the excavated parts of Herculaneum. Much that has been said about Pompei applies also to its sister town. There were *thermae,* a theater, a *forum,* a *basilica,* a *palaestra,* and other public buildings but a complete picture cannot yet be formed of the whole city until the excavations have proceeded further. As Maiuri remarks, "The contrast between rich and elegant houses and popular habitations is stronger and more profound" in Herulaneum than at Pompei, where industry and commerce had a more equalizing influence.[25] At Herculaneum the larger portion of an *insula* was occupied by two or three spacious and sumptuous houses, and the rest by more modest dwellings, often with shops, pressed together in a narrow space that made the addition of upper stories necessary. It is interesting to observe that in a few cases these smaller houses intruded between the larger ones when and where the owners of these latter had to sell part of their property, a process that can also be noted in many towns of the Middle Ages. The most opulent houses occupied the brow of the promontory where the beautiful view over the sea and the breezes could be enjoyed from the verandahs, terraces, loggias, and siesta rooms. These residences rose and extended

25. A. Maiuri, *op. cit.,* p. 15.

85. **Southern elevation of houses on the hill above Herculaneum.**

"upon the massive bastions of the scarped counterforts down the steep slope of the underlying lava. . . . Along the axes of those verandahs and those loggias run porticoes and internal corridors in order to carry the reflection of the distant glare of sky and sea into the most secret and intimate corners of the house."[26]

An interesting example of a house for craftsmen and their families has been discovered at Herculaneum. This is the so-called *Casa a Graticcio,* House with Trellis-work. This may have been typical of the cheaper dwellings built in poorer material and simpler technique. Its structure consisted of a combination of a timber or trellis framework filled with lime-mortar and covered with stucco and rough plaster. (Vitruvius, II. 8.) These houses had two separate flats, one on the ground floor accessible through a passage, the other entered through a door and over stairs. Their rooms received light from an inner courtyard, and the inhabitants had to share the water from a well.

26. *Ibid.,* p. 16.

The *decumanus maximus,* more than 36 feet wide, was closed for vehicular traffic just as the area around the *forum* at Pompei. It had many shops and workrooms and may perhaps be compared to a pedestrian mall. A suburban quarter developed between the town and the harbor which was reached through the *Porta Marina.* Along the road leading down to the sea were tombs, suburban *thermae,* and religious buildings.

Herculaneum must have been a sleepy, pleasant town whose inhabitants were mainly engaged in fishing, whose artisans seem to have produced chiefly luxury objects, apart from the usual goods needed for daily consumption. There was no large-scale industry and commerce and therefore the number of *nouveaux riches* and freedmen was but small. Herculaneum may have been one of the seaside towns favored by wealthy people where they could spend their *otium* after retirement in beautiful surroundings, close to nature and without the intrusion of the hustle and bustle of a big city.

86. Street in Herculaneum.

87. Casa a Graticcio in Herculaneum.

Roman colonial cities cannot be included in the City Survey. With few exceptions they all show the characteristic gridiron layout and the usual public buildings. Towns such as *Timgad* (Thamugadi) in Algeria are interesting because we know something about them, but they are not particularly important in the general context of a history of city planning. They do not add much to our understanding of the basic principles of urban development under Roman rule. However, the plan of Timgad may help to complete the picture sketched on the preceding pages.

Timgad

88. Map of Timgad showing the walled-in town, approximately 400 by 360 yards, built by Trajan about A.D. 100 for discharged legionaries. The extraordinary rigidity of the gridiron layout may be due to this paramilitary purpose. It is unimaginative, and the placing of the *forum*, the theater, and other public buildings does not relieve the monotony of this standardized specimen of Roman city planning.

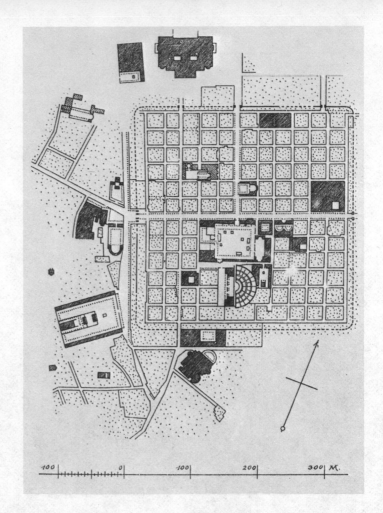

THE CHRISTIAN ERA

Trieste. The territory of Trieste was divided by the Peace Treaty of 1947 into two zones—one with a predominantly Italian, and the other with a predominantly Yugoslav population. This interim agreement was replaced by a final settlement in 1954 that returned the Italian zone, including Trieste, to Italy.

Trieste, situated at the foot of the Carso, occupies the flat expanse adjoining the bay and partly reclaimed by the draining of ancient salt ponds and the slopes of the hill crowned by the castle. The new town, at the shore, is laid out on a regular ground plan whereas the streets of the old town, huddled around the hill, are steep, narrow, and winding—adapting their course as well as possible

89. View of Trieste from a 14th-century mural in the apse of the cathedral of S. Giusto.

90. Porta Cavana and the Piazza del Sale at Trieste in 1500.

91. Plan of Trieste in 1838 with the regular new town and the irregular old town on the slopes of the hill crowned by the castle.

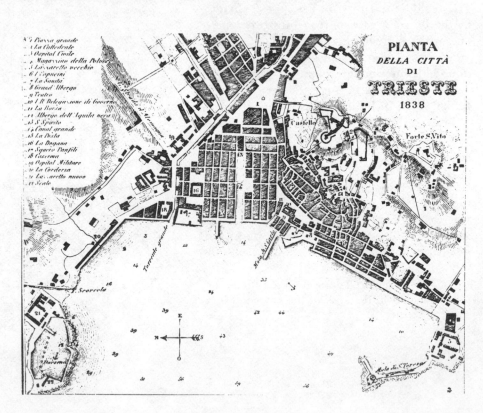

92. The Piazza del Teatro Verdi at Trieste in 1800. The building opposite the theater is slightly recessed from the street, thus allowing the formation of a small square and emphasizing the importance of the theater as a public institution.

to the irregularity of the terrain. This contrast is reminiscent of Lisbon; after the earthquake of 1755 the reconstructed part on the flat land along the river bank was laid out on a regular ground plan distinctly different from the older town on the hilly terrain with its irregular streets.

The site has been settled since prehistoric times by people who built a refuge on what is now known as the hill of S. Giusto. In the fifth or fourth century B.C. Celtic tribes occupied this stronghold and gave it the name of *Tergeste*. This place was first mentioned in 178 B.C. when the Romans, who had founded Aquileia three years earlier as a bulwark against the Celts and Istrians, took possession of *Tergeste* as the base for their advance into

Istria and made it a Roman *municipium*. In 33 B.C. it was fortified with walls and towers. Under Trajan (A.D. 96-117) the town had reached considerable importance judging from the numerous public buildings. It had a *basilica,* a *forum*, a capitol on the hill of S. Giusto, a theater outside the walls, and a *necropolis*. The March of Friuli was incorporated in the Carolingian Empire. In 1202 Trieste was captured by Venice. The conflicts resulting from this event led finally, in 1382, to the decision of the municipality to place itself under the protection of Leopold III of Austria though retaining its own government and laws. This semi-independence gradually developed into annexation by Austria, a rule that did not end until 1918.

207

Palmanova, Province of Venezia. This fortress town, halfway between Udine and the sea, was built by Venice as protection of its territory against Turkish invasions and Austrian expansionism. Work started in 1593, and after a short time (early in the 17th century) Palmanova was regarded as one of the important strongpoints in this part of Europe. Its design is often attributed to Scamozzi. In any case, its external shape and interior layout were conceived as a whole and its construction proceeded accordingly in one uninterrupted operation. The plan of Palmanova expressed the principles of the Ideal Cities of the Italian Renaissance which, like the fortresses, were also preconceived as an integrated whole, a static entity that was not to be changed in extent or structure. Two trends met in these designs: the needs of military engineering and the rigid formality of geometric regularity.[27] Social considerations played no part in this conception.

Radiating from the hexagonal central *piazza d'armi* three roads led to three strong gateways, at the northwest to Udine, at the northeast to Gorizia, and at the south to the sea. The difference between the inner and outer diameter is striking: within the ramparts it is 2,400 feet, and including the moats, bastions, and the like, it is 5,400 feet, a telling proof of the importance and the advanced technique of the fortifications. The street system is a combination of radial and concentric principles, the latter following in their broken course the lines of the hexagonal central square.

27. Cf. p. 125.

93. Plan of Palmanova in the 17th century. Engraving by Joan Blaeu from *Nieuw vermeerderd en verbeterd Groot stedeboek van geheel Italia. . . .*

94. Map of Pordenone in 1860.

Pordenone, Province of Friuli. Pordenone, the Roman *Portus Naonis,* from which Pordenone's name was derived, is situated in the middle of a fertile plain, at the foot of the mountains, halfway between Udine and Treviso. A castle, possibly dating from the time after the Hungarian invasions (899-942), rose on the navigable river, the Noncello, the ancient *Naonis,* near or on the site of the future town. At this time, the March of Friuli was one of the vitally important strategic areas that had to be defended against invasions from the north and east by the petty counts and marquises who had taken possession of the land. This explains why during this period numerous castles were erected at strategic points where they could guard the waterways and roads and protect the commerce that slowly began to develop, and to stimulate the life of the small settlements growing up under their shelter. Pordenone was one of these places, and its origin can doubtlessly be traced back to the trading activities at the landing place on the Noncello. The castle of Pordenone was repeatedly mentioned during the Middle Ages in this particular respect: In 1232, in connection with the granting of tolls to a trader Ulrico Pitter, it was referred to as *"turrim nostram et mutam in Portusnaonis;"* ("our money-changing tower at Pordenone"); and again in a record of the following year the

river traffic on the Noncello, Meduna and Livenza, which linked the region with the sea, was described as passing at the foot of the castle near the bridge crossing the river at this point.[28]

Both the castle and the ancient bridge have disappeared. Since the first years of the 14th century the function of the castle, as the stronghold protecting the town, has lost its importance. Pordenone relied on its own defenses. It was enclosed within walls, later reinforced by towers and barbicans, and surrounded with a wide moat whose water was supplied from two streams, the Molini in the northeast and the Codafora in the west, which was joined to the Noncello in the south, thus

28. A. Beneditti. *Breve Storia di Pordenone.* 1956. P. 11 and *passim.*

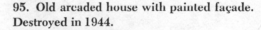

95. **Old arcaded house with painted façade. Destroyed in 1944.**

closing the circuit. Most of the houses were built of wood. The streets were tortuous and narrow, some hardly 3 feet wide. After a fire in the year 1318 that destroyed large areas, the town was reconstructed in stone. The most opulent buildings, decorated with murals, were erected in what today is the Corso Vittorio Emanuele. An anonymous Pordenonese writer of the 17th century (1687) described his town as

. . . surrounded by walls with 12 towers which were one mile and a half long and including the suburbs three miles. The shape of the circumference resembled a prostrate human figure whose head was the Borgo S. Giovanni up north; whose arms corresponded to the Borghi S. Antonio and S. Gottardo to the west and S. Carlo to the east, whereas the town itself was the body and the Borghi S. Giuliano and S. Gregorio to the south were the legs. It had four gates two of which had double drawbridges with three retrenchments [ritirate] and four posterns for underground escapes, now walled-in.

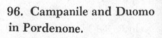

96. Campanile and Duomo in Pordenone.

210

97. Square with the Palazzo Comunale at Pordenone. Steps lead up to a church in the background. Painting by M. Moro, 1845.

In 1428 the original charter of Pordenone was reaffirmed by Duke Frederick V of Austria. It recognized particularly the importance of commerce as the main factor in the development of the town since Roman times, more important even than the agricultural activities in the surrounding countryside. Pordenone was favored by the net of waterways of the Noncello, Meduna, and Livenza, an advantage that none of the other rivers of the region could offer. In order to handle the increased traffic, the ancient port on the Noncello was improved and enlarged in 1493 by *mastro* Perino, a mason from Padua, with a *"muro scarpato cum uggere"* 47 *passi* (paces) long, 10 to 11 *passi* high, and three *pietre* (stones) wide. The only overland route, connecting the Alpine villages with Friuli in the 16th century, was the *Canale del Fella*, the so-called *Strada del Ferro*. Three annual fairs were held, the most frequented of which being the *fiera di S. Marco*. This was a "free" market; bread and wine were sold without tax. There were also "free" weekly markets for grain and other agricultural products.

Toward the end of the 14th century the growing commercial activities led to the practice of lending money at interest, less politely called usury. This was generally prohibited by the Church as immoral with the effect of throwing business into the hands of non-Christians, the Jews. If statutes issued in 1438 give a correct picture of the situation, usury was forbidden inside the walls and apparently not interfered with outside the gates—certainly an unusually ingenious way to preserve the moral integrity of the urban population. These scruples seem to have prevailed only for a short time. Since commerce and financial transactions inevitably connected with it were more important to the community than industry, the restrictions were revoked in 1452 and "business as usual" was restored.

However important commerce was for the well-being of Pordenone, the development of industry could not be neglected. The most valuable natural resources were the ample availability of running water. These advantages had to be utilized. Consequently, public water mills for grinding grain were installed in 1328. Three furnaces for the production of iron and copper followed. Workshops for knitting wool and four paper mills were established, the oldest mill dating from 1460. In 1789 this industry had become so important that eight paper mills were in operation. Silk and cotton weaving was furthered and ceramics were produced.

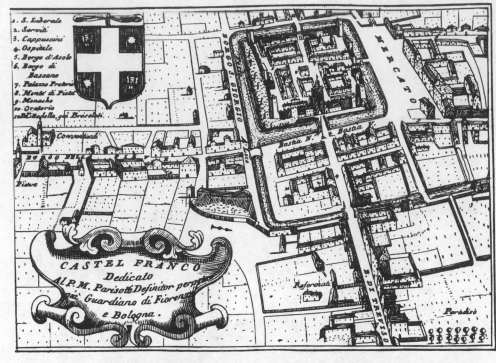

98. View of Castelfranco Veneto, showing the fortified square town and the outlying quarters partly surrounded by a moat and the market outside the walls. Engraving from *L'Atlante Veneto* by Vincenzo Coronelli, 1695.

Castelfranco Veneto, Province of Venezia.
Castelfranco stands on the Musone River along whose course from Asolo in the north to its mouth traces of a primitive society have been found. Several factors led to the choice of the site for the founding of a town—the generally favorable geographical location, the mild climate, a good water supply, the fertility of the soil, and the flat terrain. The rise of Castelfranco in Roman times was stimulated by its commercial and industrial contacts with Padua and Asolo at the terminal of the *Via Aurelia* and by its situation at a point where the spheres of interests of these two towns met. Its own production and export consisted mainly in agricultural commodities whereas textiles, finished woolen goods, and the famous cloaks were imported from Padua. After the barbarian invasions had destroyed the political and commercial centers of the *Via Aurelia*, the economy of Castelfranco began to revive, focused on the feudal domains of the prince bishop of Treviso.

In 1199 the people of Treviso decided to fortify Castelfranco as an outpost against the threatening attacks by Padua and Vicenza. Walls were raised, towers and gates erected, and a moat dug out. Although it is usual to speak of Castelfranco as a new foundation dating from the year 1199, the assumption is not

correct. The site had been inhabited before, as has been shown. What did happen was that the existing open settlement was used as the nucleus for the layout of a strongly fortified and permanently garrisoned place. The response to the challenge of Treviso came in 1210 when the Paduans founded Cittadella seven miles to the west. Both actions were dictated by the distrust of neighboring and rival communities, each convinced that it was threatened and had to defend itself against the aggressive hostilities of the other—a not unusual political game played throughout history. One's own case is always justified and blameless, while the other's is always wrong and evil.

The fortifications of Castelfranco enclosed a square area. They consisted of brick walls rising on a steep earth rampart thrown up from the spoil of the moat. There were three gates, and the interior layout followed the line of the walls. If the existing records are correct, these fairly simple fortifications took ten years to build and employed 1,000 laborers, apart from 500 bricklayers under the supervision of a master mason and four assistants. After the completion of the work, a hundred "families of good birth" were settled in the fortress, each receiving the usual grants of building plots and possibly of houses—al-

212

though this latter is doubtful, since in almost all known similar cases the newcomers had to erect their dwellings themselves—and perhaps of outlying farmland.[29] They were exempted from taxes and other burdens, and the new Castelfranco was declared a *colonia affrancata;* hence its name derived from *castrum francum.* The figures mentioned above concerning the duration of the construction of the fortifications, and apparently of the houses and streets and of the workers employed, should be taken with reservation. They seem to be excessive and, in any case are confusing—just as the information about the administrative setup is not quite compatible with the needs of a relatively small town. However, the discrepancy might be explained by the territorial extent of Castelfranco that included 14 *castelli* and 27 villages. For Treviso the place was obviously of paramount importance: it sent special representatives to Castelfranco, two consuls and twelve guardians, and introduced its own civil and penal codes to the satellite community.[30] Castelfranco was besieged by

the Paduans in 1215 and 1220 and a little later fell into the hands of Verona.

This period coincided with the revival of trade and industry in Castelfranco, favored by tax exemptions and special privileges, a development that proceeded successfully despite the restricting remains of the feudal economy. Numerous workshops, shops, inns, and lodging houses were built in stone inside and outside the walls, gradually replacing the old wooden structures. Venetian rule (1339) gave a fresh impetus to the commercial life of the town and to the growth of the population, stimulated by modern banking and credit methods mostly initiated by people from Tuscany and by Jews established in the Treviso area. With the fall of the Republic of Venice (1797) the social structure changed. The influence of the middle classes made itself felt and with it the commercial, industrial, and agricultural activities experienced a further prosperity. Factories for the processing of agricultural produce and the manufacture of consumer goods were founded, a new beginning that continued after the incorporation of Venezia in the Italian state (1869).

29. After J. Bradford. *Ancient Landscapes.* 1957. P. 267.

30. *Ibid.*

99. View of the walls and one of the gate towers of Castelfranco Veneto from the area beyond the moat. An 18th-century painting.

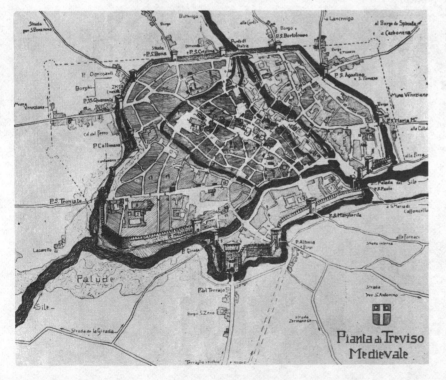

Cittadella

100. Cittadella is situated 7 miles to the west of Castelfranco Veneto. The sketch (based on an air view) shows, in contrast to the square rival fortress, the circular fortifications with four gates and a moat, and the gridiron layout of the interior somewhat artificially pressed into the oval *enceinte*.

Treviso. A Bronze Age settlement probably existed on the site of the future Treviso within a triangle formed by the Sile River, its tributary Cagnano, and the natural elevation of Sant' Andrea. This triangle gradually grew into a trapezoid in the midst of a very fertile and productive region. Its location close to the sea and navigable rivers and on the oldest and most important roads to the Alps made this first urban proto-Venetian settlement a trading and agricultural center of some significance. In 91 B.C. Roman *Tarvisium* became a *municipium* laid out on the usual gridiron plan that later changed to a polygon. Outside the

walls there were *villae*, farms, and workshops of craftsmen.

Christianity was introduced about A.D. 50 and the first church was built shortly afterward. Treviso was spared the ravages of the barbarian invasions of the fifth century owing to its reputation as a neutral town. The increase of population in the following centuries made the extension of the urban area necessary. Suburbs grew up around hospitals and convents outside the walls. In the 11th century the domain of Treviso stretched to the territory between the Brenta and Valdobbiadene and to a line between the Brenta and the Musone. The houses of the artisans and traders, who lived outside the walls, had a fortresslike character with thick walls, high towers, and grilled windows as protection against raids by hostile people, and may have served as refuges for the population of the surrounding country.

The *Comune di Treviso* was instituted in the middle of the 12th century and recognized in a charter given by Frederick I in the year 1164, containing among other privileges the unusual permission to construct arcades in order to facilitate trade: *porticus in viis regalibus aedificare et perpetuo possidere, ita tamen ut non sint solaria, vobis omnibus concedi-*

101. Plan of medieval Treviso. The dark inner line marks the ancient Roman area. Traces of the Roman street system are clearly recognizable. From A. Marchesan. *Treviso Medioevale.*

mus.[31] During the 13th century economic progress continued: Roads and houses were built, new quarters laid out, canals constructed, churches and convents erected, and the fortifications extended and strengthened with eleven gatetowers and a wide moat. However, in the course of time these fortifications proved inefficient in view of increasing political complications. It was therefore decided about 1509 to call in an experienced military engineer. The choice fell to Fra Giovanni Giocondo from Verona. His main concern was to modernize the defense system and to adapt it to the demands of the changing military techniques. The principal features of his plan were a retrenchment of the inhabited urban area to a smaller perimeter; the reinforcement of the

enceinte encircled by wide moats; and hydraulic devices by which the waters of the Botteniga and Sile could be raised to inundate the surrounding plain, thus considerably extending the defense perimeter around the town. The old walls were cleared of all unnecessary superstructures; the towers were lowered or pulled down; the eleven gates were reduced to three; a glacis was laid out; and bastions were added. These were the last great fortifications constructed by the community and the last great collective effort of the inhabitants of Treviso. During the following centuries—in spite of the involvement in the political quarrels of the great powers—the humanities, arts, and sciences flourished, a pleasant phenomenon and significant reminder of an all too much neglected insight that cultural achievements are independent of political power struggles.

31. "We grant all of you permission to build arcades along the royal esplanade and to keep them in perpetuity without, moreover, paying any ground rent."

Vicenza, Province of Venezia. Vicenza is situated at the mouth of a wide alluvial "corridor" between the Berici and Lessini Mountains—that is, the natural route of communication from Lombardy to eastern Veneto. Topographical conditions have played an important role in the origin and growth of Vicenza, although difficulties caused by underground flow

102. View of Palladio's Basilica and the surrounding quarter.

of water prevented the erection of buildings in some parts of the city. The first settlement was established on the Bacchiglione near its confluence with the Retrone which is navigable from that point to Padua. The original settlers, who left traces on the site of the future city, were the Euganei mixed with Italics, as can be deduced from pile dwellings and the *necropolis* of Angarano. These tribes were believed to have been forced to withdraw to the mountains, thus giving rise to the 34 *civitates* of the *Euganeae gentes*. In all probability Vicenza was founded by the Veneti. It was successively occupied by Etruscans, Gauls, and Romans.

Roman *Vicetia*—the oldest reliable reference to it dates from the time soon after 177 B.C.—was governed by *quatuorviri*. Its population belonged to the *Menenia* tribe and seems to have experienced a considerable prosperity under the Empire. The Roman city was surrounded by an approximately rectangular *enceinte* and traversed from east to west by the *decumanus maximus,* part of the *Via Postumia,* now the Corso Palladio.

In the first centuries of our era Vicenza was incorporated in the diocese of Milan and later, in the fifth century, it was dependent on the metropolitan of Aquileia. In the following centuries Vicenza suffered repeatedly from invasions by the barbarians that made advisable the construction of fortifications with strong towers and a deep moat. In 1183 the city was recognized as an independent community. By the year 1500 its population numbered 30,000 inhabitants; then it seems to have declined, not rising again until the first half of the 18th century.

103. Map of Vicenza in 1680 under Venetian rule. The fortifications have been extended (top right). The division of the town into two parts on either side of the Bacchiglione is clearly visible.

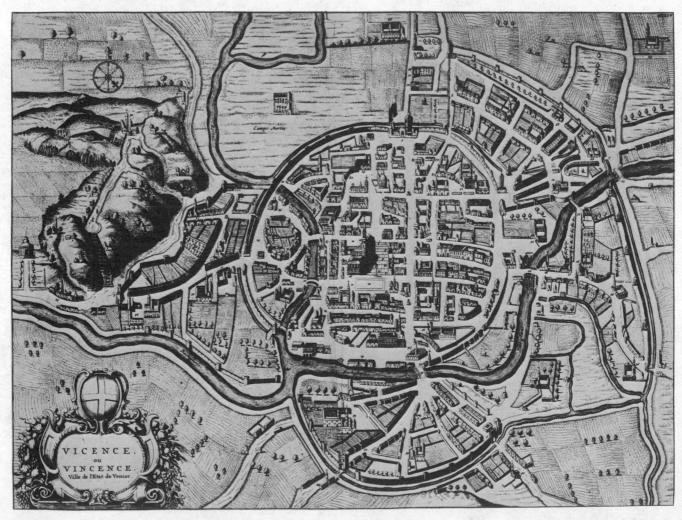

VICENCE.
ou
VINCENCE.
Ville de l'Etat de Venise.

104. The oldest map of Venice, designed in the 14th century and published by the architect Tomaso Temanza in 1780. The drawing shows the main features of the layout of the city as it was supposed to have been in 1141.

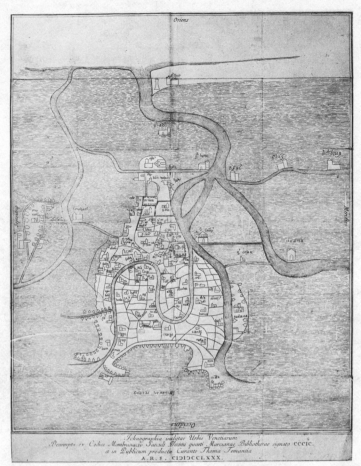

Ichnographia antiquae Urbis Venetiarum
Promptis ex Codice Membranaceo Saeculi Decimi quarti Marcianae Bibliothecae signato CCCIC
et in Publicum producta Curante Thoma Temanza
A. R. S. CIƆIƆCCLXXX.

Venezia. The origin and earliest history of Venice are intimately connected with the rise and fall of the city of Aquileia founded in 181 B.C. by the Romans as bulwark against the Celts and Istrians. Situated northwest of Roman *Tergeste* (Trieste), it was connected with the sea by a deep-water channel through the lagoon of Grado. Today it is a small village six miles inland owing to the accumulation of debris swept down from the Alps by the rivers. It was the predecessor of Venice. The selection of the site was dictated by its favorable geographical position at the head of the Adriatic and the meeting point of important overland routes. With the west it was connected by the *Via Postumia* leading from Cremona to Verona and *Concordia* and terminating at Aquileia. With the south it was linked by the *Via Popilia* via *Patavium* (Padua) and *Concordia*, and with the western shore of the Adriatic by a road running south as far as *Epidamnus* (Durazzo-Durres). Highways led to the north, to *Juvavum* (Salzburg), *Ovilava* (Wels), *Lauriacum* (Lorch), and *Vindobona* (Vienna).

This favorable situation made Aquileia a commercial and military center of great importance. It was a naval base where part of the Roman fleet was stationed, and as the capital of the province of Venetia of *Gallia Cisalpina* it ranked under Augustus as the fourth town of Italy after Rome, Milan, and Capua. It was said that under Hadrian its population numbered over 300,000 people, a figure almost certainly exaggerated but indicating the existence of a large number of inhabitants and a considerable importance and prosperity. In A.D. 452 it was conquered by Attila and, after a stubborn resistance that lasted three months, razed to the ground. The inhabitants fled to

the lagoons which stretched from Grado in the north to Comacchio in the south—that is, about 18 miles north of Ravenna, where, together with fugitives from Padua that had suffered the same fate, they founded the coastal settlements of Heraclea, Grado (*Aquileia Nova*), Caorle, Torcello, Burano, Murano, Malamocco, Pellestrina, and Chioggia. Of these places Grado, Heraclea, and Malamocco seem to have been leading until the population began to concentrate on the Rialto-Giudecca islands which were to be Venice in the eighth century.

The geographical situation of the islands was exceptionally favorable, although only small parts remained permanently free from the encroachment of the sea, cultivable land was scarce, and drinking water was not available. But they had the great advantage that the tide flushed the lagoons daily and that the inhabitants could rely on fowl and fish and on the urgently needed salt. Located at the eastern end of the largest lowlands of Italy,

217

where the Mediterranean penetrates farthest north in the European mainland, the development of the islands was assured from the very beginning of their occupation. The plain of Lombardy has been formed by the debris carried by the Po, Ticino, Adda, Adige, Brenta, Piave, Livenza, Tagliamento, and Isonzo, and the bed of boulders of which its substratum consists has been covered by a layer of rich alluvial soil. Since the rivers tend to flow eastward, the coast has been gradually extended in the same direction, so that cities like Ravenna and Aquileia, once flourishing seaports, are now many miles inland from the sea. The strong current at the head of the Adriatic, running from east to west, has deposited the silt from the rivers in long banks or *lidi* extending parallel to the shore. In the course of thousands of years, some of these *lidi* emerged above the sea level forming the ac-

105. Venice in 1500. Bird's-eye view by Jacopo de' Barbari. The urban area is closely

tual shoreline behind which large lagoons of fresh water from the rivers and salt water from the sea were formed. Venice is situated approximately in the middle of this chain of lagoons. Since the soil is a quaggy mud, the buildings had to be carried by piles driven deep into the ground.

The artery of Venice is the Canal Grande running through the city in the shape of the letter S and dividing it into two parts. It was in all likelihood the bed of a river emptying into the lagoon near Mestre. From the Canal Grande the smaller canals lead in all directions. Their course follows the line of the original channels between the islands along which the inhabitants built dykes of plaited osiers. The Canale della Giudecca separates the city from the island of the same name. The length of the canals has been estimated at about 28 miles, that of the footpaths at approximately

ilt up and the main structural divisions are clearly distinguishable.

90 miles, and the number of bridges at between 350 and 400.

The adaptation of the environment to the natural conditions has made unique demands on the courage, ingenuity, perseverance, and artistic genius of the Venetians. Their response to this challenge has been unsurpassed. Out of the raw materials of a precarious existence they have created a unity of natural and man-made beauty, a harmony of collective and individual achievements, which in its complexity and organic clarity, its realistic immediacy and rational coordination under most difficult and unusual conditions, represents one of the high points of human greatness—and of failure. Venice is not an utopian dream come true. It is an Ideal City actually built, not one merely conjured up on the drawing-board by theoreticians indulging in speculations about empty geometrical forms and regimented rigidity. True, the social problems of a community of human beings were not solved by the Venetians. But neither would they have been solved by the dreams of the utopians or the exercises of the drawing-board architects of the Renaissance. Have they ever been solved? The beauty, the brilliance, the artistic grandeur of Venice had to be paid for with despotism, corruption, slavery, and the horrors of a tribunal that could successfully compete with the Inquisition in its brutality, hypocrisy, and secret crimes. The external splendor could become a reality only by adapting the earthly aspirations "to the tenets and needs of this world" dissolving the essence of religious and human confessions. One is tempted to ponder, in this connection, the dialogue between the Grand Inquisitor and Christ found in a draft of Dostoevsky's *The Brothers Karamazov* after his death: "Hadst Thou taken the world and Caesar's purple, Thou wouldst have founded the universal state and have given universal peace." This counsel rejected by Christ was eagerly followed by the rulers and the dominant minority of the Republic of Venice, a fact that should not be forgotten when we are fascinated and enchanted by the aesthetic wonders of this city. Human perfection and human imperfection, human ideals and human vagaries, both these trends have created Venice.

In the light of these considerations, the cult of the Evangelist Mark as the patron saint of Venice assumes a particular significance. Here we have the whole panoply of religious devotion shielding and enhancing the temporal aspirations of the citizens. This cult as a formative power in the history of the city should not be underestimated. We know how often the sepulchre of a saint has played a decisive role not only in the origin of cities but also in their later development, and how around the tomb of a patron saint the bishop's residence with the church was built as the nucleus of an urban community.

When the bishop of Aquileia was forced to flee to the safety of the lagoons and established his see at Grado, the Langobards installed a new bishop at Aquileia. This resulted in a century-long dispute between the two bishops about the validity of their offices and the title of patriarch. Since, according to an old belief, all patriarchates had been founded by apostles—Constantinople by St. Andrew, Jerusalem by St. James, Rome by St. Peter, to mention but a few—the rivalry between Aquileia and Grado led almost automatically to the claim that an apostle was the founder of one of the two communities.[32]

Toward the end of the eighth century, a legend conveniently turned up that St. Mark as emissary of St. Peter had founded the bishopric of Aquileia. Thus history was made, and Aquileia seemed to be the victor. An attempt to subjugate Grado, which would also have meant the end of Venetian independence from the mainland, was thwarted and almost simultaneously the remains of the saint were miraculously transferred from Alexandria, where he had been martyred, to Venice. This happened in 827-28. The prestige of Venice was assured and hence the charismatic aura of St. Mark spread its protecting and glorifying wings over the fate of Venice. The body of the saint was not entombed in the church of Grado but hidden by the Doge in the chapel of his palace

32. H. C. Peyer. *Stadt und Stadtpatron im mittel-alterlichen Italien.* 1955. Pp. 8-24.

on the Rialto where it was safe from theft, the likelihood of which had to be seriously considered.

For two centuries nothing was heard of the cult of the saint. It was not until the year 1000 that sources began to mention him as the patron saint of Venice. The *victrix vexillum,* the flag of St. Mark, became the ensign of the Venetian armies. The investiture of a Doge took place under the sign of the saint in S. Marco. He had to enter the church barefoot, to prostrate himself before the altar before receiving the staff as symbol of his office to the accompaniment of the *laudes*:

> *Christus vincit, Christus regnat,*
>   *Christus imperat.*
> *Domino nostro dei gratia inclyto*
>   *duci Venetiarum salus, honor,*
> *Vita, et victoria. S. Marce,*
>   *tu illum adiuva.*

At about the same time coins were struck, one side of which carried the inscription *Venecia* and the name and the effigy of St. Mark. In records of the 10th and 11th centuries the loyalty oaths of the subjugated cities mentioned the name of the Doge first. In the 12th century this was changed, the saint's name occupying the first place followed by that of the Doge and sometimes by the name of the Community of the Citizens of Venice. It is obvious that the Venetians of this period used the name of their patron saint as a political instrument to further their sovereign rights, apparently convinced that resistance to a saint and his church was less likely to be successful than resistance to temporal authorities. The mosaics in S. Marco, depicting the legend of St. Mark, date from the 13th century, when his cult had reached the acme of general recognition. It is characteristic that on these representations the Doge and the other officials always appear as servants of the apostle. Toward the end of the same century the winged lion, the ancient symbol of St. Mark, became the symbol and the insignia of authority of Venice. It is doubtful that without the uniting power of the patron saint the history of Venice would have been the same as it was under the shelter of his protection and inspiration. He

106. Glass shop in Venice. From a woodcut of the Procession of the Doge on the Piazza di San Marco. Original by Jost Amman (1539–91).

was the invisible city builder and the sovereign lord of Venice. It is one of the "ifs" of history about which we are so fond of speculating: what would have been the fate of Venice, if the remains of St. Mark had not been transferred to the Rialto but had been laid to rest on the mainland?

And yet we should ask: was the religious devotion of official Venice to the saint sincere, or was it merely a convenient cloak behind which the political game could be played with less impropriety? It is interesting to note what Ruskin remarked on this aspect of Venetian history in *The Stones of Venice*:

The most curious phenomenon in all Venetian history, is the vitality of religion in private life, and its deadness in public policy. Amidst the enthusiasm, chivalry, or fanaticism, of the other states of Europe, Venice stands, from first to last, like a masked statue; her coldness impenetrable, her exertion only aroused by the touch of a secret spring. That spring was her commercial interest— this the one motive of all her important political acts.

In other words: Temporal power and material profit, not religious zeal, were the prime

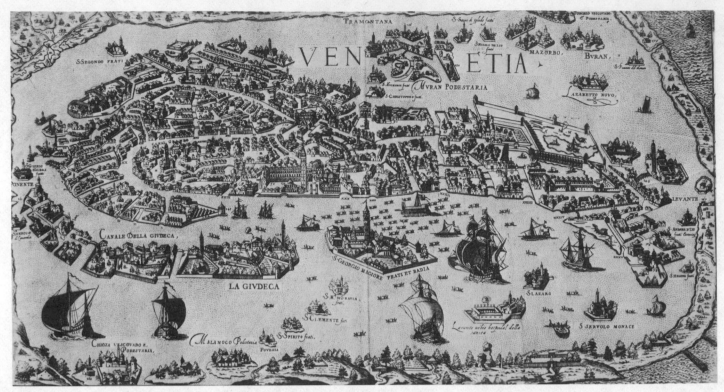

107. Venice at the end of the 17th century.

movers of the aspirations of the ruling élite of Venice. Religion was the opiate of the people and the welcome handmaiden of the political manipulations of her rulers.

It is against this background of all too human imperfection, of the inevitability of complementary contrasts making up the bewildering complexity of life that the outward form and physical structure of Venice should be viewed. The refugees from the mainland who had sought safety on the islands of the lagoons were probably not the first settlers. Their predecessors were fishermen, more or less independent owing to their poverty and their inaccessible site. This population was increased occasionally and in desultory fashion by newcomers from the mainland, who were hardly inclined to join the islanders as permanent inhabitants. They returned to their original homes when the threat of barbarian invasions had passed. But on each occasion some of the refugees stayed on. It was only after many repeated incursions and after the invasion of A.D. 568 that they finally gave up any hope of returning to the mainland, settling permanently on the islands. Thus the population began to increase rapidly, making a living

by producing salt and other commodities and by commerce which their ships made possible. The 12 lagoon townships, in which the islanders lived, were the nucleus of the State of Venice. "Beyond the reach of the barbarians, who had no vessels—forgotten by the Romans and their successors the Ostrogoths—they maintained their independence under the administration of tribunes, named by the assembly of the people in each of the separate isles."[33] These people were convinced that they were "born independent," a self-deception that nevertheless exerted a strong influence upon their character and the future history of Venice. However, internal rivalries and external threats of piratical attacks from the opposite coast of Dalmatia made a union of the separate island communities unavoidable. In A.D. 697 the citizens of the different islands assembled at Heraclea and elected a governor under the title of Doge for life. The first Doge was Paolo Luca Anafesto, who ruled from 697 to 716 and succeeded in repulsing the attackers and bringing the Lombards to acknowledge the independence of the Republic,

33. J. C. L. Simonde de Sismondi. *A History of the Italian Republics.* Everyman's Library. 1907. P. 23.

222

increasing its wealth and setting Venice on its course to greatness and prosperity.

In this connection, a letter written in the early sixth century by Cassiodorus, the minister of Theodoric, and addressed to the *tribuni maritimorum,* is of particular interest. He remarked that "men may live without gold or silver but not without salt." In enlisting the services of the Venetians for the transport of wine and oil from Istria to Ravenna he referred to them as "possessing many ships" and as being "equally at home on sea and land" and having "the opportunity, when barred from the sea by raging winds, to choose a safer route to travel by way of charming rivers." He went on to describe how "their boats, when partly concealed from a distance, seem to glide across the meadows; and since they are drawn by ropes, the natural order of things is reversed, and men help ships with their feet." He then speaks of the islands

where the tidal ebb and flow alternately covers and uncovers the face of the fields and men have chosen to live like waterfowl, protecting themselves from the onset of the sea by defences of twisted osier. The only wealth of the inhabitants consists in fish;

so that rich and poor live on equal terms, and the same kind of food and shelter does for everyone. Envy is unknown to them, and their only rivalry finds outlet in the exploitation of their saltworks. Instead of ploughs and sickles they roll their cylinders, and from this source arise all their profits, since all the world has need of salt, and by means of salt the Venetians may possess what they themselves do not produce.[34]

It would be interesting to describe in detail the unfolding of the political and economic organization of Venice and its impact upon the growth and structural development of the city; to compare the role of the Venetian oligarchy with the minority rule of patrician families in other parts of Europe; to discuss the rationalization of the commercial methods of the administrative setup; and to relate these and other problems to the emergence of the external form and the layout of pedestrian and water traffic in Venice. As tempting and as rewarding this might be, the scope and character of this history could not be expanded *ad infinitum* without serious disadvantages to

34. Quoted from G. Luzzatto. *An Economic History of Italy from the Fall of the Roman Empire to the Beginning of the Sixteenth Century.* 1961. Pp. 33-34.

108. Old view of the Canal Grande near the Chiesa degli Scalzi.

clarity and adherence to the subject—that is, to city planning as such. There is a super-abundance of excellent scholarly works available that may usefully be consulted, a small selection of which has been included in the bibliography. As part of a general City Survey dealing with the whole of Italy, each individual city can receive only restricted space and treatment, a self-imposed limitation particularly regrettable in the case of Venice.

Population data for Venice vary, although not so much as for many other cities. According to J. C. Russell, whose estimates are generally reliable, Venice had in 1540 about 131,000 inhabitants.[35] J. Beloch has calculated their number for 1552 at about 158,069 including men, women, children, the clergy, the poor in the hospitals, and the Jews.[36] At the same time the population of Venetia numbered approximately 600,000. In the following centuries the population declined to about 143,000 in the first quarter of the 17th century, if Beloch's figures are accepted; to about 139,000 at the end of the 18th century; and to about 133,000 in the 1880's. All these figures should be taken as indicating the general trend of population changes, not as exact data; the methods by which they were compiled were not at all perfect and varied too much at different periods.

Venice is the only city in which pedestrians and other traffic are completely separated. This ideal solution was of course possible only in the unique conditions of this water-bound and water-borne city. For traffic on the canals there were the gondolas, mentioned as early as 1094, perfectly adapted to the narrow and winding waterways with their flat bottoms. They were only 4 to 5 feet wide and curved out of the water at both ends with ornamental bows and sterns. In order to suppress undue luxury in their outfit the Grand Council issued an edict in 1562 prescribing black as the general color for all gondolas. For the pedestrians there were the *calli*—the lanes, alleys, and streets; the *campi*—the squares; the *fondamente*—the quays; and the *corti,* the courtyards—all creating a harmony of contrasts; the narrowness of the *calli,* and the width of the *campi,* the extension of the *fondamente,* and the seclusion of the *corti*—a harmony heightened by the *chiaroscuro* of light and shade, the vibrant air over the *calli* and the waterways, and the restless reflection of the buildings in the canals.

Venice is a *medieval* city created by the exigencies of nature and by man's ingenuity in expressing his longings in a language of form —in stone and space—that was the essence of medieval group consciousness and medieval empathy into the actuality of a given situation. There were no preconceived perspective views, no deliberately placed terminating viewpoints, no prearranged architectural compositions, no enforced or artificial grandeur. And yet everything was spontaneously subordinated to one goal, to the preservation of the human scale and of an extraordinary intimacy reflecting the immediacy of social life. The casualness of the environment responded to the unpredictable vagaries of daily life. The accidental views, the asymmetry, the surprises of the layout, the marvelous sense of spatial relations and the almost complete neglect of organized unity, the multiplicity of viewpoints within a narrow compass—in short, the majestic polyphony of individual accents, of projecting and receding volumes, the ever-renewed unfolding of the architectural melody, all these features together created the unique atmosphere of medieval Venice and her organic unity. It was this permanently changing picture, this ever-renewed and never completely fulfilled expectation, the fleeting vistas, and the intriguing contrasts of light and shade that intensified the curiosity of the visitor, driving him on to explore the next phase of what he could suspect but not yet clearly perceive, and which altogether were so characteristic of the medieval secret of city building. Humble houses alternated with patrician palaces, corresponding to the diversity of human relations and inescapable entanglement of the social classes.

The dwellings of the patricians, of the middle classes, and of the common people have all left their imprint on the city, each in its

35. *Late Ancient and Medieval Population.* 1958. P. 126.
36. "La popolazione de Venezia nei secoli XVI e XVII," *Nuovo Archivio Veneto,* 3, 1902. Pp. 5-49.

particular manner. The palaces have changed their architectural physiognomy in the course of the centuries, from the early *casa fondaco*, doing double duty as warehouse and dwelling place, to an aristocratic residence, when the patrician became a *grand seigneur*, a merchant prince administering his business through agents and employees. The main room of these buildings was a large rectangular hall accessible from the vestibule by a stairway and with two aisles projecting in the form of an U, or one aisle forming an L with the hall. All these types were arranged around an inner courtyard with external though covered staircases leading to the upper floors. In contrast to many other towns of medieval Italy with their fortresslike palaces and but few windows because of the rivalries and fights among the feudal families, the Venetian residences of the patricians were open, graceful buildings with large loggias and ample fenestration, an appearance they maintained until the 18th century owing to the social tranquillity of this commercial metropolis. The *casa fondaco* had

probably its origin in actual *fondachi*, counting houses, distinguished from the private dwellings by the large space given to the storerooms. In some cases the whole building consisted of storerooms for wheat or other commodities, such as the Fondaco de' Tedeschi or the Fondaco de' Turchi.

The houses of the wealthy middle class were a sort of compromise between the patrician dwellings and the habitations of the common people, although with more similarity to the former in their architectural conception, materials, and general appearance, yet designed for several apartments on three or four floors. The houses of the common people were more uniform, more expressive through their serial repetition and their simple plain surfaces than through architectural finesse. They were vertically subdivided, one floor for one family, whereas the *corti* were used as the social open-air gathering place by all inhabitants of the house.

Finally, there were the *scuole,* the seats of the corporations, of the shoemakers, gold-

109. Old view of the Piazza San Marco and the Piazzetta.

smiths, masons and others, often situated on or near one of the *campi* in the vicinity of a church and mostly quite modest in their outer appearance—in contrast to the *scuole* of the religious confraternities devoted to charitable work, with their monumental grand marble staircases and murals by the most famous of the Venetian painters.

Lewis Mumford has drawn attention to "the system of functional zoning."[37] As he correctly remarks the Venetians were no doubt unaware of the implications of their actions which were dictated by the grouping of the islands around the core city. They followed their instinct for rational organization of the urban structure and almost by chance created not a new type of city but a greatly improved version of what had been rudimentarily inherent in every more important medieval town—namely the concentration of the trades in streets and quarters. Here we have the germ of "functional zoning." Venice merely did the

same on a larger scale, favored by the natural conditions of the site. The cemetery was moved out to the island of Torcello, the glass industry to the island of Murano—where it was established by an edict of the Grand Council in 1255. That the Arsenal, on which the very existence of Venice depended, was located not within the inner town but at its eastern end on a separate island was only logical. It was a shipyard and munitions works for the provisioning and outfitting of the vessels and their crews. In the 15th century it employed 16,000 workers and was in charge of 36,000 seamen. Shipbuilding was partly a private and partly a public enterprise, the latter concentrated at the Arsenal and the former dispersed in smaller shipyards or *squeri* in Venice itself, Chioggia, and on other islands. The workers in the Arsenal were all wage laborers whereas in the private industry a form of artisan organization prevailed.[38]

Each residential quarter had its *campo* with

37. *The City in History.* 1961. Pp. 321-25.

38. G. Luzzatto, *op. cit.,* p. 108.

110. Scuola di S. Rocco in 1768.

some public buildings forming an integrated part of the city without losing its individual identity. The houses were grouped around the social center, the *campo* with its school, guild-hall, church, and fountain. This is, in broad outline, the organic system of the layout of Venice, of this open and yet contained city, of its restricted space that throughout history kept the population small, and of its unity in multiplicity.

In this connection it may be pertinent to note that the two weekly markets of St. Paul and St. Mark were of a purely local character, and that the annual fair of the Ascension Day never attained international importance but remained a complement of the religious festival.[39]

The Piazza San Marco, the heart of Venice, has grown only very slowly and gradually into this role.[40] Originally the square, the orchard of the early Byzantine church of St. Mark, was an irregular open space surrounded by medi-ocre buildings, stables, and butchers' shops. At this time, horses were still used and it was no unusual sight to find them tethered to the trees in the square, which served as market square, forecourt to the church and the Doge's palace, and as the central "attraction" of the Venice before the year 1000. In 1176 the square was widened to about double its size by filling in the canal at the west end and by the moving back of St. Mark's. It is probable that, apart from general considerations for the extension of the square, the yard of the stonecutters and other workers employed at the rebuilding of the church and the *campanile* demanded more space. A large public latrine occupied a corner of the place which still remained a rather un-inviting area, an appearance that did not change much during the next few centuries. An over-all idea for its layout was still missing. The square was still a market, only partly paved, and stables and horses remained a common sight.

It was not before the last years of the 15th century that a comprehensive reconstruction of the square began. It was then completely paved with bricks. The clock tower was erected over the entrance of the *Merceria,* the shopping street leading into the square, and the *Procuratie Vecchie* and other buildings were constructed. The butchers and bakers had to give up their shops and stalls in 1536 and move to other quarters in favor of the new library by Sansovino. The shape of the square, as we know it today, was slowly taking shape. The stone-cutters' yard, the trees, and the latrine were removed, and many other improvements were planned and carried through. The history of the square is interesting but its significance for the wider issues of city planning should not be overestimated. The square as a whole, the architectural ensemble of the buildings, their relationship to the canals, and the interdependence of the Piazza and the Piazzetta are together and individually jewels of beauty and artistic sensitivity of past generations which have not yet been matched in our time. The Piazza is still a living reality spanning centuries—and this is perhaps its greatest achievement.

Now there is the danger that Venice may cease to exist—either as a city in the lagoons or a city of unspoiled character. In the latter case man would be the destroyer: commercial interests threaten to "revitalize" and to "bring Venice up to date." In our rapidly vulgarized world this is a serious possibility. Nature is the other danger. The city is sinking and the islands on which it stands are subject to subsidence. The only effective way to check this development would be to block the channels from the lagoons to the Adriatic Sea and make the lagoons a lake. This would create difficulties in the disposal of sewage, an action that now is left to the ebb and flow of the tides. Since the Bronze Age the area has sunk approximately 20 feet, and since Roman times 5 to 6 feet. Should the pressure of commercial interests grow and threaten to become a reality then it may be preferable to let nature do its work, and let us hope as quickly as possible.

39. G. Luzzatto. "Vi furono fiere a Venezia?" In: *Recueils de la Société Jean Bodin.* V, La Foire. 1953. Pp. 267-79.

40. Cf. pp. 131-33.

111. Air view of the Piazza San Marco and the Piazzetta.

112. Square in a densely built-up district of Venice.

113. Two squares and their surroundings in the heart of Venice.

114. Campo SS. Giovanni e Paolo in Venice.

229

115. Rio di San Salvador. A narrow side canal with the *campanile* in the background.

116. Rio della Panada.

117. Another view of the Rio della Panad

230

118. Garden at the corner of two canals near the Fondamenta della Misericordia.

119. Air view of Venice.

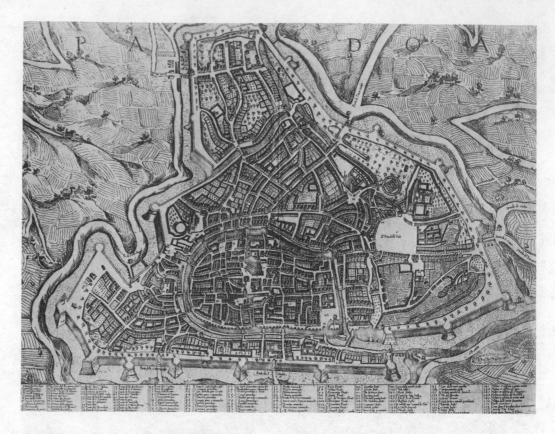

120. Map of Padua in the 16th century. The oval area of the inner town is surrounded by the Bacchiglione. Traces of the Roman gridiron plan are still distinguishable. In contrast to many medieval cities, Padua was relatively spaciously laid out, even in its oldest parts. The outer districts, near the fortifications with simple bastions, seven gates, and a moat, show large open spaces. The main public buildings are concentrated in the central section of the old city.

121. Palazzo della Ragione, the *juris basilica* (1172–1219), between the Piazza delle Erbe in the foreground and the Piazza dei Frutti, surrounded by a closely built-up area.

122. Air view of Padua with the Prato della Valle in the center.

Padova (Padua). The ancient *Patavium,* on the Bacchiglione River which once served as the moat surrounding the walls, is said to have been founded by Antenor, brother of Priam:

> *Hic tamen ille urbem Patavi*
> *sedesque locavit*
> *Teucrorum et genti nomen dedit,*
> *armaque fixit*
> *Troia.*[41]

Under Augustus, Padua was the most prosperous town of Northern Italy. After the fall of the Empire, it shared with Rome the decline of its power and economic prosperity, the deterioration of its once fertile countryside and of its trading activities. Barbarian invasions and feudal anarchy destroyed most of the remnants of the Roman period. It was not until the 13th century that an upward trend set in and a free republic was founded. Agriculture and stock breeding revived. Commerce and industry, especially the manufacture of

woolen goods, paper, and glass, were developed on a modest scale. The university was founded in 1222. It established the fame of Padua as the most eminent seat of Italian scholarship.

The few traces of the regular Roman street system gradually disappeared, and medieval buildings and a maze of narrow roads began to cover the urban area. The increase of population made an extension of the walls and the incorporation of the extramural nuclei necessary. Prosperity continued to rise under Venetian domination. A systematic development of the surrounding region was set on foot: Reforestation, specialized farming, and a general improvement of agriculture supported by an efficient system of irrigation.

Within the urban area important renovations were begun initiated and supervised, in the 18th century, by Andrea Memmo, procurator of the Republic of S. Marco. He promoted the construction of arcades *"onde la città sembri quasi nuova come Bologna"* (giving the city almost a new appearance like Bologna). Apart from the architectural value the arcades efficiently separated the pedestrian and vehicular traffic.

41. Virgil. *Aeneid.* I. 252. "Here Antenor actually found a place where Trojans might settle and named the city Padua. He gave its people a Trojan name and hung his arms on the walls."

233

123. Air view of the Basilica del Santo with the statue of the Gattamelata at the edge of the square.

But the most important work connected with the name of Memmo was the reclamation of the Prato della Valle. The name means "the Meadow of the Valley." It was a marshy area, then outside the walls where the cattle market was periodically held. A plan was worked out by Domenico Cerato whose center was an elliptical enclosure with a central island connected by four bridges to a circular avenue adorned with 82 statues of professors and students of the University of Padua and other persons highly regarded by the city.

Apart from this work Memmo furthered the economic development of Padua by the construction of navigable canals, landing places, warehouses, and other installations.

The decline of Venice ended the prosperity of Padua and aggravated the difficulties of the following period (1797-1813) during which the French and Austrian occupation impeded any serious economic activity. It was not until 1842 when the first railway line was inaugurated that an improvement set in.

Rovigo. The territory between the Adige and the Po in the easternmost part of the Po Valley was originally covered by alluvial deposits of sand and clay and an abundance of water. Hence its ancient name *Policinium*, later modified to *Polesino*, and finally to *Polesine*, meaning "Land emerging from the water." The Adige separates it on the northern side from the province of Padua; the Po separates it from the provinces of Ferrara and Mantova in the south; in the east it stretches to the Adriatic Sea, and in the west the old riverbeds of the Castagnaro and Tartaro mark the boundaries with the province of Verona. In the 15th century an important reclamation

work was carried out: a canal was dug to receive the surplus water of the Tartaro and lead it to the sea. In the 16th century the first and more systematic reclamations were undertaken: Porto Viro was constructed, consisting of a canal about 6.21 miles long through which the waters of the Po could find an outlet to the Adriatic, toward the Sacca di Goro, where they divided into several branches, forming the actual delta of the Po River.

The first inhabitants of *Polesine* were Venetian-Illyric tribes. In the fourth century B.C. Greek traders arrived, exchanging wool and amber for local materials. In the same century the territory was invaded by Gallic tribes and

124. Porta di S. Bortolo in Rovigo dating from the 13th century.

people from Syracuse, who occupied it for almost two centuries. At the end of the third century B.C. the Romans appeared on the scene. Industry, commerce, and agriculture were developed, and roads were built: the *Via Athesis* along the Adige, the *Via Annia* from Bologna to Padua, the *Via Popilia* from Rimini to *Altinum,* the *Via Altinate* from Rome to Aquileia, and the *Via Volane* linking the *Vìa Annia* with the *Via Popilia*.

Around A.D. 900 a fortified castle was built in the small settlement of *Rodigo,* which became the most important center of the Polesine territory. The town flourished. In 1483 Marino Sanudo (1466 to 1533), the Venetian historian, could write in his *Itinerario in terra ferma:* "Roigo, terra belisima, casizata magnifice" with its "mure altissime et

125. Map of Rovigo in the 16th century. The town, on the Adigetto Canal, is here seen surrounded by fortifications with bastions and a moat whose water was supplied from the canal. The building density seems to be rather low. A certain spaciousness is characteristic of the general layout, if the map is not too simplified or distorted. The main square occupies approximately the center of the urban area near the canal. The castle, part of the fortifications, is situated at the bottom corner (left). Suburbs extend on either side of the town.

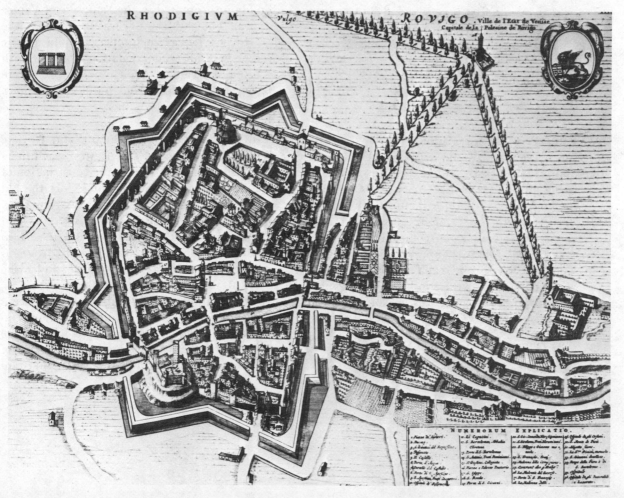

126. Old view of gatehouses at the periphery of Rovigo on the road from Padua in 1845.

grosse; arzeri et spalti fortissimi; belle, grande et spese case; la piazza molto grande, larga et longa; palazzi ben compositi; et il forte castello con spalti et torre," but adding with characteristic Venetian malice: *"Sed hoc transeat."*[42]

The name of the actual town of Rovigo appeared for the first time in A.D. 838. A century

42. "Rovigo set magnificently in the landscape . . . with its very high and strong walls; arches and very powerful ramparts; large houses with thick walls; the great square, wide and long; palaces beautifully designed; and the castle fortified with ramparts and towers."

Este, Province of Padua. Situated at the southwest base of the Euganean Hills about 8 miles north of the Adige, Este's geographical history is of particular interest.[43] Originally the river flowed close to the town. In A.D. 589 the riverbed rose and a catastrophic flood changed its course. In connection with this event the Lombards interrupted the river at Cucca Veronese and canalized its course, diverting it more to the south of the Euganean Hills away from the towns of Cologna, Montagnana, and *Ateste* (Este) toward Legnano,

43. Information on the historical development of Este was kindly supplied by Dr. Angelo Limena of Este, and the mayor of the city.

236

later it was no longer regarded as a *villa* but as a *curtis*—indicating, according to medieval usage, a small urban center, well laid out and fortified. During the following centuries it was involved in the wars between Milan, Mantua, and Venice, and other local feuds, but was finally incorporated in the Republic of Venice (1515). The 18th century was the Golden Age of Rovigo. It was an intellectual and artistic center with an academy dating from the 16th century, a theater where Goldoni's plays were performed, and numerous public institutions.

Vangadizza (Badia), Lendinara, and Rovigo. Thus the existence of the *Atestini* was fundamentally changed and only the construction of a short connecting road could restore the old vitality of their town. This crisis caused by nature and alleviated by man's ingenuity and efforts led to the restoration of the *Agro Atestino,* the rural surroundings of *Ateste,* as a new topographical entity when, under the Holy Roman Empire of the German Nation, Northern Italy was divided into feudal territories. These changes modified the environment and created new conditions which were turned to full advantage by the inhabitants of the region. The turbulent river Agno-Brancaglia (Frassine), flowing down from the Lessini Mountains, was directed to Este, the ancient road Mantua-Padua-Venezia regained its importance, and the land was irrigated by canals.

The vineyards and orchards that today cover the country date from the Middle Ages. They were planted on long lines of sand dunes in which the ancient cemeteries were located. A salient point of the topographical history of *Ateste* which should not be forgotten is that in pre-Roman times the town was a seaport with almost the same advantages as *Atria* (Adria) about 22 miles to the southeast, at the mouth of the Po, and that the *Atestini* were engaged in seaborne commerce and could use overland routes for travel to Istria, while protected against attacks from the south by the Po. The Etruscans never invaded Venetia, and the Romans never conquered this region but resorted to a peaceful penetration through an understanding with the inhabitants in 184 B.C.

The earliest history of the *Atestini*—who may be regarded as a branch of the Bolognese Villanovans—their burial customs by crema-

127. Castello di Este. Woodcut of the year 1480 in the *Cronica de la antiqua cittade de Ateste* by Pre Hieronimo Atestino.

tion, and beautiful weapons and implements, are outside the scope of this work. Suffice it to say that the *Euganei* were the first occupants of the site of Este, that they were followed by the *Illirici* in the tenth century B.C., and by the Romans in the second century B.C. whose rule lasted to the fourth century A.D., when Attila destroyed the city. After this event Este disappeared from history until the family of Este received the town and the surrounding

128. View of Este in 1775 showing the Euganean Hills in the background, the Castello (c) on the slopes of the central hill, the Borgo S. Pietro (S top left), and the Borgo S. Martino (14 center), the Torre and Ponte della Porta Vecchia (24 center), and one canal running through the middle of the urban area, and another one along the periphery (foreground). Engraving by Girolamo Franchini.

territory as a fief from the emperor in the 11th century. In the 13th century Este was taken over by Padua. It passed to Venice in 1405 and remained under her domination until Napoleonic times. Then it fell to Austria and, finally, became Italian in 1866.

The first nucleus of the Neolithic period were pile dwellings of the primitive tribes of this region known as *Ateste,* which around 1180 B.C. became an important stronghold of the pre-Aryan people of the *Euganei.* This river culture, based on hunting and collecting of food, was a closed economy without any particular political characteristics. The arrival of the paleo-Veneti toward the year 1000 B.C. changed the habitat of the earlier settlers by introducing metals, a more developed pottery, cultivation, and specialized handicrafts, and bringing with them the mode of living in fortified places, refuges, similar to those of the *Istri* and *Illirici* in the region around *Tergeste*

(Trieste). The southernmost promontory of the hills was their natural stronghold, and commerce and traffic moved along the Adige. A paved footpath from this hill down to the river has recently been discovered. In the fifth century B.C. these primitive beginnings of rudimentary city life were spreading over the whole area between the mountains and the Adige Plain, embracing a free community with a common language, religion, and blood relations, united in their struggle for life and in their rituals of burial, and protected by the fortified places on the hills.

Under Roman rule Este gradually lost its political and cultural autonomy and was successively transformed into a *castrum,* a *municipium,* and a *colonia.* Dykes were built to regulate the Adige during its course through the urban area, and three bridges were constructed, the principal one in stone as a link in the Roman arterial road from *Mutina* (Modena), to *Hostilia* (Ostiglia), *Ateste, Patavium* (Padua), Aquileia, and *Tergeste* (Trieste). These improvements were followed by the abandonment of the clusters of primitive huts, and the shifting of the settlement to the west of the fortified hill where the Adige bifurcated to the heights of the present Torre, with one branch now disappearing in the Calaonian marshes and the other proceeding to Solesino (*Solum Atesinum*) and the Adria. Thus the first actual city of *Ateste* was established between the hill and the bifurcation at right angles to the river, and the Roman gridiron system, still visible today, could be applied in the planning of the new community. The nucleus on the hill assumed the function of the Roman *presidio,* the garrisoned stronghold, whereas the city extended on the plain. A temple to the Dioscuri, the protectors of navigation, was erected and later another to Augustus as the guardian deity of peace. The *forum,* the center of the civic and commercial activities, was laid out at the foot of the *castellum.* In a short time the entire life of the city was Romanized, including the arts and crafts, the language, and the economy. The regional autonomy and characteristic indigenous culture disappeared. When the Roman

129. The Torre Civica (24 in Figure 128) built in 1690. It replaced an older medieval gate tower.

130. View of Este, showing the characteristic linear layout of the city with the main streets running parallel to each other.

Empire fell and Este was destroyed by Attila, the inhabitants fled to Monselice, Chioggia, and Rialto (Venice), and what had been a flourishing Roman city sank into oblivion.

Around the year 1000 Este began to revive under the lordship of the House of Este, one of the oldest of the reigning families of Italy. The rulers bore the title of Marquis of Italy— that is, of Margrave of the Empire, *Marchio Sancti Imperii*. The urban area spread toward the east of the former Roman city. Three nuclei, the so-called *terzieri*, developed: S. Tecla, S. Martino, and S. Pietro. These suburbs were originally isolated entities connected with the urban center only by narrow, sparsely inhabited tentacles. Later expansions included the Borgo Nuovo, the Borgo S. Stefano, the Borgo di Torre, and the Borgo S. Fermo, all grouped around the central area with the castle and finally enclosed by strong fortifications with a terreplein, eight towers, and a moat.

Under Venetian rule (1405-1797) a lively building activity set in. Civic edifices, churches and monasteries, and villas of Venetian patricians were erected. The city expanded in all directions. Agriculture flourished, and the arts and crafts revived. From the beginning of the 18th to the present century the urban area remained more or less the same, and only minor alterations were executed.

Verona. The fortifications of old Verona belong to five different periods. There were the walls built by Gallienus (A.D. 260 to 268); the walls on the left bank of the Adige, probably constructed during the reign of Charlemagne; the walls of the Scaligers, the ruling family of Verona during the Middle Ages; and the walls designed and erected by Michele Sanmicheli

131. An old map of Verona, showing part of the city and the river bend. The regular Roman layout is clearly visible even in this greatly simplified representation.

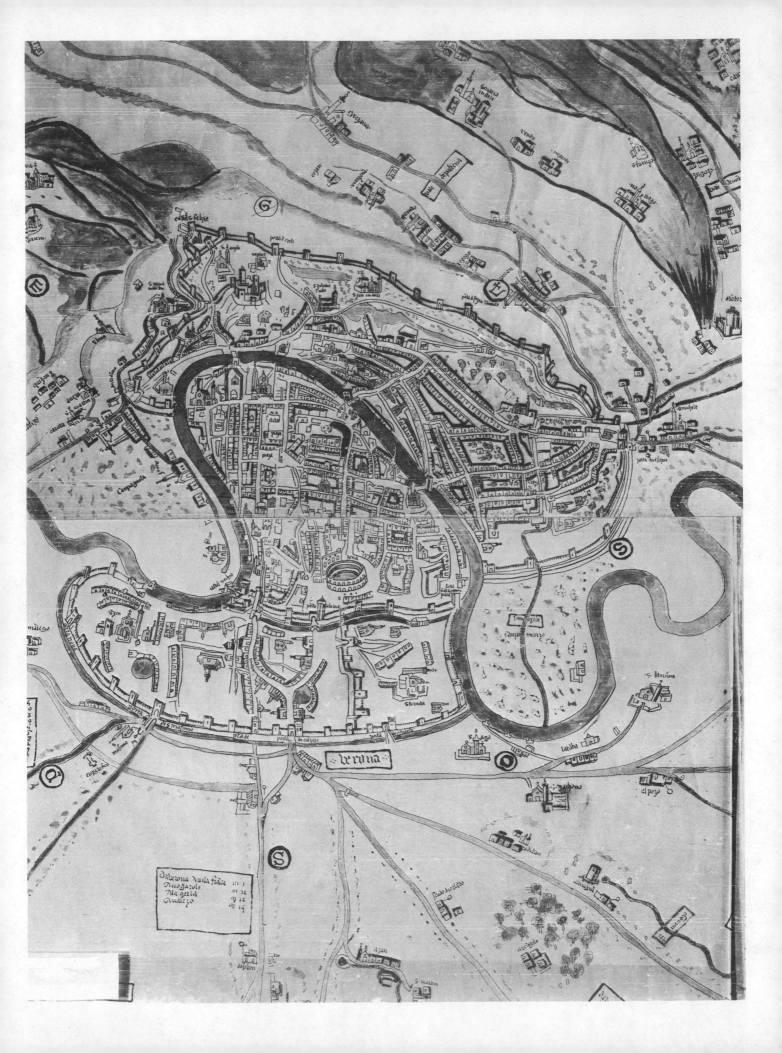

132. *Opposite:* Verona in 1439, from a large map comprising the whole of Verona in the Archivio di Stato di Venezia. The combination of the natural protection by the river and the man-made defenses provided by the walls enclosing the districts outside the river bend shows the strategic importance of the place. The medieval walls are simple, strengthened only by towers and strong gates; they follow, at least in part, the configuration of the terrain, forming in certain sections a double line of defense.

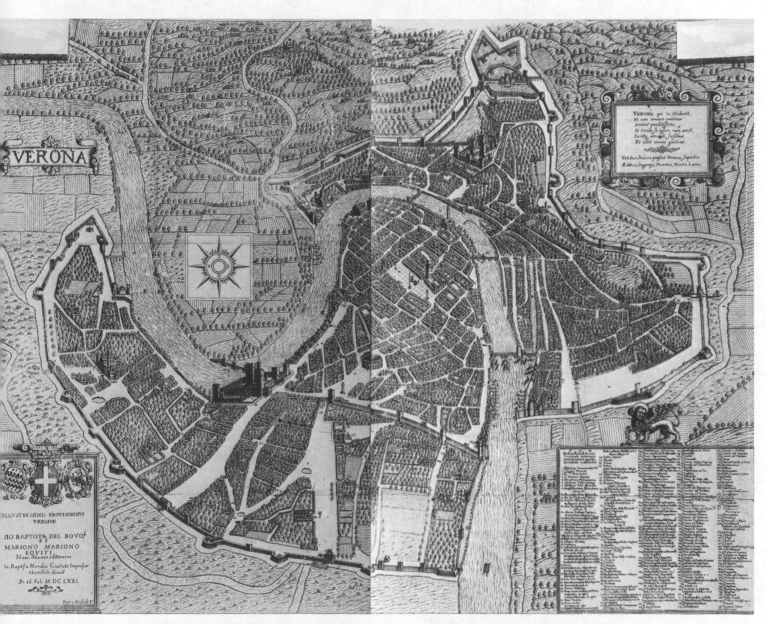

133. Verona in 1671. The circumference has not greatly changed. The course of the fortifications follows to a considerable degree the line of the medieval walls, but the *enceinte* is now strengthened by bastions, ravelins, and other defense works. The castle stands on the river. *Fora*, the squares, are distributed over the town, and the double lines of fortifications have been preserved.

241

134. Piazza delle Erbe, the old *forum*, with the tower of the city hall at the corner. The huge white umbrellas over the market stalls almost hide the fountain in the center, as well as the *tribuna;* the latter served in the Middle Ages as the site where the newly elected *Capitano del Popolo* was publicly invested with his office and sentences of condemned criminals were delivered.

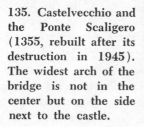

135. Castelvecchio and the Ponte Scaligero (1355, rebuilt after its destruction in 1945). The widest arch of the bridge is not in the center but on the side next to the castle.

(1484-1559) after 1527, with bastions and other contemporary improvements. In modern times Verona was strongly fortified by the Austrians in 1814 as one of the famous quadrilateral formed by the fortresses of Mantua, Peschiera, Legnago, and Verona.[44]

The valley of the Adige from the Dolomites to the low country, between the exit of the river from the mountains and the swamps of the plain, is relatively narrow. This together with the situation of Verona at the fall line, that is, at a point where the Adige passes from the rocky zone to a more gentle course in the lowland, makes the city a particularly im-

44. For early and Roman Verona, cf. p. 187.

portant focus and strategical center. Verona stands in the middle of the region that stretches in a great semicircle from the west to the Venetian plain in the east as the guardian of the route over the Brenner—a position that explains why, throughout the centuries, its rulers paid the greatest attention to the strength of the fortifications. Like many other fortress towns its growth was constricted by the girdle of the walls and, in this special case, by the naturally strong protection of the Adige flowing in a wide bend around the urban area. Nature and man worked together to make Verona an almost impregnable stronghold in a politically singularly sensitive location.

Trento. The remote origin of Trento dates back to an Ibero-Ligurian settlement on or at the isolated Doss Trento, the site of the later Roman *Verruca,* rising on the right bank of the Adige to a height of over 300 feet above the city.[45] This was, in all probability, the cradle of the Roman *Tridentum* that grew up on the left bank of the Adige at an important

45. Information partly supplied by Signor Antonio Zieger.

meeting point of roads from west to east across the Val Sugana and Giuducarie. According to an inscription of the year 23 B.C., the site was occupied by the Romans about 40 B.C. and fortified to guard a bridge and a ferry connecting both banks of the river. The center, on the left bank of the Adige, developed rapidly, furthered by its location on the *Via Claudia Augusta Padana,* continuing as the Atesian road eastward to *Atesis* (Stelvio Pass). In the

Tabula Clesiana (A.D. 46) *Tridentum* was recorded as *"splendidum municipium"* and as a flourishing *"colonia Romana."* It was the northernmost *municipium* of the tenth region of Italy and the most important urban center on the route from Verona to *Augusta Vindelicorum* (Augsburg). Originally the territory of *Tridentum* was not large. Toward the end of the fourth century it began to expand following upon the missionary work of S. Vigilio, whose activities extended to the regions of Verona and Brescia, thus laying the foundations for its territorial inclusion in the future diocese comprising this northern frontier zone.

In the barbarian invasions the eastern part of the city was destroyed. The inhabitants fled and huddled around the *Verruca*. Theodoric, who considered the Doss Trento as *"munimina Italiae et claustra provinciae,"* as "bulwark of Italy and key of the province," exhorted the people to build houses and to surround the place with solid walls. After the return of more peaceful times the eastern part of the city was rebuilt and became the center of the region and the fortified focus of the frontier zone. In A.D. 774 Trento was made the capital of the *Marca Tridentina,* and with the help of the ducal court its commercial and economic activities were developed as befitted an important city in so strategical a position as Trento on the arterial road from Germany to Italy through the valley of the Adige. In A.D. 952 the city and the surrounding region were incorporated in the Holy Roman Empire. In 1127 Trento was elevated to the capital of the episcopal principality that extended as far as Pontealto in the Engadine.

New walls were built in 1212-1215 enclosing a larger area for the greatly increased population that had begun to settle in Trento in connection with the opening of silver mines in the neighborhood. In the 15th century comprehensive urban renewal took place. Streets were straightened, wooden arcades removed to permit the widening of many roads, new houses erected and decorated with murals, and churches and palaces built even outside the walls. The modernization of the city continued in the 16th century, stimulated by the selection of Trento as the seat of the Ecumenical Council (1545-1563). To this event Trento owed its world-wide fame, ranking it almost among the political capitals of Europe, and also its economic prosperity and renown as a center of handicrafts and the arts. In the 18th century this upward trend continued, supported by a prospering agriculture and viticulture, by the establishment of silk and lumbering industries, and the growing influx of artisans and craftsmen attracted by the favorable economic conditions the city could offer.

In 1814 the Trentino was annexed to the Austrian province of Tirol. In 1919 it was reunited with Italy.

136. Map of Trento in 1580 showing the semicircular fortifications based on the Adige, the rather regular layout of the interior with the two foci, the castle and the cathedral, and numerous open spaces toward the periphery.

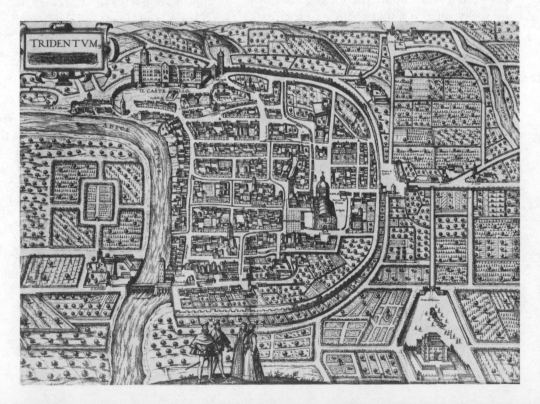

244

137. View of Trento against the background of the mountains. Numerous towers of churches and public and private buildings rise above the low houses of the burghers. The extension of the urban area is more or less the same as a hundred years ago. The picture of the city is somewhat distorted, not entirely congruent with its actual shape. Engraving of 1680.

Como. Como stands at the southern end of the western inlet of the Lake of Como. About a pre-Roman occupation of the region no reliable data are available. The Romans under the Consul M. Claudius Marcellus arrived in 196 B.C., conquered the *Insubres* and *Comenses* and erected on the site of the *Comum oppidum,* inhabited by Celtic tribes—mentioned by Livy (*Ab Urbe Condita,* XXXIII)— their new city which they called *Novum Comum,* laid out on the usual ground plan of a *castrum* walled in on all four sides. In the times of Caesar, who sent 5,000 colonists to settle there in 59 to 58 B.C., another larger town was established whose walls enclosed an area of about 61.8 acres. This may have been the third circumvallation since the existence of a pre-Roman, walled-in, smaller settlement cannot be ruled out. Traces of these first walls have been discovered about 9 feet under the present level of the city. Much later, in the 12th and 13th centuries, new walls were constructed enclosing a larger area. This medieval town was called *città murata,* the walled-in city, retaining the essential characteristics of the regular Roman layout still evident today. Roman

Comum had jurisdiction over a wide region extending, in the north, to the Alpine watershed and, in the south, to the *municipia* of *Bergomum* (Bergamo) and *Mediolanum* (Milan).

As the starting point for the journey over the much frequented Spluga (Splügen) and Julier Passes *Comum's* favorable development was assured. It was endowed with temples, baths, a *forum,* and a theater, splendid arcades, and a library—and, on its outskirts, *villae* of merchants and patricians, stately tombs, and votary altars dotted the countryside and the shores of the lake. In brief, *Comum* became a typical provincial town with all the attributes regarded by the Romans as indispensable for spreading their influence and culture over conquered races. Very early in its history the two suburbs of *Vico,* later Borgo Vico, and of *Coloniola* grew up giving the urban area the shape of a "crab," of an *urbs cancrina,* mentioned in a hymn as early as A.D. 533.

Christianity reached Como in the fourth century. In 1127 the city was sacked by the Milanese, who almost razed it to the ground, with the exception of the religious buildings.

245

It was rebuilt under Frederick Barbarossa. New fortifications with strong towers were constructed about 30 feet beyond the old walls, and a castle on Mt. Baradello was erected as added protection against new attacks. *Extra moenias,* outside the walls, in the direction to Milan, the suburb of Porta Torre di Milano or S. Bartolomeo was formed, changing the shape of the town from that of a "crab" to one of a "lobster," a similarity retained until the middle of the 19th century.

The internecine struggles among the contesting factions which, during the 12th century fought for the control of the city, led to the erection of numerous residential towers that not only changed the architectural character of the palaces of the nobles to private fortresses but turned the skyline of the city into a thicket of threatening symbols of violence and discord. At about the same time the civic center moved from the site of the ancient *forum* in the center of the walled-in urban area to the lakefront, where a harbor was constructed east of the bishop's palace (1225). This new center was enclosed within the fortifications around 1335. When this harbor proved to be insufficient, a second harbor was created approximately in the middle of the lakefront—that is, equidistant from the two walls running down to the lake. Considerable danger to the city was caused by the bridge of Lecco, built in 1335, at the point where the Adda leaves the lake. This resulted in a rise of the water level of about 6 feet and forced the municipality to build up the ground level especially close to the edge of the lake, where the buildings had been partly submerged by the water.

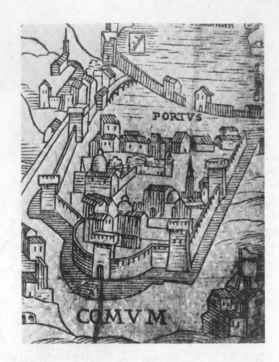

139. View of Como, showing the walls, the harbor, and the symbolic indication of the interior with houses and churches. From *Larii Lacus Descriptio* by Paolo Giovio (1559). (*Larius* was the old name of Lago di Como.)

When Como was incorporated in the dukedom of Milan, the fortifications lost their military importance. The moats were filled in and turned into gardens (1442), but at the beginning of the following century were again filled with water by the French, who restored, improved, and extended the walls, demolishing houses for this purpose and making Como a strong fortress. Many new buildings, palaces, churches and convents, and numerous dwell-

138. View of *Comum Civitas Lombardie.* In the background, crowning the hill, the castle of Baradello and at its foot a church, probably the Church of S. Carpoforo. This view of Como is particularly interesting as a symbolic representation of The City. The walls are the main characteristic of urban life, the manifestation of the sphere of law, security, and order. Without walls no city was worth the name. The *civitas* makes man free and releases him from the recklessness and lawlessness of the countryside. The right to build walls was one of the most precious privileges of the Middle Ages. This view of Como expresses in its primitive simplicity the idea of the city, the superior status of the citizens, and the material and symbolic importance of the walls. From the *Supplementum Chronicarum* by Fra Jacopo Filippo da Bergamo (1490).

ing houses were erected in the course of the 14th to the 16th centuries. The population increased from 11,000 inhabitants (2,048 families) to almost 16,000, of whom about half lived within the walled city and the rest in the suburbs. Under Spanish rule in the 17th century a general decline set in. The number of citizens decreased, the government of the city deteriorated, the wool and silk industries suffered; in addition the Black Death of 1630 together with floods which destroyed many houses, decimated the population. This situation was remedied by the Austrian administration. Commerce revived; the wool and silk industries were restored, and people returned to the city. In 1790 the fortifications were finally dismantled; the moats were filled in and replaced by a wide tree-lined boulevard encircling the urban area. Marshy tracks were reclaimed for public gardens. The foundations for a vigorous industrial progress were laid, stimulating the increase of the population and the growth of the city. The first comprehensive development plan was worked out in 1855.

140. View of Como (1630–40), showing the main features of the ancient Roman layout, the unusually high towers of the fortifications, the still rather low building density, some of the churches, and the harbor in the center of the lakefront. Painting possibly by G. P. Recchi in the Episcopal Palace.

141. View of Como with the suburbs grown up around small parish churches. From *Teatro delle Città e Porti Principali* by V. Coronelli (1698).

247

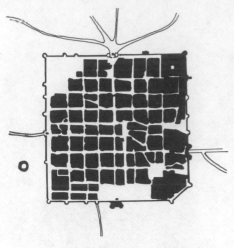

142. Roman Torino.

Torino (Turin). Turin's geographical position in the center of Piedmont—at the mouth of the principal valleys of the Piedmont Alps, on the left bank of the Po, and at its confluence with the Dora Riparia—has been a fundamental factor in its origin and development.[46] The *Colli Torinesi* on the right bank of the Po and the Po itself have always presented a formidable obstacle to communication between southern and northern Piedmont; but in the neighborhood of Turin communications are easy for a short tract of flat land between the amphitheater of Rivoli, formed by morainic deposits, and the hills. It was here on this stretch of flat country hardly more than seven miles wide, that Turin was founded. The topographical conditions have made Turin a "city of the Plain." Limited on the north by the Dora and on the east by the

46. For the following, ample use has been made of the publication by P. Gribaudi, "Lo sviluppo edilizio di Torino dall' epoca romana ai giorni nostri," *Torino*, No. 8, August 1933.

143. Torino in 1572. Engraving by G. Caracha.

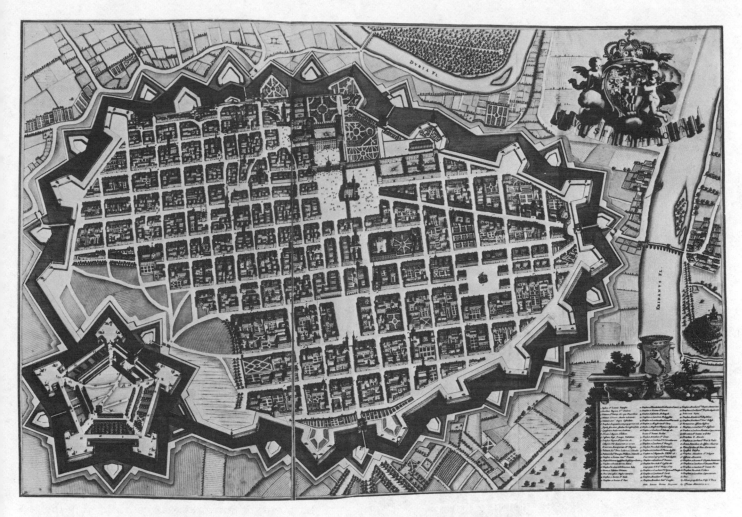

144. Torino in 1680. Plan designed by Borgonio for the *Theatrum Statuum Regiae Celsitudinis Sabaudiae*, Amsterdam 1682.

Po, Turin occupies a strong natural position owing to its elevated situation. The terrace on which it stands slopes down to the Po: The periphery of the city, on the *stradale di Francia,* is almost 850 feet above sea level; the Piazza Castello about 720 feet; the Piazza Vittorio Veneto and the bridge over the Po about 670 feet. The drop from the highest point of the urban area to the lowest point in the east, the median level of the Po, is approximately 207 feet. This configuration of the terrain had a far-reaching influence upon the industrial development of the city: a great quantity of water power was always available through the numerous canals from the Dora and Stura. Although the terrain of Turin seems to be perfectly flat, toward the east it is sloping down to the Po in slight and wide undulations, a

feature particularly evident in the streets closest to and parallel with the Po.

Turin was founded by the Ligurian tribe of the *Taurini* on the site it has occupied throughout its history. After the death of Caesar in 44 B.C., the *Triumviri* conferred Roman citizenship upon the inhabitants and named the town *Colonia Julia Taurinorum.* In 28 to 27 B.C. Augustus elevated it to *Colonia Augusta Taurinorum.* The city was laid out on the usual checkerboard system modeled on that of the Roman *castrum.* The rectangular area, surrounded by walls, was divided into four parts by the *cardo maximus* or *principalis* leading to the *Porta principalis dextra* at the south and the *Porta principalis sinistra* at the north, and by the *decumanus maximus,* the *via maior* or *praetoria,* crossing the former at

249

right angles, with the *Porta Praetoria* at the east and the *Porta Decumana* at the west. The *insulae*, divided by *cardines* and *decumani*, corresponded to the encampments of the various army divisions. The *praetorium* or *curia* was placed in the center of the city, not near the *Porta Praetoria* as in a *castrum*. The walls had a length of 9,435 feet, and the urban area covered 13.06 acres, equal to 180 Roman *jugeri*. Roman Turin was, therefore, larger than Aosta or Rimini, almost of the same size as Bologna, two-thirds smaller than Milan, and about one-seventh the size of Aurelian Rome. At intervals of 225 feet, strong towers rose; five

145. Torino in the 19th century.

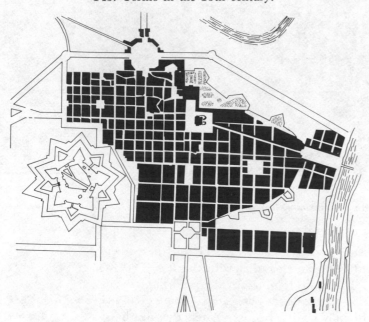

146. Torino today.

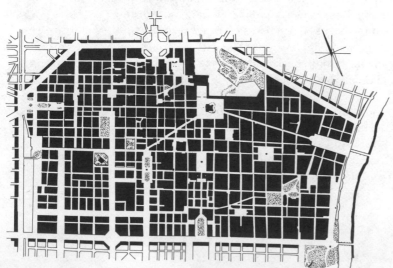

protected the corners of the walls, two each major gate, seven the southern side, and six each the other three sides except the northeast. The streets were 15 to 24 feet wide, including the raised sidewalks for pedestrians, and were paved with large slabs of gneiss. The houses, at first small and with only one story, were built of pebbles from the Stura laid in lime; later they were better constructed and larger. The confines of the Roman walled, rectangular city remained the same until the 17th century; even when the walls were reconstructed in the 16th century the *Cittadella* or "fortress" was regarded as representing the true circumference of the city.

In the Middle Ages suburbs grew up around churches and convents such as San Donato and Colleasco in the west; the suburbs of the Porta Doranea around the church of San Giorgio in Val d'Oc, and of San Biagio dei Crociferi and San Lorenzo in the north. In the 11th century the Roman walls were reinforced. The chronicler della Novalesa, writing in the middle of the 11th century, recorded that Bishop Annulo *"fuerat haec siquidem civitas condensissimis bene redimita, turribus, et arcus in circuitu per totum deambulatoriis cum propugnaculis desuper atque antemuralibus.*[47] Barbicans or outworks were constructed in the 14th century, and two bastions were added in 1461. In 1467 the defenses were again improved, and in 1537 strengthened once more during the French occupation. At about the same time, in the 16th century, the first modern bastion, called *degli Angeli,* later *Santa Giustina* and then *San Lorenzo,* was constructed in the northeast of the city, accessible only from the *Castello.* The improvements continued during the following decades.

From the French domination Turin emerged weakened and humiliated. The court, the senate, the university, and other public institutions had left the city. However, in a few years the community recovered and Cardinal Bonelli, the papal legate, could report to Pius V that Turin was

47. "It was indeed an extremely well-built city, with numerous towers encircling it, archways all about it, and passageways with ramparts above them and protecting walls."

147. Piazza San Carlo in the 18th century. Painting in the Museo Civico, Torino.

a city of 5,000 hearths and 30,000 souls, densely populated, with two to three families living in one house. It is not ugly though one does not see many palaces and the houses are not very beautiful. The small Dora passes almost through the whole city, along the middle of the street, leaving the sides dry, and helping to keep the city cool and clean.

The ruler, Duke Emanuele Filiberto, immediately set out "to adorn the city with ornate buildings considering that this would be of the greatest importance to the greatness of the city." In 1573 he issued a decree permitting

every person, who has a house or site in Turin and wants to improve and to embellish his possession with a noble and respectable building, to compel his neighbor to sell him part of his house or land necessary for the execution of the work, paying only the assessed price plus one quarter though with the obligation to begin building within a year and to finish it within three.

This ambitious plan proved to be a failure owing to the poor economic conditions which anybody with more insight would have taken into account. As a man of war, Filiberto was insensitive to everything outside his narrow field of vision: ostentation and power were his main preoccupations. Even if his plan had materialized, it would have helped only the well-to-do. He apparently never realized that the lot of the common people and their miserable housing conditions should have first claim upon public assistance. It was therefore not surprising that he was more interested in fortifying his city, a task not wholly unjustified since France and Spain had never made a secret of their hostile intentions. Consequently he ordered the construction of three new bastions and commissioned Francesco Paciotto di Urbino in 1563 to do the work. Paciotto applied in practice the theoretical principles

251

of Giorgio Martini, the great Italian military engineer and inventor of the so-called *fronte bastionato*. In 1574 the Venetian ambassador reported to the senate: "The duke is justified when he speaks of the *cittadella* as the most beloved matter and the most precious jewel in his treasury." The fortifications were indeed the glory of Italian military engineering and served as a model for many modern fortresses all over Europe.

With the construction of the new *enceinte* Turin lost its ancient rectangular shape, although *"la vera e propria città"* always remained for the citizens the core enclosed within the Roman walls beyond which it did not grow until the next century. Then, under Carlo Emanuele I as capital of a strong, disciplined and united state loyal to its dukes and kings, Turin became the political, intellectual, and economic center of Piedmont, and expanded rapidly. The first architect entrusted with the design for his "New City" by the duke (1606) was Ascanio Vittozzi. He was succeeded by Carlo di Castellamonte, a military engineer, and later by his son Amedeo di Castellamonte, who died in 1683. All build-

ings and development schemes of any importance in Turin were designed and, as far as they were executed, supervised by these three architects between 1585 and 1683. Their work, strongly influenced by Francesco Borromini and Giovanni Lorenzo Bernini—though by no means of the same high quality—and directed by duke Carlo Emanuele I, changed Turin from an overcrowded city with narrow winding streets to a provincial metropolis, dignified in appearance, and laid out in accordance with preconceived plans. Turin became the city of squares which we know today.

But whether this was an actual aesthetic and social improvement may be debatable. The spontaneous variety, the small-scale intimacy, and the personal immediacy disappeared. Rigidity, regimentation, repetition, and large-scale and uniform architectural compositions became the order of the day. The era of the *l'état c'est moi* spirit, of ostentation and hollow grandeur was approaching. The first project was the rebuilding of the Piazza Castello after a design by Vittozzi and begun in 1606. Two years later, in honor of the wedding of his two daughters, the duke ordered the con-

148. **Piazza San Carlo in 1721. Engraving after a design by Juvara in the Museo Civico, Torino.**

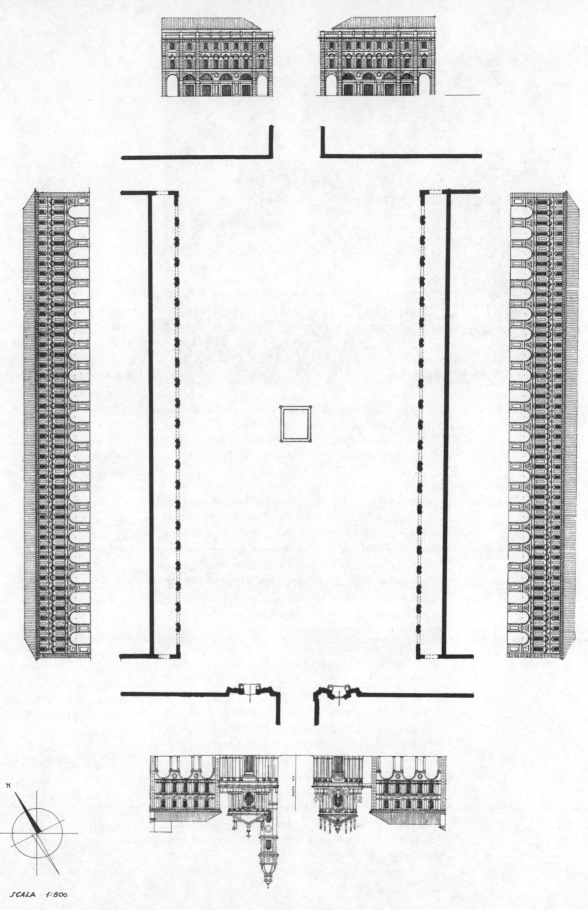

SCALA 1:500

PIAZZA SAN CARLO

149. Plan of the Piazza San Carlo and of the surrounding buildings.

150. Piazza Castello at Torino after the design by Ascanio Vittozzi. Engraving from the *Theatrum Statuum Regiae Celsitudinis Sabaudiae*, 1682.

struction of arcades, surmounted by a continuous balcony, in front of the houses around the whole circumference of the *piazza*. This initial step was followed in 1612 by a decree permitting the owners of the buildings to add two stories on top of the arcades, all conforming with their windows, balconies, and decorations to a design by Vittozzi but with the obligation to transfer the arcades to public ownership.

The so-called Via Nuova, now renamed Via Roma, was regulated and became the main artery of the "New City," and the Porta Nuova, later called Porta Marmorea, originally built in wood, was reconstructed after a design by Carlo di Castellamonte. The new district, in the southern part of the city, contained ten building blocks and was afterward enclosed by five bastions (1632). In 1620 the "New City" was inaugurated with a great ceremony. A splendid procession, led by the duke and the prince, clerical dignitaries, the municipal authorities, and the Venetian ambassador, set out from the Piazza Castello to the "*strada nuova* and entered the 'New City'

through the *Porta di San Carlo*. Thus the 'New City' was inaugurated with music, to the sound of trumpets, drums and flutes, and to the accompaniment of a salute from eight cannons."[48]

In the following year a *Magistrato delle Fabbriche* was established, meeting once every week to discuss and supervise the building program. But continuous wars that impoverished Piedmont and especially Turin interfered with the duke's ambitious plans. He was accordingly obliged to have recourse to granting ample privileges and exemptions as incentives to all those who despite the economic difficulties were willing to take an active part in the rebuilding of the capital. Consequently in 1621 an edict was issued listing twelve privileges, among them the immediate naturalization of foreigners, certain financial alleviations in respect to debts incurred for private reasons, the permission for merchants and artisans to exercise their profession with special registration, and a number of other incentives in connection with the building of new houses. However, these advantages were counterbalanced by the obligation that "all new constructions should keep to the design of the Consigliere Conte di Castellamonte," a regulation that imposed the style of one single architect upon the whole building activity of the city.

Vittorio Amedeo I continued the work of his father. In 1633 the *Regolamento per la misura delle fabbriche* was issued, stipulating that only architects of established reputation and admitted by the *primo ingegnere* Carlo Castellamonte were to be entrusted with work in the "New City," and that all buildings fronting on to the Via Roma should have uniform façades with shops on the ground floor, a second story with identical windows, a third story with decorated windows and cartouches, and a top story surmounted by a simple cornice. Why particularly qualified architects were needed for this regimented uniformity is not quite comprehensible.

Similar regulations were applied to other

48. Archivio Comunale di Torino. *Ordinati,* Vol. 171, 7 dic., 1620.

parts of the city. The Madama Reale, Christina di Francia, took special interest in the building of the Piazza San Carlo or Piazza Reale, Following the established rule and the taste of the time, she ordered all façades of the surrounding houses to be of the same design prescribed by Carlo Castellamonte. In order to avoid any difficulties she granted concessions for large tracts of the adjoining terrain to a banker, a nobleman, a general, and other wealthy people, who could be relied upon to adhere to the prescribed design and to make the most of this remunerative business. This was neither surprising nor blameworthy. The society of this period rested securely on the principle of "the two nations," the wealthy and the poor. Montesquieu expressed this general condition when he wrote: *"Il faut bien qu'il y ait du luxe. Si les riches n'y dépensent pas beaucoup, les pauvres mourront de faim."*

The Piazza San Carlo is considered to be one of the most beatiful squares of Europe. It is undeniably an interesting example of Baroque planning; it has undoubtedly a certain elegance and dignity; it is the perfect expression of the architectural ideas and ideals of the time. But it is open to doubt whether these qualities justify ranging it with the really great creations—the Piazza di S. Pietro, the ensemble of squares at Nancy, the Plaza Mayor at Salamanca, the squares around the cathedral at Santiago de Compostela, or the unpretentious yet wonderful squares in nu-

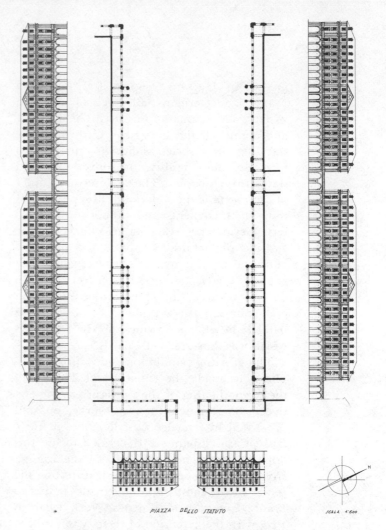

PIAZZA DELLO STATUTO   SCALA 1:500

151. Plan of the Piazza dello Statuto in Torino surrounded by uniform houses.

152. Piazza Castello with Palazzo Reale and Palazzo Madama in the 17th century. Engraving by G. Tasnière in the Museo Civico, Torino.

merous small towns of Spain, Italy, England, France, and Germany, all jewels of intimacy, variety, and dramatic intricacy. The elegance and dignity of the Piazza San Carlo were the trappings of a society suffocating in its own formality and rigidity, its conventions and standardized habits. The architectural order of the *piazza* is the order of dead repetition of individual elements and proportions, of external symmetry reaching its climax in the two identical churches flanking the main axis at one end of the square. The rectangular area is about 505 feet long and 228 feet wide. In order to conceal the many projecting garrets and chimneys Juvara planned a continuous balustrade on the cornice of the buildings which was, however, only partly executed.

The growing population and political complications made the extension of Turin and the strengthening of the fortifications imperative. A development plan was worked out and submitted by Amedeo Castellamonte in 1656. Duke Carlo Emanuele II decided to use this opportunity to make his capital the leading city of Italy, the seat of public institutions, the center of the most important roads leading to France, and a strong fortress. Work began in 1673 with the extension of the city toward the Po, and two years later regulations were issued permitting the owners of new buildings a certain freedom in the decoration of their houses but retaining the provision that they should be three stories high. However, in general the principle of uniformity and repetition was maintained. Palaces, churches, and an arsenal

were erected, and the fortifications were improved.

After the war with France, in which Turin was considerably damaged (1706), Filippo Juvara, the disciple of Carlo Fontana, was called in as architect and adviser. Though numerous plans and buildings can be attributed to him, the general trend towards regimented architecture continued with but a few minor exceptions. At the beginning of the second half of the 18th century the dismantling of the Roman walls began. A Congress of Architecture was convened in 1779 to consider the state of the buildings, the width and possible realignment of the streets, and other problems of public interest. Its recommendations were submitted to the government but the great time of Turin was over and nothing spectacular resulted from this Congress.

The population of the city, which had grown to 94,000 in 1791, decreased to 65,000 in 1808. After the battle of Marengo (1800) Napoleon ordered the demolition of the fortifications. Following the close of the Napoleonic Wars the areas of the demolished fortifications were used for the construction of new residential districts. During the 19th century several extensions took place and internal ameliorations—the paving of streets, the improvement of the water supply and sewerage system—were set in motion. Slum clearance was begun in 1885, and by the end of the century Turin had assumed the appearance and the structure of an open and monotonous modern city.

153. **Map of Genoa and the surrounding territory.**

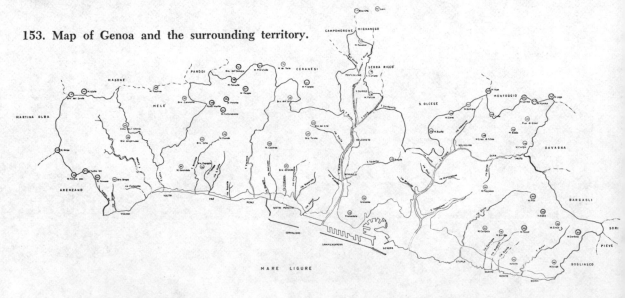

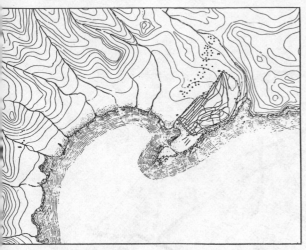

154. Pre-Roman Genoa.

Genova (Genoa). If one were to draw a dividing line between the Ligurian Alps and the Ligurian Apennines, the mountain pass of Giovi (1,386 feet) would be the most correct point. Between Savona and Genoa the slopes are steep but the hills are generally rounded. The arc of the mountain ranges forms a wide curve following the coastline around the territory of Genoa bordered on the west by the Cerusa and Leiro rivers, and further west by the Lupara, separating it from the small community of Arenzano. The most important watercourse is the Polcevera rising at the Giovi Pass and receiving the Verde River near Ponte-

decimo. There are very few flat areas along the coastal zone. The land is mostly rugged and hilly and the majority of the urban centers are situated at the mouths of the valleys. Their population is engaged in industrial, commercial, and maritime activities. Genoa, the focal point of the region, lies at the most northerly deep-water bay of the coast, separated from the Po Valley by the narrow ranges of the Apennines, and protected by them toward the north. In antiquity the *Via Julia Augusta*, running parallel to the coast and later called *Via Francigena*, connected Genoa with the west, the *Via Postumia* with the north, and the *Via Aemilia* with the south. The scarcity of cultivable land and of raw materials for industry turned the energies and the interests of the Genoese people in their search for expansion and economic opportunities toward the sea. As early as the 11th century they established trading posts in Syria and Palestine; they traded with Southern France, Barcelona, and Islamic Spain, with North Africa, and Sicily; they established colonies on the Aegean Sea and the Black Sea; and around 1300, they made pioneering voyages to the Channel ports of Bruges and London.

According to medieval legends Genoa was founded by Janus (Giano), son of Saturnus,

155. Roman Genoa.

1 - Porta di Sant'Andrea
2 - Via Ravecca
3 - Salita del Prione
3 - Discesa alla Marina di Sarzano
5 - Piazza Sarzano
6 - Chiesa di Sant'Agostino
7 - Chiesa di San Donato
8 - Vico Vegetti
9 - Piazza San Silvestro
10 - Piazza S. M. in Passione
11 - Via di Mascherona
12 - Quadrivio di Valoria su Canneto il Lungo
13 - Via di Santa Croce
14 - Mura delle Grazie
15 - Torre Embriaci
16 - Santa Maria di Castello
17 - Via Giustiniani
18 - S. M. delle Grazie, già SS. Nazaro e Celso
19 - SS. Cosma e Damiano
20 - Piazza di San Giorgio
21 - Canneto il Curto
22 - La Ripa
23 - Il Mandraccio
24 - Molo Vecchio
25 - San Marco al Molo

156. Quarters around the Sarzano Hill. Reconstruction from a map of Genoa of 1656 preserved in the Palazzo Rosso.

258

king of Italy, who gave his name to Genoa (Giano—the gate of northern Italy—Genoa). Archeological studies have revealed that a pre-Roman settlement of the Ligurians existed on the site of the future Genoa, a hypothesis that has been confirmed by excavations in the *necropolis* of S. Andrea dating from the fifth and fourth centuries B.C. The first nucleus of the actual city was the hill of Sarzano, *Arx Jani,* rising as an isolated cone on the western side of the great arc of the hills opening to the sea and intersected by brooks and rivulets. This site was certainly chosen for its favorable defensive position and its proximity to the sea. Thus these two factors determined the character of the settlement as an *emporium* and an *oppidum,* as a trading center and a fortified place. The latter function was particularly evident in the layout of the streets crossing one another in the center and connecting it with the exits at the periphery, a system always regarded as especially adaptable to the needs of defense. The people traded with the Phoenicians, Carthaginians, and Gauls, using their favorable geographical situation as a bridge between the North and the South. We may assume that Ligurian Genoa was surrounded by two lines of concentric walls, remains from a temporary Bronze Age refuge that had preceded the *oppidum* on the same site. The land around the *oppidum* was owned by the people of Genoa and their neighbors, the Langenses—Viturii, living in the Polcevera Valley. Disputes about the rights of ownership seem to have arisen between them until a decision was made by arbitrators in 117 B.C., who determined the extension of the *ager privatus* and of the *ager poplicus* of the Langenses, obliging them to pay for the latter an annual rent to the *publicum Genuam.* The *ager compascuus,* the common pastures, was owned and used collectively by both parties. This arrangement was based on a sort of federal organization including colonies and *castella,* united for the defense of the market settlement against invaders from the sea. It was a concept of joint defense in the interest of the urban center that later was accepted as an integral principle of the constitution of the Italian communities of the Middle Ages.[49]

The layout of the earliest quarters around the Sarzano Hill can be deduced from the map of Genoa of the year 1656 preserved in the Palazzo Rosso, which may be regarded as the first detailed and reliable plan of the city. A careful investigation has shown that this map differs only in parts from the ancient layout of these quarters. The walls enclosed an elliptical area—doubtlessly corresponding to the earliest primitive *oppidum*—the longer axis measuring 750 feet and the shorter one 315 feet. This inner ring around the top of the hill was surrounded by a second *enceinte* on the slopes marking the confines of the Ligurian-Gallic settlement. As already mentioned, the main streets radiated from the center to the gates and then broke off, leading to springs that supplied water for the town. A decree of 1314 referred to this arrangement as *"extra murum civitatis in roche Sarzani ante portam civitatis."*[50] Thus the Ligurian town developed around a central fortified nucleus on the top of the Sarzano Hill. It was a flourishing place when Hannibal sacked it in 205 B.C. and a source of rich booty for him.

49. P. Barbieri. *Forma Genuae.* 1938. P. 8.
50. *Ibid.,* p. 10.

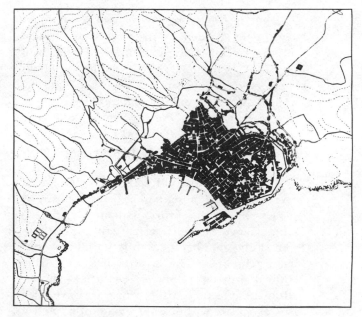

157. Genoa in 1200.

158. View of Genoa in 1581, showing in a greatly simplified manner the high building density in the ancient central part of the city and the many open spaces toward the periphery. The walls of 1536 are clearly visible in the foreground. Drawing by Antonio Lafréry (Rome 1573). Printed replica by Claudio Duchet.

Roman Genoa covered an area of about 28.4 acres divided by a checkerboard system of streets. The port was improved; the fortifications were modernized; public buildings were erected; and squares were laid out: the *Piazza Mercato* and the *Piazza Foro* outside the walls; and the *Piazza Pubblica*, the civic center, inside the walls—works that earned the Romans the recognition as *salvatores portus et moduli*.

Early Christian and Byzantine Genoa spread over an area of more than 52 acres enclosed by new walls (tenth century) without any appreciable change in the street pattern but with an increasing number of public buildings, especially churches. The growth of the city continued in the following centuries. In the Romanesque period the urban area extended to 133.5 acres within walls of almost 5,000 feet

circumference, and to 302 acres in the years from 1155 to 1600. New quarters along the shore grew up to the east and west of the old city. The new extensions were partly spreading toward the mountains, along the line of the *Thalweg* (the road through the valley) without resulting in better communications with the interior. Genoa remained a city oriented toward the sea. It would be wrong to assume that the extensions of these centuries and the reconstruction of the fortifications enclosed a densely populated area. On the contrary, there were large tracts of open spaces with cultivated fields and gardens and only thinly built-up districts.

In the 17th century Genoa's growth persisted. The urban area increased to over 2,224 acres, a development that continued steadily until modern times (7,940 acres in 1874) due,

260

especially in its later expansion, to industrialization, railway connections, and improvements of the port.

The history of Genoa was filled with wars and internal strife. In the 12th century she fought against the competition of Pisa that threatened her overseas commerce from Sardinia and Corsica, a conflict not decided in favor of Genoa until Pisa was finally and decisively beaten in the sea battle of Meloria (1284). Endless internal quarrels between the partisans of the Ghibellines and Guelphs, involving foreign powers, went on throughout the 14th and the following centuries, a plague not even the revolution of 1339—overthrowing the exclusive rule of the patricians and installing a doge for life—could bring to an end. The only steady element in this chaos was, characteristically, the *Banco di S. Giorgio,* the commercial bank, which might have been capable of stabilizing the situation and making Genoa a mercantile-aristocratic community if the great powers had "left her alone." Peace was eventually restored by the admiral of Charles V, Andrea Doria (1528). But the power of Genoa was already declining. The Turks conquered her colonies in the East; the French fleet bombarded the city (1684), and

imperial troops occupied Genoa in 1746 until they were expelled by a popular revolt. Napoleon abolished patrician rule and instituted the Ligurian Republic, to be handed over to France in 1805 and incorporated in the Kingdom of Sardinia in 1815.

Genoa is an instructive example of the distinguishing social factors which were instrumental in the formation of urban communities in Italy in contrast to the countries north of the Alps.[51] The city was respected as a space *sui generis* by the invaders, as a walled-in "container" with a special legal status superior to that of the countryside. The walls were the material and ideal symbol of the *civitas.* It was, therefore, more than a mere expediency if a conqueror destroyed the walls of a city that had opposed him; it was a deliberate and official act of degradation, a meaningful humiliation by reducing the city to the status of a *vicus,* that it should be called a village, *"vicos has civitates nominare praecepit."*[52] On the other hand, the *civitas* enjoyed the per-

51. G. Mengozzi. *La città italiana nell' alto medio evo. Il periodo langobardo-franco.* 1914. *Passim.*
E. Ennen. *Frühgeschichte der Europäischen Stadt.* 1933. Pp. 223-308. *Passim.*
52. *The Fourth Book of the Chronicle of Fredegar.* Cap. 71. Translated by J. M. Wallace-Hadrill. 1960.

159. Map of Genoa in 1656. The first detailed and official plan of the city showing the street system, many of the prominent sites, and the fortifications of 1536. The plan was executed by order of the *Padri del Comune* and used in 1785 as basis for the reconstruction of blighted areas. The design was made by the chief engineer Giacomo Brusco in 1785, using the preceding work of eight architects. The original from which this copy was made is in the Palazzo Rosso, Genoa.

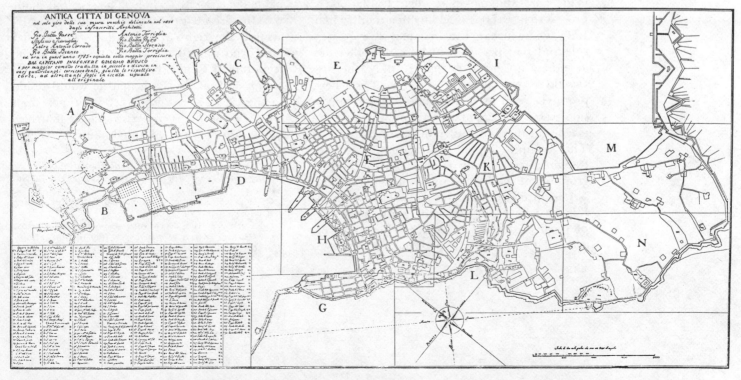

160. Map of Genoa in 1766 based on the work of Giacomo Brusco.

soñal and particular protection of the conqueror—if it had not resisted him—by acknowledging that it was an enclave where peace was guaranteed through a special legal conception. It was this concept of urban peace that was taken over by the Langobards and made part and parcel of their legislation, a process that was possible only in a country like Italy where urban life had played a greater role and had persisted to a much higher degree than in Central Europe. In Italy "the city was there"; it had not to be created as a new prototype, and its relationship to the countryside was a continuation of conditions recognized and more or less stabilized in antiquity. The beginning of the formation of urban communities in Italy is characterized by the grouping of the inhabitants in *vicinantiae* and *portae* in contrast to the *emporia* of Central Europe where the merchant guilds were the politically decisive element. The charter granted to the citizens of Genoa in A.D. 958

was addressed to *"omnibus nostris fidelibus et habitatoribus in civitate Januensi,"* making residence in the city the basis of the legal privilege that declared the house of every Genoese as immune.[53] The granting of such a privilege presupposed a collective body capable of acting as a whole. The essential point was that residence in the city automatically assured the right of citizenship. The feudal lord, who wanted to become a citizen of the Republic of Genoa, had to accept the *habitaculum* and take an oath that he would reside in the city, at least for a certain time: *"Ego ero habitator huius civitatis Janue."*[54] Further, the legally recognized inhabitants of Genoa

53. L. Schiaparelli. *I Diplomi di Ugo di Lotario di Berengario II e di Adalberto.* 1924. I, pp. 325 ff. No. XI.

C. Imperiale. *Codice Diplomatico della Repubblica di Genova.* 1936, No. 1, p. 3.

54. Oath for the acceptance as citizen of Genoa, 1138. *Historia Patriae Monumenta Liber iurium reipublicae Genuensis.* II, No. 1.

262

were guaranteed the undisturbed ownership of their land *infra et extra civitatem*. This meant that Genoa was a community dominated by agrarian interests or, in other words, that it was in its leading social strata a *synoicism* of feudal landowners, who administered their landed property from the city. This was in striking contrast to the social position of the feudal lords north of the Alps, who remained intimately connected with the rural life of their manors or their castles outside the cities. For the Italian noble it was merely a change of residence, not of status, when he settled in the city as a citizen. It is therefore not surprising that all accords of Genoa with subjugated nobles began with the obligation of the *habitaculum* and that they further include a stipulation to take part in the wars of the city with a certain number of soldiers, and the requirement that their children marry Genoese citizens.

The confirmation of the prescriptive law of the Genoese of the year 1056 reveals the already far-advanced mobilization of landed property inasmuch as numerous paragraphs refer to the acknowledgment of the sale of landed property, a clear indication of the tendency to[55] invest the proceeds in commerce. The changeover from the city as a cosettlement of landed and martial nobles to a mercantile city-state was a slow and gradual process that became more marked not before the 11th century when an increasing number of the patrician families of Genoa turned to mercantile activities. Their capital was accumulated not only from the sale of their land but also from their participation in the wars against the Saracens. From this small but important group of men originated the power élite whose members enjoyed the great advantage of a much better education and higher culture than their rural counterparts in the countries of Northern Europe. This superiority together with their financial influence put them in a strong position for the leading offices of the city-state. From their ranks the consuls were elected. In 1155 there were ten consuls in Genoa who directed the administration and who, in the course of time, became authoritarian rulers of their city-state, the leading bankers, merchants, and shipowners. This social class so characteristic of medieval Italy, with its ambitious individualism and its aggressive political partiality, was the main source of the political unrest which created an atmosphere conducive to internal strife, violence, delinquency, and suppression. Even if we ascribe a good deal of Dante's hatred of Genoa to his Florentine origin, to the apparently unavoidable eternal distrust between members of an out-group and an in-group, the curse, which he uttered against the Genoese, may have been not wholly unjustified.

> O Genoa, where hearts corrupt and rot,
> Lost to all decency! Will no man hound
> Thy whole tribe from the earth and
>   purge this blot?
>   (*Hell*. Canto XXXIII, 151)[56]

L. Curtius has excellently described the mentality out of which the clash between individualism and social conformity arose:

From this interweaving of the contrasts of natural sociability and egohood of the personality developed the Italian life of the Piazza, of the city, political party, and parliamentary struggle where individualism finds everywhere a far greater opportunity for its rhetorical, scheming talents soliciting clients and followers though subject to far more complex bonds than, for instance, in Germany or England.[57]

"Genuensis, ergo mercator." This was the essence of the credo of the wealthy Genoese. The lower classes were excluded from this lucrative business—as everywhere. A middle class that could have sustained and consolidated the economic activities and calmed down the political antagonism was almost totally missing.

The humbler and overpopulated quarters of Genoa have been vividly described by Dickens in all their stark reality, painfully contrasting with the opulence of the palaces and gardens of the patricians.

---

55. *Codice Diplomatico della Repubblica di Genova.* III. Pp. 6 ff.

56. The Penguin Classics. 1953.

57. L. Curtius. *Deutsche und Antike Welt.* 1950. P. 476.

The way lay through the main streets, but not through the Strada Nuova, or the Strada Balbi, which are the famous streets of palaces. I never, in my life, was so dismayed!

The wonderful novelty of everything, the unusual smells, the unaccountable filth (though it is reckoned the cleanest of Italian towns), the disorderly jumbling of dirty houses, one upon the roof of another; the passages more squalid and more close than any in Saint Gile's, or old Paris; in and out of which, not vagabonds, but well-dressed women, with white veils and great fans, were passing and repassing; the perfect absence of resemblance in any dwelling-house, or shop, or wall, or post, or pillar, to anything one had ever seen before; and the disheartening dirt, discomfort, and decay confounded me. I fell into a dismal reverie. I am conscious of a feverish and bewildered vision of saints and virgins' shrines at the street corners—of great numbers of friars, monks, and soldiers—of vast red curtains, waving at the door-ways of the churches—of always going up hill, and yet seeing every other street and passage going higher up—of fruit-stalls, with fresh lemons and oranges hanging in garlands made of vine leaves. . . . The majority of the streets are as narrow as any thoroughfare can well be, where people (even Italian people) are supposed to live and walk about; being mere lanes, with here and there a kind of well, or breathing-place. The houses are immensely high, painted in all sorts of colours, and are in every stage and state of damage, dirt, and lack of repair. They are commonly let off in floors, or flats, like the houses in the old town of Edinburgh, or many houses in Paris. There are few street-doors; the entrance halls are, for the most part, looked upon as public property, and any moderately enterprising scavenger might make a fine fortune by now and then clearing them out.[58]

58. Charles Dickens. *Pictures from Italy*. 1846. Pp. 9, 12.

161. Despite the passing of more than twenty centuries the original Roman checkerboard system has been preserved, as the plan of ancient *Ticinum*, superimposed upon that of present-day Pavia, shows. The *insulae* and small lots for houses only little more than 13 feet wide, and the ancient subdivision with 18 square, one-story houses on each side of the *insulae* can still be observed.

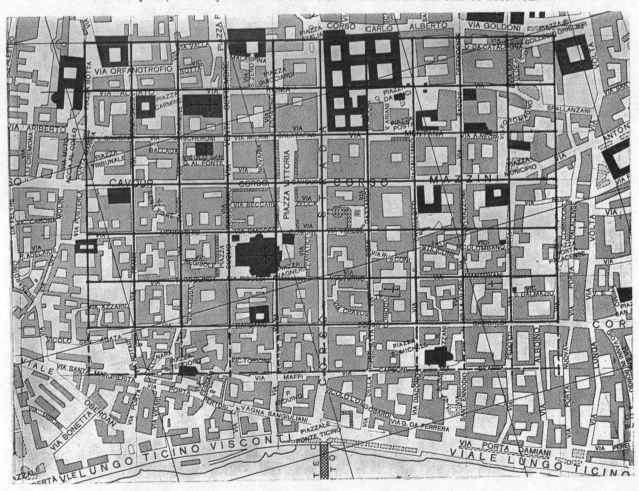

162. View of Pavia with the principal public buildings and numerous towers, but still without the bastioned walls, and groups of soldiers and horsemen. Mural in S. Teodoro attributed to Bernardino Lanzani.

Pavia. Pavia is situated on the left bank of the Ticino, about three miles above its junction with the Po. The site was particularly favorable for settlement. It had the double advantage of being protected from possible floods while at the same time using the river for navigation. Moreover, a terraced spur, jutting out from the surrounding terrain, made the crossing of the river at this point possible. It is probable that the site was occupied in neolithic times, judging from archeological discoveries. However, investigations have not yet been concluded and it is therefore still too early to decide how far these remains can be related directly to the origin of Pavia.[59] According to tradition reported by Livy, Pliny, and Ptolomy the ancient *Ticinum* was originally founded by the Celtic *Laevi* and *Maricii*. It was made a *municipium* about 23 B.C. and developed on a checkerboard plan.[60] Under Roman rule *Ticinum* was a nodal point of the

59. Excavations are conducted by Professor A. Stenico of the University of Milan.
60. G. A. Mansuelli. *I Cisalpini.* 1963.

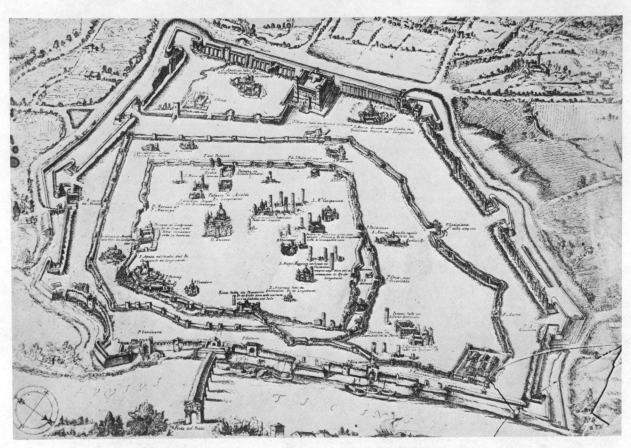

163. Map of Pavia within its threefold lines of fortifications and some of the public buildings and towers. Copy of a plan by the architect Bernardino Claricio in 1585.

North Italian road system and already an important town at the crossroads of the strategic routes from *Mediolanum* (Milano) to the Ligurian coast linking it through the *Via Postumia* to *Augusta Taurinorum* (Torino), *Placentia* (Piacenza), and *Laus Pompeia* (Lodi) and to *Brixia* (Brescia) at the foot of the Alps. The only memory of the Roman period that has survived the centuries is the checkerboard layout and remains of the sewerage system. The regular Roman plan was apparently greatly admired in the Middle Ages: The *archipoeta* of Frederick Barbarossa celebrated Pavia as *digna laudibus et topographia* evidently alluding to its geometrical structure. And later, in the 14th century, Opicinus de Canistris, who was commissioned to design a plan for Pavia, used for his work the exact

subdivision of the Roman layout.[61] His design confirms recent investigations by Professor G. Tibiletti of the University of Pavia, who was able to fix the exact measurements of the 80 squares, *iugeri,* which the Romans had applied symmetrically for the division of the urban area through the *cardo* and *decumanus.*

The successive extensions within the so-called Spanish fortifications of 1500 proceeded in three stages, as can be seen in the maps of Corte and Claricio, and were in large parts executed in the Middle Ages. What is usually called the *centro storico* of the city coincided with the course of the Spanish *enceinte* as defined in the time of Opicinus. Later modifica-

61. R. Salomon. "Aftermath to Opicinus de Canistris," *Journal of the Warburg and Courtauld Institutes,* XXV, 1962. *Passim.*

266

164. Map of Pavia at the end of the 16th century by Ludovico Corte.

tions were concerned with the extension of the outer defense system, the construction of the castle, the addition of bastions, and the adaption of the peripheral extensions to the Roman layout of the center city.

Ticinum was destroyed by Attila, rebuilt by Theodoric, and raised to the capital of the Lombard Kingdom under the name of *Papia,* probably of Celtic origin—*"quae alio nomine Papia appellatur."* (Paulus Diaconus II. 15.) It was the seat of government of the *"Regnum Italicum"* until the 12th century. The numerous towers of the nobility dominating the skyline of the city date back to the 11th and 12th centuries. These structures were built of brick with vents only for apertures; their primary function was defense and their symbolic value the demonstration of power, fearlessness, and

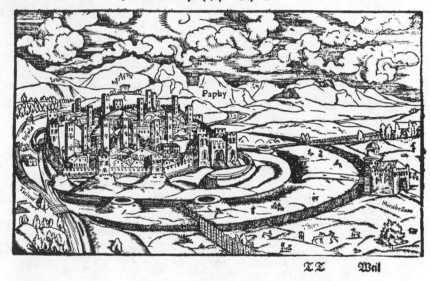

165. View of Pavia from the northeast with the Castello di Mirabello in the foreground and the Parco Visconteo. This rather imaginative representation is contained in the *Itinerarium Italiae* edited by Schott in 1610.

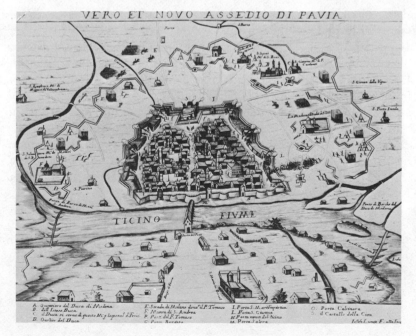

166. View of Pavia in 1658 during the siege by the French within the fortifications reconstructed by the Spaniards. Engraving by Jossefo Lunge after a design by Pauole.

267

167. View of Pavia from the south, with the walled-in suburb on the other bank of the river still showing the medieval character with modernized fortifications. Engraving of 1761–62 from *Lo stato presente di tutti i popoli*.

bellicosity. Other characteristic features of this period were the *voltone,* the big arches at the end of important streets which could be used to close entire quarters. Further, there were the so-called *xenodochii* of the monasteries serving as hospitals and as inns for the high dignitaries of the Church on their visit to Pavia. The population of Pavia in the 13th century is said to have numbered about 20,000 people. The castle, at the northwest of the urban area with an adjoining hunting park, begun in 1359 by Galeazzo Visconti, became

as the seat of the court one of the cultural centers of Europe. The university was founded in 1361 and the cornerstone for the *Certosa,* 5 miles from the city, was laid in 1396.

With the fall of the Duchy of Milan in 1525 began a period of decline for Pavia. Only the university upheld the fame of the past glory of the city. The major additions to the urban scene of the 16th century were the Ghislieri and Borromeo Colleges by Tibaldi (Pellegrino Pellegrini 1532-96) in cooperation with local architects.

Milano (Milan). Situated on the small river Olona and in the center of the fertile plain of the Po near important Alpine passes, and connected by canals with the Ticino, Po, Adda, and Lake Como, Milan's history and growth have been directly influenced by its extraordinarily favorable location. Throughout the centuries it was the coveted prize of the ambitions of foreign and local rulers, and the meeting point of merchants, traders, artisans, and artists.

The ancient *Mediolanum* was the chief city of the *Insubres,* a Celtic tribe of *Gallia Transpadana.* They called their new city after the name of a village in their homeland *Gallia Transalpina. Mediolanum* was taken by the

Romans in 222 B.C. and made a *municipium* in 49 B.C.

After the conquest the Romans established a camp on the site as a strongpoint guarding the roads from Lodi, Bergamo, Como, Novara, and Pavia, which were converging on the former Gallo-Celtic town. The location at the focal point of these important connections was the main stimulus of the growth of the city as a commercial center of first-rate importance, of large markets and storehouses, and of a thriving community life.

The original Roman camp was small, enclosing a square whose sides measured about 1,800 feet and which was placed diagonally in relation to the four points of the compass. The first walls were constructed of wood and earth, later reinforced by masonry rising on a mound whose lower part was uneven and marshy. On this lower site a suburb developed, protected and dominated by the 60 to 80 towers of the *castrum*. Toward the end of the Republic the original fortifications were replaced by a larger *enceinte* enclosing the suburbs that had grown up during the preceding centuries. The exact course of these walls is now known through careful excavations, but while the crossing point of the *cardo* and *decumanus* has not yet been identified, certain assumptions can be made on the basis of the traditional usual layout of Roman cities as to the location of a mint, palace, *forum, basilica,* and the baths.

This second *enceinte,* irregular and winding, was about 2.2 miles long with six main gates and three postern gates, not more than 180 towers, and a service road running parallel to the walls. The military value of these fortifications may be doubted, and it has been suggested that they might have been more a

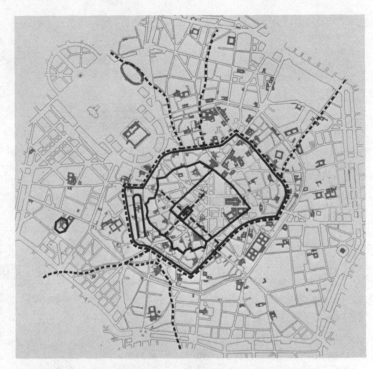

168. Plan of Roman *Mediolanum* with the original square *castrum* in the center and the extensions of the Imperial period.

169. An unusual pen-and-ink drawing of the 18th century, showing the reconstructed walls and the Roman monuments in the 11th century.

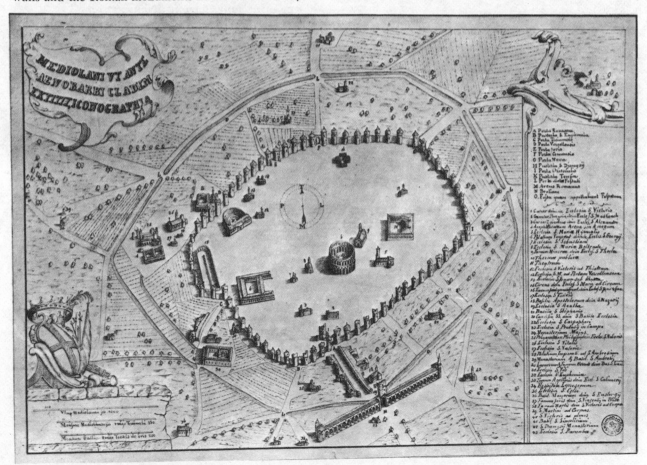

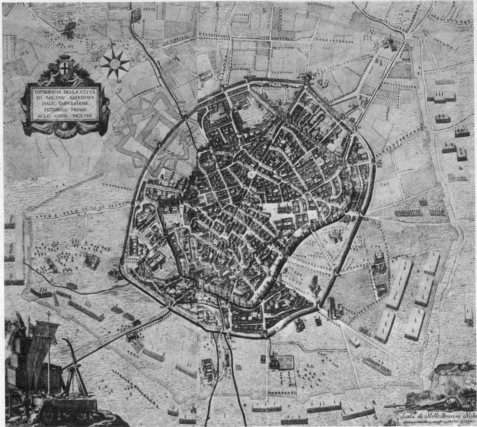

170. Map of Milano in 1158, showing large open spaces near the periphery and a densely built-up center.

171. Sketch by Leonardo da Vinci of the center of Milano. The secant lines may indicate the canals. From the *Codex Atlanticus.*

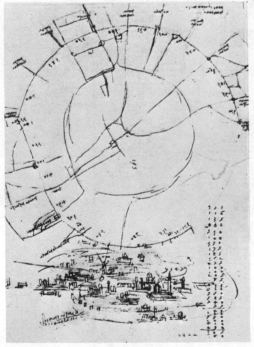

traditional symbol of protection, especially during the time of the *Pax Romana,* than a genuine and efficient defense system.

Mediolanum continued to grow and at the time of Ambrosius, Bishop of Milan from 373 to 397, a further extension—the third—of the fortifications had to be planned and executed. It enclosed fields and gardens and churches and monasteries that had grown up outside the walls. In connection with this work two streets were superimposed, more or less parallel to the walls of the *castrum,* upon the "diagonal" Roman layout of the urban area.

The population of Milan at this time has been grossly overestimated. Figures of 600,000 to 700,000 are fantastic speculations, especially if compared with a population of 154,000 inhabitants in 1854 living in considerably better economic conditions and in a city surrounded by a well-drained and cultivated countryside.

In the ninth century after the destruction of the barbarian invasions Milan began to recover. The walls were restored and inside the walls a sort of public park, the *Brolo Vescovile,* was laid out. At the same time the first agglomerations, the *contrade* developed in the interior: these were the nuclei of districts settled by poor people searching for security and protection in the proximity of the houses of powerful families. The merchants began to gather near the markets around the Piazza della Basilica di S. Tecla, and the artisans and craftsmen, the armorers, boatbuilders, saddlers, goldsmiths, and others established themselves as groups in different streets—an experiment in functional zoning characteristic of medieval communities all over Europe. This increase of industrial activities was accompanied by the construction of numerous warehouses and workshops.

Under the pressure of the threatening attack by the Emperor Fredrick Barbarossa in the 12th century the fortifications were again strengthened and extended, enclosing the outlying suburbs. The line of defense was doubled through the addition of an outer moat. These defenses withstood the siege but the city was forced by famine to surrender; the citizens, whose houses were destroyed, moved to the four provisional suburbs of Noceto, Vigentino,

Carrara, and S. Siro alla Vepra. After the victory of Legnano in 1176 the walls were reconstructed, a work that took nine years to complete. Six gates with strong towers and double archways were built, each gate corresponding to the main street of the six sections of the city, apart from the Porta Tosa and 12 postern gates with single openings.

About one hundred years later, Milan was said to have had about 6,000 wells, 70 *piazze*, "*coperti*," where the nobles could meet their clients, 400 ovens for baking bread, 290 churches, and 11 hospitals. Once more the walls were strengthened, this time by Azzone Visconti, and a double ring of streets was laid out on both sides of the walls, the outer one about 50 feet wide, the inner one 36 feet.

In 1368 the Visconti built the citadel of Porta Giovia as substitute for the old Rocchetta di Porta Romana. This castle was destroyed but later rebuilt by Gian Galeazzo Visconti which was also destroyed by the people in 1447. The present edifice is the work of Francesco Sforza. Somewhat later the *Broletto* was transferred from the area of the arch-

172. **Map of Milano in 1589 with the citadel, the inner moat, and the outer bastioned fortifications.**

bishop's palace to the district of the merchants, where, together with the surrounding square, it formed a civic center of major importance. Almost simultaneously the first *conca*, basin, was laid out at the Ponte dei Fabbri as part of the moat system where the large blocks of stone for the building of the cathedral could be unloaded. The moats and the crenellated walls were at this time still the main defense. There were no bastions: the introduction of long-range firearms was still far off.

The citadel was situated astride the walls. A large triangular area outside the walls, the glacis, was kept free of buildings. This was to be the later *Piazza d'armi*. When under Spanish rule (1536-1706) the city expanded in all directions, this triangular area was maintained as an open space for maneuvers and artillery practice. It determined the "ivy leaf" shape of the city and was conserved as the only green "lung," the present park.

Both French and Spanish rule, the former lasting from 1499 to 1525, were negative and colorless. Neither contributed to the welfare of the community. Their only interest was the strategic importance of Milan, and the

173. Sketch by Leonardo da Vinci for a city on different levels. From the *Codex Atlanticus*.

174. Map of Milano in 1737 showing the "ivy leaf" shape, the citadel with large open spaces surrounding it, and the irregular layout of the inner city.

272

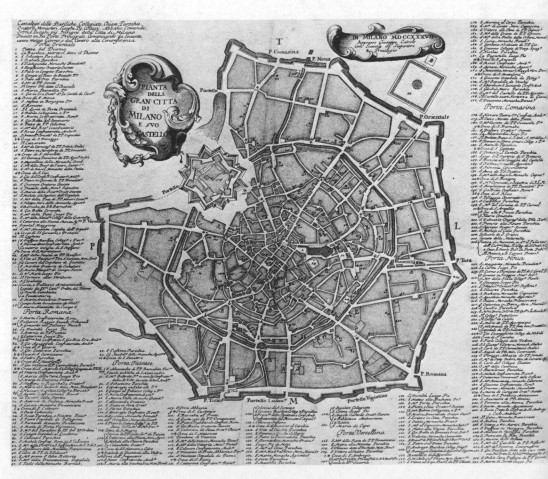

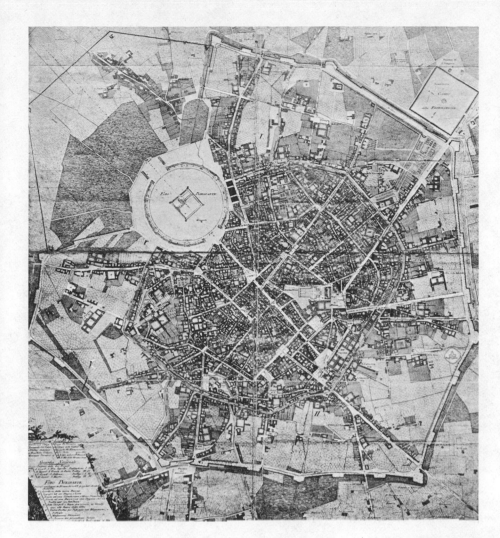

175. Development plan of Milano approved by Napoleon in 1807, indicating the intention to cut straight streets through the mass of houses in the medieval districts and to open up the center around the cathedral.

strengthening and extension of the fortifications. The result of this preoccupation with purely military considerations was an *enceinte* that was far beyond the actual needs of the city and the financial capacity of the citizens. However, a number of public buildings were erected and sponsored by the leading families, such as seminaries, schools, churches, which had a certain influence upon the layout of the streets in a few sectors of the city. Special attention was paid to the redevelopment of the Piazza del Duomo. More than 130 designs were submitted. The Austrian administration was just as unimaginative as its predecessors. Problems of urban improvement were neither understood nor tackled.

This changed under Napoleon. A grandiose project for a *Foro Bonaparte* was worked out— apparently too grandiose even for Napoleon, who suggested limitations. The citadel was to

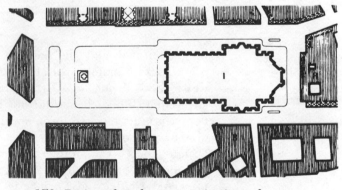

176. Project for the reorganization of the Piazza del Duomo with continuous arcades and public buildings. Middle of the 19th century.

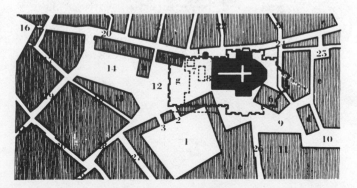

177. Piazza del Duomo in its original irregular layout.

273

178. Design for the new Piazza del Duomo in Milano only partially carried out.

be demolished and on the site a circular *piazza,* with a diameter of almost 1,000 yards, was to be laid out *"alla Bernini"* as the new city center. This scheme did not materialize, not even in its reduced form, nor did the plan of 1807 presented by the first *Commissione di Ornato*—the City Planning Commission, that provided for a great circular road around the preserved citadel and for a series of arterial roads and squares. This would have ensured a systematic loosening-up of the urban area and prevented the unfortunate radial and concentric development. It might have restored something of Leonardo da Vinci's vision of "a great and beautiful city" with straight streets lined by buildings of the same height, and a clear separation of streets into three groups at different levels: those with arcades

and closed to vehicular traffic reserved for the gentry; those for "the people" and the vehicles; and those for the stables and latrines. But it is perhaps no loss that this hierarchical antisocial plan has remained on paper.

In the 19th century various projects for the Piazza del Duomo were ventilated. Two schools opposed each other, one led by Amati suggesting a radical departure from the irregular layout and replacing it by a large rectangle with arcades and an *exedra* opposite the cathedral (1839); the other led by Cattaneo defending the irregularity of the square and its spatial discontinuity as it was at the time. In 1859 a lottery raised two million lire to cover the expenses for the reorganization of the square. With this step the modern era of Milan's city planning began.

274

Novara. Novara is situated on an elevation rising from the alluvial plain traversed by the Agogna and Terdoppio rivers. The favorable topographical conditions of the site attracted settlers at an early time. It soon became the center of a population living in dispersed settlements on the marshy terrain of the surrounding region. These first inhabitants, the Ligurians, were followed by Celtic tribes who invaded their territory about 400 B.C. Roman penetration began around 225 B.C. and reached its full impact between 201 and 190 B.C., when the existing settlement was made first a Latin, then a Roman *colonia* and finally became an important *municipium* and a political center at a crossing point of communications from the Po Valley to the Alps and from Milano to Torino. The Roman walls, dating from the second and third centuries, indicate that already at this time *Novaria's* urban development had been assured. Barbarian invasions in the fifth century (A.D. 452) necessitated the reconstruction of fortifications to defend the Christian community. In A.D. 669 the Langobards overran the territory and established the Dukedom of Novara. They were defeated by Charlemagne, who instituted a feudal system under a count. After some time, however, he had to share his rule with the bishop. Since the clerical regime was less oppressive than the

feudal domination, the people favored the bishop and recognized him in his double role as secular and clerical ruler (as Vescovo-Conte). Under imperial protection the bishops extended their dominion and jurisdiction as far as the Alps in the north and to Mortara and Vigevano in the south, with the Ticino and Sesia rivers as frontiers.

In 917 Berengar I granted a charter to Novara permitting the bishop to hold two annual fairs and a Saturday market, and to construct castles and fortifications. About the middle of the 12th century Benedictine monks built a convent and the church of S. Bartolomeo, and began to reclaim the land, introducing intensive cultivation and making Novara a model agricultural center. The *Comune di Novara* was probably constituted in 1137. Since the year 1000 Novara experienced a steady growth: the population increased, spilling over to the suburbs and outskirts of the town; numerous houses, churches, and schools were erected within the walls; and economic and agricultural progress proceeded apace. This population movement was accompanied by the grouping of the artisans and craftsmen in so-called *paratici* according to their professions based on written articles of association, *statuti*.

By the end of the 13th century the *comune*, administered by a *podestà*, elected for one

179. Old view (no date) of Novara within its fortifications and with the castle. The original regular Roman layout is not visible in this greatly simplified (and incorrect) picture.

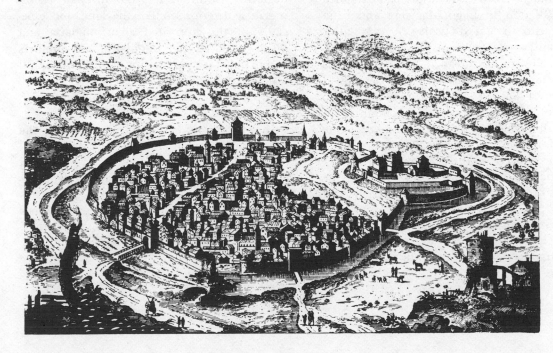

275

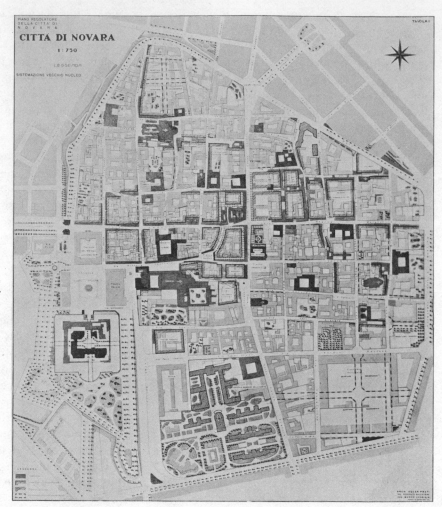

180. The ancient nucleus of Novara showing parts of the original regular layout.

year and assisted by two consuls, had extended its jurisdiction to Lago Maggiore and from Lago Cusio to Val d'Ossola. In 1357, after continuous strife between Novara and Monferrato, Novara was invaded by the enemy; its urban center and countryside were devastated and unrest ensued until in 1450 Francesco Sforza of Milano appointed a committee to revise the constitution and to modify the *statuti* for town and country. The first coaches were introduced in the 15th century, raising difficulties in rendering roads suitable for vehicular traffic that had hitherto been used only by pedestrians and mules.

Under Spanish rule (1535-1737) a decline set in. The government failed to provide even the most urgent necessities. Public works were neglected; the canals fell into disrepair, resulting in a deterioration of the land and especially of the cultivated areas; malaria and plague reduced the population in numbers and exposed it to hardships of all kinds. In all respects the Spanish administration was inadequate, riddled with corruption and inefficiency.

In 1738 Novara was incorporated in the Kingdom of Sardinia, a change leading to economic and cultural recovery. Novara's history was a succession of wars, violent upheavals, invasions, and more-or-less unsuccessful rulers, but it survived like many other small towns of Italy involved in the ups and downs of events on which they had hardly any direct influence.

276

181. Map of Vigevano with the Rocca Vecchia, a part of the fortifications, and the Palazzo and Piazza Ducale in the center of the town. From *Piante delle Città, Piazze e Castelli* by Don Giovanni Battista Sesti. Printed by Agnelli, Milano 1707. A Castle; B Tower; C Rocca Vecchia; D Passage from the city to the Rocca Vecchia; E Demolished citadel; F Porta Nova; G Porta de Val; H Porta di Strada Pavesa; I Porta della Rocca Vecchia; K Porta del Vescovato; L Porta di Milano; M Porta de Cesarini; N Porta di San Martino; O Duomo e Piazza.

Vigevano, Province of Pavia. Vigevano, about 25 miles southwest of Milano, was one of the little Residence Towns which owed their historical reputation to the artistic maturity of an autocratic ruler, a familiar figure in the Italy of the Renaissance. It originated as a center of the *Viginti columnae,* later called *Vicus Gebuin,* from which the name *Viglevanum* was derived. In Roman times it was a *castrum* that seems to have played a certain

182. Piazza Ducale and Torre del Bramante at Vigevano. Note the white pattern in the pavement underlining the structural dimensions of the square and separating the footpaths from the cobbled "passive" area of the square.

277

role as a nucleus of the military conquest of *Gallia Cisalpina*. Latin writers mostly ignored its existence. It was first mentioned in records of A.D. 816 as *Vicogena,* and in A.D. 902 as *Viccolonne*. In 1277 it became part of the Dukedom of Milan, an event marking the beginning of its great splendor and prosperity. The ancient castle was rebuilt in 1347 by Luchino Visconti, who transformed it into a stately residence. Francesco Sforza made Vigevano the seat of his magnificent court, and Ludovico il Moro continued the work of his predecessor. He called in Bramante and Leonardo to take part in the creation of the Piazza Ducale. The supervision of the actual work was entrusted to the architect Guglielmo da Camino. It was finished by Ambrogio de Curte. The result was one of the most harmonious squares of this period, combining intimacy and nobility, elegant gracefulness and unspoiled unity. Three sides of the *Piazza* were closed by uniform buildings with uninterrupted arcades on the ground floor. The fourth side was occupied by the cathedral whose façade was, however, not built until the

17th century. In 1492 Ludovico il Moro ordered the demolition of the original market square. The *Piazza* that was to replace it was not intended as a public meeting place but as the forecourt of the palace, the space under the arcades being reserved for the workshops of craftsmen and artisans brought in from Milan for the exclusive service in the palace. That the *Piazza* was planned as part of the Sforzesca and not as a public square for the benefit of the town is evident from its lack of organic relationship with the streets of the surrounding urban area.

As to the park outside the town but connected with the palace in the center through a passage to the ancient castle, the *Rocca Vecchia,* an inscription on a tablet speaks of *Vilis gleba* and *ditissima tellus*. Great efforts were apparently devoted to the reclamation of land through the construction of canals and other improvements on which, as seems probable, Leonardo proffered his advice. The planting of mulberry trees, the importation of silkworms, and the raising of sheep may have been due to his initiative.

183. Piazza Ducale and cathedral in Vigevano.

Bergamo. Bergamo is situated at the junction of two valleys, the Val Brembana and the Val Seriana through which the Brembo and the turbulent Serio flow respectively. The town consists of two parts, the *Città alta* on the hills, at an altitude of 1,200 feet, strongly fortified by the Venetians (1561-88), and the much larger *Città nuova* on the plain, about 400 feet below.

The earliest settlement on the site of the ancient city (*Bergomum* according to Pliny, *Vergamum* according to Paulus Diaconus; in Langobard and Frankish times *Pergamum*)

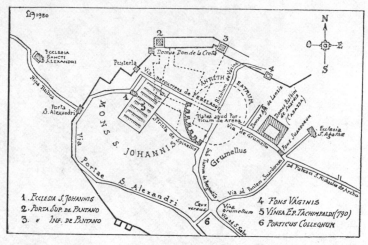

185. Map of Bergamo Alta, showing the area on the hill of S. Giovanni about A.D. 1000.

184. Ideographic view of Bergamo in the 15th century, emphasizing the material and symbolic importance of the walls as the essence of the town.

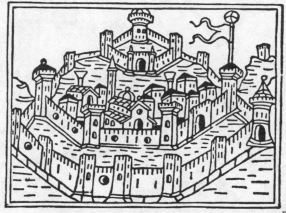

186. Map of Bergamo in 1251.

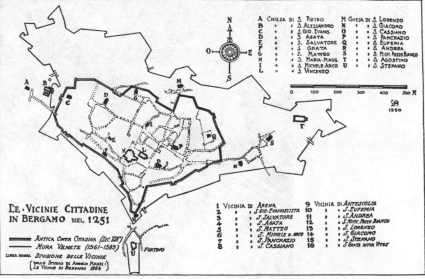

was founded by the *Orobii* whose civilization preceded that of the Etruscans. It was conquered by the *Galli Cenomani* in the fifth century B.C., who occupied it until in 197 B.C. it fell to the Romans.[62] In 49 B.C. the inhabitants received Roman citizenship from Caesar. Regarding etymology an interesting hypothesis may be mentioned, namely that the name Bergamo was derived from the god *Bergimo, Bergimus Caenomanorum Deus;* considering that the *Cenomani* were of eastern Gallic or Germanic origin, Bergamo may have originally meant *Berg-e heim,* "home on the mountain."

Roman *Bergomum* covered an area of about the same size as the medieval town. It had three gates corresponding to the directions to Milan, Brescia, and Como, a *forum,* a market, a capitol, temples, an amphitheater, a *hos-*

62. L. Angelini. *Il Volto di Bergamo nei Secoli.* 1951. *Passim.*

N. Sacchi, *Il Piano Regolatore di Bergamo.* 1951.

C. Traini. *Fascino di Bergamo.* 1953. *Passim.*

279

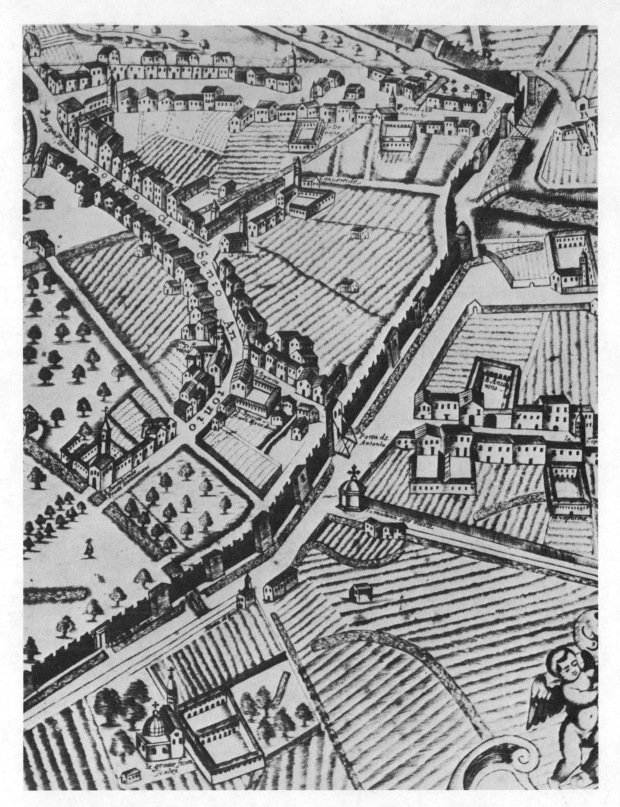

187. The districts of S. Tommaso, Galgario, and S. Antonio of Bergamo at the middle of the 17th century, showing the large open spaces of the urban area near the walls and parts of the suburbs. From an engraving by F. Scolari in the Uffizi Tecnini in Bergamo.

280

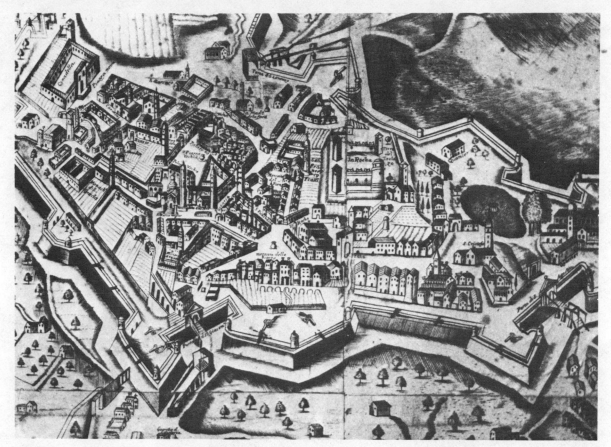

188. The central district of Bergamo Alta and the Venetian fortifications, showing numerous towers, the principal public buildings, and a generally high building density. From the same engraving as Figure 187.

pitium magnum, and aqueducts—in other words, all the features of a Roman provincial city. There were four suburbs: the *Fabricianum*, the *Pompolianum*, the *Praetorium*, and the *Crotacium*.

In the fifth century the Roman walls were still standing and seem to have provided a fairly efficient protection against attacks. However, in the following centuries Bergamo was occupied by foreign armies. The courts of the conquering rulers formed three successive nuclei around which the town developed. In A.D. 776 Charlemagne installed a count as lord of Bergamo with the explicit obligation of recognizing the authority of the bishop in religious matters; he granted the resumption of minting, already begun in the Lombard period, and of zinc and silver mining in the valleys of the Brembo and Serio. After the devastation of the city in A.D. 894 the walls and towers of the defense system were recon-

structed; the church of S. Alessandro was rebuilt, and churches and the bishop's residence were erected.

A poem by Mosè del Brolo (about 1130) entitled *Pergaminus* described Bergamo as a city surrounded by suburbs, defended by walls with four gates, with fountains, and a few towers of the noble families (their number increased later during the civil wars), with narrow and tortuous streets and small squares, and several public buildings—but still without a city hall. In the two following centuries the economic activities of the free *Comune* increased. Markets were installed, first for animals and later for produce. A new water supply was organized, *Fossatum Communis Pergami* (1190-1210) which served the industries, especially those based on the processing of leather and wool; and agricultural production and mining was further developed.

In 1339 the Visconti assumed the mastery

281

189. Palazzo della Ragione at Bergamo with fountain.

190. View of the Fair at Bergamo with stone buildings (1732–40).

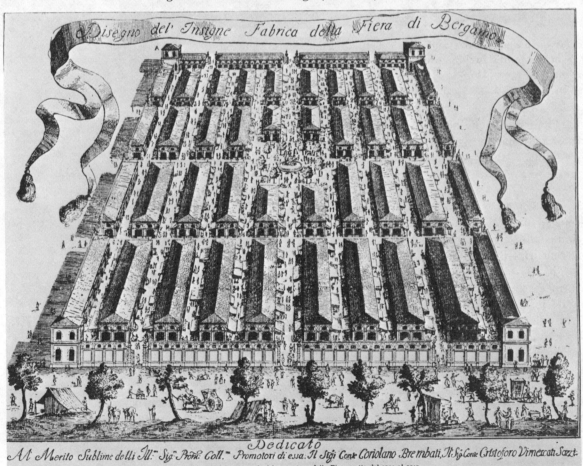

over Bergamo and, as was fitting for a bellicose family, one of their first works was the
strengthening of the fortifications and the
castle. At the end of their turbulent reign and
after losing the war with Venice, they ceded
Bergamo and Brescia to the Venetian Republic (1428). The preoccupation with the maintenance and improvement of the fortifications
during all these centuries never abated. The
new construction of the walls, after 1561,
lasted 30 years and necessitated the destruction
of numerous buildings. During this time new
suburbs grew up and many more houses and
palaces were built inside the walls. About 1630
the population numbered 27,000 of whom
9,000 were killed by the Black Death in the
same year. Disorders followed. Class distinc-
tions intensified; internal strife increased; the
middle class began to leave their houses in the
upper town and move to the suburbs, gradually gaining the upper hand in the struggle
with the nobility. Bergamo developed into an
important economic center for West Lombardy, trading with the Valtellina in Switzer-

191. Detail from the fountain in the
Piazza Vecchia at Bergamo.

192. Piazza Vecchia in Bergamo.

land, Bavaria, and parts of Austria in contrast
with Como, Pavia, and Cremona whose fortunes declined.

In this connection the history of the fairs
of Bergamo is of particular interest. The first
documentation dates from A.D. 908, the year
in which King Berengar, who had previously
sacked the city, granted to the bishop, as an
expression of his "peaceful" intentions, the
right to hold a fair—provided that the proceeds were ceded to the canons of S. Vincenzo.
This privilege was confirmed by Barbarossa in
1158 despite protests from the citizens. It was
not until 1428, at the beginning of Venetian
rule, that this privilege passed to the community. Barracks for the fair were built toward the end of the 15th century. Then

283

193. A symphony of roofs and cupolas. The cathedral and the surrounding area in Bergamo.

temporary structures were burned down in a great fire in 1591 resulting in damage amounting to 16,000 gold *scudi*. However, this disaster did not discontinue the fairs. Venice granted special tax exemptions to maintain and further the important economic activities of the city famous for its products throughout Europe. In 1731 permission for the erection of permanent stone buildings was given and one year later, after some difficulties, the community agreed to the condition that none of the shops or storerooms was to be run by local innkeepers or people engaged in basic industries. The result was that weavers, traders in metals and other raw materials and agricultural products, innkeepers, and dealers in garlic, onions, and small articles stayed away, building instead temporary huts outside the fairgrounds. The construction of the new fair began in 1732 and was completed in 1740. It consisted of nine long streets crossed at right angles by five shorter streets, with a central square adorned with a monumental fountain (today the Piazza Dante) and 540 shops in rows built back-to-back. It covered an area approximately 545 feet long on each side and had offices of sanitation, criminal investigation, overseers of the fair and the products. The plan and the buildings are attributed to the architect Giambattista Caniana (1671-1754). The complex was a self-contained entity: for the first hundred years no shop had a door to the outside. Later the south side was opened up and direct communications with the neighboring district were established. The festive atmosphere of the fair attracted daily theater performances, circuses, all sorts of shops and vendors, menageries, and innumerable visitors from many lands. What had begun as a strictly commercial enterprise finally turned into an amusement park for the populace. When in the course of time the buildings depreciated, they were used for housing poor and deprived families. All the structures were completely demolished in 1922.

Piacenza. The site of Piacenza, a short distance from the right bank of the Po, was occupied by prehistoric tribes, later by Etruscans and Celts. In 218 B.C. the Romans founded the *Colonia Placentia,* at the same time as Cremona, as a strongpoint against the Gauls. Its strategically favorable situation, surrounded by a fertile hinterland on the Lombard Plain near a vital crossing of the Po, at the beginning of the *Via Aemilia* and close to other military routes, made it a very important road center. After a short time it was elevàted to a strong *municipium* whose regular layout is still intact in the nucleus of the town. The first expansion of the original Roman layout took place toward the west, still preserving the gridiron plan of the Roman camp. At this time the population amounted to about 3,000 people, a number that later increased to almost 6,000. The Roman town covered an area of about 86.45 acres.

Hardly anything is known about the intervening period between the end of the Roman occupation and the early Middle Ages. In the

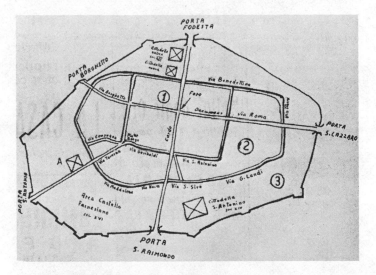

194. Map of the development of Piacenza from its foundation to A.D. 1500. 1. Roman period; 2. Medieval period; 3. Modern period; A. Citadel of the 14th century.

fourth century Piacenza was regarded as the capital of Emilia. The successive occupations by Goths, Byzantines, Lombards, Franks, and Germanic peoples did not impede its progress. From the sixth to the 12th century the population increased, possibly to 15,000 in A.D. 1000, suburbs grew up on all sides, and new fortifications were built, giving the town an oval shape along the east-west axis, whereas at the north the danger from inundations of the Po restricted the expansion. The area of the medieval town may have been something like 741.3 acres. Strong citadels guarded the gates in the north, south, and west.

In the 13th and 14th centuries economic activities prospered. Fairs and periodical markets were held. The guilds of the bankers and merchants traded with Europe and the East, and the wool and later the silk industries flourished. No records are available that agriculture played a significant role during this period, though irrigation works were in operation. The university was founded in 1248 together with important professional *collegi*. The town was divided into four quarters, each with its own church, and the jurisdiction of the town spread to the surrounding countryside.

In the 14th century, after the fall of the *Comune*, Piacenza was incorporated in the Lombard state of the Visconti. A strong new citadel was built on the Po. This political dependence diminished the importance of Piacenza and resulted in efforts of the leading noble families to regain something of their former influence. Under the rule of the Sforzas, at the beginning of the 16th century, a further extension of the city took place. The fortifications were rebuilt and modernized under the direction of the local architect Fredenzio Tramello with bastions and five gates giving the city an approximately octagonal shape (1542). A strong pentagonal citadel, *la cittadella nuova,* was constructed by the military engineer Domenico Giannelli of Siena (1547) in the south, which, in the following centuries was to be the most potent defense of Piacenza. The *enceinte* enclosed all

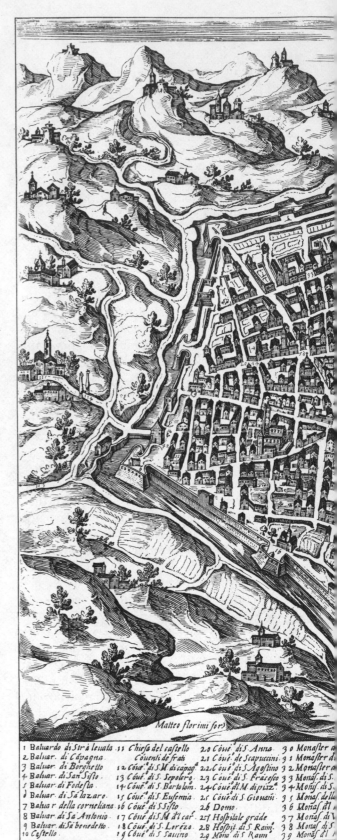

Matteo florimi for)

1 Baluardo di Strà leuata
2 Baluar. di Càpagna
3 Baluar. di Borghetto
4 Baluar. di San Sisto
5 Baluar. di Fodesta
6 Baluar. di Sà lazaro
7 Baluar della corneliana
8 Baluar. di Sà Antonio
9 Baluar. di Sà benedetto
10 Castello

11 Chiesa del castello
    Conuenti de frati
12 Côuê. di S. M. di capag.
13 Côuê. di S. Sepolcro
14 Côuê. di S. Bartolom.
15 Côuê. di S. Eufemia
16 Côuê. di S. Sisto
17 Côuê. di S. M. à'l car.
18 Côuê. di S. Lorēzo
19 Côuê. di S. Sauisto

20 Côuê. di S. Anna
21 Côuê. de Scapuccini
22 Côuê. di S. Agostino
23 Côuê. di S. Frācesco
24 Côuê. dl M. di pizz.
25 Côuê. di S. Giouāi
26 Domo
27 Hospitale grāde
28 Hospit. di S. Raim.
29 Moña di S. Raim

30 Monaster a
31 Monaster d
32 Monaster
33 Monas. di S.
34 Moñaſ. di S.
35 Moñaſ. della
36 Moñaſ. d'l
37 Moñaſ. di V
38 Moñaſ. di S.
39 Moñaſ. d'l

286

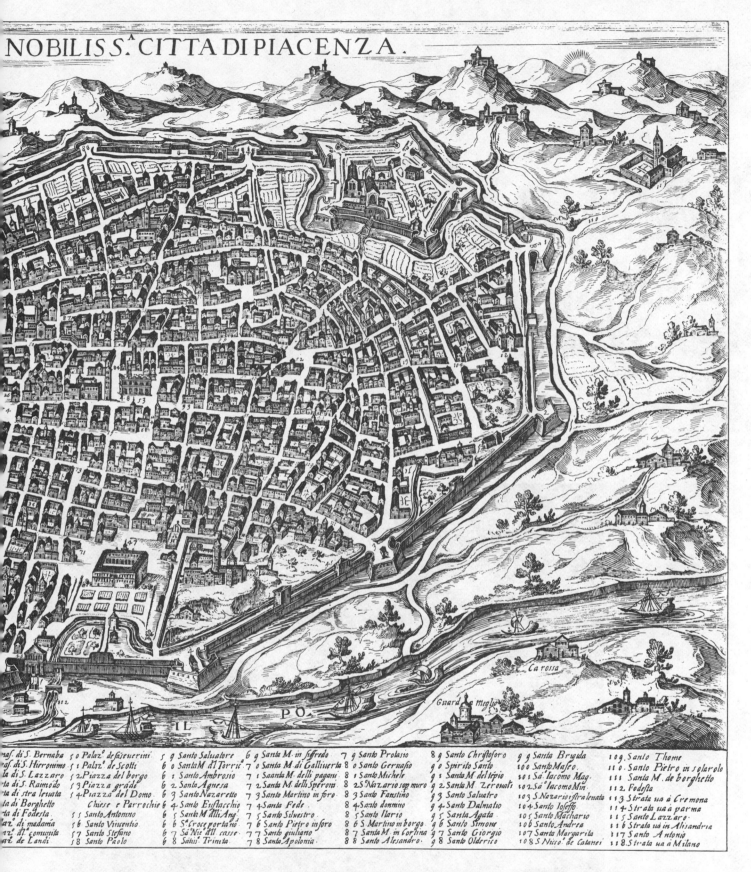

NOBILISS.ᴬ CITTA DI PIACENZA.

IL PO.

Ca roſſa

Guardia a Meglio

...naſ. di S. Bernaba	50 Palaz.ᵉ deſaſeuerini	59 Santo Saluatore	69 Santa M. in ſuffredo	79 Santo Protaſio	89 Santo Chriſtoforo	99 Santa Brigida	109 Santo Thome

naſ. di S. Bernaba — 50 Palaz.ᵉ deſaſeuerini — 59 Santo Saluatore — 69 Santa M. in ſuffredo — 79 Santo Protaſio — 89 Santo Chriſtoforo — 99 Santa Brigida — 109 Santo Thome
naſ. di S. Hieronimo — 51 Palaz.ᵉ de Scotti — 60 Santa M. d'l Torri' — 70 Santa M. di Galliuerta — 80 Santo Geruaſio — 90 Spirito Santo — 100 Santo Maſco — 110 Santo Pietro in ſolarolo
di S. Lazzaro — 52 Piazza del borgo — 61 Santo Ambroſio — 71 Saanta M. delli pagani — 81 Santo Michele — 91 Santa M. del tępio — 101 Sā.ᵗ Iacomo Mag. — 111 Santa M. de borghetto
di S. Raimodo — 53 Piazza grāde — 62 Santa Agneſa — 72 Santa M. delli Speroni — 82 S. Nazaro ſop muro — 92 Santa M. Zerenati — 102 Sā.ᵗ Iacomo Min. — 112 Fodeſta
di ſtra leuata — 54 Piazza del Domo — 63 Santo Nazaretto — 73 Santo Martino in foro — 83 Santo Fauſtino — 93 Santo Saluatio — 103 S. Nazario iſtra leuata — 113 Strata ua ā Cremona
di Borghetto — Chieſe e Parrochie — 64 Santo Euſtacchio — 74 Santa Fede — 84 Santo donnino — 94 Santo Dalmatio — 104 Santo Ioſeffo — 114 Strata ua ā parma
di Fodeſta — 55 Santo Antonino — 65 Santa M. alli Ang.' — 75 Santo Siluestro — 85 Santo Ilario — 95 Santa Agata — 105 Santo Macharo — 115 Saeto Lazzaro
az di madama — 56 Santo Vincentio — 66 S.ᵗᵃ Croce porta nō — 76 Santo Pietro in foro — 86 S. Martino in borgo — 96 Santo Simone — 106 Santo Andrea — 116 Strata ua in Aliſandria
di comunita — 57 Santo Stefano — 67 Sā Nic.ᵒ all caſſe — 77 Santo giuliano — 87 Santa M. in Cortina — 97 Santo Giorgio — 107 Santa Margarita — 117 Santo Antonio
de Landi — 58 Santo Paolo — 68 Sātiſs. Trinita — 78 Santa Apolonia — 88 Santo Aleſandro — 98 Santo Olderico — 108 S. Nico.ᵒ de Catanei — 118 Strata ua ā Milano

195. View of Piacenza with the fortifications of the 16th century.

196. Old view of the Piazza Boselli in the 19th century.

197. Air view of Piacenza showing the oval outline of the urban area, the gridiron street system of the Roman period in the center, and the medieval and Renaissance additions.

suburbs and a population that had grown to about 30,000 inhabitants and was to remain stationary until the 19th century. This extension was conceived for a much greater population than the city had at the time of its execution: it contained large open spaces for gardens and orchards. A major renewal was carried out in the southeastern quarter of the city: an arterial road, the Strada Gambara, now Via Farnese, was laid out (1540) intended for the erection of palaces and religious institutions. It was dominated by the church of Sant' Agostino, inspired by Vignola's architecture, and a great monastery and two convents in the local style of Piacenza.

In the 17th and 18th centuries the civic and economic life of the city continued its favorable development. The fairs were revived attracting visitors from all over Europe. Around the Palazzo Farnese a veritable commercial quarter grew up, and a civic center came into existence near the Piazza Grande, the cathedral, and the Vie Diritta and Calzolai. The courtly life of the Farnese with its international connections and its pompous public entertainments, the building of numerous palaces and churches, the introduction of progressive methods of agriculture, contributed to endowing the city and the surrounding rural area with an atmosphere of great vitality and a certain nobility of manners—enjoyed and sustained by the upper strata of society.

In the 19th century Piacenza began to take on a neoclassical appearance. After the unification of Italy a sort of slum clearance, long overdue, was undertaken in the ancient nucleus of the city. Banking and commercial activities, the backbone of urban prosperity since the Middle Ages, continued to prosper but the true economic basis of the social and economic life shifted to agriculture.

Generally speaking, the street system of Piacenza is a mixture of all periods from the original Roman layout through the Middle Ages, the Renaissance, and the following centuries with but few changes and opening up of new arteries. The building density is highest in the center decreasing toward the periphery where single-family houses with one floor predominate. Monasteries and convents are almost all situated near the periphery. There are only a few squares within the central city; others are situated in the outlying quarters at the crossings of streets. Medieval public buildings have survived in the inner city on the Piazza Grande and close to the cathedral. The majority of the industrial districts are located on the outskirts, although industrial establishments have invaded other parts of the urban area.

Cremona. The earliest occupants of the site, on the left bank of the Po, were possibly the Gallic *Cenomani*. In 222 or 218 B.C. the Romans conquered their territory and founded the Latin *colonia* of Cremona which was, however, not populated by Roman citizens but by *peregrini*, aliens without Roman citizenship. The town soon assumed an important military function as bridgehead on the Po, and the original inhabitants were joined by Romans who formed the famous *cohors cremonensis*. Cremona was one of the most prosperous Roman towns of Northern Italy with a population estimated at 30,000 persons including children, women, and old people, a number that is probably somewhat exaggerated though it may also refer to the inhabitants of the im-

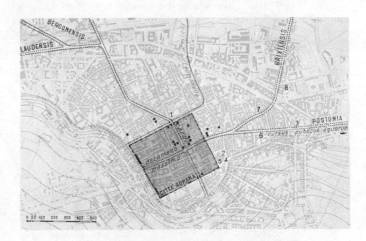

198. Plan of Roman and early Christian Cremona (222 B.C. to A.D. 553).

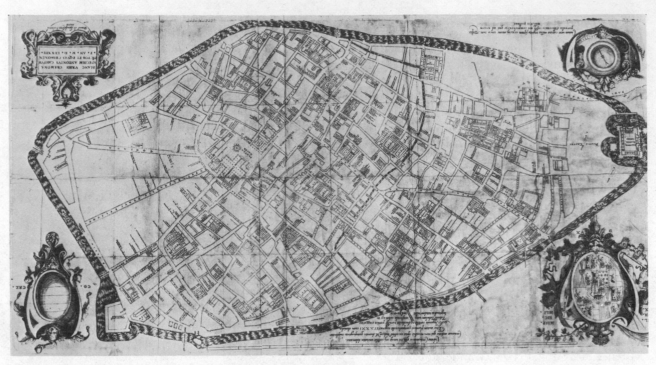

199. Map of Cremona in 1583 by Antonio Campi.

mediate hinterland. No details are known of the topography of Roman Cremona except that it was walled in, had a rectangular circumference, four gates, and the usual grid-iron layout. Its elevation to a *municipium* involved no changes of any importance; the town could not expand either to the west, south, or east since the Po skirted it in the west and then turned to the south and, for a short distance, to the east. In antiquity a large part of the space now occupied by streets and squares was under water. In A.D. 69 Cremona was destroyed by the troops of Vespasian. Although he ordered its immediate reconstruction it never regained its former prosperity. In the third century A.D. the town expanded toward the northeast and northwest, though rather tardily. Landing places were installed on the banks of the river. An inscription on a Roman stone slab, now in the apse of the cathedral, records that there existed near the landing places a *statio equorum,* where goods were loaded and unloaded. This *statio* was private property. Another, *cursus publicus equorum,* was located at some

distance on the Po and was particularly frequented by travelers arriving on the *Via Postumia* who wanted to continue their journey on the river. The riverside area was inhabited by humble folk, freed slaves, fishermen, boatmen, and porters.

Early Christianity was embraced especially by the poorest population living outside the walls. The first church was built on the highest point of the bank of the river, the *Rupe*—the rock—where a pagan temple to Mefite had stood. In A.D. 451 Cremona became the seat of a bishop followed by the erection of two churches, S. Lorenzo and SS. Maria Filippo e Giacomo later combined in the Basilica di S. Lorenzo (A.D. 999).

In 553 the Byzantines established a large entrenched camp immediately outside the walls whose function was to control the important crossing of the *Via Postumia* with the Po near the *Bergomensis* and the *Laudensis*. At this time a bridge did not exist; the only way across was by ferry. Nearby was the so-called *cataulada,* a combination of Greek and neo-Latin meaning "large encampment." It was

290

separated from the town by a tract about 120 feet wide, traversed by the *Cremonella,* at that time a branch of the Po. The *cataulada* was divided into two parts almost equal in size (each about 11.5 acres). The eastern section was occupied by the *exercitales,* that is, by people organized in military contingents with their families who were allowed to cultivate state land and to transmit it to their children with the obligation to take up arms in case of war. The *exercitales* were of different origin: there were the *bucellari* or *mercenari,* the mercenaries; the *Alemani;* and the *Giussani* or *Popolari,* the Romans or rather Italians. The western section of the *cataulada* was reserved for the Greeks, who in all probability represented the mobile troops. The camp was connected with the extramural zone of the town in the southeast by a road called by the Greek term *cumaina* or *cumania,* meaning "lapped by water." It continued through the Roman town to the so-called Byzantine suburb at the south where the nonmilitary Greeks had founded churches dedicated to their saints. This suburb was probably also the quarter of the Greek merchants. Its layout repeated more or less the regular street system of the walled-in Roman town. Other trading activities were carried on by the *exercitales* of the *cataulada* in the *mercato,* in Greek the *parlasso,* east of the camp.

Thus the Roman town was hedged in at the north and south—on the west it was limited by the Po—by extramural settlements partly military and partly commercial and religious in character. That a trading settlement, a *vicus,* developed outside the walls of a Roman camp was not unusual, nor was it uncommon for suburbs to grow up around churches or monasteries. What made the expansion of Cremona, on the lines described above, of particular interest was the origin of the outlying districts from a camp and the combination of the trading activities with a military organization.

In A.D. 603 the Lombards occupied and sacked Cremona. The *cataulada* lost its purpose and the Greeks were demilitarized. The mercenaries sought new employment with other rulers and became *arimanni*—that is, *exercitales* of the Lombards, thus holding on to their rights as the legal owners of the land they had occupied. It is probable that the Lombards built a fort at the church of S.

200. Piazza del Duomo in Cremona with the Baptistery begun in 1167 and the Palazzo Comunale and the former Palazzo dei Giureconsulti.

Michele near important roads and the *cursus publicus equorum.* In A.D. 753 the former Byzantine camp was taken over by Benedictine monks, who erected there the church and monastery of S. Silvestro. The southwestern area of the camp, formerly occupied by Greek troops, was turned into a market, probably for meat, and land was given by the monks to the butchers.

At the end of the seventh and during the eighth century the Po continued to shift its course. The new, low-lying land became public property which in the 13th and 14th century was sold to private individuals by the *Comune.*

In the first decennium of the seventh century the major development of Cremona proceeded in the suburbs but in the eighth century the resurgence of urban life spread to all parts of the city. In the ninth century the bishop built a fortified castle, surrounded the episcopal precincts on the *Rupe,* where the cathedral stood, with strong walls, and constructed a citadel at the east gate. From 916 onward the bishops combined in their person the clerical and lay overlordship of the city. As preparation against possible attacks by the Hungarians walls with towers were erected around the urban area. They were destroyed by fire in 1113. The merchants, joined by the non-Catholic population which was still numerous, resented the autocratic rule of the bishops since they were more preoccupied with temporal than with spiritual problems. They rebelled against the double role of their lords and demanded greater autonomy. As a demonstration against the intolerant attitude of the bishops the non-Catholic section of the population—mainly consisting of *Alemani* who were adherents of Arianism—built the church of S. Agata (1077) in the *cataulada,* a sanctuary almost regarded as the cathedral of the ancient military camp. This district, together with the area reclaimed from the Po, was later called *Cittanova* and its inhabitants were known as *populares.* They maintained a considerable autonomy even after the walls of the Roman city had been demolished, the formerly outlying parts united with the an-

cient nucleus, and the name of Cremona extended to the whole settled area.

New walls were constructed with a perimeter of about 3.5 miles between 1169 and 1187 enclosing still marshy land—the Porta Mosa zone—in the east, later used for the layout of four arterial roads, and also sandy and gravel tracts not suitable for immediate occupation. The urban area within these fortifications was sufficient until the 19th century and the walls, although restored and strengthened several times, remained fundamentally the same following the original outline. With changing military tactics Cremona lost its strategic importance. Finally, in the 20th century the fortifications were dismantled. The zone of the defense perimeter was used for housing without fear of inundation, since the Po had shifted its course about half a mile farther south.

The population of Cremona—that is of the area within the old walls—declined from several ten thousand inhabitants in the first century A.D. to a few thousand under Lombard rule. In the seventh century A.D. the Roman town was almost deserted, a fate shared with numerous other places during this period. With the revival of city life and the establishment of the *Comune* at the end of the 11th century, the population began to increase. The walls of the 12th century, allowing for this growth, enclosed an area that provided ample space for vegetable gardens, orchards, and fields to maintain the food supply in case of sieges, and also for the construction of new houses. Toward the end of the 13th century Cremona was again one of the larger cities of Northern Italy, politically influential and an important commercial center with a large number of artisans.

Until the 12th century most houses had roofs of straw. This changed in the following centuries. New brick houses with tiled roofs and public edifices were erected. Wealthy merchants and nobles, especially in the 15th century, built mansions with large gardens. Under Spanish rule this promising development came to an end. The population decreased to less than 10,000 inhabitants after it had been decimated by the plague of 1630. By the end of the 16th century about a quarter of the urban area was occupied by churches and religious institutions. At the same time navigation of the Po, a very important element in the economic life of the city, declined, resulting in great losses to the local merchants. Apart from the mansions of the nobility most houses were inhabited by craftsmen and artisans: They had usually a shop and a back room on the ground floor and two rooms on the first floor with a *loggia* and outer stairway from the courtyard. When the family increased more floors were added.

According to the available data—which are, however, not too reliable—the population numbered in 1763 to 1768 about 25,000 people; in 1820 about 24,500; and in 1855 approximately 26,500. Toward the end of the 18th century, and especially in the 19th century, many houses of the artisans were pulled down and replaced by more modern and larger buildings.

Only the history of Cremona can explain the agglomeration of heterogeneous elements that make up the physical and architectural structure of the city; why the cathedral is not situated in the center of the Roman nucleus; why the principal streets seem to follow an entirely irrational course; why the civic center does not correspond to the topographical conditions; why large open spaces were preserved within the *enceinte*; and why many streets vary greatly in width and are narrow even where traffic is dense.

Mantova (Mantua). Situated 88 feet above sea level on an almost insular site, Mantua is surrounded by three lakes formed by the river Mincio, the Lago Superiore on the west, the Lago di Mezzo stretching from north to east, and the Lago Inferiore on the southeast. The city, of Etruscan origin, was one of the *dodecapoli padana* later included in the lands of the Gallic tribe of the *Cenomani*. In the Roman period its territory never extended for more than 15 miles. Mantua was probably the birthplace of Virgil, who tells us that it derived its name from the nymph Manto.

Ocnus, son of fate-telling Manto and the Etruscan river, who gave to Mantua her walls and his mother's name. Mantua has a wealth of ancestry, not all of one lineage. She comprises three clans, each composed of four communities [the dodecapoli padana] all of which accept Mantua as their capital city; but it is from the Etruscan stream that she draws her strength.[63]

In A.D. 401 Mantua was destroyed by Alaric. A historically obscure period followed until it submitted to Henry IV, from whom it received ample privileges (1091). A record of 1126 mentions for the first time Mantua as a *Comune*

63. *The Aeneid*, X, 198. Penguin Classics.

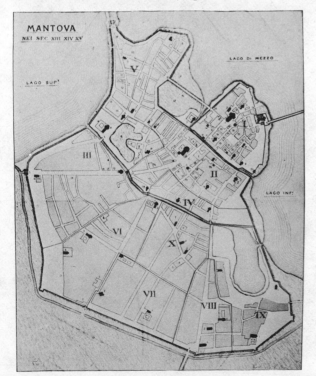

201. Map of the development of Mantua from the 13th to the 15th century. I. Città Vecchia with the cathedral and other churches, palaces, and public buildings. II. Città Nuova with the Palazzo del Comune, public buildings, and some of the *piazze*. III. Quarter of S. Giacomo. IV. Quarter of S. Martino. V. Quarter of S. Leonardo. VI. Zona dei Monticelli. VII. Zona del Redevallo. VIII. Zona della Fiera. IX. Zona dei Campi Santi. X. Zona di S. Egidio.

293

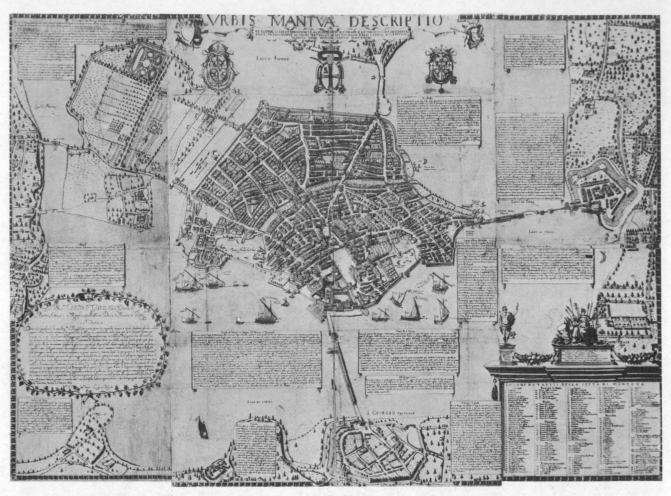

202. Map of Mantua in 1627.

204. Air view of Mantua with the Castello di S. Giorgio in the foreground.

203. *Opposite:* Air view of the Palazzo Ducale in Mantua.

205. Air view of Mantua with the modern quarters.

governed by five consuls and 26 *arimanni*[64] though the actual power remained in the hands of the bishops until, after long and violent struggles between the clergy and the patrician families, the rule of the Church was

64. The *arimanni* were Lombard peasant-warriors stationed in permanent and strategically important fortified places. They were subject only to the king, who provided them with land sufficient to guarantee their livelihood and legally recognized as hereditary and inalienable property. The land was partly cultivated and partly used as pastures. The rest was kept as woodlands for fuel and the supply of building material. They were freemen and as such frequently called upon to act as judges dispensing justice and settling disputes. It was a system somewhat similar to that applied by King Henry I for the protection of the southeast frontier of Germany. He also relied on peasant-warriors installed in fortified places as did Maria Theresa many centuries later in the eastern borderlands of her empire.

296

ended in 1235. A century of internecine feuds followed. It was not until the Gonzagas established their authority in 1328 that the great era of Mantua began and the city took a leading part in the political, military, and cultural activities of Northern Italy, which reached its acme in the 15th and 16th centuries. The comprehensive renewal, directed by Giulio Romano as *prefetto delle acque e degli edifici*, earned Mantua, according to Vasari, the name of "Nuova Roma." Alberti, Mantegna, and other artists were called in by the Gonzagas and contributed to the fame and splendor of the court and the city. Under the rule of Guglielmo (1559-87) over 50 new buildings were erected and the population is said to have grown to 43,000 inhabitants, including a large

Jewish community that had found refuge in Mantua from the persecutions of the Inquisition. However, this efflorescence came to an end with Vincenzo II (1589-1612), who sold most of the precious paintings of the art collections assembled by his predecessors, squandering the treasures of the state with utmost extravagance. After a few decades the decline was obvious: the population had been reduced to a quarter of what it had been; the fields were neglected; and the former vitality of urban life had gone. In 1707 the Gonzaga dynasty disappeared when the political power passed to Austria. Three years later the duchy became the hereditary property of the House of Austria and in 1738 was incorporated in the unified realm of Lombardy with a representative in the *Consiglio d'Italia* at Vienna. In 1796 Mantua fell to Napoleon, then passed again to Austria, later to France and was finally absorbed in the United Kingdom of Italy.

Population figures for Mantua show a rather fluctuating development.[65] The following summary gives a fairly accurate account.

1478	8,795	(after about 10,000 people died of the plague)
1494	22,000	
1559	36,196	
1592	31,422	
1625	29,710	
1632	8,015	(after the plague and sack of the city)
1742	19,859	
1816	25,516	
1863	29,729	
1911	32,692	
1960	61,721	

65. Supplied by the Mayor of Mantua.

Parma. Although definite archeological data are not available, it may be assumed that pile dwellings of the Bronze Age culture of *Terremare* existed near or even within the area occupied by Roman Parma. The Roman *colonia* of Parma was founded by the consul Marcus Aemilius Lepido in 183 B.C. on a site that was possibly not the same as that of the *colonia Julia Augusta Parma* of the Empire. From discoveries of ancient street pavements, made in connection with the construction of sewers in 1940, it was possible to reconstruct the size, shape, and layout of the Roman town. It approximated a square with sides of about 1,200 feet, and streets running southeast to northwest parallel to the *Via Aemilia* and the *decumanus,* crossed at right angles by other streets. The *forum* was situated at the intersection of the *decumanus maximus* and the *cardo maximus.* The distance between the *decumani* was 149.2 feet and between the *cardines* 182.4 feet—that is, less than that of the present

206. Map of Parma in the 16th century, showing the defense system with bastions, moat, and five gates; the urban area traversed by the Parma River; and three bridges.

297

207. The Teatro Ducale (now the Teatro Regio) in Parma at the middle of the 19th century with an enclosed forecourt.

streets. There were four gates at the end of the *decumanus maximus* and the *cardo maximus*: the *Porta Romana,* the *Porta Parma,* the *Porta Montana,* and the *Porta Padana.* The layout was therefore developed on the usual gridiron system without any major alterations. In the first century A.D. a theater was constructed outside the walls, southeast of the large oval-shaped amphitheater. Toward the end of the Roman Empire Parma was destroyed in the barbarian invasions.

During the reign of Theodoric Parma was rebuilt and extended, especially toward the south (end of the fifth century). By the middle of the sixth century, after the defeat of the Ostrogoths, the city passed under Byzantine rule through a period of splendor that earned her the name of *Crisopolis,* the Golden City, though whether this was due to her eminent position and magnificence or to the more sober fact that it was the seat of the state treasury is not clear. This "Golden Age" did not last long. When the Byzantine domination ended, a new decline set in accompanied by a considerable disorganization of the physical structure of the ancient Roman town and a retrenchment of the walled-in urban area especially in the south. In A.D. 983 the Benedictine monastery of S. Giovanni Evangelista was founded at the northeast and later the convent of the Benedictine nuns of S. Paolo at the north, both outside the walls.

As in many other towns these monastic institutions were the nuclei around which settlements grew up. The cathedral was begun in 1061, replacing the old one that had been destroyed by fire. In the same century many more monasteries were built to the north and east of the town, which ended at the Parma River in the west, at this time, flowing about 300 feet more to the east than today.

In the 12th century the fortifications were extended along the northern side and partly at the east. In the year 1179 the Parma changed its course again this time 300 feet to the west, leaving a dry area where later the Palazzo della Pilotta (1597) was constructed by the Farnese but never completed, near the old stone bridge, called the Bridge of Theodoric. The area beyond the Parma west of the river, called *Capodiponte* (bridgehead), was soon occupied by numerous houses and thirty years later (1627) the walls were moved almost 2,100 feet to the west of the river—to a line that remained unaltered for several centuries and within which numerous churches were erected in the 12th and 13th centuries. During the 13th century many important buildings were executed: the old Palazzo del Comune; the Convent of S. Francesco (now a prison); the two *Palazzi* of the Capitano del Popolo (later the *Governatore*) and of the *Auditore Civile* on the north side of the Piazza Principale; and the *Palazzo* of the notaries and the criminal court on the east side of the *Piazza* (1287-88).

At the middle of the 14th century Parma passed under the domination of the Duchy of Milano ruled by the Visconti, and later the Sforza. Luchino Visconti fortified the gates and bridges and began in 1354 the construction of a new strong *enceinte* with bastions and moats that took about thirty years to finish and remained more or less the same until the end of the 19th century. The *Castello,* not to be confused with the *Cittadella,* was built in 1471 on the site of the later Giardino Ducale.

In 1546 Parma came into the possession of the Farnese and was, together with Piacenza, handed over by Pope Paul III (Alessandro Farnese) to his son Luigi Farnese, assassinated in 1547. He was followed by eight dukes of the Farnese family. In 1550 a new bridge was constructed over the Parma in continuation of the bridge of Theodoric on which houses had been built after the river had changed its course. These houses were demolished in 1553 and the Ponte dei Salari was constructed about 300 feet upstream. The Giardino Ducale, begun in 1560 by Ottavio Farnese, covers about 49.4 acres (today the Giardino Pubblico). Work at the *Cittadella,* still existing in its original form, was started in 1591 at the south of the city outside the walls under the direction of the military engineer Smeraldo Smeraldi, obviously influenced by the citadel of Antwerp: it had the same pentagonal shape with five bastions at the angles and five curtains connecting them.

After a conspiracy of some of the nobles against Duke Ranuccio I in 1610, all patricians living in the surrounding countryside were obliged to have mansions in the city. Many palaces were built in the zone east of the Parma, called *Parma Nuova,* and on the other bank previously known as *Capodiponte.*

The vast Palazzo Farnese, commonly called La Pilotta, consists of a group of buildings including, apart from the palace, the Academy, the Picture Gallery, the Library, and the Farnese Theater (built in 1618, opened in 1628 on the occasion of the marriage of the duke with a princess of Tuscany, and designed by Giambatista Aleotti, a disciple of Palladio). It was bombed during World War II but has recently been restored. Dickens, who visited it in 1844, described it as

. . . a large wooden structure of the horse-shoe shape; the lower seats arranged upon the Roman plan, but above them, great heavy chambers, rather than boxes, where the Nobles sat, remote in their proud state. Such desolation as has fallen on this theatre, enhanced in the spectator's fancy by its gay intention and design, none but worms can be familiar with.[66]

After the extinction of the House of Farnese in 1731 and after 15 years as part of the Napoleonic Empire the Duchy became the property of Marie Louise of Austria, the consort of Napoleon, who reigned from 1815 to 1847. During this time the Teatro Ducale, later the Teatro Regio, and the Palazzo Ducale, now the *Prefettura,* were built (destroyed in 1944 and not reconstructed).

66. Charles Dickens. *Pictures from Italy.* 1846. Pp. 22-23.

208. Air view of the center of Parma with the cathedral precincts in the foreground.

209. View of the islet of La Frata, the nucleus of the Forum Alieni by Alfonso Maresta (1778). The following illustrations are from the same source.

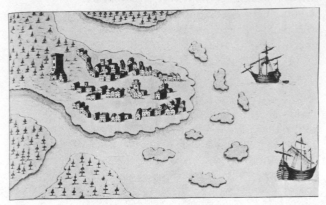

210. The Isle of Ferrariola, where refugees from La Frata sought shelter about A.D. 310.

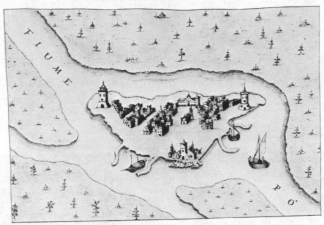

211. Ferrara Transpadana with the pontoon bridge from Ferrariola.

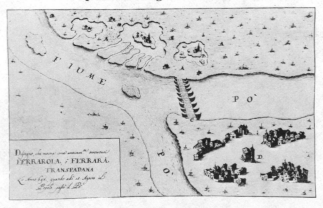

Ferrara. The origin of Ferrara is shrouded in mystery but enlivened by legendary speculations according to which it was founded either by Pelasgians from the eastern Mediterranean calling it *Massalia* as indicated by Polybius or by Trojans.[67] It is assumed that an Etruscan and then a Gallic settlement existed at *Codrea,* a focal point in the network of communications where the Po divides into three branches, and that later perhaps a second center was founded on the left bank of the river on the site of the present quarter of San Giorgio which may have been the *Forum Alieni* mentioned by Tacitus and by Boccaccio as existing since 222 B.C. This Roman marketplace is the only reliable point of reference in the otherwise rather nebulous history of the origin of Ferrara. In any case, this is more probable than the hypothetical assumptions connected with the Pelasgians or Trojans, who are more likely to have founded the nearby port of Spina further east in the sixth century B.C. This port declined in the second century B.C. and finally disappeared almost at the same time the *Forum Alieni* was established.

The Roman nucleus of the *Forum Alieni* was located on an islet in the Po called *La Frata* or *Ferrata.* It consisted of a group of houses arranged around a market square as revealed by excavations (1911). However, at a certain moment all further information about this early settlement stops, although according to unverified tradition the inhabitants were said to have abandoned the islet in the fourth century A.D. We hear again of an island *Ferrariola,* formerly called *Vico Abenza,* in the middle of the Po near Consandoli, probably identical with the present Voghenza, where refugees from Ferrara settled about A.D. 310. But this latter conclusion is by no means certain: Voghenza had been inhabited since Roman times, became an episcopal see in A.D. 330,

67. F. Borgatti. "La piana di Ferrara nel 1597," *Atti e Memorie della Deputazione Ferrarese di Storia Patria.* Vol. VII, No. 1. 1895.

G. Righini. "Come si è formata la città di Ferrara," *Atti e Memorie della Deputazione Ferrarese di Storia Patria.* Nuova Serie, Vol. XIV. 1955. Pp. 55-96.

B. Zevi. *Biagio Rossetti, architetto ferrarese, il primo urbanista moderno europeo.* 1960. Pp. 138-233.

and was destroyed in the fifth century by the Huns. *Ferrariola* was probably one of the settlements created by people overrun by the barbarians. Its center corresponded with the ancient Roman *forum* and later with the monastery of S. Giorgio whose church was elevated to the cathedral of the city in 657.

At this time only a few huts of fishermen and two churches stood on the left bank of the Po where the future Ferrara was to develop. A pontoon bridge was thrown from *Ferrariola* Island to the left bank to enable the inhabitants to flee from the invaders (A.D. 698), and to find safety behind the walls of the defense works constructed on the left bank of the Po to protect Ravenna against Lombard attacks. *Ferrariola* was almost completely abandoned, although the church of S. Giorgio was maintained.

During the following centuries an intensive urban development took place along the riverfront with a considerable increase in commerce and communications since the area further inland was too marshy and unsuitable for building. In this period an important project was launched on the initiative of Archbishop Felice of Ravenna: the Po was divided into two branches, the Po di Volano and the Po di Primario (709). By this time the name of Ferrara was firmly established; it was mentioned in a charter given by Astolfo, King of the Lombards, in A.D. 753 or 754. At the end of the ninth century the existence and development of the city was assured. A canal was constructed about 880 diverting the stagnant waters in the marshy area to the Po. It was crossed by three bridges connecting the newly

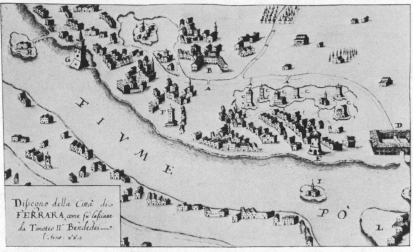

212. Ferrara about A.D. 800 with the new canal and the two castles (E and G).

gained land with the older settlement on the river bank. On the new tracts a riding school and numerous fortified mansions with towers were erected, and on the river the Piazza di S. Paolo was laid out.

Reclamation continued in the tenth century. Another canal was dug and more land added to the urban area. The building density increased; palaces and warehouses were erected. The city expanded along the river mainly between the two strongholds, the Castello dei Cortesi in the east, also called *Castrum Ferrariae,* and the Castel Tedaldo in the west (984), probably on the site of an earlier structure belonging to the Marquess of Canossa.

As protection against attacks by the troops of Countess Matilda of Canossa trying to regain possession of the castle of Tedaldo, walls were constructed along the southern side of the city. These defenses were partly destroyed in the fighting but reconstructed after a short time. In the 12th century the crisis had been

213. Ferrara after the reconstruction, showing a high building density and new walls.

overcome. With the passing of the feudal regime and the institution of Ferrara as a free *Comune* a period of prosperity and expansion began. Commerce and crafts flourished, and awareness of civic pride and consolidation of urban unity stimulated the citizens to cooperative efforts in the development of their community. At the beginning of the 13th century the urban area of Ferrara extended for about .621 mile along the river between the two castles, and for .310 mile inland. The cathedral, begun in 1135 and finished in the second half of the 13th century, exerted a considerable influence as the religious and physical symbol upon the reorganization of the city: the cathedral square became the nodal point of a number of new streets. To the north a new quarter was laid out, centered on what is today the Via Cairoli. The walls, surrounding the northern part of the city, were adapted to the redevelopment of the interior without fundamentally changing the medieval character of the community. Outside the walls a triangular

open space was created, the *pratum bestiarum,* where cattle were assembled and slaughtered. Apart from its religious significance, the new city center soon assumed political, social, and economic functions. In 1283 the Palazzo del Signore was built opposite the cathedral and along its side the Piazza del Mercato was laid out with guildhalls, warehouses, and taverns. During the following centuries more space was added to the urban area, extensions primarily dictated by political, military, and economic considerations. Tremendous efforts were made to overcome the difficulties of the terrain but these efforts were unrelated, haphazard, and without a comprehensive development plan.

Ferrara remained a medieval city without a personality until Biagio Rossetti designed the extension that was to be known as *Addizione Erculea* or *Terra Nuova,* and may be regarded as one of the first systematic city planning projects of the Renaissance.[68] Since the 13th century the Este had been rulers of Ferrara and

68. For details, see B. Zevi, *op. cit.,* pp. 142-49.

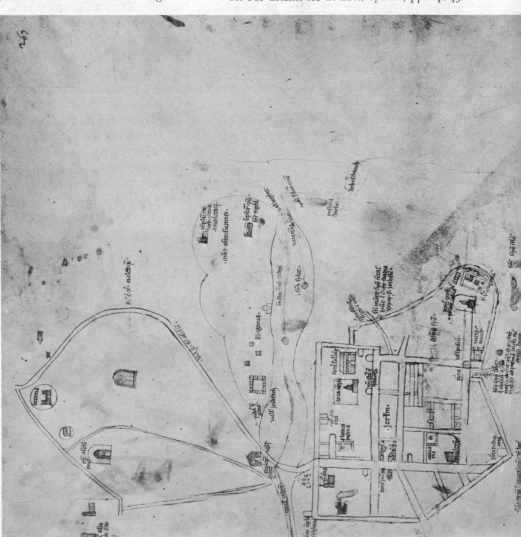

214. Schematic representation of Ferrara, clearly expressing the essential characteristics of the urban structure and form. It shows Ferrara with a suburb at the west at a time after the year 1326 when the *palatium comunitatis* was built in the center of the town. The sharp separation of suburb and town reflects the continuous fight between rivaling factions in the first decade of the 14th century. To the south of the town, at a point where the Po di Primaro and the Po di Volano branch off, is situated the island of S. Antonio, later incorporated in the urban area. Between the Volano and Primaro is the suburb of S. Giorgio, the site of the early cathedral of Ferrara. The picture is particularly interesting because it shows the situation of Ferrara in relation to the waterways, the main justification of its medieval existence. The drawing is the most ancient representation of Ferrara and is contained in the Vatican Codex 1960, 267.

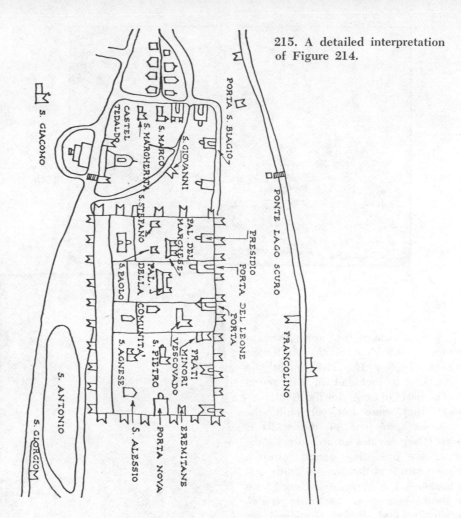

215. A detailed interpretation of Figure 214.

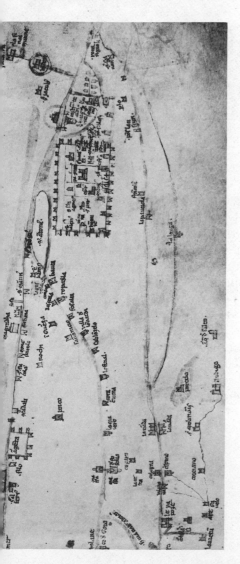

the splendor of their court attracted numerous artists, humanists, architects, and poets. The war with Venice (1482-1484) convinced the ruler Ercole I that the existing fortifications were insufficient and that a new extension with stronger walls was urgently needed. Moreover, since 1480 the population had increased, especially through the influx of a large number of Jews from Spain. The territory of the *Addizione Erculea* was soon occupied by the growing population but the war with Venice had shown how easily it could be overrun by an enemy. The political miracle, as Zevi points out, was that Ercole decided to further the immigration, to make Ferrara numerically a strong city, and to expand its economic activities. In order to realize his plans and not to dilute their effects like *"a macchia d'olio"*— spot of oil—or to intersperse poor quarters among stately buildings, he undertook to lay out a new city on the vast territory at the

303

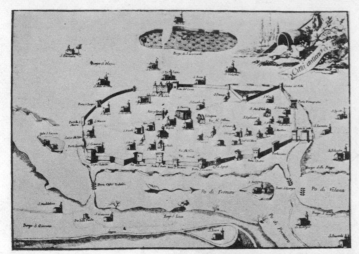

216. Ferrara in 1395, showing the triangular *pratum bestiarum* at the north outside the walls. Design attributed to Bartolino da Novara, engineer of the Este in the second half of the 14th century, and elaborated by Frizzi in the 19th century.

217. The old and the new town of Ferrara at the time of the *Addizione Erculea* (1498). The river mouth of S. Antonio is included in the southeastern part of the fortifications. Although they were not yet built, the whole northern part of the walls is shown. They enclose an area double the size of the preceding period. (In the picture north is at the top and south is at the bottom.) The map is reproduced from the fourth volume of the *Storie di Pellegrino Prisciani* in the Municipal Archives of Modena (MS. 130).

north of the urban area.[69] The supervision of this project was entrusted to Biagio Rossetti. It involved the unification of the ancient and the new cities and the transformation of the old moat of the Giovecca into an arterial road.

The ideological impetus behind this vast enterprise was the longing to emulate other cities embellished by magnificent churches and sumptuous palaces, and the desire of the noble families not to live any longer in the narrow and tortuous streets of the medieval quarters. And, as Zevi remarks, a psychological reason certainly played an important role: the need to impress the people with the grandeur of

69. *Ibid.*, p. 144.

military parades along imposing straight avenues. Finally, there was the social problem of class distinction: medieval streets were the sanctuary of the pedestrian whether wealthy or poor; but wide and straight roads could be used by people on horseback and later by carriages, and pedestrians had to guard against being harmed. Moreover, the transition from a small-scale communal economy to a commercial large-scale era, from a democratic broadly based to a mercantile economy directed by a small power élite initiated privilege of an oligarchy of a lucky few. It was this fact that found its visual crystalization in the plans for the new city.

218. View of Ferrara at the beginning of the 16th century after the *Addizione Erculea* had been finished. It shows the preservation of large parts of the ancient northern walls and the Porta dei Leoni (center of the picture). A woodcut from the *Annotazioni istoriche* by Alessandro Sardi in the Biblioteca Estense of Modena (MS. Itl. 408, F.3.17).

219. Silver plate of the reliquary of S. Maurelio in the Church of S. Giorgio in Ferrara of the first years of the 16th century. It shows the two branches of the Po di Volano (left) and the Po di Primaro (right), with the Church of S. Giorgio between them, and the southeastern corner of the city on the left bank of the Po di Volano; part of the walls on the left, and the so-called mura di Borso built by Borso d'Este.

Rossetti's plan provided for two axes crossing each other at right angles—today the Corso Vittorio Emanuele, between the Porta degli Angeli in the north and the *Castello* in the center, and the Corso di Porta Po continuing as Corso di Porta Mare and connecting the two gates respectively. At the intersection of these two streets four palaces were erected, the Palazzo de' Diamanti being the most interesting of these. It was built by Rossetti (begun in 1492 and not completed until 1567). The whole area was surrounded by walls with 16 towers and three gates. Special taxes were levied upon the population, even on the employees of the Court and the members of the university, and the landowners of the Duchy were ordered to supply peasants for this work. The plan was conceived and executed on a gridiron system. The streets were wide, the Corso Vittorio Emanuele measuring 48 feet, of which 36 were reserved for the roadway and 6 on either side for pedestrian walkways, sep-arated by large stones from the road. This was the principal street leading to the *Castello* and was lined with gardens and palaces. The Corso di Porta Po was 6 feet wider but the houses flanking it and the surrounding streets were less stately than those of the Corso Vit-

torio Emanuele. The main square, the Piazza Nuova, was situated not on the intersection of the arteries as Ercole wanted but at a distance in the northeastern part of the new city.

Zevi emphasizes the independence and life-centered approach of Rossetti toward his task, the avoidance of the two extremes, of abstract and theoretical rationalism, banal empiricism, and of predetermining every detail of the

220. Air view of Ferrara with the old city (in the foreground) and new quarters.

221. Perspective view of Ferrara, the earliest attempt to show the entire city. It dates from the first year of the pontifical rule and shows the last features of the extension in the Este period just before some modifications were carried out, such as the construction of the Cittadella. The map is dedicated by its author Giacomo di Novo to the Pope in 1598 and revised in 1602. Biblioteca Comunale di Ferrara.

222. Piazza Nuova, today Piazza Ariostea, from Antonio Frizzi's *Guida del forestiere per la Città di Ferrara*, 1787. At the left the street leading to the Porta di S. Giovanni, now the Porta Mare.

urban aspect—and, on the other hand, of the convenient faith in "spontaneous" growth. He did not intend to build an Ideal City but a city for ideal living. This is especially evident in the relationship of the streets to the fortified periphery. In the Ideal Cities the structure of the fortifications determined the layout of the streets—that is, the city was built from the outside in. Rossetti rejected this principle. His walls followed the natural configuration of the terrain, avoiding the geometrical rigidity that made the fortifications of Ideal Cities oppressive enclosures dictated exclusively by military considerations; the streets he designed did not run up against the powerful barrier of the walls and were not subordinated to their structural exigencies. Instead he created a plan organically held together by a dynamic equilibrium in which the inhabited area was the main or determining factor. "It was a continuous dialogue between the regular pattern of the streets and the natural and expressive course of the walls." [70]

As is so often the case, good intentions and principles were not enough to produce excellent results. Rossetti's plan is interesting and valuable as a counterpoise to the unimaginative rigidity of the theoreticians and the dictatorial demands of the military engineers, but it cannot be regarded as a major masterpiece of Renaissance city planning. A brave attempt to break away from a fashionable dogma, it nevertheless remains a rather uninspiring attempt to vitalize the gridiron layout and to adapt it to the manifold aspirations and activities of the community as a whole. Rossetti was not the architect of the people but the exponent of the ruling oligarchy, which may explain and excuse the shortcomings of his work.

At the end of the 16th century a certain stagnation set in, followed by a decline. "The duke is most negligent of embellishing the city," wrote the secretary of the Florentine Orazio della Rena.[71] Ferrara, *La Gran Donna del Po,* became "a mature woman" in full exuberance of her charm but resting on her laurels, on the *maniera grande,* and pride in the House of Este. There were 58 great palaces, 15 large churches, 35,000 inhabitants, and the beautiful Isola Belvedere created by Alfonso I at the beginning of the 16th century. At this time Ferrara was one of the noblest and most celebrated cities of Italy. Everywhere it was enlivened by verdure, in the streets, in private homes, and on the periphery encircling the city. At the north there was the Giardino del Padiglione; at the west, a long tract planted with trees near the water twined like a garland along three-quarters of the interior of the walls.

On January 28 of the year 1598, the last Este left Ferrara. The next day Cardinal Pietro Aldobrandini, nephew of Pope Clemens VIII, entered the city and placed the "Holy Keys" of the pope on the four towers of the *Castello.* The eagles, the emblem of the Este, ceded their place to the *Sante Chiavi.* The papal rule was not popular and could be maintained only by a strong Austrian garrison which was withdrawn in 1859. In the following year Ferrara was united with the Kingdom of Sardinia.

Ferrara! in thy wide and grass-grown streets,
Whose symmetry was not for solitude,
There seems as 'twere a curse upon the seats
Of former sovereigns, and the antique brood
Of Este, which for many an age made good
Its strength within thy walls, and was of yore
Patron or tyrant, as the changing mood
Of petty power impell'd, of those who wore
The wreath which Dante's brow alone had
    worn before.
       —LORD BYRON, "Childe Harold's
        Pilgrimage," Canto IV, xxxv.

Modena. Modena stands on a low plain in the southern part of the Po Valley between the Secchia and the Panaro. It was traversed by the *Via Aemilia,* the main artery of Emilia Province. Situated at the confluence of numerous canals which in time have been transformed into streets, Modena had the appear-

---

70. *Ibid.,* p. 147.
71. Quoted after G. Righini, *op. cit.,* p. 83.

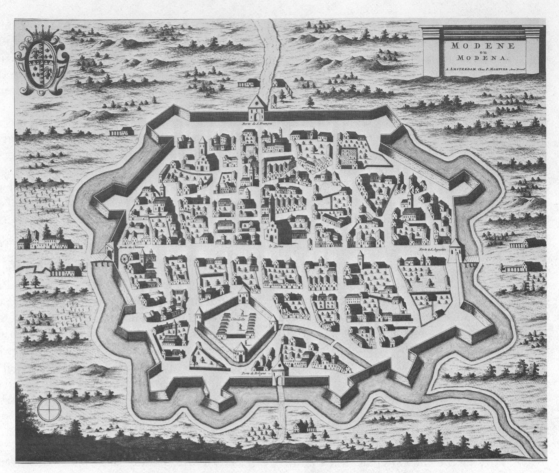

223. Plan of Modena from Joan Blaeu's *Nieuw vermeerderd en verbeterd Groot stede-boek van geheel Italie* . . . , published in Amsterdam in 1724.

224. Map of Modena in 1790, with the citadel and the adjoining Piazza d'Armi and the regular layout of the *Addizione Erculea* north of the ancient center.

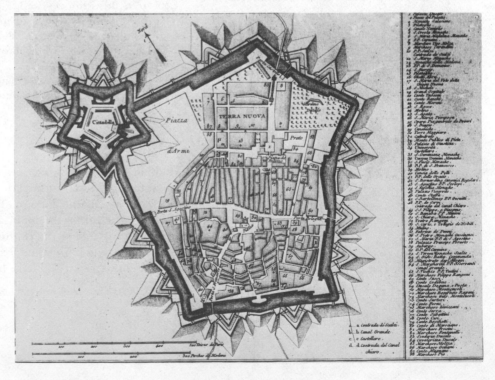

ance of a waterside city. Of Etruscan origin Roman *Mutina,* called by Cicero *firmissima et splendidissima colonia,* was the earliest Roman colony in this region of Italy (183 B.C.). It was soon made a *municipium.* Its gridiron layout has been preserved in the central area of the present city. The first religious buildings of the Christian era rose outside the Roman walls—*extra moenia*—including the residence of the bishop.

When the Roman town was destroyed by the barbarian invasions the citizens moved to a new site several miles to the northwest. The privileges granted by the emperors to the bishops were restricted to the episcopal precincts forming a nucleus around the cathedral. When in the ninth century walls were constructed by Bishop Leodoino the population began to settle in the new town, taking advantage of the greater security and the prospects of peace and constructive work.

After A.D. 1000 Modena developed vigorously. By 1071 a new and wider *enceinte* was built by Bishop Eriberto, whose course is still preserved, at least in parts of the Rua Muro. The first communal institutions were evolved in the feudal period under the rule of Matilda, Countess of Canossa. In 1099 the reconstruction of the cathedral was begun by Lanfranco and finished in the 13th century by Comacini masters. Outside the walls suburbs grew up which, in a short time, had become so important that in 1188 new advance fortifications (the so-called *terragli*) with drawbridges had to be constructed. Internal feuds led first to the erection of numerous towers and later to their destruction. At the end of the 13th century the Este, rulers of Ferrara, built a fortified castle in Modena, which they had conquered. This foreign stronghold was later destroyed by the people and the overlordship passed to the Bonacolsi of Mantua, who in 1327 initiated the construction of the third circumvallation in place of the *terragli.* This wall was, however, not completed by the Este until 1361 after their return to Modena in 1335. Under their rule building activities remained limited in the 15th century, but population increase and

225. The center of Modena with the Duomo (1099–1184) and the Torre Ghirlandina.

the growing self-esteem of Modena as the capital of the duchy made an extension of the city imperative. Ercole II therefore ordered the construction of a powerful ring of fortifications strengthened by bastions around the ancient nucleus (1546-56). The result was less fortunate than the *addizione Erculea* at Ferrara a century before. An organic unity of the new and the old city, as it had been achieved at Ferrara by Biagio Rossetti, was missing. Thus Renaissance Modena was severed from the rest of the community, a disadvantage felt particularly in the ancient nucleus by the reduction of the gates for military reasons from twelve to four. At the same time the "Canal Grande" was filled in to be converted into the most elegant street of the residential district. In the true spirit of the 17th century —the era of local and national potentates who while overestimating their self-importance never concealed their conceit, vanity, and vul-

311

gar ostentation—the Este built the immense Palazzo Ducale, later the Palazzo Reale. It proved too large for the small dimensions of the city and the Duchy but served as a symbol of self-glorification for the House of Este, and by its mere existence aggravated the contrast in the atmosphere and scale of the medieval and Renaissance-Baroque areas of the city. Its architect was Bartolomeo Avanzini, a pupil of Bernini.

In the 18th century, under the rule of Duke Francesco III, a comprehensive plan was carried out for a civic center: Surrounding a large square a group of public buildings was arranged consisting of museums and the important Biblioteca Estense, a large hospital, and a house for workmen. However, this redevelopment did not affect other parts of the city. The new street, extending on both sides of the square, dissected the urban area as an alternative to the narrow *Via Aemilia* running parallel to it through the old city. After the Napoleonic invasion a *piano d'ornato,* a plan for purely decorative purposes, was developed: arcades were built to widen the narrower streets depriving them of their characteristic atmosphere without any sanitary gains.

The usual deterioration of the architectural values of the preceding periods, through the impact of the Industrial Revolution, was the work of the 19th century. The old center underwent far-reaching modifications; the fortifications of the Este and the citadel, built in the 17th century, were demolished; the unity of the *Piazza* of Francesco III was destroyed, and a sort of slum clearance was undertaken in one of the central quarters. The population numbering 130,000 moved to the peripheral districts, whereas in the central city it decreased to 20,000. Today the ancient center of Modena is no longer the actual hub of the city where decisions are made. After decennia of neglect and insensibility a sense of responsibility is emerging, a willingness to remedy the sins of omission of the past.

226. **Air view of Modena, showing the old part and the *Addizione Erculea* and the outline of the ancient walls.**

227. Pisa in the 17th century. Engraving from Joan Blaeu's *Nieuw vermeerderd en verbeterd Groot stedeboek van geheel Italie . . .* , published in Amsterdam in 1724.

Pisa. The earliest settlement on the site of the future Pisa was situated between the Arno and the Ausar on a headland, but alluvial accumulation moved the coastline about 4 miles out to sea in the tenth century (7 miles today). Ancient *Pisae* was possibly founded from *Pisa* in Elis on the Peloponnesus. The first historically reliable reference dates from 225 B.C., the year in which a Roman army landed from Sardinia at this point of the coast. In 180 B.C. Pisa became a Roman colony and under Augustus received the name of *Colonia Julia Pisana.*

Even with the receding sea and the shallowness of the water at the mouth of the Arno, the harbor was serviceable, offering space for shipbuilding and a fleet. The rise of Pisa to one of the first ports and commercial cities of the Mediterranean and to the main rival of Genoa in the Tyrrhenian Sea set in at the beginning of the 11th century, furthered by its leadership in the fight against the infidels. In 1025 the Saracens were ejected from Sardinia; in 1030 and 1089 they were defeated at Tunis;

their navy was destroyed in 1063 at Palermo; the Balearic Islands were conquered in 1114; and participation in the crusades heightened the prestige and the power of the Pisan community. The 12th and 13th centuries were the Golden Age of the city. Its commerce extended over the whole of the Mediterranean. Pisa had stations at Constantinople, Antioch, Sidon, Alexandria, and Cairo. At this time it was a market for products from the Orient. Its main industry was cloth making. Water, indispensable for industrial activities, was supplied through canals and aqueducts.

Pisa was ruled by an aristocratic minority that sided with the Ghibelline party. After a war of 14 years with Genoa the power of Pisa was crushed in the battle of Meloria (1284). Corsica had to be ceded in 1300 and Sardinia was transferred by the pope to the kings of Aragon in 1320. Internal feuds weakened the city. In 1421 Florence acquired the town of Livorno situated on the coast. Pisa became subject to Florence. Its harbor was silting up, sealing its fate as a maritime power.

314

228. *Opposite:* Palazzo dell' Orologio in Pisa.

Pisa's first and only complete fortifications were constructed in the second half of the 12th century.[73] In a lagoon-city, protection by walls was not a primary necessity. It is possible, though not definitely proven, that a Roman fort, the *oppidum triangolare,* at the port was the nucleus of medieval Pisa.[74] When the sea receded, defense through canals and fortified towers was at first considered sufficient. The few access roads were protected by gates and gate-towers until the intervening gaps between the gates were closed by walls. This work was begun in 1156. Bernardo Maragone has described the earliest fortifications in *Annales Pisani,*

Fecerunt barbacanas circa civitatem Pisanam et Kinticam et inceperunt civitatem murare et compleverunt murum civitatis a turre, ubi posuerunt leonem marmoreum usque ad turrem que est supter pontem Ausaris.

And in the following year (1157):

Circumierunt totam urbem Pisanam et Kinticam ligneis turribus et castellis et bitischis pro timore Frederici Regis Romam venientis.[75]

73. Cf. also pp. 96-99.

74. W. Braunfels. *Mittelalterliche Stadtbaukunst in der Toskana.* 1953. Pp. 54 ff.

75. M. L. Gentile (ed.). *Gli Annales pisani di Bernardo Maragone.* 1936. "They built fortifications around the city of Pisa and Kintica [the port of Pisa], and they began to wall in the city, completing the city wall from the tower where they erected a marble lion to the tower above the Ausaris bridge." . . . "[They] surrounded the entire city of Pisa along with Kintica with wooden towers, fortresses and parapets, for fear of King Frederic who was coming to Rome."

The building of the walls was begun at many points at the same time and, in contrast to the later fortifications of other cities in Tuscany, the gates did not project beyond the height of the walls. The *enceinte* enclosed an urban area that was sufficient for all later centuries. It determined the definite size and shape of the city as a finished product, as a complete entity. According to tradition Bonannus, the architect of the cathedral, may also have been the constructor of the walls although no definite proof has been offered so far.

The driving power behind the political, economic, and artistic efflorescence of Pisa during this period was Coccus, who as consul dominated the administration of the city for 18 years and may be regarded as one of the great promoters of urban renewal in the earlier history of Tuscany. Maragone reports almost year for year his contributions listing the baptistery, the walls, the canal, several bridges, the arsenal, two towers at the harbor, the first Palazzo Comunale of the Province, the citadel Ripafacto with its strong defenses, and many more buildings.[76]

Several *Breves* have been preserved which testify to the constant care of the municipal administration for the maintenance and improvement of the public buildings and the beautification of the city. A few of these regulations may be mentioned. The *Breve* of 1286 contained a detailed order to keep the walls

76. W. Braunfels, *op. cit.,* p. 56.

free from encroachments, a malpractice that in many cases had resulted in deterioration of the efficiency in the defense system. In Pisa it was therefore requested to leave a road of 20 feet free inside and a tract of 60 feet outside the walls.[77] A *Breve* of 1162 instructs the *capitani murorum* to administer an oath to the masons in charge of the construction of the walls, a procedure somewhat akin to making them "chartered surveyors." Projecting structures, oriels and other parts of the buildings narrowing the width of the streets were looked at askance by the authorities. After a fire of 1158, a *Breve* was issued in 1164 at first forbidding all projecting parts which were mostly of wood on the banks of the Arno, and later reducing them in depth. The height of oriels above the streets was fixed to avoid impediment of traffic; in less important streets permission for projecting parts was made dependent on the consent of the neighbor although arcades were not affected by any regulations especially not, if they were more than 40 years old. In the course of time the extension of projecting parts was related to the width of the street: for instance, in the 14th century roofs could project up to a third and balconies up to a quarter of the width of the road. [78] As early as 1164 it is known that the main streets on both banks of the Arno and several others had to be paved. In the *Breve* of 1286 this directive became law, leaving it to the contractors to use bricks or flag-

stones. Looms were not to be placed in the streets except in the case of women operating them in front of their own homes.

The layout of Pisa in general and in detail is quite irregular, seemingly without any system. The cathedral square, the spiritual center of the city, is situated at the extreme northwest corner outside the residential area. This may have been dictated by the fact that already in an early period the lagoon had formed solid dry land suitable for building. The ensemble of the cathedral, the baptistery, the *campanile,* and the Campo Santo must have been for the inhabitants of medieval Pisa like a castle, a religious stronghold, protecting and dominating their city like a citadel. And just as the situation of a castle outside of or at the end of the city was not felt as an architectural or symbolic disadvantage, the eccentric location of the sanctuary was rather an attraction, a meaningful reminder of the divine essence spreading its blessings and magic spell over the daily life of the citizens. From their congested quarters they walked through narrow streets to the wide open square, making their visit to the cathedral an extraordinary event, an elating experience removed from the hustle and bustle of their ordinary existence. The city was like an annex of this castle of God. In Assisi something similar was done and, if we so wish, even at Versailles, though with the slight difference that here it was the Roi Soleil, not God, to whom obedient subjects paid reverence.

77. *Ibid.*, p. 63.
78. *Ibid.*, p. 111.

316

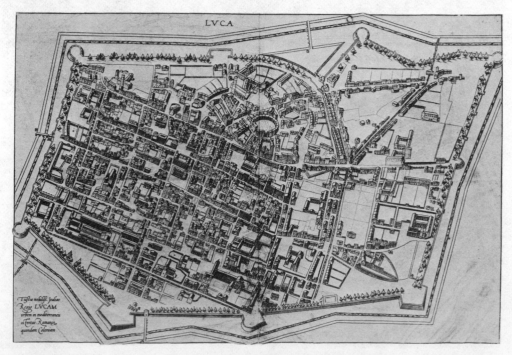

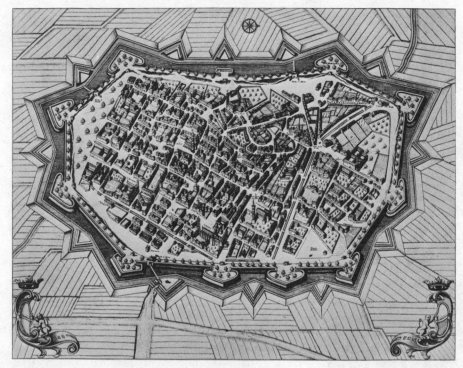

230. Map of Lucca at the end of the 17th century within the same circuit of ramparts now strengthened by bastions, making the city a "Flemish Fortress". Engraving by Pierre Mortier.

Lucca. Lucca is situated in the fertile valley of the Serchio, between the Apuan Alps in the north and the Pisano Mountains in the south. The river played a considerable role in the life of the town for three reasons. Protection from floods was difficult; defense against enemies was facilitated; and water supply for agriculture, industries, and handicrafts was available. In prehistoric times the region around Lucca was an alluvial plain of the Serchio with little land emerging from the water and much swampy ground. This period was followed by a ramification of the river in numerous branches and changes of its course resulting from the opening of the narrow valleys of the Serchio and Saltocchio toward the Lucchese Plain. Finally, in the historical period, the Serchio divided into three directions,

229. *Opposite:* Map of Lucca about 1580, showing approximately the same perimeter as in the following century (1645). At the east, along the Condotto Pubblico, suburbs of artisans have grown up. Large open spaces, with gardens and mansions, are preserved within the walls. Engraving in the Archivio di Stato at Lucca.

the most important branch skimming the site of Lucca at the southeast and leading in its last part approximately to the Ozzeri Canal, the ancient *Auser*. In the Middle Ages the riverbed rose owing to considerable deposits carried by the river, and land for cultivation was formed. The first regulation of the watercourse was undertaken in 1495. The embankment of the Saltocchio took place between 1562 and 1569, and the final regulation of the Serchio was carried through by Lorenzo Nottolini (1777-1851), directing its downward flow south along the foot of the hills at the north, where it received the waters of several smaller streams, although these works did not guarantee absolute protection against floods.

The availability of ample water resources made the defense of Lucca relatively simple through the use of wide moats, the surrounding marshes representing a major obstacle to attacks and sieges.

The economic development of the city was greatly stimulated by the abundant water supply. Irrigation was promoted and water was led since medieval times through the *Condotto Pubblico* close to the urban area as

317

the indispensable source of the many industrial activities, such as the spinning mills of the Via dei Fossi situated within the walls.

The origin of Lucca (*Luca*) dates back to the Etruscan period when the hydrographical conditions, still in the course of consolidation, were not very inviting. The first settlement may have been more like a military encampment, almost like a raft, a *zattera,* protected by the waters of the lagoon and anchored close to the *terra firma* with its hills and mountains. It was a location that dictated the original function of Lucca as the "bridgehead" at the meeting point of the mountain zone and the open country with the main Italian roads. From Florence a branch of the *Via Cassia* led to the *Via Aemilia Scauri* and hence to Lucca and further to *Pisae* and *Luna.* At the crossing of the roads there was a so-called *Mansione,* a resting place. From Poggibonsi the *Via Clodia* ran via Pontedera to Lucca, continuing to Parma. Another road reached Lucca from *Pisae.* Thus the situation of Lucca as the nodal point of a vast network of important routes made it a first-class traffic center in the Roman period.

Roman Lucca, first an *oppidum,* then a *municipium,* had four gates and nine posterns, the *Via Cassia* penetrating through the east gate, the Porta di S. Gervasio, following the *decumanus* to the Porta S. Donato in the west then crossing outside the walls the *Via Aemilia Scauri.* The *Via Clodia* reached the city from

231. Old gate at Lucca.

232. Air view of Lucca, showing clearly the unchanged shape of the medieval city.

233. Air view of the square on the site of a Roman amphitheater at Lucca and the densely built-up surrounding quarter.

the south through the Porta di S. Pietro Maggiore, following the *cardo,* and left it through the northern gate, the Porta di S. Frediano, proceeding to Parma. The site of the Piazza S. Michele at the intersection of the *decumanus* and *cardo* has always been the center of the city. The amphitheater was situated outside the walls at the Porta di S. Vincenzo; the theater was located west of the same gate within the fortifications. In the course of time the ruins of the amphitheater were used for the establishment of shops and houses, leaving

the interior as an open space. The perimeter of the Roman city amounted to 2,732 yards, occupying an area of about 96.4 acres, with a population of approximately 10,000 inhabitants.

The medieval fortifications of Lucca were built in the second half of the 13th century with a minor extension of the earlier walls of the ninth century toward the south and major extensions at the west, east, and north, including several suburbs and the Roman amphitheater. This *enceinte,* finished in 1260, was constructed in regular rows of square stones and reinforced semicircular towers about 35 feet high, four gates, and eight posterns. The gateways were protected by two battlemented lateral towers and two advanced towers, drawbridges, and enormous wooden doors, defenses worthy of the flourishing community with a prospering economy, especially in silk manufacture, banking, and commerce. Lucca was the first town of Tuscany whose economic influence spread beyond its own territory, and also the first town of Italy manufacturing silk. Its unchallenged supremacy in this field for more than 100 years came to an end only after political unrest forced numerous merchants and craftsmen to emigrate. These refugees established similar industries in Florence, Bologna, Venice, and Genoa. However, this loss was not too severely felt: the commercial class of Lucca had always included more merchants than manufacturers and as such it was a leading element in the trade of Western Europe, in particular with France, until the beginning of the 19th century. Lucca had been an important economic and political center since the later Lombard era. It had a mint, and its coins were legal tender all over Italy. It was engaged in the manufacture of luxury cloth, and its leading merchants were wealthy and influential, so much so that they could induce the Emperor Henry IV to grant them complete exemption from duties on all their transactions in the markets from Pavia to Rome.[79]

Numerous religious buildings were erected

79. G. Luzzatto. *An Economic History of Italy from the Fall of the Roman Empire to the Beginning of the Sixteenth Century.* 1961. Pp. 58, 96.

inside and outside the walls. The urban area was gradually filling up though large open spaces were still left particularly in the northern part near the periphery. In 1322 a citadel, *l'Augusta,* was constructed by order of Castruccio Castracani, after a design by Giotto covering almost one quarter of the city. It was surrounded on the outer side by the existing walls and toward the interior by new ramparts. However, this stronghold was destroyed by the people in 1369 after the end of the domination of Lucca by Pisa.

In the first half of the 16th century a comprehensive extension of the city was begun but not completed until 1650. This *enceinte* corresponded to the actual circumvallation still existing today. The extension enclosed large areas in the northeast, the south, and the west where parts of the old walls were used and strengthened by large circular towers protected by escarps. Three bastions were added to this elaborate defense system. From 1544 to 1575 numerous military engineers were employed in this work: from Modena, Pesaro, Urbino, Civitali, Milano, and Salerno, and private citizens made considerable contributions, such as 60,000 cartloads of stone by a Ludovico Penitesi. In 1571 Flemish engineers were consulted as particularly experienced experts in the contemporary problems of military engineering. It is interesting to note that work continued without an over-all plan, but in the end the defenses were completed in accordance with the Italian principles of an *"aspetto definitivo bastionato all'italiana."*[80] The ramparts consisted of 12 curtains, 10 bastions with buttresses and a platform with double escarps on the exterior side and on the interior with an embankment 90 feet wide at its base. The city was defended by 124 cannons of large caliber placed in the bastions, and by two other ones of 12,000 pounds each. The bastions had subterranean storerooms for provisions and ammunition connected with the top of the bastions by spiral staircases and were accessible from the city by ramps. A moat almost 100 feet wide, 12 demilunes, and a glacis completed the fortifications. The expenses were considerable, involving an outlay of 900,000 scudi. Five to six million bricks were used alone for adjusting the disparities between the different parts of the walls.

At this period several suburbs, mostly inhabited by artisans and craftsmen, existed. The population numbered about 30,000 citizens.

Lucca is a rare example of a city that can look back on an uninterrupted urban tradition responding in an almost miraculous way to the challenge of the various periods without substantial modifications in its physical structure. From the military-oriented needs of an *oppidum* Lucca developed to the complex religious-oriented city of the Middle Ages with its intimate and intense daily life, its economic activities, and its unison of individual and corporate responsibility. The spatial organism and unity of the city were maintained even under the stress of far-reaching functional changes, a fact especially evident in the preservation of the 17th-century fortifications until today.

In the 19th century the walls were transformed into gardens and the bastions were planted with trees. In the 20th century Lucca expanded; new quarters grew up outside the walls; but the ancient city remained confined within the girdle of the old ramparts.

80. I. Belli. *Le Mura di Lucca.* 1954. P. 10.

Pistoia. Pistoia stands on a slight eminence at the northern end of a wide longitudinal valley of the Apennines near the Ombrone, a tributary of the Arno. The Roman name *Pistoriae* has given rise to an interpretation probably connected with the fact that the clay soil in the vicinity of Pistoia, used for the production of building material, had to be beaten—*pinsere terram*—before it was burnt—*ut torreatur*—in the kilns (*fornaci*) like bread by the bakers—the *pistores*. However, this assumption as to the origin of the name of

234. Map of Pistoia in 1657. The Roman *castrum* with its regular layout is clearly visible in the center now occupied by the cathedral and the baptistery. The course of the Roman and medieval walls is preserved in the inner ring of streets and partly in the direction of the intermediate roads (center right). The Renaissance fortifications with bastions, towers, and four gates surround the urban area with the highest building density in the center and a gradual loosening-up toward the periphery. The roads, leading to the gates, do not start from the center with the exception of one fairly wide connection—if the design does not distort the proportions—with the Porta Lucchese (bottom right). Since this gate was regarded as the most beautiful one of the city, the streets around it were paved. A statute of 1296 reads: "We decree . . . that the men and persons [who live] at the Luccese gate, from the old gate as far as the circular gate at Luccese, all along the street in a straight line, whatever [part] a person owns and is responsible for paving . . . at his own expense with good, fired bricks, so that the Luccese gate may be more beautiful than all the other gates of the city of Pistoia."

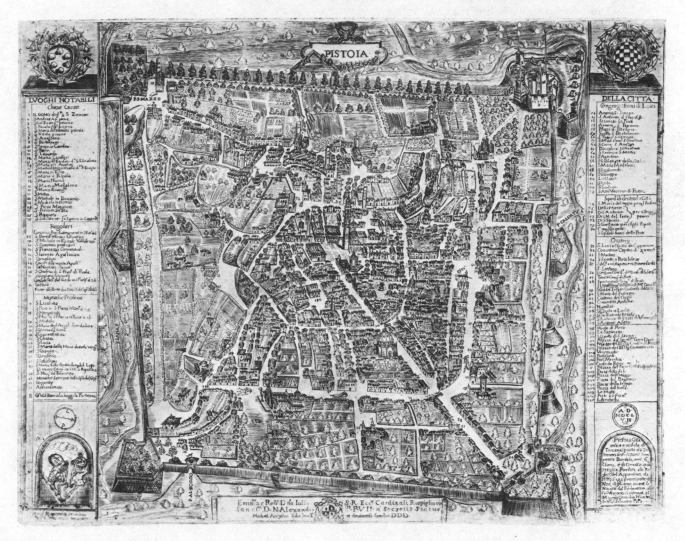

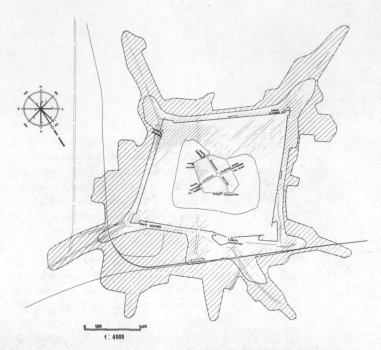

235. Development of Pistoia from Roman times to the present.

236. View of Pistoia at the end of the 18th century, with the rugged skyline and the mountains in the background.

PISTOIA.

Pistoia is too vague to serve as conclusive evidence, although it is interesting and might contain a grain of truth.

A Roman settlement existed on the site of Pistoia since the first decennium of the second century B.C. This was later made an *oppidum,* at first protected by earthworks and after some time by walls. Under the Empire Pistoia was an important military and commercial center with a large territory, a fact evident from the presence of *Duoviri iuredicundo* in the city. The *ager pistoriensis* included not only the plain and the surrounding hills but also fields, meadows, and parts of the land for pisciculture.

The Goths who occupied Pistoia left the Roman *oppidum* and its walls intact. The Lombards who followed them preserved the extension of the *ager pistoriensis* and of the *Diocesi* but extended the urban area and founded—outside the Roman walls but inside the new fortifications which were built under their rule—monasteries and churches in the eighth and following centuries. After a long period under the rule of the emperors of Germany Pistoia became a *Comune* (1085). However, the oldest record mentioning the constitution of the communal government dates from the year 1105. In the 12th and 13th centuries the municipal organization passed

322

237. Old view of the cathedral and the Palazzo del Comune, begun in 1294 and not completed until 1336.

238. Air view of the cathedral square in Pistoia.

through three different phases—the *periodo consolare;* the *periodo consolare-podestarile;* and finally the *periodo podestarile.* In the 12th century the urban area, restricted in its development by suburbs and clusters of people who had settled around the monasteries and churches of the Lombard era, had to be expanded. Fortifications were constructed enclosing the larger territory needed for the growing commerce and industries and the increasing population. Overcrowding, lack of open spaces, and bad housing conditions made this extension imperative—the more so as the citizens wished to have gardens and orchards forming oases of green providing additional food and relieving the depressing monotony of the grey mass of stone that their city had become.

With the rise of commercial activities the first banking institutions, the *banche reali,* were established, extending their activities to many parts of Europe and lending considerable amounts of money to the kings of England and France, and to other princes. But internal strife and the consequent decline of the power and prestige of Pistoia weakened its resistance to outside interference. Finally, authority was given to Florence and Lucca to reform the city (1293-95). Pistoia lost its individuality. As the anonymous author of the *Storie pistoresi* wrote, the city was "half denuded *(mezza igunda)* of people and means," and another writer described it as a "ruined countryhouse" a *"villa disfatta."* But in spite of these misfortunes a modest industrial activity continued especially in the manufacture of textiles and silk.

After the end of the Florentine domination Pistoia passed under the rule of Lorraine (1737) and began to recover something of her former prosperity. Iron was manufactured, and agriculture and commerce revived.

Prato, Province of Firenze. Prato stands on the mouth of the valley of the Bisenzio, at the extremity of a plain that has been occupied since the prehistoric era. In ancient times this plain was marshy. The inhabited centers and roads connecting them were therefore restricted to the margins of the plain and the

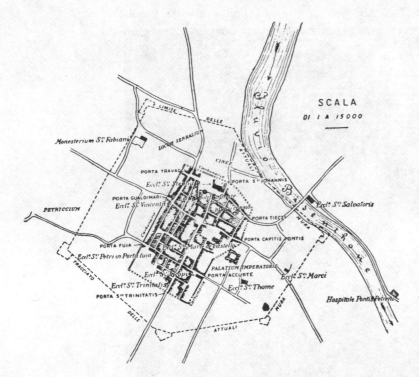

239. Map of Prato at the end of the 12th century showing the nucleus, the Borgo de Cornio, and the later additions within the walls of the 12th century.

324

241. View of Prato in the 18th century after the walls had been reinforced by bastions.

240. The Castello dell' Imperatore in Prato founded in 1248 by Frederick II as part of the fortifications, and the church of S. Maria delle Carceri built by Guiliano da Sangallo (1485–91).

foothills. The Roman road that linked Florence with other settlements ran through this area. Between Prato and Florence marks of the Roman centuriation dividing the land into a checkerboard pattern are still visible from the air.

It is probable that the site of Prato and its surrounding territory were occupied by Etruscan tribes, as recent excavations seem to confirm. No definite evidence has so far come to light that would indicate the foundation or the existence of a town as the predecessor of Prato in Roman times; rather it may be assumed that the population was dispersed over the plain, the hills, and the Bisenzio Valley without any focal point as a rallying center. However, this loose grouping of the population does not exclude the possibility that the territory was organized in some sort of *pagus* or *vicus*.

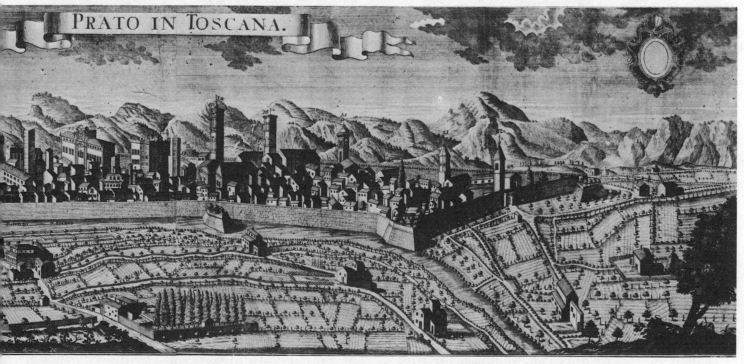

PRATO IN TOSCANA.

242. Piazza Mercatale in Prato at the beginning of the 20th century, laid out in the form of a pear and formerly surrounded by arcades and terraces where the shops of traders and artisans were located.

The oldest record dating from A.D. 998 mentioned a *Borgo de Cornio* that may have been the predecessor of Prato. This name was preserved throughout the Middle Ages, alternating with that of Prato for the settlement on this site. It is not unlikely that the *Borgo de Cornio* was identical with a Lombard *fattoria*, a cluster of farmhouses, an idea put forward by V. Carlesi and based on the fact that the record of A.D. 998 speaks of a *curtem*—meaning, according to a *glossarium* of the 13th century, *"villa, habitatio rustica, aedificiis, colonis, servis, agris, personis etc., ad rem agrestem necessariam instructa; alias colonia dicta."* ("A farm, or country dwelling, provided with everything for the necessary pursuit of agri-

243. Map of Prato in 1750 with the bastioned walls. Large open spaces have been preserved near the periphery and even in the heavily built up center of the city.

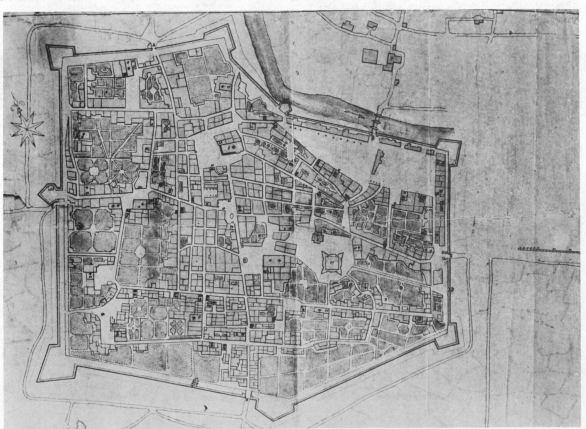

culture, buildings, farmers, slaves, land, and people; in other words, a colony.")[81] *Curtes* can therefore be identified with the Roman *latifundia* on which the lord lived in his fortified mansion. It is this fortified residence that may have been the nucleus of the *Borgo* from which Prato originated. The name of Prato meaning *pratum,* a grassy area, occurred for the first time in 1035 in some documents of the cathedral chapter of Pistoia.

Before the fortifications of the 14th century were constructed Prato had begun to spread down to the river with the large tract of grassland, the *Mercatale.* This vast open space at the Bisenzio had received its name from the fairs held there twice a year since earliest times. The square was separated from the river by battlemented walls protecting it against floods and enemies.

81. Quoted after S. Bardazzi. *Piano Regolatore Generale. Relazione Storica.* N.d. From V. Carlesi. *Origini della città e del Comune di Prato.* N.d.

With the increase of the population and the development of industry and commerce, suburbs grew up around the city. Work on the fortifications proceeded so slowly that in 1380 Florence ordered them to be completed in 18 months. Prato has essentially remained a medieval city confined within its ancient walls, with a high building density, though even in the immediate vicinity of the Piazza del Duomo gardens and orchards have been preserved. The sack of Prato by the Spaniards in 1512, the fall of the Florentine Republic, the decline of the woolen industry, and other disadvantageous factors resulted in a general deterioration of urban life and a stagnation lasting far into the 18th century preventing any major building activities. The craft guilds were abolished in 1770 and in their stead a *Camera di Commercio, Arti e Manifatture,* with its seat at Florence, was established to revive the commercial and industrial fortunes of the city.

Firenze (Florence).   Firenze, *Fiorenza,* in Latin *Florentia,* is situated on both sides of the Arno in a moderately broad valley, widening considerably toward Prato and Pistoia in the northwest, and surrounded at the north by spurs of the Apennines and at the south by the Monti di Chianti.

The area around the site of Florence was first settled by Etruscans, who planted a settlement on top of the hill overlooking the valley and called it *Faesulae* (Fiesole). About 200 B.C. the inhabitants of this hilltop settlement decided to found a town in the valley that would protect the crossing of the Arno and be in a better position to take advantage of the main Roman routes especially after 187 B.C. when the *Via Cassia* was continued via Arezzo and *Florentia* to Bologna. In 90 B.C. *Florentia* and *Faesulae* received Roman citizenship. Having fought against Sulla, *Florentia* was leveled to the ground in 82 B.C., and so completely destroyed that the identification of the actual

site of the Etruscan settlement has given rise to a prolonged debate among historians and archeologists without producing definite results. Whatever the final decision may be, the new *Florentia* was founded as a Roman colony, probably at a short distance downstream from the Etruscan place where present-day Florence is situated. The urban area of Roman *Florentia* was small, covering an irregular square whose sides were approximately 1,500 feet long. There were four gates in the middle of each side through which the main north-south and east-west roads entered the town. The *forum* was located at their intersection in the center of the walled-in area and corresponded to the Mercato Vecchio of the Middle Ages, the Piazza Vittorio Emanuele of today. A Roman bridge was constructed over the Arno at the point where the Ponte Vecchio still crosses the river and where the Roman bridge carried the *Via Cassia* from one bank to the other. Although *Florentia* was never

327

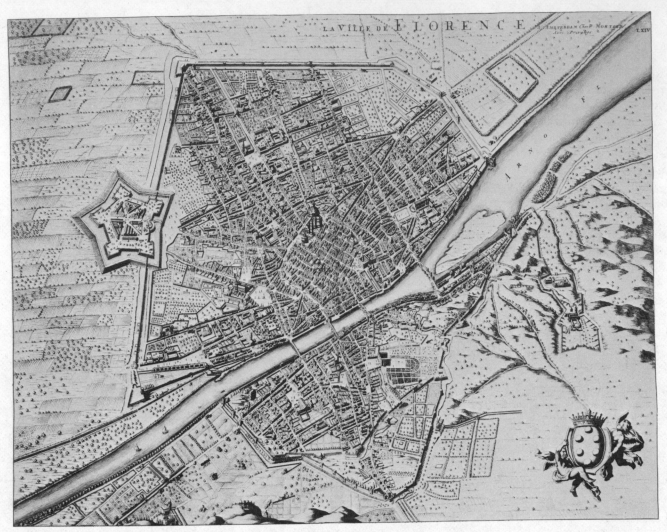

244. Plan of Florence from Joan Blaeu's *Nieuw vermeerderd en verbeterd Groot stedeboek van geheel Italie . . .* , published in Amsterdam in 1724.

more than a rather insignificant provincial town, it had all the usual ingredients of the standardized Roman accoutrement—an aqueduct, theater, baths, and temples. Nothing of this modest panoply has survived. However, a certain expansion took place: suburbs grew up and an amphitheater was built in the eastern suburb which apparently had a relatively large population.

About the history of Florence in the early Middle Ages our knowledge is rather scanty, in particular about its physical development. One can be fairly certain, however, that Florence remained an unimportant town until the beginning of the 12th century.

It is beyond the scope of this work to include even a very condensed history of Flor-

ence. Problems of city planning are its main subject.[82] Suffice it to say that Florence was the prototype of a community that rose from humble beginnings, through a long period of modest existence, to one of the leading cities of Europe, torn by internecine feuds, involved in the political machinations of the great powers, reaching the pinnacle of cultural excellence, and producing some of the greatest artists, humanists, poets, and patrons of art, literature, and learning the world has ever known. However, a heavy price had to be paid for these achievements, a price that entailed

82. The literature on Florence is almost unlimited. Some of the books mentioned in the Bibliography contain comprehensive and very detailed lists of old documents and other source material as well as works by modern writers, to which the reader is referred.

328

the moral degradation of man, the debasement of liberty and independence, the tyranny of ruthless adventurers, and the neglect of the natural aspirations of the common people. Florence was in her heyday the dorado of individualism, of the discovery of individual initiative by a few, rarely in the best interests of the many, but in the long run creating results and a greater number of eminent personalities than all other cities of Italy put together. It is this sustained and almost contemptuous individualism, this self-seeking glorification, that have made Florence a city of subjectivity, of individual ostentation—in brief, of isolated masterpieces of architecture radiating an all-pervading atmosphere of refined brilliance without binding the isolated achievements together by large-scale development plans as in Rome, to mention only the most prominent example.

Florence's history of city planning, in a strict sense, is unexciting, far less inspiring than that of many smaller and less famous towns of Italy. The greatest accomplishment of Florentine individualism was the creation of an atmosphere of unsurpassed beauty, of an enravishing sophistication contained in the narrow space of its ancient walls. The media through which this was done are individual buildings and a few, very few squares and remains of the medieval layout, the palaces, the churches, the cathedral with Brunelleschi's dome, the dress rehearsal for Michelangelo's S. Pietro, the Piazza della Signoria, the Piazza SS. Annunziata, and the subconscious but always present awareness of the sculptures and paintings in the churches and galleries, and of the great names connected with the history of the city. In this respect Florence is the supreme example of the vital role of the imponderable emanations, of "such stuff as dreams are made on," more important than realistic comprehensive planning. All this is far removed from the romantic enthusiasm of the Victorians, who never understood the true nature of Florence, but it is very much the essence of the penetrating atmosphere of this unique city. And let it be emphasized: the atmosphere is, after all, the most important value that city planning can produce, more important than grand vistas, impressive squares, or ostentatious groups of public

245. Panorama of Florence. Detail from the mural *La Madonna della Misericordia* in the Loggia del Bigallo (14th century).

329

buildings. This fact has to be recognized—especially today, when pragmatic primitivity is brushing aside everything that cannot be touched, seen immediately, or experienced directly.[83]

In the course of the centuries three different circumvallations were built—the Roman walls, the fortifications of the 12th century, and finally those of the end of the 12th and the beginning of the 13th century. The Roman walls enclosed an area, although small in extent, that was sufficient during the early Middle Ages. As more recent excavations have revealed, a Byzantine inner defense system was constructed within the Roman *enceinte* protecting a narrow rectangle around the Mercato Vecchio, the ancient *forum,* thus reducing the size of the Roman town which had become too large for the dwindling population. This defense system did not consist of a continuous girdle of walls but was apparently a rather casual mixture of still-existing parts of temples, baths, aqueducts, of whatever masonry

was still standing, and of connecting sections of walls built of the most diverse material; of columns, sculptures, and other remains from the Roman period.[84]

The revival of commerce in the 12th century and the increase of population resulted in the development of suburbs along the roads extending from the gates. In the second half of this century the outlying quarters had grown quite considerably. It was therefore decided in 1172 to include them in a new ring of fortifications, expanding the urban area by three times that enclosed by the first walls and adding an approximately triangular space on the left bank of the Arno. The walls around this new addition, not begun until 1254, were completed only in connection with the third *enceinte*—that is, after 1284. Though a plan for the whole work seems to have been prepared, the circuit of this second girdle is rather irregular, following the natural growth of the town. The actual construction was preceded by temporary palisades and moats: *"E*

83. Cf. pp. 99-102.

84. W. Braunfels, *op. cit.,* p. 60.

246. Piazza della Signoria in Florence in 1498 and the burning of Savonarola at the stake.

247. General view of Florence in 1470 by an unknown artist.

primo so chiuse con fossi e steccati . . . e poi si feciono l'altra mura."[85] The gates, whose number was increased from 4 to 12, owing to the growing traffic, were built first. As already noted, the municipal administrations were concerned to prevent encroachments upon the defense systems. In Florence this led to the imposition of a special tax for any violation of the existing regulations.

It was not until the construction of the third *enceinte* that the walls were kept completely free of any encroachments by private buildings. They were protected by an ordinance of 1323. An inscription, now in the Bargello, records that the road along the interior of the walls was "16 ells wide [one Florentine ell = 0.583 meter]; the walls including the moats

35 ells; and the outer road 13 ells and a half."

Giovanni Villani (c. 1275-1348), Florentine chronicler and one of the overseers of the construction of the fortifications, has left us a detailed description of the greatest work the community of Florence had ever undertaken.[86] "In order that the memory of the greatness of the said city be always kept alive . . . we shall give an ordered account of the building of the said walls together with the measurements made by myself, the author, who, in behalf of the commune, served as official of the walls."

The Roman walls had enclosed an area of 79.1 acres, the walls of 1172 about 259 acres, and the third walls enclosed an area of 1,265 acres. Their total length was 9,300 yards; their average width, 6.53 to 9.84 feet, and their

85. R. Malespini. *Croniche.* (cap. 56.) Ed. Tellini. Florence. 1818.

86. *Historie Fiorentine* or *Cronica Universale*, VII 39; VIII 31; IX 10 and 256.

248. View of the Badia and the Palazzo del Podestà. The Badia of Florence, founded in the 10th century, was rebuilt in the 17th century. The Palazzo del Podestà, or Palazzo del Bargello, dates from the second half of the 13th century. From *Vedute Fiorentine* by G. Zocchi, 1754.

331

height about 38.34 feet. There were 73 towers 75.4 feet high and 15 gates. Villani records that the walls were intended to give the city a regular shape and that the two principal axes, from the Porta Romana to the Porta San Gallo and from the Porta al Prato to the Porta alla Croce, were almost equally long and crossed each other in the center at the Mercato Vecchio. It seems that regularity was a main concern of the builders: great efforts were made to construct the walls as regularly as possible of the same stones in all sections and to keep an equal distance of 200 ells between all the identical 73 towers. Only the gates were differently built—a decision that led to a lively controversy, as Villani reported (X 219) of the Porta S. Frediano: "Compared with the other gates of Florence it was shapeless, wherefore the officials, who had authorized the beginning, were greatly criticized." It seems that the designs for the gates were exhibited at the offices of the responsible officials so that they could be inspected by the people and that a lively discussion about their value took place.

Villani closes his description with the words:

And thus we find that the new circle of walls measures, on the right bank of the Arno, seven thousand seven hundred *braccia* [about the equivalent of an ell]. And this section possesses nine gates—that is, four master gates and five posterns, each with a tower of sixty *braccia* and with a barbicon in front of it. And along the wall rise forty five towers, counting also those of the gates.

The area enclosed by the new walls was sufficient for a large increase of population and contained ample open spaces for gardens and orchards.

The population, living within the third ring of fortifications (in the urban area of 512

249. View of the square and the Church of San Michele e San Gaetano Berteldi, formerly of the Padri Teatini. From *Vedute Fiorentine* by G. Zocchi. 1754.

250. Palazzo Vecchio at Florence as seen from the Uffizi.

hectares), has been estimated for the year 1381 as 54,747—that is, 107 per hectare and for 1424 as 37,788 corresponding to 73 per hectare; for 1551 as 59,557.[87]

The rule of Florence over its territory was strongly affected by the struggle between the Guelphs and the Ghibellines and by the riots between the nobles and the *popolo*. Florence was mostly dominated by the Guelphs, the party of the great merchants and the industrial interests in opposition to the Ghibellines, whose power and influence derived from their landed property in the surrounding country. This distinction, admittedly oversimplified and generalized, nevertheless helps to explain the antagonism between the urban and the rural forces and their influence upon the re-

87. J. C. Russell. *Late Ancient and Medieval Population.* 1958. Pp. 60, 127.

333

lationship of the city to the countryside. In 1289 villeinage was abolished in the *contado* of Florence, a decision that struck at the roots of the Ghibelline power who wanted to keep their cheap labor on the land; whereas it aided the Guelph merchants and industrialists who needed workers for their textile trade. The result was a considerable influx from the countryside into the town, an increase of population that has been estimated at five times its previous size. The power of the Ghibellines rested on their strongholds in the country. It was not surprising therefore that the Ghibelline nobles were playing with the idea of creating a new *civitas Florentia* in the *contado* by forming a strong organization based on their castles. Florence responded to this challenge with the construction of small walled-in places to which the population was attracted by certain privileges. Villani reports (XI. 97) that in 1336 Florence ruled over Pistoia, Arezzo, and Colle Val d'Elsa with their territories, and over 18 *castelli* in the *contado* of Lucca, and 46 in her own territory. The nobles were reduced to their estates in the marginal regions. A few decades later the last great families were subdued and forced to reside in the city of Florence. However, even before this enforced *inurbamento* the greater convenience and the social amenities of urban life had induced some of the rural nobles to leave their lonely tower residences in the country and to settle in the city.

As builders and owners of castles they brought with them from their rural past the habit of living in residential towers, an aggressive spirit, and crude manners. They erected the first towers in Florence in the 11th century. A century later their number had increased to almost 150, mostly concentrated in the narrow space around the Mercato Vecchio. A veritable race ensued to build taller and taller towers until in 1254 quite a number of towers had reached the height of 200 feet or more and had to be reduced to an even height of 96 feet—a leveling process symbolic of the growing strength of democratic influence of the *Primo Popolo*. The material from the demolished parts of the towers was used for the walls on the south bank of the river. (Villani

IV. 31.)[88] Today almost all these private towers have disappeared. The skyline of Florence is broken only by a few public buildings projecting over the solid mass of the houses. The towers of the feuding noble families were private fortresses belonging to a past that is difficult for us to recapture, but possibly easier to understand if we compare them with the skyscrapers of our own time as symbols of power, prestige, ruthless ambitions, status-seeking, and unbounded self-glorification.

The material prosperity of Florence was derived from commerce and industry. The leading merchants were members of the Calimala guild, named after the street where their shops were located. Their main trade consisted in the importation of cloth from England, France, and Flanders, an activity that often included financial transactions. In the 13th century they widened their business by developing an industry for processing imported textiles for the local market and the Levant. The most important craft guild was that of the cloth makers. By the early 14th century it had become the greatest industrial organization of Florence and probably of Italy. Villani tells us that its looms produced more than 100,000 pieces per year in 300 workshops, at first of a rather modest quality but thirty years later, when the production had declined to about one third, delivering cloth of so superior a quality that it could be prized as equal or even superior to the best material from Flanders and France.[89]

The guild of merchants represented the most influential element of the rising classes and the most active promoters of the prosperity of the city. The more they combined commerce and banking the more their standing and wealth increased, gradually absorbing members of the feudal society who were not averse to taking part in the lucrative business of trade and commerce. Thus the barrier between the warriors and the traders was gradually lowered, and a new kind of aristocracy came into being that was to play the leading

88. W. Braunfels, *op. cit.*, p. 52.
89. G. Luzzatto, *op. cit.*, pp. 97-98,

334

role in the cultural and commercial life of Florence.

The importance of commerce and its growing expansion stimulated Florence to seek a direct outlet to the sea, involving her in hostilities with Pisa and resulting in Pisa's almost total subjection to Florence. Though the Arno may have had a greater volume of water in the Middle Ages than today because of the larger extent of the forested areas, it could not be used for navigation up to Florence. This explains the conflict with Pisa, without which it could not develop a mercantile fleet and expand its commerce.[90]

As has already been stated, it is not the purpose of this work to present a complete history of Florence. We have to restrict ourselves to the narrower subject of city planning proper. It may be argued that the organization of the municipal administration should be considered in this connection. However, even this would lead us too far away from our immediate task.[91]

In 1421 Giovanni dei Medici was elected *gonfalomiere* of justice. With his ascent to power begins the period of the greatest pros-

90. W. G. East. *An Historical Geography of Europe.* 1956. P. 318.

91. Readers may be referred to the numerous works dealing with this aspect of urban development contained in some of the books mentioned in the Bibliography from which may be singled out E. Ennen's *Frühgeschichte der Europäischen Stadt,* 1953, pp. 270-293. This work offers an excellent and comprehensive list of relevant source material and modern literature on this subject.

251. Ponte Vecchio at Florence. The original bridge was built by Taddeo Gaddi in 1345.

perity and splendor of Florence. Under the rule of the Medici, who had amassed enormous wealth through successful banking speculations, Florence, especially under Lorenzo il Magnifico, became the leading city of Renaissance Italy. It attracted a galaxy of humanists, artists, poets, and scholars—standard-bearers of the new and wider outlook emerging from the narrower confines of preceding centuries. But this social superstructure, with its excessive spending and ostentatious pomp, had to be supported by the acquisition of ever-increasing financial means from which the lower classes were of course excluded. Money-making and avarice spread. Alberti has

sketched a vivid picture of these ambitions and of the gap between the receipts and expenditures that could never be bridged:

The priests want to surpass all others in splendor and magnificence; want to trade a great number of well-groomed and beautifully adorned horses; want to appear in public with a great retinue. From day to day their propensity for idleness and arrogant wickedness increases. Although fortune has endowed them with abundant means, they are always discontented and without any thought of saving, without any economy; they are only intent on how they can satisfy their incited greed. Receipts are always lacking; expenditure is always larger than their regular income. Thus they are

252. Map of Florence and the Valley of the Arno.

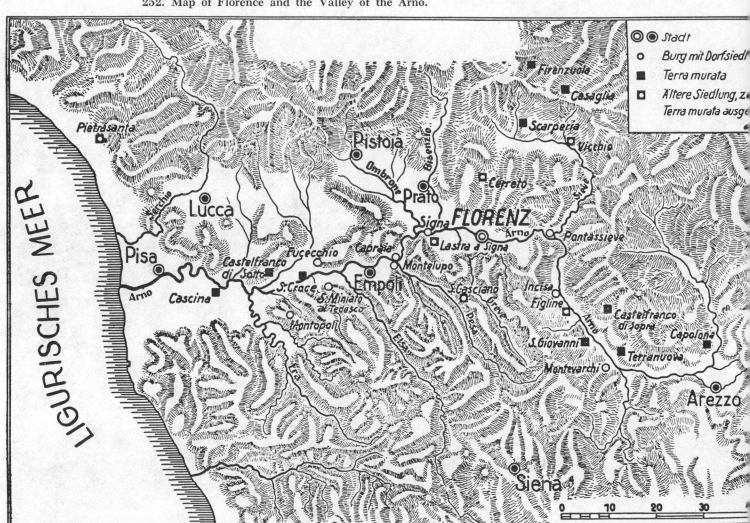

forced to hunt up what is missing from some other sources.[92]

All this was nothing unusual. It has happened in all lands and at all times, but at Florence the triumph of culture and corruption, of learning and violence had reached an unusual refinement—an excellence of spiritual manifestations which almost totally overshadowed the suffering and degradation of the common people. The great building activity, the material prosperity sustained by banking and trade in woolen cloth, the accumulation of riches by a small minority did not result in the improvement of the living conditions of the masses. Their quarters remained what they always had been—overcrowded slums. Time and historical romanticism have woven a thick veil that has hidden this unpleasant truth from generations of uncritical admirers of Florence. But the life of a city cannot be measured by positive achievements alone—not even if they are as brilliant and unique as in the città dei fiori. What we know from existing records and other old documents of building regulations, layout of new streets, sanitary installations, and the inspection of buildings confirms the neglect of the quarters of the poorer classes. The city planning of Florence consisted in the creation of individual masterpieces; it was not a comprehensive urban renewal of the city as a whole.

And yet there is a redeeming feature, a lesson of utmost importance for the history of city planning and one that Florence more than most of the great cities of the past can teach us. It is the atmosphere of a city, the milieu, the general setting, the image it evokes in the mind of its citizens, the all-pervading totality of these intangible emanations that creates the individuality of an environment, its drama and variety, intricacy and intimacy, its contrasts and attractions. All these imponderable qualities together were the magnet that made Florence the cradle of the Renaissance, the gathering place and the center of attraction of great men in a far more immediate and efficacious way than material, coordi-

nated manifestations embodied in large-scale development plans could ever have done.

The foundation of walled-in country towns by Florence is of considerable interest.[93] It was not merely a political move directed against the feudal lords of the contado but an important step toward the unification of city and surrounding country, one of the goals of every Italian major municipal administration. This urban "imperialism" was not restricted to Italy, where it continued as a legacy from antiquity. It can be observed in almost all parts of Europe and was expressed in the territorial ambitions of numerous cities, even small towns, bent on adding a sizable rural hinterland to their urban area. Florence used this device during a relatively short space of time, mainly between the years 1284 and 1306. Political and economic motives went hand in hand: the feudal system and influence were to be broken and the expansion of the urban economy was to be secured and strengthened.

The foundation of the terre murate, the walled-in country towns, was the most potent instrument for combining the suppression of feudal anarchy and the extension of the political and economic domination of Florence over a wider region.[94] Until the second half of the 13th century the building activity of the Comune outside the walls was mainly concerned with the fortification of existing castles and rural settlements, and with the maintenance of citadels in subjugated towns. The terre murate and the construction of roads and bridges linking them together introduced a new and active method characteristic of the enterprising spirit of Florence at this period. A terra murata was a new foundation systematically laid out like all similar foundations in newly conquered territory. The bastides of France are the best-known examples. Basically, the terre murate repeated the principle of a Roman colonia with a few modifications. The two first foundations were Santa Croce and Castelfranco di Sotto, formed

92. L. B. Alberti. I Libri della Famiglia. G. Mancini (ed.). 1908. P. 265.

93. Cf. p. 334.

94. M. Richter. "Die 'Terra Murata' im Florentinischen Gebiet," Mitteilungen des Kunsthistorischen Institutes in Florenz, Vol. V, No. 6. 1940. Pp. 351-378, passim.

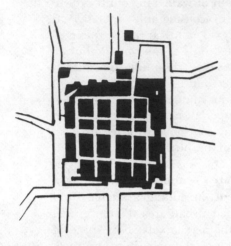

253. Plan of Castelfranco di Sotto.

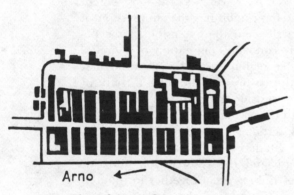

Arno ←

254. Plan of Santa Croce.

255. Plan of Castelfranco di Sopra.

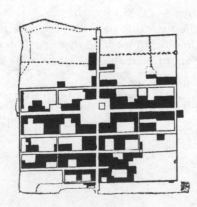

338

by four rural parishes—the four gates of Castelfranco were called after them—and testifying to the independent and energetic action of the countrypeople. In other cases some of the villages and market towns of the upper Arno Valley applied to Florence—that had already appointed a special administrative section for this purpose—to establish one or two *terre,* expressing the hope that this would lead to their emancipation from feudal rule. The most important places were founded on the initiative of Florence alone, such as San Giovanni Valdarno and Castelfranco di Sopra, Scarperia (1300), and Firenzuola (1330)—a name suggested by Villani as symbol of the intimate relationship between the new town and the mother city.

The military defeat of the feudal lords was made complete by social measures: villeins were settled in the new towns, thus depriving the lords of laborers, and were declared free of any obligation toward their former masters. The legal basis for these steps was a decree of the Republic of 1289 that prohibited the feudal lords from buying or selling peasant-serfs, *fideles.* The danger that the liberation of the serfs could result in a growing influx into the city was an additional reason for settling them, sometimes by coercion, in the new towns. The extension of the urban jurisdiction was one of the essential goals: *"Pro honore et jurisdictione comunis florentie amplianda et melius conservanda,"* as one of the edicts put it. But apart from the political incorporation of the *contado* economic considerations played a considerable role, especially the safeguarding of the food supply and the improvement of agriculture.

The new settlers were exempted from all taxes, in most cases for ten years, but were obliged to build houses on land supplied free of charge by the *Comune* and to take part in

256. Plan of Firenzuola.

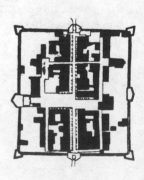

the construction of the fortifications. Whether the new lot of the settlers was as much of an improvement as they had hoped for may be questionable. It is more likely that they merely exchanged the despotism of the feudal lord for the tyranny of the *Comune* and the rational dictate of the emerging capitalistic system. The supervision of the foundation and the subsequent activities were entrusted at first to one or two and later to six representatives of Florence. Their job was the choice of the building site, the evaluating of its price, the layout of the streets and squares; the building of churches, gates, and bridges; the selection of the settlers, the distribution of the work, and other related duties. These supervisors played the same role as the *locatores* in Northern Europe, who were employed by the feudal lords in connection with the settlement of the large regions east of the Elbe. In general, sites on plains were preferred in contrast to the fortified castles of the feudal lords, which were almost without exception situated on hills, although in a few cases elevated terrain was chosen—for example, at Castelfranco di Sopra or Scarperia.

The existing overland routes were, so far as possible, protected by one of the new foundations: Scarperia and Firenzuola guarded the route to Bologna; Cascina and Castelfranco di Sotto the road to Siena; Castelfranco di Sopra and San Giovanni Valdarno the valley to Arezzo. Within the walled-in area the roads continued as the main streets, dividing it into equal parts and crossed in the center by another street at right angles. The rest of the mostly narrower streets and the walls ran parallel to these axes. The four gates were located at the entry of the overland routes. Symmetry and regularity dominated the layout in most cases focused on a central square, a precursor of the Ideal Cities of the Renais-

sance. Some of the *terre murate* have been attributed to Arnolfo di Cambio—for instance, Castelfranco di Sopra and San Giovanni.

The walls were constructed in stone and strengthened mostly by square towers following the example of Florence. The gate-towers were especially strong and often of a high artistic quality as at Firenzuola, *"per ornare la città di dentro e il contado di fuori, pro honore comunis florentie."*[95]

None of these "Ideal Cities" developed into an important center. Some stagnated and became quiet little country towns, and others were abandoned. Like many *bastides* of France and England they fulfilled a temporary function. When the purpose for which they had been founded lost its importance, they ceased to be of any value to the Republic; but as symbols of a new trend in city planning, of a purposeful procedure in the founding of urban communities, and of the political and social changes that were emerging, they are of particular interest and deserve a place in the history of urban development.

95. "To adorn the city within and the surroundings without in honor of the Florentine community."

258. Plan of Terranuova.

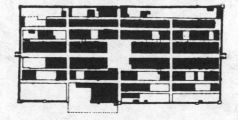

257. Plan of Scarperia.

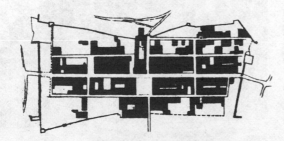

San Gimignano, Province of Siena. This small hilltop town, overlooking the Elsa Valley, is situated not far from Volterra, one of the principal centers of Etruscan civilization in Italy. Although quite a number of Etruscan remnants have been found in the vicinity of San Gimignano, its Etruscan origin cannot definitely be ascertained. Tradition has it that two young Romans, Silvo and Muzio, built a fortress on the site where later San Gimignano rose. This fortress or military camp was first called Castello della Selva, Citadel of the Wood, and changed its name later following a siege by Totila. After a twenty-year fight against Volterra, San Gimignano became a free *Comune* governed by consuls, then by a *podestà*, by *capitani*, and finally by a *Consiglio Generale*. In 1353 the town submitted "vol-untarily" to Florence, a decision arrived at with a majority of only one vote and after a long and heated debate embittered by the violent local feuds between the Guelph Ardinghelli and the Ghibelline Salvucci.

San Gimignano, surrounded by strong walls possibly since the eighth century, developed along three winding streets steeply rising to a center formed by three squares—the Piazza della Cisterna, the Piazza del Duomo, and the Piazza dell' Erbe communicating with one another through narrow and intricate lanes. Each one of these three streets led down to a gate in the north, south, and east respectively. Of the over 70 towers, which the noble families had erected in the 12th, 13th, and 14th centuries, 13 are still standing. The towers, which are all square with but a few narrow and long slots, were exclusively used as defensive annexes of the palaces not for residential purposes. However, it is very doubtful whether their defensive value was the main reason for their construction. It is much more likely that prestige, wealth, and boastful aggressiveness were the driving powers that made it imperative for every noble family to be the owner of these threatening symbols of superiority.

259. Map of San Gimignano.

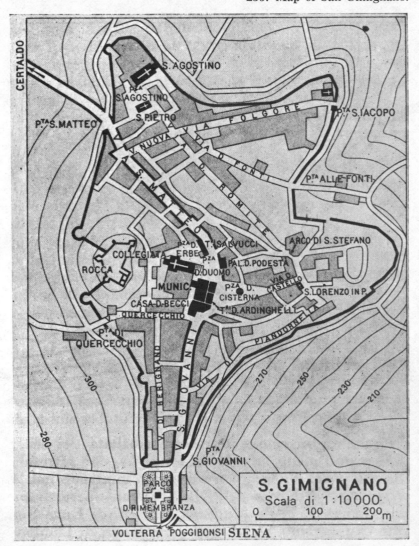

260. Piazza della Cisterna in San Gimignano.

261. San Gimignano blessing the town. Detail from the painting by Taddeo di Bartolo in the Museo Civico, San Gimignano.

This explains the fierce competition among these feudal ruffians to build towers higher than all the others, a rivalry finally checked by a law that no tower should be higher than the tower of the Palazzo del Podestà—that is, more than 156 feet.

San Gimignano was not a town of burghers but a town of nobles, not of aristocrats of the spirit and the soul but of warriors embracing force and violence, cunning, passion, and hatred. Theirs was an existence that was not satisfied with the peaceful recognition of their social status as leading citizens but demanded obedience from others and an outward demonstration of their own antisocial mentality. This ideal of life created the Romanesque cities of which San Gimignano is one of the most expressive symbols with its enormous towers, each a self-contained unit, and all together creating an aggressive and artistic unity of unusual strength and ruthless insolence.

262. Piazza del Duomo in San Gimignano.

263. General view of San Gimignano.

264. One of the main streets in San Gimignano, a narrow canyon lined by uninterrupted rows of houses.

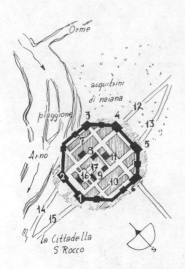

265. The second octagonal *enceinte* of Empoli (1336).

Empoli, Province of Firenze. Empoli, about 25 miles west of Florence, was and still is an important nodal point on which roads from all directions converged. Once it was also a landing place of some significance:

North of the walls of Empoli, on the banks of the Arno, land many boats from the riverside settlements of Valdarno and the lower Val d'Elsa. Hundreds of thousands of kilos of grain are stored in the warehouses to be sent during the year to Florence together with other commodities. This river traffic has created two types of activities, those of boatmen and carters.[96]

The territory of Empoli is bounded on the north by the Arno and on the south by small hills, only a few rising above 300 feet. Before the 18th century the immediate neighborhood of the urban area was marshy on three sides, continuously exposed to inundations of the Arno and its tributaries.

96. Quoted from Guerrini after *Il Piano Regolatore Generale del Comune di Empoli.* 1956. P. 5.

Empoli was first mentioned in 1015, the year its inhabitants rebelled against Pisa and established a republican government under the protection of Count Guidi. The first *castello* of Empoli was situated about a mile from the present town. It was destroyed in the rebellion against Pisa. The inhabitants were scattered among the *castelli,* small towns, villages, and the *Cittadella* of the surrounding country. The actual origin of Empoli dates back to 1119 when the Contessa Emilia, wife of Guido Guerra I, donated a tract of land on which the people of the former Empoli could build their homes: *"ubi eorum casas aedificent et castras reaedificare faciant."* Local autonomy was encouraged and merchants, who did not yet represent a political force, were attracted; and a zone, protected from the inundations of the Arno, was established. The market that gradually developed was one of the most famous in all Tuscany, owing to the favorable situation of the town in the center of an important traffic network. In connection with the growing commerce six *casamenti* were set up which soon grew into small urban aggregations surrounded by rectangular walls. They were situated on the main roads which met at the center—*il canto*—of the urban area.

A second *enceinte,* this time octagonal in shape and with six gates, was constructed in 1336. A third ring of fortifications was built at the end of the 15th and the beginning of the 16th century, enclosing the town within a rectangle. The gates of the earlier walls were retained, making the defense of the town easier and attacks more difficult. The walls

266. The third rectangular *enceinte* of Empoli. Mural in the Palazzo della Signoria in Florence.

were reinforced with a large embankment and a wide moat.

Since the 14th century the wool industry, and later the textile industry, was the main occupation of the citizens. In 1551 the population numbered about 4,900, of whom 1,730 lived in the urban center; in 1731 there were 7,170 inhabitants, including 2,640 in the inner city. For the year 1818 the figures were 9,700 and 4,000 respectively.

267. Siege of Empoli in the 16th century showing the third *enceinte* and the densely built-up urban area. Mural by Giorgio Vasari in the Palazzo della Signoria in Florence.

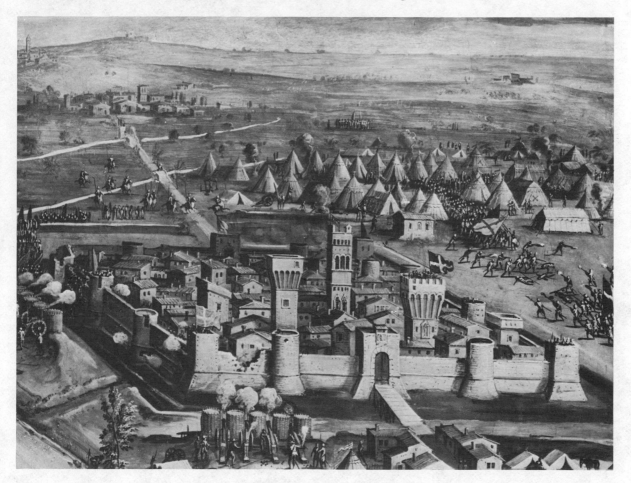

Rimini, Province of Forli. Of the remote origin of Rimini nothing is known that would allow us to draw definite conclusions as to its date and its earliest occupants. The first, more reliable evidence seems to confirm that Rimini, the ancient *Ariminum,* was a colony of the Umbrians, whose civilization in eastern Emilia was concentrated in the valley of the Marecchia. However, the Umbrian town did not occupy the same site as the later Rimini. Finds that would appear to belong to this civilization have been discovered far from the sea, on the hills that surround the Rimini of today. With the conquest of the Po Valley about 390 B.C., the region of Rimini, part of the so-called *Ager Gallicus,* passed to

345

268. View of Rimini in 1450, showing the Marecchia River with the Ponte di Tiberio, the walls, the citadel of Sigismondo Malatesta, the *Rocca*, the port, and in the foreground a ship with bulging sails. This oldest view of Rimini is from a bas-relief by Agostino di Duccio on a pillar in the third chapel on the right in the Church of S. Francesco, the Tempio Malatestiano, renovated after a design by Leone Battista Alberti.

269. View of Rimini in the 17th century. From Braun and Hogenberg, *Civitates Orbis Terrarum*, 1638.

270. The Rocca Malatestiana in Rimini built by Sigismondo Malatesta (1437–46). It had six towers, four bridges, moats and dungeons, and earthworks, underground passages, barracks, and armories. In the center stood the residential palace, square in shape, with a triple protection of gates, battlements, and bulwarks.

271. Borgo S. Andrea outside the walls in the southwest of the urban area. It is now a densely built-up district at the edge of Rimini.

the Senonian Gauls, who had to yield it in 295 B.C. to the Romans. The district that extended from *Sena Gallica* (Senigallia) to Rimini, or more precisely from the river Esino to the Rubicon, was incorporated in the Roman state, and in 268 B.C. Rimini became a Roman colony with a population somewhere between 6,000 and 10,000 inhabitants. It was situated in a strategically favorable position, at the extremity of the lands occupied by the Boii, a Celtic people, and protected by the Adriatic and the *Arimnus* (Marecchia) and *Aprusa* (Ausa) Rivers. In 220 B.C. it was connected with Rome by the *Via Flaminia;* in 187 B.C. with Piacenza by the *Via Aemilia;* and in 132 B.C. with Aquileia and beyond to *Noricum* and *Pannonia* by the *Via Popilia.* Under Augustus *Ariminum* flourished and was one of the most important towns of Italy. It was divided into seven *vici.* Its port was a base for part of the Roman fleet. Naval yards, potteries, public buildings, and communal institutions were established. Augustus, who took a great personal interest in the development of the town, gave it the name of *Colonia Augusta.* In gratitude to Augustus the people of *Ariminum* erected a triumphal arch in his honor in 27 B.C.

Under Byzantine rule Rimini was the northernmost town of the maritime *Pentapolis,* the other four being Pesaro, Fano, Senigallia, and Ancona. At the middle of the eighth century it passed with the whole exarchate under the dominion of the Church, thus establishing a juridical and political situation that remained more or less unchanged until 1860. In the 13th century Rimini was a free *Comune.* The bitter struggles between the partisans of the Guelphs and Ghibellines, which date back to this period, ended in 1295 with the victory of the Malatesta, who ruled until in 1528 the population rose against them and joined the Papal States.

272. Air view of Rimini showing traces of the Roman street system in the center and the outline of the Malatesta fortifications.

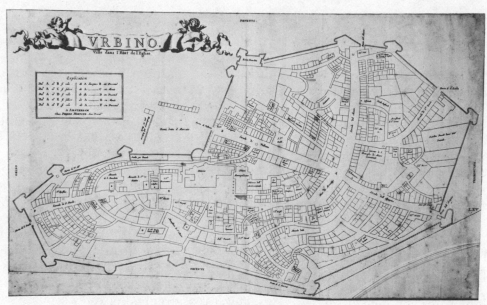

273. Map of Urbino showing the adaptation to the configuration of the terrain of the numerous narrow and winding streets within the walled-in urban area. Engraving by Pierre Mortier, 16th century.

Urbino, Province of Pesaro and Urbino. Urbino, the ancient *Urvinum Metaurense*—the name is derived from the river *Metaurus*—is situated on the summit of an abrupt hill surrounded by barren heights. Remains of pre-

Roman fortifications have been discovered near the archbishop's palace, which may have been part of the original *castrum*. Of the Roman period, traces of a theater and *thermae,* supplied by an aqueduct, have been ex-

274. Air view of Urbino with the Palazzo Ducale at the right.

cavated. Urbino was involved in the Gothic wars and remained under Gothic rule until it was conquered in the sixth century by Beligarius. Later it passed to the Exarchate of Ravenna and to the duke of the Pentapolis Annonaria. In the 12th century urban life revived, and with it the renewal of the ancient Roman center around the cathedral. Since the 13th century Urbino, under the rule of the Montefeltro, experienced its greatest development, reaching its culmination in the 15th century with the great building activity of Federigo di Montefeltro (1444-82) and his son Guidobaldo (1482-1508). It surpassed the neighboring courts of the Malatesta at Rimini and the Sforza at Pesaro. The splendor of the court of the Montefeltro and their patronage of the arts and literature attracted numerous artists, among them Paolo Uccello, Piero della Francesca, Melozzo da Forli, and even painters from abroad, such as Justus van Gent. The house where Raphael was born and lived during his boyhood is now a small museum.

The main industry of the state of Urbino during the 16th century was the manufacture of majolica, mostly for the dukes.

In 1626 Urbino and its dependent towns of Pesaro, Fano, Fossombrone, Gubbio, Castel Durante, and Cagli, along with about 300 villages, were incorporated in the Papal States.

The town is dominated by the Palazzo Ducale, built by the Dalmatian architect, Luciano di Laurana (1465-82). The irregularity of the palace was dictated by the uneven terrain and technical considerations of construction.

275. Air view of the densely built-up urban area of Urbino and the fortifications.

276. As a continuous layer of dark-brown tiles, the roofs of Urbino, gently undulating over the compact mass of houses, express materially and symbolically the Mediterranean habit of close-togetherness, almost unbroken cohesiveness of houses, and a well-knit community.

279. View of Senigallia after the reconstruction under the Rovere family in the 15th century.

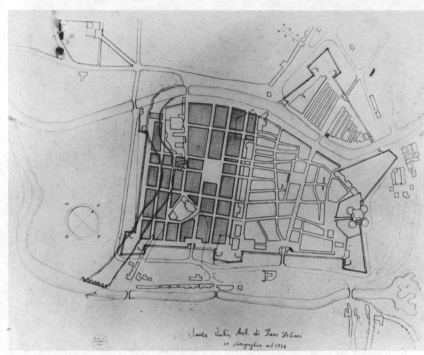

277. Map of Senigallia in 1758, with the upstream extension that took place during the 18th century.

278. Street scene in Senigallia in 1792.

352

Senigallia, Province of Ancona. No reliable evidence as to the origin and the site of Senigallia is available. It may be assumed, however, that several centuries before the Christian era small groups of fishermen settled in the marshy area at the mouth of the Misa and that, at the end of the fifth century B.C., it was constituted as a community of the Senonian Gauls. It became a Roman colony in 283 B.C., the exact site of which cannot yet be identified but it probably was situated within the boundaries of the later urban nucleus. The city was destroyed by Alaric in A.D. 409.

With the revival of urban life and of industrial and commercial activities in the tenth century, Senigallia began to recover. An ancient map of the walls of the town of the year 1264 shows that the walled-in area comprised virtually the whole territory between the bend of the Misa and the Penna extending toward the sea, possibly up to the present Rocca Roveresca. During this century the famous fairs were established. Senigallia was again destroyed in 1264. It is said that only the cathedral, the bishop's residence, and a few churches were saved. Two centuries of decline followed, reducing the city to a few houses in a region that had become swampy and infested by malaria. In 1300 Senigallia was incorporated in the Papal States and fortified. Finally, in 1445 Sigismondo Malatesta, *Gonfaloniere* of the Church and *Vicario* of the territory, began the reconstruction of the city in which only 36 houses, nine towers, the cathedral, and the residence of the bishop had been left standing. In order to attract new inhabitants Sigismondo granted far-reaching privileges which seem to have been effective;

a considerable influx of immigrants, especially from Lombardy, resulted. New fortifications were constructed, and in 1471 the embankment of the Misa was begun. In 1474 Sixtus IV assigned the lordship of the city to the Rovere family. After 1631 Senigallia became part of the duchy of Urbino. During this period work on the fortifications continued and the street system was improved and completed. Houses and public buildings were erected and new churches founded. The fairs gained in importance, and in the 18th century the city expanded upstream, adding a new district to the original nucleus. From this time until the year 1860 no substantial changes of the urban structure took place.

Fermo, Province of Ascoli Piceno. Fermo was founded by the *Picentes* about the same time as Rome, or possibly even earlier. After their defeat by the Consul Cornelius Sempronius it lost its independence and became as *Firmum Picenum* the first Roman headquarters in the region (271 B.C.). Following the battle of Philippi (42 B.C.) it was made a Roman colony. Situated at the intersection of roads to *Pausulae* and *Asculum,* it also was connected with the coastal town of *Castellum*

280. View of Fermo in the 17th century. The walls follow the contours of the hill and the streets are adapted, at least in part, to the configuration of the terrain. The building density is generally low with many open spaces distributed over the urban area.

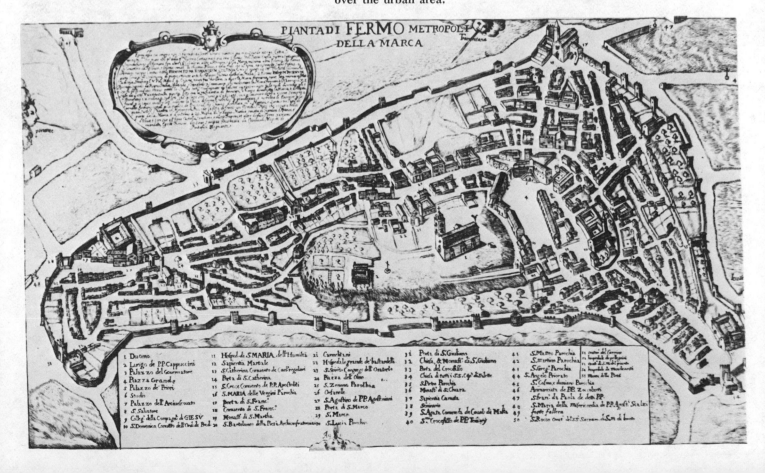

Firmanum. In the tenth century it was the capital of the *Marchia Firmana,* and in 1199 was constituted as a free *Comune.* In 1550 Fermo was transferred to the rule of the papacy.

The history of Fermo is the same as that of many other small Italian towns. Involved in the upheaval of the outside world and the quarrels of feuding parties, it suffered from wars and other misfortunes, was destroyed and rebuilt, recovered and again declined. But behind the girdle of the protecting walls the daily life of the ordinary citizens went on in all its simplicity and accustomed routine.

Fermo is situated on a hill whose summit was occupied by a citadel until 1446. The cathedral stands near the summit, a landmark visible from afar.

281. Plan of Ascoli Piceno from Joan Blaeu's *Nieuw vermeerderd en verbeterd Groot stedeboek van geheel Italie . . .*, published in Amsterdam in 1724. The plan shows clearly the situation of the town on the peninsula between the rivers, the walls at the edge of the steep river banks, and the fortifications on the neck of the peninsula. At the right the city ends at the foot of the Hill of Annunziata, where the citadel of Pius IV was built to hold the turbulent city in check.

Ascoli Piceno. The ancient *Asculum* was the chief town of *Picenum.* Situated in a strategically favorable position on the *Via Salaria*—one of the more important communications between the Adriatic and Tyrrhenian Sea—it occupied a site on a plain at the confluence of the Tronto and Castellano, where it was protected on three sides by the precipitous banks of the rivers and, on the fourth, by a steep height. It had an almost ideal defensive position: a peninsula formed by the rivers and a

282. **Palazzo dei Capitani del Popolo with the Torre Civica at the Piazza del Popolo opposite the Church of S. Francesco in Ascoli Piceno.**

relatively narrow neck that could easily be fortified by a wall between the rivers, as was actually done in the Middle Ages. A comparison with Bern, Switzerland, is not out of place; here the same conditions determined the choice of the site for an important town. The Romans who conquered *Asculum* in 268 B.C.

were well aware of the strategic value of the place. They developed it on the basis of their usual gridiron plan with the streets running parallel and perpendicular to the main direction of the rivers. The walls followed more or less the irregular banks of the rivers. The *Via Salaria*, entering the town through the

areas near the bridgeheads. Due to its strategic position, Ascoli was contested by Goths, Byzantines, and finally by Lombards, who conquered it and united it with the duchy of Spoleto. Eventually it passed to Frederick II, and later to the papacy. In the 13th century Ascoli obtained a certain communal autonomy that was retained until the 16th century. During this period the Roman street system was modified by an overlay of medieval alterations that softened the classical rigidity of the layout. New streets, radiating from the Porta Gemina and the Ponte Solestà, were constructed through the oldest medieval section of the town. Two main centers of urban life developed: the commercial center, the Piazza del Popolo, on the site of the ancient *forum*, with the market and the residence of the *Capitano del Popolo*; and the political center, the Piazza Arringo, with the palace of the bishop and the mansions of the nobles where public assemblies took place. Each of the two centers had its religious "consecration"; the former through the Church of S. Francesco and the latter through the cathedral. During the Middle Ages the architectural configuration of the two squares was irregular and spontaneous. This changed in the 15th and 16th centuries when the communal setup assumed a more dictatorial form and state bureaucracy became more absolute. Then, a more systematic planning from above began and the city assumed the character still observable today in the central part.

In 1445 Ascoli liberated itself from the rule of the Sforza and was incorporated in the Papal States. The institution of the *Capitano del Popolo* was abolished and the traditional separation of the communal powers disappeared. The Palazzo dei Capitani was taken over by the magistrates of the city and the antithesis between Piazza del Popolo and the Piazza Arringo came to an end. The next fifty years were a period of peaceful reconstruction and an intense building activity. Under the

Porta Gemina and leaving at the Ponte di Cecco, became the *decumanus* within the urban area, and the road to Fermo, the *cardo,* crossing the Tronto over the Ponte Solestà.

After the fall of the Roman Empire the social life of the town declined. The reduced population concentrated in the least exposed

357

governorship of Raniero dei Ranieri the Piazza del Popolo was surrounded by arcades (1507-1509); the Loggia dei Mercanti, at the side of the church of S. Francesco, was constructed (1509-13); the architect Cola dell' Amatrice designed the rear façade of the Palazzo del Popolo (1520) and the façade of the cathedral (1529).

In 1535 the last chapter in the autonomy of Ascoli was enacted. Nobles barricaded themselves in the Palazzo del Popolo. The papal governor ordered it set afire. The rebels were exterminated and the revolt was suppressed. The first reaction of the pope was the restoration of the ancient *forte dei Malaspina* and

in 1564, under Pius IV, the citadel Pia on the hill of the Annunziata was constructed dominating the city, and the Palazzo del Popolo became the residence of the papal governors. From this moment the physiognomy of the city, politically and architecturally, was definitely settled with the exception of the replacement of the Roman bridge of Cecco by a new bridge (1578) and the layout of a street leading in a straight line from the new bridge to the Piazza Arringo, cutting through a zone mostly occupied by gardens. Finally, the two medieval buildings, the Palazzo Arringo and the Palazzo Comunale, were combined behind one façade, a work executed in 1638.

284. Piazza del Popolo in Ascoli Piceno with the Church of S. Francesco. The principal street of the ancient city passes alongside the church without destroying the unity of the square or leaving a sense of a vacuum at its two corners.

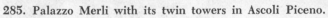
285. Palazzo Merli with its twin towers in Ascoli Piceno.

286. Palazzetto del Bargello and the Piazzetta Omonima at Gubbio.

Gubbio, Province of Perugia. Gubbio, the *Ikuvium* of the Umbrians, the *Iguvium* of the Romans, the *Agobbio, Ugubio,* and *Agobio* of the Middle Ages, names derived from *Jove,* rises on the west side of Monte Ingino in the shape of an irregular trapezoid. The Mountains of Gubbio, spurs projecting from the main system of the Apennines, have since prehistoric times provided limestone for the city's buildings, giving it an iron-grey look and the byname *Città di Pietra*.

In the prehistoric period the present plain was covered by a lake. The first inhabitants therefore settled on the southern sides of

287. Gubbio in the 16th century. The Palazzo Ducale (A top left of center); the Piazza Grande (C) with the Palazzo del Magistrate (D) in the center; the large Piazza del Mercato (N bottom center). The original Roman layout is clearly visible as are the two streets forming a "V" (right of center in the lower part). The fortifications follow the contours of the hill and large open spaces are preserved near the periphery. Engraving by Pierre Mortier.

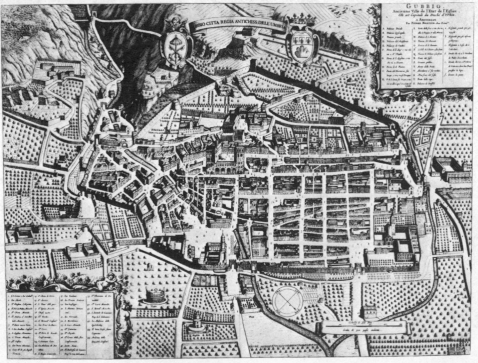

the Monti Calvo and Ingino, halfway up the slopes—where they were sheltered from the inclement climate and protected from wild animals and hostile tribes. Between the rocks and in the safety of the caves they found natural refuges or built primitive huts of branches from trees and stone and adapted the terrain to their needs, fortifying it with walls of large rocks.

During the following period when the Umbrians established themselves in *Ikuvium,* their religious and political center, and when the lake was reduced to marshes, the settlement was transferred to the foothills of Monte Ingino, the site now occupied by the lower part of the present city. Here it was protected by the natural defenses of the rivers Camignano and Cavarello—at this time still fast-flowing, but now only minor streams—and the barrier of Monte Ingino in addition to strong walls with three gates.

In Roman times the place became a *municipium* and the capital of the *Clustumina* tribe. It was laid out on the Roman gridiron plan with *decumanus* and *cardo* except for two divergent streets forming a V, an irregularity that can also be observed in the Roman nuclei of Paris and Bologna, indicating other than

Roman influences in their origin. Gradually the city expanded on the plain toward the south. This zone was developed by contractors and *equites* with a theater, swimming pools, and streets with mosaic pavements. Outside this area there was the *necropolis* with mausoleums, tombs, and *stele*. This district, which was the wealthiest and least protected, was repeatedly sacked during the barbarian invasions. Even today it shows the deliberate efforts that were made to adapt its layout to the configuration of the terrain.

During the period of the barbarian invasions Gubbio suffered greatly. Finally in 1191 Henry IV gave permission to rebuild the city on the mountain. Here systematic use was made of the natural terraces and other projecting parts of the "Hill Ubald the Blest selected" (Dante, *Paradise,* XI, 44).[97] As a free *Comune* Gubbio experienced in the 14th century its greatest prosperity. The numerous buildings which today still give it its medieval character and general layout, date from this period. Few structurally important changes were made during the Renaissance.

97. St. Ubald had selected this place for his hermitage before he was bishop of Gubbio.

Perugia. Perugia stands almost a thousand feet above the valley of the Tiber. From the center, situated on a site where several ridges meet, the town spreads outward along their summits and slopes. Its four ramifications, extending for a relatively long distance, are separated from one another by deep valleys. The whole of this very irregular area was surrounded by fortifications constructed in the Middle Ages and included remains of the walls of the Etruscan period.

The Etruscan *Perusia* was one of the twelve cities of the Confederacy of Etruria. After the rebellion against Rome it was forced to sue for peace in 294 B.C. Although the city was burnt to the ground by Octavian in 40 B.C. it was rebuilt almost immediately and became a Roman colony with the name of *Colonia Vibia Augusta Perusia.* The extent of the

Etruscan city is still perfectly identifiable within its massive walls surrounding the summit of the hill and containing the urban area until the Middle Ages. The interior layout cannot be reconstructed but it may be assumed that one major artery crossed the city from north to south connecting the two more important gates, the Porta della Via Vecchia and the Porta Marzia. Only a few churches and monasteries were erected outside the walls. The appearance of the city itself must have been very modest: the majority of the houses were small and of wood.

In the 12th and 13th centuries more churches were built within the walls and numerous houses were erected, gradually filling the central part of the city. Suburbs grew up and the social and economic life developed favorably. This was the period during which

Perugia: sviluppo urbano dal periodo etrusco-romano al 1955

epoca etrusco romana
dal sec. V al 1250
dal 1250 al 1400
dal 1400 al 1550
dal 1550 al 1870
dal 1870 al 1955
opere demolite

Rappresentazione nel rapporto 1:7.500

289. Detail from a painting by Meo di Guido da Siena (beginning of the 14th century)—the oldest view of Perugia, showing the Piazza Grande in its primitive aspect with the Palazzo dei Consoli at the left (demolished at the beginning of the 16th century) and the ancient cathedral with the *campanile* (demolished in the 15th century). In the Galleria Nazionale dell' Umbria in Perugia.

288. *Opposite:* Development plan of Perugia from the Etruscan-Roman period until 1955.

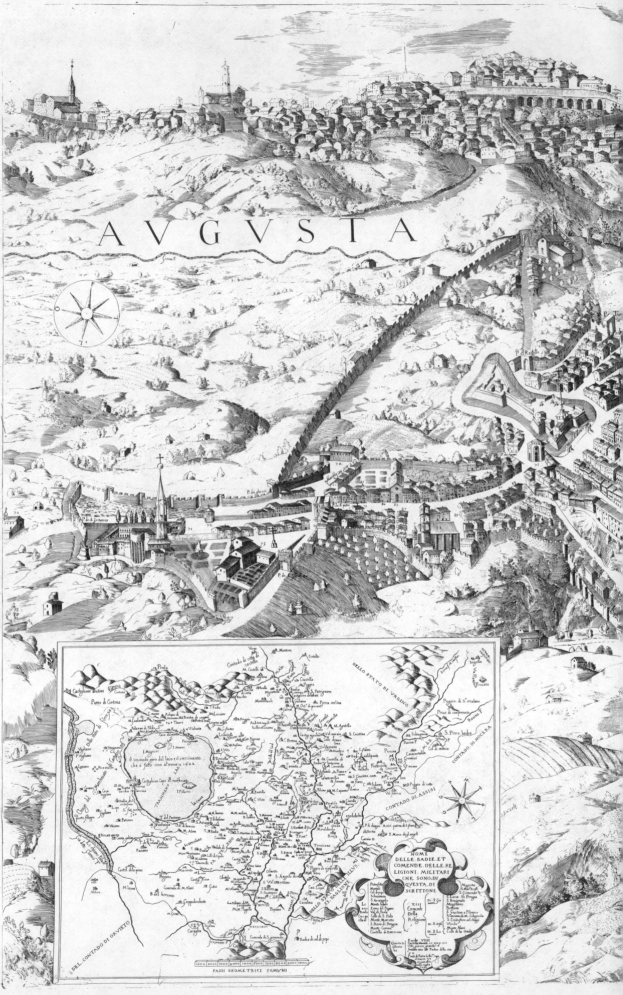

290. Perugia in 1602, clearly showing the irregular spread of the city over several hills and the high building density in the center of the town. Engraving by Livio Ensebi.

AVGVSTA

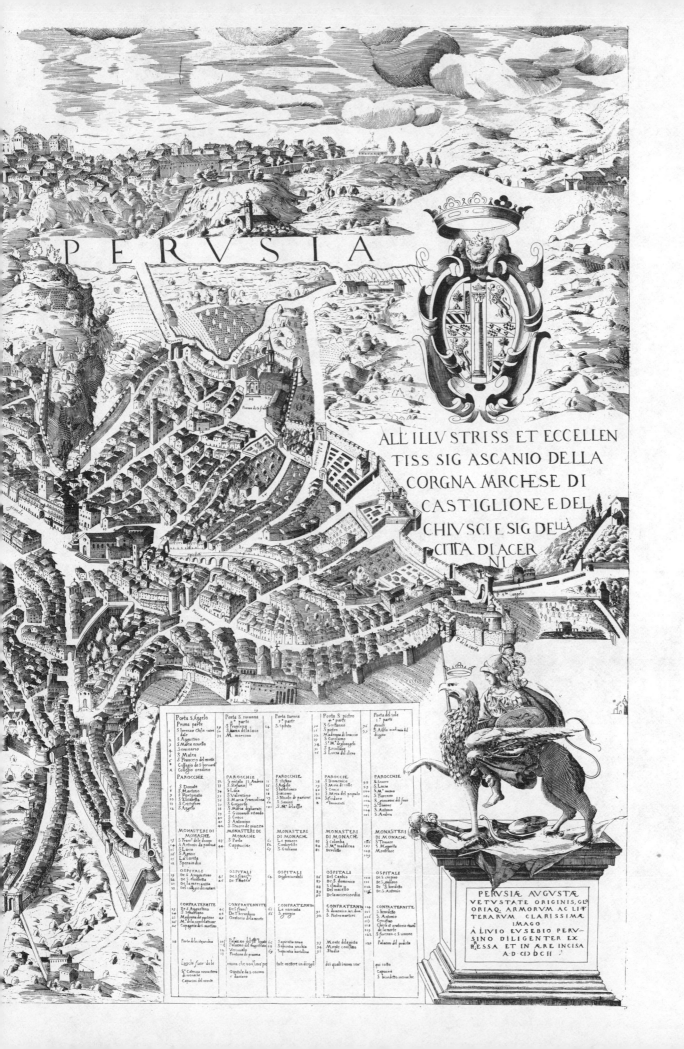

291. Porta della Mandorla at Perugia.

Perugia reached its greatest prosperity and splendor. The network of streets was improved; public buildings multiplied; strong mansions with towers and elegant palaces began to line the streets of the old town. However, the basic physical structure of Perugia remained almost unchanged during the following centuries. The changes that did take place were mostly negative. The houses grew higher, making the narrow streets darker and unhealthy; the elegant *campanili* were truncated; the beautiful buildings of the earlier centuries were tampered with, and the character of the city was gravely impaired both in general and in detail.

292. Il buon Governo. Mural in the Palazzo Comunale in Siena by Ambrogio Lorenzetti.

Delineabat D. V.

Breue totius Hiſtoriæ Senarum Argumentum
Orlando Malauolta Auctore

SENAM Vrbem Ætruſcis uictis, à principio Romani habuerunt; Quò Colonia P. Corn. Ruſino et Marco Curio Dentato Conſſ. deducta, eam per Præfectos gubernabant; A quorum Dominatione declinante Imperio, cum reliquis Italiæ Populis ſub Erulorum Regis Odoacris occidit poteſtate; Quo à Theodorico ſuperato, Gothi eam tenuerunt; Hos Græci Narſette Duce expulere; Eos Longiubardi, ſub quorum Rege Pertari in ſexta Generali Synodo, iuſſu Agatonis Papæ Anno Dñi DCLXXVI. Conſtantinopoli acta, interfuit Vitalianus qui ſe ſubſcripſit Sanctæ Senenſis Eccleſiæ Epiſcopus, qua dignitate à Iohanne primo antiquitus ornata fuerat Ciuitas, quæ ſub Deoclitiano Principe ab Anſano Chriſti Fidem acceperat, Longo-

bardorum potentia in Carolum cognomento Magnum ceſſit, a quo Libertate donata, primum Nobiles Remp. inſtituere; Quæ, poſt nobilem illam Montis Aperti Victoriam diſcordiis Ciuilibus agitata, in paucorum potentiam ex Ariſtocratica, tunc in Democraticam commutatur; Vnde pernicioſa MONTIVM nomina exorta ſunt; Nam, poſtquam Conſulare ius Nobilium ceſſit, ex ordine populari, Vigintiquatuor, deinde Sexaginta, mox Triginſaex, tum Quindecim uirorum Collegia ad breue tempus Remp. geſſerunt; Neq; Nouem uirorum Poteſtas ultra Septuaginta annos diu ualuit; Quod in popularem licentiam lapſa Duodecim uiros ſucceſſores habuit; Et illi poſt non multum tempus Reformatores; Sublatiſq; Vicecomitum ac nonnullorum Ciuium Tyrannide; Reuocatiſq; pluries exulibus, ſæpe forma Reip. immutata eſt: Demum (cum Ciuilibus, tum externis armis feſſa) iterum ſub Monarchiam reuerſa a Magno Ætruriæ Duce fœliciter gubernatur.

293. View of Siena—a thicket of towers rising above the chaotic mass of the low houses. Engraving by Orlando Malauolta.

Siena. Siena has developed from the center of three hills spreading not unlike Perugia outward along the ridges. This natural configuration into three parts has played an important role in the internal organization of the city. The nucleus of medieval Siena was situated on the highest point of the southern sector of the city called *Castello Vecchio*.[98] Its

gentle slope joins the two ridges converging on this point from the north and east respectively at the crossroads called Croce di Travaglio. F. Schevill believes that this name may refer to a cross erected at the meeting point of the three spurs or to the cruciform shape of the intersection branching off in different directions. *Travaglio* may be a corruption of the Latin *trium vallium*.[99] The Croce di Travaglio is located opposite the Loggia della Mercanzia and immediately above the Piazza del Campo in the depression between the

98. It is by no means certain that Roman Siena, which was destroyed in the Gothic wars, occupied the same site as medieval Siena. It has been suggested by Giovanni Cecchini that the Roman town stood several miles away from the later Siena.

G. Cecchini. "Dove era la Siena romana?", *Il Campo di Siena*, VI, No. 271, 1957.

99. F. Schevill. *Siena. The History of a Medieval Commune.* 1964. P. 276.

367

southern and eastern ridges. This natural configuration has determined not only the physical but also the social and political structure of Siena.[100]

The division of Siena into three sectors is very old and in any case not unusual. Most cities had four quarters or sometimes more. Siena belonged to the group that was divided into three, others being Pisa, San Gimignano, and Volterra. The three sectors of Siena were called *terzi*. The southern *terzo* was named Città; the eastern S. Martino, and the northern Camollia. The building density was highest in the center where the three ridges met and was thinning out along the ridges. From this subdivision into three parts, dictated by nature, developed the tripartite organization of the administration. There were three consuls or the multiple of three; a new *podestà* had to establish his residence in a *terzo* different from that of his two predecessors; or the government of a political party had to consist of nine or fifteen members drawn equally from each of the *terzi*.[101] This principle of equal representation was observed in many Italian towns. What makes its observance in Siena particularly interesting is that it had grown out of the physical conditions of the site—as possibly also in some other cities—on which medieval Siena developed.

The legend that ancient Siena was founded by Saena, the son of Remus, brother of Romulus, can be discarded as an invention. What we now know makes it certain that it was an Etruscan town, then fell to Rome, and that it was made a Roman colony under Augustus with the name of *Saena Julia*. Whether *Saena* indicates any connection with the Senonian Gauls as founders has not yet been corroborated by reliable evidence. Of premedieval Siena only a very few relics have been found.

It was not before the eighth century A.D. that Siena began to recover from the devastations of the barbarian invasions. When the Lombards arrived and incorporated the conquered regions of Italy in their kingdom Siena was an insignificant market center consisting,

100. Cf. pp. 102-105.
101. F. Schevill, *op. cit.*, p. 277.

294. Il Campo in Siena. Engraving made in 1717.

296. View of Siena taken from the *campanile* of the cathedral.

like so many other towns of this period, of a loose conglomeration of dilapidated huts and inhabited by a greatly reduced population. However, since the seventh century it had been the seat of a bishopric. Since that time the fate of Siena was closely associated with the rising influence of the Church and the episcopate. In the following centuries the city passed through a period of internal feuds until it became a free *Comune* in 1125 and the most powerful rival of Florence. The involved history of the wars with Florence and the internal struggles between the bishops, nobles, and the people lies outside the scope of this work. Suffice it to say that by the end of the 13th century the oligarchic government of IX was set up—after a reduction from 36 members—that for about seventy years ruled Siena successfully. Peace and prosperity returned, trade flourished, and a great building activity set in.

In 1348 Siena was hit by the plague. The population, which had reached about 50,000 in the city and possibly double this number in the *contado,* may have been reduced by 50 per cent or more.[102] In 1399 Siena fell under the rule of the Visconti. It changed hands several times until it was annexed by the duchy of Tuscany in 1559.

102. W. M. Bowsky. "The Impact of the Black Death upon Sienese Government and Society," *Speculum,* Vol. 39, No. 1, 1964.

295. *Opposite:* View of Siena in 1873, showing the spread over the ridges from the center, the fortifications, the sites of the showpieces such as Il Campo, and the generally indifferent layout of the city as a whole.

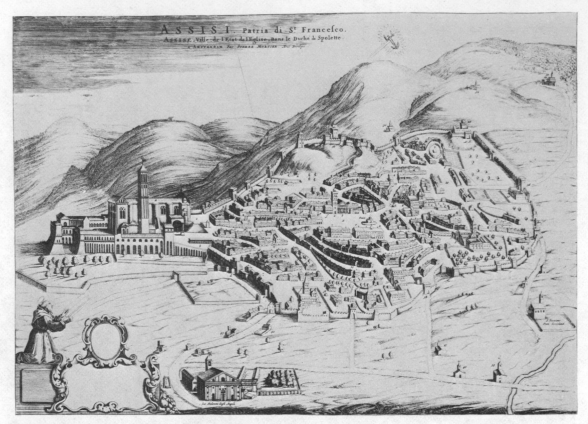

297. View of Assisi from Joan Blaeu's *Nieuw vermeerderd en verbeterd Groot stedeboek van geheel Italie . . .*, published in Amsterdam, 1724.

298. Air view of the church and monastery of S. Francesco and its connection with the town.

Assisi, Province of Perugia. Assisi, the Roman *Asisium,* is situated on a spur of Monte Subasio. The monastery and the double church of S. Francesco, rising on a mighty substructure at the edge of the mountain, dominate the town, which seems to be hardly more than an appendix of this Fortress of Faith. It is this relationship between the small urban community and the imposing group of religious buildings that endows Assisi with a unique beauty and a symbolic power of unusual and inescapable impressiveness. Many churches and monasteries have been built outside numerous towns but none have created so intimate a connection with the homes of the inhabitants and retained the aura of the saint in whose honor the shrine had been erected. Linked to the town by a narrow viaduct resembling a causeway between an island and the mainland, the two diagonal streets leading from the forecourt of the church to the town are like two strong sinewy arms holding both together. The streets continue in the main direction along the spur on which all the principal roads of this small community follow as far as possible the natural configuration of the terrain. The Piazza del Comune is situated on the site of the Roman *forum* near the cathedral which stands on a rising slope. The streets and stairways leading to it are tortuous

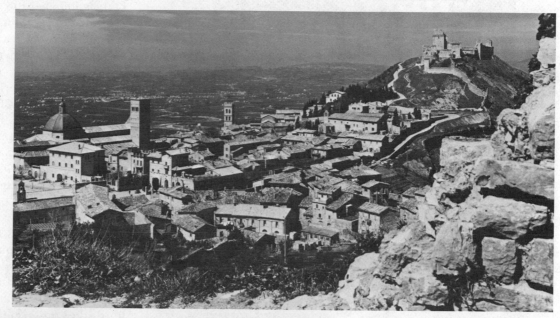

299. The town of Assisi and the Rocca Maggiore on the summit of the hill, the secular counterpart of the religious complex at the other end of the spur.

300. Scalette vicolo S. Andrea, one of the narrow stairways surmounting the difficulties of the site in Assisi.

373

301. Piazza del Comune in Assisi, with the temple of Minerva, now a church, the Torre Comunale (1212–1305), the Palazzo del Podestà, and a fountain.

and narrow; they enter it, especially at the eastern end, on different levels. The shape of the *Piazza* is long and of moderate width, conditioned by and adapted to the restricted space available on the top of the hill.

Assisi was involved as many other small and large towns in the struggles of the outside world and in local feuds. Under Roman rule it was a flourishing *municipium*. Christianity was introduced in the third century by the first bishop S. Rufinus. After a long period of decline, it recovered in the 11th century. It was razed to the ground in 1198. In 1202 the war with Perugia broke out in which Francis took part and was taken prisoner. In 1208 Francis founded the Order of the Franciscans dedicated to absolute poverty and renunciation of the world, and received his stigmata in 1224. He died in 1226.

The 13th century was for Assisi a period of revival and prosperity. The churches of S. Francesco and S. Chiara were built, others were restored; palaces and houses were erected. But at the same time the internecine feuds continued: many houses still had a small door, the so-called *porta del morto,* high above the street level which could be entered only by a ladder and by one person at a time. In 1319 the Ghibelline party made itself master of the town and Assisi passed under the rule of Perugia only to be conquered in rapid succession by the Visconti, Montefeltro, and Sforza and to be exposed to further misfortunes. This period of anarchy and violence did not end until the 16th century. The town was exhausted and sank to the level of a subdued provincial center.

Spoleto, Province of Perugia. Spoleto stands on a hill at the southern end of the valley of the Topino which joins the Tiber near Assisi. The upper part of the town is about 500 feet higher than the lower, a difference in altitude that had a considerable influence upon the physical structure of the urban area. It is possible that the name of ancient *Spoletium*

has been derived from the word *spur,* meaning "city," and that this etymological relationship may refer to a primitive Etruscan settlement. Between the sixth and fifth centuries B.C. polygonal walls were constructed, about a mile and a half in length, surrounding an area that in the Middle Ages included a large part of the residential district, and for strategic reasons

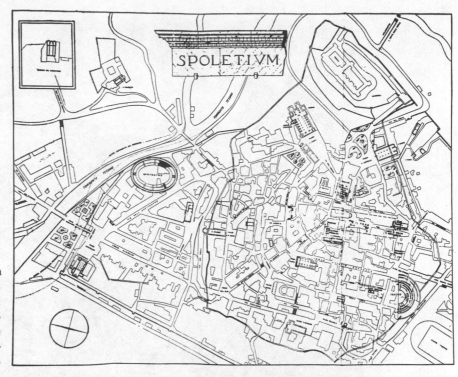

302. Map of Roman *Spoletium*. The *forum* is at the right center and traces of the Roman street system are visible in the vicinity.

303. View of Spoleto in 1599 with the medieval walls, the Rocca (top center), the Piazza, and a fairly low building density especially toward the periphery. The map may, however, be oversimplified. From *Theatrum Urbium Italicarum*, Venezia, 1599.

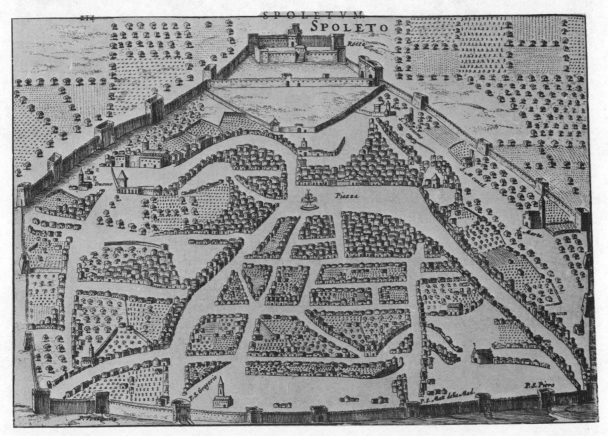

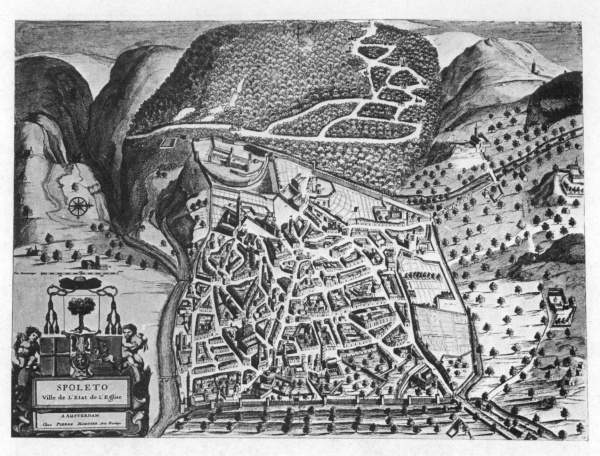

SPOLETO
Ville de L'Etat de L'Eglise

A AMSTERDAM
Chez PIERRE MORTIER Aux Bariège

the site of the ancient *acropolis,* where later the *Rocca* was built (1364). Hardly anything is known of the Umbrian period.

In 241 B.C. *Spoletium* became a Roman colony. The walls were reconstructed *in opera quadrata.* Allied to Rome, it resisted Hannibal and after the close of the Punic Wars was regarded as one of the most loyal colonies —as Cicero put it, *"in primis firma et inlustris."* In 90 B.C. *Spoletium* was elevated to a *municipium* governed by *quattuorviri* and the local senate. It suffered greatly in the civil wars, flourished in the times of Constantine, was involved in the Gothic Wars, and was occupied by Beligarius in A.D. 537. It was besieged and occupied by Totila in A.D. 545, who fortified the amphitheater, not the rock above the town, making it the citadel, a function it fulfilled until 1364 when it was destroyed and replaced by the present *Rocca.* Roman remains have been preserved as well as traces of the Roman gridiron layout. The

forum occupied the center of the town, today the Piazza del Mercato, situated on a man-made flat space paved with limestones.

In 1155 the prosperity of the city (now a free *Comune*), and the intensive building activity following a considerable increase of population, came to an end. After the suppression of a revolt of the citizens against Barbarossa and the Guelph duke, Spoleto was completely destroyed. One hundred towers were torn down and almost all the monuments, testimonies of past glory, were burned. However, the city recovered. New defensive works were set on foot (1297), suburbs were developed, new districts within the walls laid out, the urban area administratively reorganized in twelve *vaite,* new towers and numerous houses built, the Piazza Maggiore enlarged, and hospices for orphans established. A sense of order—today we would call it systematic planning—began to dominate all municipal activities that continued into the 17th and

376

304. *Opposite:* View of Spoleto and surroundings in 1663. The urban area within the walls has been built up more densely. Engraving from Joan Blaeu's *Cosmographia* published in Amsterdam, 1663.

305. Piazza del Duomo in Spoleto with a stairway leading down to it from the higher parts of the town.

18th centuries. The medieval appearance of the city was gradually adapted to the conditions and the tasks of a new age whose most influential representatives were the nobility and the high clergy. A consciousness of urban pride was awakening. Air and light for the new mansions and public buildings, a general longing for more spaciousness, for more openness to enhance the effect of the important buildings, became the order of the day. The rise of the middle class slowly changed the appearance and structure of many streets. Shops were installed on the ground floor and many houses had outside staircases to reach the upper apartments.

Todi, Province of Perugia. Todi, the ancient *Tuder,* rises on a steep hill above the left bank of the Tiber. Umbrians, Etruscans, Romans followed one another during the early history of the town. Alternating between ex-

306. Piazza del Popolo and the three Palazzi Comunali in Todi.

377

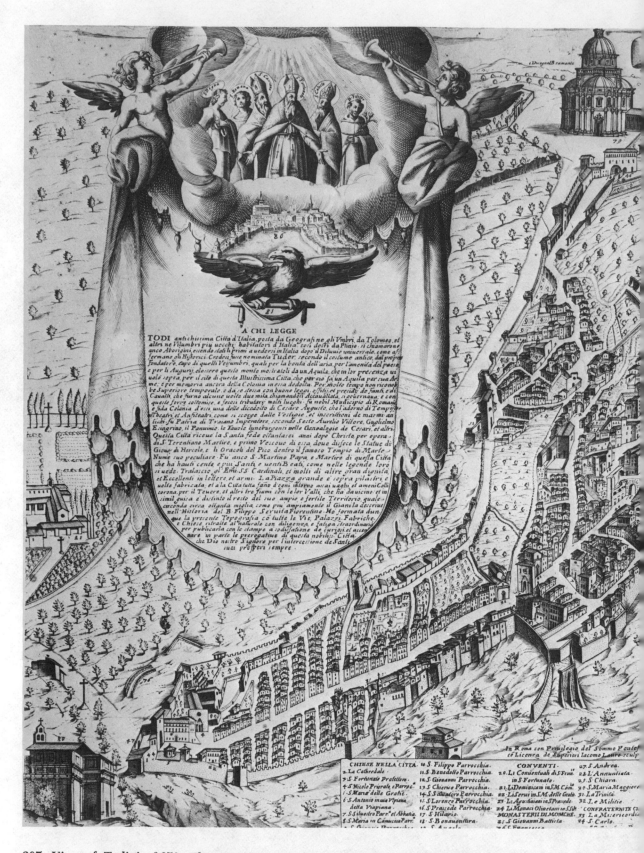

307. View of Todi in 1650. The approximately triangular core of the walled-in urban area covers
the slopes and the top of the hill extending outward along a smaller and a larger spur. The center of the

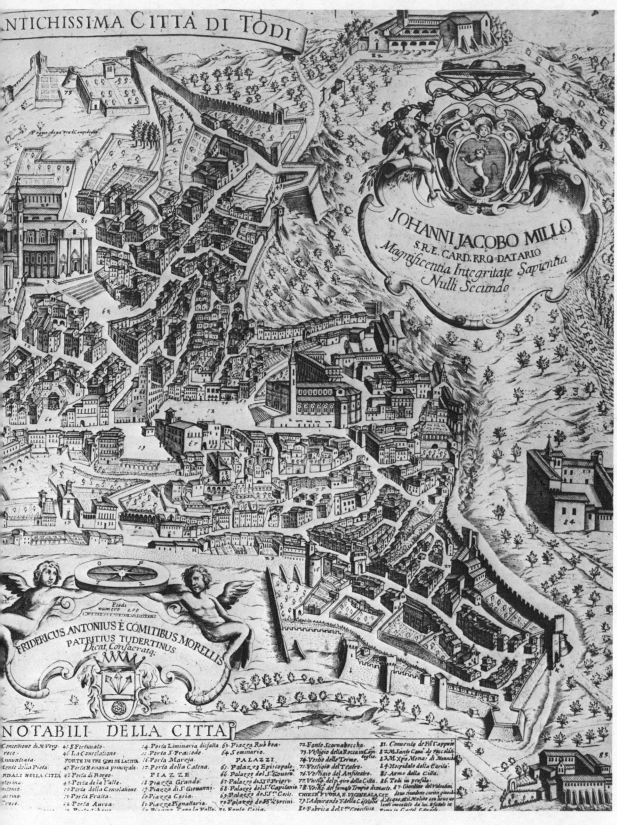

 NTICHISSIMA CITTÀ DI TODI

JOHANNI JACOBO MILLO
S.R.E. CARD. RRO DATARIO
Magnificentia Integritate Sapientia
Nulli Secundo

FRIDERICUS ANTONIUS È COMITIBUS MORELLIS
PATRITIUS TUDERTINUS
Dicat Consacratq:

NOTABILI DELLA CITTA

town is occupied by the main square and the principal public buildings. The streets follow more or less the contours of the terrain.

ternal wars, internal feuds, prosperity and decline, tyrannical rule and quest for liberty, the daily life of the ordinary citizen went on within the narrow orbit of the small town in all its immediacy and personal preoccupations.

309. Map of the development of Viterbo from the 11th to the end of the 13th century.

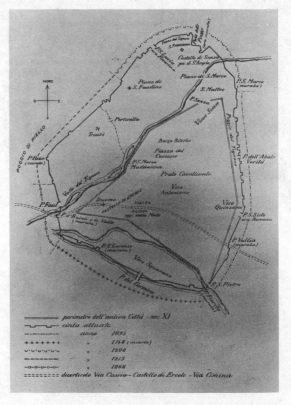

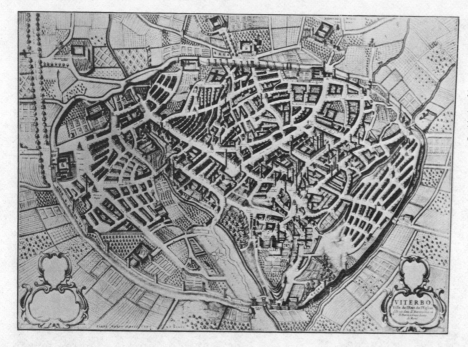

310. View of Viterbo at the end of the 16th century, showing numerous towers in the center and a diminishing building density toward the periphery.

Viterbo. Viterbo, situated on the *Via Cassia* where it was joined by the *Via Ciminia,* stands on the lower slopes of Mt. Cimino dominating a fertile plain that extends to the west and north. Its site may have been occupied by an Etruscan settlement. It was a situation particularly favorable for defense: Located between the valleys of the Urciono and the Mattezza the steep volcanic ash slopes provided a natural protection on two sides so that only the third had to be strengthened by walls and moats. It is possible that the original Etruscan village called *Surrina* had been destroyed in the fourth century B.C. by Gauls and Romans and that a *Surrina Nova* was founded nearby by the displaced inhabitants. This new settlement was apparently conquered and destroyed in turn during the barbarian invasions. The surviving rest of the population seems to have returned to the first site and established themselves on the ruins of the original village.

Viterbo was first mentioned by name in A.D. 741 when it was visited by Pope Zaccarias I. In 773 the Lombards erected a castle on the site which was later taken over by the Church at the time of Charlemagne. Tradition has it that the actual origin of Viterbo dates from a decree by Desiderius which united within the walls the four hamlets of Fanum, Arbanum, Vetulonia, and Longula, and that the first letters of these four places—F.A.V.(U.)L.—were contracted into the name of *Faul,* referring to the lower part of the town in the Urciono Valley. At first only a small group of houses gathered around the castle on the narrow rock. This small settlement developed favorably, and by the end of the tenth century it seems already to have gained a certain importance, surpassing the older localities of the region. Immigrants from the north and neighboring districts contributed to its growth and after a relatively short time the place assumed the appearance and the social and political elements of a genuine town. By the end of the 11th century it was surrounded by walls and became a free *Comune* (1095) and a powerful city, which, in the last decades of the 12th century, dominated all of the surrounding territory.

The building density was highest around the castle and the cathedral that had been erected nearby. From this core the inhabited area extended in several directions, whereas the open spaces and the only sparsely settled parts were situated near the periphery. A charter was granted in 1167. In the course of

311. **Old houses in the medieval quarter of S. Pellegrino in Viterbo, a splendid example of unity in diversity and spontaneous irregularity.**

the 13th century far-reaching privileges were conferred on the city by Frederick II; it was proclaimed the provincial seat of the "Patrimony of St. Peter" given by the Countess Matilda of Tuscany to the papacy. Gradually the dispersed structure of the city was consolidated. The thinly built-up quarters were more and more densely settled and certain functions were transferred from the nucleus around the castle and cathedral to other parts. The markets were probably first situated in the lower districts. The municipal offices, previously dispersed over the city, were concentrated in the main square of the community after imperial rule had ended in 1247. In 1354 the fort—the original focus and later the core of the city—was moved to a site near the Florentine Gate where it could play a

more efficient role in the defense of the place. A mint was established, and an annual fair was held. This rapid development was favored by the attraction of the healthy climate, an ample supply of excellent drinking water, the fertility of the hinterland, the situation at the *Via Cassia*—the most frequented road to Rome—and the population of the suburbs, consisting of sturdy peasants who could be called out as soldiers at a moment's notice to help protect the city.

The highest density of population was in the San Pellegrino quarter where a number of medieval houses have survived. Here many nobles had their residences and parts of the old street pattern have been preserved. In other quarters the streets are more regularly laid out and the houses were more orderly sited. Gradually the appearance and structure of Viterbo changed. Streets became wider and straighter and houses were more systematically aligned with the streets. Symmetry and repetitive arrangements and motives began to dominate, and Renaissance forms replaced the medieval architectural elements.

Population estimates compiled by E. T. Price[103] have produced the results shown in the table for the period from 1225 to 1871.

103. "Viterbo: Landscape of an Italian City," *Annals of the Association of American Geographers*, Vol. 54, 1964, p. 252.

Anagni, Province of Frosinone. Anagni, the ancient *Anagnia*, rises on a hill dominating the fertile valley of the Sacco. In prehistoric times it must have been almost inaccessible. The rock and the enormous walls made it an impregnable fortress crowned by the strong castle of the leader. Owing to its position in a fertile district and its strategic importance it became the capital of the *Hernici* and the seat of the assembly of the Hernican towns. It was conquered by the Umbrians and in 306 B.C. by the Romans, who made it a colony and reconsecrated it to the deities of Lazio Province.

After A.D. 1000 Anagni was a powerful community with a well-organized administration. Toward the end of the 13th century it occupied a predominant position in the history of medieval Italy not only because it had given, in the short span of one hundred years, four popes to the throne of St. Peter but also because it had taken an active part in all important historical events of the 12th and 13th centuries.

Anagni was razed to the ground by the duke of Alba about 1556, never to be restored to its previous glory.

312. *Campanile* and cathedral at Anagni on top of the hill, on the site of the ancient *acropolis*.

Year		Population
1225		20,000 able-bodied men
1272		9,000–12,000 total
1445		9,000
1538		7,200
1635		9,720
1640		11,326
	Commune	
1736	12,375	
1833	14,612	
1853	16,344	
1871	20,637	

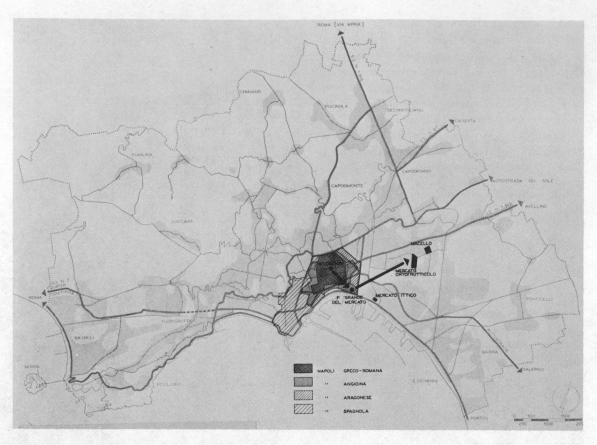

313. Plan of the historical development of Naples.

Napoli (Naples). The first settlement on the site of Naples was founded from Cumae, the Kyme of the Greeks west of Naples at the *Via Domitiana,* and was called *Parthenope* or *Palaeopolis.* Cumae itself had been settled in the eighth century B.C. by colonists under the leadership of the *oikists* Hippocles of Kyme and Megasthenes of Chalcis, two small towns on the island of Euboea. Later arrivals from Athens and Chalcis did not join the earlier pioneers at *Paleaopolis* but decided to build a new town, which they called *Neapolis* in contradistinction to the old town of *Palaeopolis.* The reasons for this decision are not quite clear. One explanation for the foundation of a new town may be the idea of limitation that dominated Greek city planning and especially the foundation of new colonies. The group of colonists sent out from the mother *polis* under the leadership of an *oikist*

was limited and the size of the colony laid out by this group was adapted to the number of its members and the available food supply from the surrounding country. Every extension would have upset not only this balance but also the very idea of restricting the colonial *polis* to its original size. It may well be that these considerations prevented the acceptance of new colonists by the already established community and forced them to build their own new town.

In 328 B.C. *Palaeopolis* was besieged and occupied by the Romans as punishment for the incursions of its inhabitants upon the Campanian allies of Rome. *Neapolis* surrendered without resistance and became a *civitas foederata.* This event marked the end of *Palaeopolis* and the beginning of the rise of *Neapolis.*

The favorable situation at the northern

384

shore of the Bay of Naples with its excellent harbor secured for *Neapolis* a leading role among the colonies of *Magna Graecia*. Its maritime trade spread beyond the immediate approaches to the Bay of Naples and finally to most of the coastal towns of the south.

Neapolis was divided into four regions called Montagna, Palatina or Campana, Nilense, and Termense. Three *decumani* each 19.41 feet wide ran from east to west and were crossed at right angles by a number of *cardines* following each other at an average distance of 125 feet.[104] The gridiron plan may have been influenced by the layout of Thurii, which is said to have been at least partly the work of Hippodamos. However, this possibility is based on an *ex post facto* speculation that thus far cannot be substantiated and probably never will be. Hippodamos' role as a city planner is by no means clear. He was first of all a theoretician—a political scientist

104. N. Galdo. *Relazione Illustrativa del Nuovo Piano Regolatore.* Published by the Comune di Napoli, Ufficio Tecnico, 1955-58, Vol. I, p. 24. Also for the following.

G. Russo. *La Città di Napoli dalle Origini al 1860.* Two volumes. 1960. *Passim.*

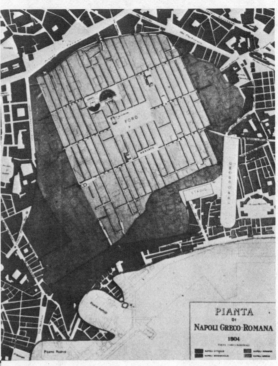

314. **Map of Greco-Roman Naples.**

315. **Map of Naples in the 11th century.**

385

we would call him today. That the regular layout of Greek cities can be ascribed to his ideas can be accepted, but this is not the same as his active participation in city-planning schemes as a practical expert or consultant. However this may be, the regular layout of Greek colonies was accepted practice. Numerous colonies were founded on a systematic plan preconceived as a whole instead of growing up haphazardly. Since a colony was restricted in size and in the number of its settlers (as mentioned above), and since it was the expression of the will of one person, the *oikist,* it was only natural that elementary ideas, such as systematic regularity, could arise in many places independently of one another. It is one of the strange preoccupations of archeologists and art historians always to search for external causes that have influenced human creations instead of accepting the fact that certain fundamental ideas and reactions are the same under similar conditions.

After the fall of the Roman Empire Naples was repeatedly attacked by the armies of the barbarian invaders, suffering grievously until in the eighth century an independent government under a duke was installed that lasted for almost four hundred years. During this

period Naples consolidated her social and economic institutions and became, according to Edrisi, the most populous city of the Mediterranean, allegedly with a population of 60,000 (?) inhabitants in the last decades of the ducal regime. The urban society consisted, as in most other cities, of the upper class of the nobles and high officials, the professional and commercial people, the clergy—as usual, a social group keeping apart from the rest of the population—and of the *milizia* with a more hereditary character. Apart from these strata there was *il popolo* with its various trades, each profession concentrated in the same street and associated in *consorterie* organized on the model of the ancient *scholae.*

During the high Middle Ages Naples remained almost completely within the confines of the Greco-Roman period—that is, within the walls constructed by the Emperor Valentinian III in A.D. 450 only short sections of which had been extended. Along the shore, outside the southern walls, new alluvial land had formed that was retained for some time as public property. At the east there was the *Campaniano* where the marshland, the *padule,* was gradually taking shape irrigated by the small river Sebeto. At the north there was the

Capo di Clio with the roads to Capua and Nola, and numerous *villae*, estates, and some suburbs. At the west roads led through the hills to Soccavo and Pianura and Pozzuoli respectively.

With the establishment of the Angevin dynasty as the government of the Kingdom of Naples in 1266 the role of Naples changed: the city became the capital of the kingdom and the seat of the Court. The population increased to 60,000 inhabitants. Merchants from Catalonia, Marseille, Pisa, and Florence rivaled in catering to the needs of the new state and its rulers. The number of officials and lawyers grew rapidly. Naples became the living symbol of the prestige, the dignity, and the power of the dynasty, whose munificence, capriciousness, or wisdom decided the fate of their Residence City. But the actual development was lagging behind these superficial ambitions. However, a few new districts were developed to house the growing population and the foreign merchants. These latter were allocated special quarters. The French were assigned a section to the east of Castelnuovo where the "Piazza Francese" is still situated; the merchants from the provinces were settled on the site called "Rua Provenzale" where

later the Palazzo Reale was built; and the Catalans and Genoese were established in the "Rua Catalana" and "Loggia ai Genovesi" respectively. But the new districts covered only a very small area insufficient for the increase of population. Their layout was chaotic and the buildings badly constructed and designed. All this contrasted strongly with the numerous splendid churches and convents erected in the older quarters and especially with the great interest and energy devoted to the building of the new royal palace as the nucleus and center of a district with sumptuous mansions for the princes of the blood and other high dignitaries of the regime. Self-glorification and showpiece architecture have always been the antithesis of social awareness and responsibility.

Somewhat more serious efforts for the improvement of Naples were made by Alfonso II of the Aragon dynasty. His plan aimed at (1) the enlargement of the city through the extension of the gridiron street system, the alignment of the existing streets, and the elimination of porches, corners, and projecting parts; (2) the construction of an aqueduct; (3) the building of fountains and drinking places for animals at intersections and other

317. Map of Naples in 1566 by
Antonio Lafrey in the Museo
di S. Martino, Naples.

318. Piazza della Carità at the Porta
Reale in Naples in 1697.

319. Detail of Lafrey's plan showing
La Porta di Chiaia, the Borgo S. Spirito,
and the Quartieri Spagnoli.

388

places suitable for watering the streets; (4) the erection of a large edifice to house all the tribunals and the offices of the royal administration. At the same time the fortifications were rebuilt, enclosing a larger area than heretofore (1488-1499).[105] In general, the authorities were more inclined to cooperate than to prohibit, to further actively what had to be done than to procrastinate.

But the Spanish administration waited too long. The population grew; the city grew; and the misery of the common people grew beyond tolerable conditions. The Baroque was not an age for the masses, less so than any other era, and the Spanish viceroys were the last to admit that the lower classes had a right to share in the blessings of a more humane existence. For them the Kingdom of Naples was a recruiting pool of soldiers and officers, and this attitude was strengthened by the general apathy and emptiness of the lives of the population. Consequently the contributions of the Spanish regime to the fate of Naples during the 16th and 17th centuries were inefficiency, regimented dullness, and unimaginative indifference.[106] Only the absolutely necessary was done and the creative grandeur of the Baroque bypassed Naples. There is no need to describe in detail what was not being done. The most telling facts are the growth of the population and the increase of the urban area. Nor is it of particular interest to describe the times from the end of the Baroque period to the 19th century. It was "still more of the same."

The following figures are of importance for the historical development of a city cast in the role of a capital without having the social and economic qualifications for this function. The figures should be accepted with some reservations. They are based on estimates by various scholars and only in a few cases on the results of an official census (1547, 1688, 1742, 1770, and 1804).[107] The dates for the different epochs are related to the population figures, not to the actual duration of each epoch.

	Approximate Size of the Urban Area	Population
Greek Epoch (7th to 3rd century B.C.)	60 hectares	30,000
Roman Epoch (328 B.C. to A.D. 536)	100	35,000
Ducal Epoch (753 to 1139)	100	50,000
Angevin Epoch (1282 to 1440)	200	40,000–60,000 45,000 after the Plague of 1399
Aragonese Epoch (1480 to 1500)	200	75,000–120,000
Spanish Epoch (1505 to 1688)	350	
1505		130,000
1547		212,106
Before the Plague of 1656		365,000
1688		186,769
Bourbon Epoch (1742 to 1860)	500	294,241
1742		338,095
1770		443,421
1804		

105. G. Russo, op. cit., pp. 62-68.
106. C. Beguinot. "Una preesistenza ambientale a Napoli: i 'Quartieri Spagnoli'." Quaderno di Urbanistica N. 5. Per il VI Convegno Nazionale di Urbanistica, Lucca. 1957. Passim.

107. N. Galdo, op. cit., p. 18.
G. Russo, op. cit., pp. 22-23.

Sorrento, Province of Napoli. According to some historians the Teleboi founded Sorrento in 753 B.C. and erected temples to the Sirens and to Minerva at the extremity of the slopes of Capo di Massa. They were followed by the Picentini, Greeks, Samnites, and Romans. Strabo (I. 22) mentions the place as *Sireon* or *Sirenusium* after the Sirens, who, according to tradition, had dwelt there. But from Roman times onward it was known as *Surrentum,* its territory extending from Capo di Massa to the Sarno River. The original nucleus was situated on a rocky platform above the sea, which en-croached upon the cliffs and left only a narrow strip of beach for settlement. The site was bounded by two ravines running down into the Marina grande and the Marina piccola.

In the days of the Roman Empire *Surrentum* was adorned with temples, a theater, public baths, a *forum,* and numerous patrician *villae.* It was the favorite residence of Augustus, Antoninus Pius, and Marcus Aurelius. After the fall of the Empire it was an autonomous duchy until absorbed by the Kingdom of Naples in 1133.

320. View of Sorrento in the 17th century, rising above the cliffs and surrounded by walls on all sides. The regular Roman layout is still visible and also the two small ports. Modern copy from G. B. Pacichelli. *Il Regno di Napoli in Prospettiva.* . . . Napoli, 1703.

321. View of Amalfi.

Amalfi, Province of Salerno. Amalfi is said to have been founded by people from Melfi (Province of Potenza). Its name may have been derived from this town. First mentioned in the sixth century, it was apparently an important place in the seventh, governed by its own doges. It rose to great prosperity and influence. The *Tabula Amalfitana,* which were recognized until 1570, were for centuries the maritime code of the Mediterranean. By the end of the ninth century it was a walled town; its doges were honored with the title of Defenders

322. Via P. Capuano at Amalfi.

tended their activities to all parts of the then known world. Pressed into a narrow space between rock and sea, maritime trade was the natural outlet for the nobles, who were not only warriors and politicians but far-sighted merchant-adventurers sending their agents everywhere, founding branch offices and retaining for themselves merely the general direction of their far-flung commercial enterprises.

In 1131 Amalfi submitted to count Roger of Sicily, and a few years later was attacked by the Pisans. Amalfi was forced to capitulate. Its power declined. In 1343 it was almost totally destroyed by a great inrush of the sea that demolished most of its buildings, the arsenals, and harbor.

Amalfi rises in terraces on the steep slopes of Monte Cerreto at the mouth of a deep ravine. Hans Christian Andersen has described the extraordinary narrowness of the town in *The Improvisor:*

The city lies, if I may say so, singularly piled upon itself. The streets are little passages between tall houses, and right through them. Now one comes through a door into a long landing-place, with small openings on the sides leading into dark chambers, then into a narrow lane between brick-work and walls of rock, step up and step down, a half-dark labyrinth of dirty passages. I often did not know whether it was a room or a lane in which we were. In most places lamps were burning; and if it had not been so, although it was midday, it would have been dark as night.

of the Faith for their services in the fight against the Saracens. About the year 1000 it was said to have had 50,000 inhabitants and to have founded colonies in Byzantium, in Asia Minor, and Africa. Its merchants ex-

Monte S. Angelo, Province of Foggia

323. This small town stands on the top of a hill and is surrounded by walls. The main church B occupies the center. The palace F is situated near the walls, and the citadel M is part of the fortifications. Since the fifth century it has been a pilgrimage center in reverence to the archangel Michael. Old view of Monte S. Angelo. Date unknown.

324. Andria was founded in 1046. It was the favorite residence of Frederick II. The town is surrounded by a circular *enceinte*. The palace B stands near the cathedral A. A square H is laid out near the walls. Churches and monasteries are situated outside the fortifications. Old view of Andria. Date unknown.

Molfetta, Province of Bari. Molfetta was incorporated in the realm of Frederick II, who invited the town to send representatives to a general parliament at Foggia (1240). It was sold by Charles V to the duke of Termoli in 1522, sacked by the French in 1529, and became a free city in 1806.

The walls surrounding the town were the first line of defense. The interior layout of the urban area offered the second or rather the ultimate defensive obstacle in case the walls were overrun. The principal, curvilinear streets changed their course unexpectedly from section to section or branched off like "the spine of a fish," *spina pesce,* jutting out two by two like "bayonets," *baionette,* but all leading in the direction of the *Largo Castello* at the harbor. There were few arteries and few squares.

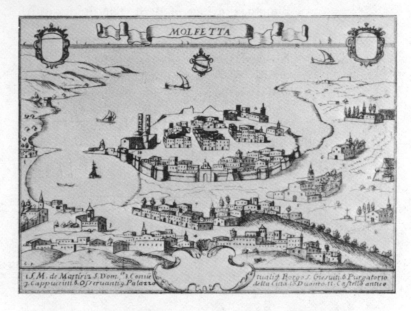

325. In this greatly simplified view of Molfetta the second vallation has disappeared. The cathedral (10 left) stands near the port. A suburb has grown up and churches have been built outside the walls. From G. B. Pacichelli, *Il Regno di Napoli in Prospettiva . . .* , Napoli, 1703.

393

326. View of Bitonto with its walls dominated by the cathedral.

Bitonto, Province of Bari. The site on which Bitonto, the ancient *Butuntum,* developed has been occupied since the Neolithic period. No exact information as to the date of the origin of the urban nucleus is available. It is likely that it grew up on the southeastern part of the present city. The root *bhot* or *bhotros* from which the first syllable of *Butuntum* has been derived meant in old Italic "construction," and the ending *-ntum* was common to many towns of the Messapii, who inhabited the region of the southeastern peninsula of Italy, the "heel" (Tarentum, Metapontum, Hydruntum, and others). *Butuntum* was the center of the Messapii or, as Pliny called them, of the *Botontini* living in rural settlements and *castra* scattered over the countryside. The pre-Roman *necropoleis* have been discovered around the primitive, inhabited nucleus.

Under Roman rule *Butuntum* became a *municipium* and stopping place on the road from Benevento to Brindisi. During the Byzantine and Saracen period the town remained confined within its walls. It began to expand after the Norman conquest in 1078 toward the northwest, assuming a trapezoid shape in whose center the cathedral was erected. In the following centuries the walled-in area was gradually built up with public and private edifices, whereas outside the walls, churches and monasteries arose. Apart from a few arteries the streets of the interior formed a maze of narrow and tortuous alleys, passages, and short roads. From the year 1799 onward extramural development increased. The new quarters and streets spread radially out from the center, making it easier for the agricultural workers to reach the *campagna bitontina* and facilitating the important production of the famous *olio di Bitonto.*

327. View of Altamura at the end of the 18th century.

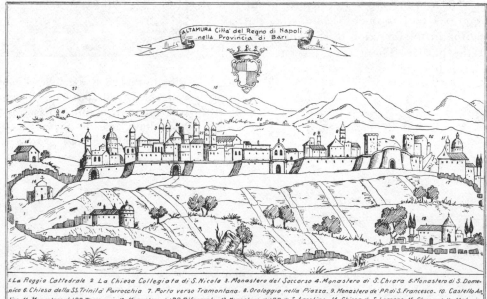

394

Altamura, Province of Bari. The site of Altamura in central Puglia has been occupied since about 1000 B.C. as recent excavations have disclosed. It flourished from the seventh to the fifth century B.C., as can be deduced from numerous finds of tombs, pottery, and the strong megalithic walls. It was destroyed at the beginning of the third century B.C. and remained uninhabited until medieval times. Between 1220 and 1230 it was rebuilt by order of Frederick II on the site of the former *acropolis* and resettled by a mixed population of Latins, Greeks, and Hebrews from the neighboring districts. At the end of the 13th century it was fortified by walls and a citadel. In the following centuries it passed under the rule of several families the last of which being the House of Farnese of Parma. It received its charter as a city from Clemens VIII in 1485.

Within the medieval walls the streets were narrow, irregular, and winding with numerous ramifications and small squares. There was a ghetto, the *Giudecca,* typical of the separation of the Jews in the Middle Ages. The modern development (19th century) proceeded along rectilinear streets radiating from the gates of the medieval fortifications.

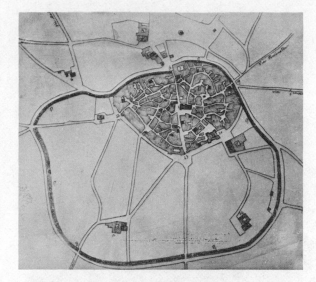

328. Map of Altamura at the end of the 18th century. The cathedral occupies the center of the town at the principal street running straight through the urban area. The street pattern on the left is more or less focused on the main street, whereas that on the right shows traces of a concentric layout.

329. Development plan of Manduria from the earliest period to modern times.

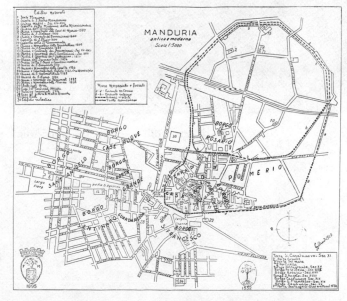

Manduria, Province of Ionio. Manduria's origin dates back to 1500 B.C., the period in which indigenous tribes began to settle in this fertile region of the Salentina Peninsula. They were followed by the Messapii, who established a permanent settlement on the site occupying an area with a perimeter of about 2.1 miles and enclosed it with powerful walls extending for more than 3.1 miles. These defenses were surrounded by an outer moat about 12 feet wide and 18 feet deep dug in

395

330. Gate of the 16th century in Manduria.

the rock. The threefold walls consisted of large rectangular solid blocks of marine gravel piled on one another without cement. Another moat, as large as the outer but less deep, formed the innermost line of defense. Streets beginning at the gates—so far six gates have been discovered—divided the inhabited area of the interior. Traces of the roads are still visible, among them a circular road following the line of the walls. Beyond the gates the streets continued as country roads passing large *necropoleis* of various epochs dug into the rocks.

In 209 B.C. Manduria was destroyed by the Romans. From this time until the 11th century A.D. hardly any information about the fate of the town has been preserved, although we know that it was devastated by the Goths and Saracens. It was finally rebuilt about 1090 by the Normans among the ruins in the southwestern part of the Messapic town, and called *Casalnovo.* Around the small parish church groups of modest houses began to grow up, their roofs touching each other, and the upper stories accessible over outer stairways. Narrow and tortuous lanes, blind alleys leading through arches, and small squares divided this mass of buildings which local chroniclers called *La Terra.* From this maze of houses and streets a complex of a distinct character stood out: no windows or chimneys, only blank walls. This was the ghetto still perfectly preserved with the synagogue.

In the 15th and 16th centuries the ring of the ancient walls became too restrictive. Suburbs grew up in the west and east where soon mansions with large courtyards, balconies, and rich doorways and windows were erected by the noble families. In the 17th and the following centuries the town expanded farther from the ancient site, mainly to the west and southwest. The new quarters had wide and straight streets almost all lined by one-story houses and large gardens, a development worthy of the misguided ideas on city planning of the 19th century.

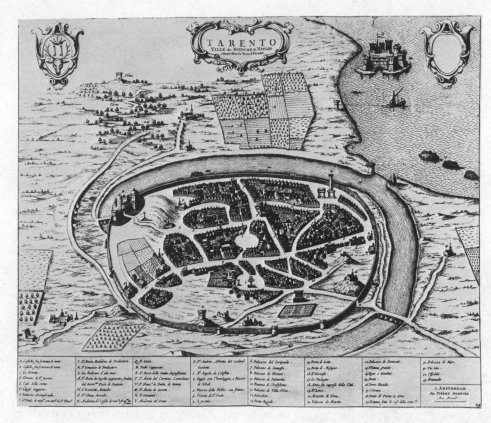

331. View of Taranto from Joan Blaeu's *Nieuw vermeerderd en verbeterd Groot stedeboek van geheel Italie . . .*, published in Amsterdam, 1724.

Taranto, Province of Ionio. The present town of Taranto stands on an island which, in antiquity, was a peninsula until its isthmus was cut through in the Middle Ages. It is now connected with the mainland by a bridge that separates the outer harbor, the *Mar Grande*, from the inner harbor, the *Mar Piccolo*. The rocky island was the site of the citadel and the old town. The restricted space resulted in a very high building density with narrow streets and lofty houses.

Tarentum was founded by Sparta in 707 B.C.

The settlers had been illegitimate children who as grown-ups resented their inferior status. When they became too troublesome they were dispatched to establish a colony.[108] This they did. Their settlement occupied the site of the present town. *Tarentum* was conquered by the Romans in 272 B.C. In A.D. 927 it was destroyed by the Saracens, rebuilt on the narrow space of the island, and in the following periods repeatedly changed its rulers.

108. J. Boardman. *The Greeks Overseas*. 1964. P. 178.

Small Towns of Apulia. These small urban places have almost without exception their origin in premedieval times, that is, they were founded in the process of colonizing the region as strongpoints of defense or as economic centers of fertile districts. Most have grown around a nucleus spreading outward, more or less equally in all directions—just like a *mac-*

chia d'olio—a "spot of oil." In general, the nucleus was left intact in its original ground plan whereas alterations and additions took place only outside this inner "precinct." As in many other parts of the Mediterranean region, where people live closely together and houses line the streets in uninterrupted rows even in villages, proximity and the preserva-

397

332. *Troia.* One main street runs throughout the whole length of the town giving it coherence and form. Elements of conscious planning are obvious.

333. Air view of the center of Manfredonia.

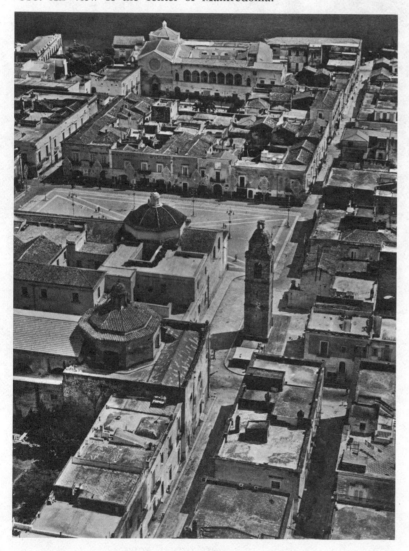

tion of the human scale have always been essential characteristics of the Apulian towns. Thus a strong feeling of neighborliness, which is not the same as a community feeling, developed and the social life remained confined to the immediate neighborhood, strengthening conservatism, interest in the little things of daily life, and satisfaction with an environment restricted to the narrow vicinity. Private life spilt over into the street and intimacy—how deep is it in reality?—between neighbors has heightened the cohesion of these small groups. Thus the stimulus for outward extension is missing and the self-sufficiency of the precinct dominates.

There are rarely towns that have been deliberately or systematically planned. Most places have grown up spontaneously though by no means haphazardly. In many cases the influence of nature, the configuration of the terrain, and location on the coast are obvious factors seen at first glance. These small centers cannot boast of marvelous buildings or of grand development schemes. Their contribution to the history of city planning is modest, though of a particular modesty, of a human simplicity spontaneous and direct, a type that does not raise sophisticated artistic problems but is nearer to "folk art." They are simply *there,* have always been there—that is the lesson and the overwhelming impression of these unpretentious and yet significant places.

A few plans of these towns follow.[109]

109. The plans are published by kind permission of the author from E. Minchilli, "Classificazione e Forma delle Città in Puglia," *Giornale del Genio Civile,* No. 3-4, 1958.

334. *Manfredonia* was founded in 1263 by King Manfred, who laid the first stone in a solemn ritual to which he had summoned astrologers from Sicily and Lombardy. It was laid out on a preconceived checkerboard plan and first mentioned in 1272 as a new town for the inhabitants of destroyed Siponto.

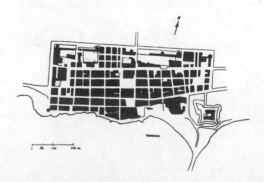

335. *Arnesano.* The town, laid out on a regular ground plan, has derived its name from the Greek word *arne* (sheep), referring to the fertile pastures of this district.

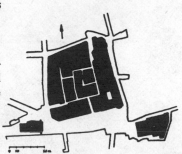

336. *Muro Leccese.* Arnesano and Muro Leccese show a certain regularity of layout and a tendency to keep from spreading beyond the original dimensions of the site.

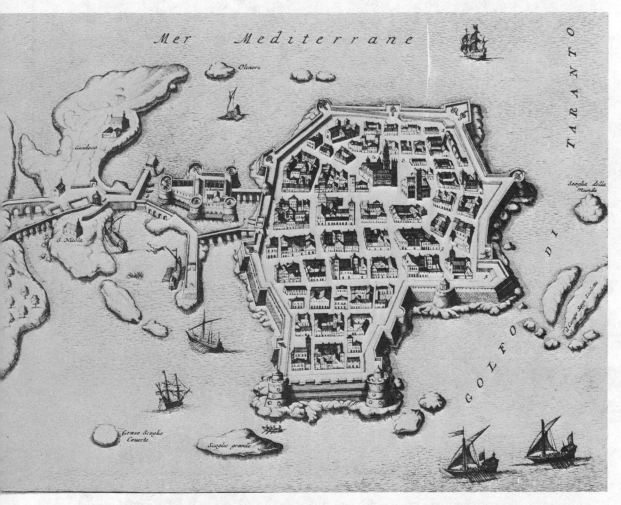

337. *Gallipoli,* the Greek *Kallipolis,* preserves almost unaltered its ancient character as an island town. Old view from Joan Blaeu's *Nieuw vermeerderd en verbeterd Groot stedeboek van geheel Italie . . . ,* published in Amsterdam, 1724.

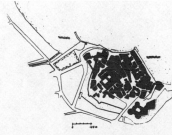

338. *Otranto.* Otranto's importance stems from its situation and function as a port connecting southern Italy with the East and especially Greece, although it could not compete with Brindisi.

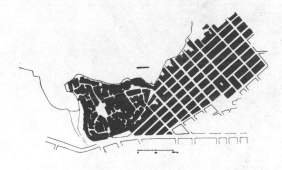

339. *Castellaneta.* View of the ancient walled-in nucleus of Castellaneta in the 18th century.

340. *Polignano a Mare.* Contrast between two eras: the original nucleus, spontaneously grown up, and the 19th-century dull, pretentious, and stereotyped addition.

341. *Putignano.* Concentric development around the original nucleus, which is still clearly distinguishable.

400

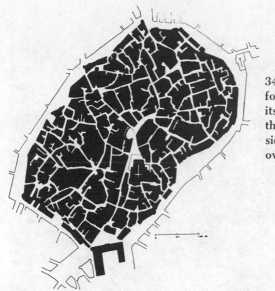

342. *Martina Franca*. Founded in A.D. 927, fortified in 1300, the town has grown within its walls seemingly unsystematically. In reality the layout is the result of functional considerations and of the primacy of the houses over the streets.

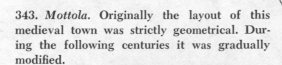

343. *Mottola*. Originally the layout of this medieval town was strictly geometrical. During the following centuries it was gradually modified.

344. View over the roofs of Alberobello.

Alberobello, Province of Bari. The Mediterranean habit of living closely together in compact settlements—sometimes with up to 20,000 inhabitants—is one of the reasons for the numerous "village towns" characteristic of Italy. Alberobello is one of these places in Apulia that deserves particular attention as the center of the region of the *trulli*.

Trulli are square or circular houses with a conical roof constructed of flat slabs of limestone without mortar or cement. The origin of the word *trullo* is not clear. It has been suggested that it is derived from the Greek *tholòs,* or from the Latin *turris,* later also from *turulla, trulla,* and *trullum,* meaning "small tower." In any case, the *trullo* dates back to a very early period and belongs to that group of human habitations that respond with an elementary directness and simplicity to the

human need for shelter and protection. In almost all parts of the world the basic form of the *trullo* can be found—in caves of Asia, in beehive huts of Africa, in peasant homes of Estremadura, in the igloos of the Eskimos, in the yurts of Mongolia, and in the fortress churches of Bornholm. It is the primeval cave feeling that has created the all-round, protecting shell of these abodes.

The original *trulli* consisted of a single circular room with a conical roof. Today, many *trulli* have several rooms and combine the flat and the conical roof as a solution more easily adaptable to many-roomed houses.

346. Street in Alberobello.

402

345. *Opposite:* View of the Valle d'Idria with the *trulli* around Martina Franca.

347. In Alberobello one finds a marvelous rhythm of ascending and descending lines, of circular and vertical surfaces, of plain walls, of the rough texture of the roofs, and of white and dark surfaces.

Messina. Numerous legends and enchanting myths are woven around the origin of Messina, telling how Sicily was separated from Calabria by a stroke of Poseidon's trident; how Cronos' sickle gave the port its shape and the city its Greek name, *Zancle;* how it was visited by Ceres and Proserpina, Zeus and Orion, how Hercules and the Argonauts passed the site, and how Odysseus sailed between the rocks where Scylla and Charybdis dwelt. The much more prosaic fact about the origin of Messina is that the slopes of the *Promontorium Pelorum,* the promontory of Faro, were occupied in prehistoric times by *Sicano-Siculi* settlers, first living in caves and later in oval or rectangular huts. Certain archeological finds indicate that a primitive contact may have been established between the local population and the eastern Mediterranean, possibly resulting in an exchange of the agricultural products of Sicily for manufactured goods through Phoenician, Cretan, or Greek traders from Argolis.

The actual *Zancle* was founded about 730 B.C. by settlers from Cumae and Chalcis, who are said to have been "pirates." The *Siculi* probably retreated to the hills and the interior to evade the Greek invasion and to maintain a certain independence. However, Hellenization proceeded, though slowly, and was completed by the end of the fifth century B.C. The first town was probably situated to the south of the harbor, but conclusive evidence on this point is not available.

Hardly anything is known about the Greco-Roman city of Messina. We may, however, distinguish two stages of development: the period of the first Greek city lasting from

403

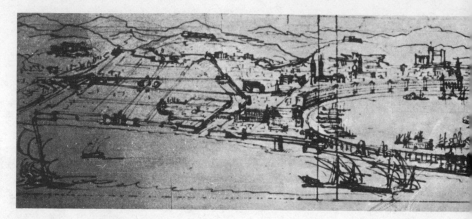

348. The oldest view of Messina, by an anonymous artist of the 15th century. Although a highly imaginary representation, it nevertheless indicates some of the characteristic features: the harbor, the compact form of the city, and its rise on the slopes of the hill. From a codex in the Biblioteca Nazionale di Roma.

730 to 396 B.C., the year in which it was destroyed by the Carthaginians; and the second period of the Greco-Roman city beginning after the rebuilding in 396 B.C. by Dionysos of Syracuse and ending with the subjection to Rome in 241 B.C. as a *civitas foederata*. It is likely that this later city was laid out on a gridiron plan but definite evidence is lacking.

After the fall of the Roman Empire, Messina passed to Byzantium and was allowed to have its own independent municipal administration. There was but little building activity except for the erection of churches. From A.D. 843 to 1061 the city was under Saracen rule. New agricultural methods were introduced and ordinances issued that radically affected the distribution of population and the mobilization of economic resources of the region, although the principal interest of the new rulers was to use Messina as a fortress.

Under the Normans, who conquered Messina in 1061, a lively building activity took place. City life grew more complex, industries flourished, and the arts and crafts were encouraged. Strong fortifications with numerous towers were constructed. The population increase was so great that an extension of the walls became necessary. Finally, after a visit by Charles V (1535) a far-reaching decision was made. The existing medieval walls were abandoned and a new, much larger *enceinte* was built to protect the city against attacks by the Turks. Messina assumed the aspect of the structure of a big city with a population that is said to have reached 50,000. To a traveler arriving by sea Messina must have made a

404

349. Project for the redevelopment of Messina by Filippo Juvara (1685–1735). Note the transformation of the Palazzo Reale into a park; the new arsenal, and, in general, a trend to unification and organic juxtaposition. The project was never realized. Original in the Biblioteca Nazionale di Torino.

great impression: enclosed at the lower end by the battlemented walls of the harbor; half-hidden houses only gradually visible through the many gates; and the city fanning out over the slopes toward the summit of the hill.

The excellence of Messina's geographical position has determined its historical continu-ity against all the adversities of nature. Its port has heightened its military and commer-cial importance despite its lack of natural resources.

Messina was partially destroyed by an earth-quake in 1783, and totally ruined by one of the most disastrous earthquakes in 1908.

350. View of Messina in the 16th century, with the walls built by Charles V.

351. View of Syracuse from Joan Blaeu's *Nieuw vermeerderd en verbeterd Groot stedeboek van geheel Italie . . .*, published in Amsterdam, 1724.

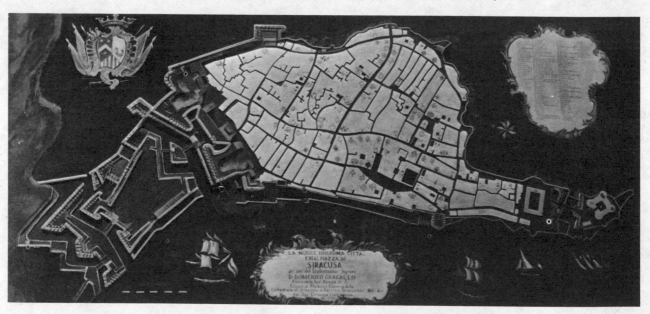

352. Relief map of Syracuse by Giuseppe Costa (1763).

353. Air view of Syracuse.

Siracusa (Syracuse). Ancient Syracuse consisted of four separate towns called *Tetrapolis* until *Epipolae* was added by Dionysios I (405-367 B.C.) and the whole complex was then known as *Pentapolis*.[110] The earlier towns on the mainland, *Achradina, Tyche,* and *Neapolis,* occupied the rising ground and the flat part between the sea on the east and the hills of Epipolae on the west. Ortygia, facing the mainland towns, was an islet now connected by causeway with the mainland.

The earthquake of 1693 reduced Syracuse to ruins. The city was rebuilt. Numerous Baroque palaces and churches of no great artistic value were erected. The general plan is not noteworthy.

110. See pp. 603-604.

Noto, Province of Siracusa. The first settlement that may be considered as the predecessor of Noto was situated about 10 miles to the north of the present city. It had been transferred to this less accessible site for strategic reasons by the *Siculi,* who called it *Neas,* the "New" town, a name the Greeks changed to *Neaton* and the Romans to *Neatum* and

354. View of Noto before the earthquake of 1693, showing the heartlike shape of the city, its situation on a rocky steep spur, and its irregular layout with wide streets and several squares. Engraving in the Biblioteca Comunale at Noto.

407

355. Air view of Noto as laid out on Landolina's plan.

Netum. It was then successively dominated by Arabs, Normans, Swabians, and Aragonese and enjoyed important privileges.

The medieval town rose on the site of the ancient *Netum* on a spur with steep rocky slopes. It had the shape of a heart. At the north it was linked to the surrounding mountains by a narrow isthmus protected by a strong castle. At the south a mule track led from the valley to the center of the city. In the 17th century it had a population of 20,000 inhabitants before the earthquake of 1693.

356. The cathedral and the Corso Vittorio Emanuele at Noto.

Chronicles tell us of flourishing industries, stately palaces, beautiful houses, sumptuous churches and monasteries, splendid monuments and fountains. A wide street ran through the whole length of the city from the eastern to the northern gate. Even if we accept this glowing description only with certain reservations as a piece of local propaganda, it is probable that Noto was a pleasant and appealing city.

This city was destroyed by the earthquake of 1693. A new Noto had to be built. The choice of the site encountered considerable difficulties. The citizens, who wanted to rebuild it on the ruins of the old town were overruled by the Court of Madrid, which on the recommendation of Cardinal Giudice, Viceroy of Sicily, decided in 1702 that the new city should be laid out near the sea and 10 miles to the south of the old Noto, and that the new buildings already erected on the site should not be pulled down as intended.

A development plan was worked out by Don Giovanni Battista Landolina and two engineers for a population of about 10,000 people. Landolina did not see the execution of his design. He died during the plague that befell the city in 1693, killing 3,000 persons. His scheme, based on a checkerboard plan, was carried out only in part, and later completed and modified by the Jesuit priest Fra Italia—most likely identical with the architect Fra Angelo Italia da Licata (b. 1628).

The plan, following the fashionable ideas on city planning and greatly influenced by the publications of the theoreticians of this period, is a typical drawing-board product of an unimaginative mind. What makes Noto interesting are the individual buildings, their scale and gardens, their grand sweep, their contrasting volumes and flowing lines, and the play of light and shadows in its ever-changing variety. In short, a splendid Baroque city on the fringes of European civilization.

358. Via Corrado Nicolaci at Noto, with a continuous rhythm of balconies and a superb, short vista toward the concave façade of the church.

357. The Chiesa Immacolata and Belvedere SS. Salvatore at Noto.

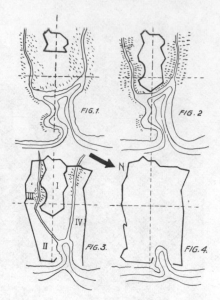

359. Sketches of the development of Palermo. Fig. 1. Phoenician period; Fig. 2. Roman period; Fig. 3. Swabian period; Fig. 4. Baroque period.

ably and when it became more powerful, it assumed the title of *Res Publica Panormi*.

In A.D. 831 Palermo was conquered by the Saracens and made the new capital of Sicily with the name of *Burlima,* an event that ushered in a period of great building activity and city planning connected especially with the name of Abu Hasan. He reconstructed the fortifications (938-947) which had been torn down by his predecessors and built a citadel. We have a description of the Palermo of this period by Ibn Hauqual, a tenth-century Ara-

Palermo. The earliest occupation of the site is attested by the discovery of a neolithic settlement and a *necropolis* at the foot of Monte Pellegrino. *Panormus* is said to have been founded by Phoenicians in the eighth century, at a time when Sicily was inhabited by the *Siculi* in the east, by the *Sicani* in the west, and the *Elimi* in the southwest. When the Greeks began to colonize the island the Phoenicians withdrew westward and established *Panormus* as one of their strongpoints on an oblong hill about three quarters of a mile long and 1,500 feet wide between the Papireto and Cannizzaro rivers. The peninsula on which *Panormus* stood was at this time surrounded on both sides by the sea reaching almost to the cathedral which is now far inland. The place was chosen by the Phoenicians as a base for their trade and commerce and for its excellent strategic position guarding the harbor and the routes to the interior. The name *Panormus* is Greek and means "all harbor," παν ὅρμος. Thus, Palermo was from the beginning a fortress and a port town.

After the end of the Carthaginian rule *Panormus* was taken by the Romans (254 B.C.). The city was divided into two sections—*Paleopolis,* the old Phoenician settlement, and *Neapolis*—separated by a wall and palisades from each other. The new town was laid out on the unhealthy and marshy terrain at the foot of the Greek *acropolis*. The people lived in the new quarter whereas the healthy quarter of the *acropolis* was inhabited by nobles and dignitaries. *Panormus* developed favor-

360. The oldest representation of Palermo in 1189. The upper left section shows a pleasure garden with trees and animals; the next section, to the right, contains nine lamenting figures; the third a group of seven persons; and the fourth another group of twelve people. On the right, in the upper half, is the Cappella Palatina; in the lower half, other groups of people are depicted, each representing a definite period and district of the city. From the *Liber ad honorem Augusti* by Pietro da Eboli contained in the Codex 120 of the year 1195 in the Municipal Library of Bern.

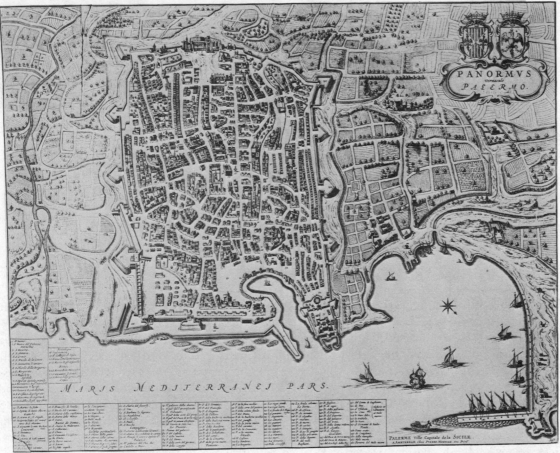

361. Plan of Palermo from Joan Blaeu's *Nieuw vermeerderd en verbeterd Groot stedeboek van geheel Italie . . .* , published in Amsterdam, 1724.

bian geographer, a short summary of which follows.

Palermo is divided into five districts: The first is the actual city surrounded by high walls; here live the merchants and here is the great Friday Mosque, formerly a Christian church. The second, called *Halesah*, is also walled in. This is the residence of the sultan. Here are neither markets nor storehouses but baths, a mosque of moderate size, the prison, arsenal, and houses for officials. The third, more important and more populated, is the harbor district. South of the city orchards and gardens are situated. Money changers and spice merchants have their markets outside the walls just as the tailors, armorers, and coppersmiths, and grain merchants have established themselves in this quarter. Butchers have their shops inside the walls. There are said to be more than 150, who seem to be rather wealthy judging from the size of their mosque. The quarters along the seashore are inhabited by rough people, quarrelsome soldiers, a dissolute rabble, and juveniles who insult decent women.

This somewhat confusing description can be reduced to the fact that there were four quarters:

1. The *Cassaro* (Roman *castrum*. Arabic *Kasr*) in Roman times divided into *Paleopolis* and *Neapolis*.
2. The *Halesah, Kalsa.*
3. The quarter of the Mosque and the *Borgo Nuovo* long since unified with the west of the *Kalsa.*
4. The *Schiavoni*, the harbor district.

Under Norman rule (since 1072) Palermo reached its greatest prosperity and splendor, and under Frederick II was an intellectual center of considerable importance. A new Palazzo Reale was built, around which a quarter for the nobility and court officials grew up. In front of the palace a vast *piazza* was laid out from which three streets branched off.

411

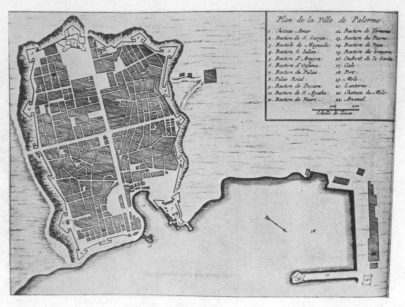

362. Map of Palermo in 1719 clearly showing the new arterial roads, the fortifications, and the intricate system of the medieval quarters. From *Description de l'Isle de Sicile, et des ses Côtes Maritimes avec les Plans de Toutes ses Forteresses . . . .* by P. del Calléjo y Anguló. 1734.

During the following centuries the harbor was drying up, and a new commercial quarter, between the two rivers, developed. It was not until the 16th century that the rather spontaneous growth of Palermo gradually began to give way to a more "systematic" renewal. The two great thoroughfares—the Cassaro (today the Via Vittorio Emanuele) and Maqueda —were planned and laid out under Spanish viceroys. They cut straight through a labyrinth of alleys, lanes, and narrow, tortuous streets and intersected at the Quattro Canti, in the center of the city. Whether this "systematization" was an improvement may be doubted. It was certainly a contribution to the general dullness of the inner section of Pa-

363. Air view of the harbor and center of Palermo with the two thoroughfares and the Quattro Canti.

lermo. But a new scale was introduced, and the sedan chair was replaced by opulent carriages. The oblong city of the Middle Ages was gradually transformed into the square city of the Baroque. The Roman system of *decumanus* and *cardo* meeting in the center was restored, and the drawing-board city builders had the satisfaction that their "system of coordinates" divided the urban area into four neatly delimited quarters—in theory. This attempt at "systematization" failed. The overcrowded quarters remained overcrowded and the new straight arteries remained an empty demonstration of futile ambitions. Fortu-

nately the greatest asset of Palermo, its physical location, could not be systematized. The city, surrounded by a vast semicircle of mountains, with the Monte Pellegrino on the west and the Capo Zaffarano on the east, stands on a small bay. Behind it the Conca d'Oro rises gently to Monreale, crowned by its cathedral. The whole of this "Golden Shell" is a garden of olive groves and orange trees, of palms and almonds, and flowers. It is this unique beauty of a unique situation that has reserved for Palermo a place among the great cities of the world.

Cefalù, Province of Palermo. The name of the ancient *Cephaloedium* was derived from the Greek word *kefale*, meaning "head" and referred to its situation on a headland. On the origin of Cefalù no reliable data are available. The medieval town was laid out under Roger II, a work begun in 1131 concurrently with the erection of the cathedral. On the crest of the hill above the town a Saracenic citadel stood on the site of the ancient Greek fortress.

364. Air view of Cefalù. The original regular layout has been preserved just as the very high building density indicated in Figure 365.

365. View of Cefalù with the cathedral, the fortifications extending to the shore, and the citadel on top of the hill. The regular layout indicates it was founded according to a preconceived plan.

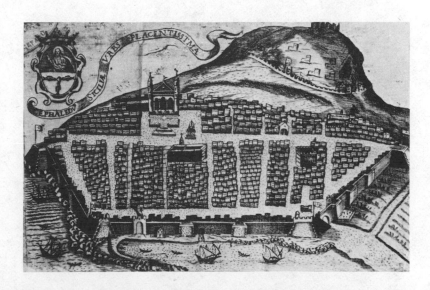

Roma (Rome). Over the centuries a vast number of scholarly and general works have been published on the history of Rome in all its manifold aspects. This flood of relevant and irrelevant information renders superfluous any attempt to retell the story of a city that is said to be eternal. The author confesses that he has approached the subject with considerable trepidation—not because he is overawed by the quantity or quality of the available scholarly research or by the historical complexity of the development of Rome, but because he has to restrict his own contribution to the physical transformation of Rome that has been going on throughout the millennia. Although concentration on this single aspect was unavoidable, the author admits that this restriction is open to criticism. However, in an International History of City Development dealing with many countries and a great number of cities, certain concessions to the scope and character of the work as a whole have to be made.[111]

As far as possible the following discussion has been grouped around contemporary plans

111. For details, see pp. 28, 55-56, 60, 144-154, 156-157, 160-179.

366. Topographical map of Rome.

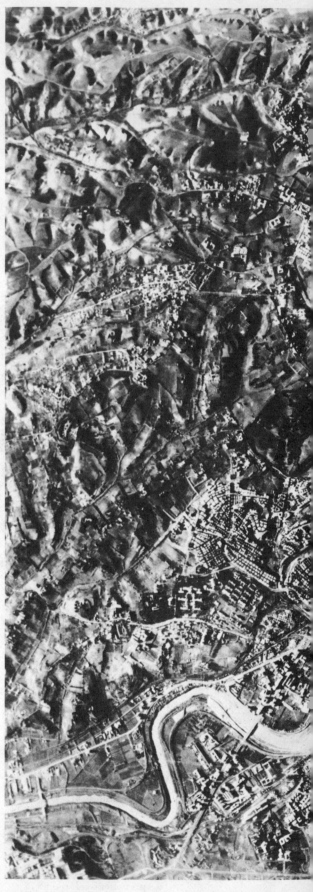

367. Air view of Rome and immediate surroundings

or maps illustrating earlier stages of development. For further information readers are referred to the bibliography containing works that offer detailed documentation on the history of Rome and numerous publications on first sources. To anticipate a criticism often made by those who rely almost exclusively on written records in their judgment of a scholarly work, it should be emphasized that the visual documentation through maps and old views is of equal importance and value, and should be regarded as indispensable original source material. This aspect of scholarly research cannot be stressed too strongly, for historians are too easily inclined to dismiss old maps and views as "not sufficiently reliable," a bias that can be explained only by their imperfect training in the interpretation of visual documentation.

With these reservations in mind the following description of the physical growth of Rome is offered, leaving it to the reader to consult other works if he wishes to have more information on other problems of the history of Rome.

368. Reconstruction of the prehistoric hut on the Palatine. The hut was relatively large, 12 by 16 feet, and was sunk about one yard into the soil. Its posts, fixed in holes in the ground, supported the roof and a small porch.

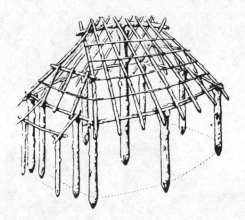

The Site. The irregular configuration of the terrain was one of the main factors determining the physical, political, and social structure of Rome. The lower parts, interrupted by ridges—the seven hills of the city—consist of volcanic ash partly solidified into hard tuff. Numerous eruptions in the Alban Hills had filled an inland lake, creating an uneven plateau. On one of the hardened lava streams flowing down from the craters in the course of time, which almost reached the gates of Rome, the *Via Appia* was laid out. Earliest Rome grew up on the hills, not in the valley of the Tiber. Later, especially during the imperial period, the city spread over the lower sections until it covered the entire area of the *Campus Martius* in the bend of the Tiber.

Rome's situation, approximately in the middle of the long axis of the Italian peninsula and almost halfway between the eastern and western Mediterranean, was particularly favorable as the only access to the interior along the Tiber—the coasts of Etruria and Latium being flat and without any natural harbors. The nucleus of Rome, the Palatine Hill, dominating the first ford where the Tiber could be crossed at the Isola Tiberina, was the natural focal point for the population and for the natural lines of communication. Here, in an excellent defensive position, the earliest settlement arose whereas the Capitoline Hill was crowned by the *arx,* the fort, and the areas near the river were occupied by the commercial quarters and warehouses. The residential districts were preferably developed on the hills where they enjoyed salubrious air and were safe from inundation. The street system, especially some of the principal arteries, was likewise conditioned by the irregularity of the terrain. The *Via Sacra* followed the watershed between the Palatine and the Velia connecting the depression of the *forum* with that of the *Colosseum.* The slope of the Palatine, with the least gradient, was used for the access road to the Palatine Hill and the *Alta Semita* followed exactly the ridge of the Quirinal. Apart from these factors the irregularity of the site influenced the gradual development of the city and the simultaneous existence of the early villages in different locations.

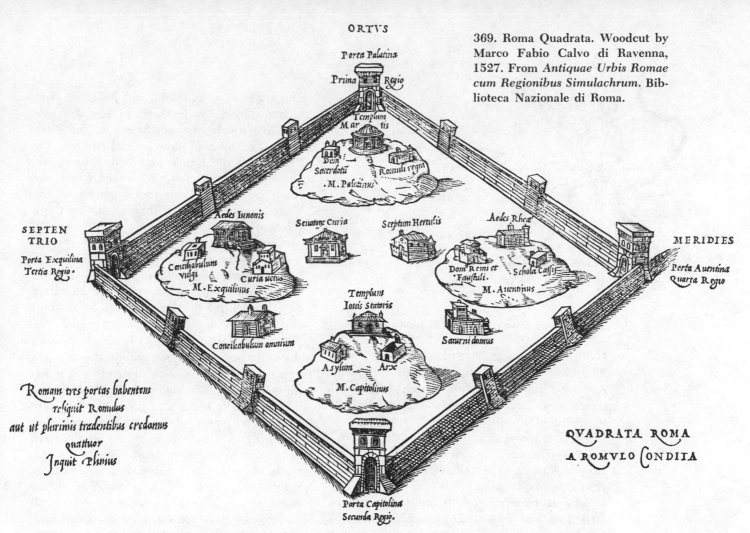

369. Roma Quadrata. Woodcut by Marco Fabio Calvo di Ravenna, 1527. From *Antiquae Urbis Romae cum Regionibus Simulachrum*. Biblioteca Nazionale di Roma.

The Earliest Settlements. It is likely that the Alban volcanos, still active before the year 1000 B.C., prevented the occupation of the site of Rome by settlers until this date. The earliest settlers were shepherds and agriculturists coming from the north—that is, from southern Etruria—who erected their primitive huts on the Palatine and possibly on the Capitoline and Esquiline hills. About the eighth century they were followed by people from the Sabine Hills. This later group occupied the Quirinal and the Esquiline ridges. These separate villages were probably protected by palisades and ditches, the usual defenses of this period around hilltop villages and refuges.

The question of *Roma quadrata*, the name given to the settlement on the Palatine, is still a controversial subject. Various theories have been put forward but none is totally convincing. In any case it is unlikely that there existed a settlement laid out on a square ground plan with streets crossing each other at right angles. It is more probable that the term of *Roma quadrata* was a later invention possibly connected by tradition with the *mundus*, the sacred pit, in the center of Roman cities. However, the sacred place—and for that matter *Roma quadrata*—was not situated in the center of the Palatine but at the periphery in front of the temple of Apollo. The tradition of a *Roma quadrata* on the Palatine as the nucleus of Rome seems to die hard.

Tradition also has it that the first stone walls, around the entire city, were constructed by Servius Tullius (578-534 B.C.). Recent archeological investigations by the Swedish archeologist Gösta Säflund (begun in 1932) have revealed that the so-called Servian wall was not built in the sixth century B.C., and that only small sections of primitive defenses existed at the time of the Etruscan kings. What is certain is that the fortifications were reconstructed in stone at their full length of about 3.7 miles after the sack of Rome by

417

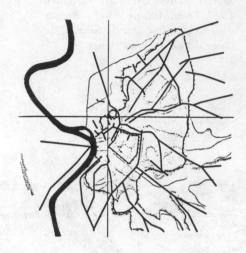

370. Map of the earliest and Republican Rome.

Gallic tribes under Brennus in 387-386 B.C. The *Cloaca Maxima,* the Great Drain, draining the *forum* depression, that had hitherto served as a cemetery, has also been attributed to Servius Tullius.

The destroyed city was rebuilt though apparently without any systematic plan, for, as Livy tells us (v. 55. 2), the reconstruction proceeded without plan, resulting in a rather chaotic agglomeration of houses along irregularly laid out streets. Here are Livy's own words:

People began in a random fashion to rebuild the City. The state supplied tiles, and granted everybody the right to quarry stone and to hew timber where he liked, after giving security for the completion of the structures within that year. In their haste men were careless about making straight the streets, and paying no attention to their own and others' rights, built on the vacant spaces. This is the reason that the ancient sewers, which were at first conducted through the public ways, at present frequently run under private dwellings and the appearance of the City is like one where the ground has been appropriated rather than divided.

In plain words: the rebuilding proceeded chaotically and made Rome a disorganized city, which it has remained until the present day.

Under Servius Tullius the urban area, covering about 704 acres was divided into four *regiones*—the *regiones Sucusana* or *Sub-*

urana, Esquilina, Collina, and *Palatina,* later to be extended to the Aventine Hill and several districts in the northeast. At the same time, the center of the city shifted from the Palatine to the *forum,* and numerous public buildings were erected, such as the *Regia,* the residence of the kings, the sanctuary of the Vesta, the *comitium,* at the foot of the Capitoline Hill, and the temple of Jupiter Capitolinus, Juno, and Minerva.

Republican Rome. In 456 B.C. a law was promulgated assigning the Aventine Hill to the *plebs,* thus giving it a particular character as a residential district, a fact that perhaps explains why it was not included within the *pomerium* until the time of Claudius. During the early period of the Republic the outward appearance of Rome was probably not much different from that under the Etruscan kings. The public buildings and private houses were simple and primitive, evoking the impression of a military city. And so it was the citizens assembled in the *Campus Martius* at the moment when they were warned of attacks from neighboring Etruria. The expansion of the Roman state after the middle of the fourth century B.C. was accompanied by a considerable building activity that continued throughout the following centuries. Far-reaching reconstructions were required after great fires had destroyed large parts of the city in 241 B.C., 213, 210, 192—the year in which Rome was visited by an earthquake—in 178, and 111.

In the second century B.C. the first systematic urban renewal, especially of the *forum* and the quarters along the Tiber, was undertaken. Numerous public buildings were erected by the leading exponents of the new oligarchy as visible signs of their wealth, influence, and desire for popularity. The urban area expanded, having remained almost unchanged since the fourth century. The population had steadily increased for several centuries. According to Beloch,[112] whose figures are still the most reliable, the Roman territory had a population of 130,000 in 508 B.C.; 103,000 in 474, 152,000 in 392, 270,000 in 234,

112. J. Beloch. *Die Bevölkerung der griechisch-römischen Welt.* 1886.

394,000 in 125, and 910,000 in 70 B.C. However, even these figures should be accepted with reservation.

The increasing social differentiation, that went on for a long time, gave rise to the formation of clearly distinguishable quarters for the lower and the upper classes. The *plebs* occupied the Aventine and the Caelius whereas the ruling minority preferred to live near the political center, the Palatine. Other districts of the central zone such as the *vicus Tuscus* and the *Subura* were inhabited by small traders and artisans. Here the building density was relatively high and the houses modest, though more opulent residences were not infrequent as has been testified for the *Subura*, especially later under the Empire, just as on the Quirinal and Viminal. Gardens covered large spaces on the Quirinal, the Pincio, the *Campus Martius,* and above all along the banks of the Tiber.

During the last decades of the Republic activities connected with urban renewal were dictated, apart from the natural growth of Rome, by the political ambitions of the rulers. As Strabo said, "The ancient Romans were so preoccupied by the great problems that they neglected the embellishment of their city. Without disregarding the great problems the modern Romans, especially those of today are embellishing it with magnificent monuments" (V. 3.8), and, we should add, neglected the deteriorating quarters of the lower classes— concentrating their attention almost exclusively on public buildings, that is, on show-piece architecture, in their own political interest.

Imperial Rome. A survey of the innumerable plans through which cartographers and artists of later centuries have tried to recapture the physical structure of ancient Rome seems to suggest that Rome consisted only of public buildings. In vain one searches for any indication of how the residential districts were laid out and what the street system was like. The fragments of the *Forma Urbis Severiana,* the plan of Rome engraved in marble between A.D. 203 to 211 and placed on the wall of the library in Vespasian's Forum in the reign of

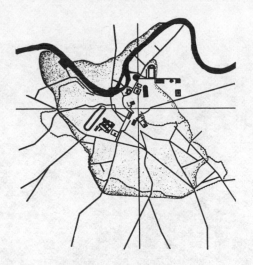

371. Map of Rome at the time of Augustus.

Septimius Severus, have been badly preserved. Of more than a thousand pieces only 712 have been fitted together, constituting more or less larger sections. But only 41 of these pieces have been identified and localized with certainty, making it almost impossible to draw definite and detailed conclusions from this unique topographical document.

A plan of ancient Rome by Gotfridus van Schayck published between 1620 and 1635, which attempts to reconstruct the layout of the urban area in more detail, can hardly be regarded as a serious contribution to our knowledge of Rome in the imperial era. Its highly diagrammatic design and the standardized representation of the houses lining the rather imaginary layout of the streets are obviously unsuitable as reliable evidence. We have to resign ourselves to the fact that we know next to nothing about the detailed structure of the residential districts of Imperial Rome, and that the available information refers almost exclusively to public buildings— a drawback that makes it impossible to analyze the physical structure of the city as a whole.

The area of Rome was from the earliest times divided into the urban zone proper—the *urbs* with its *continentia aedificia,* the actually built-up zone, and the suburbs. This followed conventional practice. It developed out of the social and economic conditions that everywhere were conducive to the grouping of outlying districts around the core. The two zones had different administrative and juridical or-

419

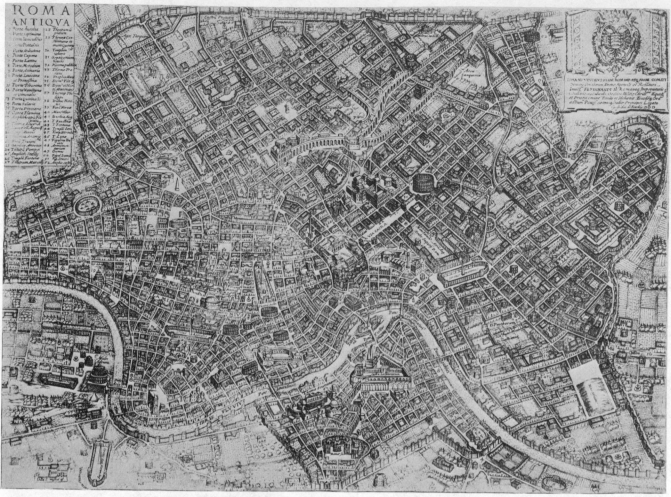

372. Plan of ancient Rome. Engraving by Gotfridus van Schayck published between 1620 and 1635. Copy in the Biblioteca Nazionale di Roma.

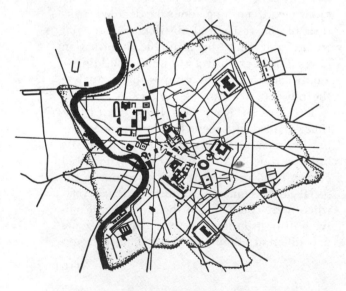

373. Map of Rome in the Imperial period.

ganizations and were marked off against each other by *cippi,* landmarks, along a line delineating the *pomerium,* which coincided from the beginning with the circuit of the walls as it had been laid out in the foundation rites of the *limitatio.* This line separated the *imperium domi* from the *imperium militiae*— that is, the civil administration of the municipal authorities from the military administration of the army authorities. Within the *pomerium* no burials, military maneuvers, nor executions were permitted. It was only natural that outside the *pomerium* the poorer population erected its primitive huts just as today the *bidonvilles* of the squatters occupy the "no man's land" around the fast-growing cities of Latin America.

The land was classified as *publicum, sacrum*

and *privatum.* The public land could be granted or sold to private persons. There were no laws that would permit its expropriation for public purposes; the state had to buy land in the open market, sometimes involving such considerable sums as 100 million sesterces for the enlargement of the Forum Romanum (Forum Julium). Within the *pomerium* the city was divided·under Augustus into fourteen *regiones* and 265 *vici*—later, under Diocletian, increased to 300 to 400. Each region was administered by an *aedilis* or *tribunus plebis* or a *praetor,* who was later replaced by a *curator,* and the *vici* by *vicomagistri.*

Under Caesar two important laws were promulgated: the *Lex Julia Municipalis* dealing with the regulation of traffic, the maintenance of the streets, and the sewerage system, the water supply, the police, the food supply, and precautionary measures against the outbreak of fires;[113] and the *Lex Julia de modo aedificiorum.* This latter established certain standards for the construction of buildings. The scarcity of space had resulted in the erection of ever-higher buildings using timber as building material instead of more solid structures of stones or bricks, a neglect that had frequently caused the rapid spread of fires. The *Lex Julia* therefore prescribed the use of tiles for the roofs and an *ambitus,* the space between the sides of two adjoining buildings or *insulae,* of 28.75 inches, an order that was later emended to permit party walls, *parietes*

113. Th. Mommsen. *Inscriptiones Latinae Antiquissimae.* 1863. Part I: Instrumenta publica populi Romani.

374. **Rome's regions under Augustus. Woodcut by Marco Fabio Calvo, 1527.**

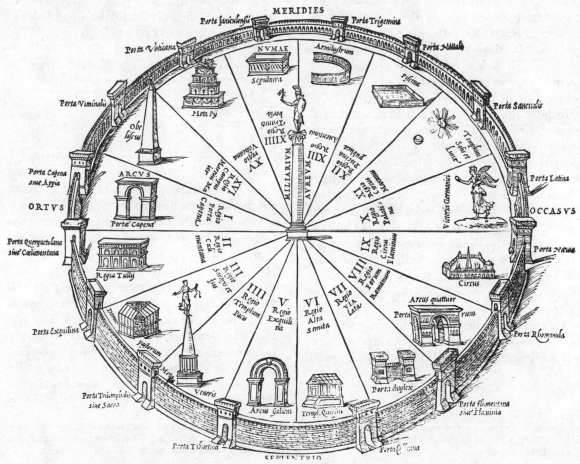

communes—possibly because of the more economic use of space, provided these walls were not thicker than 17.7 inches. A further regulation limited the height of the houses to 70 feet—that is, to 6 or 7 stories.[114]

The abolition of the *ambitus* involved the reversal of an ancient religious custom intimately connected with the foundation of cities and the ever-present protection of the home by the gods. In ancient Rome each family, particularly the patricians, had an altar with an eternal fire where the *penates,* the house gods, were worshipped. This sacred place, the hearth, was surrounded by an enclosure originally a hedge, a wooden fence or a stone wall, for dwellings situated in the open country. When the houses were built closer together in the cities, they were kept separated from one another by a space, however narrow. In early times a party (or common) wall would have been regarded as a sacrilege. Consequently, a free space was kept between two houses and consecrated to the god of the enclosure. This is the religious meaning of the *ambitus.* In time this practice declined but the original idea of "insulated" houses lived on in the name of *insula,* an isolated home not contiguous to the neighboring buildings.

In later times *insulae* was used as a term for houses with several apartments, *domini insularum* or, according to the translations in the glossaries, *synoikia,* as opposed to the single house, a *domus.* The average size of a Roman *insula* as indicated in the *Forma Urbis* varied. It has been estimated at 306, 208, 246, and 200 square meters, and by Gerkan at 148 square meters. On the basis of 222 or 211 square meters the area of Rome, built up in *insulae,* has been calculated at 9,860,000 square meters from the number of *insulae* computed at 44,300 or 46,602.[115]

To complete and possibly to revise the picture, though only to a minor degree, the excellent investigations of Professor J. C. Russell

may be quoted.[116] According to the *Regionares* there were about 307 city blocks, *vici,* at the middle of the fourth century A.D., about 1,790 houses, *domi,* and between 44,200 and 46,200 apartments, *insulae,* figures that differ slightly from those mentioned above. The area of an average apartment house was approximately 300 square meters. If this figure is multiplied with 44,200 the result is 1,326 hectares. This result, however, is impossible, since the total area of Rome was only 1,386 hectares. Consequently *insula* can only mean, according to Russell, an apartment or hearth, not an apartment house. His conclusion seems to be convincing, although it contrasts with the definition of *insula* as given above. It is obvious that the term *insula* has been used rather indiscriminately and that this explains the greatly different estimates. On the basis of 3.5 persons for an apartment and 10 persons for a *domus* Russell arrives at a total of 172,000 and an average density of 125 per hectare. Yet this figure should be related to the noninhabited areas which Russell gives as

Streets	138 hectares
Campus Martius	60 "
Gardens	98 "
Public buildings	84 "
Warehouses	24 "
Tiber River	22 "
	426 hectares

This would leave only 970 hectares or about 200 persons per hectare.

It is probable that the city of Rome was larger in the first century A.D. than in the fourth century. According to Pliny (Nat. Hist. III. 66) its perimeter was in A.D. 74 about 13,200 paces. At 1.48 meters to the pace this would be about 19,500 meters, corresponding to the length of the Aurelian Wall. The city area was, therefore, about the same that it was two centuries later—that is, about 1,380 hectares. It would lead us too far to go into a detailed examination of other estimates. Useful references can be found in J. Carcopino's *Daily*

114. F. Castagnoli, C. Cecchelli, G. Giovannoni, and M. Zocca. *Topografia e Urbanistica di Roma.* 1958, pp. 61, 110. Vol. XXII of *Storia di Roma.*

115. *Ibid.,* p. 167.

116. J. C. Russell. *Late Ancient and Medieval Population. Op. cit.,* pp. 64-65. The figures are given in the decimal system according to Russell.

Life in Ancient Rome,[117] which may be consulted for further information. Russell's final conclusion is that a population of 350,000, at the time of Augustus, is not improbable and that this would mean about 250 persons per hectare. "If the population was actually concentrated in less than 1,000 hectares, as seems likely, the number to the hectare rises to 350 and one understands the need for apartment houses." Admittedly all this is rather confusing, but it may yet give an indication of the size of Rome and its population.

The close attention of the municipal administration to details as expressed in the various building laws was not met by a corresponding determination to pursue a systematic policy of city planning in general. As we have seen, this lack of foresight dated back to the rebuilding of Rome after the sack in 387 B.C. When the tribunes "were urging the *plebs* unceasingly to quit their ruins and emigrate to a city ready to their hand at Veii, Camillus [the dictator and conqueror of Veii] went up into the assembly, attended by the entire senate" (Livy V. L. 8) and convinced it in an impassioned speech not to emigrate and not to rebuild the city elsewhere in a more organic and contemporary manner. The meeting ended with the famous words *"Hic manebimus optime"* and Rome was rebuilt "in a random fashion." Sentimental attachment to the past was stronger than unconventional and bold actions. Political expediency triumphed as usual over reason and the exciting adventure of a new beginning.

Rome continued on her way of disorder, of neglect of the justified ambitions of the masses, and in the self-deception that innumerable unrelated details would make an organic whole. This stubborn, emotional pursuit of unregulated growth is the more astonishing because it fundamentally contrasts with the systematic layout of almost all cities founded by Rome in the provinces and even with the traditional idea of a *Roma quadrata* and the elaborate ritual connected with the foundation. It seems that Rome was inescapably chained to the fate common to all capital cities of the world, with the unique exception of Peking, which contained the germs of unsystematic growth from the very beginning. Rome failed like all the other capitals to develop a tradition of moral responsibility, social awareness, or community spirit. Instead of these creative forces she overestimated as the seat of political power the exigencies of political ostentation, and preferred to succumb to the selfish machinations of speculators and unenlightened politicians, who were by no means qualified to judge the problems connected with the complex physical development of a metropolis.

This was the situation that faced Caesar in the last years of his life. There were four major problems that had to be solved: the expansion of the residential area; the adaptation of the residential districts and the street system to the needs of a capital city; the modernization of the public services and public institutions, in particular the extension of the *forum*; and the improvement of the communications between the various parts of the city and especially of the new quarters with the urban center.[118] There were three possibilities for the extension of the residential zone. The most natural solution would have been an extension toward the east where the arc of the higher hills was farthest away from the river and the unhealthy areas. However, this was exactly the reason why the upper classes preferred this district and erected numerous *villae* in this part of the city. To evict these powerful families from their properties was impossible—even for Caesar. Moreover, a continuous belt of gardens and open spaces extended to this zone, regarded as "intangible" and therefore to be preserved. On the other hand, there was the possibility of extension toward the south, toward the Aventine, the plebeian quarter. This had to be ruled out because the people living there worked in the nearby port and storehouses, the *horrea*, in the docks and workshops connected with the

117. 1961. P. 16.

118. L. Quaroni. "Una città eterna." In: *Roma città e piani.* Edizioni di "Urbanistica." N.D. Pp. 27 ff.

423

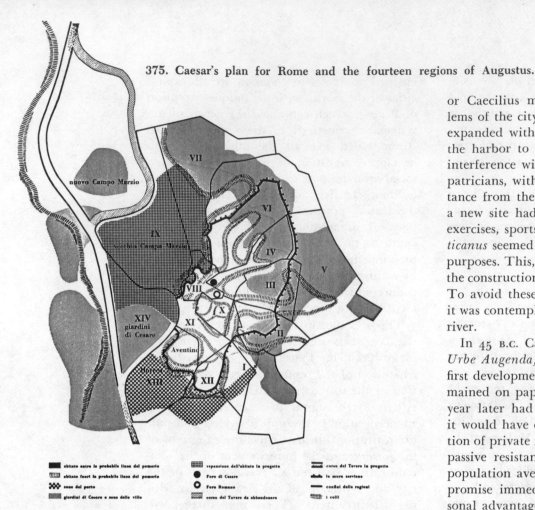

375. Caesar's plan for Rome and the fourteen regions of Augustus.

nuovo Campo Marzio

VII

VI

IX

Vecchio Campo Marzio

IV

VIII

V

III

X

XIV
giardini
di Cesare

XI

II

Aventino

I

XIII

XII

abitato entro le probabile linea del pomerio
abitato fuori la probabile linea del pomerio
zone del porto
giardini di Cesare e zona delle ville

espansione dell'abitato in progetto
Foro di Cesare
Foro Romano
corso del Tevere da abbandonare

corso del Tevere in progetto
le mura serviane
confini delle regioni
i colli

port facilities, which could not be transferred elsewhere. There remained the *Campus Martius*—that is, the expansion toward the north beyond the *pomerium* between the Quirinal and Capitoline hills. This was the zone for military exercises and, in case of siege, the field for active defense. This latter possibility could be discarded as most unlikely during Caesar's time. The size of the *Campus Martius* was large enough to satisfy the housing needs of the present population and of a later influx of immigrants and officials, who were expected to settle in the capital the more the administration of the Empire grew in complexity and extent. Moreover, the *Campus Martius* was a perfectly level plain permitting a regular street system and near enough to the *forum* to relieve the pressure upon the center city and to establish convenient communications between them.

The zone of the *Campus Martius* appeared to Caesar and his Greek architect Pomponius

or Caecilius most suited to solve the problems of the city: the residential area could be expanded without transferring the docks and the harbor to another location, without any interference with the belt of the *villae* of the patricians, without unduly increasing the distance from the center.[119] On the other hand, a new site had to be developed for military exercises, sports, and games. The *Campus Vaticanus* seemed to be the best choice for these purposes. This, however, would have involved the construction of new bridges over the Tiber. To avoid these difficult and expensive works it was contemplated to divert the course of the river.

In 45 B.C. Caesar promulgated the *Lex de Urbe Augenda,* which may be regarded as the first development plan of Rome. The plan remained on paper. Even if Caesar's death one year later had not prevented its realization, it would have encountered the strong opposition of private interests—just as today—and the passive resistance of the great majority of a population averse to all changes that did not promise immediate tangible results and personal advantages—just as today. However this may be, *"talia agentem atque meditantem mors praevenit"* (Suetonius. *Caesar.* 44. 4).[120]

With Augustus began the age of imperial vulgarity, of shameless political propaganda, of a mediocre standardized architecture, and of hoodwinking the people with *panem et circenses*. It was the show that mattered. The *Res gestae divi Augusti,* recording all the public works of the emperor—among other things he restored over eighty temples—is one of the most embarrassing documents of self-glorification left to posterity. It does not say a single word about a coherent urban policy for the metropolis and of large-scale plans for the improvement of the lot of the common people. What else does his empty boast that "he had received a city of brick and left it a city of marble" mean, but that he regarded the public buildings as his greatest achievement? Dicta-

119. *Ibid.*, p. 30.
120. "But he was cut short in the midst of all his projects by death."

424

376. Map of the Campus Martius. Engraving by Giovanni Battista Piranesi, 1762.

tors have always indulged in ambitious building programs if for no other reason than to eclipse with their new edifices the works of their predecessors and to immortalize their own name. Mussolini and Hitler did the same, and the "swashbuckling *condottiere*" Augustus was a past master in this field—and a cunning bureaucrat.

Like all bureaucrats who expect and encounter opposition, Augustus preferred the indirect approach to the problems of the metropolis. Consequently, he abandoned Caesar's comprehensive development plan, as outlined in the *Lex de Urbe Augenda,* dismissed this predecessor's architect, and transformed that plan into one for the administrative reorganization of the city. The diversion of the Tiber was given up and the systematic development of the *Campus Martius* as a residential area now less pressing because the zone of Trastevere had been "ceded to the Roman people," was approached indirectly and presented as "the idea of a Rome of the future" in this part of the city. Consequently a number of public buildings were erected in the *Campus Martius*: the Pantheon, the temple of Bonus Eventus, the *Arc Pacis,* the *Thermae* of Agrippa, the theater of Marcullus, the *Porticus Octaviae,* and other buildings. In this way a *fait accompli* was created, the aversion of the citizens to the development of the *Campus Martius* silenced, and a grand opportunity for the erection of public buildings exploited to the full.

This indirect procedure should not surprise us. It is used today: shopping centers, the cathedrals of a materialistic society, are built in deteriorating residential areas or a department store is located in a rundown district as the first step toward urban renewal.

The other action through which Augustus tried to improve his capital city was an administrative reorganization. The urban area, now greatly increased by the inclusion of new districts, among them the *Campus Martius* in the metropolitan region, was divided into fourteen *regiones,* a measure explained as dictated by the need for administrative decentralization. The *regiones* were subdivided into *vici,* whose size varied from 34.6 acres in the peripheral region V to 1.73 acres in region VIII, the central city, and to 989 acres in region XIV. The sizes of the *vici* were adapted to the density of population: hence the small *vicus* in the center and the large *vici* in the less populated peripheral zone.

In the purely practical sphere, the restoration of the old and the construction of new aqueducts and the regulation of the Tiber should be mentioned, as well as the establishment of five brigades whose members, called *vigilantes,* were organized in seven cohorts.

When they were faced with their greatest challenge, the *vigilantes* failed miserably—whether through inefficiency or through the magnitude of the disaster or by order from the highest authority, is impossible to decide, just as the origin of the great fire that broke out on July 18 in A.D. 64 and destroyed large parts of Rome will probably remain forever uncertain. Whether it was deliberately set by Nero or happened by accident is of no interest in this connection, but Tacitus' description contains so many relevant details that a condensed summary may not be out of place.[121]

A dreadful calamity followed in a short time after, by some ascribed to chance, and by others to the execrable wickedness of Nero. The authority of historians is on both sides, and which preponderates it is not easy to determine. It is, however, certain, that of all the disasters that ever befell the city of Rome from the rage of fire, this was the worst, the most violent, and destructive. The flame broke out in that part of the circus which adjoins, on one side, to mount Palatine, and, on the other, to mount Cælius. It caught a number of shops stored with combustible goods, and, gathering force from the winds, spread with rapidity from one end of the circus to the other. Neither the thick walls of houses, nor the inclosures of temples, nor any other building, could check the rapid progress of the flames. A dreadful conflagration followed. The level parts of the city were destroyed. The fire communicated to the higher buildings, and, again laying hold of inferior places, spread with a degree of velocity that

121. *Annals.* XV. 38-43. Translation by A. Murphy. 1836.

377. Model of Imperial Rome at the time of Constantine. The district around the Colosseum.

nothing could resist. The form of the streets, long and narrow, with frequent windings, and no regular opening, according to the plan of ancient Rome, contributed to increase the mischief. The shrieks and lamentations of women, the infirmities of age, and the weakness of the young and tender, added misery to the dreadful scene. Some endeavoured to provide for themselves, others to save their friends, in one part dragging along the lame and impotent, in another waiting to receive the tardy, or expecting relief themselves; they hurried, they lingered, they obstructed one another; they looked behind, and the fire broke out in front; they escaped from the flames, and in their place of refuge found no safety; the fire raged in every quarter; all were involved in one general conflagration. . . . During the whole of this dismal scene, no man dared to attempt any thing that

might check the violence of the dreadful calamity. A crew of incendiaries stood near at hand denouncing vengeance on all who offered to interfere. Some were so abandoned as to heap fuel on the flames. They threw in firebrands and flaming torches, proclaiming aloud, that they had authority for what they did. Whether, in fact, they had received such horrible orders, or, under that device, meant to plunder with greater licentiousness, cannot now be known.

During the whole of this terrible conflagration, Nero remained at Antium, without a thought of returning to the city, till the fire approached the building by which he had communicated the gardens of Mæcenas with the imperial palace. All help, however, was too late. The palace, the contiguous edifices, and every house adjoining, were laid in ruins. To relieve the unhappy people, wan-

427

dering in distress without a place of shelter, he opened the Field of Mars, as also the magnificent buildings raised by Agrippa, and even his own imperial gardens. He ordered a number of sheds to be thrown up with all possible despatch, for the use of the populace. Household utensils, and all kinds of necessary implements, were brought from Ostia, and other cities in the neighbourhood. The price of grain was reduced to three sesterces. For acts like these, munificent and well-timed, Nero might hope for a return of popular favour; but his expectations were in vain; no man was touched with gratitude. A report prevailed, that, while the city was in a blaze, Nero went to his own theatre, and there, mounting the stage, sung the destruction of Troy, as a happy allusion to the present misfortune.

On the sixth day the fire was subdued at the foot of mount Esquiline. This was effected, by demolishing a number of buildings, and thereby leaving a void space, where for want of materials the flame expired. The minds of men had scarce begun to recover from their consternation, when the fire broke out a second time with no less fury than before. This happened, however, in a more open quarter, where fewer lives were lost; but the temples of the gods, the porticoes and buildings raised for the decoration of the city, were levelled to the ground. The popular odium was now more inflamed than ever, as this second alarm began in the house of Tigellinus, formerly the mansion of Æmilius. A suspicion prevailed, that to build a new city, and give it his own name, was the ambition of Nero. Of the fourteen quarters, into which Rome was divided, four only were left entire, three were reduced to ashes, and the remaining seven presented nothing better than a heap of shattered houses, half in ruins.

The number of houses, temples, and insulated mansions destroyed by the fire cannot be ascertained. But the most venerable monuments of antiquity, which the worship of ages had rendered sacred, were laid in ruins: amongst these were the temple dedicated to the moon by Servius Tullius; the fane and the great altar consecrated by Evander, the Arcadian, to Hercules, his visitor and his guest; the chapel of JUPITER STATOR, built by Romulus; the palace of Numa, and the temple of Vesta, with the tutelar gods of Rome. . . .

Nero did not blush to convert to his own use the public ruins of his country. He built a magnificent palace, in which the objects that excited admiration were neither gold nor precious stones. Those decorations, long since introduced by luxury, were grown stale, and hackneyed to the eye. A different species of magnificence was now consulted: expansive lakes and fields of vast extent were intermixed with pleasing variety; woods and forests stretched to an immeasurable length, presenting gloom and solitude amidst scenes of open space, where the eye wandered with surprise over an unbounded prospect. This prodigious plan was carried on under the direction of two surveyors, whose names were Severus and Celer. Bold and original in their projects, these men undertook to conquer nature, and to perform wonders even beyond the imagination and the riches of the prince. They promised to form a navigable canal from the lake Avernus to the mouth of the Tiber. The experiment, like the genius of the men, was bold and grand; but it was to be carried over a long tract of barren land, and, in some places, through opposing mountains. The country round was parched and dry, without one humid spot, except the Pomptinian marsh, from which water could be expected. A scheme so vast could not be accomplished without immoderate labour, and, if practicable, the end was in no proportion to the expense and labour. But the prodigious and almost impossible had charms for the enterprising spirit of Nero. He began to hew a passage through the hills that surround the lake Avernus, and some traces of his deluded hopes are visible at this day.

The ground, which, after marking out his own domain, Nero left to the public, was not laid out for the new city in a hurry and without judgment, as was the case after the irruption of the Gauls. A regular plan was formed; the streets were made wide and long; the elevation of the houses was defined, with an open area before the doors, and porticoes to secure and adorn the front. The expense of the porticoes Nero undertook to defray out of his own revenue. He promised, besides, as soon as the work was finished, to clear the ground, and leave a clear space to every house, without any charge to the occupier. In order to excite a spirit of industry and emulation, he held forth rewards proportioned to the rank of each individual, provided the buildings were finished in a limited time. The rubbish, by his order, was removed to the marshes of Ostia, and the ships that brought corn up the river were to return loaded with the refuse of the workmen. Add to all this, the several houses, built on a new principle, were to be raised to a certain elevation, without beams or wood-work, on arches of stone from the quarries of Alba or Gabii; those materials being impervious, and of a nature to resist the force of fire. The springs of water, which had been before that time intercepted by individuals for their separate use, were no longer suffered to be diverted from their channel, but left to the care of commissioners, that the public might be properly supplied, and, in case of fire, have a reservoir at hand to stop the progress of the mischief.

It was also settled, that the houses should no longer be contiguous, with slight party-walls to divide them; but every house was to stand detached, surrounded and insulated by its own inclosure. These regulations, it must be admitted, were of public utility, and added much to the embellishment of the new city. But still the old plan of Rome was not without its advocates. It was thought more conducive to the health of the inhabitants. The narrowness of the streets and the elevation of the buildings served to exclude the rays of the sun; whereas the more open space, having neither shade nor shelter, left men exposed to the intense heat of the day.

To burn down a city in order to rebuild it on a large scale, may not have been the most commendable or the most humane method, but it was certainly a very efficient and radical device to create a *tabula rasa* on which a new beginning could be made without too many obstacles. After all, cities have frequently been burned down by enemy action in the course of the centuries and have risen again as greatly improved and better-planned communities— as the examples of Coventry, Hamburg, and Dresden have recently demonstrated—but in the case of Rome it was rather awkward that the fire was not started by an enemy. The attempt to lay the blame on the Christians, an internal enemy, is unconvincing, although it has a strange resemblance to the *Reichstag* fire of 1933 which the Nazis started in order to inculpate the Communists and thereby seize power. In any case, the obliteration of large parts of Rome was a blessing in disguise. It made a reconstruction on modern lines possible; it was in effect a gigantic slum-clearance project. And history seems to have repeated itself: Just as after the sack of Rome in 387 B.C., when the building of a new city was debated, Nero was, according to Tacitus (XV. 40) "seeking the glory of founding a new

capital and endowing it with his own name." After Suetonius (*Nero.* 55) its name was to be *Neronopolis.*

The rebuilding of Rome involved formidable problems far beyond those connected with the replanning of the devastated regions. A large-scale forced transfer of population had to be carried through with all the attendant material and moral difficulties; work and supply had to be reorganized; enormous quantities of building material had to be transported to the metropolis; and vast sums were needed to repair the damage. All this did not prevent the emperor from indulging in megalomaniac ideas. He did not hesitate to build his *Domus Aurea,* whose garden, lakes, and palaces extended from the Palatine down to the valley of the Colosseum to the Esquiline. Fortunately, this monstrous conglomerate was destroyed by his successors and the grounds were restored to public use. In contrast to the sensible plan for the rebuilding of Rome as described in broad outline by Tacitus, the *Domus Aurea* was a symbol of the vulgarity, parvenuedom, decadence and extravagance, which, from this time onward, were to be the hallmark of the imperial metropolis—increasing the social antagonism, involving the people in the general moral decline and undermining all respect for the authorities.

It is one of the great mysteries of history how this hollow edifice could survive the next few centuries. The cult of bigness and prodigality, the all too human admiration and unthinking acceptance of even the worst excesses, provided they are pompous and impressive enough, may be one explanation. But the more tangible reason may have been that life in the provinces continued more or less on its old course of modesty and decency. However, the social and political structure was not only undermined from above. It was at the same time undermined from below. While the sumptuous palaces on the Palatine were still standing in all their splendor, while one magnificent public building followed the other, the catacombs of the Christians began to spread underground. A new religion was born and the cult of the divine emperors was

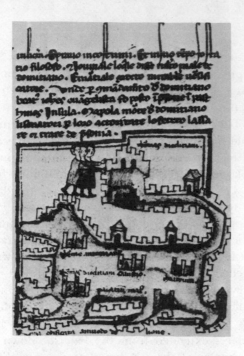

378. Ancient Rome in the form of a lion. Animals were often used as symbols of cities in the early Middle Ages. Rome's symbol was a lion, the king of beasts, indicating the supremacy of Rome over other cities. The design shows a lion with a raised tail, three men at a battlemented wall, and a number of public buildings. Miniature from the end of the 13th century in the Staats- und Universitätsbibliothek, Hamburg.

challenged by an other-worldly power, humble and yet irresistible, relying exclusively on its spiritual force, and appealing above all to the hitherto dispossessed masses.

The rebuilding of Rome after the fire of A.D. 64 was the last great enterprise of the pre-Christian era to be planned and executed on a grand scale. The Aurelian Wall (A.D. 272), hastily constructed against the invasions of the barbarians, can hardly be regarded as a constructive contribution to city planning. It merely marked the confines of the largest extension of the metropolis.

Christian Rome. The period from the final century of the Roman Empire to the return of the pope from the exile in Avignon in 1376 was one of decline, retrogression, and general dissolution. In the fourth century the Campagna was more and more deserted. Malaria spread from the coast inland. In 410 Rome was sacked by Alaric; in 455 by the Vandals; in 537 she was besieged by the Goths, who cut off the water supply of the city by damaging the aqueducts. One catastrophe followed another. Poverty and misery created conditions that were to be repeated only once—during the move of the papal court to Avignon when the population sunk to less than 30,000 inhabitants. The monuments of antiquity were used as quarries or their columns and sculptures were carried off to be used in other buildings. Shops and workshops were installed in the ruins and sarcophagi served as water tubs—even as troughs for pigs. For centuries Rome was like a large limepit into which the most precious marble was thrown for the production of mortar.[122] Rome survived this self-destruction supposedly because she knew that she had the duty to be eternal and not to disappoint generations to come.

What was going on in these centuries was the transition from one civilization to another, a process that not only involved a spiritual readaptation to new ideas but also a physical shift of the center of gravity from the inner city to the periphery, to S. Giovanni in Laterano in the southeast and to the *Civitas Leonina* and the Castel S. Angelo, the mausoleum of Hadrian, in the northwest. A gradual structural reorganization of the previously centralized city took place, based on the formation of the Christian parishes as focal points of the slowly emerging new administration. Defense considerations played a considerable part in this development. The an-

122. After F. Gregorovius. *Geschichte der Stadt Rom im Mittelalter.* 1903, III. P. 568.

430

cient *arx,* the Capitol, could no longer fulfill its original role as a center of defense. The Castel S. Angelo was incomparably more suited for this purpose with its strong walls and compact form, especially because it was near the *Civitas Leonina* which had been surrounded by walls by Leo IV (847-55). Both together, the Castel S. Angelo and the *Civitas Leonina* on the Vatican Hill, formed the nucleus of the papal power, the *borgo,* the fortified area, in which the papal offices, the papal residence, and the cathedral were concentrated.

Dangers from without and feuds within the city made a steady development impossible. Internal strife between contending parties for a long time prevented a coherent organization of the urban area. Instead, the city was split up into small fortified quarters and fortified houses from which the rival factions conducted their internecine battles. The removal of the papacy to Avignon left Rome virtually without government. Feudal anarchy reached its climax and misery, poverty, and depopulation increased. It was not until the return of Gregory XI from Avignon in 1376 that conditions began to improve.

The population increased to 40,000 inhabitants in the middle of the 15th century; to 100,000 in 1600; and to 123,000 in 1655. The main work of reconstruction took place between 1450 and 1650. The northwestern part of the urban area on the Vatican Hill and in the bend of the Tiber as well as the narrow belt from S. Giovanni in the southeast toward the *fora* and the Capitol were more and more densely built up. This development gained momentum in the 16th and 17th centuries and extended to the north and the northeastern sector.[123]

The plans that were envisaged and partly carried out were strictly utilitarian adapted to what was "possible" and most needed. They were free from any ambitions to build an Ideal City and to apply the drawing-board schemes of the Italian theoreticians to the practical rebuilding of the eternal city. The

123. For details see *Topografia e Urbanistica di Roma,* op. cit., pp. 352, 354, 364, 381, 411, 436, 438.

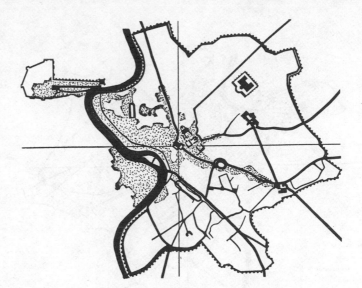

379. Map of Rome in the 12th century.

principle followed by the popes and their architects was to create a network of arterial roads and to leave the secondary streets and quarters traversed by them untouched. Obelisks, fountains, and columns were erected at strategic points. In short, Rome was "Haussmannized" in advance of Haussmann, al-

380. Rome at the beginning of the 15th century showing a multitude of public buildings, the walls, the river with the islets, but no private houses. Anonymous miniature in a private collection.

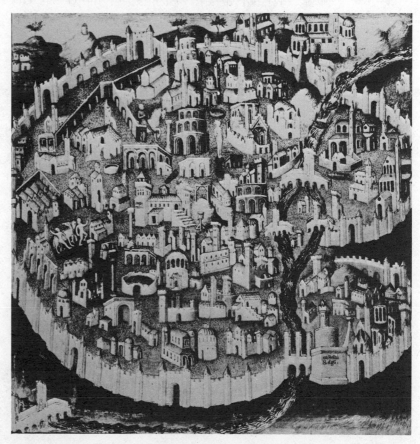

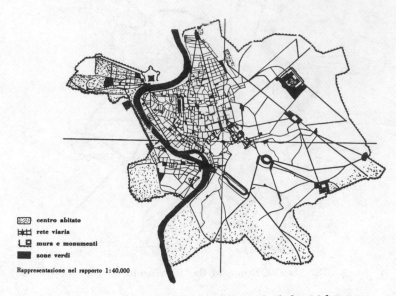

381. **Rome at the end of the 16th century.**

though with immeasurably better taste and artistic talent than in the Paris of Napoleon III. It was a rebuilding from above, a pompous spectacle to be admired by the people but not made for their benefit.

The arterial roads, insofar as they materialized, produced a certain unification of Rome but not an organic whole. Why the admiration of the plans of the popes is almost a "must" is difficult to understand. They were a rather haphazard conglomeration of unrelated details, splendid in individual and partial achievements but lacking the coher-

ence that alone raises city planning to a supreme art. Rome has remained a city of fascinating and marvelous details, of unsurpassed beauty in some sections and of distressing ugliness in others.

Leonardo Bufalini's plan of Rome in 1551, the first more detailed representation of Rome to be published, shows that the inhabited area covers approximately only one quarter of the Aurelian city. Giovanni Battista Nolli's plan of 1748 shows an extension of the inhabited area toward the east, and Giovanni Falda's plan of 1756 a further extension in this direction and, in general, a greater building density. These plans like many others are interesting and should be studied in detail, though with reservations as to their accuracy in respect to the street system, the width and the course of the streets, and the relative size of some of the public buildings. They represent subsequent stages of development of papal Rome different in extent, character, and political importance.[124]

Real concern for the masses was just as nonexistent in papal Rome as in imperial Rome. What was offered them was a Splendid Misery,

124. It may be appropriate to point out again that we are here dealing with problems of city planning in general, not with individual buildings or individual features such as streets or squares. As far as this latter was deemed important, it has been mentioned in the general part preceding the City Survey.

382. *La Roma Grande* of Sixtus V. The plan for the Rome of Sixtus V was designed by Domenico Fontana. It was based on the system of the great axes from Trinità dei Monti—Santa Maria Maggiore; Santa Maria Maggiore—Santa Croce in Gerusalemme; Santa Maria Maggiore—San Lorenzo; San Giovanni—Colosseo.

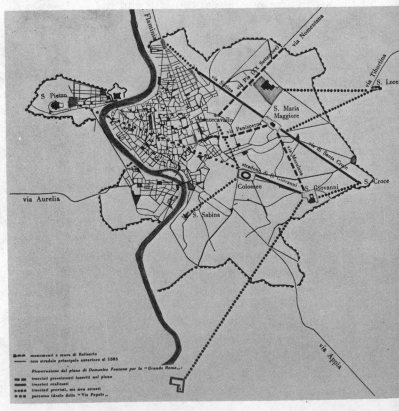

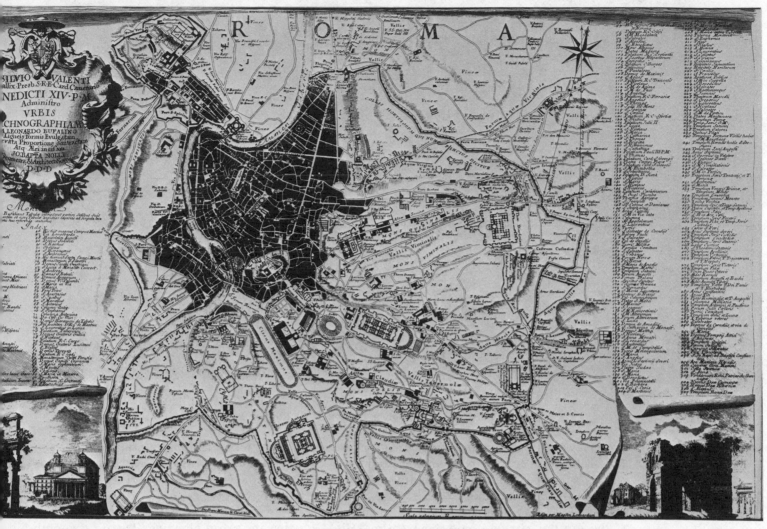

383. Plan of Rome in 1551 by Leonardo Bufalini.

a pompous show without economic basis, a show in which the common people remained passive onlookers, tolerated as admirers of the pageantry enacted by the high and mighty. The common people were provided with grand architectural perspectives but no social perspectives; great architecture but no great hopes for the future; sanctimonious lip service and promises for "mansions in the sky" but no decent houses on earth. Imperial Rome had been a city of monuments. Papal Rome remained more or less the same, a city of monuments and avenues. The show went on. The performers remained the same. The audience remained the same.

No better symbol of papal Rome can be presented than the schematic plan of the streets projected by Sixtus V: Streets and monuments—nothing else!

That this statement is not an exaggeration has long since been proved. When Count Philippe-Marcellin-Camille de Tournon arrived in Rome as Napoleon's governor of the city, he found a population of about 200,000 inhabitants living on charity, local commerce, and patronage, or on financial support from the Church, and international transactions. It was a city of consumers, not of producers, a city without properly equipped streets, without parks, without public services that, at this

433

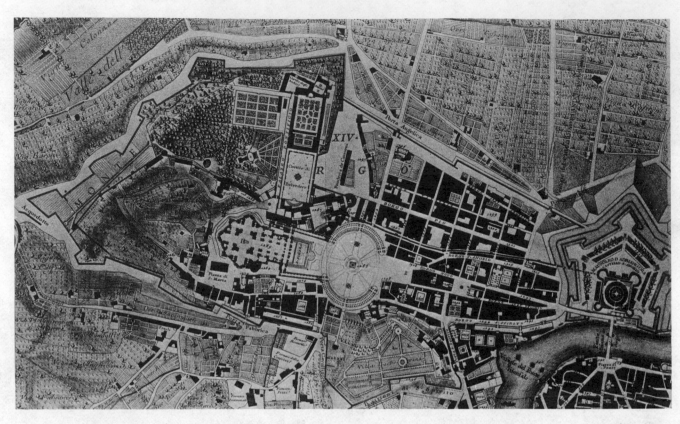

384. Sections of the plan of Rome in 1748 by Giovanni Battista Nolli, the so-called *Pianta Grande*. Biblioteca Nazionale di Roma.

time, were already commonplace in other capitals; a city the majority of whose houses were in a wretched condition. A building industry to speak of did not exist.[125]

The governor faced a task that demanded the greatest circumspection and energy. His plan was to solve two problems at the same time—the rehabilitation of the slum quarters and the employment of the inhabitants in constructive works. However, the lack of funds and of skilled labor defeated his purpose and forced him to abandon these projects. Instead he tried to relieve the situation by the employment of unskilled labor in less expensive

schemes for which only a minimum of valuable material was needed. He resorted, therefore, to the usual expedient of selecting works that involved the excavation and construction of large earthworks as the preparation for a systematic urban planning. Toward the south the whole archeological zone from the *Via Appia* to the *fora* and the Piazza Venezia was chosen as a suitable field of action and, at the northern end of the Corso, the Piazza del Popolo was to be regulated and two parks laid out. These works were to be carried out by paid workers and not by convicts as previously. These were excellent intentions, partly realized though not leading to a comprehensive development of the city as a whole as their originator had hoped for.

125. L. Quaroni, *op. cit.*, p. 68.
F. Castagnoli et al., *op. cit.*, pp. 474-79.

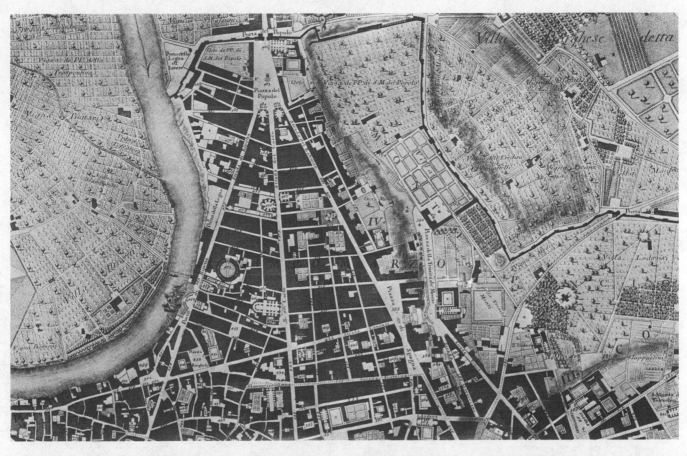
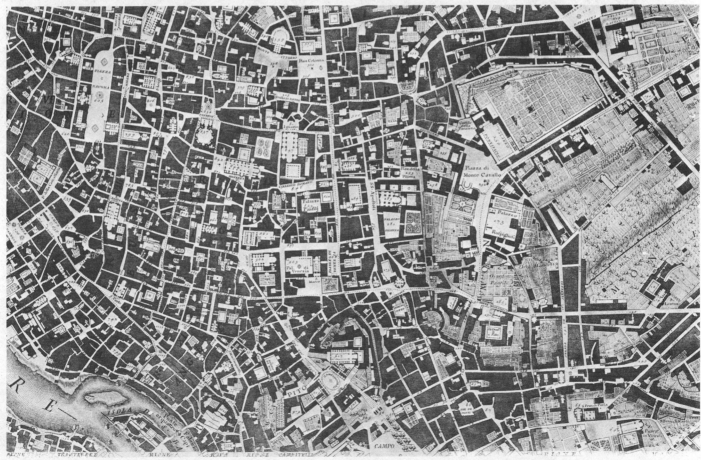

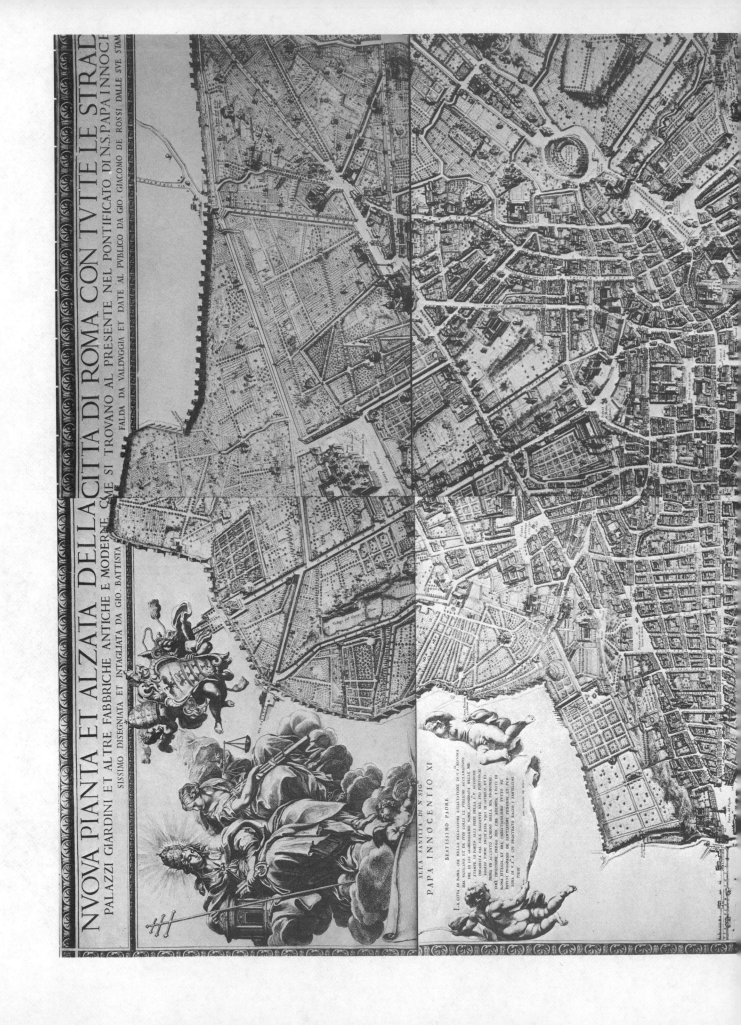

385. Plan of Rome in 1756 by Giovanni Battista Falda. Copy of the Biblioteca Sarti in Rome.

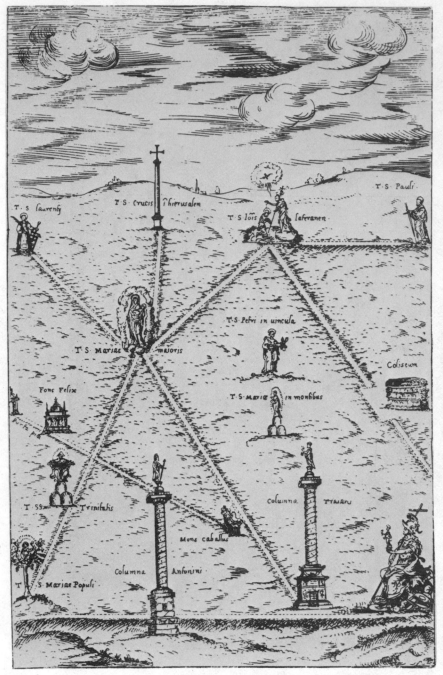

386. Schematic plan of the arterial roads of Rome projected by Sixtus V in the Biblioteca dell' Istituto di Archeologia e Storia dell' Arte in Rome. The center of the design is Santa Maria Maggiore symbolized by a statue of the Virgin.

387. Air view of St. Peter's and the bend of the Tiber.

388. Air view of Rome with the Piazza del Popolo in the foreground and the three arterial streets radiating from it.

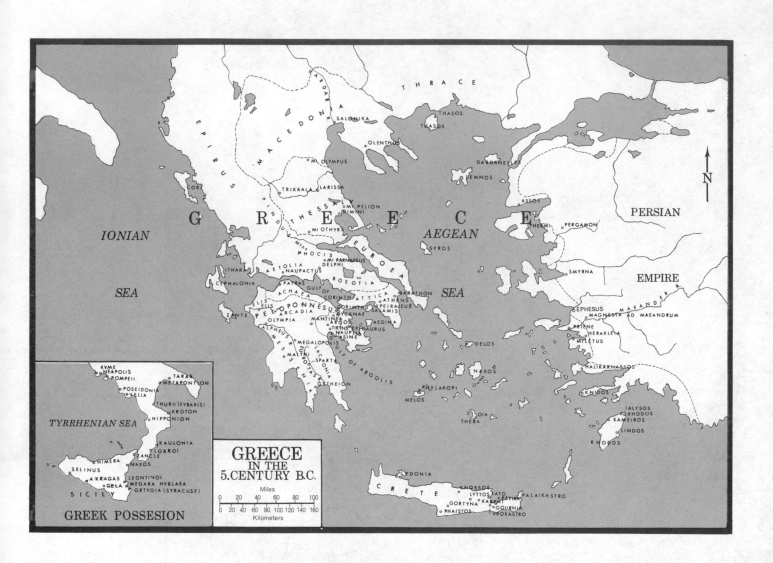

THRACE

EPIRUS
MACEDONIA
SALONIKA
THASOS
THASOS
OLYNTHUS
MT OLYMPUS
DARDANELLES
LEMNOS
ASSOS
TRIKKALA LARISSA
G R E E E C E E
MT PELION
DIMINI
THESSALY
MT OTHYS
THERMI
PERGAMON

PERSIAN

IONIAN

SEA
AEGEAN
SYROS

PHOCIS
MT PARNASSUS
DELPHI
ETOLIA NAUPACTUS
ITHAKI
CEPHALONIA
PATRAS
ACHAEA GULF OF CORINTH
ELLIS
ZANTE
ELLIS PELOPONNESUS ARCADIA
OLYMPIA
ALPHEUS MANTINEA
MESSENIA MEGALOPOLIS
MALTHI
SPARTA
TAIGETOS
GYTHEION

EUBOEA

BOEOTIA
MARATHON
ATTICA
ATHENS
CORINTH PEIRAIEUS
MYCENAE SALAMIS
ARGOS AEGINA
TIRYNS EPIDAURUS
NAUPLI ASINE
GULF OF ARGOLIS

SMYRNA

EMPIRE

EPHESUS
MAEANDER R
MAGNESIA AD MAEANDRUM
PRIENE
HERAKLEIA
MILETUS

SEA

DELOS

NAXOS
HALIKARNASSOS

KNIDOS

PHYLAKOPI
MELOS
OIA
THERA

IALYSOS
RHODOS
KAMEIROS
LINDOS
RHODOS

CYDONIA
C R E T E
KNOSSOS
LYTTOS ATO DIKTIA PALAIKASTRO
GORTYNA KASRO
GOURNIA
PHAISTOS VROKASTRO

N

GREECE
IN THE
5. CENTURY B.C.

Miles

0   20   40   60   80   100

0 20 40 60 80 100 120 140 160
Kilometers

ANCIENT GREECE

Evil is a form of the unlimited, and good of the limited.

ARISTOTLE

GREECE IS A COUNTRY of small plains and short rivers, of small valleys and short mountain ranges, of deep inlets and numerous islands. This small-scale landscape has furthered regional isolation and localism and given rise to separate communities each a more-or-less self-contained unit. Overland communications were difficult, whereas the sea offered an easy and wide field of expansion. These peculiar physical conditions of their homeland prevented the Greeks from forming a land empire. The rugged nature of the terrain drove them to the sea, impelling them to spread their culture along the shores of the Mediterranean and beyond, and to found a maritime commonwealth. The great extension and variety of the indented coastline rivals the diverse topography of the land surface.

Millions of years ago a primeval ocean called "Tethys" covered the Mediterranean and large regions beyond its present shores. Its marine sediments were deposited in the Greek mountains as sandstone, slate, and limestone. The mud bottom of the Tethys ocean solidified in the course of time and formed roughly horizontal layers. When in a later period toward the end of the Archaeozoic era, these horizontal layers were lifted up by pressures in the crust of the earth, mighty folds were formed and mountains came into being. Their rocks, now exposed to sun and air, gradually decomposed and were worn down; the highest peaks were lowered and the depressions were filled with the alluvial material which again solidified in the course of millennia. Thus the high mountains were transformed into a low and undulating massif whose remnants are still visible today in the so-called Thracian block, in the smaller Cycladian block, and the Laconian block, the Peloponnesus. This ancient massif was bent and broken in the course of ages and a large part of its surface dipped beneath the sea. In the Pliocene period other movements of the crust of the earth formed new folded mountains, the Alps, the Carpathian and Balkan Mountains, the Himalayas, and also the mountains of Greece. Only the most ancient foldings, the "blocks" mentioned above, remained unchanged because their greater age had made them so strong that they resisted the renewed pressure. These new uplifted rocks disintegrated again and were leveled and fractionalized by uplifting and sinking to an extent far surpassing the old folding and overthrusting. At this time the Mediterranean was formed. Its waters penetrated from the Atlantic Ocean deep into the new depressions and covered the whole of western Greece. Greece and Asia Minor were still connected. In the Newer Tertiary period and the Quaternary era Greece and Asia Minor were separated and the Mediterranean assumed its present shape. The Strait of Gibraltar was opened. The archipelago of the Cyclades remained as the highest part of submerged mountains.

The Land

445

Although today the formerly active volcanos are dead, earthquakes are not infrequent in Greece, especially in the zone stretching along the northern margin of the Peloponnesus to Corinth, Melos, Santorin toward the coast of Asia Minor. Limestones are generally hard and splinter easily. Rain water sinks into the earth and flows underground, leaving the surface dry and barren. These conditions are widespread in Greece and are called *Karst* phenomena after the *Karst* limestone district of Yugoslavia near the Adriatic coast. The soil is mostly thin and caves, swallow-holes, and underground rivers are formed. The rain water tends to dissolve the limestone, thus producing the uneven topography so characteristic of many regions of Greece. The gullying and the subsequent dissection have so broken up the Thessalian plateau that the most fantastic, almost inaccessible and isolated rock columns were formed. These gigantic "sugar loaves" are 85 to 300 feet high and of an iron-gray or reddish-brown conglomerate of gneiss, slate, syenite, and greenstone. The summits of these pinnacles are crowned by the Meteora monasteries, which can be reached only by an arrangement of ropes and nets worked by a windlass—or by almost perpendicular ladders. The narrow area makes a compressed arrangement of the buildings inevitable, but each monastery has its cells for the monks, a church, a refectory, and a water cistern. Water flowing over the edge of the fault blocks molds sharp notches in the upper part of the precipice. Thus at the eastern side of the Taygetus in the southern Peloponnesus, which falls steeply toward the much lower Eurotas Valley, deep canyonlike gorges are cut into the rocks by water rushing down from the snow-capped mountains, performing its work of erosion.

The distribution of settlement is dependent on the food potential of the small landscapes dispersed over the whole of Greece. The relative degree of fertility of those restricted compartments, which are more or less sharply separated from one another, determines the structure of settlement in general and in detail, making them self-sufficient units based on agriculture or fishing or both. The olive was and still is an important product, and the grape was cultivated in many parts of the country. This self-sufficiency—called by the Greeks *autarkeia* or autarchy—was one of the basic factors on which the ancient city-states developed. It made possible their limitation in size and spirit and was a potent force in preserving their political independence. The city-states of antiquity were not industrial towns as those of Medieval Europe; they were rural towns inhabited by farming people with the exception of such trading centers as Corinth and Athens. The mountainous areas are unsuitable for settlement; they are the domain of the shepherds with their flocks of sheep and goats. Small coastal plains, larger valleys, and baylike widen-

389. Rock formations in Thessaly crowned by the Meteora Monasteries.

ings at the entrance of side-valleys form the main part of the fertile land on which the city-states grew up. The alluvial plains near the coast penetrate deeper inland only in a few cases—for instance, in the Argolis Peninsula and around Athens—and continuous coastal belts such as around Corinth are rare. The mountain chains, bordering the river valleys, extend for the most part directly to the coast. The larger plains of Thessaly, Boeotia, and Aetolia in the interior, and the large *polje* of Arcadia are also traversed by ridges, not dissimilar in character from the natural compartments which have been formed in the Peloponnesus by the ridges between the valleys of the Inachos, Euratas, and Pamisos.

The clearing of the forests has changed not only the face of Greece but also her economic and social structure throughout the centuries. The growth of the cities and the increase of population gave rise to an intensive deforestation, especially around cities and towns. Originally large parts of Greece were well wooded, as numerous references by classical writers testify. Oak and beech groves were distributed over the mountains and highlands. Homer and Thucydides tell of forest fires that destroyed many trees; and Plato describes in the *Critias* (V) how the trees disappeared from the soil of Attica to be used for the roofs of houses, rendering Attica a "naked upland." He says: "What now remains compared with what then existed is like the skeleton of a sick man, all the fat and soft earth having been washed away, and only the bare framework of the land being left." He indicates how this destruction of the woodlands led to the failure of springs and streams because the bared slopes could not prevent the rapid runoff of the rain. And only a century later Theophrastus mentions "that the supply of ship timber . . . was very limited, and that only the forests of Macedonia and Thrace remained fairly abundant."[1] Timber was needed in very considerable quantities for the numerous fishing and transport vessels and the navies, and the more their size increased the more timber had to be provided. Strabo in his *Geography* (XIV.6.5) refers to Cyprus, which may be characteristic of other parts of Greece:

Timber was required for the construction of the fleets, as the sea was now navigated with security and by a large naval force; but when even these means were insufficient to check the growth of timber in the forests, permission was given to such as were able and inclined, to cut down the trees and to hold the land thus cleared as their own property, free from all payment.

However, there were large tracts which were still well wooded, although heavy inroads had been made into the forests. Only when the population began to emigrate to the East and other

448

1. E. C. Semple. *The Geography of the Mediterranean Region.* 1932. P. 289.

parts of the Mediterranean region in the later centuries and when the birth rate declined, were the demands for timber lessened and the forests given a respite. But during the Middle Ages the fear of invading nomads, of Slavs and Turks, drove the population into the mountains and gave rise to renewed clearings of the woods while the deserted lowlands became swampy, and the once-fertile soil turned into unproductive wasteland. The demands of Venice for timber for her navy—especially in the neighborhood of her naval bases of Chalcis, Naupactus, Corinth, Nauplia, the southern tip of Messenia, and on Crete—also contributed greatly to the denudation of the forests and subsequently to the drying up of springs and rivers. As at all times water supply was an essential prerequisite of the distribution of settlements; this had far-reaching consequences for their development. Many villages and small towns stagnated or were even abandoned.

Water and fertile soil, proximity to or remoteness from the coast, safety and insecurity of the sea traffic, and the conditions of overseas trade were more powerful agents than man's determination in the fluctuating fate of many settlements. Most of the ancient and later places are situated near the principal roads and cultivable areas. The fortified castles of Mycenae stood preferably at the edge of the plains; the medieval villages were hidden away high above the lowlands as protection against the hostile invasions that followed the main roads. The monasteries of the Byzantine period sheltered in remote valleys or, like the group of monastic communities on the peninsular promontory of Athos, in the seclusion of the sacred mountain. All these monasteries were fortified. In general, isolated hills and mountain sites were preferred for settlements by the invading groups that followed each other in the course of the centuries. They were conquerors and, conscious of the fact that they were not peaceful and friendly newcomers, they preferred sites that were easily defensible, such as the castles of Mycenae or the towns of the Dorians. After Alexander the Great these elevated strongholds often whole groups of them, or only a small part—were surrounded by walls. This trend continued during the Byzantine, Frankish, and Venetian periods when the castles were fortified with strong walls and lookout towers—and later, in the 17th century, with bastions which increased the safety of these places apart from their natural defensive strength on isolated and steep mountains. The plains were occupied by the oldest pre-Grecian inhabitants and later by subjugated agricultural laborers who lived in dispersed settlements.

The climate of Greece has remained unchanged at least since the beginning of the historical period—that is, about 1000 B.C. It is a moderate Mediterranean climate with three seasons only: the period from March to June, the growing season, when the crops are maturing; the dry months from July to October; and

449

the rainy season, lasting from November to March. January is the coldest month, and spring, beginning in the second half of March, is short; the hot season arrives while the high mountains are still covered with deep snow. The controversy over whether the climate has changed in historical times has been decided in favor of a theory of stability in climatic conditions, thus discarding the notion that rainfall fluctuations were the cause of the decline of the Roman Empire and of the depopulation and subsequent decadence of the Mediterranean civilizations. All the facts that can be deduced from our knowledge of ancient tillage methods and other data reinforce this conclusion.

The causes of decline are to be sought not in a changed climate but in denudation of the hillside soil, deforestation with the failure of springs, destruction of irrigation works by barbarian or nomad attack, collapse of orderly government under repeated barbarian inroads, and possibly to the exhaustion of the soil, causing agricultural decline.[2]

The difference of climate and vegetation between the regions west and east of the Pindus and the mountains of Arcadia is marked. The coastal landscape of the western Peloponnesus resembles Southern Italy, while the eastern part has much less rainy days. Therefore the western rivers have a permanent flow of water whereas the eastern rivers are intermittent, running in deep notches. The contour of the mountains in the west is gentler and more rounded as a result of the heavier rains and the western winds, while the eastern peaks are more rugged and broken, and the woods are larger and more dense—for instance, the Sacred Grove of Olympia, the oak forest of Mount Pholoe in Arcadia, or the forests of Aetolia and Epirus. Weather was, as Semple put it, "a despot to the ancient Mediterranean folk, and the weather was governed by the winds."[3] As an old adage expressed it, *Annus fructum fert, non tellus;* the season produces the crop, not the soil. Hence the winds were important and their direction decided the harvests, food or famine, heat or cold, and aided or hindered navigation. In antiquity eight to twelve different winds were distinguished and named not according to the direction whence they blew but according to force, temperature, humidity, source, and season. The eight more generally known were inscribed on the Tower of the Winds at Athens. This ancient distinction is still known today among the seamen and peasants of the Mediterranean. Even in winter the northerly and northeasterly "trade winds" prevail. The cooling and moderating influence of the great sea basin of the Mediterranean is of the greatest importance, especially in the hot season, and the distribution of the rainfall is a consequence of this large "Inland Sea." The whole of the rain falls in winter; there is none between May and October.

2. E. C. Semple, *op. cit.,* p. 100.
3. *Ibid.,* p. 93.

Corn is cut in June and July. The most common vegetation is the evergreen scrub, the *maquis,* and the few spots with their beautiful plants are widely dispersed like oases among this ubiquitous cover of the land.

The easy access to the sea reduced the need for communications by land, the more so as the relief and the indented coastline made overland routes difficult. This explains why the Greeks were not road builders like the Romans. The sea was the lifegiving power and on its influence rested the culture and the economic development of Greece. The Greeks were originally not a seafaring people. They were inland dwellers who had come from the grassy steppes of the North. It was not free choice but necessity that forced them to take to the sea: the soil of their country was not too fertile and their land was barren and rocky, which as noted above drove them to search for new homes overseas. For them Poseidon was an angry and resentful god. But the Greeks had no choice. They nerved themselves and set out to colonize the shores of the Mediterranean. The generally calm weather, the rare currents, and the numerous islands of the Aegean, numbering over 480, made navigation easy even for the little and primitive ships of the early Greeks.

Five major geographical regions may be distinguished: the islands, the Peloponnesus, Central Greece, Northern Greece, and Macedonia and Thrace.

1. **The islands** have exerted from the very beginning a profound influence on the formation of the cultural and political development of Greece. The archipelago of the Cyclades stretches as a broken bridge between the Greek mainland and Asia Minor to the south of the Aegean. Almost in the center of this group lie the islands of Syros and Delos. Further south, another semicircle of islands extends from the extreme south of the Peloponnesus to the southeast of Asia Minor with Crete, the seat of the earliest great Aegean civilizations of the Minoan period. Crete covers an area of 3,328 square miles while Naxos, the largest of the Cyclades, has an area of only 173 square miles, Syros of 31 square miles, and Delos of a bare 1 square mile. Both Syros and Delos played a prominent part at successive periods of Greek history. Syros was the commercial center of the Cyclades during the Aegean Copper Age (3000-2400 B.C.). This trade consisted mainly of useful rocks such as obsidian and marble, and of metallic ores. The resources of these islands were limited and this, combined with the safe and easy navigation between the numerous islands, was a stimulus to establish contacts with other peoples. Syros' influence declined when Crete rose to prominence in the Bronze Age and the principal sea lanes shifted farther south. A third bridge between Europe and Asia Minor is formed by the Northern Sporades, with Lemnos as the largest island extending to the

Dardanelles and thence to the Black Sea. Apart from these main groups there are many islands near the coast, and numerous peninsulas. Euboea and Cythera, Salamis and Aegina belong to the first category, while the latter enclose innumerable bays and gulfs offering excellent shelter for small fishing and coastal boats and in some cases for larger vessels The Ionian Islands off the west coast of Northern Greece include Corfu, Leukas, Cephalonia, Ithaka and Zante, and others.

2. **The Peloponnesus.** Its shape has often been compared to a hand with four fingers. The thumb is the Argolis Peninsula, the other three fingers being formed by long promontories. The most easterly of these promontories is separated from the Argolis Peninsula by the Gulf of Nauplia. The Gulf of Corinth to the north extends deeply into the land to the Isthmus of Corinth, only about 4 miles wide at its narrowest point. It was never a real obstacle to the connection with the Gulf of Aegina to the east, for boats could be hauled across the portage of the Isthmus. Now the Corinth Canal has made the Peloponnesus an island. It has been suggested that the sea has played but an insignificant role in the life of this region. This is true, and its explanation can be found in the obstacles which topographical conditions created in establishing easy contact with the sea. Ports are few and often not well related to the settlement areas. The land consists of more-or-less isolated compartments. Even the basin of Sparta, whose fertile lowland extends relatively near to the coast, is not open to effective communications which would facilitate the transport of goods. This remoteness from the main stream of development may be offered as one of the reasons for the contrast between Athens and Sparta. Athens had all the advantages which were generally connected with a successful settlement of the mainland of Greece: a rocky hill as refuge, a fertile plain, and a good port. This third factor was mostly missing in the Peloponnesus.

The central upland is encircled by lowland basins alternating with uplands and mountains. To the south there extends a *Karstic* region with streams flowing underground and water disappearing into deep chasms. In antiquity the basins were the given sites for settlements located near spring water. The main rivers are the Alpheus and the Eurotas. Olympia on the lower Alpheus, Patras on the Gulf of the same name, and Corinth are the most important towns of the northern Peloponnesus. The fertile land around Corinth is closely related to the sea. Corinth owed its importance in antiquity to its command of the sea and of the land route, the latter being the only access to the Peloponnesus from the north. The Argolis Peninsula, though mostly barren and mountainous, possesses in the fertile basin of Argos an historical area of greatest significance. A pass connects it with

Corinth, and the regions of Mycenae and Tiryns are witnesses of its connection with Crete. The modern town of Argos occupies the site of the ancient one. The basin of Sparta, in the center of Laconia, covers an area of less than 50 square miles and is surrounded by mountains. Its connection with the sea leads over a difficult road across the Taygetus. In general the Aegean coast of the eastern promontory is inhospitable, thus increasing the isolation of Sparta. Messenia to the west is less inaccessible and barren than Laconia. It has several ports and the mountains are lower. The climate is milder and the soil fertile.

3. **Central Greece** extends from the Gulf of Corinth and Aegina to the Othrys Mountains in the north. The central mountain massif, which is the continuation of the Pindus range, has a general north-south direction. Three ridges branch off this eastward: the Othrys range, Mt. Oeta, and farther south a ridge originating in Mt. Parnassus and ending in the promontory of Sunium. The narrow valley separating Mt. Parnassus from the Giona contains the sacred town of Delphi. The most southerly of the depressions is the plain of Attica on the Gulf of Aegina. To the north follows the plain of Boeotia with its front on the channel cutting it off from the island of Euboea. A third depression, at the southern base of the Othrys range, opens toward the Gulf of Lamia which has its equivalent on the west coast in the Gulf of Arta. All these depressions are fairly fertile and contain modern towns located in some cases on the same sites as the old ones. The plain of Attica consists of the basins of Athens and Eleusis. The land route passes from the north through the plain. Numerous ports on the northern shores of the Gulf of Aegina give easy access to the sea.

4. **Northern Greece.** The character of the land changes north of a line running from the Gulf of Arta in the west to the Othrys Mountains in the east. The small-scale landscape of the south, with its great variety of detail, gives way to a large-scale and broader uniformity, and the olive groves are replaced by oak forests. The western region contrasts sharply with the eastern. The west, Epirus, is mountainous and backward, whereas the east, Thessaly, is fertile and its plains are surrounded by hills and mountains. Epirus is mainly a *Karstic* upland with sheep rearing. There are no good ports, and communications by land are difficult. Fertile lands exist on the northern shore of the Gulf of Arta and in the upland basins. Ioannina is the main town. The two lowland basins of Thessaly are centered in the west around Trikkala and in the east around Larissa being connected by the Peneios River with the Vale of Tempe between Mt. Olympus and Mt. Ossa. Mt. Pelion rises farther south on the same ridge. Mt. Olympus is part of the Macedonian upland and stands be-

tween the basins of Thessaly and the plain around the important port of Salonika.

5. **Macedonia and Thrace.** The seaport of Salonika is the natural center of this region. It is an important nodal point with connections to Belgrade, Monastir, Istanbul, and Athens. The Vardar passes through the Salonika plain in its lower course. In general, it is a low-lying area covered by debris from the hills surrounding it, mostly marshy and in large parts favorable for the production of wheat, tobacco, maize, rice, and cotton, while on the dry and higher land vines, fruit and mulberry trees grow. A depression mainly consisting of lakes extends at the base of the peninsula.

CHAPTER 8

THE 19th CENTURY has played a prominent part in misunderstanding and misinterpreting Greek culture and Greek thinking. A superficially idealistic picture emerged which represented Greek society, art, and thought as almost the final achievement of humanity. The Greeks were regarded as the rationalists *par excellence,* as the "Ideal Men," and their art, philosophy, and social institutions as ultimate truths. This uninformed enthusiasm had its origin in the exciting discoveries which the spade of the archeologists had brought to light. The reaction against this shallow idealization set in at the beginning of the 20th century. Then it was discovered that the Greeks had the same complex human characteristics of all men at all times and in all lands, that rational and irrational trends, primitive and cultured mentality shaped their mental behavior and therefore all their actions. It is indeed true that the Greeks made "man the measure of all things," that the gods were given human shape, and that an awareness of the ideal man developed, but this fact does not in any way diminish the importance of the irrational, the demoniac and orgiastic, the emotional and passionate, which were always present in the Greek character. It is obvious that this complex mental setup, this "Inherited Conglomerate," as Gilbert Murray has called it, had a profound influence on the attitude of the Greeks to their environment. They had gone through successive stages of development from primitive and magical religious movements to an unfettered search for truth and intellectual purity. The deposits of the earliest elements always remained a reality. They were not displaced by the new; they were absorbed into the emerging changes, or persisted side by side. At the end of the Archaic Age the "Inherited Conglomerate" was "historically intelligible as the reflex of changing human needs over many successive generations, but intellectually a mass of confusion."[1]

The Greeks' interpretation of the universe gradually moved away from unquestioning belief to the search for comprehension, although it never rid itself completely of the fetters of mythical limitations. As Professor Butterfield has expressed it in *The Origin of Modern Science,* Greek experience of Nature "has the door half-way open to spirits." It remained an eminently personal world and thought was not fully emancipated. Macrocosm and microcosm were intimately interwoven, and man symbolized the general in his individual being. Greek symbolism was a concrete, direct symbolism which came to life in visible form, not through complicated analogies. Thus the *polis* was the symbolic expression of the local society, and the only correct form of its synthesis with the cosmic order. But this Greek symbolism retained strong affinities to earlier periods. Nature was filled with gods and demi-

1. E. R. Dodds. *The Greeks and the Irrational.* 1957. P. 180.

The Greeks and Their Environment

gods, with beings similar and related to man. But in contrast to primeval magic, which derives its *raison d'être* and power from its unchangeableness, Greek symbolism was not a rigid pattern; its openness to change, its permanent re-creation endowed it with a strong and direct realism that attuned it ever anew to life.

Man was the center of life on earth, and the earth the center of the universe. Concentric spheres surrounded the earth; the outermost sphere, as the sea of divine harmony, caused the revolution of the celestial bodies. But in this universe motion had to be created by a mover, and the bodies had to possess souls and aspirations giving matter itself mystical qualities. This Aristotelian system consisted of continuous matter without any void. Here we have the explanation why Greek architecture did not consciously create space and space relations, and why Greek cities were mere accretions of individual elements rather than the result of coherent and integrated spatial conceptions.

The symbolic dreamland of Aristotle and his disciples was, however, not the sole emanation of the Greek spirit. It still belonged very much to the sphere of the "Inherited Conglomerate."

390. The Ptolemaic universe with the earth in the center surrounded by concentric rings in which the heavenly bodies move. From an old atlas of astronomy.

Other tendencies were also at work and show how the old and the new, the emotionally conditioned and the intellectually conceived existed side by side. For

A new belief-pattern very seldom effaces completely the pattern that was there before: either the old lives on as an element in the new—sometimes an unconfessed and half-unconscious element—or else the two persist side by side, logically incompatible, but contemporaneously accepted by different individuals or even by the same individual.[2]

Thus Anaxagoras outraged orthodox opinion of his time by suggesting that the sun was a mass of incandescent metal; and Aristarchus of Samos, the "Copernicus of Antiquity," proclaimed that all planets, including the earth, revolved about the sun. Both men were persecuted for their scientific convictions.

The Aristotelian cosmology, like all primitive conceptions of the universe, was shaped by the terrestrial experience of man in spite of its great advance over preceding ideas. It reflected the events on earth as they influenced man's thoughts and actions or were created by him. The heavens merely served as a limiting enclosure for the earth—that is, for man—and were kept in motion by imaginary powers. The inside of the universal sphere was filled with some sort of matter. There was no vacuum. Outside this sphere there was a great nothingness. Matter and space were simply two different aspects of the same phenomenon and both were coterminous. In Aristotle's own words,

It is plain, then . . . that there is not, nor do the facts allow there to be, any bodily mass beyond the heaven. The world in its entirety is made up of the whole sum of available matter. . . . This world is one, solitary and complete . . . there is neither place nor void . . . beyond the heaven.[3]

What a profound confidence; and what a simplicity of mind! This *horror vacui* led Aristotle to maintain not only that there could not be a vacuum in fact on earth but that there could not be any vacuum anywhere in principle, for Nature would always so operate that a vacuum was impossible. This conception should be borne in mind, if Greek art and city planning are to be fully understood. It will go a long way toward penetrating into the essence of the Greek gift for the plastic arts. The Greek temple is a sculpture and Greek cities are agglomerations of sculptural elements.

The animistic basis of Aristotle's ideas is clearly evidenced when he discusses space and motion. There is no distinction between organic and inorganic nature:

Primitives and children do not draw the same hard and fast distinc-

2. E. R. Dodds, *op. cit.,* p. 179.
3. *On the Heavens.* I. IX.

457

tion that we do between organic and inorganic nature, between living and lifeless things. The organic realm has a conceptual priority, and the behavior of clouds, fire, and stones tends to be explained in terms of the internal drives and desires that move man and, presumably, animals. . . . Much of the appeal of the Aristotelian doctrine must lie in the naturalness of the perception that underlies the doctrine.[4]

But this is not all: apart from its animistic trends there is a definite tendency to discuss space in terms of a "life space," in contrast to modern space which is

. . . homogeneous and isotropic; it has no "top" or "bottom," "east" or "west." Primitive space, in contrast, is more nearly a life space: the space in a room, or in a house, or in a community. Each position is a position "for" some object or "where" some characteristic activity occurs. . . . Primitive space is the active dynamic space of everyday life.[5]

Or, as we would say, it is a social space.

The conception of infinity and of space as a formative element is entirely irreconcilable with these ideas. Their moral application is perfectly expressed in Aristotle's words: "Evil is a form of the unlimited, and good of the limited."[6] And this again is the clue to the limited size of the *polis;* to the small scale of Greek buildings; and to the clearly circumscribed sculpture. What can be taken in at a single glance, what can be experienced in reality and with direct intensity—that is the primary goal of the Greek artists. Therefore, the emphasis is on human society, and the environment exists solely for satisfying its needs. Man is supreme. It is characteristic that Aristotle classified democracies according to the bases of their subsistence. But all the great achievements of the Greeks in modifying their environment did not lead to a systematic study of the scope and character of these changes. Instead a rather complacent notion of a golden past seemed to be a more convenient explanation when Nature did not yield everything that was expected of her and when a certain degeneration from this Golden Age became all too obvious. The alternative to this glorification of the golden past and to the subsequent decline was the theory of cycles, of historical ups and downs introducing a notion derived from the life cycle of an organism.[7] But through all statements which have come down to us runs as the guiding notion the tacit assumption of man's supremacy. Strabo made perhaps one of the most pertinent remarks in this respect: "As regards the various arts and faculties and institutions of mankind, most of them, when once men have made a beginning, flourish in any latitude whatsoever, and in certain instances even in spite of the latitude."[8] This would seem to be a complete rejection of environmental influences and an exclusive emphasis on man as the one-sided reshaper of his environment.

458

4. T. S. Kuhn. *The Copernican Revolution.* 1957. P. 96.
5. *Ibid.,* p. 96.
6. *Nichomachean Ethics.* II. VI. 14.
7. C. J. Glacken. "Changing Ideas of the Habitable World." In: *Man's Role in Changing the Face of the Earth.* W. L. Thomas, ed. 1956. P. 71.
8. II. 3. 7.

This statement shows the supreme value attached to man's actions and aspirations and the scant importance of Nature as an independent and formative agency.

Both the irrational and the rational lived side by side in the Greek soul. And how could this have been otherwise? It was the 19th century that created a perverted idea of the Greek mind, of a bland yet elated happiness, an unquestioning and undeviating rational intellect serving as the omnipotent guide to a godlike existence. The real picture is quite different. The Greeks were ordinary human beings like their fellow-men. The dark forces of their earlier stages of development lived on as powerful opponents of their reason, and the primeval, prerational urges surged into the reality of their daily life. As Professor Dodds has shown in his admirable book *The Greeks and the Irrational,* the heroes of the Homeric Age were so intensely aware of the unforeseen, of the inexplicable, that they could explain them only as the work of outside forces, of demons, of the Erinyes, or of one of the Olympians. He shows convincingly the gradual transition from a "shame culture" to a "guilt culture." In a "shame culture" to which the Homeric Age clearly belongs,

the highest good is not the enjoyment of a quiet conscience, but the enjoyment of *tīmē,* public esteem . . . and the strongest moral force which Homeric man knows is not the fear of god, but respect for public opinion, *aidōs.* . . . In such a society, anything which exposes a man to the contempt or ridicule of his fellows, which causes him to "lose face," is felt as unbearable.[9]

In the Archaic Age the outside interventions were regarded as punishments for the sins of human beings and this, together with the extreme insecurity of this period and the relaxation of the patriarchal family ties, brought about the change toward a "guilt culture." As Professor Dodds explains:

No doubt general social conditions account for a good deal. In Mainland Greece (and we are concerned here with mainland traditions) the Archaic Age was a time of extreme personal insecurity. The tiny overpopulated states were just beginning to struggle up out of the misery and impoverishment left behind by the Dorian invasions, when fresh trouble arose: whole classes were ruined by the great economic crisis of the seventh century, and this in turn was followed by the great political conflicts of the sixth, which translated the economic crisis into terms of murderous class warfare. It is very possible that the resulting upheaval of social strata, by bringing into prominence submerged elements of the mixed population, encouraged the reappearance of old culture patterns which the common folk had never wholly forgotten.[10]

Men became vulnerable by their sense of guilt and open to new

459

9. E. R. Dodds, *op. cit.,* pp. 17 ff.
10. *Ibid.,* pp. 44 ff.

ideas which endowed every individual being with a soul that might search for its own experience in the deeper layers of the subconscious. The concept of supernatural interference with the individual was replaced by individual absorption into the supernatural. Shamanism, though in a modified form, survived in the mental complexity of the Greeks. These ideas had reached the Greeks through

the opening of the Black Sea to Greek trade and colonisation in the seventh century, which introduced the Greeks for the first time to a culture based on shamanism. . . . These new elements were . . . acceptable to the Greek mind because they answered to the needs of the time, as Dionysiac religion had done earlier. Religious experience of the shamanistic type is individual, not collective; but it appealed to the growing individualism of an age for which the collective ecstasies of Dionysus were no longer sufficient.[11]

And in this connection it is suggested that even Plato's Guardians were a sort of rationalized shamans, whose power would derive not from the subconscious but from intellectual insight.

Out of this welter of seemingly contradictory ideas emerged in the Classical Age, "the Inherited Conglomerate." The reaction against this bewildering complexity led Socrates and Plato into the deceptive belief, so common to most intellectuals, that knowledge is the panacea for all ills and that it will induce men to do the right thing; although they were not totally unaware of the inescapable impact of the irrational. It seemed that at the end of the fifth century Reason was to emerge triumphantly as the sole life force and that the irrational subconscious was to fade away into oblivion. But this all-too-human expectation was one of the innumerable illusions which mankind fashions out of its facile optimism and its dreams. The unpredictable powers of the irrational had not lost their vitality. They surged up again and again as astrology and mystery religions from the East. Today we know that reason and emotion, conscious intellectual efforts and subconscious emotional urges, balanced classicism and overflowing romanticism exist side by side and with the same justification, and that Greek civilization can be understood in all its complexity only if both these streams are recognized as equal life forces shaping its ideal and material emanations. Behind the idea, behind the structure and the appearance of the *polis,* behind the relationship of the buildings to each other, to the streets, and to the city as a whole, all these trends were operative and together created the language of form through which the Greeks expressed their ideal of civic life.

The geographical conditions of Greece were not favorable to political unity. The small scale of the landscape, the valleys separated from one another by mountains, the islands more-or-less

460

11. *Ibid.,* pp. 142 ff.

self-contained, and the lack of easy intercommunications in general furthered the rise of small political units with a strong local character and self-government. It is impossible to give a definite answer to the problem of whether this environment was the sole cause of Greek disunity or merely a congenial challenge to the inherent incapability and even disinclination of the Greeks to abandon their fragmentary political system. However this may be, the bonds that united the Greeks, apart from their racial and linguistic homogeneity, were religious coherence, common gods, and identity of political institutions—that is, of the *polis*. The logical outcome of this attitude was the Panhellenic institution, the Olympic Games, which took place every fourth year and were consecrated to the highest common god, to Zeus. Their significance transcended the political divisions and fortunes of the Greeks and even survived the end of Greek independence.

The spiritual unity of the Greeks, the world-wide and positive acceptance of life in all its infinite variety embraced the whole gamut of experience from life-denying to life-asserting responses to the challenge of their environment. Even in their positive acceptance of the world the Greeks remained aware of the fragility and the questionable ambiguity of human existence, an attitude Nietzsche described as the pessimistic keynote of their emotional disposition. But the Greeks understood how to discipline these urges which welled up from the deepest layers of the unconscious, and to sublimate them in austere and meaningful forms of expression. This achievment was accompanied by and absorbed into a consummate ability to blend these emotions with perfect sobriety and a distinct rationalism. It is, therefore, not surprising that the initiator of the rational checkerboard cities, Hippodamos, became one of the first thinkers who, not as a statesman but as a planner and mathematician, developed a theory of an ideal state and society.

The perfectionist trends which were so strongly embedded in the Greek character were also causes of its limitation. Perfectionism made difficult a concept of the world as anything other than a finite and static system despite the acceptance of the irrational as a living force. However, this juxtaposition of the seemingly irreconcilable was not peculiar to the Greeks. It was an all-too-human experience which the Greeks shared with all other peoples. But the fact remains that their horror of infinity and of a void, their disinclination to reshape their environment fundamentally and systematically, and their dislike of a large social space within which daily life could be lived were outstanding features of their response to the challenge of environment. Man was the measure of all things, but only man in his physical limitations. It is characteristic that they had no word for "space," that which is not. They restricted their colonization to the coast

461

and did not penetrate into the hinterland. Wherever they went, they carried their conception of the small, limited *polis* with them. Their spirit of adventure was intimately interwoven with their sense of perfection and limitation. It did not close the door to reason and rational explanation. Their scientific notions evolved from form and matter, not from mass and energy. They were masters of geometry, not of dynamics. They had no zero in their number system. Their architecture remained a plastic art. True, the Dionysian tendencies did exist and played a considerable role, but the visible form in which they expressed their artistic aspirations was "space-less," limited, and solid. The venture of a few of their thinkers into the realm of a searching and speculative interpretation of the universe was looked at as an un-Greek activity. Men like Democritus, Aristarchus, and Anaximander outraged orthodox opinion. In their search for ideals the Greeks did not and could not pass over the threshold which restricted their ideas and their spirit to the small and narrow world of daily existence. But within these limits they tried to live up to their ideal and to reconcile the rational and the irrational, the Apollonian and the Dionysian tendencies which made up their complex character. Their city-states were limited in conception and in reality approached this ideal with an almost naïve simplicity. But it would be wrong to single them out as one of the culminating achievements of city building. The cities of China and India, of the European Middle Ages and the Italian Renaissance, settlements of African tribes or of the South Sea islanders reached perhaps a higher degree of perfection and social integration. The influence of Greek city building on the succeeding periods was virtually nil, while Greek architecture remained for many centuries and almost up to the present not a living and formative force but a misunderstood and unsuited ideal of the timid pattern-book architects. The Greek cities could not exert a more lasting influence because they lacked perhaps the most formative element of city design—a clear idea of space and space relations. They were, like the temples, sculptures; sculptures consisting of numerous more-or-less independent units. They grew by accretion, not by spatial unity and spatial extension. The Greek ideal lived on in architectural formalism: individual elements were used as a secondhand language of form by the Romans, by architects of the Renaissance and the Baroque and, finally, by those of the 19th and 20th centuries—who had nothing to lose but their pattern books.

462

EVERY SOCIETY, except our own, has had a clear idea of the Ideal City. And almost every society has failed to translate this ideal into bricks and mortar and to leave to posterity a pure and unadulterated physical image of the Ideal City which philosopher-statesmen or architect-planners had made the goal of their vision. The Greeks were no exception. The people that possibly came nearest to their ideal were the Chinese, whose cities, in spite of all their shortcomings, embodied to an exceptionally high degree the theoretical principles which religion and reality had taught them. The Greek *polis* was far from being an Ideal City as the nineteenth-century enthusiasts believed it to be. Their fallacies, some of which are still alive today, led them to assume that life in a Greek city-state was perfect and that we would have found many congenial and highly attractive features in a Greek city. That may be so, but it depends on the particular type of men who would have liked to live in these cities.

Alfred North Whitehead made a pertinent remark when he suggested that the modern man who would really feel at home in these ancient places is a professional heavyweight boxer—who would have no difficulty ignoring the petty rivalries within the city and between the city-states, or the slavery on which the economic life depended. Such a man would not feel frustrated by the stuffiness of the small-town atmosphere or by the parochial narrowness of the people. It is one of the most misleading assumptions that the spirit of the few outstanding individuals, about whom history tells us so much more than it does about the life of the ordinary citizens or the slaves, percolated deep into the mind of the masses and shaped their communal life in all its manifestations. Today as in the past, the higher the so-called leaders stand in the cultural and social hierarchy the farther they are removed from the ordinary run of men whose lives make up the actual stuff of history. The ordinary men and women who lived in the Greek city-states remained excluded from the goings on in the esoteric circles of the select few. We cannot recapture their thoughts or the motivations of their actions in daily life. We can only try to see them as ordinary human beings and to understand their daily existence as nothing extraordinary, guided by routine within the narrow compass of small towns. We should therefore not ascribe to the Greeks or to their lives in urban surroundings anything that raises them above the level of other city dwellers. Rather we should see both their actions and their city-states as simple responses to the modest needs and aspirations of daily life. As Spinoza says,

I have taken great care to understand human actions, and not to deride, deplore, or denounce them [or, we may add, to glorify them].

The Polis and the Region

I have therefore regarded human passions, like love, hate, anger, envy, pride, pity, and the other feelings that agitate the mind, not as vices of human nature, but as properties which belong to it in the same way as heat, cold, storm, thunder, and the like belong to the nature of the atmosphere.[1]

Neither overestimation nor denigration are justified.

With these reservations in mind we shall outline some of the basic trends which brought the Greek *polis* into being. There is ample evidence in literature and in speeches that have been handed down to posterity as to what the Greek thinkers demanded of their Ideal City. There is also quite an impressive array of facts why this ideal goal always eluded the Greeks or could not be maintained when and if it seemed to be within reach.

The *polis* was, as Arnold Toynbee put it, "juridically a 'state' and emotionally a 'country,' while its people were a 'nation.' "[2] It is this threefold connotation which makes it ambiguous to translate *polis* as city or town or state. It had something of all these properties without attaining perfection in any one of them —if we apply our own standards. Thucydides, who used the term *polis* for groups of unfortified villages as well as for fortified towns, suggesting an uninterrupted development from the early village community to the fully grown city-state, explained the origin and development of the *polis* as follows:

It is apparent that the country now called Hellas was in early times insecurely occupied and subject to frequent movements of population as each community found itself dispossessed by ever more powerful invaders. In the absence of trade and free intercourse by land or sea every community depended on its own territory for the necessities of life. There was no superfluity of wealth, and no cultivation of fruits, because they never knew when they might be dislodged from their unfortified habitations; nor were they reluctant to move, being confident of obtaining anywhere the means to satisfy their immediate needs; and hence their towns were not distinguished by size or other marks of power. Such migrations were always most frequent where the best soil was to be had. . . . The fruitfulness of these regions favoured the accumulation of wealth, which promoted in turn destructive civil factions, thereby inviting foreign attacks. Attica, on the other hand, preserved from discord by the poverty of her soil, remained in uninterrupted possession of the same people. . . . The early Greeks, like the barbarians of the islands and coasts, had taken to piracy as soon as they learned to sail the seas. . . . They raided and ravaged the unfortified groups of village communities, gaining the greater part of their livelihood in this way. . . . In regard to towns, those founded in the later period and possessed of some surplus wealth were all fortified and situated by the sea on

1. B. de Spinoza. *The Political Works*. Edited and translated by A. G. Wernham. 1958. P. 263.
2. A. J. Toynbee. *Greek Historical Thought From Homer to the Age of Heraclius*. 1924. Pp. XXIV-XXV.

narrow necks of land in order to facilitate trade and strengthen their hold on their neighbours; but the earlier foundations, being exposed to the attacks of pirates, were located at a distance from the sea.[3]

This is an excellent comment on the material causes of city development. The ideal reasons may be summed up in the words of Aristotle: "The city is the highest of all forms of association and embraces all the rest." And an old legend described how Zeus sent down to the first city dwellers, who were inexperienced in the art of city life, his divine messenger Hermes bearing in his hands Reverence and Justice as the ordering principles of cities and the bonds of friendship and conciliation. For the Greeks, the city-state was the logical development from the family, the tribe, and the village to the higher form of existence liberated from the rhythm of Nature and superseding the blood relationship of the family and the clan. The gregarious instinct, that most powerful agent of congenial companionship, drove the Greeks into the *polis* which, according to Aristotle, "comes into existence for the sake of mere life, but exists for the sake of the good life,"[4] and which is held together by mutual reverence and justice.

In early times pastoral wealth was the most adequate form of possession: the unstable conditions of this period forced the people into a more-or-less migratory way of living, whereupon it was relatively easy to take their flocks and herds with them,[5] while the general insecurity had a detrimental effect on more permanent settlements and therefore on tillage. Consequently, agriculture was in the backward areas mainly confined to cereals, which yielded a quick return. City life was regarded as superior to life in the open country, which appeared to the inhabitants of the *polis* as barbarous. When Strabo wrote about the Iberians of Spain he remarked: "The majority of the Iberians are village-dwellers, and as such are uncivilized."[6] He knew that the Greeks had also lived in open villages.

It was only relatively late, after the Persian Wars, that people came together from many communities into . . . the city. . . . And I might almost say that, with only a few exceptions, the other Peloponnesian places named by the poet were also named by him, not as cities, but as countries, each country being composed of several communities, from which in later times the well-known cities were settled.[7]

The process of urbanization developed in stages by "the combination of villages into a town, the combination of towns into a city."[8] The most prominent of open settlements was Sparta, which consisted of several villages "after the old Hellenic fashion."[9] This "old Hellenic fashion" which was a doubtful privilege in-

3. *History of the Peloponnesian War.* I. 2-5. 7.
4. *Politics.* 1252b. 29.
5. G. D. Thomson. *Studies in Ancient Greek Society.* 1949. P. 349. Also for the following.
6. III. 4. 13.
7. VIII. 3. 2.
8. G. D. Thomson, *op. cit.,* p. 350.
9. Thucydides. I. 10.

duced the Spartans to force the inhabitants of Mantinea to disperse their city and to live in villages, an anachronistic revenge of narrow-minded militarists. However, after the defeat of Sparta, Mantinea was restored as a city and a new one was formed at Megalopolis from the towns and rural settlements of the region. The inhabitants of Megalopolis came from a number of small places and from the surrounding country. All the old hamlets and dispersed settlements were deserted and absorbed into one large *polis* area. However, the new settlers were not numerous enough to fill the great expanse of Megalopolis. At the same time the *polis* of Ithome (then called Messene and walled in about 250 B.C.) was founded for the helots of Messene.[10]

The origin of the *dêmos* was the village community which was identical with the clan. Aristotle defined the *polis* as "a union of clans and villages,"[11] of *géne* and *kômai*. The term *polis* means therefore the city-state, the city itself, and the region with its villages which belonged to the city. The *acropolis,* to anticipate another factor of city development, was "a natural stronghold, such as would have been a good site for a village settlement in the troubled times described by Thucydides."[12] The citadel and the lower town, the *acropolis* and the *asty*, were the two distinctive parts of the city proper. In the earlier period of Greek history the tribes settled in one place only for a certain time. They retained their coherence ideally and materially—that is, each settlement was inhabited by one tribe and (if we may draw comparative conclusions from other tribal examples about which sufficient evidence is available) was subdivided according to clans. This grouping survived into later times: if we read of a *tetrapolis* such as the Island of Zakynthos or the town of Marathon, or of a *pentapolis* at Syracuse, it means that several tribes or several clans had formed a confederacy and that their originally more-or-less self-contained units had gradually grown together without losing too much of their identity.

In the choice of the site and the units parceled out to the clans the quality of the soil and the availability of water were of major importance. Good defensive positions were preferred. It is probable, though we have no conclusive evidence for these earliest settlements in Greece, that the clan of the tribal chief occupied the best site, with the compound of the chief in the center serving as refuge for the other families of the clan in times of unrest—or that the whole settlement was protected by some sort of enclosure, by palisades or ramparts, behind which the inhabitants of the other villages could find safety when threatened by other tribes. It is also possible that there was an open space in front of the chiefs house where the heads of the clan would assemble. This may have been the primitive and earliest precursor of the *agora*.

10. E. Kirsten. "Raumordnung and Kolonisation in der griechischen Geschichte." In: *Historische Raumforschung II*, 1958. Forschungs- und Sitzungs—berichte der Akademie für Raumforschung und Landesplanung. P. 39.

11. *Politics.* 1281a. 14.

12. G. D. Thomson, *op. cit.,* p. 352.

But again it should be emphasized that no material evidence is available, although certain conclusions *a posteriori* may be drawn from neolithic settlements in other parts of the world as to the physical structure of these tribal settlements. Fields and pastures surrounded the villages, the former as open holdings of each family and the latter belonging to the community as a whole. The interrelationship of the villages of the same tribe and of the clans to the tribe was based on a hierarchical principle descending in importance from the village and the function of the tribal chief to those of the chiefs of the clans, and finally to the heads of the households.

These earliest communities were self-contained and self-sufficient. This changed with the introduction of metal tools produced locally or supplied by itinerant smiths.[13] This led to a greater efficiency and a certain division of labor. In the course of time a class of specialists grew up who were not engaged in cultivation but had to be supplied with food by the other members of the village community. This presupposed that agriculture had reached a sufficiently advanced stage of development where a surplus of agricultural commodities could be produced. Not only better tools but also better organization was needed. Consequently the economic power of the chief increased and in his hands an accumulation of capital began to develop in the usual form which we know also from other countries. In this way his standing as the protecting leader endowed with magical powers grew together with his charisma. The tributes and labor services he received were the economic basis of this ascendancy and with these privileges his prestige was enhanced. It was a sort of chain reaction, leading from modest beginnings to the exalted position of the kings with all its concomitant effects: the acquisition of large parts of the land; the receipt of the greatest share in loot; the use of slave labor resulting from victorious wars; and the beginning, though on a very small scale, of trade. It has been suggested that

the exchange of commodities grew imperceptibly out of intertribal hospitality. . . . Each parting gift constitutes a claim on the recipient to be honoured at some future date. . . . Acceptance of this is a pledge of security for the transaction that follows. It is at the same time a perquisite for the kings—an impost of trade. This explains why barter develops under the chief's control.[14]

In the process of this development the self-sufficiency of the villages gradually disappeared. An intercommunity barter conducted by the chiefs and the artisans spread over wider areas. Production for one's own village was superseded by production for outside villages on a commercial basis. The meeting place

13. *Ibid.*, p. 355.
14. *Ibid.*, p. 356.

of the central village was used as a market square; the central village itself developed into a market town; and the villages depended more and more on the production of this new economic unit in their midst, their own home industries continuing although on a reduced scale. The chiefs grew richer and the clansmen poorer. A landed aristocracy came into being and with it the enclosure of its land. The tribal settlements became cities and the cities became states with a landed aristocracy as the dominant minority,

surrounded by a poverty-stricken peasantry in dependent villages. The new unit was the expression of a new division of labour, agrarian and industrial which, once established, promoted further divisions of labour and thereby raised human life to new levels of complexity on a slave basis.[15]

The following centuries saw the struggle of the landowners against the rising merchant class. When the former prevailed, urbanization was slow; when the latter predominated, urbanization gained a firm foothold and its development was accelerated. But behind these changes another revolution was going on which was of an infinitely greater significance. It was a revolution in the human sphere: the ties of blood loosened and gave way to elective affinities, to absorption into the urban society which lived under the protection of a god.

The individual member of this society was deeply embedded in this civic community and even his family life was subordinated to the communal existence. The *polis* was limited both ideally and physically, thus creating the embracing framework within which all its inhabitants could establish an immediate and personal relationship. It was this merging of the private and public life which prevented a stagnation through the deadening influence of bureaucrats and priests. The citizen of the *polis* spent the greater part of the day in the *agora* or in the gymnasium which was held to be just as indispensable for a town as water, *agora,* theater, and municipal buildings. The extraordinary expansion which radiated from the city-states during the colonial period was the direct result of the limitation of the *polis.* The structure of the *polis* in general and in detail aimed at a balanced limitation within which man was the measure of all things. Hence the demand of Aristotle that the population of a *polis* should not exceed the largest number which suffices for the purposes of life and can be taken in at a single view. This predilection for smallness, this abhorrence of bigness, runs like a golden thread through the whole of Greek thinking. A Greek town was conceived in a manner not too dissimilar from a sculpture which also can be

15. *Ibid.,* p. 358.

taken in at a single glance. It explains why the *polis* did not grow beyond narrow limits—quite apart from certain practical considerations such as food or water supply—and why new *poleis* were founded when the limits of expansion which were regarded as appropriate had been reached. The Greek city was conceived as a limited entity where the whole population could assemble in the theater, the *agora,* the council house, and where the voice of the orator could be heard by every citizen. The temples rose on moderate elevations; the council house, with the hearth of the town, stood at the market square; and the market was situated in the lower parts of the country where the roads from the interior and the coast met. The houses of the citizens huddled together on a small area. Numerous examples exist where these principles were applied. There was, for instance, Kyme on the Campanian Gulf in Italy; when this had reached what was considered an appropriate size, Puteoli was laid out a mile away; then the first Neapolis; and when this also reached its limit a new Neapolis sprang up in the immediate neighborhood, so that the earlier "Newtown" became Palaeopolis.

The city-state could develop only at the expense of the biological family. That is, the ties of blood were subordinated to elective affinities, and family life was superseded by the demands of communal existence as a politically active member of the *polis.* "Of all the activities necessary and present in human communities, only two were deemed to be political and to constitute what Aristotle called the *bios politikos,* namely action (*praxis*) and speech (*lexis*)."[16] Gradually speech became more important, for it was through speech that, in the opinion of Greek thinkers, people could be influenced and violence be avoided. Talking and arguing were the essence of man as a *zoon politikon.* Slaves and barbarians remained outsiders whose life was deprived of that most precious privilege of the full citizens of the *polis,* of "the central concern of all citizens to talk with each other."[17] Yet this overriding devotion to the public sphere did not lead to an abnegation of the private life and the home. But it was not respect for private property, as we understand it, but "the fact that without owning a house a man could not participate in the affairs of the world because he had no location in it which was properly his own."[18] In contrast to the household whose very essence was the fulfillment of the natural wants and needs of its members the political life as a citizen of the *polis* meant freedom and both, the private and the public realm, were dependent on each other inasmuch as the smooth working of the household and the efficient handling of its daily needs were the prerequisites of political freedom. In other words, attending to the management

16. Hannah Arendt. *The Human Condition.* 1959. Pp. 24-25.
17. *Ibid.,* p. 27.
18. *Ibid.,* p. 30.

of home life should not interfere with the free exercise of the political privilege and participation in the public life of the *polis*. Consequently, the *polis* consisted only of equals, in the strictest and ideal sense, while the household rested on inequality, on the rule of its head over the rest of the family. The only life worth living was the life of the free citizen of the *polis*, who was free from work and the restrictive pursuit of practical activities, and independent of the ideal and material success which the needs and wants of the biological family would impose upon him. It is, therefore, not surprising and goes a long way toward the understanding of the status of women and slaves, both belonging to the same category of "laborers," the first as the guarantors of the continuation of the family, and the latter as the instruments through which the daily needs of life were maintained. Slavery was not introduced as a source of cheap labor or profit. It was regarded as the essential means to free the life of the full citizen of the *polis* from laboring under necessity, to prevent him from becoming a "working animal."

The transformation of the early clansman into the citizen of the *polis*, from a family man into the *zoon politikon*, was a long process. Only gradually the new type of Greek townsmen evolved out of the raw material of human beings which the old groups had formed. These men had come to the city because they felt that life was more worth living there than in the country, and that the material and ideal powers of the city-state would gain by concentration and cooperation. Military considerations, especially protective needs, played only a secondary role in the early period. Then the people who lived in small groups scattered over the land would retreat into the more inaccessible parts of the country when danger threatened. However, it was safer to live permanently under the protecting shelter of an *acropolis* than to flee to a safe place every time an enemy approached.

The actual driving force in the formation of the *polis* was peace, not war. The citizens did not protect their living space by walls, at least not at the beginning. The *acropolis* alone was walled in. Walls were built only later when a more advanced stage of urban development had been reached and civic pride deemed this necessary as an outward sign of importance. It is characteristic that the Spartans never built a *polis* but lived in open villages, a way of life that was perfectly in keeping with the interests of their ruling class of landed nobles. This development is almost the opposite of that of the medieval town which was from its very beginning fortified.

Life in the *polis* went on mostly outside the house. In the medieval town the house was the home of the burgher and men gathered only for special purposes in public. The houses of the *polis* jostled each other; there were no gardens, or only interior ones within the house. The town of the early Middle Ages was a garden city and the private garden an instrument of segregation and privacy. The colonnades of the *polis* were the embodiment of community life; originally *agora* meant "assembly" and later "assembly place," but not "market place." The market square of a medieval town was first of all a space for a definite economic purpose and in many cases the *raison d'être* of the town. Out of the club life of the Greeks developed the spirit of the city-state; out of the narrow sphere of the guilds grew the spirit of the parochial burgher.

Up to the time of Alexander the Great the *polis* was in most cases a coastal town not more than one day's journey from the sea. Consequently the Mediterranean was the field of extension of the *polis*. Except in a few cases the typical medieval town was an inland town and expanded either through its own enlargement or by spreading a territorial hegemony over its hinterland. The surrounding region was an integral part of the *polis* whereas the medieval town formed a kind of utilitarian association with its hinterland within the territory of the state.

The very essence of the *polis* was not its physical situation or appearance. It was the living interaction of the citizens, their mutual contact through speech and action. The people were the *polis* and wherever they were, they carried the idea and the spirit of the polis with them. "Wherever you go, you will be a *polis*." The *polis* existed in its physical embodiment solely as the space which had to be delimited and organized so that within it men could act and deliberate. Consequently the actual situation of the *polis,* its physical existence, did not evoke the same patriotism as we know it today or as the Romans attached it to their cities. This ubiquity of the spirit of the *polis* and the creative synoicism of the Greeks enabled them to believe that they could do the extraordinary and could do it permanently because the *polis* was always and everywhere present offering in spirit an inexhaustible abundance of opportunities to do great deeds, at the same time excluding the frustrating experience of ineffective actions and empty speech.

The organization of the *polis,* physically secured by the wall around the city and physiognomically guaranteed by its laws—lest the succeeding generations change its identity beyond recognition—is a kind of organized remembrance. It assures the mortal actor that his passing existence and fleeting greatness will never lack the reality that comes from being seen, being heard, and generally, appearing before an audience of fellowmen.[19]

19. Hannah Arendt, *op. cit.,* p. 198.

This is the true reality of the *polis,* the sharing of the political space with others, the living presence among other men.

The idea of Aristotle was a static and balanced society which would retain a perfect equilibrium without dynamic transformation. This was the ideal to which his utopian successors reverted in their own time. The reality was, however, quite different. Great social upheavals shook the Greek city-states and changed Greek society. The *polis* came into being and developed, like the majority of other towns, by migration from outside. It consisted, therefore, of numerous heterogeneous elements. It is true that these movements from the country to the towns were sometimes prevented—for instance, in Corinth about 600 B.C., where the country people were forbidden to leave their land because this would imperil the food supply. However, these attempts proved unsuccessful in the long run, for as in other periods the way from the country to the towns led from servitude to freedom. In this respect the antagonism between town and country did exist in ancient Greece but it did not result in an outspoken political fight because both town and country formed a territorial unity.

But a division of labor set in at the moment when the economic structure of the town began to be detached from the village economy. The country supplied the food and the town fulfilled the political, cultural, and industrial tasks. Together with this division of labor a social stratification set in: the country people were not full citizens. They were mostly poor and their plots were small, or else they were slaves. This social differentiation and suppression was aggravated when the barter economy was replaced by a money economy, however primitive this may have been. The country people were unable to adapt themselves to these economic changes which increased their servitude and poverty. On the other hand, the *polis* never lost its character as an overgrown agricultural village despite its industrial activities. The majority of its population were cultivators who maintained the contact with the countryside, not craftsmen or shopkeepers. The agrarian character of the *polis* was one of the reasons why trade guilds did not play the same decisive part as they did in the medieval towns. Apart from this, the widespread use of slave labor and the generally small scale of production made the association of free craftsmen difficult. If there were any guilds at all, they were primarily religious and had no ambition to control working conditions or trade practices.[20] Moreover, specialized occupations tended to be hereditary in the tribal society. This may have been another reason why purely professional associations did not find a fertile soil in Greece where these ancient memories might have lingered on.[21]

20. H. Michell. *The Economics of Ancient Greece.* 1957. P. 142.
21. G. D. Thomson, *op. cit.,* p. 332.

The ideal citizen of the *polis* was the landowner and cultivator. The rise of the city and the extension of its territory were directly dependent on the fertility of the soil and the available food supply. Thus the interdependence of town and country operated in economic and social, political and cultural fields. And apart from these tangible influences, other more imponderable elements came to the surface with the migrations of the peasants to the towns. These tillers of the soil were still nearer to the chthonian forces and still embedded in their primeval and magical omnipresence. Their absorption into the urban society modified its spirit in a subtle and gradual process in which they themselves were transformed and swallowed up by the more rational clarity of urban thinking. Out of this mutual penetration in the deeper layers of the conscience grew a new bond between the most valuable creations which the *polis* has left to posterity: the mystery cults; the Greek tragedies which unveil the primordial motives of human actions; the Greek temple which not only embodies the rational lucidity of Hellenism but also enshrines and, at the same time, subdues the demonic and mystical intensity which again and again breaks through in the religious rituals. The temple is the symbolic crown of the *polis;* the *agora* is its political center. Both together express the duality of the *polis*: secular awareness and communal coherence enfolded by religious piety and spiritual sublimation.

CHAPTER 10

Distribution
of Settlement
and
Colonization

THE DORIAN MIGRATION which marks the actual opening of the historical epoch on the Greek mainland, Crete, and Rhodes began with the annexation of territory by the invaders, who occupied only contiguous areas of the most fertile land—for instance, in Sparta (about 900 B.C.) and later when the Spartans conquered Laconia and the interior of Messenia (820-720 B.C.). The original inhabitants were restricted to the less fertile soils which they had cultivated before the invasion. To these regions withdrew also all those groups that did not want to be absorbed by the Dorians. Thus a separation of the Dorian and non-Dorian (*perioikoi*) population developed not only in Laconia and Messenia but also in Thessaly and Elis and possibly in Boeotia. The land occupied by the Dorians alone was divided up into lots, *klaroi,* which, at least theoretically, were supposed to be equally fertile. The Dorian immigrants established themselves either in existing or new settlements—the latter being the case in Sparta—from which they cultivated their land as warrior peasants.[1] The principle of this internal colonization, that is, the occupation of the most fertile land taken from the conquered peoples and its division into lots, was maintained when the colonization spread to other countries. It formed the basis of the instructions emanating from the Delphic Oracle through which the *eunomia,* the harmony of the mode of living, among the colonial settlers was to be preserved. The colonists had to keep together and establish their mastery over the natives as they had done at home, employing the same methods as the Spartans, who "were not individuals willing to accommodate themselves to an existing pattern of life, but a community bringing their own pattern with them and determined to preserve it."[2] They transferred their stratified society to the colonies, following the example of the Spartans who, as a minority, had to live among hostile neighbors. "There were the 'Spartiates', the only true Spartans, on the top; the *perioikoi* ('neighbours') below them—a class that was free but with no political rights; and at the bottom the *helots,* not personal slaves of the Spartans, but serfs of the Spartan community, most of them working on the land."

Up to the fourth century B.C. Greek colonies were planted exclusively within a coastal belt with the same climatic and food conditions which the settlers knew from their homeland—that is, where vines and olives would grow. These limits explain the restriction of the colonization only to parts of the Black Sea coast and the avoidance of the Upper Adriatic exposed to the *bora,* the severe north wind that blows from the *Karst* region, and of certain stretches of the Spanish littoral zone open to the con-

1. E. Kirsten. "Raumordnung und Kolonisation in der griechischen Geschichte." In: *Historische Raumforschung II.* 1958. Forschungs- und Sitzungsberichte der Akademie für Raumforschung und Landesplanung. Pp. 27 ff. Also for the following.

2. H. D. F. Kitto. *The Greeks.* 1951. P. 90.

tinental climate. Almost all alluvial plains of the coastal regions of the Dardanelles, the northern zone of Asia Minor, the Crimea, and intermittently the west coast of the Black Sea, the east coast of the Adriatic, and the coast of the Provence were occupied by Greek colonies.

This means: the Greeks did not search for a complementary addition to their food supply but for its extension. Their foundations had the same agrarian character as the *poleis* of the mother country: they were not towns but communities according to their political autonomy, more exactly *Gemeindestaaten* [city-states], with a peasant population (living on their own work in the fields but more often on that of their serfs, the *helots*). Trade and commerce did not at all play the same role as for the inhabitants of the central European towns since the Middle Ages. The colonization supplied the emigrants (*apoikoi*) with farm land which the homeland could no more offer. However, it did not include the whole territory of the new homeland but only the cultivated areas interspersed like oases and compartments in the limestone mountains.[3]

Another type of colonial expansion was the occupation of capes or small islands which were near hilltop settlements of the natives—for instance, in Sicily, at Thapsos, Megara, Messina (Zancle), Ortygia, the later and older part of Syracuse, on the dunes of the south coast of Sicily, on Ischia, on the peninsula of Tarentum (Taranto) and Otranto; also in Spain and in France at Massilia (Marseilles) and Nicaia (Nice), and at numerous points of the Black Sea. All these foundations were in good defensive locations and were therefore at first without farmland. They were intended as trading points where goods could be bartered with the natives. Land could be acquired later and then only with the help of the local inhabitants as described by Herodotus (IV.156. 8) for the settlement of the island of Plateia. The following stage, the development from trading points to agrarian settlements, led to the foundation of Leontinoi and Akragas in Sicily, Hipponion, Poseidonia (Paestum), and Neapolis (Naples) to mention just a few. This process was accompanied and made possible by the acquisition of cultivable land and a gradual dissociation from the mother *polis*.

Distribution of settlement and colonization are intimately connected with the demographic aspects of Greek history. Evidence on the increase or decrease of population in ancient Greece is very meager. Conclusions cannot be based on exact data but can only be deduced from the general course of historical development and indirectly from a cautious evaluation and correlation of archeological discoveries which are, however, by no means complete.

Actual population figures of ancient Greece do not exist, for

3. E. Kirsten, *op. cit.*, p. 32.

the numbers mentioned by Greek writers cannot possibly be considered reliable, as careful investigations have shown. However, on the basis of calculations of food supply and food consumption—to give but one instance—the population of Attica toward the end of the fourth century may have been about 233,000. The population of all Greece in the same period may have been about two and a half million, which corresponds roughly to the population figures for the beginning of the 20th century. It seems further that between the Persian and the Peloponnesian Wars the population increased due to better living conditions and growing wealth, and that this increase was mainly made up of slaves. The decrease of population during the Peloponnesian War resulted not only from heavy casualties but also from the plague that befell Athens. It may also be assumed that the poorer quarters of Athens and the Peiraieus suffered more than the richer. After the war the population rose again, mostly due to an influx of foreigners and slaves and to the mercenary soldiers who were employed instead of citizens. From 338 to 313 B.C. the number of citizens dropped, probably because many emigrated to the countries conquered by Alexander and to the newly colonized Thrace.[4] It is, however, open to doubt that infanticide played an appreciable role in the downward trend of population or the retardation of a population increase. Infanticide was practiced but apparently not on a considerable scale.

As to the interaction of population numbers and colonization we are also without statistical data. We know that new foundations sprang up all over the Aegean and beyond, but we have no exact knowledge of how many people migrated to the new colonies. This movement lasted from the middle of the eighth to the middle of the sixth century. It would be wrong to assume that the colonists were mostly citizens of the mother city. Such an exodus would have seriously affected the social and economic structure and the safety of the mother city. It is much more likely that a considerable number of the pioneer settlers joined the enterprise as volunteers from other parts of Greece or had been resident aliens in the city which promoted it. Miletus, for example, is said to have founded 80 to 90 colonies. It would have been far beyond her population capacity to send out only her own citizens. It is much more probable that she, like other cities, was the organizer and sponsor, especially in the incipient stage, selecting the site and providing transport, rather than being the supplier of the bulk of the colonists herself. That these tendencies existed is obvious from a report by Thucydides: when in 435 B.C. Corinthians refounded Epidamnus, the present Durazzo in Albania, they searched publicly for colonists, promising equal treatment to all who were willing to take part in the enterprise from

476

4. *Ibid.*, pp. 21-23.

wherever they might come.[5]

The pre-Hellenic civilization of the South Aegean, which lasted for about one thousand years before its dissolution in the 12 century B.C., was the common possession of a fairly large population spread over a wide region. Its economic basis was an agriculture which had reached a relatively high state of productivity and organization that lent itself to a certain degree of centralization and surplus economy. This may be concluded from the inventories, storerooms, and other relevant finds in the palaces of Crete and, by way of comparison, with similar institutions in Egypt and Babylonia where the temples served as storehouses and as a kind of economic clearing house. However, this basis did not guarantee a steady and sufficient supply of agricultural commodities and must have affected, as the fluctuating fortunes of such small country towns as Gournia or Palaikastro show, the prosperity and density of population.[6]

The distribution of settlements and the cultivation of terraces of the Minoan, Hellenic, and medieval and modern periods suggests that the cultivated area of Minoan Crete was probably rather larger than that of later periods, and the population greater; for there is no reason to believe that the fertility of the soil has been diminished, or the methods of farming improved, since the Minoan Age.

About the distribution of settlement and population on the mainland into which Minoan civilization advanced during the Late Minoan Age, between 1600 and 1400 B.C., we know even less. In general, we may assume that Laconia and Attica were settled late, the former only in parts and the latter, after a slow beginning, more extensively while Argolis was occupied at an early date and apparently quite intensively. It is probable that this movement resulted from overpopulation in Crete and in some of the other islands. It is fairly certain that in the Third Late Minoan period, that is, after the destruction of Knossos about 1400 B.C., the Aegean settlements of the mainland type spread to Southern Italy, to Syracuse, and Tarentum in the west; to Lemnos and Thessaly in the north; and to Cyprus and Philistia in the east. This process continued for three centuries and eventually reached the western coast of Asia Minor. It is also likely that in the Late Minoan Age patriarchal clans of horse breeders invaded mainland Greece from the Danubian grasslands or the steppes of Southern Russia. Why did these apparently nomadic and pastoral peoples move southward into what is now Greece? It is still too early to discount the theory that periods of a minimum or decreasing rainfall were the reason why these tribes left their homes. This may have been so but we should await more conclusive evidence than has been offered so far.

5. Thucydides. I. 27.
6. J. L. Myres. *Geographical History in Greek Lands.* 1953. P. 182. Also for the following.

In any case, what little we know is sufficient to prove that the Greeks had to build their civilization on a soil where before them other peoples had flourished, built their settlements, spread their influence to other shores, and reshaped the natural environment by terracing the slopes, cutting irrigation channels, and cultivating their fields. Perhaps the most important reclamation was the draining of the Copais in Boeotia in the Minoan period. At that time it was a fertile district while in the Greek era it had turned into swamps; or the roads of Minoan Argolis which were "almost disused in historic times;[7] or the Pylos of Nestor which was no mean city in the 13th century B.C., although the Greeks of later periods did not even know the exact place where it had stood.

The early migrations of peoples which spread over Greece had brought with them a mixture of races that led to interbreeding and intercultural adaptations. The Greeks were fully aware of these facts and knew that they were of "mongrel ancestry." This early period, with its open frontiers and the invasion of foreign elements, is in striking contrast to the seclusion of Greece from the 12th century B.C. to the third century A.D. Several theories have been advanced for this seemingly inexplicable phenomenon one of which is "that a free Greece needed a strong Macedon. Only with the northern passes closed by a hardy half-barbaric neighbour, could the Greek cities in the south live out their life-histories unmolested."[8] This is an attractive and quite acceptable explanation especially if considered together with other factors such as the diminishing population pressure in the regions north of the Greek peninsula and the growing coherence and increasing strength of Greek civilization during its formative period.

The colonial movement of the Greeks did not come into being like a *deus ex machina.* It continued the earlier migrations through which Cyprus and the islands and the coast of the Aegean were settled. But it differed from them inasmuch as the colonies of the later period owed their existence to a mother city and retained sentimental ties with it, even though they were politically independent. The origin of the Greek colonies, or rather the *causa causans,* was commercial only in some cases. Generally they were not established as trading posts like those of the Phoenicians or Carthaginians or those of Miletus on the coasts of the Black Sea. The Greek colonies were founded as *poleis,* imitating the mother city in its social, political, and economic structure. They were the result of various causes: the tendency to keep the size of the mother city small; the foresight to maintain a balance between food supply and population; political discontent; a spirit of adventure; promotion of trade;

7. J. L. Myres, *op. cit.,* p. 186.
8. *Ibid.,* p. 187.

redundancy of people; political ambitions of the mother city; and many other factors.

The development of the Greek colonies was rapid. Obstacles, which faced later European settlers in other countries, did not exist or were easily overcome by merging with the nation. Thus race, color, and climate were meaningless and did not appear to the Greek mind as possible difficulties that might retard or complicate the foundation and growth of their new settlements. The peoples whom the Greeks encountered were either on a similar cultural level or of a race related to the Greek, or physically not too different. Thus it was accepted as natural that the population of the colonies would consist mainly of natives. The climate was congenial to the Greek colonists in the whole of the Mediterranean region, which has exceptionally uniform climatic conditions. Finally, all Greek colonies before Alexander the Great were coastal towns like the mother cities. All these factors together were favorable to Greek colonization and explain its success and duration.

Greek colonization in its narrower sense—or rather its tremendous impetus—had run its course during the sixth century. It seems that by this time the majority of the sites suitable for colonization had been occupied and that Carthage and Etruria in the West and Persia in the East opposed further expansion, at least on Greek terms. The Greeks who set out from their homeland took with them their political ideas and their devotion to the ideal of the self-sufficient and self-contained *polis*. These ideals they upheld in the new lands as long as the mother cities maintained those principles. But colonial expansion defeated, at least to a degree, its own purpose. The basis of the old self-sufficiency had been an agriculture which provided virtually all the commodities that were needed, and what was not produced on the farms such as iron tools and the like could be acquired in the town. The more the colonies spread to regions like Scythia, for instance, which could supply corn in exchange for olives and wine, textiles and metal work, the more land could be turned over from corn growing to the old mixed farming practice which had worked so well in favor of self-sufficiency. This change in farming established the old conditions—though only for a short time—for the trade between the corn-growing countries and the city-states continued to increase but at the cost of a certain specialization and a reduced self-sufficiency. In the course of time this commercial intercourse led to a growth of Greek industries particularly in the ports where the raw materials arrived. These expanding industries and the distribution of goods needed workers, full-time workers, who could not remain part-time farmers. This development created many new jobs at home and

479

consequently reduced the number of those who sought their fortune in new lands.

Overpopulation is a relative term depending on the degree to which men are able to adapt their environment to their needs. The problem is rather one of distribution and how this distribution of population and settlement can be carried through. It is obvious that the attitude of the Greeks was in this respect like that of other peoples conditioned by what they regarded as feasible, and what they liked or disliked. As they held strong views on what was desirable they clung to their ancestral ideas and to their ancestral soil as long as possible, being disinclined to open up new regions if these were too dissimilar from their homeland. Consequently their field of action remained in the coastal areas of the Mediterranean and these restricted areas appeared to them "full to overflowing," while in reality the vast hinterland was to them a *terra incognita*. They were genuinely convinced that by the middle of the sixth century the limits of colonial expansion had been reached. So they turned, as it were, inward and began to intensify the urban industries at home.

Colonization on a grand scale began again under Alexander the Great, this time spreading over the interior of all the conquered land from the Aegean to India. If we take as a basis of calculation Aristotle's demand that the ideal *polis* should have as an optimum population 10,000 free male citizens, a figure of one million for every hundred of the new foundations would be a fairly correct estimate; this does not include the slaves or the fluctuating population of aliens. Compared with this renewed outburst of colonization under Alexander and his successors—the majority of the cities were founded within a hundred years after his death—the period from 200 B.C. to 200 A.D. was almost an anticlimax, although the movement did not come to a complete standstill.

The total population of Greece has been estimated as a little above four million including one million for Macedonia. It seems that this figure remained more or less stationary for the next century. But in the second century the downward trend became rather pronounced. Polybius ascribed this decline to a slackening of the moral standards, to the overestimation of material gains and possessions, the love of ostentation and leisure—all of which operated, in his view, against marriage and the rearing of children.[9] By the end of the first century B.C. this downward trend had become so serious that Augustus made it his foremost task to survey the human and natural resources of Greece, to revive family life, and to stimulate marriage. He had some success, but even with the *Pax Romana* it was a short-lived interlude. The decline could not be arrested.

9. Polybius. XXXVI. 17.

The distribution of the Greek city-states and their colonies over the Mediterranean region is very irregular. They cluster on the eastern shores of the Greek peninsula and to a lesser degree on the west coast of Asia Minor while only a few are dispersed along the eastern shores of the Adriatic. Around the Black Sea the Greek settlements were fairly numerous, all founded by Miletus; on the south coast of Asia Minor and on the coast of Syria Greek settlements were almost totally absent, as on the African coast. Sicily and Southern Italy present a different picture with numerous Greek foundations. The reasons for this great contrast were partly political and partly environmental; political inasmuch as other powers would have encountered and checked the Greek advance, and environmental because of physical conditions which the Greeks were unwilling or unable to overcome. Before the ascendancy of Rome the Mediterranean was essentially a Greek world. Its influence in the West extended to Massilia (Marseilles), Ampurias, and Southern Spain.

If we look back at the history of Greek settlement as a whole one misconception should be revised. The spread of Greek settlement moved in cycles; it was not a purely maritime process. The first stage was an overland movement carried forward by people from the interior of the Eurasian Continent over land routes and land frontiers, destroying the Minoan civilization and sweeping on to the islands. The second stage was a maritime movement originating from the Greek nucleus around the Aegean and spreading to the west, north, and east. The third stage was an overland expansion in the wake of Alexander's conquests. The impact of all three movements on the ancient world was tremendous, and after its power was spent its influence remained a formative force of European and to a lesser degree Asian civilizations. In all these regions the idea of the *polis* became a living example of the Greek way of life; its architecural forms lived on in Roman buildings; Greek philosophy and political ideas shaped Roman and medieval thinking; the cosmology of Aristotle remained the only accepted dogma till it was dethroned by Copernicus and Giordano Bruno.

But Greek city planning had no lasting effect. It had to give way to the rigid Roman military camp which soon became the standard layout for all Roman cities. This change was a symbolic act. The motivation for the planting of Greek cities all over the Mediterranean region was the peaceful spread of an ideology. The colonies like the mother cities remained independent political units, restricting their influence to their immediate hinterland on the coast. However, the foundation of Roman cities and colonies was motivated by conquest and with the definite purpose of providing nodal points of the Roman administration. The sphere of influence of the Roman cities extended over large territories. They were not only the visible signs of Rome's greatness but also strongholds and garrison towns from which the subjugated peoples could be governed and kept submissive. The military camp, this disingenuous demonstration of military rigidity, was the obvious form for these purposes. The fact that it owed its origin to a religious ritual and symbolism does not diminish its military significance. Many actions and beliefs which had a noble and sacred origin were debased in the course of time and misused for vulgar and dangerous ends. Why should the original Roman city be an exception? The *polis,* on the other hand, never lost its essential meaning and physical appearance even when it had deteriorated to a stereotyped pattern. The Greek checkerboard plan was something entirely different and cannot be compared with the seemingly similar Roman layout. Why this is so will be explained in another connection.

Greek colonization proceeded under the supervision of the mother city. It was a systematically planned social and economic enterprise. It was not carried into effect by individual pioneers, to be gradually developed by groups of subsequent newcomers. A colony was conceived from the outset as a *polis* limited in extent and numbers, as a self-contained entity, which was to retain its initial structure and stable equilibrium. Each of the first colonists received a site for a house within the walls and a share of the land outside the enclosure. Head colonists supervised the layout of the city and the distribution of the land. The number of inhabitants was fixed in relation to the available food supply. The city could grow within these limitations. If the population increased beyond these predetermined restrictions, a new *polis* was founded. Drinkable and sufficient water, fertile soil, timber for ship-building, and a good harbor were essential prerequisites for the choice of the site, which was to be in a territory with peaceful and amenable natives willing to cultivate the fields in recompense for "protection" by the colonists against hostile interference.

The general Greek term for colony was *apoikia,* whereas *cleruchy* meant originally an Athenian colony although this name was later used rather more indiscriminately, and *emporion* as applied exclusively to trading posts. No clear line can be drawn between colonies established on individual initiative with the approval of the State and those founded as official enterprises of the community. Both types existed together and played a decisive role in the spread of Greek colonization.[10]

The intimate dependence of the colony on the mother city was symbolized by the religious ritual according to which the colonists lighted the sacred hearth in the colony with fire brought

10. A. J. Graham. *Colony and Mother City in Ancient Greece.* 1964. Pp. 4 ff. and *passim* for the following.

by them from the sacred hearth, the *hestia,* of the mother city. The religious character of founding a new colony was also evident in the obligation to consult the Oracle at Delphi. In the course of time the priests may have acquired a considerable amount of geographical knowledge that they used for advice to the colonists. However, the main purpose was to obtain the sanction of the god and to transfer the religious symbolism that enhanced the mother city to the new colony. Thus the Oracle at Delphi combined the role of a practical advisor with that of a religious patron.

The actual organization of the colonial enterprise was entrusted to an *oikist* whose status and task were in some respects not too dissimilar to those of the *locator* in the early Middle Ages, when numerous settlements were laid out in the great colonial movement spreading from the west to the east of Northern Europe.[11] It seems that in the early period of Greek colonization the *oikist* had almost autocratic, even monarchical power or was an instrument of the ruler of the mother city as long as it was dominated by a tyrant. On the other hand, he did not even take part in the organization and foundation of the imperial colonies of the fifth century: The democratic colonies of Athens were clearly not suitable places for a monarchical *oikist.*[12]

The colonies were planted along the great north-south and west-east trade routes and especially where important spheres of interest merged—for instance, Rhodes, Byzantium, Syracuse, and Alexandria. In search of Egyptian grain Greek like Phoenician traders before them sailed to the Delta of the Nile.

They spread a veneer of Mediterranean culture and Greek speech over the Delta. This district became the seat of steady maritime activity, however, only when the old Milesian factory at Naucratis on the Canobic arm was converted into the one open treaty port of Egypt by Psammeticus about 620 B.C.; and again after 330 B.C. when Alexander the Great built the Greek city of Alexandria on the western rim of the Delta beyond the reach of Nile silt. But this active port was wholly Greek with a large cosmopolitan population; it was in no sense Egyptian. Its maritime enterprises were directed by the Greek dynasty of the Ptolemies.

Conditions were similar at the mouth of the Rhone where they

determined the permanence of the port of Massilia: a situation forty miles southeast of the Rhone mouth, parallel spurs of the Provence hills enclosing its harbor, deep water close inshore, sufficient proximity to a river highway opening up a productive hinterland, and again a coastwise current here setting westward and carrying off the Rhone silt toward the competing port of Narbo.[13]

The hills were ideal for an *acropolis* and the port was pro-

11. See Vol. I, pp. 103, 123, and 468 of *The International History of City Development.*

12. For details of the changing role of the *oikist* and for Foundation Decrees see A. J. Graham, *op. cit.,* pp. 29-39 and appendices.

13. E. C. Semple. *The Geography of the Mediterranean Region.* 1932. Pp. 129, 161.

tected from the blasts of the *mistral*. Colonies of the type which had a particularly favorable strategic location remained under the strict control of the mother city as dependent *poleis,* called *cleruchies.* They resembled the Roman military colonies and were strongholds for further expansion. The colonies which Pericles founded in the Chersonesos and Lemnos belonged to this category. Good harbors were preferred as protection against hostile tribes; and double harbors with two entries which made navigation independent of the direction of the winds such as Knidos, Perinthos on the east coast of Thrace, Cyzicos in the Propontis, and Mytilene in Lesbos on an islet connected by a bridge with the main island and a harbor at either end of the channel. The situation at Syracuse was similar where the small island of Ortygia was united with the mainland of Sicily by a mole and later by a bridge.

Alexander's colonization was an instrument of his social and cultural policy. The cities he founded were to be a source of imitation for the barbarians and, as such, centers from which Greek civilization was to spread to the surrounding country. He believed his mission was to carry Greek culture to other lands and to break down the barriers between the Greeks and the conquered peoples. Purely commercial or military purposes could have been fulfilled by fortresses, garrison towns, or fortified outposts, but cities offered a life different from these ephemeral and *ad hoc* foundations—they brought the essence of Greek civilization, the community life within a city, to lands which, in the opinion of Alexander, had nothing similar to offer. His cities were thrown open to the native population and although our knowledge in this respect is still vague in detail, his general policy seems to have aimed at an end of segregation. Alexander's intentions did not survive his death. His successors, who followed his example as a colonizer and founded numerous cities, reverted to the original Greek habit of excluding foreigners. Their ambition was to immortalize their name, and the foundation of cities appeared to be a singularly impressive means to attain this goal. They founded cities, military colonies, and trading posts, or simply renamed existing cities or rebuilt them. However, their record as founders of cities should be regarded with some reservations: they did build cities but certainly fewer than they hoped posterity would believe.

Roman colonization was motivated by the need of administrative centers and of providing land for Roman citizens. Most of the Roman colonies were revived on existing Greek sites. Only a few were new foundations. War veterans were settled by the emperors either in semirural colonies or as citizens in the cities. In Achaea

Augustus made a great change, sweeping the decaying cities and villages of Ambracia, Amphilochia, Acarnania, Leucas, and the greater part of Aetolia into the great city which he built to celebrate the victory of Actium, Nicopolis. This vast synoicism, which exceeded the most ambitious efforts of the Successors, was justified in that it created one very flourishing city, though at the expense of many little towns which were rendered desolate.[14]

The Byzantine emperors made efforts to redress the unequal distribution of cities in the different provinces. Where city life had developed spontaneously, urban communities were numerous. Where provinces had been divided into city territories by the Roman administration, cities were few and far between. The remedy seems to have been the suppression of smaller communities which were economically desolate and the amalgamation of others which were not viable. In general the suppression of smaller communities and the foundation of new cities in the larger territories were mainly for administrative convenience.

The *polis* of classical times was the result of a long process of development. Urban settlements in the Aegean region date back to the third millennium. The pre-Doric centers of the Mycenaean civilization were fortified places, citadels, and residences of the ruler, surrounded by an open settlement, the *asty*. The Hellenic *polis* was probably initiated on the eastern coast of the Aegean by emigrants from the Greek mainland; either they had conquered existing settlements or established new ones and this new type of community gradually spread to the mainland, the original home of the refugees. There is hardly any doubt that the small-scale and closer landscapes of Greece furthered the foundations of small towns with a limited agricultural hinterland. But, as pointed out, this was not the only cause:

The succession of Phrygian, Lydian, and Persian conquests of the *poleis* in Anatolia proved that the area could be quite well integrated into larger realms, if the power and the will to do so were given. While the topographic factor must not be rejected, the numerical smallness of the refugee groups who settled in Ionia also affected the form in which they had to organise themselves. That the circumstances of the first foundations were somewhat extraordinary is suggested by the terminology. The "tribes" which constitute the *polis* are called *phylai,* while the language has another term to signify a tribe settled on a territory, *ethnos.* Hence, the conjecture is plausible that the *phylai* of the *poleis* were originally military units, perhaps ship companies, as they may have been formed on occasion of a transmarine migration to Anatolia.[15]

This suggestion is very interesting and pertinent; it would add another and rather utilitarian explanation to the more idealistic causes which made and kept the *polis* limited in number of

14. A. H. M. Jones. *The Greek City from Alexander to Justinian.* 1940. P. 65.
15. E. Voegelin. *Order and History.* Vol. II: *The World of the Polis.* 1957. P. 119.

inhabitants. Although the tribal institutions weakened in the course of time, the *polis* never completely lost the traces of its origin. It remained a "halfway-house" between a community of citizens united by a *conjuratio,* to follow Max Weber, in fraternities like the towns of the European Middle Ages and a tribal settlement. The citizen of the *polis* remained entangled in the tentacles of his tribal origin only half-conscious of himself as an individual and only half-awake beneath the veil of animism and illusion. His society was never split into lonely human atoms as our modern society. The tribal bond and the incompletely developed individualism prevented the growth of the *polis* into a nation-state which could come into being only when and where the atomization of society had reached an advanced stage.

CHAPTER 11

I N *THE REPUBLIC* Plato gives an interpretation of the rise of the *polis* that should warm the hearts of every rational economist. He says:

A city comes into being because individually we are not self-sufficing but have a variety of wants. Then, as men have many wants and many persons are needed to supply them, one takes a helper for one purpose and another for another; and when these partners and helpers are gathered together in one habitation the body of inhabitants is termed a state. These men give and receive in exchange because they think it is to their advantage. Our mutual needs will, it appears, lead to the formation of the state.[1]

Aristotle enlarges this one-sided explanation by his famous statement that man is by nature a political being and therefore cannot exist in solitude but needs the state to make life worth living.[2]

While the division of labor, the exchange of goods leading to the rise of merchants and shopkeepers, and the introduction of a money economy and hired labor are all stages of development familiar to liberal thinkers of the 19th and 20th centuries, the emphasis on the dominating role of the state and subordination of the individual to the state are incompatible with modern political theory, although not with the practical experience of the last decades. The Ideal State of the Greeks remained an utopia although it persisted in occupying the minds of philosophers and some statesmen. In a way each colonial expedition was at least toying with this idea and the political system of Sparta was an attempt at the practical implementation of an Ideal State. The acquisitive instinct and the profit motive appeared to Plato as utterly irreconcilable with his perfect society although it was based on slavery. If there is any excuse at all for this inconsistency, it may be found in the fact that slavery was a universal feature of the social and economic systems of antiquity and that it existed not long ago in the United States and is still in evidence today in some countries of the Middle East. Greek economy without slavery is unthinkable. On the average a well-to-do household employed three slaves and only the very wealthy had more, sometimes as many as fifty.[3] In agriculture relatively few slaves were employed due to the fact that the farms were generally small and the seasonal character of the work made it an unremunerative investment to feed slaves the whole year round. Slaves in the employ of the states were numerous as policemen, navvies, minor officials, and mine workers.

The Phoenicians, predecessors of the Greeks as traders, used silent barter as a method of exchange with primitive peoples but also had trading posts in the Nile Delta and perhaps on the coast of Asia Minor. The earliest type of trade took place without

Trade and Industry

1. II. 369 B.
2. *Politics.* 1252 B and 1253 A.
3. H. Michell. *Economics of Ancient Greece.* 1957. P. 161.

487

direct contact on neutral ground where a sacred truce protected both parties. This sacred character of the market persisted in one form or the other for thousands of years, not only in primitive societies but also in highly advanced civilizations. It was still alive in the Middle Ages as the *Marktfrieden,* the peace of the market, or as in Russia where sometimes the churches served as storehouses and where the goods were weighed in the aisles; or in certain privileges of the places where markets were held. A further step was in the establishment of a fortified post near a town and at a good landing place where a warehouse could be built—for instance, the "Milesian Fort" in Egypt which enjoyed "some measure of extraterritorial rights."[4] However, it is certainly a misreading of historical facts to regard trade as the primary stimulus of Greek colonization.

What attracted the Greek pioneers to a new life overseas was the possibility of acquiring in the colonies land which they were denied at home. The growth of population and the repeated subdivision of the family plots had made the existence of many farmers precarious. In the new settlements there was at least a fair chance to begin afresh and to hope that the struggle for survival would be successful. Two types of colonial enterprises served as safety valves: purely agricultural colonies, called *apoikiai,* founded by free associations of landless peasants or people who needed an outlet for their energies and spirit of adventure; and systematically planned *poleis* called *cleruchies,* under the direct guidance of a mother city, as already mentioned, located at politically and commercially strategic points on which trade, especially in grain and timber, and garrisons could be based. Although both colonization and trade were intimately related to each other, there was no clearly formulated colonial or commercial policy. Greek colonies often developed into trading centers but they were not founded as such except in rare cases. They became trading colonies if they were planted on sites which favored commerce or which had been trading posts before.

Gradually the commercial activities increased and the Peiraieus and other Greek ports had a fairly considerable overseas trade. Athens was not a big industrial center receiving large quantities of raw materials and exporting finished goods. After the Persian Wars, her main exports were olive oil, wool, wine, and marble; her principal imports consisted of grain and timber. She was essentially an *entrepôt* like other places, for instance, Aegina, Corinth, and Naucratis in Egypt. The great commercial importance of Miletus was to a considerable degree the direct result of the favorable position at the mouth of the Maeander which was navigable for 150 miles inland. It was protected by islands and was a natural *entrepôt* for the coastal trade, the in-

4. *Ibid.,* p. 212.

terior of Asia Minor, the Black Sea, and Egypt. The river plain with its wheat fields, the hills with vineyards and orchards and pastures for cattle, and the sheep which delivered the excellent Milesian wool were commercial assets of the greatest value. The trade of Miletus penetrated in the north far inland to Rumania and South Russia and in the south to Egypt.[5]

Greece did not have what today are called heavy industries. The industrial activities, which came nearest to this definition, were mining and shipbuilding. The Greeks were superior artists and artisans in some fields, but not skilled craftsmen. Their industries worked on a small scale and were only of secondary importance to the growth of the cities. Trade—that is, grain trade—had but an indirect influence on the rise of the *poleis* inasmuch as it made them more independent of the local food supply, which as the sole source would have quite seriously limited their growth. The main industries of leatherworking, pottery, spinning, and weaving, of the manufacture of clothing, and the auxiliary activities of winegrowing, production of olive-oil and foodstuffs, carpentry, building, and the metal trades could all be operated with a relatively small number of workers, the more so as quite a number of them were carried on as home industries. The exchange of these goods for overseas imports proceeded over four main routes radiating from Athens and Corinth: past the coasts of Macedonia and Thrace to the Dardanelles and Bosphorus into the Black Sea; via Crete to Egypt and thence to Cyprus and Rhodes; to the coasts of the Adriatic through the Gulf of Corinth; and over the Isthmus of Corinth to Sicily, the west coast of Italy, Gaul, and Spain. Overland trade was insignificant for two reasons: water-borne transport was cheaper and the roads were bad.

All in all, neither trade nor industries were of the same importance in the development of cities as in medieval Europe or in China or India, to name but a few examples. This is not to say that they did not influence the physical and social structure of the *poleis*; but it does mean that essentially the Greek cities remained limited in size. Their inner coherence and relatively balanced composition was not disrupted by industrial or commercial expansion as in the later periods of European history. When the pressure of population grew too strong, the solution was the foundation of a new city but not the absorption of the surplus population into industry. If and when industries and commerce increased, this increase remained within manageable limits, except perhaps at Athens.

It has been explained that everything "unlimited" was contrary to the essence of Greek feeling and thinking—it was "evil." Certainly this deep-rooted dislike of excessive expansion and the similarly outspoken passion for smallness and limitation is what

5. *Ibid.*, pp. 240 ff.

worked against the uncontrollable growth of the cities through industrial and commercial expansion, quite apart from certain practical considerations and factors inherent in the technical capacity of the period. The artisans and craftsmen processed the raw materials that were given them. They worked for a customer and only then for the market. Living place and working place were under the same roof; their houses huddled together and the built-up residential area was small. Production for a surplus economy was of secondary importance. The *polis* was and remained above all a consumers' association. Hence the *polis* did not know an industrial producers' policy, and hence also the insignificant role of the guilds and, above all, the absence for a long time of expansive forces which would upset the ideal of a static balance, however different the reality may have been. In general the Greek way of life was simple and even severe; it did not demand large industries to supply the necessities of life or innumerable luxury goods. Ancient Greece remained agricultural throughout her history. She has never become—not even today—an industrial country.

Let us examine, though only in a very condensed and simplified survey, the main sequence of transformations through which the material culture of the Greeks—that is, their industrial development—has passed and how Greek society responded to the stimuli of environment and ideologies. The barbarian tribes, probably Greek-speaking Indo-Europeans who invaded Mainland Greece about 1800 B.C., brought with them their own traditions. They dislodged or subjugated the early inhabitants and merged their own agricultural and industrial customs with those of the indigenous peoples.[6] They restored the ancient townships and set about to increase the manufacture of armaments. Pottery became a specialized industry. From 1600 B.C. on numerous products and techniques were introduced to Greece from Crete. The old villages grew into citadels where the war lords stored the wealth which they had plundered or bartered from the Minoans who could not compete with their superior weapons. The next step was to bring Minoan craftsmen, by persuasion or force, to their courts. Thus a surplus wealth accumulated and Minoan techniques were transferred to the mainland. In the end Crete was conquered and the Mycenaean culture replaced the Minoan civilization.

The fortified castles, the "cities," of the rulers of these semi-barbarous and militaristic tribes were small but almost impregnable strongpoints dominating the surrounding country. Mycenae, the capital, covered only 11 acres but the population must have considerably increased by this time, judging from the cemeteries in the hillsides. Life in these "fortress-cities" was very dif-

6. V. G. Childe. *What Happened in History*. 1952. P. 169. Also for the following.

ferent from the "mercurial" temper and the bustle in the wall-less (open) palace and port of Knossos. The might of the rulers was based on and derived from the new type of weapons which were far superior to anything their adversaries or their own people could pit against them. The surplus wealth which the princes had acquired was invested in luxury goods; it was not used in public works. But this wealth remained within moderate proportions: the princes were after all petty rulers of poor valleys and could hardly aspire to the profits the merchants could make by trade in the raw materials needed for armaments and other goods.

After 1400 B.C. Mycenaean trade expanded and especially pottery was exported in quantity to Troy, Asia Minor, Syria, Palestine, Egypt, Sicily, and Southern Italy. It was accompanied by migrations of Mycenaean folk in search of a fuller life which the narrow world of the Mainland valleys and small citadels could not offer. In the 14th and 13th centuries Mycenaean society became poorer and workmanship declined. The luxury industries of the princes and nobles became redundant. Iron swords replaced the expensive bronze rapiers. The Mycenaean cities reverted to what they had been before—more-or-less self-sufficient villages. But certain crafts and skills survived. However slowly and precariously, the Greeks of the Iron Age could build the foundations for their Classical period on the remnants of the preceding civilization.

The barbarians had not demolished the whole Minoan-Mycenaean edifice. In fact, here as everywhere, the invasions merely gave the final push to fabrics already tottering through internal decay. In the most favourable instances, particularly in Greece itself, they just swept away top-heavy superstructures to make room for more progressive additions to a fundamentally healthy building. The substantial achievements of the Bronze Age were on the whole saved. By 1000 B.C. recovery was beginning. The losses were more than made up in the next five centuries.[7]

The highly developed crafts, which had flourished in the Mycenaean economy, had disappeared. The citadels of the rulers, where surplus wealth had been accumulated, had been abandoned. The cities that survived were virtually villages, different only inasmuch as the presence of potters, smiths, and a few other craftsmen added a professional element to the rural structure of their society. They were almost self-sufficient; trade was practically nonexistent. The majority of their inhabitants lived by subsistence agriculture and fishing. The scarcity of land and the growing population drove the landless peasants overseas to join the pioneer settlers in the new colonies. These new foundations were a welcome market for the trade and industry of the home-

7. V. G. Childe, *op. cit.*, p. 187.

land and soon offered an outlet other than emigration for the younger sons of the farmers.

This rebirth of industrial activities which began in the eighth century gained momentum in the seventh century. At the beginning Aegina and Corinth were probably leading in the mass production and export of cheap commodities; then followed Athens and other coastal towns. Pottery was the main export but other activities must also have contributed to the increasing commerce, and by the sixth century numerous small farmers were able to turn from subsistence farming to specialized cultivation—especially of vines and olive trees. This reduction of the area under the plow forced the cities to import grain in increasing quantities. It has been estimated that by the fourth century the volume of grain imports into Attica was four times the home production.[8] This made it possible to support a population which was considerably larger than the number that could have been supplied by their own home production of foodstuffs. The population of Athens in the fifth century had increased to about 300,000. Athens was not the only city to profit from this development. In the sixth century Samos, for instance, covered within its walls an area of about 400 acres, with large open spaces. Miletus, which was replanned in 480 B.C., covered 222 acres, including 52 with parks and gardens. Selinus, whose *acropolis* enclosed originally only about 21 acres, was extended in the sixth century to over 48 acres. Megara Hyblaea, on the east coast of Sicily, spread over 150 acres, and Syracuse was still larger.

The goods which paid for the imports of foodstuffs were produced in small and independent workshops with only a small number of workers and a certain degree of specialization of labor. However, these small industries could not absorb the surplus rural population. The wealth accruing in the cities from these industries was used to employ slaves. Although the number of slaves in industry should not be overestimated—in Athens, for instance, with the largest and most numerous industrial enterprises, there were about 115,000 slaves in the fifth century—slavery operated against the expansion of industry. The wages of the slaves were just enough for their bare existence; their purchasing power was virtually nil and therefore did not contribute to an expanding economy. Moreover, slave labor had a degrading effect on industry. Industrialists preferred to invest their profits in farming and money lending instead of plowing them back into industry. Gordon Childe makes the further pertinent remark:

The Greek "industrial cities" were not only cleft internally into contending classes, but were also opposed to one another as autonomous

8. *Ibid.*, p. 198.

States continually dissipating real wealth in internecine wars that benefited only the slave-dealers. It is this state of perpetual internecine warfare, itself partly due to the class struggle (in as much as slavery prevented the productive employment of surplus population) and in turn aggravating it (by replenishing the slave-market), that appears in history as the occasion for the ruin of the classical economy and the collapse of the policy it supported.[9]

The rising merchant class contended with the landed nobles for the power in the city-states. It invaded the higher executive offices. The poorer classes got more and more restless demanding a voice in the conduct of their *polis*. Gradually they succeeded, at times with the help and at others without the support of men motivated by personal ambition or by concern for the general welfare. These self-styled leaders, called tyrants, had mostly made their fortune from commerce or industry or financial transactions, and often spent great amounts of their wealth on public works and new industries. Most were overthrown by democratic upheavals. For as Descartes expressed it more than two millennia later: "It is senseless, if one single person plans to reform a State by changing everything down to the foundations and overthrows it only to rebuild it again." When democracy was finally established the old clans lost their political influence, the municipal offices were thrown open to all full citizens, and to enable them to fulfil their new functions efficiently they received a compensation for their work in the public interest. Thus democracy and economy were closely interrelated and all citizens could take an active part in the management of their own affairs. However, there were serious lacunae in the setup of this democratic government by the people and for the people. Women were excluded and remained secluded; and resident aliens were not allowed to share the new democratic privileges. The time needed for the political activities was largely gained at the expense of women, aliens, and slaves who had to do the work for the full citizens of the *polis*. They were the ruling class excluding the influence of all other inhabitants. After 450 B.C. the hitherto expanding market began to contract and the antagonism between the poor and the rich grew more violent adding to the interstate conflicts internal strife and an intensification of economic contradictions.

A major economic and social crisis was averted, at least partly, by the conquests of Alexander the Great. New markets and new fields for colonization created new opportunities and a diversion from internal conflicts. Industry was given a fresh outlet and a new stimulus; trade prospered aided by the unification of large territories, currency reforms, and improvement of navigation. Transport by land and sea became faster and more efficient. And just as the raw materials and manufactured goods spread over

9. *Ibid.*, p. 201.

ever-widening areas, persons of all races became more mobile, carrying their customs and experiences to other lands. Not only material goods but also ideas, scientific and technical discoveries, and philosophical insights flowed through these new channels of intercourse. The main beneficiaries from this expanding economy were the middle class, the landowners, and tenant farmers, who employed other people for cultivating their land; the owners of workshops and shops, ships and warehouses; the moneylenders and the middlemen who hired slaves or workers. The small farms worked by peasants were gradually giving way to large capitalistic farms, and public works were executed by contractors instead of by individual craftsmen and artisans. In all spheres the scale of enterprise was widening and an international economy replaced the parochial one of the city-states. And even something like a universal brotherhood of men, though but an isolated flight into the rarefied atmosphere of uncompromising morality, saw the light of day. An ordinance of a shrine to Agdistis at Philadelphia declared:

Let men and women, slave and free, coming into this shrine swear by all the gods that they will not deliberately plan any evil guile or baleful poison against any man or woman; that they will neither turn to nor recommend to others nor have a hand in love-charms, abortives or contraceptives or doing lottery or murder; that they will steal nothing but be well-disposed towards this house.[10]

No distinction between men and women, between free and slaves! All are equal—at least within this temple, for in reality they were not, else there would have been no need to mention it.

Slavery remained an essential institution of a society that could not know better. It worked against applied science, for the large reservoir of manpower made labor-saving devices unattractive—prerevolutionary China is another example—and stabilized the internal purchasing power on a very low level. By 200 B.C. it was obvious that the classical economy was unable to cope with the ever-increasing complexity of the social and economic problems. The population of old Greece declined and families were deliberately kept small by abortion and infanticide. Internecine wars between the innumerable units of the Hellenistic world further reduced the population, and external wars aggravated the general lawlessness. Adventurers, robbers, and pirates were encouraged by the states

to nest in the disputed frontier zones. The multiplication of these parasites was only a symbol of social disorders which denied an adequate livelihood to peaceable peasants and artisans and extolled vio-

10. Quoted after V. G. Childe, *op. cit.*, p. 258.

494

lence and slaughter in the name of patriotism as the highest expression of manly virtue.[11]

But "patriotism is not enough," even if directed toward better ends. The economic anomalies inherent in the coexistence of numerous and small political units made them easy prey for Roman determination and ruthlessness. Greece and most of Alexander's empire were reduced to the status of dependent provinces. A new chapter was opened in which Greece played but a subordinate role.

11. *Ibid.*, p. 259.

CHAPTER 12

The Polis

RURAL AND URBAN SETTLEMENT of a region are interdependent. The one cannot be understood without the other. This holds good also for the city-states which comprised the city proper and the surrounding countryside. Unfortunately our knowledge of the distribution of settlement of the rural population in ancient Greece is rather incomplete. No data are available apart from almost meaningless references either so general or so vague that they cannot serve as a basis for an exposition of the physical structure of the rural settlement that would not be open to serious criticism. Why this is so is difficult to say. It may result partly from the ephemeral nature of the rural buildings which were built of short-lived and therefore easily perishable material—this applies also to the houses of the city dwellers although, in this case, the street plan and parts of isolated buildings which often survived allow us to draw certain conclusions as to their size, layout, and character—and partly from the preoccupation of scholars and archeologists with the *polis* proper and their all too common misapprehension of the fact that the physical structure of a village is a reliable guide to the understanding of its social and economic fabric.

Whatever the reasons for this deplorable lack of information, the fact remains that the land question and the way in which the peasants of ancient Greece had distributed and built their settlements were of paramount importance to the fate of the *polis*. It is therefore appropriate to summarize the little we know that is relevant in this particular connection before we turn to the description of the cities, of their layout, size, internal arrangement, and transformations.

As everywhere and at all times the land question was an important political factor. Its satisfactory or unsatisfactory solution depended as much on social conditions as on the physical structure of the country. How an ideal city-state should be developed has been set out by Plato in the *Laws* (V. 745):

In the first place, the city is to be located as nearly as possible in the centre of the territory. . . . Next, the whole area, including the city, is to be divided into twelve portions, starting from an enclosed sanctuary of Hestia, Zeus, and Athena, which shall be called Acropolis. These portions are to be equal and adjusted in extent to the quality of the soil. Altogether 5,040 holdings are to be described, and each of them is to be divided into two parts, one in the city, the other at a distance. . . . The citizens themselves shall then be divided into twelve groups.

The lots were held by the heads of families belonging to the same tribe. This ideal distribution was constructed on actually existing procedures and to that extent it may give an indication of how the land of a city was organized. From other sources it is evident that the holdings in the countryside were subdivided into two parts to be cultivated in alternate years. It is probable that crop rotation did not exist before the fourth century. The family estate was owned in perpetuity by the family descending from one of the founders of the *polis*. Of course, the family land was subdivided in the course of time but this corresponded to the simultaneous division of the family itself. But the principle remained that the land could not be disposed of; that "the land owns the man, or rather the group of men, who dwell on it. . . . The land and the dwellers on it are one."[1] There were exceptions to this rule: farms changed hands but this transfer was legally subordinate to the inheritance by kinship.[2] "In developed Greek law . . . private, individual property existed, and a man could in very large measure do as he liked with his own."[3] But property could not be transferred to a daughter. The tendency was to keep the land of the family or the clan indivisible.

If we look at the *Iliad* and *Odyssey* we find the land tenure to have been somewhat as follows. The people, under their king or baron, lived in a *polis*, a word which later meant "city," but in Homer is often quite a small place. Small or large, it was essentially a group of houses, generally surrounded by a wall, if not always, and normally in a position naturally strong. All around it lay fields and meadows, cultivated by the citizens or used for the pastures of their beasts. But if we look for the owners of these fields, we find that generally they have no individual owner . . . but that some system existed by which strips of the land were assigned to various members of the community, not, apparently, as their property, but for them to plough and reap, and presumably enjoy the fruits of, until a re-division took place.[4]

The underlying principle was to preserve the essential idea which had given rise to the city-state: that it had originated in a union of joint families. Its synoicism was founded on the individual *oikoi* as the social cells of the community. These ideas were clearly illustrated by the procedure applied in new colonies. The land was equally divided into as many plots as there were colonists to be settled and then parcelled out by lot. Although it is still an open question, it is probable that something like a village community as we know it from Central Europe developed on this basis of equal shares for all, and that the villages thus constituted were surrounded by open-field systems consisting of strips. And a further tentative conclusion may be drawn from this first assumption: the peasants lived in villages, not in isolated farms in the middle of their holdings as a division of the land equal in size and quality was impossible. That this is a reasonable probability may be deduced from the character of the early cities.

1. H. J. Rose. Primitive Culture in Greece. 1925. P. 174.
2. G. D. Thomson. *Studies in Ancient Greek Society.* 1949. P. 314 and *passim.*
3. H. J. Rose, *op. cit.,* p. 175.
4. *Ibid.,* pp. 179-80.

Even as late as in the time of Thucydides—he was born about 460 B.C.—the city consisted of a number of villages which possessed a certain degree of social and economic homogeneity, that is, at least the rudiments of a community.

How the villages were laid out and how their houses were grouped, whether they were mainly compact or street villages, we do not know. We are slightly better informed about the crops raised and for what animals pastures were used in the different landscapes of ancient Greece. But these features of rural life are outside the scope of city planning. We have also a certain amount of data on irrigation from which we can gather, for example, that terrace agriculture was applied at a fairly early date for vineyards and gardens, thus extending the crop area and helping to conserve the water supply.[5] The embanking of rivers for flood control was known to and practiced by the Greeks of the Homeric Age. The draining of the swamps was another method of enlarging the cultivable area. Reclamation schemes—for instance, in Boeotia—date back to legendary times. The reclamation of Lake Copais has already been mentioned. In this connection it may be relevant to mention Plato's description of how the citizens of his model republic built aqueducts to irrigate their outlying gardens[6] and conserve the water supply and dammed the mountain torrents so that the water "might produce streams and fountains for the fields below them and for all places, and thus cause the driest spots to possess water plentiful and good."[7]

It is clear, however, from what we do know of agriculture in ancient Greece that the Greek farmers adapted themselves successfully to the difficult conditions of their country. For instance, recent investigations in Attica in the coastal plain south of Athens have revealed the remains of ancient field systems consisting of terraces and boundary walls.[8] These fields adjoined the sites of ancient demes and were spaced at about equal intervals. As far as the investigations have shown, the quality of the terracing can easily equal that of modern times. But with all their efforts and dexterity, they could not meet the food requirements of the growing population. Emigration was therefore the obvious solution. This movement, coupled with the need to relieve unemployment at home and the attraction which the opening up and conquest of new territories offered, started the Greeks on the road to colonization and scattered them over the whole of the Mediterranean world. The new colonies imitated the structure of the mother cities and spread Greek culture far beyond the boundaries of the narrow limits of the Aegaean.

It would have been desirable to give a comprehensive description of the structure of rural settlement in ancient Greece as has been done for other countries and to show the interaction of village and town, their interdependent distribution, and the

5. E. C. Semple. *The Geography of the Mediterranean Region.* Pp. 440 ff.
6. *Critias.* XIII.
7. *Laws.* VI. 761.
8. J. Bradford. "Fieldwork on Aerial Discoveries in Attica and Rhodes. Part II. Ancient Field Systems on Mt. Hymettos, near Athens," *The Antiquaries Journal,* Vol. XXXVI. Nos. 3-4. 1956. P. 172.

mutual influence on their origin and development from early times onward. The history of rural settlement in ancient Greece has yet to be written, not only in terms of agrarian reforms or methods of cultivation or the relation of class, tribe, and state but also in relation to the villages, their dependence on the cities, and on the causes and changes that made them what they were and placed them where they were. As this is a history of city development, such a task lies beyond our present scope and must be left to others. It should prove a fascinating subject.

The *foundation* of the *polis* was a religious act.[9] Life and religion in antiquity were inseparable. This is common knowledge but this general statement begs another and more pertinent question: What were the origins of the sacred ritual without which the Greeks, like other ancient peoples, would never think of founding a city? The *polis* was an association of families, of phratries, groups of families, and of a tribe, none of which was an administrative division but an integral element of the next higher unit. Further, each group existed before the *polis* came into being, the development of society reflecting the subsequent stages of the amalgamation of these individual groups and of the widening and uniting sphere of religion. In the small and primitive society of early antiquity every family worshipped its own gods. When several families joined in a group (phratry), they also united in reverence to a divinity common to the whole group without giving up their family deity. The same process was repeated on a larger scale when phratries combined to form a tribe. Tribe, family, and phratry were independent units, each with its particular god; once they were formed they did not admit new members.

But just as several phratries were united in a tribe, several tribes might associate together, on condition that the religion of each should be respected. The day on which this alliance took place the city existed. . . . The tribes that united to form a city never failed to light a sacred fire, and to adopt a common religion."[10]

Plutarch describes how at the beginning Attica was divided by families.[11] Then no city existed but each family lived independently as a closed group and had its own religion. Gradually they formed larger groups—for instance, the four villages of Marathon which worshipped the Delphian Apollo after their unification, or the people of Peiraieus and two neighboring places which erected a temple to Hercules. In the course of the centuries the numerous little groups grew together into fewer and larger associations until Theseus finally succeeded in uniting them into one city which recognized Athene Polias as their common divinity.

9. R. Martin. *L'Urbanisme dans la Grèce Antique.* 1956. Pp. 38-44. For a detailed description of regulations for the practical layout,, etc., of cities see *ibid.,* pp. 57-72.

10. N. D. Fustel de Coulanges. *The Ancient City.* 1956. P. 127. *Passim.*

11. *Theseus.* 13.

What was the origin of the sacred fire which was lighted at the formation of a city? It was a custom that had grown from the sacred duty of every family to have on its house altar an "eternal fire" which was never allowed to go out as long as the family was alive. The sacred fire was the very real symbol of the living religion of the family and this early religion was an individual worship that was observed in the house of the family, not in a temple. It was a jealously guarded private property which had to be surrounded by an enclosure around the hearth. Whatever this enclosure was—a hedge, a wall of stone or one of wood—"it marked the limit which separated the domain of one sacred fire from that of another."[12] But the fire was not only the religious, it was also the symbol of the property right of the family. From this separated and sacred enclosure Fustel de Coulanges derives a theory which is attractive but not fully supported by factual evidence—although it may be correct for the earlier periods of Greek history. He relates how at the beginning, when the people still lived in the country, the sacred enclosure encompassed the house and the fields and how the houses moved nearer together when the tribes built cities. Then the sacred enclosure became smaller and its boundary would be marked by a low wall, a ditch, a furrow, or a mere open space. But never would two houses be contiguous—that is, built without a space between, as a party wall was "supposed to be an impossible thing." In this connection he mentions, to reinforce his argument, that at Rome "the law fixed two feet and a half as the width of the free space, which was always to separate two houses, and this space was consecrated to 'the god of the enclosure.'" This would have an interesting bearing on the internal layout of the early cities and also be a plausible illustration of the tendency, often followed by rural people on first moving into a city, to retain their old habit of separate buildings.[13]

Fustel de Coulanges stresses the point—with full justification—that according to the Greeks "the sacred fire taught men to build houses." He could have gone further and stated not only implicitly but explicitly that the sacred fire taught men to build cities, for the sacred fire was a powerful agent in making man sedentary and attaching him to the spot where the cult of his ancestors had taken root. From this first step of a self-contained existence to the emergence of the gregarious spirit in ever-growing intensity was an all-too-human impulse which could not be diverted or arrested. It was an irresistible process that drew the Greek tribes together in cities. Like other peoples of antiquity they were convinced that their society was the will of the Gods. They were not aware of the man-made nature of their gods, of the fact that they projected their own social ideas onto the gods.

500

12. N. D. Fustel de Coulanges, *op. cit.*, pp. 62-63.
13. See p. 422.

As Bernard Shaw put it, "we are not in the hands of God but God is in our hands." The widening circles of a common religiosity drove men together to share in the common protection by and the common worship of the same divinity.

This longing for a communal religious experience was one of the strongest motives in the formation of the Greek cities, and it was ripe for fulfillment once agriculture had developed sufficiently to free enough people from cultivation so that they could devote their full time to other professions. It was something entirely different from the development of the towns of the Middle Ages which derived their *raison d'être* primarily from economic reasons, the need for protection, and the longing for freedom. This then was the essence of the nature of the formation of Greek cities. It was the principle on which later cities were founded and modeled. It could not always be applied in this ideal form. But basically it never disappeared completely and was transferred from the mother city to its colonies. Wherever a new social organization was established, it was consecrated by sacrifices, religious festivals, and the revival of time-honored traditions.

The foundation of a Greek city was, therefore, always a religious ritual. The will of the divinity should determine its site. Consequently, the Greeks turned to the Oracle of Delphi or, when the Pythia just happened to be more favorably disposed toward another tribe—for example, when the Messenians were looking for a site where they could build a city after their return to the Peloponnesus—they were content with divinatory dreams that would conveniently come to a priest or another suitable person. When the site was fixed with the help of the gods, the ritual concentrated on entreating them to make the new city their residence. The founders believed that their ritual would "attach the sacred beings to the soil which they themselves were going to occupy, and could shut them up within the enclosure which they themselves were about to trace."[14] This ceremony was so important that every city at least pretended to know its divine or semi-divine founder and the day and year of its foundation, even though this event had to be dated back to legendary times. The same religious rituals were observed when an existing city was reoccupied by colonists or conquerors. In all these cases the newcomers lighted their own sacred fires. Mortal men were the agents who had fulfilled the will of the gods who were the actual founders of the cities and lived in them eternally.

In theory the inhabitants could never relinquish their city, for it was the permanent residence of the gods and it was for this reason that all cities were to the Greeks, as to Romans, eternal. However, this confident belief did not prevent the all-too-human

14. *Ibid.,* p. 140.

shortcomings from bringing misfortune to a city. When this had become too obvious and wickedness threatened the community, the early Greeks tried to get rid of these unpleasant by-products of city life by using a scapegoat. Thus, at Athens they annually chose an ugly man and woman, increased their magical potency in certain ritual ceremonies, and drove them out of the city. It seems that they pretended to burn them alive, though this appears to have been more a symbolic than a real sacrifice. Or at Massilia where a criminal was kept for a year at public expense and then put to death.[15] A further consequence of this mutual contract between the gods and men was the supremacy of the city, of the state, over its individual members. State and religion were one and this double pressure deprived the citizens of individual liberty; it led to interference in the most intimate affairs of private life. At Athens and Sparta men were forbidden to remain single or were punished if they married late. They were not allowed to drink pure wine—for instance, at Locri; regulations were issued which prescribed the kind of attire or the headdress of women or the number of dresses women could take with them on a journey, this latter regulated by law at Athens; or men were not permitted to shave their beards as at Rhodes.[16] The city was omnipotent and not a place of freedom. Under whatever form of government the citizens of the *polis* lived, individual freedom did not exist, not even the idea of it—if certain political rights such as freedom at the ballot box or the admission to public offices are not regarded as synonymous with liberty. This overestimation of society and the consequent underestimation of the rights and aspirations of its individual members was largely due, as Fustel de Coulanges justifiably concluded, "to the sacred and religious character with which society was clothed in the beginning."

15. H. J. Rose, *op. cit.*, p. 150.
16. Fustel de Coulanges, op. cit., p. 220.

CHAPTER 13

GREEK CITY PLANNING had no lasting effect upon the work of future generations. Unlike Greek architecture, it was but an episode in the long history of art. Why this is so has been explained earlier. Here it may suffice to repeat that Greek cities did not and could not hand on to posterity a living tradition out of which a new and yet related form of city building could grow. Theirs was a conception too limited, too static, and above all too lacking in awareness of the creative power of space and space relations as the most formative element of city planning. As we have seen, no word for "space" existed in the Greek language. Greek artists never felt tempted to leave the sphere of the limited, to explore infinity; they did not apprehend the exciting possibilities which the symbolic representation of unlimited space could offer and which for later periods, especially for the Baroque, were the lifeblood of their artistic achievements. They could not be aware of these possibilities, for their deepest conviction was "what is, is; what is not, is not." This principle enunciated by Parmenides dominated the mind and the work of all Greek artists, including city planners. It made that "what is not" unthinkable and "what is" indivisible and continuous. It was diametrically opposite to Lao-Tse's dictum, "it is on the space where there is nothing that the utility of the house depends."

For the Greek artist the ideal medium of expression was sculpture, and therefore all his works were conceived in this spirit. The world of solid volumes, of tactile experience, was his sphere of creativity; not the world of immaterial space. It has been rightly observed that:

Time and space, to us the symbols of infinity, were barred by true classic style, sometimes by means of subtle niceties of composition, more often by obvious arrangement. In classic relief the terminal figures ordinarily turn inward toward the centre, avoiding suggestion of continuity to right or left; extension in depth is likewise cancelled by a neutral background.[1]

Thus we have two essential properties of Greek city planning: its plastic nature and the use of contrasting—that is, projecting and receding—volumes as solid means to express this nature; and the deliberate limitation, the determined containment of the intervals between the sculpture-buildings. Like the Greek temple, which stands as a sculpture in the landscape and whose interior is "spaceless," the city is an agglomeration of sculptures. This is its artistic essence. The "spacelessness" of the Greek temple is the symbol of this sculpturelike character: the *cella* is very small; it is a purely "utilitarian" room for the statue of the god, not a place for processions or the congregation of people; the early two-nave *cellae* and their consequent partition along the middle axis is

1. C. R. Morey. *Medieval Art.* 1942. Pp. 10-11.

Frontiers of Greek City Planning

proof enough that the creation of an architectural space was not a problem which bothered the Greek architects.

Thus the Greek city was an assemblage of individual elements, of block units whose number could be increased *ad libitum* by external addition. But this was not done; the idea of the *polis* forbade it. There was no main axis on which the principal buildings could have been focused; and even if there was a main street —for instance, at Selinus and Priene—the public squares and buildings were not organically related to it nor to the plan as a whole. It is illuminating, in this connection, to study the reconstructions of ancient Greek cities at Delphi or Priene: a jumble of buildings without any obvious relation to each other or to the squares and streets. The element of planning was the block unit, and just as expansion in general proceeded by the foundation of new towns repeating the pattern of the old *polis,* the internal layout of the *polis* rested on the addition of adjacent block units so long as the available area permitted it. This was a process of accretion rather than an organic extension; it strongly resembled the unconcerned behavior of a child who puts his blocks together to build a toy town without attaching any meaning to the space between them. The streets in a Greek city do not exist as space *sui generis*; they have no spatial significance. They are, as previously observed, intervals left over between the solid mass of the buildings. The result—to use once more a comparison which may help to clarify the character of the relationship between streets and houses—is something like a halfway house between the conception and function of the streets and squares and the *patios* and *plazas mayores,* the open-air interiors of Spain, and the plazas and streets of the *pueblos* of the American Indians, which like forgotten residues between the projecting and receding volumes of the houses, also resemble sculptures.

The main and general principles of Greek city planning are: limitation; "spacelessness"; inorganic internal arrangement; accretion. Neither together nor individually were these principles stimulating enough to be handed down to posterity as inspiring ideas. It is extremely difficult to decide whether Greek cities were beautiful or dull. It is more likely that they were rather nondescript in general but attractive in detail, a quality they share with other cities. Their contribution to the art of city planning is much less than that of other epochs or other countries. They suffer from the doubtful glorification which unthinking enthusiasts have bestowed upon them and from the superficial inclination to believe that a few good public buildings decide the quality of a city as a whole. However, despite our insufficient knowledge, certain basic principles of Greek city planning are evident. It is against this background that the internal arrangement of the Greek cities will have to be judged.

In neolithic times small settlements were dispersed all over the country. As usual and characteristic of this period they preferred elevated sites with a sufficient water supply and surrounded by fertile land. These isolated and open communities, which came into existence at about the end of the fourth and lasted to the middle of the third millennium B.C., were conquered and destroyed by invading tribes. New and fortified strongpoints arose on the old sites from the end of the first period to 2200 B.C. The center of these settlements was the *acropolis*, the fortified citadel, protected by several concentric walls in dry masonry "behind which the defenders stood on artificially raised causeways with aptly distributed and constructed entrance-passages of a width of only 0.85 to 1.10 meters."[2] The houses were situated outside this stronghold which served as a refuge in times of danger for the population. The same arrangement is known from other countries—for example, the castles of the *daimyos* of Japan which were also surrounded by the open settlements of their retainers and the common people; or villages in Spain which clustered around a castle on a hill; or the rural communities under the protection of a *Königsburg* in Germany. The houses between the second and third enclosure in the plan of Dimini and between the first and second wall were occupied by the immediate retainers of the chieftain, who lived within the innermost part of the citadel. The open space in front of his *megaron* was the center of the social and political life of the settlement.

In some cases hitherto isolated and dispersed settlements united, provided they were near enough to form a loose conglomeration. This happened, for example, at Marathon and Sparta. Gradually the most important and most favorably situated village assumed the function of the administrative center and of the capital of these village communities. It was mostly located at the foot of a hill and protected by an *acropolis*. In time administrative and religious buildings were erected within its precincts. Here the inhabitants of all the villages that formed the union assembled to discuss matters of common concern. The best-known example of this synoicism is Athens. It was a loose confederation of small sovereignties under the overlordship of Athens. The individual members which joined this union, either voluntarily or by force, retained their identity and political organization for a shorter or longer period but their inhabitants became citizens of Athens which was, at least at the beginning of this development, neither the head of a league of more-or-less independent communities nor a city ruling over other subject

2. A. Kriesis. "Ancient Greek Town Building," *Proceedings of the Second International Congress of Classical Studies, Copenhagen, 1954.* Vol. IV, p. 30.

settlements. She was the central city of a united state and every villager of Attica had the same political rights as the people of Athens; they were no longer Attics but Athenians.[3] In later times the Athenians thought that Theseus, the legendary king, was the creator of this union. This synoicism and the rise of one city to prominence grew out of the union of a number of existing settlements. The other possibility consisted in the foundation of a new city as the capital of a geographically and politically homogeneous area. In some cases, but by no means always, the principal community was walled in from the beginning. This distinguished the Greek cities fundamentally from those of the European Middle Ages or from those of China. In both cases a city or a town without walls was unthinkable.

Why was this not the case in Greece? Why was defense from a fortified stronghold regarded for a considerable time as sufficient, and why was urban life identified with existence within the enclosing protection of walls? It is difficult to give an unequivocal answer to these seemingly simple questions. One explanation may be that in the earlier stages of city development the whole region of which the city was the center was regarded as the unit of defense and treated as such. This assumption may find a certain corroboration in the numerous small and isolated compartments so characteristic of the Greek landscape. Another possibility is the different relationship between city and country. In Europe a strong antagonism separated the townspeople and the country-people, while in Greece the surrounding countryside and the central city grew together into a state. This regional and political union and its spirit of a common destiny may have worked against the isolation of the city by a defensive perimeter. We should keep in mind the basically different origin, idea, and goal of Greek synoicism: it was diametrically opposite to the medieval despotic dominance of the town over the countryside. At least in its ideal conception synoicism was a union of equals with the central city as a *primus inter pares*. Therefore, it may not be too far-fetched to assume that the common defense was, in early periods and even sometimes later, an equivalent, an ideal shelter, for the physical protection by walls around the city. The ruling class in the urban communities of Greece were the nobles, the landed aristocracy, who never lost their dislike of cities and maintained their rustic spirit—an attitude that was most strongly alive in Sparta, which was never protected by walls. It is understandable in this sense that Aristotle identified the defensive system of the *acropolis* with the monarchical or oligarchic system of government, and fortified cities with democracy, and that in historical sequence walled-in cities followed open settlements.

As its name implies the market square, the principal open

3. J. B. Bury. *A History of Greece.* 1955. P. 166.

space of the medieval cities, served as the center for commercial transactions. This was its actual *raison d'être,* not the need for public meetings. The *agora,* on the other hand, was above all a place for the congregation of the citizens of the *polis* where they could meet and exchange news, where politics were made and opinions formed. It was an open-air meeting hall and *"une condition primordiale de la vie en cité"*[4] It was the indispensable attribute of the political and social union which was the essence of Greek synoicism. That the *agora* was also in many cases the market square was of secondary importance. However, there were sometimes two *agorai*—for instance, in the oligarchic cities of Thessaly, where the marketplace was reserved for trade and transport and the actual *agora,* situated at the foot of a hill, was the social and political center. This development explains why, especially in the older cities, which had grown in size and population, the ancient *agora* was often very small and could hardly accommodate the great number of citizens who took part in the general assembly. How important the *agora* was for the Greeks as the symbol of urban life and civilization can be judged from Homer's remark that "the Cyclopes have no assemblies for the making of laws, nor any settled customs, but live in hollow caverns in the mountain heights;" and, as Herodotus writes, "the Persians . . . never buy in open market, and indeed have not a single marketplace in the whole country."[5] Synoicism is therefore independent of the foundation of a new town or of the existence of fortifications; it is a social and political unification which requires as its functional instrument a place where this unification can become a reality. The *agora* is therefore identical with the *polis.* Neither can exist without the other.

Just as synoicism created but the preconditions out of which a *polis* could develop and therefore had no direct effect on its physical structure, so the *agora,* in general, had no direct influence on the layout of the *polis.* It was not the functional focal point on which the *polis* was centered or which determined the street pattern. The *agora* was a self-contained space virtually without organic or aesthetic contact with the rest of the *polis.* In this respect it was not too dissimilar from the *plazas mayores* in Spain which, in most cases, were also ruthlessly cut out of the mass of houses; or from those in the Spanish colonial towns which occupied the area of one or several block units that were not built up. The early *agorai* were irregular, a more-or-less arbitrary assemblage of isolated buildings grouped around an open space. The best-known example of this type is the *agora* of the Ceramicus at Athens. A leading idea, an over-all conception is missing. It was a combination of commercial and other buildings and of a market square and social meeting place. Other

4. G. Glotz. *La Cité Grecque.* 1928. P. 27 and *passim.*
5. Homer. *Odyssey.* IX. 112.
   Herodotus. *The Histories.* I. 153.

507

ancient *agorai* were at Lato in Crete and at Elis. About this latter Pausanias remarks (VI. 24. 2): "The *agora* of Elis is not after the fashion of the cities of Ionia . . . , it is built in the older manner, with *stoas* standing independently of one another and with streets between them." The newer type aimed at regularity and cohesion. These *agorai* were enclosed on all or almost all sides. But the relation to the area of the *polis* as a whole remained still vague and unsystematic. The *agorai* at Priene, Miletus, and Magnesia are typical examples occupying the area of two, six, and sixteen blocks respectively. The streets enter the *agorai* at the corners or merely skirt them. In general the tendency is to make the *agora* an enclosed square surrounded by colonnades. But even the later *agorai,* which with their public buildings and colonnades were complete and homogeneous elements of the *polis,* did not exert any formative influence on the city as a whole or on the pattern of the streets.

The *agora* was the most original creation of Greek city planning. It had its predecessors in other civilizations of antiquity but it never achieved the same symbolic significance with which the Greeks endowed it. The history of the *agora* is identical with the history of urbanism in Greece. The *agora* was the soul, the moral exponent, the political symbol of the *polis.* It reflected in its physical form the stages of development of Greek cities, beginning with the almost anarchic and irregular *poleis* and leading eventually to the less spontaneous but more systematic layout of the regular cities. In the archaic era the *agora,* situated at the meeting point of a number of more important streets, is assimilated, in its general form and in the arrangement of its buildings, to the irregularity of the winding and tortuous streets. In this way unity in diversity is created not through an aesthetic architectural order but merely through functional practicability. When the functions of the *agora* finally crystallized in the fifth and fourth century B.C., its more-or-less loose conglomerate of numerous details changed into a composite and organic whole and a definite type was established. It effaced the importance of the *acropolis* and became the dominating element of the layout. Its site and shape were adjusted to the street pattern, yet it remained a space *sui generis,* an insertion in the road system of the *polis,* but was never made the focal point, the *point de vue,* the perspective culmination of streets leading into it as, for example, the Piazza del Popolo at Rome or the squares in front of the palace at Karlsruhe or Mannheim. The *agora* was fitted in between the streets covering several blocks that were not used for buildings.

Le but pratique de l'agora n'est jamais oublié; la place n'est jamais traitée comme un simple enjolivement du groupement urbain.

C'est la grande leçon d'urbanisme que nous permet en définitive de formuler cette étude architecturale; très exactment intégrée à la cité, l'agora est déterminée par ce cadre avec lequel elle reste toujours en harmonie. Les développements exagérés, hors de proportions, les excroissances gigantesques qui s'accrochent à la cité comme un organisme parasite n'apparaissent qu'après la décadence de la Polis; le sens de la mesure fait place à la recherche du grandiose, mais l'histoire de l'agora grecque est terminée.[6]

The *agora* is a functional organism whose structure depends on and has been formed by the political, religious, and economic activities of the *polis*. Between about 750 and 650 B.C. the evolution of the *agora* emerges more clearly from the hitherto amorphous agglomerations of functions characteristic of a *polis* still in the early formative stage, from the confused juxtaposition of the religious and political, of the commercial and social life of its citizens. The *agora* of these periods has been defined "as the medium of community self-help,"[7] but now gradually new aspects and new values begin to give another and more distinct character: the administration of justice and the organization of the judiciary. It is through these channels that the political ferment and the disappointment and complaints of the inhabitants find their outlet and are directed into the main stream of political and religious responsibility. This development, so essential to the well-being of an urban community, enriched the formation of the *polis* and was itself stimulated by the growing clarification of the idea of the *polis* and its physical structure. It was a mutual uplifting, a conciliation of the individual and the collective will leading to Eunomy and Harmony of the community, the twin daughters of Justice. These great aims could not be attained without the help of the gods and thus the actions of men and their religious devotion merged into one grand scheme. Justice and the respect for the human rights of each citizen were the driving force behind the formation of the *polis*, and the *agora* was the symbol of this ideal. From the simple place of assembly of the *laoi*, the warriors, the militant followers of a tribal chief, the *agora* grew into the role of the creative center of the *polis*, the moral and political guardian watching over the peace, the order of life, and the well-being of the community. The double function of the *agora* as the political and religious heart of the *polis* had the immediate consequence that it was also the site of public celebrations, of games connected with funeral rites and the cult of the gods, that were for the Greeks merely another aspect of political awareness. These festivals were inspired by the myths which commemorated the foundation of the *polis*, legendary heroes, and illustrious citizens.

6. R. Martin. *Recherches sur l'Agora Grecque. Études d'Histoire et d'Architecture Urbaines.* 1951. P. 545. Also for the following.

7. R. J. Bonner and Gertrude Smith. *The Administration of Justice from Homer to Aristotle.* Vol. I. 1930. P. 26.

The architectural composition of the archaic *agora* was more complex than that of the preceding period. It expressed the growing interdependence of the functions which the formation of the *polis* engendered in its buildings, their arrangement in its general plan. But everything was still in flux, and regional influences were still too strong to permit the formulation of unifying principles that would transgress local boundaries. The close contact between the *agora* as a place of assembly and a place of religious ceremonies was especially evident where the *agora* was merely a sort of forecourt, a promenade leading to the sanctuary, for instance, at Gortyna and Dreros, Crete. In this case the political was subordinated to the religious function. It is likely that the sanctuary protected the commercial activities carried on in the *agora;* but this was of minor importance, for the market was not the origin of the *agora*. In this respect the *raison d'être* of the *agora* was fundamentally different from that of the main squares in the European towns of the Middle Ages which were market squares and nothing else in their origin and the *causa causans* of innumerable urban communities. The *agora* of the earlier *poleis* did not occupy a particular important site in the layout. Often it was merely an open space around an altar or a small temple, and more frequently the junction of several streets or the extension of one of the main roads. Only gradually did it become an independent square under the growing impact of the practical needs of the developing city. At Lato, Crete, and at Athens the first buildings were erected along a street that was progressively extended.

By the beginning of the fifth century the *polis* reached its final, classical form and with it the *agora* gained not only in complexity but also in functional clarity. After their victory over the Persians the Greeks were more than ever convinced that their political organization in small city-states was superior to any other way of life. The small limited *polis* remained their ideal and all their activities and aspirations were adapted to this self-imposed and self-contained society which, according to Plato, should be based on the *isonomia,* on the equality of the full citizens not exceeding 5,040 in numbers. But the evolution of the *polis* and the *agora* did not stop; it was a continuous process and raised new problems for which new solutions had to be found. In the classical period the economic function of the *agora* developed at the expense of the political, moral, and religious functions. It became the center of commercial transactions and with this transformation a certain specialization of the public squares within the urban area took place. This specialization was the result of the economic progress which during the sixth and fifth centuries changed the character of the social and political life of the *polis*.[8] However, the economic function of the *agora* was not its oldest and original pur-

8. R. Martin. *op. cit.*, p. 283 and *passim.*

pose. The market developed, in many cases, independent of the *agora*. It began with the *emporion, "lieu d'échange neutralisé,"* situated outside the city or at the boundary line between two groups of peoples. And just as at the *agora* the gods were often the guardians of peace and order and of honesty in commercial activities

certains emporia, comme Délos ou Calaurie, n'eurent jamais d'autre protection que celle d'un sanctuaire à caractère fédéral. En quelques cas, ils attirèrent à eux la place politique, en particulier dans les cités où un équilibre devait être recherché entre deux populations de race différente; à Halicarnasse, l'agora et le centre commercial sont au fond de la baie, entre les établissements des colons grecs et des indigènes, là où la place des échanges s'était installée, dans une zone neutre; à Samos, l'agora fut établie, pour les mêmes raisons, entre les collines occupées face à face par les Grecs et les Cariens.

In these cases the market square was independent of the *agora* and had only the name in common with it. To these external markets belonged those which were organized as centers of supply for the provision of the army during a campaign. The cities of the neighborhood preferred these extramural markets to the permanent markets within the city boundaries and treated the provision of the army as a temporary enterprise independent of the food supply for their own citizens. In general the introduction of economic functions to the *agora* proper was regarded as a degradation of the original and pure idea of the *agora*, and even where political and commercial activities existed side by side in the same place, special groups of buildings were erected for the shopkeepers, traders, and money-changers. In any case, the separation—that is, the specialization of the *agorai*—was strictly maintained in the theoretical projects for the Ideal Cities and by the philosophers of the fourth century. Plato went even further. He conceived the *agora* as a place exclusively reserved for the religious function, for the improvement of the individual. In his conception the Ideal City guarantees political success through the observance of religion. The old idea of the *agora* has disappeared: the philosophers and the true leaders of the *polis* avoid the hustle and bustle of the marketplace and all other places where people assemble.[9] His *agora* remains the center of the city but it is subordinated in importance to the *acropolis*. It is surrounded by the temples but far away from the markets which are relegated to the outside of the city. The political function of the *agora* has been forgotten. Its religious significance is paramount.

Aristotle, more realistic, restores in his Ideal City at least some of the original political and religious characteristics of the *agora* but tries to free it from the blemishes with which democ-

9. *Republic.* IV. 425d.

racy, in his opinion, has soiled it. He recognizes the importance of commerce and trade but he isolates them from the moral-religious and political aspects of communal life. According to him three focal points are essential for the urban organism: the group of sanctuaries where the judges have their meals in common; the political *agora* in close proximity reserved for the citizens and prohibited to all artisans and agriculturists, if they are not summoned by the judges;[10] and another *agora,* at a safe distance and isolated from the two other places, easily accessible from the sea and the interior for the market where financial transactions take place and the agronomists and *astynomi,* the city stewards, have their offices.[11] This distinction of the political and commercial functions in different and separated *agorai* became one of the essential principles of Hellenistic city planning till after the fourth century B.C. the political and religious symbolism of the *agora* lost its significance in proportion as the independent existence of the *polis* was absorbed into the Macedonian Empire and drawn into the rivalries of the princes and leagues. The traditional political ideas of the role of the *polis* were undermined; the *agora* was deprived of its influence as a uniting factor of the communal life, being reduced to a monumental though still privileged showpiece of the physical layout of the city.

Compared with preceding periods, city planning of the fifth century stagnated. No innovations were introduced until, at the end of the century, a new movement spread from Asia Minor to continental Greece. Its initiator or at least symbolic exponent was Hippodamos of Miletus. The foundation of Thurii (Sybaris) on the Gulf of Tarentum and the plan for Peiraieus were most probably directly influenced by him. The regular plan, based on a gridiron layout of streets, was not exceptional. The origin of this layout cannot be discussed in this connection; it would lead us too far afield. Suffice it to say that in Etruscan cities and other places in the north of Italy the same principles had been applied as in the colonial cities planted by the Greeks on the shores of the Mediterranean and especially those on the Black Sea which were founded by Miletus. It is more likely that Hippodamos and his followers were primarily propagandists, not inventors of this rather disingenuous scheme that was to be the standard pattern of virtually all colonial towns for two thousand years. In other words, it was the most obvious and easiest solution where military considerations imposed a simple and speedy solution. In any case it exerted a considerable influence on city planning and consequently on the *agora* as an essential element of the city plan. The *agora* retained its importance as a privileged square within the city but not as a principal factor of the urban organism. It remained at best a component part, a certain link in the urban

10. *Politics.* VII. XI. 1331 a, b.
11. R. Martin, *op. cit.,* p. 307.

structure, and at worst a mere showpiece. It did not determine the layout of the streets or any detail of the city. It was a space left free where a number of important buildings could be erected.

What did change was the architectural articulation of the *agora* itself. It became a closed square surrounded by colonnades, a space more or less isolated from the rest of the city. The means to achieve this effect were the *stoai,* the colonnades, not unknown to the Greek architects of preceding centuries but only now used systematically as a unifying factor that would link the individual buildings, surround and limit the *agora,* and create an open-air interior. It permitted the integration of the individual buildings and functions in one grand scheme: the assembly hall, the law courts, the sanctuaries, the altars, and even the shops that adjoined the whole complex without being unpleasantly conspicuous behind the colonnades. The *stoai* facilitated communication between the buildings and also with the other parts of the *polis.* It is easy to understand that this more rigid design could only slowly be introduced to the old cities of continental Greece with their irregular street pattern. The open-air interior of the Ionian *agorai* retained a certain openness, a certain interpenetration with the adjacent streets just as the *plaza mayor* in Spanish cities includes the immediate neighborhood and yet excludes its incongruous features. This final formation of the *agora* materialized at the very moment when the idea and the existence of the *polis* began to decline.

The citadel was in many cases the original center around which a settlement grew up. It was mostly situated at the periphery on a hill or a spur, or at a certain distance from the city, as at Corinth and Sicyon. These citadels were permanently inhabited, and were not merely places of refuge in time of danger. They were the fortified palaces of the princes which were either incorporated within the city area or left outside, yet they were not integral parts of the fortifications once the city was protected by walls. New citadels were not built within those cities where local self-government was strong enough "not to tolerate a citadel within its boundaries where the enemies of its liberty could gain a foothold."[12] The original *acropoleis* were sometimes demolished because the cities did not want to retain what was for them not only a symbol but an ever-present threat of suppression.

The prerequisite for all the changes which the citadel has experienced is the existence of a wall defending the whole inhabited area of the city. A wall means that the development of the city has reached a certain stage, that it has existed before and that its circumference

12. A. von Gerkan. *Griechische Städteanlagen.* 1924. P. 11.

has not increased substantially. . . . At the time when Greece gradually began to adopt urban ways of life, experience was totally lacking and the settlements in the cólonies grew from small beginnings by permanent influx. It is therefore unthinkable that the *poleis,* which were originally only the central organs of the political union of the state, were walled-in from the beginning. . . . The possibility and necessity of a fortification which was not based on small strongpoints alone had still to be grasped by the citizens.[13]

The course of the fortifications had no direct influence on the layout of the cities. Purely military reasons were decisive. These and the configuration of the terrain determined shape, size, and structure of the walls. These factors led in some cases to extraordinarily large fortifications—for instance, around places in Aetolia and Acarnania, and around Syracuse where they were about 16 miles long. The reason for this large extension of the walls was to render the use of heavy siege equipment difficult, if not impossible, by building the walls along almost inaccessible terrain, along ridges, gorges, or coasts where defense was easy and attack difficult. These considerations explain why flat or moderately rising sites were avoided. If this was not possible, the circumference was shortened which led to the unusual circular fortifications of Mantinea and in most other cases to rectangular, almost square forms. However, in general both types were combined since most cities were situated at the foot of a hill: the walls extended far into the hilly terrain and followed, on level land, the exact boundaries of the inhabited area without any regard for a later extension. Hilltop *poleis* were rather rare; they originated in many cases from the most ancient settlements around a citadel which had grown beyond the narrower ring of the fortifications and spread to the lower slopes. To this type belonged Assos, Neandreia, and Pergamon.[14]

Too much attention has been paid to the contrasting values of the regular and the irregular cities. We shall deal with this problem later in connection with the description of individual places. However, the following remarks may be pertinent as a general explanation of the size of the regular city whose origin is connected with the name of Hippodamos of Miletus, the city planner and political theorist. He lived in the fifth century B.C. and was strongly influenced by the scientific outlook of the Ionian philosophers, who assumed that the world can be understood and excluded "the person of the 'understander' from the rational world-picture that is to be constructed."[15] They broke away from the I-Thou relationship and moved toward an I-It relationship. They conceived the world as "devoid of all the subjective qualities, the sensorial data, from which it was built." Their theories did not find a ready acceptance but it may be sug-

13. *Ibid.,* pp. 17-18.
14. A. von Gerkan, *op. cit.,* p. 111.
15. E. Schrödinger. *Nature and the Greeks.* 1954. Pp. 51 ff.

gested that their spirit exerted a considerable influence on the practical designs of Hippodamos.

The sixth century was a most remarkable period in the history of humanity. It initiated spiritual and intellectual trends of paramount importance. Gautama Buddha was born about 560 B.C.; Lao-Tse and Confucius around 550 B.C. Thales and Anaximander, both born at Miletus, belong to the same era. Why was it that the narrow fringe of Asia Minor was the birthplace of this revolutionary school of philosophers? It was a region without the centralizing tendencies of a powerful state that are often antipathetic to free thinking. It consisted of small and independent city-states, either republics or tyrannies that did not prevent freedom of thought. Its inhabitants were seafaring intermediaries between East and West. Their trade between Asia Minor, Phoenicia, Egypt, and Greece, southern Italy and southern France was not restricted to material goods but furthered the exchange of ideas. It drew its stimulus and derived its material possibilities from practical problems.

Manufacturing devices, new techniques in handicraft, means of transport, aids to navigation, methods of laying out harbours, of erecting piers and warehouses, harnessing water supply, and so on, will be among the first things one people learns from the other. The rapid development of technical skill, which results in an intelligent people from a vital process of this kind, stirs the mind of theorizing thinkers, who will often be called upon for help in carrying out some newly learned art. If they apply themselves to abstract problems about the physical constitution of the world, their whole way of thinking will show traces of the practical origin from which it started. This is precisely what we find in the Ionian philosophers.[16]

And, we may add, in their compatriot Hippodamos. It was only natural that this political thinker and architect broke away from the irrational irregularity of Greek city planning and translated his theoretical speculations into the rational regularity of a systematic layout. It may not have been chance that he planned Peiraieus, the harbor town of Athens, an eminently practical task. It was this atmosphere, this rational search for clarity which produced the scientific attitude of the Ionian philosophers and of their follower Hippodamos, offering a much better explanation of the introduction of the gridiron plan than all the "learned" speculations of art historians and archeologists.

The relationship of streets and houses in the *polis* was always the same whether the layout was regular or irregular: the houses were the primary element and the streets may be compared to a mere residue left over between the built-up blocks. The average width of the streets was about 12 feet. Almost all cities had one or several main streets mostly running parallel to the longitudinal

16. E. Schrödinger, *op. cit.*, p. 54.

axis of the *polis*. The greater width was the only feature that distinguished them from the rest. The principal street of Peiraieus was about 45 feet; at Selinus and Knidos about 30 feet. Most of the streets were unpaved, as in Athens, Miletus, Alexandria and, of course, in all smaller towns. Sanitation was poor; open or only partly covered gutters were usual. Water supply and drainage systems were highly developed. Priene, Magnesia, Ephesos, and Pergamon—the latter with a high-pressure water conduit—are among the best-known examples of the Greek period.

In general the layout of the residential quarters was compact; the streets were narrow and sometimes very tortuous; the houses crowded together; and the total effect must have been rather monotonous and nondescript. It is difficult to follow those archeologists, who have tried to regain a more conspicuous place for the Greek house. Their efforts have not been too successful. It may be conceded that a small number of houses, those which today would be inhabited by white-collar workers and the higher echelons of the middle class, were fairly comfortable, even luxurious, and aesthetically satisfactory. But the bulk of the houses for the masses had certainly no architectural or social merits. However, it was—as everywhere—this grey-brown conglomerate of houses that filled the larger parts of the *poleis*. There was nothing that could even faintly compete with the burghers' houses or with the humble abodes of the workers and craftsmen in a medieval town. The exterior, as mostly in the south, was plain. There were only a few openings; most houses had one story; and all were more or less alike. All this need not necessarily be a disadvantage. The real disadvantage is that we still know too little about the life and the housing of the common people and that our conclusions, though probably correct, would gain in precision and completeness if more factual evidence were available.

Even our incomplete knowledge, however, should be sufficient as an eternal reminder that the few showpieces of Greek cities—the temples, the *agorai,* the public buildings, the *acropoleis*—were but one side of the picture. If we forget this, it would be the same as though future archeologists who excavate London or New York were to conclude that Buckingham Palace, Trafalgar Square, Westminster Abbey, or Rockefeller Center had been almost the only formative elements of these *metropoleis*.

The Greeks were lovers of flowers and trees, of their sacred groves and gardens. But verdure, parks, and arbored walks played no part in their conception of the *polis*. There were private gardens and interior gardens in the houses of the wealthy citizens; there was the Academy of Athens with fountains, trees and walks; there were the *gymnasia* and *palaestrai* with landscaped gardens.

But all these spaces were fairly small, more or less secluded, and without any influence upon the city as a whole. Apart from rather generalized remarks by Greek poets and writers and a few historians we know next to nothing of the layout of a garden and the principles that determined the shape, character, and structure of a park. That the Greeks were a nature-loving people seems obvious. That they used nature as an element of city planning seems doubtful. That their private gardens were more a loose arrangement of individual features than a systematically thought-out whole seems certain. In any case, the few works which have made any attempt at all to treat the subject of Greek gardens cannot offer more than laboriously collected fragments from poets and writers which are really not too enlightening.[17]

17. M. L. Gothein. *A History of Garden Art.* 1928. Pp. 53 ff.
E. C. Semple. *The Geography of the Mediterranean Region.* 1932. Pp. 485 ff.

CHAPTER 14

CITY SURVEY / ANCIENT GREECE

The following selection of cities, representative of the stages through which the development of the *polis* has passed at different times and in different regions, is of necessity incomplete: our knowledge of the physical layout and appearance of many cities of ancient Greece is insufficient. This explains why famous names are missing from the survey. But we do know enough to form a fairly clear picture of Greek city planning in general. Moreover, the selective method makes it perhaps easier to avoid the one-sided emphasis on the contrast between the "regular" and the "irregular" city plans so characteristic of numerous books on this subject which, after all, is but one aspect—and certainly not the most important one—of the intricate and complex problem we have to deal with.

The cities are grouped geographically so far as possible and with due regard for historical continuity.

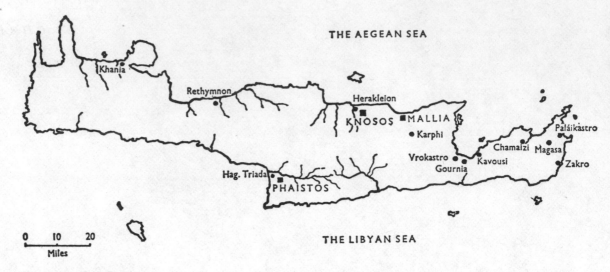

THE AEGEAN SEA

Khania

Rethymnon

Herakleion

KNOSSOS · MALLIA

Karphi

Palaikastro

Chamaizi · Magasa

Vrokastro · Kavousi

Gournia

Zakro

Hag. Triada

PHAISTOS

0   10   20

Miles

THE LIBYAN SEA

391. Map of Ancient Crete.

CRETE

"Out in the dark blue Sea there lies a land called Crete, a rich and lovely land, washed by the waves on every side, densely peopled and boasting ninety cities." Thus Homer describes the island in the Odyssey's nineteenth book.[1] These ninety "cities" had hardly anything in common with the later *poleis*. They were open settlements, often under the protection of a fortified castle, and mostly not far from the coast. In any case, Crete was thickly populated at the time of Homer—that is, about 1000 B.C. —and it is not unlikely that the population in the Middle Minoan period (about 2000 to 1550 B.C.) numbered about half a million.[2] The oldest settlements were at the edge of the fertile Messara Plain in the south. From here the settlement spread to the west and north. An almost uninterrupted chain of mountains follows the southern coast. The river valleys and the deep narrow ravines with their precipitous cliffs—in the White Mountains they reach a depth of 2,400 feet—impede the traffic. Only a few wider valleys are interspersed between the mountain ranges, apart from the plains of Messara and those of the north coast. This bold and varied relief has certainly con-

tributed not only to the dispersion and relative isolation of some of the settlements and towns but also to the tensions and separatism of the political units.

In the north the Minoans encountered peoples of the Stone Age and pressed them back to the east. They took over their settlement of Knossos which soon surpassed the older town of Phaestos. The fame of Crete, her high culture and the excellence of her arts and crafts —since the 16th century B.C. export to mainland Greece had begun—attracted invaders from the north, who occupied first Knossos and later, around 1400 B.C., some of the other settlements. The Minoans withdrew to the east and west ends of the island or to the mountains. These first Greek conquerors, the Achaeans, settled in fortified castles on hills which dominated the fertile plains. They could easily be defended without walls from the houses surrounding them which rose in terraces on the slope of the hill.

The next invaders were the Dorians, who landed on the island about 1000 B.C. As peasant-warriors they preferred the plains and forced the conquered population to cultivate the land, leaving them in their own households and on their own plots, *klaros,* and therefore called *klarotae,* an arrangement that was most appropriate to the backward agricul-

1. Translated by E. V. Rieu. 1948.
2. R. W. Hutchinson. "Prehistoric Town Planning in Crete," *Town Planning Review,* Vol. XXI, No. 3, 1950. P. 206.

ture and natural economy of the time and was adopted in several of the agricultural states of ancient Greece. The most important towns of the Dorians were Knossos, Gortyna, Lyttos and later, after 519 B.C., Cydonia in the west, a foundation of Aegean seafarers.[3] The Messara was the main settlement area of the Dorian peasants. The existing fortified castles in the small plains, the broader valleys, and on the coasts were occupied by the conquerors. Thus the Dorian invasion was split into small *poleis*. In the course of time, their rivalry and political antagonism made them mutually independent. It was above all their situation in a fertile region that raised Knossos, Gortyna, Lyttos, and Cydonia above the numerous other places.

During the eighth and seventh centuries B.C. the Dorian rulers remained open to external influences and responsive to the traditional values and achievements of the conquered. But this receptive attitude changed when it seemed to undermine the predominance of Dorian ideas, habits, and life. It seems that the Dorian conquerors feared being absorbed by the higher civilization that had preceded them, a fear that was not at all unjustified as history has proved on many occasions. Since about 600 B.C. they kept aloof from all artistic progress and even from participation in the growing efflorescence of Greek civilization. Their society began to stagnate. They retained the military organization of their peasant-warrior attitude and, like the Spartans, the militarists of antiquity *par excellence*, they lived in camps; private life ceased to exist; changes in the way of life were forbidden. It is easy to understand that this higher barbarism must have abhorred the refined culture of the Minoan period. After all, what had these primitive warriors in common with the elegant rulers of Minoan times? What could they have contributed toward the development of cities and the arts? It was only after Knossos and Gortyna had tried to unite the largest fertile areas of the island that the anachro-

nistic ideals and ideas of autonomy and autarchy began to dissolve and internal disturbances spread over the land.

From the middle of the fifth century political and economic influences from mainland Greece penetrated to Crete—first to Knossos, which was especially exposed to them through its situation on the north coast, and then to Gortyna in the south. However, it took more than a hundred years before an urban way of life was accepted as an improvement over the rustic and traditional customs and ideas of the preceding agrarian society. Gortyna was fortified about 220 B.C. Knossos was again leading and maintained its primacy as the main trading center of the island, whose importance grew through its favorable situation as a halfway house between the Macedonian states of the Ptolemies in Egypt and the Seleucids in Syria. Since 250 B.C. the cities of Crete formed leagues (*symmachiai*) with Knossos, Gortyna, Cydonia, and later Lyttos leading the various groups. The decline of its rivals, the Macedonian States and nearby Rhodes, initiated in the second century B.C. a new prosperity of the island and a revival of the cities. Only now were the strongpoints of the interior abandoned and the coastal settlements enlarged and reorganized as towns. Piracy, which had been a constant threat to the islanders, was made "respectable": it was systematically taken over by the Cretans and soon became the basis of the wealth of the coastal towns. This came to an end when Rome, in 69 B.C., began to suppress this "legitimate" buccaneering and with it the independence of Crete. After the introduction of the *latifundia* system the countryside became deserted and the small country towns declined. Gortyna, the new capital of the whole island, owed this prominence to its favorable position near the south coast which made contact with northern Africa easy.

Crete is of special importance because it was the cradle of the first European urban civilization. Almost all urban sites, excavated so far, show that the houses were crowded together along narrow lanes with gutters, and

3. E. Kirsten and W. Kraiker. *Griechenlandkunde.* 1957. P. 268. Ample use has been made of this excellent and competent work throughout the whole City Survey.

that they were rather broad and flat, and were grouped around a palace or a market square. The towns

. . . were markets by origin and became important as such through the development of industry and navigation. . . . In all these towns, shops and workshops jostled one another, particularly round the big square. . . . According to the lie of the land, the streets were tortuous or they intersected at right angles. . . . When they had a slope to cover they were not built on an inclined plane, but in horizontal sections connected by steps. In Crete they were narrow, their width varying from 4.59 to 8.2 feet and reaching 13.12 feet as an exception.[4]

The so-called Town Mosaic of the Middle Minoan period from Knossos shows the elevation of Minoan houses. They were two or three stories high and had flat roofs. The origin of Knossos and Phaistos was, in all probability, a compact village on a hill rising from the fertile plain that surrounded it, while the majority of the neolithic villages grew up in valleys with a good water supply. It is also likely that hardly any attention was paid to the layout of the street system: houses were the primary element of the towns and the streets were of but secondary importance. However, this assumption needs some qualification, for the better residential quarters at Tylissos and on Gypsadhes at Knossos were laid out in rectangular blocks with streets crossing one another at right angles.[5] At the present state of our knowledge it appears that the earliest towns developed around the house of the prince or chief, who erected it on the best site available. None of the towns was fortified. This was also typical of other islands such as the island empire of Japan: the sea and (in the case of Crete) the navy were regarded as sufficient protection. Another interesting feature is the absence of temples. But this "omission" may seem to be less surprising if we remember that the palaces were sacred as the seats of the God-King and sheltered "lustral areas," rooms for purification rites, and that the Cretans were wont to worship on the top of mountains[6] or at sacred springs. After 1400 B.C. a great disaster, probably an earthquake, destroyed the palaces and towns and put an end to the Cretan naval empire. The Minoans fled before the Achaean invaders, left the valleys, and built refuges on hills in the mountainous regions.

To this period belong the first settlements at Axós in the Ida district, at Prinias guarding the road to the Mesará, and at Góulas, at Karphi and at Vrókastro in the east. Gone was the old security, the old reliance on the fleet. The new houses were all fortified . . . they were inhabited by the remnants of the old population. . . . The divine dynasty of Minos had perished but surely the great goddess, the Earth-Mother would not desert her worshippers. Thus every Sub-Minoan town, though it had no sacred Palace, no lustral areas or pillar crypts, possessed its small civic shrine to the goddess usually in a form strongly resembling that of the simplest type of Greek temple.[7]

6. *Ibid.*, p. 208.
7. *Ibid.*, pp. 216, 219.

392. **Environment of the Palace of Knossos. A acropolis; K so-called caravanserai; P palace; Kl. P small palace; V royal villa.**

4. G. Glotz. *The Aegean Civilisation.* 1925. P. 138.
5. R. W. Hutchinson, *op. cit.*, p. 203.

Knossos. Palaces were built by the princes at Knossos, Mallia, Tylissos, Phaistos, and Hagia Triadha, all in Central Crete. These palaces were religious, political, and economic centers. They contained factories and warehouses like oriental temples or royal residences and were situated in the open country. Their central courts were reserved for private or semiprivate manifestations. Public assemblies seem to have been restricted to squares outside the palaces.[8] The court within the palace precincts was a

8. R. Martin. *Recherches sur l'Agora Grecque. Études d'Histoire et d'Architecture Urbaines.* 1951. Pp. 85 ff.

"lieu des grandes assemblées à caractère religieux, lieu peut-être aussi des représentations à grand spectacle qu'affectionnaient les Crétois, elles étaient un trait d'union entre le palais du prince et sa cité; largement ouvertes au public, placées sous la protection de quelques autels et lieux de culte, elles offrent, dans l'urbanisme minoen, l'image assez exacte de ce que sera l'agora dans la cité héllenique. Les deux aspects caractéristiques de l'agora primitive, la fonction religieuse et la fonction représentative, se retrouvent associés sur les places extérieures des palais minoens.[9]

The significance of these palaces to city planning may be compared with the relation-

9. R. Martin, *op. cit.*, pp. 94-95.

393. Air view of the Palace of Knossos.

ship of the palace and the town of Versailles: when Louis XIV took up his residence in the palace, the town was virtually nonexistent except for a few isolated houses to the south of the present Place d'Armes. Thus Knossos, the most magnificent of the Minoan palaces, often compared with Versailles, merits this comparison in a double sense: as the splendid and elegant seat of the ruler and as the agent that gave rise to the town of Knossos—but with the difference that the Minoan palace was an architectural masterpiece, refined in its grandeur and noble in conception and execution, whereas the palace of the *roi soleil* was ostentatious, almost vulgar, and badly built.

The palace at Knossos, like the other residences, attracted specialist craftsmen who worked for the prince and shared in his wealth. It was like a great household with workshops and magazines from which the needs of the Court and its attendants were supplied and whose surplus was used for trade. The economic power of the Minoan rulers must have rested to a considerable degree on trade and secondary industries, not on agricultural production.[10] The palace was surrounded by a zone of *villae* for the well-to-do people. A caravanserai was built for visitors. It was connected with the palace by a viaduct and a bridge over the Vlychia stream. The palace as such cannot be discussed in this connection. Its merits are purely architectural, and besides it lies outside the scope of this work. Unfortunately, the town of Knossos which grew up around the palace, mainly to the north, has not yet been excavated. Judging from other places we may assume that it was a compact town, very likely not systematically planned. For the same reasons the palaces at Phaistos, Mallia, and Hagia Triadha have to be excluded from this survey.

10. V. G. Childe. *What Happened in History*. 1952. P. 16₅.

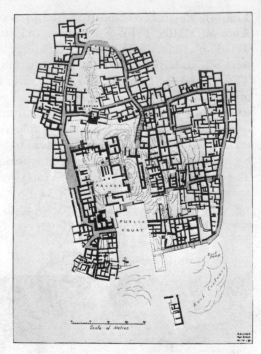

394. Plan of Gournia.

Gournia, Eastern Crete, near the Bay of Hierapetra, has been only partly excavated. Its houses are crowded together on the arid slopes of a limestone ridge. The summit is occupied by a mansion facing a large public court which may have served as a market square. Extreme use has been made of the available space. "It would seem that men were determined on no account to surrender the smallest plot of cultivable land by encroaching upon the valley to make their houses"[11] The two main streets were paved, one enclosing almost the whole site was connected with another circular road by stepped ascents.[12] The street pattern, though seemingly quite unsystematic, is rationally adapted to the complicated terrain and gives easy access to the rectangular house units. The narrow lanes and alleys are tortuous, climbing, and partly leading over stairs to the other levels. This "Prehistoric Pompei" consisted of sixty houses, mostly two-storied and covered an area of 6½

11. G. Glotz, *op. cit.*, p. 140.
12. J. O. S. Pendlebury. *The Archaeology of Crete*. 1939. P. 191.

acres. Its inhabitants were farmers, who were engaged in cultivation, cattle raising, and fishing. On the basis of agricultural raw materials weaving, leatherworking, and similar trades were carried on as well as pottery, stone and metal work for which the nearby clay, stone, and copper were used. Some of the houses had small shops and workshops. Findings indicate that the village industries were possibly concentrated in the southern quarter. A small shrine north of the palace has been identified as the "first clear example of a civic centre for worship other than the palace."[13] Although the objects found in the shrine belong to the Late Minoan period, it seems most likely that the shrine itself was built together with the village in the Late Minoan I period.

13. R. W. Hutchinson, *op. cit.*, p. 215.

395. Plan of Palaikastro.

Palaikastro, in the extreme east of Crete, on the Bay of Grandes, was a country town that gradually grew wealthy by commerce. The chief occupation of the inhabitants was cattle raising. It spread along the coast over a fertile plain at the foot of a hill. The main street, well paved and drained, was lined with large houses which were apparently owned by upper-class people who were traders and shipowners.[14] The town was built partly in Middle Minoan times. There are indications that the general plan remained unaltered for about eight hundred years.[15] The layout is not too dissimilar from that of Gournia, although it is more regular owing to its location on a more level terrain. The building density is very high and the interpenetration of the houses is very complex with a minimum of access streets.

14. G. Glotz, *op. cit.*, p. 139.
15. R. C. Bosanquet and R. M. Dawkins. "Palaikastro Excavations, 1902-1906," *The British School at Athens,* Supplementary Paper No. 1, Part 1. 1923.

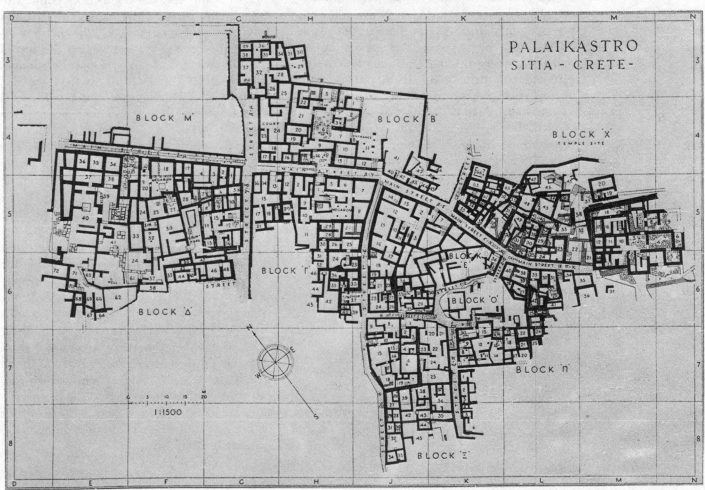

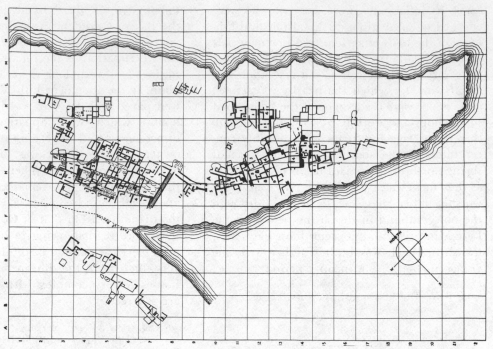

396. Plan of Pseira.

Pseira is a small island rising from the sea as a barren mass of rock some two miles off the coast of Eastern Crete opposite the plain of Kavousi. In the east the terrain slopes sharply down to the shore. A once-flourishing Minoan settlement occupied the narrow area on top of the rocks and the adjoining hillside to the south.[16] It owed its existence to the good harborage for small craft. Remains of a Roman camp have been found on the topmost ridge of the island, on the edge of the cliffs of the west coast. The settlement was inhabited by traders and seamen. The cultivable area was obviously restricted to the terraced hillsides—remains of numerous terrace walls have been excavated—and the soil was too poor for an agricultural population. It was above all the sheltered port that attracted the settlers and made them prosperous. Gournia, not too far away, but without a harbor, never enjoyed the same prosperity or similar close contact with Knossos.

In general, the town resembled Gournia but its situation was more dramatic, more spectacular. It was a "huddle of streets and houses

along the top and sides of a rocky point with long flights of steps descending at irregular intervals to the water's edge." Two main roads led to the center of the town on the top of the hill from which, just below the summit, several streets traversed all parts of the flat, built-up area. These streets along the level were unpaved; they had a more-or-less even floor of natural rock. The other roads leading down to the water had paved stepways. The houses were built of heavy, sometimes roughly squared blocks of stone. Bricks seem not to have been used.

The town was destroyed in the Middle Minoan I period. It was not rebuilt until the Middle Minoan III period. Then its greatest prosperity began and continued until the town was destroyed by the same catastrophe that visited all places in Eastern Crete. While Gournia and Palaikastro recovered from this disaster, Pseira was apparently abandoned after the end of the Late Minoan I period and remained deserted until Roman times. The Late Minoan I town had grown considerably so that the overcrowding of the top made a new quarter on the hill to the south of the harbor necessary, almost doubling the original built-up area.

16. R. B. Seager. "Excavations on the Island of Pseira, Crete." In: *Anthropological Publications*, University of Pennsylvania, Vol. III, No. 1. 1910-14. Pp. 1-38.

526

**397. Plan of the site of Vrokastro as ex-
cavated in 1910.**

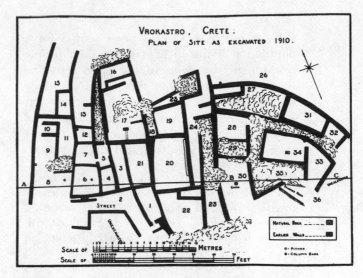

Karphi, Central Crete, in the plain of Lasithi,
built about 1100 B.C., was a city of refuge of
the early Iron Age and as such fulfilled functions similar to those of Vrokastro.[17] It was
inhabited by the remnants of the native population of Minoan stock, who had fled from
the Dorian invasion. Situated on an almost
inaccessible peak, it could be reached only
by two steep paths on the north and south
sides, the latter leading to the ruler's house
and to the shrine at the edge of the precipice
and dividing into numerous lanes and alleys.
This intricate street pattern was one of the
best exemplifications of Aristotle's demand for
an arrangement that "is difficult for foreign
troops to enter and to find their way about
when attacking." (*Politics* VII. X. 4.) The
houses rose in terraces and access, in some
cases, was only possible over the roofs of the
lower buildings, as still today in the town
Tzermiadho and other places of the eastern
Mediterranean or in the *pueblos* of the American Indians.

Vrokastro, Eastern Crete, is of interest as a
refuge settlement in a naturally protected
position.[18] It stood on a steep limestone spur
nearly a thousand feet high on the east side
of the valley of Kalo Khorio, whose north and
west faces are almost inaccessible. A winding
path leads up on the east. The south face is
connected with the hills behind by a saddle.
"The appearance of Vrokastro at the height
of its power must have been similar to that
of an Italian hilltown of to-day." The site had
obvious advantages just because of its inac-
cessibility. It was an excellent lookout from
which approaching boats could be seen while

17. "Excavations in the Plain of Lasithi. III. Karphi:
A City of Refuge of the Early Iron Age in Crete," *The
British School at Athens*, Vol. XXXVIII, Session 1937-
38. 1940.

18. E. H. Hall. "Excavations in Eastern Crete, Vrokastro." In: *Anthropological Publications*, University
of Pennsylvania, Vol. III, No. 3. 1914. Pp. 74-185.

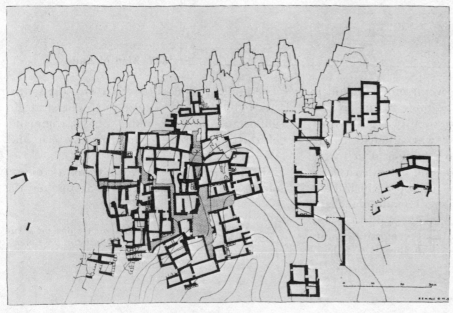

**398. Plan of the sub-Minoan
town of Karphi.**

still far out at sea. This was essential for a population living in fear of invasion: people working in the fields in the plain could be warned in time so that they could withdraw to the safety of the hill. Vrokastro was but part of an Iron Age settlement that may have spread over a large area at the foot of the rocky hill. It was its citadel and lookout.

We may suppose that at some stage at least in the history of the site the valley had been seized by invaders who had reduced their predecessors to the position of a *perioikoi* [people without citizenship but personally free and left in possession of their land] and driven them to less promising districts like Vrokastro and the hills behind.[19]

It was the Dark Age of Crete. "We seem to be back in the Neolithic Period with its life of terror, the only difference being that some building skill had survived and robber castles take the place of caves."[20] Judging from the group of houses that have been excavated, the town plan must have been similar to that of Gournia and Pseira.

19. E. H. Hall, *op. cit.*, p. 82.
20. J. D. S. Pendlebury, *op. cit.*, p. 303.

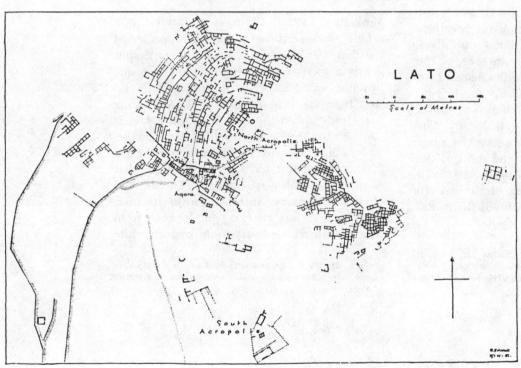

399. Map of Lato.

Lato, Eastern Crete, several miles inland, is the most interesting example of an archaic Greek town. It spread over two peaks of a rocky hill. The *agora* was situated in the saddle between the two elevations which were occupied by a northern and a southern *acropolis* respectively. The hills on which Lato stood were part of a small mountain chain extending from the sea to the southwest and only in the north joining the massif separating the plain of Laconia and Hagios Nikolaos.

The highest point of the town with the southern *acropolis* rises to 1,000 feet. The strategic importance of Lato rested on its command of the main route connecting Eastern and Western Crete.[21]

Broadly speaking, the town forms a crescent facing the sea. The rocky and abrupt terrain

21. J. Demargne. "Les Ruines de Goulas ou l'Ancienne Ville de Lato en Crète," *Bulletin de Correspondance Hellénique*, Vol. 25. 1901.

was a natural protection which needed to be reinforced by artificial fortifications only at the more exposed points.[22] The town was unevenly built up. The most densely settled parts were in the north and northwest. The terraces, which followed the contours of the terrain, were relatively narrow: they supported mostly only one row of houses and a footpath. Their walls were of an impressive polygonal masonry and continued in some places as the back walls of the buildings, as a breastwork on the roof of the houses which protected the defenders against an attacking enemy. The district around the southern *acropolis* was thinly settled and had no walls. The *agora,* in the saddle between the two peaks in the form of a rough pentagon on a large terrace, was surrounded by public buildings with porticos on the west and south, and a shrine. On the north a series of steps may have served as a small theater. Behind them stood the *prytaneion* which gave the *agora "un caractère monumental assez rude,"* as Martin puts it, *"en faisait presque une place fortifiée, bien à l'image de ces époques primitives où des rivalités violentes opposaient les villes, toujours menacées d'être partagées entre deux voisines plus puissantes."*[23] This whole group of buildings was the equivalent of the "manor house" at the center of other Cretan towns.

The adaptation of the town to the difficult terrain was perfect. It was a well-planned town, which only intense efforts and deter-

22. R. E. Wycherley. "Hellenic Cities," *Town Planning Review,* Vol. 22, 1951. Pp. 107-108.
23. *Op. cit.,* p. 229.

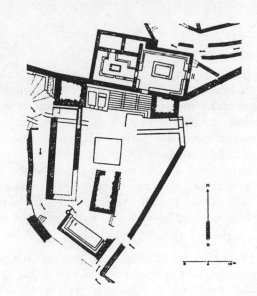

400. Plan of the Agora at Lato.

mined foresight could have created. It should cause a revision of the all too simple notion that a "planned" city has to be regular, and that all irregular cities are not planned and unsystematic.

The main roads converged upon the *agora,* cutting through the terraces. Others followed the course of the terraces, winding between the houses. The principal roads continued beyond the town and connected it with the highways. It was an ingenious system which paid the highest tribute to the skill and systematic approach of the architects who planned Lato. The relationship between houses and streets was perfect, utilitarian, and organic. The houses, clustered together, were small with narrow inner courts. Natural water supply was lacking. There were no springs. The inhabitants had to rely on cisterns.

THE ARGOLIS

The peninsula of Argolis, the landscape of the heroic age of Greece, stretches as a fertile plain between bare mountain ranges from the sea inland. The mountains converge toward the north with good communications to the Isthmus of Corinth and continue westward to Arcadia. The interior opens toward the Gulf of Nauplia in the west. In the second millennium B.C., when the mountain chains bordering the plateau were still covered by thick forests, the Argolis was the center of the prehistoric civilization of Greece whose representatives were probably invaders of a non-Indo-European race related to the tribes inhabiting the Cyclades and Crete. Our knowledge of the successive waves of tribes is still insufficient. However, we may assume that about 1900 B.C. the first Indo-Europeans ar-

529

rived at Mycenae and founded their first settlement on the *acropolis*. This stronghold remained the center of their dominion while other smaller strongpoints rose on the hills surrounding the plain which were interconnected by roads and with the ports of Corinth, Asine, and Epidaurus. These invaders, the early Helladic farmers (c. 2500 to c. 1900 B.C.), were followed by the Achaeans a couple of centuries later. The 15th and 14th centuries were a period of turmoil and rivalry.

These barbarians added their own contributions without extinguishing the agricultural, industrial and commercial traditions of their predecessors. The old townships were reconstructed. . . . Then from 1600 on . . . the Helladic villages became the citadels of rich war lords disposing of concentrated wealth . . . they persuaded or compelled Minoan craftsmen . . . to settle at their courts. . . . Eventually the Mainlanders were equipped to annex Crete, too, and the Mainland *Mycenaean* civilization usurped the dominion of the Minoan throughout the Aegean world.[24]

These semibarbarians owed allegiance to petty

24. V. G. Childe, *op. cit.*, pp. 169-70.

lords, who built their fortified castles in strong positions which dominated the neighboring country and the subject people. This civilization perished when at the end of the 12th century another wave of invaders descended from the north. The Dorian conquerors destroyed Mycenae about 1100 B.C. and swept away the few cultural achievements of their predecessors, ushering in the Dark Age of Greece. This period lasted three centuries, filled with chaotic barbarism, until hesitantly and yet irresistibly the first groping outlines of Classical Greece began to emerge. The Dorians occupied the *Larisa*, the *Burg*, of Argos and made it their fortified refuge. They established their principal settlement, which covered about the same area as the present country town of Argos. The low hill north of it they called *aspis* (circular shield), thus transferring the political center of the Argolis from the citadel of Mycenae to Argos and the coastal plain, which was cultivated by the subject earlier tribes as bondmen. Gradually they crossed the mountains in the north and settled in Cleonae, Corinth, and Megara.

Mycenae. The citadel of Mycenae crowns a moderately high rocky hill rising between two ravines.[25] Hills, outposts of the range of Arachnaeus, guard it at the east and are traversed by prehistoric roads connecting Mycenae with settlements on the Argive Plain and Corinth. Mycenae occupied a favorable strategic position overlooking the entrances and exits to and from the northern hills. It flourished during the Bronze Age and its civilization has been described by Homer. It was Agamemnon's "capital." The citadel was first occupied about 3000 to 2800 B.C.—that is, at the beginning of the Early Bronze Age. The prosperity of Mycenae began with the Middle Bronze Age (2200-1600 B.C.). Cultural contacts with Crete developed. The summit was surrounded with a wall which probably protected the residence of the ruler. A number of

25. A. J. B. Wace. *Mycenae. An Archeological History and Guide.* 1949.

houses belonging to this period have been found on the western slope and on some of the neighboring hills.

The existence of fortified castles, such as Mycenae or Tiryns, gave rise to small settlements outside their walls. This corresponds to the European Middle Ages when the rulers lived in *Burgen* on hills, around which small groups of more-or-less compact or dispersed settlements grew up. The earlier settlers were forced by the new rulers to build their enormous citadels while the retainers of the overlord settled in smaller strongholds in the neighborhood. These "subcitadels" have been identified in a considerable number all over the Argive Plain: in Nauplia, Argos, and Asine, and at the eastern edge of the Plain at Dendra all interconnected by roads. The civilian population lived in small detached groups at short distances from one another, with the graves of their ancestors surrounding their dwellings outside the fortified area which served as a refuge in times of war and unrest. Their settlements were mostly situated on low hills with a good water supply and near fertile land.

On the hills adjoining Mycenae stood settlements of varying prosperity. One on the Kalkani hill to the west of the citadel is comparatively small. A larger one has lately been identified on the top of the ridge above the Treasury of Atreus, where the houses seem to be those of a high-class residential quarter. Before the Lion Gate were some small buildings which probably offered shelter to man and beast as well as accommodation for shops and booths.[26]

The citadel was reserved for the ruler and his family, courtiers, administrators and their families and later also possibly for soldiers, slaves, and special craftsmen. Their houses were built on terraces within the walls accessible through narrow lanes and connected by a main road with the palace. It seems that no private houses were allowed to be built right up to the walls. Between the walls and the houses, which accompanied the course of the wall directly on its inside, there was nearly always a gap.

After the destruction of Mycenae around 1100 B.C., it remained uninhabited until reoccupied in the Early Iron Age. "In the court

26. A. J. B. Wace, *op. cit.*, p. 103.

of the palace small huts were built. . . . This town developed into the classical Mycenae which in 480 and 479 B.C. sent its contingent to fight against the Persian invaders at Thermopylae and Plataea."[27] This place existed until 468 B.C. when the Argives conquered it and dismantled the walls. A *kome,* a small fortified township, was founded by the Argives; it was first mentioned in 235 B.C.

In general the Early Bronze Age settlers preferred isolated and well-defensible hills as the site for their compact villages. While in the Early and Middle Helladic periods (2500-1580 B.C.) these villages were the only settlements on these sites, in the Late Helladic or Mycenaean period (1580-1100 B.C.) the hilltops were occupied by a citadel, by an *acropolis,* which protected a settlement that now spread over part of the surrounding plain. Something similar has happened at Asine, on the Gulf of Argos, to the southwest of Mycenae. Here on a rocky peninsula which was an excellent natural fortress a Bronze Age town developed where "a narrow neck of land joins the rocky *acropolis* to the mainland. The town was built in terraces obviously dictated by the steep rocky slopes" making the most rational use of the space available.[28]

27. *Ibid.,* p. 24.
28. R. W. Hutchinson. "Prehistoric Town Planning in and around the Aegean," *Town Planning Review,* Vol. XXIII, No. 4, 1953. P. 9.

401. Plan of the Acropolis at Mycenae.

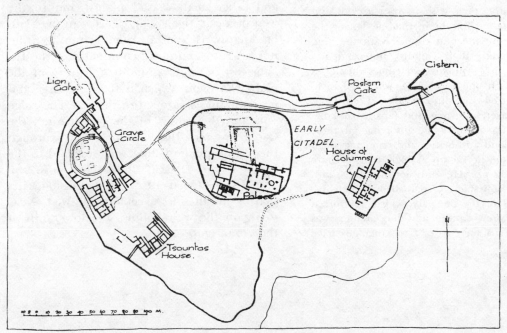

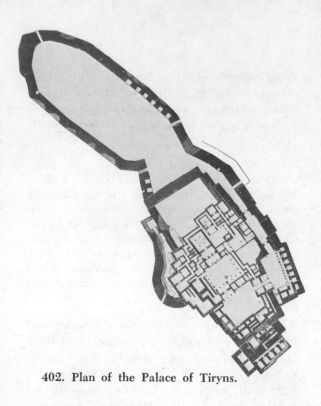

Tiryns stands on a limestone block only 75 feet above the Argive Plain. In pre-Greek times the sea reached much nearer to the citadel and Tiryns was an important settlement.[29] The citadel covered an area of 4.94 acres compared with the 7.41 acres of Mycenae and may be regarded as a second smaller residence of the Mycenaean rulers. The settlement outside the fortifications spread in Mycenaean times over the plain to the east of the hills. The citadel consisted of two parts: the southern half on the higher ground was occupied by the palace, while the northern lower part served as a refuge for the population of the neighboring settlements. Storerooms and casemates were built in the thickness of the walls which Greek tradition regarded as the work of the Cyclopes.

29. G. Karo. *Führer durch Tiryns.* 1934. P. 39.

402. Plan of the Palace of Tiryns.

ATTICA

The city of Athens and the state of Attica formed the city-state of Athens after Theseus united the townships and villages which were dispersed over the Attic countryside under the hegemony of Athens. Thucydides has described this synoicism (2. 15):

From the reign of Kekrops and the earliest kings down to Theseus Attica was inhabited in several townships, each with its own *archon* and its own *prytaneion*. Except in time of danger the *archontes* did not meet in council with the king but administered their affairs independently through their local councils. Sometimes they even went to war with one another, as when the Eleusinians supported Eumolpos against Erechtheus. Theseus, however, a strong and far-sighted king, reconstituted the country by dissolving all these local councils and authorities and removing them to Athens, where he set up a single central council and *prytaneion*. He did not interfere with their property, but merely compelled them to become members of the one city, which, reinforced from all sides, grew rapidly, and thus enlarged was handed on to his successors. The Athenians have

kept ever since a public festival, the *Synoikia,* in commemoration of the event.

Mountain ranges and isolated mountains separate the individual small plains but do not erect insuperable obstacles; low passes lead between Parnes and Pantelikon to the north Attic basin; between Pantelikon and Hymettos to the plain of Mesogaia and farther over coastal ridges to the plain of Marathon and other small coastal plains; and in the west between Aigaleos and Parnes to the plain of Eleusis. A central ridge, running from northeast to southwest, culminates in the Lykabettos, the most prominent feature of the plain of Athens, which is the only large and fertile arable area open to the sea. The ridge separates the valleys of the two streams, the Cephissos and Ilissos, which flow through the coastal plain of Phaleron westward to the sea. The rocky massif of the *Acropolis,* separated from Lykabettos by a depression, rises sharply on all sides except in the west. Near to it, on the west, follows the lower hill of the Areopagos.

532

Athens is situated in the center of the fertile Attic Plain. The three harbors of Peiraieus, Zea, and Munychia were the natural outlets in close propinquity to the city and the source of its seapower and overseas trade. The rock of the *acropolis* attracted the earliest settlers as the most favorable site; it was an exquisite stronghold endowed by Nature with indispensable requisites for defense which could hardly escape the attention of the first invaders; the surrounding country was fertile; and several springs rose at its foot. Thus food and water supply were secured and protection, without elaborate artificial fortifications, was afforded.

Ideally and materially, the *acropolis* was the core of the settlement of the Attic Plain from earliest times. The name *polis* was first used for the *acropolis,* then for the city of Athens, and finally for the city-state. In the Neolithic period modest mud huts were built at the southern slope and on top of the rock. Others were dispersed along the valleys of the Cephissos and Ilissos. Even today the names of some rivers and places recall these pre-Greek settlements. Since about 2000 B.C. the Greek conquerors subjugated the original population. They forced them to cultivate the land and to build palaces and strongholds. During this period (2000-1200 B.C.) the *acropolis* became the seat of the king and his retainers and was fortified by a cyclopean wall which followed the edges of the rock. Independent settlements were situated in the other plains of Attica which were the nuclei of small *poleis*. Numerous citadels have been discovered which date back to this period and were the seats of the followers of the king of Athens.

The early cyclopean walls of the *acropolis* represented but one stage of the fortifications. They were not identical with the so-called Pelasgicon or Pelargicon. This was apparently a wall with nine gates around the base of the citadel which enclosed the dwellings at the foot of the *acropolis* and also the springs. Thus an outer and an inner line of defense protected the citadel.

The decisive turning point in the early history of Athens was the synoicism brought

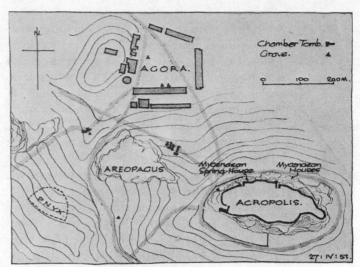

403. Plan of Mycenean Athens.

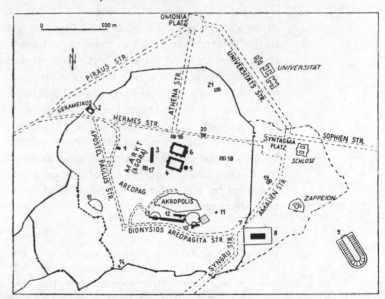

404. Ancient and present Athens.

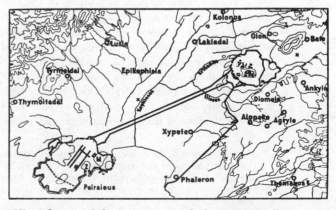

405. Athens and the Peiraieus with the Long Walls.

about by Theseus which may have taken place at the beginning of the first millennium B.C. Thucydides' description of this event has been quoted earlier. However, the synoicism which led to the unification of Attica should not be equated with the foundation of Athens or with that of other *poleis* although both, unification of a region and foundation of a city, often coincided. Synoicism was the act through which a Greek state was formed; it does not explain the origin of the *polis* in spite of the use of the word *polis* as a synonym for both.

Excavations indicate that the population increased at this time. This may have been one of the reasons why Attica was henceforth administered from Athens in twelve districts as a *dodekapolis.* A further consequence of synoicism was the settlement of the minor princes in Athens. They retained their estates in the country but lived in their town houses, preferably situated on the Pnyx opposite the *acropolis,* which from this time seems to have been the most fashionable residential quarter[30] where the first administrative buildings were erected, such as the house of the chief administrator, the *prytanis,* of the city of Athens. However, the synoicism which legend ascribed to Theseus may have been a tale probably invented by Kleisthenes, the founder of Athenian democracy.

The idea that the local chiefs were reluctant to move corresponds to the conditions of the fifth century when the Attic yeomen were notorious for their attachment to their homesteads. The *Eupatridai,*[31] on the other hand, had nothing to lose and everything to gain by residing in the city. They kept their property and increased their power . . . the authority of the early kings was undoubtedly limited by a still vigorous sense of tribal equality which even after it had been shattered, left deep down in the minds of the people a heritage of democratic ideals which neither time nor adversity could efface; and it may well have been the stirring of these ancient memories in the

new democracy of the fifth century that inspired the tradition as we have it.[32]

The move of the landed aristocracy to the city influenced not only the structure of settlement but above all the social and political development. While heretofore every free inhabitant of Attica who owned land and was a *hoplite* (a heavy-armed foot-soldier) was a full citizen, now a new class, an urban nobility with their old Mycenaean customs, joined the citizenry of the *polis.* This influx, apart from other factors, had a profound effect upon the royal power. In the eighth century it led to a severe restriction of the king's position. He had to renounce his command of the army in favor of the *polemarchos* and then also his rule to the *archon.* Finally, the kingdom was completely abolished in 683 B.C. and an official, who was annually elected from the nobility and had to attend to the religious duties of the king, was installed as *archon basileus.* With these changes the *acropolis* lost its importance as the seat of the king and the Areopagus became the center of the city. Here the oligarchic council, the successor of the aristocratic councillors of the king, met under the chairmanship of the *archon basileus.*

With the decline of the agrarian squirearchy, the rise of maritime trade and piracy, and the introduction of a money economy since about 630 B.C. nonnoble families gained the upper hand. The old nobles withdrew to their estates. The peasants, who had been evicted from their land and moved to Athens, settled in the area of the *kerameikos,* the quarter of the potters. The center of the *polis* was shifting to the northwest, to a depression that had hitherto been swampy. Since the middle of the sixth century numerous public buildings and temples were erected; an aqueduct was constructed; arts and crafts flourished; and with these changes the importance of the *agora,* the political and social center, increased as the focal point of Athenian democracy. The antagonism between country and city, which was beginning to be more outspoken, was smoothed over by making every

30. E. Kirsten and W. Kraiker, *op. cit.,* p. 80, *passim.*
31. Eupatridai were the ancient nobles who resided in the *polis* and enjoyed political privileges. They might have been, in very early times, the only full citizens of Athens.

32. G. D. Thomson. *Studies in Ancient Greek Society. The Prehistoric Aegean.* 1949. P. 365.

534

free inhabitant of Attica a citizen of Athens independent of the former restrictions of land ownership and place of residence. The smallest administrative units of this politico-social leveling-up were the *demoi,* the almost 180 villages and hamlets of Attica, as well as settlements within the urban area. Thus the contrast between country and city was minimized, at least in theory, without impairing the supremacy of Athens as the political and economic center.

The devastation of Athens by the Persians in 480 B.C. was so great that, as the story goes, Themistocles considered the transfer of the city to Peiraieus. Yet in 479 B.C. Athens was surrounded by walls. This was the first fortification of a city on mainland Greece. It made Athens the refuge to which the inhabitants of the open country could withdraw in times of war, the more so as the walls enclosed uninhabited areas. This finally ended the role of the *acropolis* as the citadel of Athens. The "Long Walls," which according to Plutarch were built by Themistocles and connected Athens with Peiraieus, were destroyed after the surrender of the city. The Age of Pericles saw the greatest triumph of Greek art and architecture. But this outburst of creative activity was restricted to the erection of individual buildings, especially on the *acropolis.* The Parthenon, the Erechtheum, the Propylaea, and other public buildings belong to this period. The city itself, after its destruction by the Persians, was not reconstructed with the same fervor or with any clear plan. The houses were superficially repaired and the streets remained what they had been before: narrow, crooked, and unsightly lanes and alleys. A great opportunity was missed. Ostentation, demonstration of local pride, and respect for the gods who could not be worshipped without their temples proved stronger than considerations for the welfare of the people. It was an evasion of social responsibility and in spite of all its beauty, in spite of all the great artistic and unique achievements, the fact is undeniable that political democracy remains mere lip service, if it is not identified with an all-embracing and dignified environment that raises the material and ideal standard of living above the mere utilitarian level.

Around 430 B.C. there were about 170,000 citizens in Attica, plus 30,000 *metoikoi*—permanently resident aliens—and 115,000 slaves. After the Peloponnesian War the sunset of Athens began. Its population decreased through plague and war. Pericles was the last aristocratic spokesman for the people. After him *nouveaux riches* came upon the political stage, Cleon, a big industrialist; Nikias, a mining magnate; and a crowd of lesser war profiteers. The spirit of the *entrepreneur* dominated the atmosphere of the city. Public buildings were erected mainly for economic purposes. More and more people of rank and distinction left the city and retired to the seclusion of their estates. Around 330 B.C. Athens had about 84,000 citizens, perhaps 35,000 *metoikoi,* and 100,000 slaves. But even in its political decline Athens remained the leading cultural city of the Greek world until, under Macedonian rule, the political and cultural pendulum swung to Asia Minor and Hellenistic ambitions and influences gained the upper hand. Athens sank to the status of a country town. It could not compete with the great designs of the Hellenistic cities. Emigration to these places set in and Athenian ideas and culture spread over the whole ancient world. People began to abandon the city. Finally Athens was conquered by Sulla in 86 B.C. and Roman interest in and admiration of Greek civilization led to a revival—though a revival of doubtful value, which like a thin and crude veneer was but make-believe, a travesty of the former deep-rooted cultural homogeneity and purposeful and spontaneous originality.

Ancient Athens, like ancient Rome, was a conglomerate of unrelated details. There was no over-all planning, not even a unifying vision of the city as a whole, as a complex entity. What then is the contribution of Athens to city planning? Even if we dispose of the all-too-simple, not to say primitive, notion that an irregular city is not "planned" and only regular cities with rigid axes and

406. Air view of the Acropolis from the south.

streets intersecting at right angles are planned, Athens cannot possibly be regarded as an integrated, deliberately controlled organism. The Greek conviction that "man is the measure of all things" was the ever-present, conscious and unconscious impulse which made the human scale the dominating formative power in all buildings, in their spatial arrangement, and in the layout of squares and prominent sites. Beyond this it resulted in an instinctive dislike of rigidity, in a disinclination to organize the urban space, as it were, in a vacuum. Preconceived plans, worked out beforehand on the drawing-board, were alien to the Greek mind. Even the gridiron layouts of Hippodamos and his followers showed a certain disrespect for axial planning: their plans were mere accretions of identical building blocks, a system that could be extended *ad libitum*. Greek city building was an "on-site" procedure focused on man. It was a spontaneous adaptation to particular local conditions, to the terrain, to its shape and contours, to its size and surroundings. And it was more than a physical adaptation to certain physical conditions. It was an identification with the whole atmosphere of a place, an empathy of greatest intensity that eliminated theoretical speculations that might diminish or destroy the immediacy, the intimate interaction of man and environment. This may explain the seemingly chaotic appearance of ancient Athens and other cities. It may be difficult for modern man of the technological age to understand this attitude, which for the Greeks was the only natural and human reaction to the challenge of their urban environment. The all-pervading human scale, the unconcern for ostentatious rigidity, are perhaps the only contribution of ancient Greece to the art of city building. Yet it was a great contribution. It must be sensed and experienced instinctively for it cannot rationally be defined.

The same principles that were valid for the city as a whole also determined the layout of individual sites. The *acropolis,* the *agora,* and an industrial district are the obvious choice to demonstrate these principles in prac-

tice. They are integral elements of Athenian planning and representative examples of Greek city planning in general, although they represent but detailed solutions within the general scheme.

The *acropolis,* the citadel, and the *agora,* the public square, were the two nuclei of Athens. The *acropolis* stood nearly in the center of the classical city. It was the starting point of its development and remained its religious symbol throughout the centuries. Originally it was the permanent fortified residence of the kings with a sanctuary, not a refuge for the countrypeople in times of danger. In the course of the centuries the defensive and residential functions of the *acropolis* ceased to be essential and were superseded by the concentration of the most prominent religious buildings. A zigzag terraced path led up to the *propylaea.* Here the visitor entered a sort of forecourt, then moved on through the court to the east end of the *propylaea,* and finally the Parthenon and the other buildings would emerge into full view. It was a gradual, indirect approach, which in a subtle way drew the visitor forward, entirely different from the perspective view of the Renaissance and Baroque where a main building or a group of buildings attracted the visitor. The Greek solution was a step-by-step intensification increasing its effect through concealment, through incompleteness, through skillful preparation and synchronized details that drove the visitor on and beckoned him to the open space in the center of the *acropolis* with its closed composition of free-standing buildings and a view over the surrounding landscape.

The *agora* lies to the northwest of the *acropolis* and north of the Areopagus. It was the civic and commercial center of Athens with the main administrative buildings. The old *agora* of the fifth and fourth centuries had fewer buildings and the central area was open with only minor monuments. In the course of time numerous buildings were added, and *stoai* and other public buildings loosely surrounded its fringes. In the Hellenistic age longer *stoai* were constructed that enclosed

538

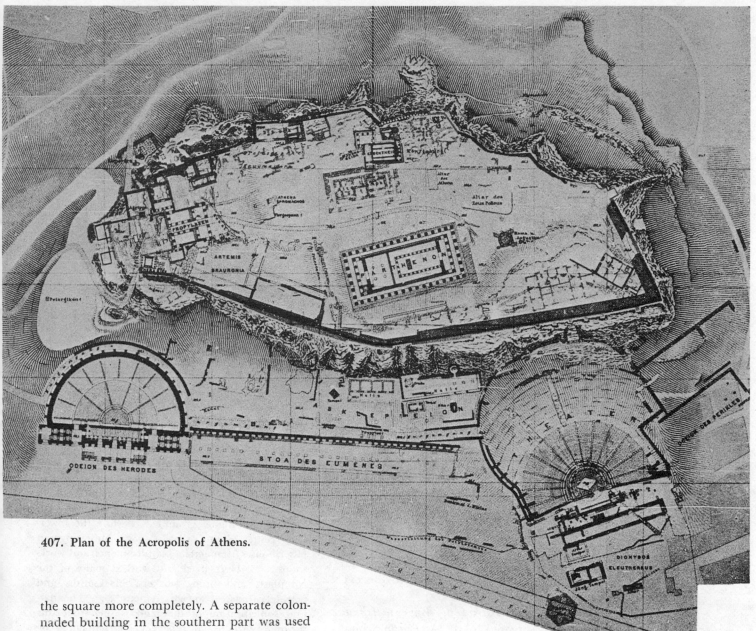

407. Plan of the Acropolis of Athens.

the square more completely. A separate colonnaded building in the southern part was used as a market. In the second century B.C. Attalos, King of Pergamon, a great admirer of Athenian culture, provided funds for the erection of a two-storied *stoa* with shops behind on the east side of the *agora*. In Roman times the *odeion,* a covered theater, and a temple of Ares were built in the middle of the square. Inevitably a site that has been occupied for thousands of years cannot convey a true impression of what it has been at a particular time. The general aspect is confused and yet the loose arrangement of the buildings, the Panathenaean street, the processional way to

the *acropolis* cutting diagonally through the *agora,* the situation near the foot of the Areopagus and the *acropolis,* and the dominating position of the temple of Hephaestus, the god of the metalworkers whose workshops were nearby—all these manifold and individual details were harmonized by the unpretentious human scale and their natural and easy interdependence. Moreover, in the fifth century B.C. Cimon, Athenian statesman and

539

408. Model of the Athenian Acropolis.

general, planted the *agora* with plane trees.[33] This factor may also have been a unifying element.

Since 1931 the American School of Classical Studies at Athens has been clearing and exploring the *agora* systematically. Their work is now complete except for a final tidying and landscaping of the site according to the evidence of ancient authorities.

An Industrial District of Ancient Athens has been investigated by the American School of Classical Studies at Athens and the results have been partially published in *Hesperia* (1951). The area lies to the southwest of the *agora* and in the depression between the Areopagus at the east and the Hill of the Nymphs and the Pnyx at the west. It measures 557.6 by 262.4 feet. The following is a condensed excerpt from the report. It gives a certain idea of the structure and layout of an industrial district in antiquity.

33. After a report by R. E. Wycherley in the *Manchester Guardian*, February 18, 1955.

The slopes of the Areopagus above Areopagus Street to the east seem in Roman times at least to have been built up with the houses of the well-to-do. . . . The dwellings of the prosperous were built on the higher ground . . . while the lower-lying center of the valley . . . was built up with lesser houses, commercial establishments, and workshops. . . . Here lived and worked many of the coroplasts and bronze-workers, blacksmiths and marble cutters, of ancient Athens. . . . The natural configuration of the land is such that this region of Athens must have been frequented by passers-by, if not actually settled, from the very earliest times. If . . . , as has been suggested by Thucydides, the early town lay to the southwest of the Acropolis, then communication with the areas to the north must have been channelled through the pass between the Pnyx and Areopagus and northward through our area, probably by footpaths . . . which later became suburban roads and with the northward growth of the town finally turned into city streets. . . . These streets, then, were early features of the Athenian landscape as well as important arteries. [The three streets are Areopagus and Piraeus Street and the street of the Marble workers.] The area was al-

540

most certainly a part of Melite or of Kollytos, both of which were demes containing workshops of various kinds. . . . The demes leading all the others in artisan metics between 420 and 320 B.C. were Melite, Skambonidai, and Kollytos. The crafts plied in the first and last of these demes were: goldsmith, worker in encaustic, cabinet maker, mason, sculptor, carver of ornamental stone work, gilder, lead merchant, brick-layer and odd-jobber. . . . The marble cutters and sculptors probably had their own workshops here, and worked under contract on the Acropolis at such state enterprises as the adornment of the Erech-theion.

As usual in the simpler quarters, the houses were closely built together, lining the narrow streets on both sides. Their width differed up to 15 feet in some parts and houses repeatedly encroached to a distance of over 5 feet over the streets. There were also Roman houses in the northwest part of the area. Here the excavations have not been sufficiently advanced to give a detailed picture.

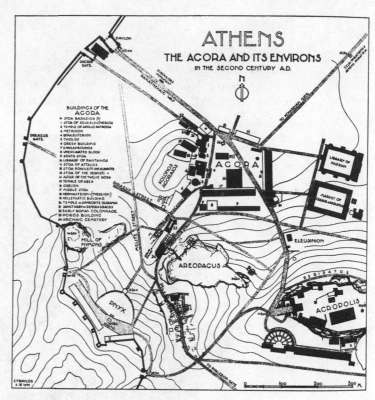

409. The Agora of Athens and its environs.

410. Plan of the industrial district of ancient Athens.

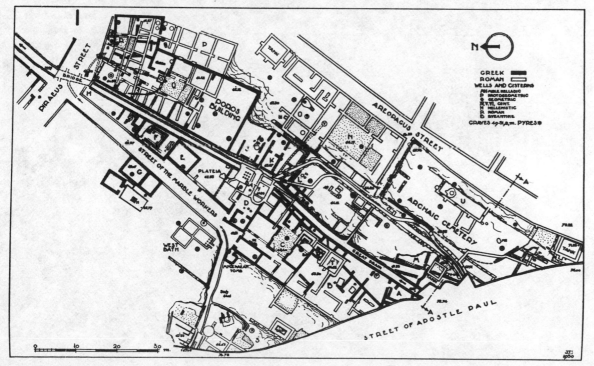

Peiraieus, the port of Athens, about 5 miles to the southwest, offered the great advantage of an almost landlocked bay and two small coves, Munychia and Zea. The town was laid out on a checkerboard plan, the first design of this type in mainland Greece—though not, as has been repeatedly suggested, of Europe. Etruscan towns were also built on a regular

542

ground plan. It was, however, the first opportunity to lay out a new town in a rational way without the obstacles that existed in the older and irregular towns—and this was the majority on the mainland. The design has been ascribed to Hippodamos of Miletus. This is possibly correct, although conclusive evidence is lacking. It is more likely that the regular scheme with its streets intersecting at right angles, which Hippodamos had theoretically worked out in his writings on political and social problems, had been summarily applied to the virgin site. Still another possibility may be suggested: a regular plan was obviously the simplest and given solution when a new town had to be built in one sweep. Historical evidence in this respect is overwhelming. On the other hand, Hippodamos was known in Attica for his theoretical studies; his ideas were "in the air." It is therefore not impossible that two trends met; the general as just mentioned, and the personal stimulated by Hippodamos' workings. He has been elevated to a prominence as town planner in modern times which he hardly possessed in antiquity. In any case, our knowledge of the ancient harbor town is too scant to permit a detailed description. We do not know whether the regular layout covered the whole peninsula; nor can it be proven convincingly that the *agora* in the center of the town, which has been rather superficially regarded as one of Hippodamos' main architectural achievements, was really his own work especially designed for this particular case. What has possibly happened was that he provided a central space—if we accept his authorship of Peiraieus at all—which was to be kept free from buildings, and that this space had a rectangular or square shape in contrast to the *agora* at Athens.[34] Finally, the layout of a harbor town was a rational enterprise, a technical task that relegated social and political considerations to a second place. There is no reason to be enthusiastic about the "revolutionary" importance of Peiraieus or to regard it as the beginning of "modern" city planning. We shall return to this problem in connection with the layout of Miletus and other cities.

34. A. von Gerkan. *Griechische Städteanlagen*. 1924. P. 54.

543

411. Air view of Peiraieus and its harbor.

Corinth lies one mile and a half south of the Isthmus which connects Central Greece and the Peloponnesus and separates the Corinthian and the Saronic Gulfs. The distance between these two inlets, which were of immense importance to the history of ancient Greece, was about 4 miles. The city therefore had two ports, Lechaeon at the west and Kenchreai at the east, the latter the better harbor. At first the goods were carried over the Isthmus by pack-animals; later ships were hauled across. Plans to build a canal are said to date back to about 600 B.C. An actual attempt was made by Nero in A.D. 67 but was given up because of a revolt in Gallia. Finally the canal was built in 1882-93 along the line fixed by Nero's engineers, whose course is still visible. Corinth also dominated the overland routes to the Peloponnesus. It was therefore in a particularly strong strategic position which it used to the full in the interest of its political and economic position. The territory of Corinth was small and not fertile. Thus the natural conditions directed its main activities toward commerce. As Strabo remarked,

Corinth is called "wealthy" because of its commerce, since it is situated on the Isthmus and is master of two harbours, of which the one leads straight to Asia, and the other to Italy; and it makes easy the exchange of merchandise from both countries that are so far distant from each other. . . . The duties on what by land was exported from the Peloponnesus and what was imported to it fell to those who held the keys [of the country]. And to later times this remained ever so. . . . And the temple of Aphrodite [at Corinth] was so rich that it owned more than a thousand temple-slaves, courtesans, whom both men and women had dedicated to the goddess. And therefore it was also on account of these women that the city was crowded with people and grew rich; for instance, the ship-captains freely squandered their money.[35]

Ancient Corinth stood on two terraces, one about a hundred feet lower than the other. Its core was in an indentation near the center of the upper terrace. The citadel Acro-Corinth rose sharply 1,886 feet above the surrounding country. Strabo describes it as follows:

A lofty mountain with a perpendicular height of three stadia [a stadium = about 606 feet] and one half; and an ascent of as much as thirty stadia, ends in a sharp peak; it is called Acro-Corinthus, and its northern side is the steepest; and beneath it lies the city in a level, trapezium-shaped place. . . . Now the circuit of the city itself used to be as much as forty stadia, and all of it that was unprotected by the mountain was enclosed by a wall.[36]

Enormous fortifications enclosed the citadel, the Lower Town, and the port of Lechaeon after long walls had been built over the whole length of 13.05 miles. The *agora,* on the terrace south of the temple of Apollo, was surrounded by colonnades. It was the meeting point of roads to the port of Lechaeon entering it through a stately *propulaion* built in Roman times, to Acro-Corinth, Kenchreai, and Sikyon. The development and layout of the *agora* have been influenced by religious requirements which centered on the temple of Apollo standing on an elevation and surrounded on three sides by *stoai.* This was the civic center of Corinth during the sixth and fifth centuries. The area had more of the character of an annex to the temple than of a secular center. It was *"un lieu de refuge intangible,"* reserved primarily for funeral rites dating back to the origin of the city. Sheltered from the encroachments of foreign religions and beliefs which merchants from other lands would bring with them, the center was sharply distinguished from those of the panhellenic cults by its sanctuary of the Isthmus. In the following centuries the *agora* spread from the north to the south, and the ancient temple precincts lost their importance as a civic center to the new and independent *agora* which had an air of *"un plan d'ensemble qui porte la*

35. VIII. 6. 20.

36. VIII. 6. 21.

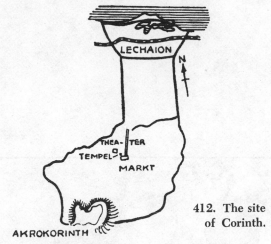

412. The site
of Corinth.

marque des conceptions nouvelles."[37] The new *agora* had shops on the north and south sides and also on the west, though somewhat recessed and hidden by other buildings. The town hall was situated behind the south *stoa*.

This Roman *agora*, 765 by 381 feet, had all the characteristic features of Roman design. It was the political and economic center of the

37. R. Martin, *op. cit.*, pp. 217, 340.

city; the spatial organization was homogeneous; its shape was rectangular; and the rows of shops and *stoai* formed a coherent whole. A *basilica,* a monumental building which contained the law courts, occupied the east side. A theater and an *odeion* were situated to the northwest of the *agora*. The contrast to the more intimate ancient Greek religious and civic center at the foot of the temple is enormous. It is not so much the difference of scale but the contrast of spontaneous intimacy and organized grandeur that symbolizes the antagonistic distinction between two civilizations, between the instinctive limitations of ancient Greece and the deliberate groupings of Rome. The temple *agora* is dominated and held together by a religious atmosphere of devotion, and the Roman *agora* by functional and utilitarian buildings. Nothing more heterogeneous can be imagined within a relatively narrow area.

413. The Agora of Corinth.

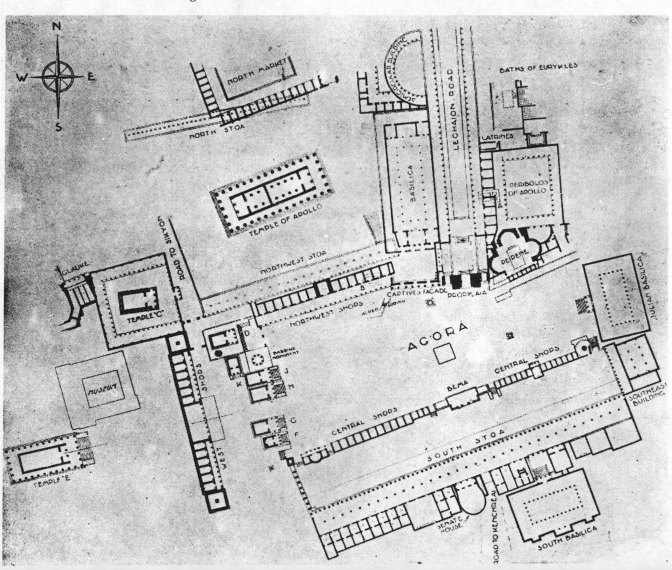

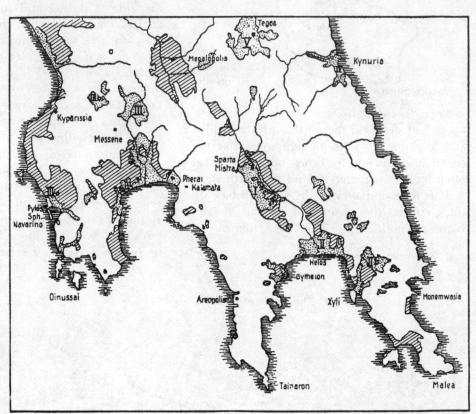

414. Map of Laconia and Messenia.

Sparta, the capital of Laconia, on the Eurotas River, 27 miles from its port of Gytheion, was situated at the northern end of the Laconian plain, dominating the only land routes into Laconia. The alluvial plain of the Eurotas including the marginal zone has no connection with the coastal plain on the Laconian Gulf. It was a landlocked region, a fact that may, at least partly, explain the particular political and social structure of Sparta, so

distinct from the development of all other Greek city-states. As repeatedly mentioned, synoicism was not necessarily connected with the foundation of a *polis*. Sparta is the exception *par excellence*. Its synoicism resulted in a "living together" in a number of villages. This "dispersed synoicism," possibly dating back to the ninth century, was organized on a regional rather than on a local basis. Remnants of neolithic settlements (before 2000 B.C.) have been found in many places of the plain and the marginal zones. According to tradition, Dorians settled in the later tenth century in four villages: Limnai, Kynosura, Mesoa, and Pitane. And indeed the fertile country around the present town of Sparta is surrounded by four hills on which vestiges of early settlements have been identified.

The invasion of the Peloponnesus by Dorian bands from the northwest was only partly successful and did not lead to a complete subjugation of the whole country. The martial customs and habits of their migratory past were therefore preserved for several generations and left their indelible mark upon the character and education of the Spartan people. State and community meant everything, and the individual was subordinated to their interests. These qualities fully unfolded when the population increased and became sedentary around 800 B.C. Amyklai was added as a fifth village to the four earlier settlements which had made up the original union. Now Sparta, an autonomous community, called herself a *polis* despite the rural structure of settlement and took over the cult of Amyklai, the citadel, the *polis*, where Apollo was worshipped as protector of the Dorian immigration.

Dorian and pre-Dorian institutions coalesced although the country was clearly divided between Dorians and Achaeans, the latter remaining in possession of the mountainous zones that surrounded the basins and the coastal plain. The Achaeans were called *perioikoi*, "dwellers around," and though they retained their personal freedom and a certain measure of independence they were under the immediate supervision of Spartan governors. Their settlements, though of a purely agrarian character, are still traceable where cultivation in the mountains was possible. The towns of Pharis, Bryseai, and Helos were abolished. This resettlement of the country was guided by a clear principle: the Spartans as conquerors occupied all the valuable land—that is, the extensive alluvial plains. Only the smaller oases in the mountains were left to the *perioikoi*. No new Dorian settlements were founded. The land was divided into equal plots or, *klaroi*—that is, entailed farms of the clans which supported several families. In contrast to other Greek city-states, the countryside was not dotted with dispersed settlements. The citizens were concentrated in the five villages and only helots and the *perioikoi* lived outside.

The militaristic character and the agrarian structure of settlement and society, which re-tained the features of the early conquering period, made Sparta a warrior state and the natural adversary of Athens. Around 750 B.C. the free citizens of Sparta numbered about 8,000. Their life proceeded within the limited world of the five villages. Gradually new tensions arose when the state began to stretch out beyond Taygetos, Parnon, and the mountainous regions of southern Arcadia. In 464 B.C. an earthquake destroyed almost all buildings, killing a considerable number of inhabitants. These losses and a century of incest so reduced the population that between 479 and 418 it fell from 5,000 to almost 3,000 full citizens. This trend continued and diminished their number to 1,000 around 370 B.C. so that incentives were offered to families with many children.

Excavations tell us very little about the physical layout of Sparta. The origin of the civic center is obscure, though literary evidence and religious tradition seem to indicate that it was located in the region of the sanctuary of Artemis Orthia. R. Martin suggests that *"la tradition aitiologique des rites de flagellation rapportée par Pausanias sert au moins à nous prouver que ce culte était commun à tous les villages lacédémoniens et qu'il faut le mettre en rapport avec le synécisme.*[38] In the course of time, but in any case before the end of the sixth century B.C., the political center moved south, to the site where the *agora* of classical times has been identified. This led to a functional division: some of the political and civic rites such as the *gymnopaidiai* (dances performed by naked boys at public festivals) were transferred to the new place while others, which were part of the ancient cult, remained attached to the altar of Artemis where they had originated. The original *agora* was extremely simple, without any decoration to distract the attention of the citizens from the grave political problems under discussion. (Plutarch. *Lycurgus* 6.) It was situated not far from the theater at the foot of the *acropolis* which occupied an isolated hill at the periphery of the *polis*.

38. *Recherches sur l'Agora Grecque. Études d'Histoire et d'Architecture Urbaines.* 1951. P. 207.

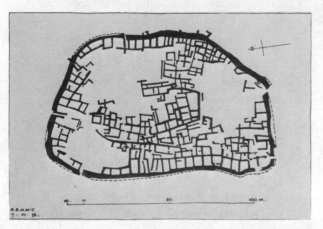

415. Map of the town of Malthi.

Malthi, Messenia, in the western Peloponnesus, can probably be identified with the classical town of Dorion. The earlier remains belonging to Dorion I and II have more or less disappeared under the layers of Dorion III. Its area, roughly oval in shape, was enclosed by a strong wall and divided into three parts. The center was occupied by the citadel standing on a terrace and fortified by an inner wall. This was the most elevated part of the *acropolis.* The citadel resembled a large elongated apsidal house and palace, consisting of an irregular trapezoid in the southern and a very large and only partly occupied northern half. The *acropolis* was enclosed by walls with storerooms. The houses within this area were inhabited by servants and retainers. The whole was reminiscent of the fortified castles at Mycenae and Tiryns. The second part of the town consisted of groups of houses irregularly arranged and partly built against the inside of the outer wall. The third part was occupied by three open spaces where the country people could shelter in times of danger.[39] The layout of Malthi was irregular and focused on the citadel. It must have been a stronghold of considerable importance in a hostile country.

39. M. N. Valmin. *The Swedish Messenia Expedition.* 1938.

Megalopolis, Arcadia, lies in a plain on both banks of the Helisson. It was founded in 370 B.C. when all Arcadian townships, forty after Pausanias (VIII. 27. 3-5), were incorporated in it. The site had been uninhabited. It may have been chosen as a neutral locality to avoid jealousy among the participating groups. Megalopolis had a double function: it was a federal capital and a bastion against Sparta. It covered a large area about 5½ miles in circumference, divided into two almost equal halves by the river Helisson. It enclosed large open spaces. We know nothing of the layout in detail except the situation of the two great centers of public life both extending over a softly undulating terrain: the federal buildings on the left bank of the river, and the *agora* with the religious and municipal buildings on the right bank. One of the hills was occupied by the sanctuary of Athene Polias and served as the *acropolis.* The principal federal buildings were the theater and the *thersilion* or parliament hall which provided shelter in bad weather when the open theater could not be used for political assemblies. Both sites were systematically laid out. The *agora* at the north on the right bank was rectangular with *stoai* at the north and east, and public buildings and sanctuaries of the townships which had taken part in the foundation of Megalopolis.[40]

40. E. Kirsten. "Die Entstehung der Griechischen Stadt," *Archäologischer Anzeiger,* Vol. 4, 1964, p. 898.

Mantinea, Arcadia, lies in a long and marshy plain. In early times it was a cluster of villages which were merged into one city between 465 and 460 B.C. This was the first synoicism which led to the foundation of the first city of Mantinea. In 385 B.C. this city was destroyed by the Spartans. They ordered the dioecism, the dissolution of the city. Only the temples and sacred buildings survived. The people were dispersed in rural settlements. In 371 B.C., after the victory of Epaminondas, the population returned. The city was rebuilt. New walls were erected. The whole layout was dominated by the requirements of defense. However, the destruction of the first city was not quite total. Apart from the sacred buildings, remains of walls and foundations were preserved. This *"nouvelle Mantinée se superposa donc à l'ancienne, enfermant dans le cadre neuf de ses remparts, de ses édifices et de ses maisons modernes, les restes vénérables qui la reliaient au passé."*[41]

Mantinea was a circular city. In the history of Greek city planning it was unique; the

41. G. Fougères, *Mantinée et L'Arcadie Orientale.* 1898. P. 133, *passim.*

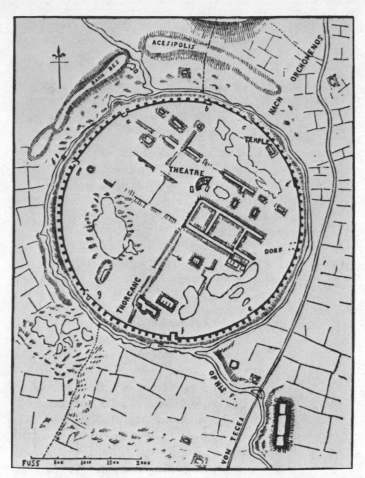

416. Plan of Mantinea.

417. The walls of Mantinea.

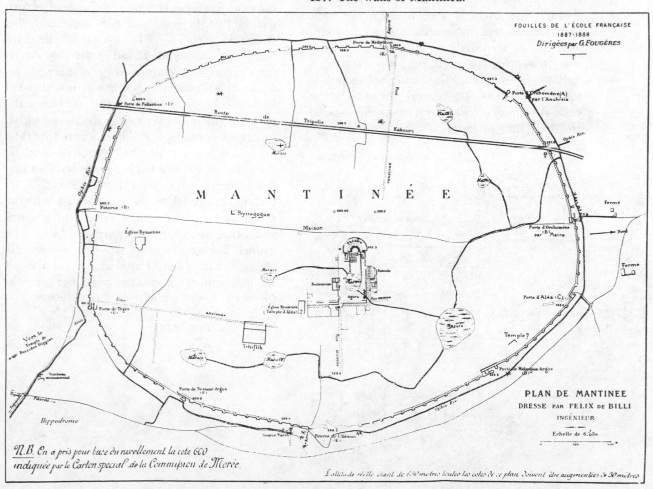

origin of this type of fortification remains a mystery. A possible explanation may be that the new theories of Hippodamos and their parody by Aristophanes who had helped to spread their knowledge had found a fertile soil in the minds of the Mantinaean architects. In the *Birds* (1004-1009) Aristophanes introduced the Athenian astronomer Meton as a quack who claims he can square the circle, proclaiming:

With the straight rod I measure out, that so the circle may be squared; and in the centre a marketplace; and streets be leading to it straight to the very centre; just as from a star, though circular, straight rays flash out in all directions.

This was, of course, meant as a parody and as such it has been justly dismissed as irrelevant. But the fact remains that a parody is sometimes more serious than a superficial observer may understand. In any case, here was a plan for an Ideal City and a pattern that had been applied in a very similar manner at Mantinea. Irrational nonsense is perhaps sometimes not too far from rational truth. Mantinea was almost, though not quite, The Ideal City of antiquity. It had all the main characteristics which were to be worked out so laboriously many centuries later by architects of the Renaissance. The defense perimeter determined everything; the streets led radially to the gates; the center was a public square, the *agora*. There were ten gates in the *enceinte* whose circular course was the shortest and best line of defense. The *agora*, though not in the very center, was near the point where the streets converged. None of these streets can now be followed along its whole length, but their beginning at the gate and their ending near the *agora* can be traced. The *agora* was an essential element of the defense system like the *piazza d'armi* of a Renaissance city. It was the place where the soldiers assembled and from which they could reach the fortifications in the shortest time. Here the commanding officer could install his headquarters and station his reserves. It is very likely that Themistocles intervened, as suggested by Fougères,[42] and advised the Mantinaeans to use the experience gained at Athens through their contact with Miletus and make their city a bulwark against their common enemy. This may also explain the pre-eminent consideration given to the defensive strength of the new city.

A circular road ran along the inside of the walls connecting the gates. The ten roads leading to the ten gates of the city continued within it and divided the urban area into ten unequal sectors. An inscription speaks of five tribes, or rather demes, which represented the five quarters of the city. It is therefore not impossible that each quarter consisted of two sectors. But there was one very large sector between the gates L and K (top left on the map) that was uninhabited and possibly covered with gardens or retained as open space. As already mentioned, the *agora* was not situated in the geometrical center of the city but at the meeting point of the radial streets where its functions could operate more efficiently. The *agora*, as shown in the reconstruction by Fougères, is the result of a long development from simple and primitive beginnings. Its rectangular interior is surrounded on the north and east by *stoai* behind which shops and other buildings are partly hidden. The council house occupies a site near the middle of the south side. At the west a number of small sanctuaries and other buildings are held together by the semicircle of the theater.

42. *Op. cit.*, pp. 376 ff.

418. The Agora of Mantinea.

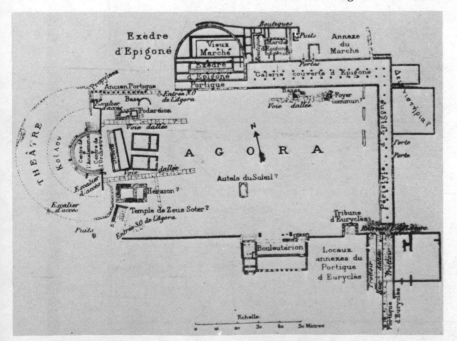

Delphi may be mentioned in this connection because in contrast to Olympia it was not only a place of worship but a settlement. It is situated in a glen about 6 miles from the northern shore of the Gulf of Corinth. It is closed in by the cliffs of Mount Parnassos on the north and by Mount Cirphis on the south. Between the two mountains a stream receives a brooklet which rises in a deep gorge at the sacred spring, the Castalian Fountain. It was a grandiose and solemn setting for the temple and oracle of Apollo.

The sanctuary stood on a site of a settlement dating back to the middle of the second millennium B.C., where according to tradition the earth goddess Gaia was worshipped before the cult of Apollo was introduced by tribes immigrating from the north. The settlement at Delphi owed its importance and wealth to the sanctuary and may have been founded by the priests or rather by their holy community. Delphi was the central Greek sanctuary uniting all Greek tribes, whose fame and influence extended beyond the European mainland to Asia Minor and even to Egypt. The Oracle was consulted by princes, tribes, and cities and played a decisive role in the foundation of new colonies. It encouraged colonization in the west along the Mediterranean shore and was a forceful political instrument which spread Greek culture, Greek *eunomia,* and Greek power to regions that had hitherto been free from alien domination.

The colonies remained attached not only to the mother city but also to the Oracle, as the adviser of their founders. The maxims of the Seven Wise Men living in the period from 620-550 B.C. and conducting the affairs of their country as rulers, lawgivers, and councillors were recorded in the temple. The most famous of these maxims was "Know Thyself," expressing the characteristically Greek emphasis on man as the measure of all things. Delphi was not only a pilgrimage center like Santiago de Compostela or Montserat, the Ise Shrine, or St. Peter's; it was a political agency of the first order which the priests used to the greatest advantage of Greece and their own power.

Greece had neither a Bible nor a Church; that is why Apollo, vicar on earth of the heavenly Father, came to fill the gap. Without Delphi, Greek society could scarcely have endured the tensions to which it was subjected in the Archaic Age. The crushing sense of human ignorance and human insecurity . . . would have been unendurable without the assurance which such an omniscient divine counsellor could give, the assurance that behind the seeming chaos there was knowledge and purpose. . . . The Greeks believed in their Oracle, not because they were superstitious fools but because they could not do without believing in it.[43]

And we may add: Without understanding the paramount role of the Oracle and the reasons why it responded to and reflected the essence of the Greek attitude to life Greek cities with their seemingly chaotic incoherence, their instinctive grouping of buildings, and the creative empathy with which they adapted the man-made to the natural environment—without understanding these qualities, the spontaneity of human reaction to the challenge of the environment and the vision of purposeful immediacy behind the seemingly unsystematic appearance of the many Greek cities, we can never really appreciate their unique place in the history of city planning.

The grouping of all the buildings in Delphi was, as in most other Greek ancient towns, irregular without any apparent coordination. A rigid and systematic regularity with axial emphasis on the main buildings was still incompatible with the original conception of a sanctuary as an integral part of the natural environment. The respect for the sacred and animistic essence of Nature, spontaneously and subconsciously transferred to the world of inanimate works created by man in honor of his gods, operated against the restriction of their autonomous independence by deliberate interrelations. As has been explained before, the arrangement of buildings, altars, and statues was like the grouping of sculptures, each of which had its own individuality and all together formed a man-made extension of the inscrutable variety of Nature. This is the reason why Delphi has been mentioned in this connection.

43. E. R. Dodds. *The Greeks and the Irrational.* 1957. P. 75.

419. Air view of Delphi.

Delphi's importance waned with the decline of uniting ideas and through the lack of an unambiguous attitude during the Persian Wars until in Hellenistic times religious scepticism undermined the respect for the Oracle and finally reduced the site to an interesting remnant of the past.

The sacred enclosure was surrounded by a wall. It rose in three terraces, beginning with the lowest terrace in the south, where the Sacred Way entered at its eastern and lowest part. This way zigzags up the hill and in a characteristically Greek fashion reaches the *temenos* almost casually without any direct relation to the great temple. There is no axial orientation, no attempt at symmetrical perspective. The Sacred Way was accompanied by numerous treasure houses and offerings which also filled the first terrace. Then it continued north to the middle terrace with the temple and finally westward to the theater, which was also situated within the enclosure. A stadium lay outside the walls to the northwest on a plateau resting on a terrace wall. The fact that the *bouleuterion* (the council chamber) and the *prytaneion* (the religious and political center with the hearth and the sacred fire where foreign ambassadors and persons who had deserved well of the community were entertained) stood within the Sacred Enclosure gave it a political character. As R. Martin suggests, *"il s'agit d'organismes plus municipaux qu'amphictioniques."*[44] Amphictyons were deputies from the city-states of Greece. The site of the *agora,* the indispensable element of a community, can probably be identified with the large open space on the lower terrace where the Sacred Way widened—that is, to the east of the council chamber and to the south of the Hall of the Athenians. The Sacred Enclosure of Delphi exhibited within a narrow area the same principles that shaped the physical structure of many Greek cities— an unsurpassed blending of man's work and nature; a perfect adaptation to a difficult terrain; unity in diversity; an instinctive coordination of numerous different elements; a dramatic concentration on the main building, the temple; and the wide embracing sweep of the semicircle of the theater, merging in the massif of Holy Parnassos towering above the Sacred Enclosure, forcefully reminding man of his insignificance and the human scale of even his most sacred works.

44. *Op. cit.,* p. 239.

Dimini, Thessalia, was a neolithic hilltop settlement. Its natural area was enlarged by terracing. It was a strongly fortified place with six enclosures in dry masonry. The dwellings clustered closely together around the innermost enclosure with the seat of the chieftain. Open spaces served as refuges for the population. The layout followed in the main the contours of the hill, which was surrounded by fertile land and had a good water supply.

420. Plan of the Neolithic hilltop settlement of Dimini.

553

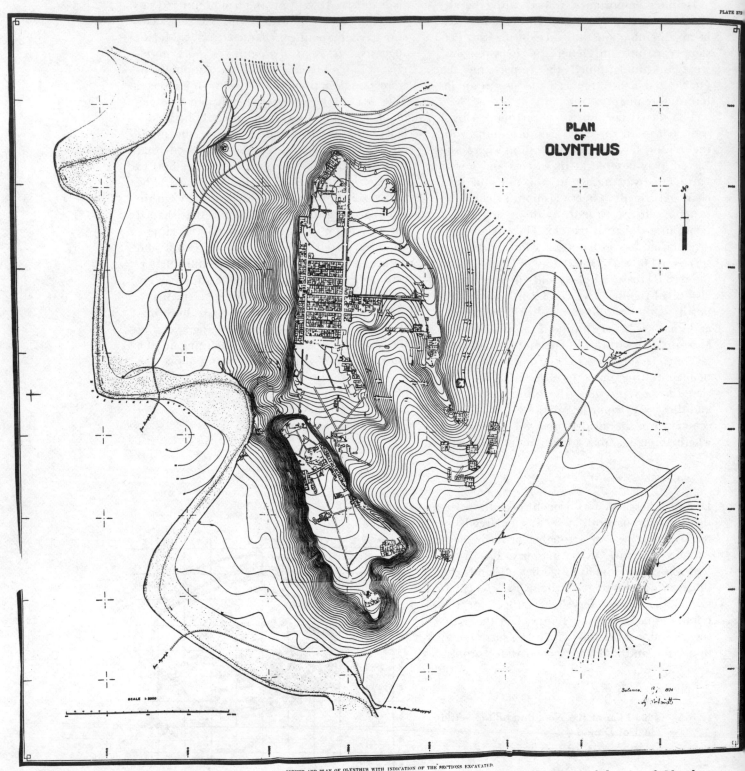

PLATE 272

**PLAN
OF
OLYNTHUS**

N°

SCALE 1:5000

Salonica, 12; 1934

SURVEY AND PLAN OF OLYNTHUS WITH INDICATION OF THE SECTIONS EXCAVATED.

421. Map of the site of Olynthus.

Olynthus lies at the head of the Toronaic Gulf on the peninsula of Chalcidice. A neolithic settlement was situated at the southern spur of the south hill which was continuously inhabited since about 1000 B.C. After the Persian Wars in 479 B.C. the ruined village of Olynthus was taken over by the Chalcidians and became one of the many towns on the peninsula. Gradually the importance of Olynthus grew until its preponderance over the other towns was firmly established. Finally, to facilitate the defense of the region, the other coastal towns were abandoned after 432 B.C. and the Chalcidians combined in one strong city at Olynthus. This synoicism was the most important event in its history.[45] A new city was laid out which covered the two flat-topped hills and the plain to the east. The old settlement area remained inhabited though in loosely dispersed groups.

The new Olynthus was laid out on a gridiron plan, the characteristic form of almost all colonial foundations. Olynthus belonged to this category, though with one important qualification: what was a preconceived design were the streets, the checkerboard plan, and of course the building blocks, not the city as a limited entity. That is, the city could grow —within certain limits—by the accretion of block units of approximately the same shape as those which the street pattern had cut out. This disposes of the idea that Olynthus, like other Greek regular cities, was conceived as a whole from the start. As a matter of fact everything remained in flux and only the similarity of the building blocks and the layout of the streets created the semblance of a preconceived and coherent idea, which was more apparent than real.

The new residential town covered an area of 3,600 by 600 feet on the flat plateau of the north hill, gently sloping down to the south, while the western edge was the natural boundary of the urban area. Here the walls followed the contours of the terrain. The main gate was in the northwest protected by a sort

of bastion. Four parallel main streets varying from 15 to 21 feet in width ran north-south and were intersected at regular intervals and at right angles by other parallel streets 15 feet wide. The streets were unpaved except for a few patches of cobbling. An unusual feature was the diagonal street, more or less parallel to the eastern edge of the south hill, which joined one of the north-south "avenues" in the southern half of the north hill. This was the connection with Mekyberna and the sea. The building blocks were occupied by two rows of houses, each group consisting of five dwelling units and separated by narrow alleys paved with cobblestones. Each house covered an area of about 2,565 square feet with five rooms, including a small bathroom and two or three workrooms and storerooms. The arrangement of the rooms varied but in most cases the houses were entered from the south through a small courtyard onto which a long shallow room opened at its north side. There were upper stories probably built over the northern part which showed in a rudimentary form the characteristic features of the *peristyle* house. Only a few buildings had shops, except some of those in the longest and widest "avenue." At the southern end of this "shopping street," at its west side, there was a hall with columns and a fountain house fed by an earthenware pipeline from a source about 9.32 miles to the north.

Public buildings and large squares were almost wholly missing at Olynthus. The social and economic conditions of the fourth century were still mainly conditioned by the agricultural preoccupation of the population. Industrial activity was restricted to small-scale manufacture with a few slaves. The contrast between rich and poor was not so obvious as in later times. There was no need for the *polis* to dull the masses with *panem et circenses.* This may partly explain why large public buildings and ostentatious squares—an indispensable feature of the later Hellenistic cities —were missing at Olynthus, and why there were only a few shops attached to the houses. However, a certain distinction did exist between the districts of the wealthy and the less

45. M. Gude. *A History of Olynthus.* 1933.
D. M. Robinson and J. W. Graham. *Excavations at Olynthus.* The Johns Hopkins University Studies in Archeology. Part VIII. *The Hellenic House.* 1938.

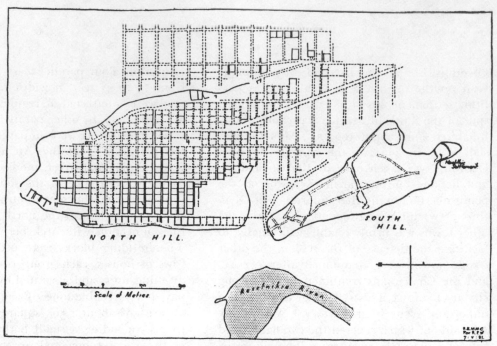

422. Reconstructed street plan of Olynthus.

prosperous. The excavations indicate that the better quarters were mainly situated to the east of the north hill. Here outside the old walls a suburbia, a *proasteion,* had grown up, not as a more open development with detached *villae* but with larger and fewer houses grouped in building blocks of the same size as in other parts of the city. This district was eventually enclosed in the fortifications. The excavations have further revealed that since 379 B.C. the city had grown more rapidly. In 348 B.C., before its destruction by Philip of Macedonia, the population may have been close to 15,000, including slaves.

On the south hill a center of shops and workshops had gradually developed near the old market square. This was the site which had been inhabited since early times and had conserved the ancient unsystematic grouping of buildings. Here at the northern end of the ridge was the civic center of the first settlement which was abandoned toward the end

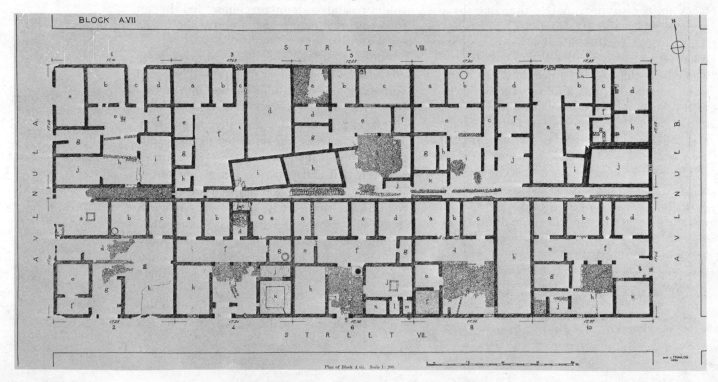

423. Houses on the North Hill at Olynthus.

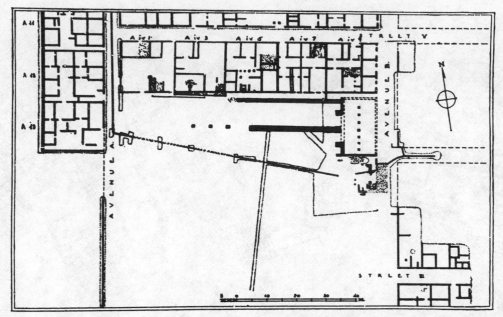

424. New Agora at Olynthus.

of the fifth century at the time of the founding of the new city, and was moved to the south of the quarter on the western edge of the north hill. Its north side was occupied by the hall, the *stoa*, already mentioned, near the fountain house. The excavators of Olynthus have suggested that this large open space may have been used for shops and possibly as a parade ground. They discard the idea that it was the new *agora* because no public buildings, temples, or altars have been discovered and the soil was neither leveled nor paved. But this argument is not too convincing. At Miletus and Peiraieus, to mention only these two examples, it took a long time before the layout and the leveling of the ground were completed. On the other hand, the type of the *stoa* corresponds to that of the colonnades of Ionian *agorai* which likewise had no office buildings or shops directly attached to them.[46]

46. R. Martin, *op. cit.*, p. 390.

THE ISLANDS

Thera is the southernmost island of the Cyclades. A great volcanic eruption at the middle of the second millennium B.C. destroyed all organic life on the island and covered the slopes and the Elias Mountain with a thick pumice layer under which remains of a Minoan settlement (1800-1500 B.C.) have been discovered. The volcanic rock with the ancient Elias Mountain rises to over 1,000 feet. The eruption left the island uninhabited for centuries until it was resettled at the beginning of the first millennium by Dorians, who were probably attracted to the site because the pumice layer offered fertile arable land and nature a fortresslike security.

The town that the Dorians founded extended along the ridge of the Messavuno Mountain and could be entered only from the Sellada, the saddle, which connected it with the higher Elias Mountain. Sandy beaches on both sides of the steep mountain permitted the mooring of flat vessels and the unloading of booty, provisions, and building material—especially marble. Some other small settlements of Dorian times have been identified on the island. The ancient port of Oia was situated to the east of the Sellada. The layout of the town was organically adapted to the terrain. The *agora* occupied the center of the ridge, a site, so it seems, deliberately chosen

557

DIE ALTE STADT

THERA

NACH DEN AUSGRABUNGEN 1896-1902

1 : 1000

ÄLTERE MAUERN   WASSERBEHÄLTER, CISTERNEN, CANÄLE

SPÄTERE MAUERN   ANTIKE FELSINSCHRIFT

ANTIKE STRASSEN und PLÄTZE   Ausgrabungsgebiet

WEIHEINSCHRE   moderner Wegrand

Nach Aufnahmen v. P.Wilski mit Ergänzungen von W.Dörpfeld, P.Sureos, W.Wilberg.

for this purpose.[47] The southern end of Messavuno was reserved for the *"agora* of the gods."

Les découvertes de Théra ont confirmé dans le détail la description qu'Eschyle fait d'un tel sanctuaire dans Les Suppliantes. *Les "autels communs" (Suppl. 222) des divinités ainsi réunies en une agora permanente s'installent de préférence sur des hauteurs ou des croupes dominant les habitats humains.*[48]

This separation of the religious and secular functions was later explicitly demanded by Aristotle (*Politics.* VII. II. 2, 3). The main street beginning at the Sellada connected these squares in the most convenient way which avoided steep gradients. It rose from 792 feet at the Sellada to 1,153 feet at the *agora* and

then dropped at the *"agora* of the gods" to 660 feet. There must have been, at the widest part of the crest, another approximately parallel street which was connected with the main street by narrow and steep lanes mostly in the form of stairways. Here and there rudimentary serpentines were employed to overcome the steep gradients of the terrain—for example, north of the market square. These steep streets and lanes were at least partly paved, because without paving they could hardly have withstood the rain. Detailed investigations have led to the conclusion that the town was surrounded by a wall.[49] This may seem unusual, for the narrow ridge which falls off steeply on almost all sides does not seem to require artificial protection except at the

47. R. Martin, *op. cit.*, p. 235.
48. *Ibid.*, p. 169.

49. F. Freiherr Hiller von Gaertringen. *Thera. Untersuchungen, Vermessungen und Ausgrabungen in den Jahren 1895-1902. 1899-1909.* Vol. I, p. 190. Vol. III, pp. 75-77.

425. General map of the town of Thera.

northwestern end where it slopes down to the Sellada.

The *agora* was merely the enlargement of the main street which widened to about 90 feet over a length of more than 300 feet. Its long and narrow shape was conditioned by the natural configuration of the terrain. It was still a long way from the grand compositions of the Hellenistic period. The development of the more distinct form of the *agora* was dependent on the corresponding growth of political maturity; and this, as has been explained, was a long, slow process. It may be pertinent to compare the *agora* at Thera with the earliest markets in medieval Europe: in both cases widenings of streets served the civic function of the market. As in Greece, market squares of a distinctive functional and architectural character developed only gradually in the towns of the Middle Ages. The *stoa basilike*, a large covered hall with a central

row of 12 columns probably erected at the time of Augustus, dominated the *agora*. It stood on the west side of the square and was the most important public building of the town. The theater, to the west of the *agora*, dates back to the Ptolemaean period and served also as a council hall. The houses of the population huddled together behind the *agora* in the western part of the town and possibly in several other groups; the excavations do not permit us to draw definite conclusions. The main street ended at the southern end of the ridge in an open space with the gymnasium (second century B.C.) and the temple of Apollo Karneios, the tribal god common to all Dorians. The situation of Thera resembles in some respects that of Pergamon. It is almost an early dress rehearsal for this later highly refined and much more complex masterpiece of the harmonious cooperation of men and nature.

559

Phylakopi, on the volcanic island of Melos, founded before 2100 B.C., was a naval base of Minoan Crete. The third subsequent town on the original site, which belonged to the Late Minoan I period, stood on a small hill. Phylakopi was the capital of Melos, a member of the Minoan Commonwealth, a center of industry and trade, and a port of call on the route to the mainland.[50] The layout of the

50. The Society for the Promotion of Hellenic Studies. *Excavations at Phylakopi in Melos.* Conducted by the British School at Athens. Supplementary Paper No. 4. 1904. *Passim.*

town was not so unsystematic as might appear at first glance. The streets crossed one another at right angles and were oriented to the cardinal points of the compass. They were narrow, only about 4½ feet wide. Several of them had rough stone drains to carry off the rain water. The houses, closely built together probably with open courts, contained from two to four rooms. The Mycenaean palace occupied the north side of a small square with a few streets running directly into it at the corners. This was the meeting point, the primitive *agora,* of the population.

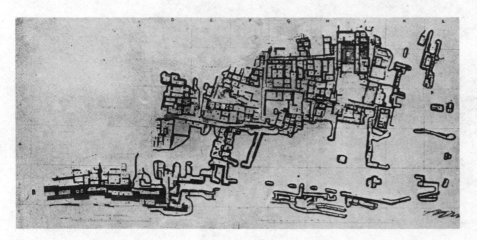

426. Plan of Phylakopi.

Delos, the Sacred Island of Apollo, has been inhabited since the third millennium B.C. It was regarded as the center of the Cyclades which were, according to the ancient belief, grouped around it in a circle, a *kyklos,* hence their name. The island rises to 350 feet in the steep peak of Mount Cynthus. As the birthplace of Apollo it was the seat of a great Ionic festival which took place at the anniversary of the birth of the god. The holy character of Delos had an unusual effect upon the fate of the island. Its dependence on Athens impeded the development of an autonomous town which would have been prejudicial to Athenian supremacy. But apart from the political influence, Athens interfered with the most personal events in the life of the inhabitants. In the sixth century, at the instigation of the Athenian statesman Peisistratus, all tombs within sight of the temple of Apollo were

removed lest they should impair its sanctity. Later, in 426 B.C., an even more far-reaching lustration was carried through by the Athenians: every tomb was removed from the island and a law decreed that henceforth, for all time, anyone about to give birth to a child or to die had to be conveyed at once from its shores. Even this was not regarded as sufficient. In 422 B.C. the Athenians expelled the whole secular population. However, this draconic measure was revoked in the following year and the inhabitants were permitted to return.

The sanctity of the island did not hinder its economic development. Owing to its favorable geographic position and the financial transactions which the wealth of the temple made possible, Delos was, in the fourth century B.C., a famous transshipment point and commercial center and since 250 B.C. the seat of trading companies from Italy. Most of the

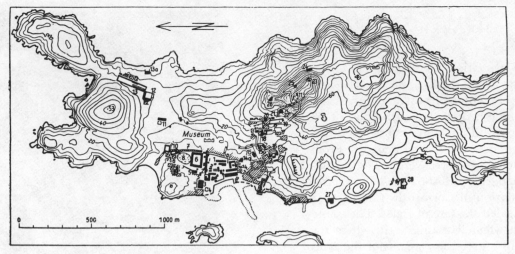

427. Excavations at Delos.

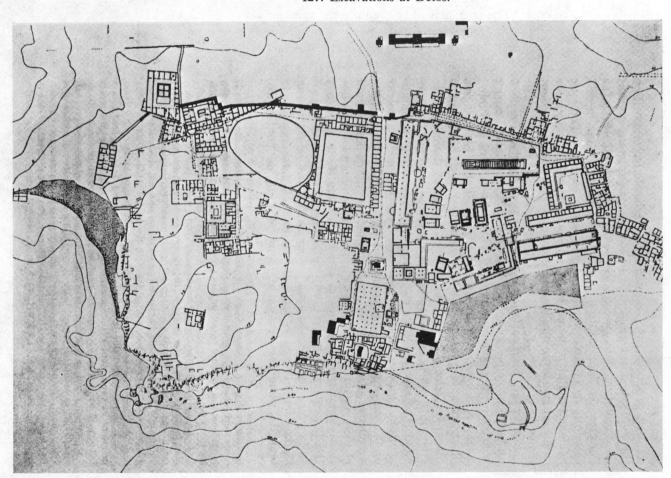

428. The Sanctuary of Apollo and the immediate surroundings at Delos.

important public buildings were erected in the third century B.C. At the same time the residential and harbor town developed. In the second century B.C. the Roman Senate, under pressure from Italian merchants resident on the island, declared Delos a free port, a decision that gave considerable impetus to the economic prosperity of the population especially after the destruction of Corinth in 146 B.C. which ended the commercial competition between the two cities. Toward the end of the second century the market, the wharfs, and the piers were enlarged for the increasing trade and traffic. After the destruction of 88 B.C. the main buildings were restored by Sulla. A second destruction followed in 69 B.C. From this blow Delos never recovered. The inhabitants were deported and the town left in ruins. The refoundation of Corinth by Caesar in 44 B.C. finally sealed the fate of Delos. The island was deserted when Pausanias visited it in the second century A.D. A few guards of the sanctuary were the only inhabitants.

The precincts of the temple, the residential town, and the district at the harbor were the three constituent elements of the Sacred Island.[51] The sacred embassies, sent annually to the Ionic festival, disembarked at the "sacred harbor" which was protected by two granite moles and a wharf built about 220 B.C. The main entrance to the sacred enclosure was situated in the immediate vicinity of the harbor. Here began the ancient sacred way which passed a small settlement of the Mycenaean period and remnants of religious buildings of the first centuries of the first millennium B.C. These buildings were grouped around a small square paved with bluish marble. The west side of this square consisted

51. École Française d'Athènes. *Exploration Archéologique de Délos*. 1909-59.
R. Vallois. *L'Architecture Hellénique et Hellénistique à Délos*. 1944.

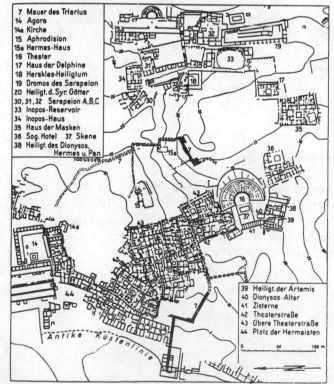

7 Mauer des Triarius
14 Agora
14a Kirche
15 Aphrodision
15a Hermes-Haus
16 Theater
17 Haus der Delphine
18 Herakles-Heiligtum
19 Dromos des Sarapeion
20 Heiligt. d. Syr. Götter
30, 31, 32 Sarapeion A, B, C
33 Inopos-Reservoir
34 Inopos-Haus
35 Haus der Masken
36 Sog. Hotel   37 Skene
38 Heiligt. des Dionysos, Hermes u. Pan

39 Heiligt. der Artemis
40 Dionysos-Altar
41 Zisterne
42 Theaterstraße
43 Obere Theaterstraße
44 Platz der Hermaisten

429. Residential district of Delos.

430. Air view of Delos.

of a terrace about 4½ feet above the pier and was occupied by a *stoa* of the Naxians which extended also along the southern side. Toward the seventh century the Mycenaean village was abandoned and the residents moved to the south of the foot of the theater hill. The most ancient statues and altars of Delos have been discovered in this square, which was the center of the earliest religious rituals and civic life.

In the course of the sixth and fifth centuries the precincts of the temple spread to the east and north. Temples and treasures were built and later, in the third century, a large, long hall bordering the *temenos* at the east. This was probably a building in which a sacred ship, possibly a *triëres,* was exhibited.

As always, the residential and commercial districts were situated outside the sacred enclosure toward the south and southeast. Most of the public buildings were erected in the third and second centuries: the *agora* of Theophrastos, the new market; the market of the Italians, of the *Rhomaioi*; the great hall remodeled by the Athenians which probably served for financial and other transactions; and the clubhouse of the merchants from Berytos (Beirut) to the northwest of the sacred lake which was a sanctuary and a commercial building at the same time. All these buildings belonged to this later period. Up to the end of the third century B.C. Delos had only one *agora* which adjoined the temple of Apollo to the south. Here the administrative buildings were situated, the *prytaneion,* and several *stoai.*

The residential district lay between the theater and the old *agora* of the Delians. It was a compact mass of houses pressed together within a small area without any preconceived plan, which had gradually grown up in accordance with the needs of the moment and the configuration of the terrain. Only a few dwellings date back to the third century, the majority belonging to the second and early first centuries. The streets were irregular and narrow, 4 to 8 feet wide, and lined on both sides by houses up to 36 feet high. They were thus narrow canyons without any other openings than the entrance to the houses. The residences of the well-to-do were distributed over the whole quarter. They had always an inner open courtyard with an *impluvium* around which the reception and private rooms were arranged. But most of the houses were simple and often primitive, especially in the main streets, with open shops and workshops on both sides of the entrance.

The harbor district, to the west of the residential quarter and extending far to the south along the shore, consisted mainly of warehouses and piers for the loading and unloading of goods which on the island had to be carried by donkeys, porters, and on barrows, just as today. It may be assumed that the famous—or infamous—Delian slave market took place near the landing place.

Delos is almost like an encyclopedia of Greek city planning, illustrating the manifold facets of its subsequent stages of urban and religious development from primitive beginnings to the complex structure of a religious and secular community, and finally to its gradual fading away into a centuries-long obscurity.

Rhodos has been settled since prehistoric times. Around 1500 B.C. several trading outposts were founded by Minoan traders from Crete. About a century later Achaean invaders from Mycenae built their fortified castles on hilltops dominating fertile coastal areas. Their presence lived on in the name of Ialysos Achaia, the hill at Ialysos, which was crowned by one of their strongpoints. The Achaeans were followed about 1000 B.C. by the Dorians, who founded small independent states with the Mycenaean castles as centers at Ialysos, Lindos, and Kameiros. Lindos, situated at the only good natural harbor, soon gained as-

564

431. Air view of the city of Rhodos.

cendancy over the other places as the base of the seaborne traffic to Cyprus, Syria, Egypt, and other parts of North Africa. Since about 700 B.C. Rhodian colonies were founded on the southern coast of Asia Minor and in the westernmost parts of the Greek world—for example, Phaselis in Lycia; Soli in Cilicia; Salapia on the east coast of Southern Italy; Gela on the south coast of Sicily; and Rhoda on the northeast coast of Spain. Rhodos also took part in the foundation of Naukratis in the Nile Delta around 570 B.C. Under the influence of Athenian political ideas the hitherto independent countries of Ialysos, Lindos, and

Kameiros united in one state, which was also joined by other neighboring islands. This unification culminated in the founding of the city of Rhodos in 408 B.C. at the northeast extremity of the island which rises fan-shaped from the sea.

The decision to build a new city as the capital of the unified state is of considerably greater interest than the endless speculations on whether Hippodamos was the actual originator of the checkerboard plan of Rhodos or whether this layout was merely an application of an all-too-obvious principle when a new city had to be planned. In any case it is most

565

unlikely that Hippodamos took part in the design of Rhodos. He was born about 500 B.C. and even if he was still alive in 408 his great age would almost certainly have prevented him from taking an active part in the foundation. It is much more likely that the Peiraieus scheme and its author had become famous and that it was usual to refer to it in a general manner as Ἱπποδάμειος τρόπος, the Hippodamian way. Thus without any deliberate intention a tradition may have developed that both —Peiraieus and Rhodos—were the work of Hippodamos. Moreover, at the end of the fifth century checkerboard plans were not unusual; for instance, Magnesia on the Maeander near Miletus. Finally, Rhodos was founded as federal capital immediately after the revolt of the island against the rule of Athens—that is, it proceeded under Spartan influence. It is most unlikely that Hippodamos, who was a staunch friend of Athens, had offered his services to the enemy.[52]

52. A. von Gerkan, *op. cit.*, pp. 48, 49.

The new city was planned for about 100,000 people. It covered an area that was five or six times the size of the medieval city. The grid of rectangular units extended from the artificial harbors to Mount Smith in the west where the *acropolis* was situated.[53] The application of the gridiron plan to a site very similar to that of Miletus—a promontory covered by a rectangularly laid out town— hardly needs to be mentioned. However, our knowledge of Rhodos is too incomplete to permit a more detailed description. The latest air photographs have revealed the street pattern.[54] But this is not enough; streets are after all only a very minor factor in the development of towns, and their importance has been greatly overestimated by the more orthodox city planners.

53. J. Bradford. "Fieldwork on Aerial Discoveries in Attica and Rhodes. Part II. Ancient Field Systems on Mt. Hymettos, near Athens," *The Antiquaries Journal*, Vol. XXXVI, Nos. 3, 4. 1956. Pp. 57-69.

54. J. Bradford. *Ancient Landscapes.* 1957. Pp. 277-286.

432. Air view of Kameiros.

Ialysos, to the west of Rhodos, has been an inhabited site since about 1400 B.C. The fortified castle on the top of the hill and the small settlement occupying its slopes have been identified and partly excavated, as the air photograph shows.

433. Air view of Ialysos.

434. Plan of the center of the town of Kameiros.

Kameiros, on the northwest coast of the island, covered a small area on the slopes of a hill. The streets were mostly laid out at right angles to each other. The triangular *agora* was bordered on one side by temples, on the other by private houses with a few shops.

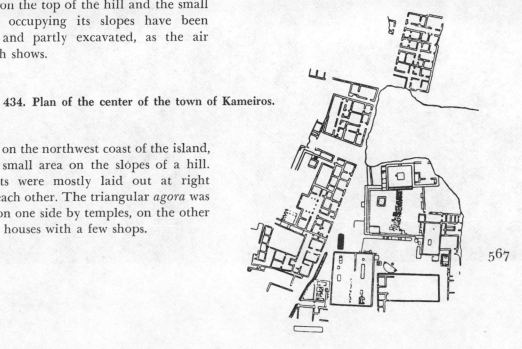

567

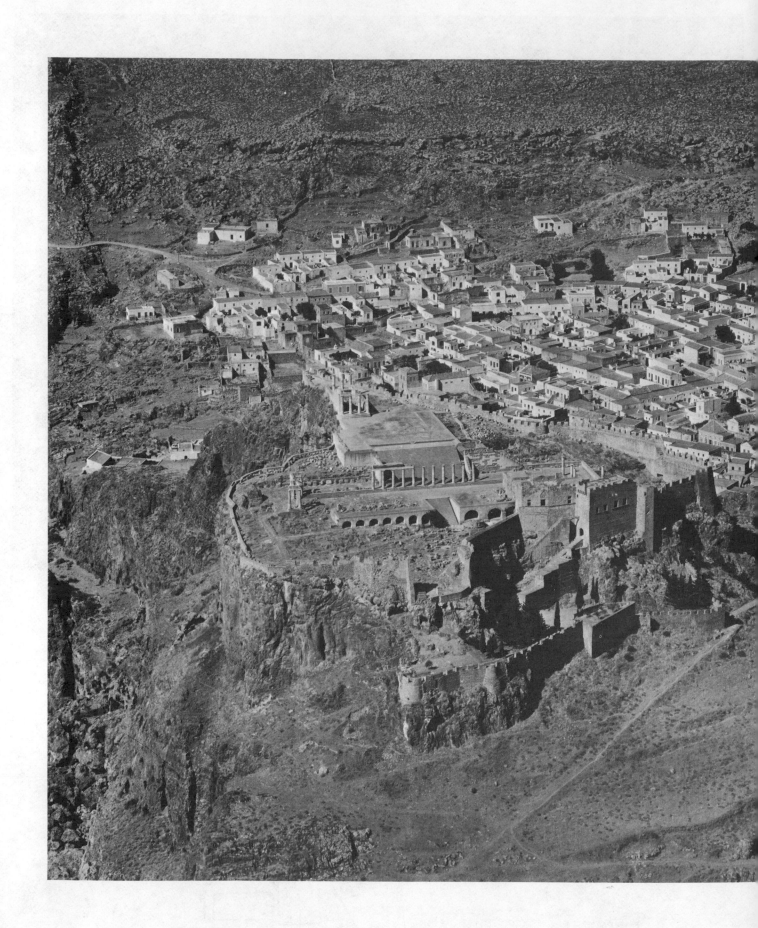

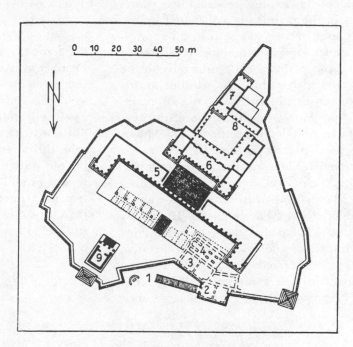

436. Plan of the Acropolis of Lindos.

435. Air view of the Acropolis of Lindos.

Lindos, on the east coast, may be mentioned in this connection because the *acropolis* and its situation on a terrace almost immediately above the sea are interesting. The *acropolis,* unlike its Athenian predecessor, was characteristic of the new Hellenistic building principles which aimed at symmetrical and axial groupings and systematically preconceived layouts.

569

Thasos, off the coast of Thrace, owed its relative importance in antiquity to a combination of favorable geographical factors: nearness to the mainland; a sheltered harbor (a great asset in a region without an appreciable number of good landing facilities); a fertile coastal plain in close proximity to the harbor; and a steep hill, the natural site for an *acropolis* dominating harbor and plain. Greeks from Paros, on the advice of the Delphic Oracle, founded the settlement of Thasos on this site between 710 and 680 B.C. which soon attracted Thracian immigrants from the mainland. The Greeks opened up gold mines on the island from which they drew annual revenues of 200 or even 300 talents (Herodotus VI. 46), which enabled them to build ships and fortifications and to engage in a lucrative trade. They connected the *acropolis* with the naval base through a massive wall 2.5 miles long. These fortifications enclosed large open spaces which may have served as refuge in times of war.[55] Since the sixth century an *agora* developed between the port and the *prytaneion*. It seems that the public buildings were erected on a street which led from the port to the *acropolis* through this district around the *prytaneion*. At the beginning of the fourth century a new plan was put forward. The *agora* was enlarged to 300 feet in length and 240 feet in width though its final regular shape did not materialize before Roman times. Despite this attempt at a systematic replanning, the old spirit proved stronger than the attraction of novel ideas: the buildings of the *agora* remained unrelated entities without any genuine unity. The residential quarters which are still being explored extended over the slopes of the hill.

55. École Française d'Athènes. *Études Thasiennes.* 1944, 1953, 1954, 1959.

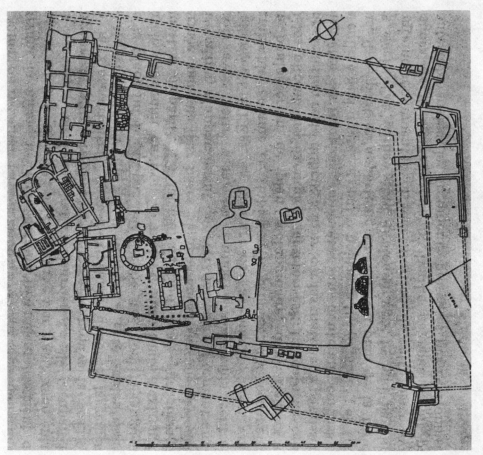

437. Plan of the Agora at Thasos.

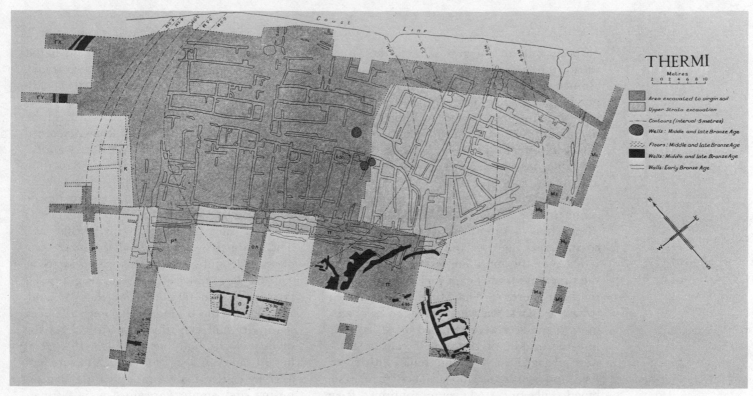

438. Plan of Thermi on Lesbos.

Thermi, on the east coast of Lesbos near hot springs, was a neolithic Bronze Age settlement. The fifth town on the same site was abandoned about 2400 B.C.[56] It was surrounded by a multiple ring of fortifications. The main street began at the south gate and was crossed by another street at right angles

leading to the west gate. Other streets branched off toward the sea. The *agora* with the main buildings lay near the center (of the excavated part) at a widening of the main street. Thermi was reoccupied in the Middle Bronze Age and, at the beginning of the 14th century B.C., fell under the influence of the Mycenaean civilization. Its existence terminated in a conflagration about 1200 B.C.

56. W. Lamb. *Excavations at Thermi in Lesbos.* 1936.

ASIA MINOR AND BEYOND

The terrain of western Asia Minor, with its great variety of landforms, its mountains and hills of different altitudes, direction, and geological structure, its deep depressions and its fertile alluvial lands, resembles that of Greece in many respects. The rift valleys, extending from the edge of the western plateau of the interior westward to the Aegean, are traversed by rivers—the Hermos, Kayster, and Maeander—bringing down considerable amounts of silt from the plateau that the ports of Ephesos and Miletus filled up, the coastline advanced in many places, and the course of the Hermos

changed repeatedly. At the coast the valleys continue as gulfs, and the mountain ranges as peninsulae or islands. Vegetation, climate, and cultivation are Mediterranean in character, as in Greece, and have made the fertile coastal belt a "second home" of the Greek people, a part of their *Lebensraum*.

At an early age, almost at the beginning of their history, the Greeks established colonies along the western fringe of Asia Minor which formed a continuous zone of Greek civilization extending from Trebizond on the Black Sea to Rhodes. Although they were not merely

571

outposts but an integral part of the Greek world, they remained colonial settlements inasmuch as their hinterland was occupied by non-Greek peoples. These first Greek colonies with their intimate contact with the European mainland differed from those of the second period of Greek colonization which, to a considerable degree, emanated from Asia Minor and spread over the whole Mediterranean.

The Aegean was the center of trade and commerce in which the Greek cities of Asia Minor took a prominent part. Here, in the coastal area, the overland routes from the interior met the most important sea routes of the time, one from Egypt and Syria along the southern shores of Asia Minor, and the other from the Black Sea where Milesian colonies—more than sixty were founded by Miletus before the middle of the seventh century B.C.—were engaged in overland trade with inner Asia and southern Russia. Then these combined traffic and trade routes continued from Asia Minor to mainland Greece and beyond to the west.

With Alexander's conquest of the Orient, Greek culture and influence spread over large parts of the interior of Asia Minor and further eastward. The center of world trade, which now stretched farther to the east and west and needed fewer stopping places owing to the improved technique of navigation, shifted to Alexandria and Antiochia and later to Byzantium. The supremacy of the Greek cities on the coast of Asia Minor declined. They had to be content with a secondary role, and although their commercial importance diminished they experienced in the Hellenistic-Roman period their greatest cultural prosperity, losing their colonial character as their hinterland was Hellenized.

It is unfortunate that the word Hellenistic continues to be used rather loosely. It is more correct to apply this term only to the period from Alexander the Great to the time of Augustus—that is, to the era from the rise of the Greek monarchies to their supersession by Rome as the supreme power in the late second and first centuries B.C. It was a period of waring states, of contending civilizations and great

cultural upheavals—an age not too dissimilar from our own. Greece and Rome, two fundamentally different worlds, confronted each other. The philosophical and spontaneous yet rational culture of Greece and the realistic and pragmatic materialism of Rome remained irreconcilable for centuries. What may appear as a synthesis was merely a mutual adaptation of surface values, which in spite of certain interesting achievements never touched the essence of either. Art and architecture changed from an introvert to an extrovert character. The instinctive certainty and the small scale of architectural compositions gave way to organized large-scale ostentation. Rigid axial layouts became the order of the day and, although at the beginning (as long as Greek sensitivity and empathy were still alive) the quality of city building was high, this trend finally ended in a showpiece architecture and a civic design that approached the embarrassing and empty *parvenue*—or philistine—products of the 19th century.

The Greek cities of Asia Minor were *poleis* in fact and in spirit. They were inhabited by Greeks and Macedonians, apart from a certain number of native people. The architectural language of form, like the spoken language of the upper classes, was Greek. Although the origin of cities such as Miletus and Priene dates back to the first half of the first millennium B.C., these cities reached their cultural and political maturity in Hellenistic times, and although their layout in principle goes back to the fifth and fourth centuries, the completion of the plans in detail took a long time to materialize. It is therefore correct to speak of the *polis* of Asia Minor and farther east as Hellenistic cities without prejudice to their origin or the beginning of their redevelopment in centuries before the Hellenistic age.

The contrast between Rome and Greece has been likened to the present antagonistic balance between Europe and America. This, however, is but one aspect of the transformation which took place in the Hellenistic period. Another pertinent comparison is the transition from the Middle Ages to the Renaissance and above all to the Baroque, from an Age of

Faith to the Scientific Revolution of the 16th century. This revolution of the mind and the outburst of activities that resulted from it were of the same epoch-making importance as the age

when Greek rationalism appeared to be on the verge of final triumph, the great age of intellectual discovery that begins with the foundation of Lyceum about 335 B.C. and continues down to the end of the third century. This period witnessed the transformation of Greek science from an untidy jumble of isolated observations mixed with *a priori* guesses into a system of methodical disciplines. In the more abstract sciences, mathematics and astronomy, it reached a level that was not to be attained again before the sixteenth century; and it made the first organised attempt at research in many other fields. . . . It is as if the sudden widening of the spatial horizon that resulted from Alexander's conquests had widened at the same time all the horizons of the mind. . . . The traditions and institutions of the old "closed" society were of course still there and still influential; the incorporation of a city-state in one or other of the Hellenistic kingdoms did not cause it to lose its moral importance overnight. But though the city was there, its walls, as someone has put it, were down; its institutions stood exposed to rational criticism; its traditional ways of life were increasingly penetrated and modified by a cosmopolitan culture.[57]

Traditional values declined and with them religion. The city gods were still worshipped as it befitted a patriotic citizen, but this was done more out of social conformity and routine than with the intention of influencing and molding the purpose of life. Against all expectations that the Ideal Age of Reason was there to stay, a slow intellectual decline set in and the irrational impulses of human nature broke through the lucid veneer of the intellect, once more gaining the upper hand, supported

by the emergence of a more-or-less uncritical mass society and all its concomitant drawbacks.

It is against this background that we should try to understand the transformation from the archaic, irregular, and spontaneous city development to the new, regular, and rational Hellenistic city design and finally to the stereotyped rigidity and hollow superficiality of the Roman period. It is characteristic that Aristotle proclaimed man should discard the old belief which counseled humility demanding him to think in mortal terms; man possesses the germ of a divine essence, the intellect, and therefore he should exist as though he were not mortal.[58] The humility that man should discard had been one of the indispensable attributes that made him build his cities on a human scale, and keep them small and limited without ostentatious demonstrations creating the illusion of a greatness incompatible with his mortal nature. This turning away from the ancient humility was a symbol of the new rational spirit that found its physical embodiment in the architectural composition of the Hellenistic cities. The intimate human scale, the introvert, narrow, and tortuous streets, the instinctive and informal grouping of temples and public buildings gradually gave way to larger and unified effects and to deliberate and cumulative coordination. The streets lost their individual character and changed to nondescript thoroughfares and axial elements of the general plan; the principal buildings became component parts of homogeneous squares. This development from spontaneous individuality to calculated planning and standardization of planning principles passed through the same evolution as the streets and houses, the squares and public buildings from the Middle Ages to the Baroque—yet with the difference that no perspective views were introduced, only short and undramatic vistas.

57. E. R. Dodds, *op. cit.*, pp. 236-237.

58. *Nichomachean Ethics.* 1177b, 1178a.

573

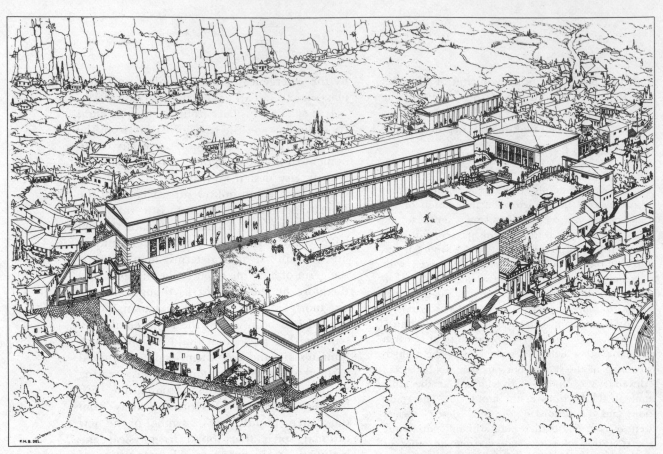

439. Reconstruction of the Agora at Assos.

Assos, situated in the southern part of the Troad, the territory surrounding the city of Troy, was founded about 900 B.C. It rose on terraces, cut into the slopes of a hill, to the summit crowned by a temple of Athena. It is mentioned in this connection because the *agora* is of particular interest. The arrangement of the buildings was similar to the principle followed at Pergamon. The *agora* was laid out on a narrow and long natural terrace as a trapezoid wider at the west than at the east end. The southern side was occupied by a two-story hall built against the slope of the terrace. The upper story, open on both long sides as a promenade from which the visitors could enjoy the marvelous view over Lesbos and the coast to Pergamon in the south, was on the same level as the *agora*. The lower story with baths was closed and stood on the natural rock of the downward slope. The north side was closed by another longer hall built against the upper slope of the terrace. The buildings were arranged in two groups—the offices and the administrative center at the east around

the *bouleuterion* which dominated this part of the *agora* with its impressive façades, and at the west a small temple at the end of the central axis of the square. The west side, like the other sides, was closed by buildings, obviously shops, open to the street and consequently independent of the *agora*.

The similarity with Pergamon was founded on historical developments: Assos had been under the dominion of the Attalids, the kings of Pergamon, for about a century, from 241 to 133 B.C. The dramatic effect of the composition of the *agora* was intended for those who entered it from the east: the divergence of the long *stoai* toward the west, and the central position of the temple rising in its full outline independent of the *stoai,* created an impression of amplitude which introduced a principle of civic design that had hitherto been alien to Greek planning. We have here the rudiments of a perspective view and also of Baroque compositions, of the Piazza del Campidoglio; of the Piazza di S. Pietro; and the Piazza di S. Marco with their divergent

574

sides and optical illusion which increased the effect of the main building and heightened its coherence with the square, subordinating it as a sort of forecourt to the principal edifice.

Pergamon, 18 miles inland, at the junction between the Selinus and the Kaikos, flourished under the Attalid dynasty. It was unfavorably situated although it had easy access to the Hermos Plain through smaller plains and over low elevations. For the direct route from the interior to the coast this way was an unnecessary *détour* which could easily be avoided because the Hermos Plain offered the more direct connection. This explains why Pergamon never became an important trading community. It owed its rise to the capital of the Roman province of Asia and later, with Ephesos and Smyrna, to one of the great cities of the province, to entirely different factors—the extraordinary strong site of the *acropolis* and the fertility of the coastal plain with easy access from the sea. Pergamon was in the first instance a political and cultural center.

The development of the town began on the summit and the upper slopes of the rocky hill, but already under the first kings its center shifted downward, while its former site was mainly given over to the *gymnasion* and the enclosures of the Hera and Demeter temples. The steep slopes and the ancient roads pre-

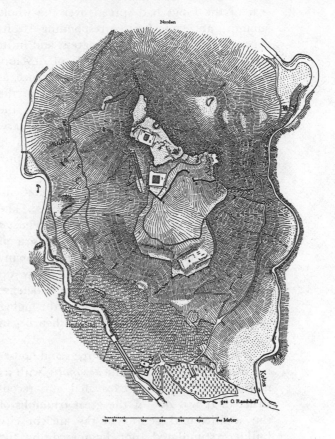

440. Topographical map of the site of Pergamon.

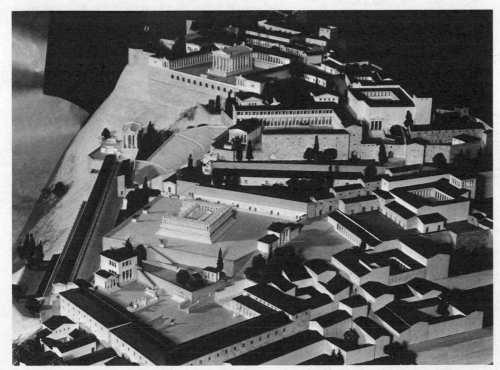

441. Model of Pergamon.

575

vented systematic planning; moreover, considerable parts of the rocky terrain remained free of buildings. In the course of time the seat of the kings had spread over the whole summit, an evolution corresponding in its causes, in the details of its progress, and in its results to the consecutive stages of development of the ancient *acropolis*—for instance, at Athens, first town, then fortified seat of the ruler with sanctuaries, and finally, after the end of the monarchy, the national sanctuary.

Although the capital of a not inconsiderable state, the excavations at Pergamon have produced no administrative building; especially on the *acropolis* not a single monumental edifice for this purpose has been identified. The site was quite unsuitable for a town. Its *raison d'être* was the *acropolis,* the fortified seat of the ruler, around which it developed as many towns of the Middle Ages which grew up around a *Burg*. When the need for defense decreased, the town descended from the higher slopes toward the plain and only then began to expand.[59]

Of the lower town and its streets and houses not much is known. But the *acropolis,* with its monuments, has been excavated and reconstructed. It was one of the great triumphs of the architectural genius of the ancient city builders stimulated, not hampered, by the seemingly insurmountable difficulties of the

59. A von. Gerkan, *op. cit.,* pp. 108, 121.

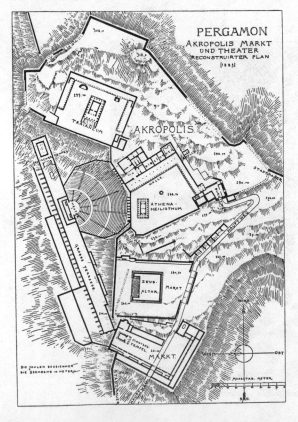

terrain. They succeeded by adapting their work to the natural configuration through terraces and substructures and by taking advantage of the natural amphitheater which the hill formed toward its northern end.[60] The main road began at the south gate of the strong wall built by Eumenes II (197-159 B.C.). Side streets, some of them with steps, branched off the main road which rose in steep and tortuous curves. A Lower Market was situated not too far from the south gate. It was an enclosed square with two-storied colonnades and shops. This *agora* was not part of the town plan but an independent unit. The upper story of the colonnades was unusual; no other market seems to have had two stories except at Assos, no doubt influenced by Pergamon. This may have been a specifically Pergamese motif, probably resulting from the need for multistoried buildings which would be in conformity with high terraces and also from a desire to make the most efficient use of the available space.

Then followed the *gymnasion* on a site which other architects less imaginative and daring than the builders of Pergamon would never have dreamt of using for a purpose that demanded a natural level ground. The Pergamenes, experts in the art of refusing to follow the line of least resistance, if there was any opportunity for coping with difficulties, created an ingenious system of terraces with substructures connected by stairways. The lowest terrace, small and irregular, was a playground for young boys; the long middle terrace, with a fountain and a temple, was for the older boys, the *ephebes*. The long building on the north side contained a race track in its upper floor. The top terrace had a two-storied colonnade surrounding a large *palaestra* and numerous rooms for various purposes. Then followed on different higher terraces a temple, probably for Apollo, and the temples of Demeter and Hera.

The road continued to rise toward the *acropolis* through the upper *agora,* which was adjoined on the northwest by a higher terrace

60. A. C. L. Conze. "Stadt und Landschaft." In: *Altertümer von Pergamon.* Vol. I. 1912-13.

442. Plan of Pergamon.

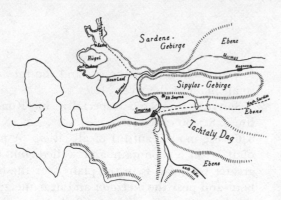

443. Map of Smyrna and environs.

with the Great Altar of Zeus, the most spectacular monument of Pergamon. The road left this enclosure through a *propylon,* passed shops and a colonnaded court, and entered the fortified gateway of the citadel with the palaces, storehouses, and arsenals. A precinct of the sanctuary of Athene, placed obliquely above the theater, was situated on the left of the interior of the gateway. On a terrace, immediately behind the theater to the east, stood the famous library which is said to have contained 200,000 volumes. The theater was built into the curve of the hill sloping down to a long terrace that united the whole magnificent composition in a grand sweep on the summit of the rock. This strong horizontal accent, beginning at the lowest point of the *agora* and ending at the theater, was the keynote of the dramatic rhythm which flowed through the tiers until it reached the uppermost crest crowned with the temple of Athene Polias. The terrace was limited on the outer side by a colonnade possibly open toward the valley and the inner side. It was supported by a two-storied substructure. At the southern end was another terrace on a lower level. Passages at the exit from the upper terrace permitted a shortcut to the upper *agora.*

Pergamon was in its final form a systematically planned entity conceived and executed on a noble scale and in a majestic spirit. It is of no small significance that within about a hundred years the area of the city increased tenfold. Under Attalos I (241-197 B.C.) it comprised 51.9 acres and under his son Eumenes II it had grown to 222.3 acres, whereas the ancient original *acropolis* covered only 22.23 acres.[61]

61. A. Conze, *op. cit.,* p. 148.

Smyrna was one of the most important cities of antiquity in Asia Minor. Its history, continuing without a break from earliest times to the present day, can be verified through records and archeological data. The configuration of the coastline in the region where Smyrna was founded and developed throughout the centuries was more varied than in the northern part of the coastal belt. The gulfs reached far inland and the peninsula projected far out into the sea. Here no continuous plain extended along the coast, and the coastal road had to cut through the mountainous peninsulae.

In spite of these unfavorable factors, low passes and valleylike depressions permitted traffic to move parallel to the coast without too much difficulty. Moreover, the three largest valleys, those of the Hermos, the Kayster, and the Maeander, reached the sea in this central part of the west coast. The first and the third of the valleys extended right up to the edge of the plateau in the interior, which was also accessible from the upper end of the Kayster Valley without too steep an ascent. These large valleys were not only the most fertile and most densely settled parts of Asia Minor but also the natural connections from the interior to the coast and therefore the traffic arteries with the most important overland routes. Thus at the mouths of these three valleys the great *emporia* of antiquity developed.

Smyrna was one of three cities that grew up at the mouth of the Hermos. The other two, Kyme and Phokaia, never reached the importance of Smyrna, though their situation was favorable. Kyme dominated the passage between the coastal hills and the mountainous country that led to one of the gulfs formed by the delta of the Hermos. Phokaia, the mother city of Marseilles, had an ideal harbor in a more advanced position than Smyrna, which lay at the head of an arm of the sea

577

and therefore more inland. As long as navigation was imperfect and made the sailing into a long and winding gulf difficult and time-wasting, Phokaia was in a more favorable situation. But later, when the initial difficulties had been overcome, Smyrna's location at the head of the gulf offered greater advantages because it shortened the more expensive and less convenient overland transport and made communication with the interior easier. Thus in time the competition between the two cities was decided in favor of Smyrna, although Phokaia remained throughout the centuries a moderately useful small port and town owing to its fertile hinterland.[62]

The most ancient Smyrna lay at the slope of the Sipylos. It was the frontier city between Aeolis and Ionia. During the seventh century it was a flourishing commercial place until destroyed about 600 B.C. by the king of Lydia. For three centuries Smyrna lost its rank among the Ionian cities, yet it continued to exist despite the disruption of Greek life and political institutions, though in a reduced form as a group of villages. It was eventually rebuilt by Antigonus (316-301 B.C.) and later enlarged and fortified. The new city was laid out on the present site on the slopes of the Pagus at the southern end of the gulf stretching over the

low ground between the sea and the hill, the small plain of the river Meles.

Smyrna prospered especially in Roman times. Strabo called it καλλίστη τῶν πατῶν (XIV. 646), the most beautiful of all cities. "A part of it is on a mountain and walled, but the greater part of it is in the plain near the harbour and near the *metroon* and near the *gymnasion*." Thus he distinguished, apart from the hill crowned by the *acropolis*, three districts at the harbor, at the *metroon*, the temple of Cybele, and at the *gymnasion*, and reported that the well-paved streets were broad and crossed one another at right angles. However, this should be understood with a certain qualification, for the city surrounded the lower slopes of Pagus like a "necklace" and a regular street system in all parts was impossible. The road from Ephesos entered the city at the Ephesian gate near the *gymnasion*. There was a stadium not far from the *acropolis*, as well as a theater on the north slopes of Pagus. The city had two harbors, an open roadstead and an inner basin which could be closed by a rope. Details of the plan and the buildings are not sufficiently known to contribute anything of particular importance to Greek city planning, but its topography is a valuable illustration of the great influence which the natural conditions exerted on the choice of the site and the future development.

62. A. Philippson. "Antike Stadtanlagen an der Westküste Kleinasiens," *Bonner Jahrbücher*, Vol. 123. 1916.

Magnesia ad Maeandrum, situated on a stream flowing into the Maeander, was said to have been founded by Thessalian and, according to Strabo, Cretan immigrants. After its destruction by the Cimmerians about 700 B.C., it was soon rebuilt by Ionian colonists. At the beginning of the fourth century the inhabitants of Magnesia decided to move their city and to regroup around the temple of Artemis on the slopes of Mount Thorax. The new city was laid out on a gridiron plan similar to those of Priene and Miletus, and the street system was orientated toward the four points of the compass. Within this system space was reserved for the *agora* as elsewhere, but religious

considerations demanded that it be associated with the sanctuary of Artemis. The actual execution of this intention did not materialize before the end of the third century when the city had acquired sufficient means to carry the expensive scheme into effect.[63] Everything indicates that the rebuilding of the city was to proceed systematically according to a preconceived plan. It should be noted that

Les liens religieux qui avaient attiré l'agora à proximité du sanctuaire principal de la cité ne

63. C. Humann. *Magnesia am Maeander. Bericht über die Ergebnisse der Ausgrabungen der Jahre 1891-1893. 1904. Passim.*

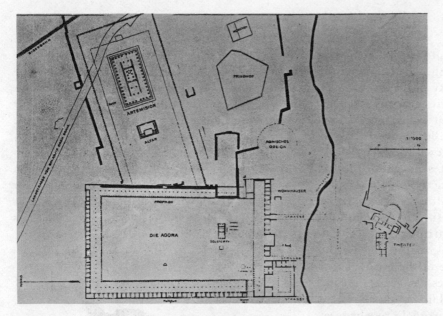

444. Plan of the Agora and the Sanctuary of Artemis at Magnesia ad Maeandrum.

jouèrent qu'un rôle minime dans la conception du plan; son orientation ne fut nullement imposée par celle du sanctuaire préexistant; la place fut intégrée, comme à Milet et à Priène, dans le réseau régulier des rues et prit ainsi une position oblique par rapport aux axes de la composition antérieure. Cet exemple de Magnésie est précieux, car il nous révèle la force d'un principe fondamental de l'urbanisme ionien qui donne la primauté au système des rues; dans le conflit qui opposait ici l'orientation des constructions religieuses et la régularité du plan orthogonal, la première fut sacrifiée.[64]

The *agora* occupied an area of six building blocks and adjoined at the east the temple precinct of Artemis which extended diagonally to the main axis of the *agora*. It covered a considerable space: over 616.64 feet long and almost 328 feet wide without the *stoai*. Behind the south *stoa*, which served as a vestibule, religious and administrative institutions and a building that was probably a *prytaneion* covered an area of three building blocks. Two

streets entered the *agora* at the southern end on either side in front of the vestibule. The public buildings were grouped together at one side of the *agora*, an arrangement that seems to indicate the predilection of the architects to treat them as an independent motif. A small temple of Zeus Sosipolis stood in the southern part of the *agora* before the vestibule. It was completely subordinated to the general composition and did not impair the character of the *agora* as an open square, nor should the *stoai* be regarded as a framework which would enhance the value of the temple as an indispensable architectural element. The temple served an important religious function that took place in the *agora* in the fourth century and was connected with the fertility cult.[65] It consisted of two phases. The second phase was common to both gods, to Zeus and Artemis who received the sacrifices in their respective temples, a ritual that was made easy by the proximity of their sanctuaries.

64. R. Martin, *op. cit.*, p. 406.

65. *Ibid.*, p. 221.

Priene, in the foothills of Mykale, was formerly situated on the coast. The swampy estuary of the Maeander, originally a wide gulf, was gradually filled in by the deposits carried down from the interior. Priene was a small provincial town without the attraction a great sanctuary or a good port would offer. It had

hardly more than 4,500 inhabitants. From east to west it measured 1,800 feet and from north to south less than 3,000 feet. The perimeter of the fortifications was only 1.55 miles and the walls were slightly more than 6 feet thick. It seems that they were built first, if we follow Diodorus (XII. 10) and Vitruvius (I. 6. 1).

The first Priene was situated on the plain of the Maeander. When this site became uninhabitable—the irregularity of the river endangered the safety of the inhabitants—the new Priene was founded about 350 B.C., more than a century after the rebuilding of Miletus. It was a "modern" Greek town with self-government and limited resources and as such it may have been typical of numerous other places of the Hellenistic period, although not many of them could boast of a similarly magnificent situation and the same architectural unity. It was a town of pedestrians, unsuitable even for horses or mules. In spite of the great difficulties, which the four successive terraces created for the architects, it was laid out on a gridiron scheme. The rock of the *acropolis* rose between two deep gorges to a height of over 1,000 feet above sea level and of nearly 700 feet above

larly over the streets, obviously following the ruts the rain water had worn in the roads. The eighty *insulae* were more or less of the same size. The *insulae* were subdivided into four building plots each 80 by 60 feet. There were six main streets and sixteen side streets. Priene, like the majority of other towns, was situated on the southern slopes of the mountain so that it was fully exposed to the sunlight for most of the day. This orientation was especially recommended by ancient writers such as Xenophon (*Memorabilia* III. VIII. 8-10).

SUMMIT OF ALAZA
CA 1000 M.

ACROPOLIS
381 M.

PLAIN OF THE
MAEANDER
6 M. ABOVE SEA LEVEL

445. Profile of the terrain of Priene.

the town.[66] It was a refuge that could easily be defended, not a citadel, for this would have been incompatible with the self-respect of a self-governing town. The connection of the *acropolis* with the residential quarters was exceedingly difficult and inconvenient. It consisted only of a very steep and rocky stairway that could not be used by many people at the same time or for the transportation of goods in case of sudden danger.

The east-west streets were more or less level but the north-south connections were steep stairways ascending over the terraces to the end of the urban area. The width of the streets varied between 10.49 feet and 14.43 feet. The main streets had a rough pavement of slabs; most of the gutters remained open, but occasionally they were covered so as not to hinder the traffic, because they ran irregu-

The *agora*, in the center of the town, covered an area of two *insulae* and was surrounded on three sides by *stoai*. The north side remained open. Here, along this side, the main east-west street passed the square and

66. Th. Wiegand and H. Schrader. *Priene. Ergebnisse der Ausgrabungen und Untersuchungen in den Jahren 1895-1898.* 1904. Pp. 35 ff. and *passim.* Also for the following.

580

446. The Gulf of Miletus in antiquity with Priene on the northern peninsula.

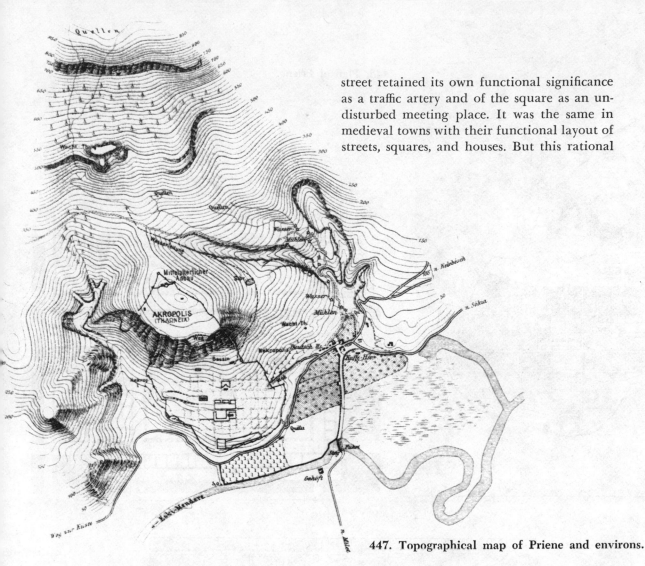

street retained its own functional significance as a traffic artery and of the square as an undisturbed meeting place. It was the same in medieval towns with their functional layout of streets, squares, and houses. But this rational

447. Topographical map of Priene and environs.

was bordered on the north side by a long *stoa* on a terrace dominating the *agora* and closing the whole composition. It was called the Sacred *Stoa* and was used, apart from its religious function, for banquets and other official business. The *agora* at Priene is a particularly interesting example because it reveals, in contrast to Miletus, a clear architectural program which was carried through in one sweep. It was conceived as a whole, almost as one building. The system of the neighboring streets was adapted to this conception and not the other way around. It is characteristic of the Greek rational approach to these problems that the main street, or any other street, never leads as a continuous axis through the center of the *agora*, which is not an extension of the street but a square bordered tangentially by a street. This difference was decisive, for a tangential

principle was abandoned in all those cases where practical usefulness was subordinated to spectacular demonstrations. The axial vistas of the Roman period and the tangential system of the Greeks are incompatible in the same sense that ostentation and culture can never be reconciled. The deliberate disregard of axial arrangements is further illustrated by the fact that the gates in the town walls corresponded with the streets but not with their axes. This principle was common to almost all Greek and especially Hellenistic fortifications. The gates were either slightly eccentric or, if the terrain permitted it, considerably displaced sideways or even at right angles to the street. Rational considerations of defense were decisive, not an enforced symmetry.

The *bouleuterion* was situated inconspicuously behind the Sacred *Stoa*. A second small

581

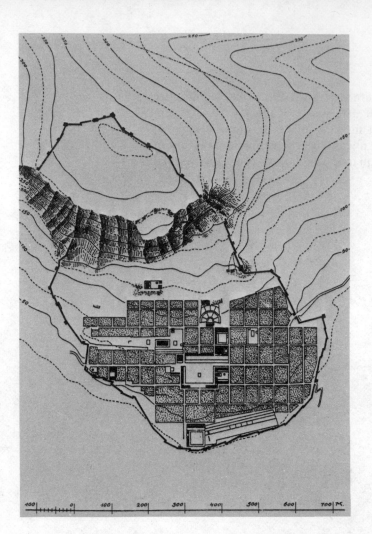

448. Plan of Priene.

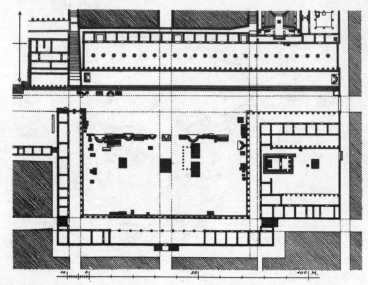

449. The Agora of Priene.

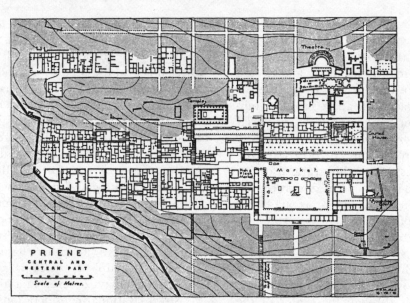

450. The central and western sections of Priene.

square, covering half an *insula*, adjoined the main *agora* at the west. This has been identified as a meat and fish market. Just as the administrative buildings were situated without any direct relation to the main streets, so the temple of Zeus stood almost isolated to the northwest of the *agora*, partly hidden behind a long hall.

Priene has been called a "banal" town. This opinion is interesting not because it is unusually superficial but because it is based on a purely two-dimensional assessment of the use of the regular street pattern on a difficult and irregular terrain. Architecture and city planning are a three-dimensional art and should therefore be judged only in this sense. To call Priene "banal" does not take into account this fundamental quality. This misguided and misleading statement is characteristic of a school of thought that regards the street system as the essence of city planning. That the gridiron plan has been imposed upon the very difficult terrain of Priene is no reason whatever for condemning it. On the contrary, it speaks for the imaginative audacity of the architects. There can hardly be a more dramatic and less "banal" arrangement than the succession of four terraces—on the highest the temple of Demeter; on the third the temple of Athene Polias, the theater, and the upper gymnasium; on the second the *agora* and the temple of Zeus; and on the first—the lowest—the stadium and the lower gymnasium. This sequence of terraces, one rising above the other to the *acropolis*, is almost too simple an illustration of the three-dimensional quality of architecture. Moreover, it should not be forgotten that since the fourth century the gridiron plan was the more-or-less generally accepted type of Greek city planning. While it was not a particularly ingenious system, here in Priene it was dramatized in a splendid manner. What was without doubt rather dull on a level terrain was turned, on this seemingly unsuitable site, to the greatest advantage. It showed Greek ingenuity at its best and an intimate interaction of man and environment that could hardly be surpassed.

Miletus was one of the oldest Ionian colonies. Of the archaic town existing before its destruction by the Persians in 494 B.C. little is known, except that it was situated at the foot of the hill of Kalabaktepe where a small settlement grew up following the arrival of Ionian immigrants. This group of settlers and the descendants of their Mycenaean predecessors seem to have lived side by side. It is possible that the harbor, the sanctuary of Athene, and the market formed a sort of neutral zone where trading activities took place. This zone was traversed by two important roads: one leading to the coast and the other, the Sacred Way, connecting ancient Miletus with the great sanctuary of Didyma.

Milet nous offre à l'époque archaique, une image assez précise de la cité des Phéaciens avec son port, son agora et son sanctuaire groupés au pied de l'agglomération principale que défendait un puissant rempart. Tout comme Ulysse, le voyageur qui débarquait à Milet, en traversant l'agora encombrée de marchandises et d'agrès, en longeant l'autel d'Athéna, apercevait les lignes sombres des remparts sur le sommet de la colline où s'étageait la ville haute.[67]

The new town was founded in 479 B.C. on a small island-like group of hills and on an isthmus-like part of a peninsula that had perhaps gradually formed from an artificial dam that may have been the first connection of the hills on the island and the mainland. A small bay between these outlying hills was the harbor of the new town. Overland routes were difficult. The mountains of Latmos were a considerable obstacle. But this barrier and the sea, which surrounded the town on three sides, provided an excellent protection against attack. The immediate hinterland was unproductive, which explains why Miletus remained mainly a coastal and colonizing trading town. The reason why it developed in this island-like situation was very probably the flat, marshy, and shifting nature of the coast of the mainland which made it unsuitable for seaborne traffic. A more advanced harbor, protected

---

67. R. Martin, *op. cit.*, p. 58.

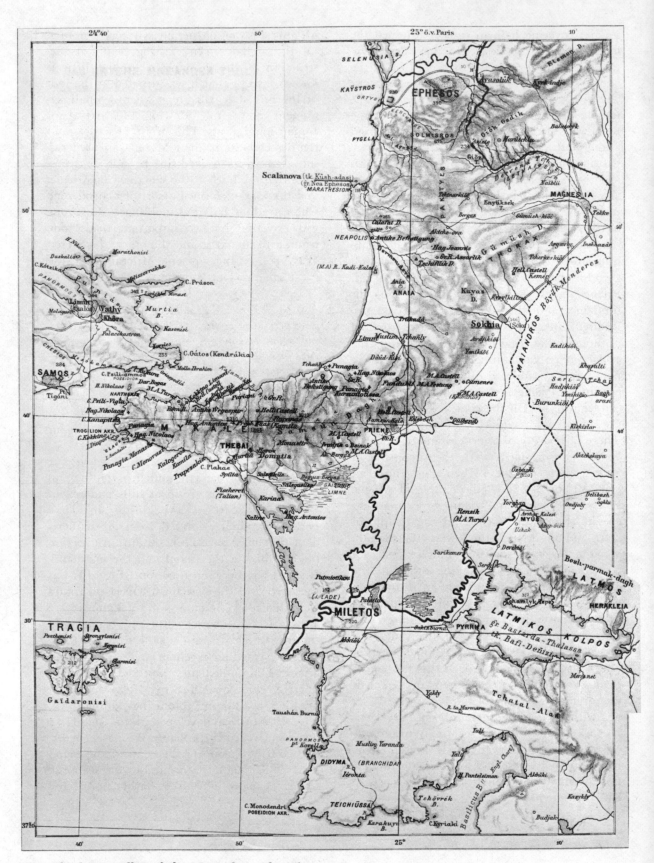

451. The lower valley of the Maeander with Miletus.

against silting, was therefore an essential necessity.

The rebuilding of Miletus was an architectural feat of the first order, although the town itself remained small for a long time.[68] It was planned from the very beginning on a large scale for an area that included not only the outer part of the peninsula to the isthmus between the harbor at the theater and the flat bay at the east, but also a terrain that offered sufficient space for a city of 80,000 to 100,000 people in the late Roman period. With its four harbors and the large *agorai*, the economic development of Miletus rested on a firm basis even though its political influence had vanished. The rebuilding of the mother city, which had played a leading role in the early colonization before the middle of the seventh century, was the last and most worthy deed of a distinguished colonial career.

The city was laid out on a gridiron plan which has been ascribed to Hippodamos. This event has been greatly overestimated as the turning point of Greek city planning and even of city planning in general. It is doubtful that Hippodamos was the inventor of the system which bears his name. It is more likely that he contributed to the clarification of a theory and suggested certain directives for its workings. Why he found a fertile soil in his home town has been explained before. Why was the gridiron scheme nothing new? The usual assumption that it can be traced back to oriental influences can be dismissed as untenable; Gerkan has proved this convincingly. The regular layout—streets crossing one another at right angles—has been, at all times, an instrument of colonization in Northern Europe, in France and Spain, and in Latin America. Miletus, which had founded eighty *poleis*, had certainly applied this simple principle to its colonies. In time the practical experiences gained in this tremendous enterprise had been elaborated to a theory of city planning from which the more recent foundations profited. Miletus was one of these later foundations. There is no reason why the Greeks, who were after all

not without imagination, should not have been the originators of this theory and its application in practice on their own soil. They understood that colonization could proceed much more easily if streets were laid out first and lots of equal size assigned to settlers. These simple yet eminently practical considerations had great and obvious administrative advantages: quarrels between the settlers were avoided and an unsystematic growth of cities could be prevented. It is doubtful if this system even appeared as something new and unusual to contemporaries or if it was regarded merely as an overdue application of principles tried out successfully in the colonies. The role

452. Map of Miletus.

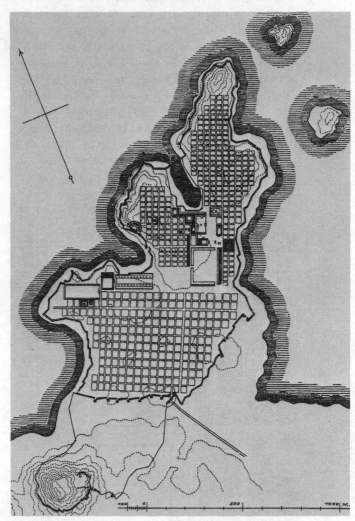

68. Th. Wiegand. *Milet. Ergebnisse der Ausgrabungen und Untersuchungen seit dem Jahre 1899. 1906-36.*

585

of Hippodamos was in all probability not too dissimilar from that of Alberti, Leonardo da Vinci, Filarete, and other theorists who developed the framework for Ideal Cities.

The plan for Miletus was conceived as a whole but executed only gradually, in strong contrast to the Athenians, who rebuilt their city piecemeal on the ruins of the old buildings and without any major change of the street pattern. The Milesians were determined to make their new city a model of Greek city planning. The whole area was handed over to the architects, who were commissioned to produce a master plan in accordance with the new ideas. Their first step was to fix the different zones, the residential quarters and those for public buildings which were built later during the following two or three centuries. The architects of the fifth century were not concerned with the details of the overall plan or with the design of the great south and north *agorai*. They merely provided in general for the space which the houses and public edifices were to occupy. This procedure illustrates the far-sightedness and realistic approach which they brought to their task. It seems that every design for a new building had to be submitted for approval by the city architect, who was responsible for the observance of the master plan.

The average width of the streets was 15 feet

and the size of the *insulae*—there were about 400—was 75 by 100 feet. They were larger in the southern part of the peninsula and had an orientation that differed slightly from the *insulae* in the northern part. There were two *agorai*, one at the west called the North *agora* opposite the theater on the northern side of the bay, and the South *agora* at the east. The zone of the *agorai* was the core of the city between the northern and southern halves. During a century this zone, which covered an area of 17.29 acres, remained free of permanent buildings and was used as a sort of building yard and dumping place where the materials for the new city were stored and other preparatory activities carried on. Toward the end of the fourth century the development of this zone was begun with the North *stoa* and carried through in successive stages. This whole area was reserved for trade. The basic measure was the unit of an *insula* and in general the street lines were kept as imaginary axes. Here stood the *bouleuterion* and other communal buildings. This adherence to the general system of the division of the terrain created a unity of scale and layout and allowed, at the same time, an imaginative grouping in general. The South *agora* covered an area of twenty *insulae*, that is, of about 642.88 by 534.64 feet. Here was the *prytaneion*, a *gymnasion*, baths, and the *Delphinion*, the temple of Apollo. The South *agora* was intended as a place for public functions, free from commercial activities which began to intrude only later. The zone of the *agorai*, separating the northern and the southern part of the city, had no organic architectural connection with the urban area as a whole. It was "simply there" but it fulfilled its function as a civic center because it occupied a site that was particularly favorable for commercial and civic activities. As has been said before, the gridiron plan was above all an assemblage of individual block units whose number could be increased *ad libitum* by external additions. The block units, not the streets, were the primary element of planning, because thinking in abstract space relations was alien to the Greeks. Theirs was the attitude of a sculptor.

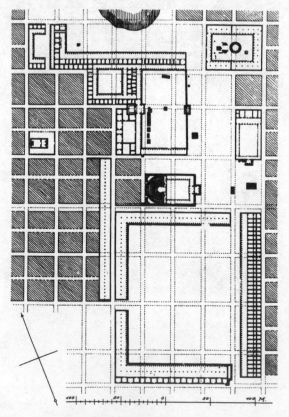

453. The Agorai of Miletus.

The streets as spatial elements in an architectural composition did not enter their conception of a city. This explains the cellular character of a Hellenistic city such as Miletus and the lack of axial interaction of its different parts.

The walls surrounded Miletus on all sides also along the sea front. When the uninhabited southern part between the city and the Kalabaktepe was abandoned, a transverse wall was built along the base of the peninsula which shortened the defense line from 5,904 feet to 1,640 feet.[69] The new wall could be directly controlled and better guarded than the older fortifications which extended at a greater distance, including the hill. This was an advantage because there was always the possibility that the mercenaries were unreliable or that opposition groups within the city would create disorders. The southern side of the fortifications was decidedly the weakest link in the whole system, and the new wall had actually decreased the strategical value—for now the enemy could take advantage of a wide plain which sloped down to the north, thus facilitating the bringing up of siege engines and permitting the enemy to dig in on the Kalabaktepe where they could overlook the whole city. It was therefore essential to erect along this line a first-class protection, and the transverse wall was indeed an outstanding achievement of the Hellenistic science of fortifications. The 1,500 foot long wall was divided into eight curtains with nine gates. The curtains were arranged obliquely to each other and thus formed alternatively re-entering and salient obtuse angles. Moreover, one end of the curtain was always drawn back, thus leaving an entrance at one side that was protected by a tower.

The history of the growth of Miletus is of interest because it illustrates the development from primitive beginnings to a large and prominent city. The oldest, the fortified Late Mycenaean settlement, was situated about 450 feet south of the bay at the theater which was the main harbor of the peninsula.[70] The other bay, more to the north—the Bay of the Lion—became important only later when the whole peninsula was inhabited. The Mycenaean settlement dominated the two roads from the west and the south and the harbor. The next stage was the settlement of the Kalabaktepe, which can be traced back to the Ionian immigration. In the following period the character of settlement changed. The hill had been occupied by an agricultural tribe and served as a strongpoint in its fight with their neighbors at the theater harbor. At first the settlement spread to all sides at the foot of the hill while the area at the harbor remained only thinly settled. But the possession of the harbor gained an ever-increasing importance and consequently the settlement grew along the coast, characteristically along the western shore. This stage began at the middle of the eighth or at the beginning of the seventh century. The leading principle of this early development was the connection of the fortified hill with the harbor by an uninterrupted belt of settlement along the coast and the road.

After the catastrophe of 494 B.C. Miletus was depopulated. The inhabitants had been killed or deported, or had fled to the fertile plain as the northern coast had been occupied by the Persians. Only after 479 B.C. did Miletus again begin to organize as an urban community. The first vestiges of this revival led once more to the Kalabaktepe, which offered obvious advantages to the small band of Milesians who had survived before they received reinforcements from the returning fugitives or from other sources. The old fortifications could easily be repaired; the settlement was compact; building material was available from the ruins of the earlier buildings; and, above all, this site did not restrict the systematic development of the new city. With the erection of the transverse wall the hill and the plain at its foot were excluded from the urban area proper. Miletus was now a big city. Its population increased and the population density grew. Trade and commerce flourished. But the extension of Miletus remained within the limits which the master plan had laid down.

69. A. von Gerkan. "Die Stadtmauern." In: Th. Wiegand, op. cit., Vol. II, Part 3. 1935. P. 53.

70. Th. Wiegand, op. cit., Vol. I. 8. 1925. Pp. 113 ff.

Herakleia, at the foot of Mount Latmos, situated at the head of the Latmic Gulf, was a small town with an extraordinary individuality.[71] It stood on a mountainous site in the midst of a wild landscape, a *Felsenmeer*, of dark granite. Here, in this solemn and rugged environment, a town was built with regular streets and fortifications which ran for almost one mile over precipices and steep slopes rising from the sea to a height of nearly 1,500 feet. Ridges extend in various directions from the summit of the mountain massif. The most important of them forms a barrier against the valley of the Maeander, protecting the inner part of the Latmic Gulf from filling up and becoming a swamp. The urban area proper lay on a ridge of moderate height, sloping down toward the south and finally narrowing to a small peninsula where a fortified castle stood atop a rocky hill rising steeply above the sea. The town ascended the mountain slope in a narrow strip which was so interspersed with rocks that the streets could only be laid out with great difficulties. The first

71. F. Krischen. *Die Befestigungen von Herakleia am Latmos.* 1922.

455. *Opposite:* **The outer walls of Herakleia above the citadel.**

fortifications enclosed an area out of all proportion to the size of the actual town but included the dominating points of the terrain. This *enceinte* had a length of 4 miles and 65 towers. When the northeastern part of this circumvallation was abandoned, a transverse wall was erected and a citadel. About 20 towers were built during this period. Finally, those parts of the citadel facing the town were demolished so that only a wall 2.80 miles long with 50 towers remained. The walls had an open passage on the inside for the defenders behind the parapet. Stairs led at certain intervals to this passage. The towers were square and round and had one lower and one upper story. There were numerous gates, varying in width from 6 to about 8 feet.

According to Gerkan[72] the town became the capital of the Carian Empire in 301 B.C. and was then called Pleistarcheia after the Carian king. It was conquered in 295 B.C. and named Herakleia. After 285 B.C. it gained its autonomy and abandoned the disproportionately large fortifications because it lacked the requisite number of soldiers to man them.

72. *Griechische Städteanlagen.* 1924. P. 15.

454. View of Herakleia from the south.

Halikarnassos originally occupied only a small island close to the coast. When in the course of time this island was joined to the mainland, the town extended and the older town of Salmacis was incorporated. In this southernmost part of the west coast of Asia Minor the mountains reach down to the sea without any larger plains or valleys. The coast is cut off from the more important overland communications. Despite the unfavorable situation a few seaports flourished in this ancient region of the Dorian colonization although they could not rival with the Ionian foundations. These towns had to rely for their food supply on the seaborne traffic which followed the coastline and proceeded farther to Egypt and Syria through the narrow passage between the mainland and the islands of Rhodes and Kos. The towns, which grew up on the peninsula of the mainland, served as stopping places. These mainland ports were Halikarnassos and Knidos. Halikarnassos was situated at a sheltered bay of a headland projecting to the north of Kos. It dominated the only road—by no means an important trade route—to the interior and to the town of Mylasa where several other roads leading to different parts of Caria met. This hinterland of Halikarnassos, a mountainous arid region, was thus not entirely isolated.

In spite or perhaps because of its secluded situation, which could easily be defended against the interior, the Carian princes selected Halikarnassos during the Persian period as their residence. It is doubtful whether this event led to a replanning of the town. Vitruvius (II.8) praised it as a perfect city. He said of Mausolos, the most famous of the Carian rulers, that

he realised that the situation of Halikarnassos was by nature strong and very favourable for a convenient depot and trading centre [*emporium*] and a sheltered harbour. The place has the curved shape of a theatre. Downtown, that is at the harbour, he established the market [*forum*]; farther upwards, in the centre of the semicircular space he drew, like a passage [*praecincto*] a wide street . . . ; but high up on the summit [*arx*] he erected in the middle a temple of Mars with a colossal statue. [Mausolos built the royal palace according to his own plan.] From there one sees to the right the market, the harbour and the whole town; but to the left a secret harbour which was so hidden by the mountains nobody could see or know what was going on there while the king could give his orders from the palace to the sailors and marines without anyone noticing it.

This is all Vitruvius tells about the town. In any case, we may conclude that the *agora* and the commercial center were situated at the head of the bay in a neutral zone between the settlements of the Greek colonists and the indigenous people.[73]

73. R. Martin, *op. cit.*, p. 284.

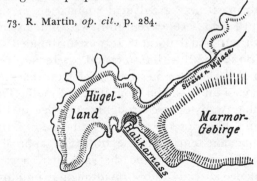

456. **Map of Halikarnassos and environs.**

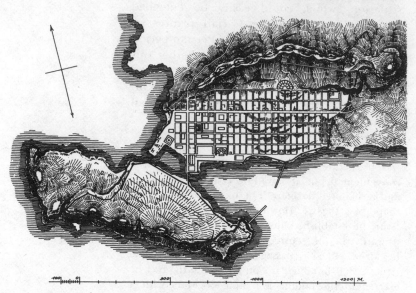

457. Plan of Knidos.

Knidos had even more unfavorable overland connections than Halikarnassos. It lay at the extremity of a 43 mile long and mountainous peninsula, virtually without any connection with the hinterland. It stood partly on the mainland and partly on an island connected in antiquity by a causeway and a bridge forming two bays which were used as harbors, a situation much preferred in antiquity, for the two harbors provided shelter from wind and weather. Knidos was probably founded by Lacedaemonian colonists. It was laid out on a gridiron plan on a terrain which resembled Priene in many respects. The main streets running west-east were fairly level, while the side streets were mostly built as stairways. The *insulae* were 175 by 100 feet and the streets 15 feet wide. One broad street traversed the town from east to west. It was crossed by another main street connecting the urban area with the island. *Agora,* theater, *odeion,* temples, and public buildings completed the picture of a typical small and prosperous town of Hellenistic times.

The archaic Knidos was probably restricted to the island of Triopion, where the sanctuary of the Dorian League had been built. The extension to the mainland may belong to the period after the Persian Wars or to the fourth century.

Marisa (Maresha. Tell Sandahanna), Israel, about 12 miles west of Hebron and 21 miles southwest of Jerusalem, stood at the border between the Judaean Hills and the Plain of Shephelah on a site near the present Beit Jibrin. It was a Seleucid foundation of the third and second centuries B.C. and an important nodal point.[74] It was surrounded by a double wall with towers and covered an area of about 6 acres measuring 520 feet from east to west and 500 feet from north to south. The inner wall followed roughly the edge of the *tell.* The outer wall was farther down the slope and encircled the hill. The approach to the town was from the east where a gate opened directly into a quadrangular building with chambers on three sides whose east wall was part of the surrounding fortifications. Its purpose is not clear, but it may have been the barracks of the town garrison. The main street "A," running east-west for a distance of 350 feet from the "barracks" to the houses along the west wall, was partly paved and had a maximum breadth of 20 feet. Three side streets, 7 to 18 feet wide and ending as a *cul-de-sac,* branched off from the main street to the north and three others to the south. What seems to have been the most important block of the town adjoined the main street at the south. It covered about 140 square feet and included two courts which may have been places of public assembly. The rooms at the southwestern side of this block may have been government offices. The houses, laid out around open courtyards, were closely built together. Many of the rooms were irregular. The general impression is that the available area has been used fairly systematically and rationally.

74. F. J. Bliss and R. A. S. Macalister. *Excavations in Palestine. During the Years 1898-1900.* 1902. Passim.

459. *Opposite:* **Plan of Marisa (Tell Sandahannah).**

458. Relation of Dura-Europos to the trade routes with Syria.

460. The Hellenistic Agora at Dura-Europos.

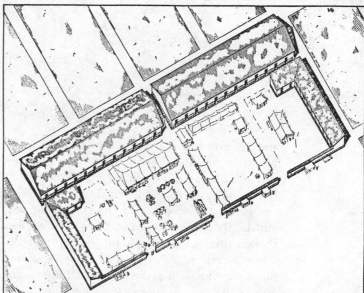

Dura-Europos, according to the first reference available, was founded about 280 B.C. by Nicanor, a general of Seleucus, as one of the fortress colonies which protected the Euphrates route and in particular the river crossings. He called it by the Macedonian name Europos. It is possible, however, that the site had been inhabited before, since the word *Dura* is Assyrian derived from *dûru,* meaning a fort or burgh.[75] For the Seleucids this route was of great importance, for it was the lifeline between Greek Syria and Asia Minor and the Persian satrapies in the East. The protection of this connection by strongpoints was not the only means of guaranteeing its safety. The defenders should be Greeks and the region had to be Hellenized. Consequently, Dura

75. M. I. Rostovtzeff. *Caravan Cities.* 1932. P. 93. *Passim.*

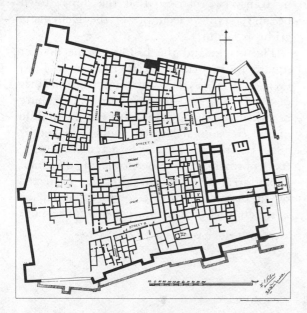

was populated with Greek soldiers who were also prosperous landowners. This was a procedure that has often been used in history in different lands and at different times. The Chinese settled soldier-peasants in the northwest to protect their frontiers against nomad incursions; Maria Theresa followed the same principle along the Hungarian border; and the Czars did the same against the Cossacks in the south, thus giving rise to the origin of numerous towns.

That this policy was successful and Hellenization took root, may be concluded from the fact that the population continued to speak Greek after Dura had become a Parthian fortress. Dura was thus primarily a fortress

591

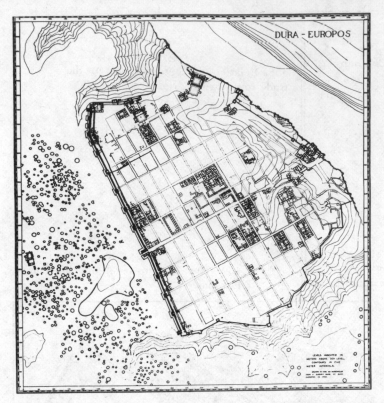

461. Plan of Dura-Europos.

and agricultural colony, and as such its main function was the defense of the river, of the surrounding country, and of food production. It was not a large commercial center, at least not in its earlier days. At the end of the second or the beginning of the first century B.C. Dura came under Parthian control and became the seat of a Parthian garrison. At about the same time it may have gained importance as a center of caravan trade, followed by a period of great prosperity. After the foundation of Palmyra, Dura profited from its favorable position at the nearest crossing place of the Euphrates and the most northerly Parthian fort. It became the point of departure for the caravans from the Euphrates to Palmyra and the receiving center for the goods sent from Palmyra. The garrison was responsible for the safety of the roads, a fact that attracted the caravan merchants to Dura for shorter or longer stays. The Macedonian landowners developed into "Levantine merchants," who provided the caravans with all the various necessaries and in return levied taxes.

The citadel of Dura was built on top of a cliff above the Euphrates, and the town was laid out on a piece of desert land sloping down

to the river between two natural depressions to the north and south, surrounded by strong walls. Although the exact size of Macedonian Dura has not yet been established, it was most likely smaller than the city of Roman and Parthian times, occupying only a limited space on either side of the Euphrates caravan road protected by one or two forts built on the site of the later citadel. The ruins discovered on the citadel hill are of pre-Roman date, probably belonging to the Hellenistic age and to the Seleucid or early Parthian period.

Two different suggestions have been advanced as to the development of the citadel. The top of the hill may have been an area of habitation and the surrounding cliff unfortified. "In the early Parthian times a fortress-palace was probably built on the edge of the cliff above the ruins of the Hellenistic structure" or "the walls of both the town and the citadel were built in Hellenistic times."[76] The palace had a large courtyard open to the people. "Here, seated before a monumental entrance, the king or his representative would pass judgment and enforce law and order." The two caravan routes determined, at least partly, the layout of the town. One, running along the river, probably formed the main road of the lower town, while the other one defined the topography of the upper town, passing through the Palmyra gate, continuing within the town as the main street toward the citadel, and dividing the upper town into two unequal parts. It was intersected by transverse roads so that the upper town became a typical example of the Hellenistic gridiron layout.

The origin and the history of the market square are still confused. It seems clear, however, that it was laid out after the outlines of the *insulae* had been defined. The square occupied an area of eight blocks in the middle of the city and measured about 524 feet by 482 feet, or slightly over 5.80 acres, accounting for approximately 5 per cent of the total urban area. The shop buildings were erected on the north side of the square separated by a street, each containing twenty-four shops

76. M. I. Rostovtzeff, *op. cit.*, pp. 171-73.

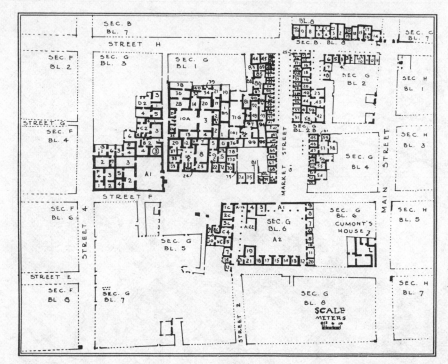

462. Plan of the market center of Dura-Europos.

with storerooms. Other shops occupied parts of the eastern and western sides. A wall connecting the southern end of these buildings separated the northern from the southern part of the square, the latter most likely reserved for temporary booths.

Conception and plan of the *agora* are Hellenistic, an assumption confirmed by the details of the building technique employed in the surrounding halls. The original plan of Dura was based on block units of 100 by 200 feet, separated by streets of 18 feet. However, these basic subdivisions were used flexibly

to meet the requirements of circulation, and the rectangular grid, though perfectly regular, was skillfully adapted to the particular features of the site. . . . The Dura plan . . . falls into place as an exemplar of a uniform and standardized Seleucid planning system which employed the same unit and the same proportions in varying simple multiples as the circumstances required. The development of such a system was the natural outcome of what was in the early Hellenistic period very literally a mass production of cities.[77]

77. M. I. Rostovtzeff and others (ed.). *The Excavations at Dura-Europos.* Preliminary Report of the Ninth Season of Work, 1935-36. Part I. 1944. Pp. 25-26.

History repeated itself many centuries later when the Spaniards built their stereotyped towns in Latin America.

The Hellenistic central square was first of all a market, not a political *agora*. Gradually this commercial function enveloped the whole area. Shops and houses encroached more and more upon it; by the turn of the first and second centuries the open area which had been enclosed by the halls had shrunk to about half its original size and the former access streets had mostly been replaced by others. The Hellenistic market square had developed into an oriental bazaar which

as an expression of concentrated urban economy is the antithesis of the *agora* or open market place. It is essentially a close-knit, permanent nexus of streets lined with shops. Behind or in connection with the shops there may be dwelling places, places of manufacture, or warehouses, but the essential is the avenues of circulation and the crowded places of sale. The open, public place is fundamentally foreign to it.[78]

78. *Ibid.*, p. 53.

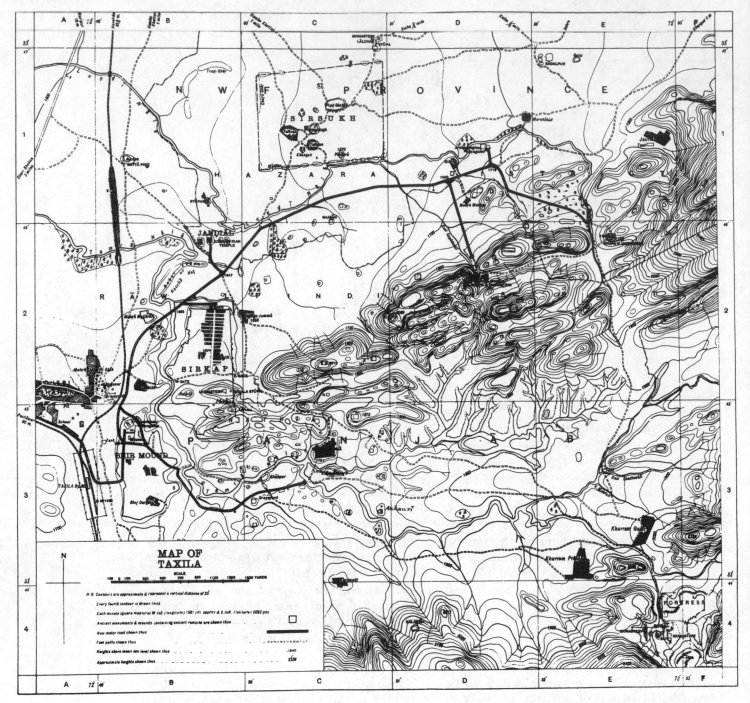

463. Map of Taxila and environs.

Taxila, Pakistan, Punjab, east of the Indus River and about 20 miles northwest of Rawalpindi, was in antiquity the meeting place of three important trade routes from Hindustan and Eastern India, the "royal highway"; from Western Asia; and from Kashmir and Central Asia. The city's fortunes were intimately linked to these highways. To them it owed its origin and later prosperity and, when they were diverted and trade with foreign countries was interrupted, its final decline was inevitable.[79] It was described by Arrian in his *Anabasis of Alexander* (V. 8) as "the greatest of all cities between the Indus and the Jhelum"; and by Strabo in *Geography* (XV.

79. J. Marshall. *Taxila.* 1951. Vol. I, p. 2 and *passim.*

28) as extremely fertile. It stood at an altitude of about 1,700 feet in a valley that was 5 miles wide at its mouth and 11 miles long. At the western end of this valley, separated by a distance of 3½ miles from one another, were three separate cities—the Bhir Mound city, the Sirkap city, and the Sirsukh city as they are now called. The first city was destroyed and rebuilt three times before the Bactrian Greeks transferred it to the site of Sirkap. The earliest settlement on Bhir Mound dates back to the fifth and sixth centuries B.C. or earlier.

All these ruined cities were irregular. Their streets and houses were planned haphazardly. This was in marked contrast to the later city with its more or less regular layout. Alexander the Great reached the Punjab in 326 B.C. but the Greeks who accompanied him were obviously not impressed by the appearance of Taxila. They had nothing to report because the city

had no architecture worthy the name. . . . Its streets [were] crooked, its houses ill-planned and built of rough rubble masonry in mud, which, though neater and more compact than the masonry of the earlier settlement below it, was still relatively crude and primitive.[80]

The Greek city at Taxila, at Sirkap, was laid out on a gridiron plan, the characteristic pattern of the Hellenistic period. It was a university center where mathematics and medicine, astrology and archery, and almost every religious and secular subject was taught: Taxila

owed this academic pre-eminence to its situation at the northwestern gateway to India and to the cosmopolitan character of the population.[81] The third city at Sirsukh belongs to the Kushan period, to the first centuries A.D. The earlier city was transferred from Sirkap to this site about A.D. 80.

Although in this connection only the second or Greek city is of particular interest, it may be useful to compare it with the plan of part of the earlier site because of its striking contrast to the later layout. In the Bhir Mound city the blocks of dwelling houses and shops were divided by an irregular and unsystematic network of streets and lanes. The main street running approximately north-south and fairly straight had an average width of 22 feet. The other winding streets varied from 9 to 17 feet in width. The lanes were mere passages between the houses and seem to have been part of the adjoining private property. They were sometimes *cul-de-sacs* and could not be used by the public as shortcuts between the larger streets. Small open spaces were distributed over the town area. The houses were built around an open courtyard with the rooms arranged on one or more sides.[82] At the beginning of the second century B.C. the city of Taxila was moved by the Bactrian Greeks to the northeast, to the Sirkap site. This new city remained occupied for three centuries, when it was again transferred farther northeast to the site of Sirsukh. It is probable that the older cities were at least

80. *Ibid.*, p. 20.

81. *Ibid.*, p. 43.
82. *Ibid.*, pp. 89, 91-92.

464. Map of Sirkap.

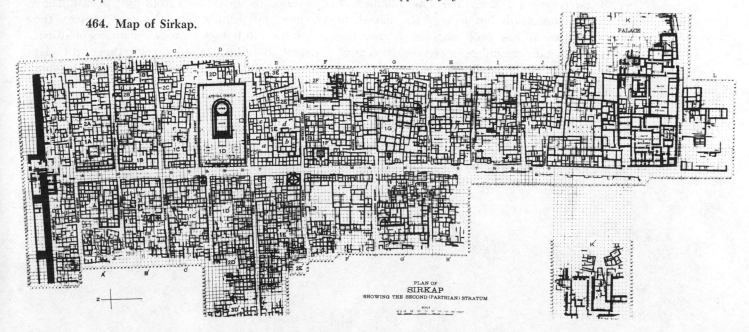

PLAN OF
SIRKAP
SHOWING THE SECOND (PARTHIAN) STRATUM
SCALE

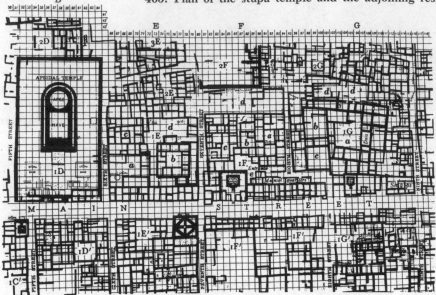

partially inhabited for some time when the new ones had already been in use.[83]

The site was ideal for a Hellenistic regular city. It occupied the extreme end of a spur with a small sharply defined plateau. It offered a considerable area of level ground on which the gridiron scheme could easily be laid out. Low defensive hills, which could partly be included in the defense perimeter, provided a natural protection. Several streams guaranteed a supply of water, at the same time adding to the efficiency of the defenses. The walls were about 3½ miles long and 15 to about 21 feet thick. They enclosed three ridges of the spur, an isolated flat-topped hill, and the low, level plateau. The streets intersected one another at right angles, the main street running north-south and the side streets east-west between building blocks about 120 feet long disposed at fairly regular intervals. The number of gates is uncertain but it is likely that there were four. It has been established that the northern gateway did not open on the central axis of the main street but a little to the east of it. This arrangement, as already mentioned, was not uncommon in Greek cities. It had the advantage that any sudden onrush of invaders could be more easily checked.

The isolated flat-topped hill in the southwest of the city was the *acropolis* and one of the main reasons why the Greeks selected the Sirkap site. The plan of the excavated area shows the city as it was in the first century A.D. when it had been rebuilt by the Parthians after an earthquake along much the same lines as those employed by the Greeks.[84] The following description, based on Sir John Marshall's report, recreates the appearance of the city at a time when two civilizations had merged and produced a result only rarely encountered. About A.D. 50, a decade after the great earthquake, Taxila had been reconstructed. Most buildings were plastered and whitewashed or painted in yellow, blue, red or green, as is still the habit in some of the present-day cities of the Near and Middle East. Shops in the low houses, with one or two rooms and often with a veranda, stood on a high plinth lining the main street on both sides although not in a continuous row. Narrow side streets traversed the urban area from west to east. Temples and shrines were dispersed between the shops and houses. Domes and spires of stūpas and Buddhist temples rose above the flat roofs of the low buildings. At a distance the royal palace stood out in its white and gleaming splendor against a background of hills to the south. The private houses, usually accessible from the side streets, were situated at the rear of the shops and shrines. Near the walls simple houses, probably for the soldiers who guarded the fortifications, were located.

83. *Ibid.*, pp. 112 ff.

84. *Ibid.*, pp. 139 ff.

But in the fashionable residential quarter the houses of the well-to-do were large and opulent. Between the palace and the North Gate there was the district of the governing classes with their slaves and attendants. These houses were two-storied and flat-roofed as a precaution against earthquakes. Nearer the palace the residences had inner courtyards and may have served as public offices. The palace, visible from all parts of the city and rising above the surrounding lower buildings, was "like a glorified private house." It had several courts, for private and public audiences and for the guards, apart from the residential quarters, and a private chapel. It was a relatively unassuming structure but its layout, in general and in detail, resembles not only the Pakistan palaces at Assur, Dura, and Nippur and early Sasanian palaces but also the ancient Assyrian palaces of Mesopotamia.[85]

The third city may be briefly mentioned. It stood about a mile north-northeast from the northern wall of Sirkap. When the Kushan invaders, in about A.D. 80, transferred the city of Taxila to this new site of Sirsukh, they may have followed a tradition that called for crowning and symbolizing their conquest of the country by founding a new capital. But a more cogent reason may have been a plague which shortly before their arrival had killed half the population of the Sirkap city. Sirsukh was an irregular rectangle of 1,500 by about 1,100 yards with an extramural area, possibly for the temporary use of the caravans and also for permanent dwellings of low-caste people and lepers.[86]

85. J. Marshall, *op. cit.*, pp. 140-41.
86. *Ibid.*, p. 217.

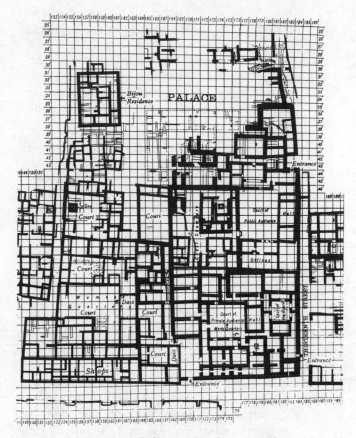

466. Plan of the royal palace at Sirkap.

The city of Taxila is one of the most fascinating melting points of two civilizations each with a long cultural tradition of city building. It is like an open-air museum where the subsequent stages of development can be studied in close proximity, and where seemingly irreconcilable features, such as Greek shrines and Indian stūpas, were welded together through the force of a language of form free of compromise and aware of its own intrinsic value.

Begram, Afghanistan, about 45 miles north of Kabul, at the confluence of the Ghorband and Panjshir rivers, is the name of a small town which stands on the site of the ancient royal capital of Kapisa.[87] Immediately at the

87. R. Ghirshman. *Bégram. Recherches Archéologiques et Historiques sur les Kouchans.* 1946.
J. Hackin. *Recherches Archéologiques à Bégram.* 1939.

junction of the two rivers was "the Ancient Royal Town" covering an area of about 600 by 300 feet and fortified by earthen walls revetted on both sides with unbaked bricks. It seems that this place had been built by Graeco-Bactrian kings in the second century B.C. The ancient royal town was situated on a rock called Bordj-i-'Abdallah. It was pro-

597

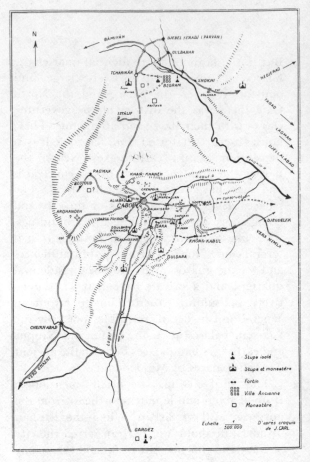

467. Map of Begram and environs.

tected at the east by a steep slope; at the north and west by the two rivers; and like a peninsula was united with the surrounding country only on one side, in this case at the south.

A une date postérieure, palais et citadelle furent transportés à 500 mètres plus au Sud, dans un autre rectangle orienté de la même façon, mais de proportions plus vastes (150 × 450 mètres). Le nouveau quadrangle était réuni au premier soit par le rebord abrupt du plateau, soit (au Sud-Est) par d'épaisses murailles faites de grandes briques crues . . . ; et cette troisième enceinte devait protéger les bazars, qu'on nous dit avoir été si richement fournis, ainsi que les résidences urbaines des principaux habitants. L'ensemble de ces circonvallations se développe sur 2 kilomètres 500 de circuit. Alentour s'éntendaient les faubourgs où vivait le menu peuple, puis les cimetières encore plein de jarres funéraires.[88]

The place was difficult to defend and the bastion, known as Bordj-i-'Abdullah, was probably until the destruction of the town a *"véritable réduit de défense."* In spite of the still rather insufficient excavations it seems that the layout of the ancient town resembled that of Taxila (at Sirkap) and Dura-Europos— that is, it may have been a rectilinear plan. In Dura-Europos and Begram the longest and most exposed side was the most strongly protected; the other sides of the walls followed the contours of the terrain. In either case an *acropolis,* the military center of the town, rose on a cliff overhanging the river and defended the approaches from this side, and the main gate was situated near the middle of the wall facing the land side, from which the main street led through the town to the river.

Taxila and Begram are of particular interest because they show how far Greek principles of city planning had penetrated eastward and how they were adapted to local conditions.

88. A. Foucher. "Notes sur l'Itinéraire de Hiuan-Tsang en Afghanistan." In: *Études Asiatiques Publiées à l'Occasion du Vingt-Cinquième Anniversaire de l'École Française d'Extrême-Orient.* Vol. I. 1925. P. 270.

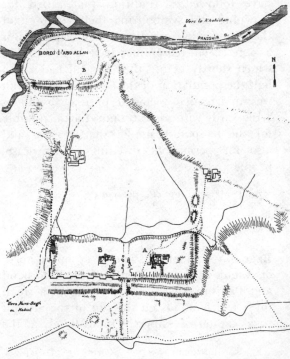

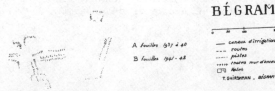

468. Plan of Begram.

Magna Graecia, Southern Italy and Sicily, was for the Greeks what America was for England in colonial times: a field of expansion and political prestige and, at the same time, a testing ground for the colonial skill of the motherland. When the Greeks arrived in the early eighth century their main interest was trade and their first contacts were with the inhabitants of Etruria and Latium. Here they found better markets than in the more primitive regions of the south, and here the first Greek colony on the mainland, Kyme, was founded about 750 B.C.[89] The site of Kyme was protected by a swampy lake against the interior and by an *acropolis* which dominated a long, sandy beach where Greek ships could easily berth. The immediate hinterland was relatively poor. Its soil was not particularly fertile, a fact that suggests the colony was most likely intended as a station for trading with the Etruscans and other peoples of the surrounding region.

Kyme was founded from Ischia where an earlier settlement had been established by Greek colonists. This settlement was abandoned after earthquakes and a volcanic eruption, but there is no indication that these events were connected with the foundation of Kyme. It is certain that the Greeks had at least a vague knowledge of the coastal areas of Sicily before they sent out the first colonists. In the Mycenaean period, between 1400 and 1000 B.C., native settlements had been on or near the coast. Then the center of population shifted inland to mountain sites which could easily be defended and where the inhabitants were not exposed to slave raids by the Greeks. This may have been the reason, although definite proof is missing. However, the Greeks found on their arrival in Sicily native settlements on the sites of Syracuse, Megara, Leontinoi, and on the mainland of Lokroi,

Taras, and Kyme. Naxos, the oldest colony in Sicily, was founded about 734 B.C. on a site which was reached first by ships sailing down the east coast.[90] It stood on a low promontory and remained a small town. Its foundation and subsequent history were connected with Katane and Leontinoi. These three Khalkidian colonies held together for centuries and possessed the richest land in Sicily.[91] A similar interdependence existed between Zankle (Messina) and Rhegion, the twin cities on the Strait of Messina, both situated on a narrow coastal strip surrounded by high mountains and founded principally for strategic reasons —that is, to gain a firm foothold which would enable the Khalkidians to control the passage through the Straits. Syracuse was founded by Corinth at about the same time as Naxos (c. 733). It had an excellent harbor and the Greeks had been trading with a Sikel settlement on the island of Ortygia for several years. Syracuse, like the majority of Greek colonies, needed a considerable number of farmers and graziers to be self-supporting in food supply; but the main purpose of Corinth was to establish a trading town and to relieve population pressure at home.[92]

The colony, an important city from the beginning, soon spread from the island to the mainland.

The success of this historical venture and of wider trading in the west was one of the factors which transformed Corinth in a short space of time from a not very significant city to the leading state in Greece and the first to develop its trade and industries on a large scale. For over a century Corinth controlled the whole colonial area economically, and in that time the colonies made Corinth what she was.[93]

These leading colonies, including Gela on the south coast of Sicily (688), were founded within a very short time. Then several decades passed

89. T. J. Dunbabin. *The Western Greeks. The History of Sicily and South Italy from the Foundation of the Greek Colonies to 480 B.C.* 1948. P. 2. *Passim.* Also for the following.

90. *Ibid.,* pp. 8-9.
91. *Ibid.,* p. 10.
92. *Ibid.,* p. 15.
93. *Ibid.,* p. 18.

before Himera (648), on the north coast, was established. Here, in the west, the Greeks came in contact with the Phoenicians, who had occupied the western part of the island.

In contrast to the colonization in Sicily which proceeded systematically and was sponsored by a few Greek city-states the development in Southern Italy was less well organized. It simply grew and many people from both sides of the Corinthian Gulf took part in this enterprise. They were more interested in settling in a fertile region where they could cultivate the land than in commerce. The first colony was Sybaris. It was a port of call in a large and fertile plain at the mouth of the Sybaris and Krathis rivers. Poseidonia, a Sybarite colony on the west coast of Italy south of Naples in a fertile plain, became a point of interchange for the trade between Sybaris and Etruria, though this seems not to have been the primary purpose of its foundation. Kroton, founded on the advice of the Delphian Oracle, was a port of call with a fertile hinterland on the slopes and foothills of the Sila Mountains. Then followed Kaulonia, Taras with the only good harbor on the east coast, a colony of Sparta, Metapontion, and Lokroi. The Sikels and other natives were not allowed to live in the Greek colonies except possibly as slaves. As in later centuries they were, like other native peoples, cheated of their land by empty promises, broken treaties, or worthless gifts after having received the invaders as friends. At Lokroi, for instance, the colonists swore to abide by an agreement whereby they would share the land in common with the natives "as long as they stood on the same earth and kept their heads on their shoulders." However, they avoided "the consequences of their oath by putting earth in their shoes and heads of garlic on their shoulders.[94] This ruse seems to have been commonplace and proves, if nothing else, that segregation has been since earliest times a potent instrument of human self-righteousness. The Sikels lived in the countryside or outside the Greek cities and worked as slaves or laborers for their masters. This lasted for about two hundred and fifty years after the first colonies had been founded. Then it seems that a certain desegregation began to set in. But before this change the Greeks regarded the Sikels as inferior and were proud of their own descent.[95]

94. *Ibid.*, p. 44.
95. *Ibid.*, p. 193.

Taras (Taranto), founded in 706 B.C., stood on a rocky peninsula at the entrance to the only good harbor of the east coast of Southern Italy.[96] The two islands of S. Pietro and S. Paolo, called the Khoirades in antiquity, protected the outer harbor which was connected with the inner harbor by a narrow channel. The citadel occupied a small promontory between the harbors connected with the land to the west by an isthmus before it was cut through in the Middle Ages. At what date the city spread from the citadel to the mainland in the east is unknown. Around 400 B.C., the time of its greatest prosperity and power, Taras covered an area of about two square miles, apart from a suburb at the west of the Little Harbor. The *agora* was situated on the mainland, in the western part of the walled-in area and, according to Polybius (VIII. 29. 7), was accessible by three streets. Its layout seems to have been relatively loosely grouped and open, for there were several secondary openings for a number of side streets. The only definite conclusion that can be drawn from the meager information is that the *agora* was not situated in the immediate proximity of the sea, which would explain the existence of the two other squares serving as markets near the storehouses of the harbor.

96. T. J. Dunbabin, *op. cit.*, pp. 28 ff., 87 ff., 146 ff.

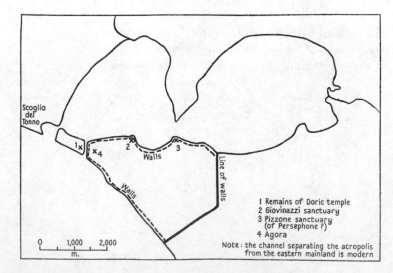

Scoglio del Tonno

1× ×4 2 Walls 3

Line of walls

Walls

1 Remains of Doric temple
2 Giovinazzi sanctuary
3 Pizzone sanctuary (of Persephone ?)
4 Agora

Note: the channel separating the acropolis from the eastern mainland is modern

0 1,000 2,000
m.

469. Map of Taras.

Sybaris and Thurii share the same fate: both are famous because so much has been written about them, and both have left hardly any traces from which their physical appearance can be reconstructed. And yet they must be mentioned in a history of city planning, if for no other reason than that the name of Hippodamos has been connected with the building of Thurii. The exact site of Sybaris is uncertain. It was destroyed by the Krotoniates in 510 B.C. who razed it to the ground and diverted the waters of the Krathis over its ruins. It was an Achaean colony founded about 720 B.C. in a region that was very fertile in antiquity. It stood between two rivers, the Krathis and the Sybaris, which originally had independent mouths but now meet several miles inland. The name of Sybaris was synonymous with luxury, an epithet that has survived the centuries to the present day. Literary evidence is ample. It tells us of

the great banquets and splendid public festivals; the elegant youth of the city; the costly wares of Ionia, the metal-work of Etruria, the rarities of the whole Greek world; the shaded streets, the well-tilled fields, the flourishing little inland towns; the care taken for health and comfort, the pride in wines and cuisine; the encouragement to foreign merchants, and the kindly contempt for anyone who had to travel.[97]

Sybaris was the greatest and most prosperous city before its destruction. It had conquered a territory that was larger than that of any other city in Southern Italy and Sicily. It founded colonies as far away as on the Tyrrhenian Sea among which Poseidonia (Paestum) was the most famous. It freely admitted citizens from all parts of Greece, and its citizen population may well have been 100,000—making a total of about 500,000. The roads were in good order and were planted with shade trees outside the city. Noisy trades were excluded and Turkish baths were introduced. This is the oldest reference to public baths.[98] Sybaris was a progressive city and it is very doubtful whether its "luxury" was really

something extravagant or effeminate or merely a deliberate attempt at raising the standard of living and improving the amenities of urban life. If the Sybarites felt that nonconformity with the austere standards of ancient Greece was an asset, they were certainly right to live as they did, and we should not be surprised that those who felt they were left behind did what people always have done: they ridiculed and denigrated the nonconformists and blamed them for something they would have been only too glad to copy—if they could possibly have done so.

For about half a century the Sybarites lived as exiles in their colonies until in 452 B.C. they tried to revive and to repeople their old city, an attempt that was brutally suppressed by the Krotoniates. But the appeal for help which the Sybarites had sent to Athens found a willing response. Pericles invited Greeks of all tribes to support the fugitives and to demonstrate the unity of the Greek world by founding an ideal city near the site of the destroyed Sybaris. Numerous colonists from various parts of Greece followed his summons and in 443, under the guidance of Athens, a large group set out to found Thurii. Two prominent men were active participants in this enterprise. They were Herodotus and Hippodamos, who belonged to the brilliant circle surrounding the Athenian statesman and who were in sympathy with his Panhellenic ideas. According to Diodorus (XII. 10) the colonists were divided into ten tribes, three from the Peloponnesus and seven from more distant regions. The city was laid out on the Hippodamian gridiron scheme with three longitudinal and four transverse streets, no doubt under the personal guidance of Hippodamos. However, the intention to make Thurii an ideal city not only in its physical appearance but also in its administration and civic unity proved to be a utopia. Dissension broke out among the tribal groups; the Delphic Oracle demanded the new colony for the Dorians, and after a few years most of the leading citizens, who sympathized with Athens, returned home.

The site of Thurii has not been excavated. We have to rely on literary evidence and con-

97. T. J. Dunbabin, op. cit., p. 76.
98. Ibid., p. 79.

jecture. We may assume that all streets were lined with houses on both sides and that there were twenty *insulae* of which about fifteen were occupied by dwelling houses and the rest by the market, temples, and public buildings. Each *insula* may have consisted of eight houses. Thus the number of inhabitants was small, about half of that of Priene, and the town was, at least at the beginning, rather insignificant.

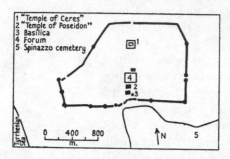

470. Map of Poseidonia.

Poseidonia (Paestum), founded around 700 by Sybaris on the Bay of Salerno, was situated near the mouth of the Silaris (Sele) River in a plain with a fairly rich hinterland. The site had been inhabited from most ancient times. A *necropolis* of the Neolithic period has been discovered and within the city itself neolithic and palaeolithic implements have been found, proof that an indigenous population lived there before the arrival of the Greeks. However, our knowledge is still too incomplete to throw much light on this early settlement. It might have been a prehistoric village which was enclosed by ditches. So far no indications have been found even after a careful study of air photographs.[99]

According to Strabo (252) the original inhabitants of the site took refuge in the mountains when the Sybarites arrived to found their new colony. Poseidonia attained a high level of prosperity due to the fertility of the surrounding country and as a center of commerce with the Etrurians. This prosperity aroused the hatred and envy of the Lucanians, who conquered it in about 400 B.C. and changed its name to Paiston or Paistos. The

99. J. Bradford. *Ancient Landscapes.* 1957. Pp. 218-27.
P. C. Sestieri. *Paestum.* 1958.

602

walls, about 3 miles in circuit, had a pentagonal shape following the outline of a shelf of limestone formed by the low rocky eminence on which the city stood. A moat surrounded the entire circuit and was crossed by bridges at the gates. The walls, as can be seen today, may be partly Roman or Lucanian, or Greek. There were four gates, apart from a number of posterns used for sorties during sieges. The largest, the west gate, had a vestibule inside and guard rooms and two towers on the outside. A bastion between the two towers was so constructed that it forced the attacking enemy to expose their right flank, unprotected by shields, to the arms of the defenders.

The two Roman streets, which crossed one another at right angles, very probably followed the lines of earlier pre-Roman streets. The three Doric temples occupied the center of the city, the *temenos*, along which led the Sacred Way coinciding with the track of an earlier Greek road from the nearby *necropolis*. As air photographs have shown, the urban

471. Traces of buried streets at Paestum identified from air photographs.

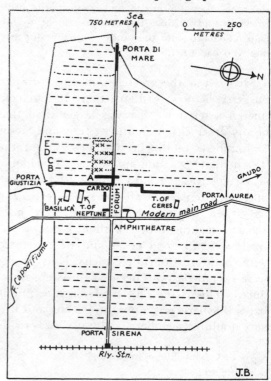

area was divided by 30 parallel lines 130 feet apart which mark the street system. The built-up area within the walls was extensive but further evidence is needed before the relationship of the Roman to the Greek streets and the size of the *insulae* can be decided. The Roman *forum* occupied the site of the Greek *agora* which divided the two parts of the *temenos*. The southern part included the two major temples, the Basilica and the Temple of Poseidon, besides some smaller temples and was dedicated to the goddess Hera, while the nothern part around the Temple of Demeter (Ceres) was probably consecrated to Athene. Further excavations and more air photographs may reveal other valuable data from which the layout and other features of the Greek city may be deduced.

Pompei and **Neapolis** do not contribute to our knowledge of Greek city planning. The ancient Greek parts are buried under the Roman ruins in Pompei and under later and modern buildings in Naples. The latter had a regular street system with unusually oblong blocks which can still be distinguished today in the modern layout. During the sixth century B.C. the Greeks were masters of the entire Gulf of Naples. They were firmly established in the strong *acropolis* of Kyme and on the hills and rocks of Puteoli (Dikaiarkhia) and Neapolis, and at the naval base of Misenum. Their rule extended southward to the extreme point of the peninsula of Surrentum (Sorrento) and to the islands of Ischia and Capri. Kyme was founded about 757-756(?) and, as already mentioned, was the oldest of the Greek colonies in Italy and Sicily intended in the first place as a trading center. Excavations have so far not produced a coherent picture of ancient Kyme. Only details of the *acropolis* and fortifications are known.

Syracuse was founded in 733 B.C. from Corinth. The island of Ortygia, the nucleus of the colony, the *nasos* (island), was at this time inhabited by Sikels with whom the Greeks had been trading before the foundation of Syracuse. However, it is most unlikely that the Sikels and Greeks jointly occupied the island. The former must have left the site at about the time of the Greek colonization. Classical Syracuse consisted of the districts of Achradina, Tyche, Neapolis, and Epipolai. It had two harbors, the Great and the Little Harbor, which may have been the main attractions for the colonists when they settled the site. From the second half of the sixth century the island of Ortygia was joined by a causeway to the mainland whose low shore extended at the southwest into a swamp. This region was the original Syrako, which gave the city its name and was settled at the same time as the island. This mainland settlement, north of the harbors, was the district of Achradina or ἡ ἔξω πόλις, the outer city.[100]

100. T. J. Dunbabin, *op. cit.*, p. 50.

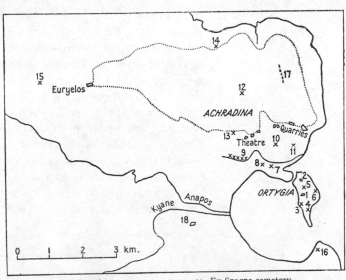

472. Plan of early Syracuse.

1. Athenaion.	10. Ex-Spagna cemetery.
2. Apollonion.	11. S. Lucia cemetery.
3. Arethusa.	12. Ottone cemetery.
4. Piazza S. Giuseppe.	13. Grotticelli cemetery.
5. Sperduta.	14. Scala Greca.
6. Wells in Via Gelone.	15. Belvedere.
7. Agora.	16. Plemmyrion.
8. Piazzale Stazione.	17. Gelonian Wall.
9. Fusco cemetery.	18. Olympieion.

Syracuse extended its territory over the whole southwest corner of Sicily. At the end of the sixth century it included a mixture of Sikel villages and military colonies; small Greek country towns and isolated Greek farms with large and small landholders living side by side. Syracuse became the commercial center of Sicily. In 485 B.C. Gelon, tyrant of Gela on the south coast, transferred his seat to Syracuse which he had occupied without opposition. He increased the population of his new residence by a synoicism which resembled more the Roman principle of granting citizenship than the procedure applied in Greek city-states. More than half of the population of Gela and people from other cities were transplanted to Syracuse and made citizens turning it into a city with a mixed population. This increase led to an extension of Syracuse. The low-lying areas were partly included in the fortifications. An *agora* was laid out near the Little Harbor and the island of Ortygia became the inner city, the stronghold of the ruler.

Akragas, founded in 580 B.C. from Gela and Rhodes, occupied a site which was by nature roughly rectangular, rising at the Rock to a height of 1,160 feet. Two torrents, known to the Greeks as Akragas and Hypsas, joined before reaching the sea. The southern side of the plateau is set off by a low, long hill running parallel to the coast. The Akragas region is a land of hills and valleys suitable for olive and wheat cultivation. It merged into the undulating tableland of the interior, one of the foremost granaries of the Roman world. Sikel settlements occupied the hilltops. Traces of the ground plans of their huts have been found—mostly circular but occasionally square.[101]

Akragas extended its influence along the Mediterranean coast toward Gela in the east and Selinus in the west and penetrated inland as far as Himera on the Tyrrhenian Sea. At this early stage the building activity in the city was insignificant. Only the walls can be traced back to this period. After the victory at Himera (482 B.C.) over Carthage, Akragas accumulated great wealth. Large numbers of slaves captured at Himera were employed in building operations, mainly temples. It seems that a veritable building craze developed, for in less than half a century nine temples were erected, among them the colossal temple of Zeus. Whereas the first phase was directed toward the conquest of power, during the second phase the state ceased to expand and was greatly weakened by continued warfare against the native Sikels and other small city-states.

The new generation with its love of luxury, art, and ostentation was criticized by its contemporaries. When Carthage returned to the attack in 406 B.C. they encountered, after the conquest of Himera and Selinus, only a feeble resistance. Akragas was pillaged and destroyed and never regained its former greatness and splendor.

The *acropolis* of Akragas was a unique fea-

473. Map of Akragas.

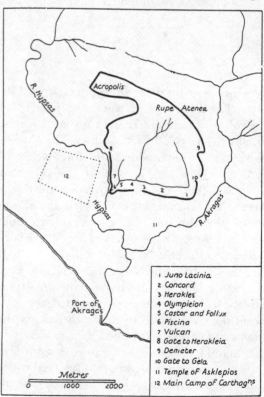

1 Juno Lacinia
2 Concord
3 Herakles
4 Olympieion
5 Castor and Pollux
6 Piscina
7 Vulcan
8 Gate to Herakleia
9 Demeter
10 Gate to Gela
11 Temple of Asklepios
12 Main Camp of Carthagns

101. P. Marconi. *Agrigento*. 1929.

ture in the colonial cities of Sicily and Italy and an anachronism "in an age when the inhabitants of old Greece were creeping down from acropolis to harbor town."[102] It was so large and strong that it could easily hold an average ancient city, and even now accommodates a town of 25,000 inhabitants. Akragas included almost from the beginning the area which it occupied afterward. The walls followed the contours of the terrain and enclosed an area of 900 acres. Residential districts for the poorer classes probably extended over the upper part of the hill, for houses of the simplest type have been found here, whereas the quarters for the well-to-do and the public

102. T. J. Dunbabin, op. cit., p. 312.

Selinus was founded in 628 B.C. by the Sicilian Megarians. Its acropolis occupied the southern extremity of a steep promontory called Terra di Pulci which, isolated at the west and east by two narrow valleys, rose about 100 feet above the sea. The site was not particularly advantageous for a city. It had poor landing facilities and the marshes at the two rivers made it unhealthy. The territory of the state formed a rectangle approximately 32.3 by 15.5 miles. Its prosperity was mainly derived from cultivation and cattle breeding. The city was sacked by the Carthaginians in 409 and after this misfortune it declined, lingering on as an unimportant small town which would have been completely forgotten if its ruins had not preserved a faint reflection of its former splendor. The great building program, which included above all the erection of the temples, was initiated toward 580 B.C. and was intended to replace the modest and primitive structures built at the time of the foundation. Selinus' ambition was to emulate its rivals and, if possible, to surpass them. As the excavators of Selinus put it, it was the

imprudente coquetterie de parvenue, qui fait parade de ses atours dans un cercle d'inquiétantes convoitises. . . . Cette fièvre de construction, qui dure tout un siècle, de 580 à 480 environ, dépasse en ardeur et en prétention, sinon en goût, le

buildings may have spread over the flat tracts of land. The southern range of hills was reserved for the temples which were lined up like a chain of pearls along the southern wall. Broadly speaking, there were three zones: one in the center almost uninhabited; another crowded with houses for the masses above, and homes for the wealthy and public buildings below; a third stretching right up to the city walls occupied by temples and shrines. The agora was in the lower part of the city. The general layout was exceptionally spacious with large open spaces within the walls. Water was supplied by a network of aqueducts hewn out of the rock or built of stone slabs and conveyed through earthenware pipes placed inside the duct or running outside parallel to it.

merveilleux effort de l'Athènes de Pisistrate, de Périclès et de Nicias.[103]

Soon the acropolis became too small for the ambitions of the citizens. The old city on the acropolis was crowded out by the sanctuaries and moved to the neighboring hill. Gradually the upper town lost its former residential character, although it was sufficiently large to retain at its flanks parts of the ancient quarters with its tortuous streets and archaic houses which must have resembled the kasbahs of oriental cities. "En bas, c'était le bourdonnement de la vie laborieuse, mercantile, industrielle et politique; en haut, la sérénité d'une atmosphère supra-terrestre, où les dieux régnaient seuls parmi la fumée des sacrifices et le murmure des prières."

The old town, which Pamilos, the oikist of Selinus, founded on the promontory di Pulci, occupied about the same area as the contracted city which was rebuilt by Hermocrates in 408. The walls of the earlier city had a circumference of 3,936 feet and enclosed a pearlike site 1,476 feet long and 426.40 to 459.20 feet wide, covering 21.74 acres. The population may have numbered hardly more than 6,000 inhabitants. Toward 580 about 7.41 acres were set aside

103. J. Hulot and G. Fougères. Sélinonte. La Ville, l'Acropole et les Temples. 1910. P. 91, passim. Also for the following.

474. General view of Selinus.

for the sanctuaries and a large terrace was constructed which served for festivals and other public activities. This was an enormous enterprise. An artificial substructure was built from the foot of the rock to the level of the new platform. Shortly before 409 the whole urban area of Selinus may have been something like 69.18 acres, with a population of about 30,000 citizens not counting slaves. The cemeteries which covered about 617.5 acres surrounded the city and its outlying district like a *ceinture funéraire* occupying all the hills in the vicinity.

The new and smaller Selinus was built on an almost unencumbered site. Only the temples and parts of the ramparts were still standing. The plateau of the *acropolis*, leveled and supported by the substructure, must have been

to Hermocrates like a drawing-board on which he could give full scope to his vision. However, it seems that this vision was nothing out of the ordinary, for he followed the contemporary fashion and planned the city on the grid-iron scheme, adapting it with only minor deviations to the still-standing temples without that spark of imagination which would have kindled into a fierce flame the ingenuity of a more creative man. The irregular outline of the site, which may have stimulated a more provocative solution, was neglected. The rigidity of a regular layout was imposed on the *acropolis*. A north-south axis, 1,394 feet long and about 29 feet wide, divided the terrain roughly into halves. It was crossed at right angles by a number of equidistant east-west streets and accompanied by other streets run-

ning parallel to it. The area around the temples in the southeastern part was kept free of other buildings except along the main street and the walls. Two squares were laid out on the west side of the north-south axis. The site of the *agora* is obscure. It is possible that further excavations may lead to an identification of its position. The whole was in fact and in spirit a perfect drawing-board achievement, a *rêverie à la mode* without the instinctive vitality which would have related the individual elements in an organic and mutually enhancing composition. This over-all failure should not, however, distract from the beauty of the temples and their relationship to one another in detail. The architects were, as so often, more creative and sensitive than the city planners.

607

475. Reconstruction of the port and the adjoining houses at Selinus.

608

476. *Opposite:* Reconstruction of the Acropolis of Selinus.

Massilia (**Marseilles**) was founded by Phocaeans about 600 B.C. on a terrace north of the Old Harbor of Lacydon. It was fortified on the landward side by a wall. The terrain sloped down in gentle terraces toward the harbor. The colony consisted of an upper town with the *acropolis* and the sanctuaries, and a lower town of the merchants and may have had a population of about 5,000 inhabitants. Its shape was rectangular and the circumference of the walls was hardly more than 8,200 feet.[104] These were the usual dimensions of the Greek colonies whose task was to trade, not to conquer. The original inhabitants, the Segobriges, and the colonists lived side by side but each group retained its independent way of life. The contacts between the Greeks and the tribes remained friendly for a long time. On the days of the Hellenic festivals the gates were thrown open and the young

104. C. Jullian. *Histoire de la Gaule.* Vol. I. 1908. Pp. 193 ff.

M. G. Vasseur. "L'Origine de Marseille. Fondation des Premiers Comptoirs Ioniens de Massalia vers le Milieu du VIIe Siècle," *Annales du Musée d'Histoire Naturelle de Marseille,* Vol. XIII. 1914. *Passim.*

Ligurians entered the town, their chariots adorned with flowers, and joined in the festivities of their hosts. It seems that the town was laid out on a gridiron scheme, but the available data are still too meager to permit definite conclusions in this respect.

During the following centuries the Massaliots established numerous daughter colonies, among them Nice, the *Town of Nike,* Antibes (Antipolis), Olbia, Tauroeis, Citharista toward the east, and in the west Arelate (Arles), Rhodanousia, and others. It was a maritime empire that gradually developed. All important foundations were ports, not only naval bases but also commercial harbors. Not a single colony was founded in the interior. Almost all these coastal towns were fortified by walls and served, apart from their general function as urban centers, as refuges for the merchants and countrypeople in times of danger and as strongpoints in the defense against pirates and brigands. They dominated the sea and land routes and for a long time were able to repulse the Ligurians, Celts, and Iberians.

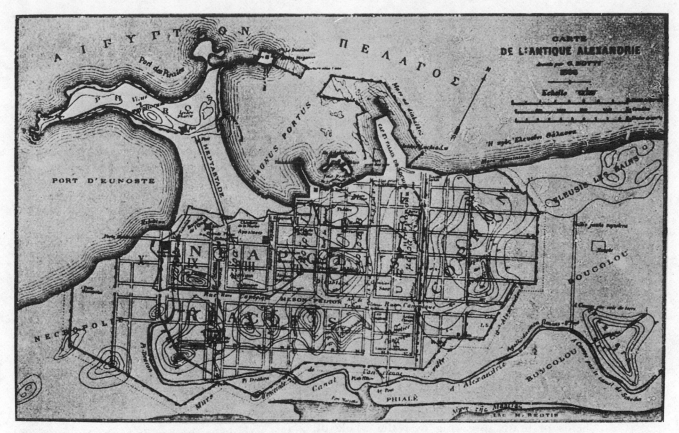

478. Plan of Alexandria.

Alexandria, Egypt, was founded by Alexander the Great in 332 or 331. Archeological data especially on the Greek period are scanty, and the reconstructed plans are unreliable. We know that Alexander's architect Deinokrates, who had accompanied the king to Egypt, designed the city, though not on the grand scale that has been attributed to him. The phenomenal growth of Alexandria belongs to later periods. At Alexander's time the Greek cities were still relatively small. The investigations, which were conducted in the nineteenth century by Mahmud Bey, are more or less useless and give an erroneous picture of the early Hellenistic city.[105] More recent excavations have shown that the street plan and the extent of the city as reconstructed by Mahmud Bey belong to the latest period of Imperial Rome.

It may be that Alexandria was intended as an equivalent of the destroyed Phoenician

477. *Opposite:* This map of Marseilles, though dating from 1824, shows the general situation and the configuration of the terrain which attracted the early Greek settlers.

105. Mahmud Bey. *Mémoire sur l'Antique Alexandrie, ses Faubourgs et Environs Découverts par les Fouilles. . . .* 1872.

611

Tyre. In any case, the expectations of the founder were not only fulfilled but surpassed, for as early as the reign of the first Ptolomies, Alexandria was (together with Carthage) one of the most important cities of the whole Mediterranean. The main reason for this success was the incomparably favorable site on the westernmost branch of the Nile which, owing to the prevailing eastern currents, was least exposed to silting. It combined the advantages of large seaports with those of an inland harbor at Lake Mareotis. It had two seaports, Port Eunostos and Magnum Portus, which were created by the construction of the Heptastadium dam from the city to the island of Pharos with the famous lighthouse. The native Egyptian population lived in the most ancient district of Rakotis, a former fishing village, in the southwest which was adjoined toward the northeast by the Greek town.

Vitruvius describes the selection of the site by Alexander in enthusiastic terms as the spontaneous stroke of a genius. "Here Alexander noticed the harbour sheltered by nature with its magnificent *emporium* together with fields of grain spreading over the whole of Egypt and the immense advantages of the giant Nile river." (II, Introduction.) But posterity may be inclined to regard the foundation of Alexandria more as a routine enterprise than as a quasi-divine act of inspiration. No doubt, the site was extremely favorable but one of the main achievements of Alexander and his successors was the foundation of virtually hundreds of new cities, Alexandria being merely one of them, although certainly one of the most ambitious creations of the period. Its layout proceeded on the recognized principle of the gridiron plan, a principle intelligently adapted to the particular conditions of the site. In any case, Alexandria made a tremendous impression on later writers. Strabo's description is famous (XVII 1. 6 ff.):

The advantages of the city's site are various; for, first, the place is washed by two seas, on the north by the Aegyptian Sea, as it is called, and on the south by Lake Mareia, also called Mareotis. This is filled by many canals from the Nile, . . . so that the harbour on the lake was in fact richer than that on the sea. The shape of the area of the city is like a chlamys [a Macedonian military cloak]; the long sides of it are those that are washed by the two waters . . . and the short sides are the isthmuses. . . . The city as a whole is intersected by streets practicable for horse-riding and chariot-driving, and by two that are very broad . . . which cut one another into two sections and at right angles.

And he continues to describe the city in the most enthusiastic terms.

Even if we reduce the various eulogies to a more sober appreciation the site of Alexandria and its spacious layout must have been impressive. It is most regrettable that the contribution, which Alexandria doubtlessly made to Hellenistic city planning, cannot be assessed in any more precise form. Although it would be inviting to speculate on the basis of the innumerable conjectures of archeologists and writers about the details of the city plan and its districts, the result would only be generalities. However this may be, Alexandria opened a new chapter in the commercial history of Greece. It was the symbol of trade with a widening world caused by the great attraction which its handicrafts exerted upon the workers in the Greek homeland and by the general shift of industry away from Greece proper that contributed to a population decline in Greece itself.[106] The center of gravity was distinctly moving toward the west not only politically but also culturally. In the process Alexandria was the harbinger of a new era which finally culminated in the grandeur of Rome.

106. W. L. Westermann. *The Slave Systems of Greek and Roman Antiquity.* 1955. Pp. 34-35.

Naukratis, Egypt, was founded around 600 B.C. on the site of an earlier trading settlement.[107] It lay about 10 miles west of the present Rosetta-branch of the Nile—that is, in the western part of the Delta. In ancient times it was accessible by the Kanobic branch which was then farther to the west. Herodotus mentioned it (II. 97):

When the Nile overflows, the whole country is converted into a sea, and the towns, which alone remain above water, look like the islands in the Aegean. At these times water transport is used all over the country, instead of merely along the course of the river, and anyone going from Naukratis to Memphis would pass right by the pyramids instead of following the usual course by Cercasorus and the tip of the Delta. [And in II. 179:] In old days Naukratis was the only port in Egypt, and anyone who brought a ship into any of the other mouths of the Nile was bound to state on oath that he did so of necessity and then proceed to the Canopis mouth; should contrary winds prevent him from doing so, he had to carry his freight to Naukratis in barges all round the Delta, which shows the exclusive privilege the port enjoyed.

Strabo also referred to Naukratis giving another geographical indication (XVII. 1. 23):

Above Momemphis are two nitre-beds . . . and the Nitriote Nome . . . Nearby, and in this Nome, is a city Menelaus; and on the left, in the Delta, lies Naukratis, which is on the river, whereas Saïs lies at a distance of two schoeni from the river.

107. W. M. Flinders Petrie. *Naukratis.* Part I. 1884-5. P. 5. *Passim.*
H. Prinz. "Funde aus Naukratis," *Klio,* Belheft Vol. 7. 1908.

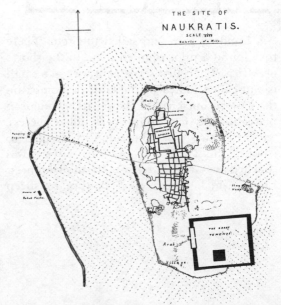

THE SITE OF NAUKRATIS.

The position of Naukratis has long been disputed but has now been identified as the mound of Nebireh or its immediate neighborhood. This mound contained archaic temples of Apollo and Aphrodite as, according to Herodotus and other writers, Naukratis did. It covered a great commercial *emporium* and was a center of Greek manufactures and trade.[108]

The excavations, though incomplete, have shown that Naukratis consisted of two agglomerations: the Egyptian town at the south and the Greek town at the north. Thus the two groups lived side by side as Amasis, the Egyptian pharaoh, intended. As Herodotus said (II. 154):

Amasis liked the Greeks and granted them a number of privileges, of which the chief was the gift of Naukratis as a commercial headquarters for anyone who wished to settle in the country. He also made grants of land upon which Greek traders, who did not want to live permanently in Egypt, might erect altars and temples.

The mound is about half a mile long, including the Great *Temenos,* and a little over a quarter of a mile wide. As far as the plan of the town has been traced it shows a mixture of a near-regular and an irregular layout. As Flinders Petrie explains (p. 35),

There are at the upper and the lower margin of the plan two sets of arrow-lines; these point to the directions of the streets, which appear to have been built from two rather different bases. The lower set of arrows is parallel with the Great *Temenos* wall, and points to the streets of the eastern side of the town more particularly; while the upper set points to a system of streets which make a small but distinct angle of about 10 or 12 degrees with the other series. This seems most likely to have been the system derived from the line of the canal which skirted the side of the city. Two such systems together show that there must have been some other element beside the canal-line to influence the builders in the earliest times; and it seems therefore to give some weight to the early age of the Great *Temenos.*

The enclosure in the northern part of the city is supposed to be the *palaestra* which was

108. W. M. Flinders Petrie, *op. cit.,* p. 4.

613

479. Map of Naukratis.

dedicated to Apollo whose temple adjoined it. The Great *Temenos* in the south of the city covers an area equal to a third of the city area. It is "the greatest of all these temenê, which is also the most celebrated and the most frequented (or conspicuous), called the Hellenion," as Herodotus says (II. 178). And he adds,

The Hellenion was built by the joint efforts of the Ionians of Chios, Teos, Phokaea, and Klazomenae, of the Dorians of Rhodes, Knidos, Halikarnassos and Phaselis, and of the Aeolians of Mytilene. It is to these states that the temple belongs, and it is they who have the right of appointing the officers in charge of the port.

This immense enclosure was the heart of the Greek race in Egypt. It was for the Greek colonists the equivalent of the Panionion, the revered center of the Ionian states of Asia Minor. The Great *Temenos*, the Pan-Hellenion, could readily hold fifty or sixty thousand people and its strong walls, 50 feet thick of solid brickwork and 40 feet high, could protect from attack. It was thus a sanctuary, a place of assembly, a refuge, and the civic center of authority where matters of public welfare were discussed. It fulfilled, therefore, the functions of an *agora* combining secular and religious purposes. Only the more private institutions of civic life, the *gymnasion,* the *palaestra,* and the *stoa,* were located in the city proper. Religious processions and festivals took place in the *temenos* which was a veritable miniature town separated from and yet an integral part of the city.

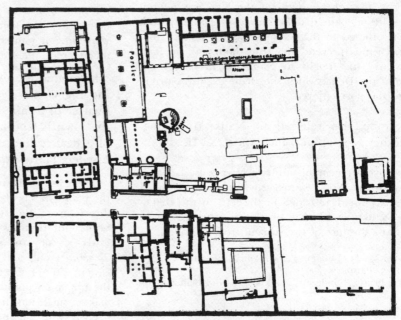

480. Plan of the Agora of Cyrene.

Cyrene, Libya, was founded about 630 B.C. by colonists from Thera, forced to emigrate around the middle of the seventh century, because of overpopulation and a long period of drought. The Delphic Oracle, consulted before the leaders of the expedition decided on this solution, advised them to found a colony in a "place between waters." The leader, a certain Aristoteles, later the first king of Cyrene under the name of Battus, set out with two hundred men and sailed to Crete. There they found a pilot who led them to the shores of Africa. Their first settlement was on a small island called Platea in the Gulf of Bomba on the eastern outskirts of the fertile Cyrenaican plateau. This first colony was not a success, and after two years the colonists decided to consult the Oracle again. The advice was couched in sarcastic terms: "If thou knowest Libya, which giveth good pasture to sheep

614

A — Acropolis Gateway
B — Corner Tower of Acropolis
C — Sanctuary of Serapis and Isis
D — Roman House
E — Unidentified Edifice
F — House of the Dionysos Mosaic
G — Rock-cut road to Fountain
H — Milestone of Hadrian
I — "Sacred Way" (sidewalk of Valley Street)
J — New Fountain (Aqua Augusta)
K — Greek Baths
L — Triumphal Arch (Antonine)
M — Unidentified Roman Building
N — Market-Theatre and Severan Propylon
O — Roman city-centre (Valley Street)
P — Christian Church (6th Century A.D.)
Q — Byzantine Defensive Wall
R — Arab Tower
S — Cathedral
T — Waterworks (Roman cisterns)
U — Circus (Hippodrome)
V — Temple of Zeus
W — Hill-top Temple
X — Tower of City Wall
Y — Archaeological Museum and Library
Z — Sculpture Museum and Circular Tomb

481. Plan of Cyrene.

better than I, then I greatly admire thy wisdom."[109] With this advice the settlers returned to Africa and transferred their settlement to the mainland, to a site called Aziris between Bomba and Derna. Here they stayed for six years. But when they learned there were even better sites more to the west, they moved on again and finally settled on the future site of Cyrene. Their Libyan guides told them: "Here, O Greeks, ye may fitly dwell, for in this place there is a hole in the heavens," meaning that there was abundant rainfall and good arable soil and ample pasture.

In the course of the next century more settlers arrived from many parts of Greece. The Libyans were driven from their land to make room for the newcomers and an Egyptian army, which had entered Cyrenaica to help the Libyans, was defeated by the Greeks about 570 B.C. After another century full of internal strife and external wars the monarchical regime was replaced by a republic. Dur-

ing this era the frontier between Cyrenaica and Tripolitania, dominated by Carthage, was stabilized. When Alexander the Great arrived in Egypt in 332 B.C. he received valuable gifts, including 300 war-horses and five four-horse chariots from the people of Cyrenaica.

We may assume that the first Greek settlers built their houses near the Fountain of Apollo on whose water supply their well-being depended. But this area, on the terrace below the Fountain, was quite restricted. Moreover, it was soon reserved for religious purposes. It is therefore likely that the houses were erected on the site of the later acropolis, which could easily be defended, and also along the sheltered valley southeast of the Fountain. This valley became later the main artery of the town plan. Since, in the early centuries, it was a muddy watercourse, the first king laid out a dry access road along the ridge of the southwest hill.

The original town plan cannot be reconstructed. Later buildings have changed it

109. Quoted after R. Goodchild. *Cyrene and Apollonia.* Published by the Antiquities Department of Cyrenaica. 1959. P. 8. Also for the following.

615

beyond hope of reconstruction. But we may conclude from historical and topographical evidence that the Hellenistic framework of the layout was not completely regular, owing to the undulating terrain. There were three main streets, the middle one following the valley between two hills and carrying the wheeled traffic from Derna and Apollonia, the fort of Cyrene. On the ridge of the southwest hill, more or less parallel to the valley street, ran the old access road which led to the *agora* and further to the gateway of the *acropolis*. The town was surrounded by walls about four miles long and enclosed two hills. The *acropolis* had separate fortifications. Roman and later buildings, erected independently of the ancient Greek structures, make it extremely difficult to identify distinct features of the original town plan and the interrelations of individual buildings. The present context of most Greek remains appears meaningless, and a reconstruction of the ancient town plan would therefore be mere guesswork.[110]

110. R. M. Smith and E. A. Porcher. *History of the Recent Discoveries at Cyrene made during an Expedition to the Cyrenaica in 1860-61.* 1864.

1   *Fountain of Apollo* (Nymphaeum)
2   *Stairway to Sanctuary*
3   *Byzantine Lime-kilns*
4   *Greek Propylea* (4th Cent. B.C.)
5   *Temple* (? of Aphrodite)
6   *Entrance to Byzantine Baths*
7   *Strategheion*
8   *Roman Propylea*
9   *Hellenistic Fountain*
10   *Temple of Hades* (Pluto)
11   *Temple of Dioscuri*
12   *Altar of Apollo* (4th Cent. B.C.)
13   *Temple of Apollo*
14   *Temple of Jason Magnus*
15   *Shrine of Apollo Nymphagetes*
16   *Fountain of Cyrene* (Roman)
17   *Greek Fountain* (disused)
18   *Temple of Isis*
19   *Grotto* (? Mithraeum)
20   *Paved Terrace*
21   *Axis Wall*
22   *Unidentified Temple*
23   *Wall of Nikodamos*
24   (*Not on map*)
    Greek Theatre and Roman Amphitheatre
25   *Unidentified Temple*
26   *Temple of Artemis*
27   *Altar of Artemis*
28   *Temple of Hecate*
29   *Baths of Trajan*
G   *Rock-cut road*
H   *Milestone of Hadrian*
I   *"Sacred Way"* (sidewalk of Valley Street)
J   *Area of New Fountain* (Aqua Augusta)
K   *Greek Baths*

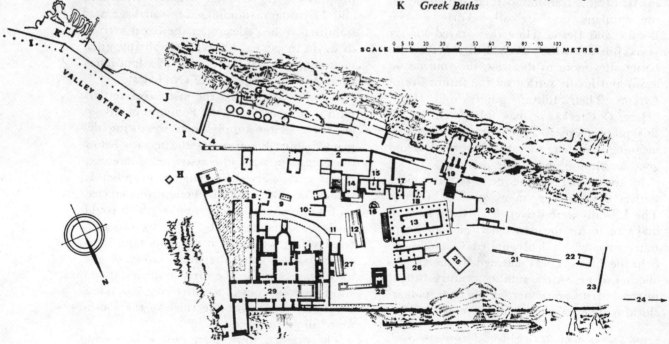

482. Plan of the Fountain and Sanctuary area of Cyrene.

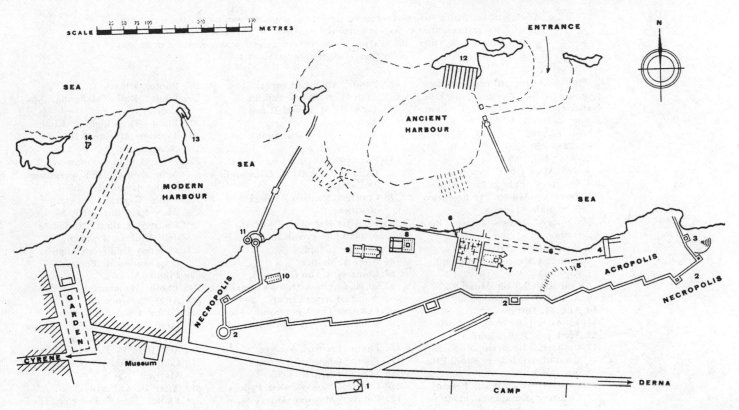

Apollonia was the port of Cyrene for more than a thousand years. It was originally a dependency of Cyrene but became autonomous in the Roman period as one of the five cities of the *Pentapolis*. The Hellenistic city walls are well preserved. The *acropolis* hill is still unexcavated. The course of the main street running east-west has been identified. The sinking of the coast has greatly changed the topographical condition of the port, but underwater explorations have revealed some information on the original layout of the harbor.

1 *Extra-Mural Church (unexcavated)*
2 *City Walls (Hellenistic)*
3 *Theatre*
4 *House with Cisterns*
5 *Rock Chambers (? warehouses)*
6 *Main Street*
7 *Eastern Church*
8 *Roman Baths*
9 *Central Church*
10 *Western Church*
11 *West Gate*
12 *Slipways on Island*
13 *Submerged Quarry*
14 *Tomb-chamber in Quarry*

Acknowledgments for Illustrations

IF NO OTHER ACKNOWLEDGMENT HAS BEEN MADE, IT SHOULD BE ASSUMED THAT
MY SINCERE THANKS ARE DUE TO THE MAYORS OF THE RESPECTIVE TOWNS AND
CITIES, FOR THEIR COOPERATION IN SUPPLYING PLANS, MAPS, PHOTOGRAPHS, AND
OTHER DOCUMENTARY MATERIAL.

The following illustrations are reproduced by courtesy of Ente Nazionale Italiano Per Il Turismo, Rome: Nos. 23, 57, 77, 78, 81, 82, 85, 86, 87, 102, 121, 123, 135, 183, 208, 228, 250, 291, 299, 300, 301, 322, 344, 345, 363.

1, 2, 3. After J. S. P. Bradford.
4. Courtesy Ente "Pro Spina," Ferrara. Museo Archeologico Nazionale, Ferrara.
5. Courtesy Museo Civico, Piacenza.
6. Courtesy M. Pallottino.
7. Courtesy Museo Archeologico, Aquileia.
8. Courtesy British Museum.
9. After J. S. P. Bradford.
10. After J. Durm.
11, 12. After J. B. Ward Perkins.
13. After J. S. P. Bradford.
17. Courtesy The Metropolitan Museum of Art, Rogers Fund, 1912, New York.
18. Courtesy J. B. Ward Perkins.
21. Courtesy Kölnisches Stadtmuseum, Cologne.
22. Courtesy W. Braunfels.
24. After A. E. Brinckmann.
25. Courtesy W. Braunfels.
26. Photo: Alinari, Florence.
28. Courtesy American Museum of Natural History, New York.
29. Courtesy Musée du Louvre, Paris.
39. After A. E. Brinckmann.
40. Photo: Alinari, Florence.
42. Photo: Grassi, Siena.
46, 47, 49. After A. E. Brinckmann.
51, 53. Photo: Alinari, Florence.
55. After A. E. Brinckmann.
56. After J. Durm.
58. Courtesy Niedersächsische Landesgalerie, Hanover.
59. Photo: Alinari, Florence.
62. Courtesy Direzione Generale, Monumenti Musei e Gallerie Pontificie, Città del Vaticano.
64, 65. Courtesy Biblioteca Apostolica Vaticana.
67. Photo: Alinari, Florence.
69. Courtesy Bayrische Staatsgemäldesamlungen, Munich.

70. Photo: Alinari, Florence.
71. After J. B. Ward Perkins.
73. Courtesy Ministero Difesa Aeronautica.
74. After I. A. Richmond and W. G. Holford.
75. From *Scavi di Ostia* by G. Calza, G. Becatti, I. Gismondi, and others.
76. Courtesy Ministero Difesa Aeronautica.
80, 81. After Overbeck, *Pompeii*.
83. After Ente Provinciale Per Il Turismo, Naples.
84. After A. Maiuri.
88. Courtesy A. von Gerkan.
89, 90, 92. Courtesy Museo Civico di Storia ed Arte, Trieste.
106. Courtesy The Metropolitan Museum of Art, Whittelsey Fund, 1949.
116. Photo: Ferruzzi, Venice.
117. Photo: Giacomelli, Venice.
119. Photo: Ferruzzi, Venice.
120. Courtesy Museo Civico, Padova.
122. Courtesy Ministero Difesa Aeronautica.
131, 132, 133. Courtesy Biblioteca Civica, Verona.
134. Courtesy U.S. Army.
143, 144. Courtesy Biblioteca Reale, Torino.
147, 148, 152. Courtesy Museo Civico, Torino.
156. After P. Barbieri.
163. Courtesy Civici Istituti d'Arte e Storia, Pavia.
164, 165. Courtesy Museo Civico, Pavia.
166, 167. Courtesy Museo Civico, Pavia.
185, 186. After A. Mazzi.
189, 191. From *Fascino di Bergamo* by C. Traini, by special permission from the Mayor of Bergamo.
197, 220. Courtesy Ministero Difesa Aeronautica.
247, 248, 249. Courtesy Museo Storico, Florence.
251. Photo: Philip Gendreau, New York.
252 through 258. After M. Richter.

261. Photo: Alinari.
264. Photo: Rollie McKenna, New York.
271. Photo: D. Minghini, Rimini.
272. Courtesy Ministero Difesa Aeronautica.
274, 275, 276. Photo: Fotomero, Urbino, with the kind permission of the mayor of Urbino.
286. Photo: Gavirati, Gubbio.
288. After *Urbanistica*, No. 30, 1960.
289. Courtesy Galleria Nazionale dell' Umbria, Perugia.
290. Courtesy Biblioteca Augusta del Comune di Perugia.
296. Photo: Alinari.
298. Photo: Aeronautica.
302. After P. Fidenzoni.
311. Photo: Goliardo, Viterbo.
313. From *Napoli. Edilizia Pubblica e Attrezzature Urbane.*
314, 315. After R. Capasso.
316. Courtesy Museo Nazionale di S. Martino, Naples.
318. After D. A. Parrino.
321. Photo: *Screen Traveler,* from Gendreau.
332, 334–36, 338, 340–43. Courtesy E. Minchilli.
347. Photo: Ramosini, Bari.
353. Photo: Maltese, Siracusa.
359. After E. Caracciolo.
366. Courtesy P. M. Lugli.
367. Photo: Fotocielo, Rome.
368. After A. Davico.
370–71, 373, 375. Courtesy L. Quaroni.
377. Courtesy Museo Civiltà Romana, Rome.
379, 381, 382. Courtesy L. Quaroni.
387, 388. Photo: Fotocielo, Rome.
389. Courtesy Royal Greek Embassy, Washington, D.C.
390. Courtesy the American Museum of Natural History, New York.
391. After R. W. Hutchinson.
392. Courtesy E. Kirsten.
393. Courtesy Royal Hellenic Air Force.
394. After H. Boyd-Hawes, *Gournia Vasiliki and other Prehistoric Sites on the Isthmus of Hiera-*

petra, Crete, American Exploration Society, 1908.

395. After R. C. Bosanquet and R. M. Dawkins.

396. After R. B. Seager.

397. After E. H. Hall.

398. After British School at Athens.

399. *After Bulletin de Correspondance Héllenique,* Vol. XXV, Pl. XX, 1901.

400. After Bullen in *Pauly's Real Encyclopädie,* Suppl. VII, 1940.

401. After A. J. B. Wace.

402. After Bossert.

403. After *Hesperia,* Vol. XVII, 1948.

404, 405. Courtesy E. Kirsten.

406. Courtesy Royal Hellenic Air Force.

407. After W. Judeich, "Topographie von Athen." In *Handbuch der Altertumswissenschaft* III, ii, 2. 1931.

408. Courtesy Royal Ontario Museum, Toronto.

409, 410. After R. S. Young.

411. Courtesy Royal Hellenic Air Force.

413. After American School at Athens.

412, 414. Courtesy E. Kirsten.

415. After M. N. Valmin.

416, 417, 418. After G. Fougères.

419. Courtesy Royal Hellenic Air Force.

420. After C. Tsountas, *The Prehistoric Acropolis of Dimini and Sehlion.* 1908.

421 through 424. Courtesy D. M. Robinson and Johns Hopkins Press. From *Excavations at Olynthus.* Part VIII, 1938 and Part XII, 1946.

425. After Freiherr Hiller von Gaertringen.

426. After *Journal of Hellenistic Studies,* Suppl. No. 4. 1904.

427, 429. Courtesy E. Kirsten.

428. After École Française d'Athènes.

430. Courtesy Royal Hellenic Air Force.

431–33, 435. Courtesy Royal Hellenic Air Force.

434, 436. Courtesy E. Kirsten.

437. After École Française d'Athènes.

438. After W. Lamb.

439. After F. H. Bacon.

440. After C. Humann.

441. Courtesy Staatliche Museen, Antiken-Abteilung, Berlin.

442. After H. Luckenbach. In J. Durm. *Baukunst der Griechen.* Part 1. 1910.

443. After A. Philippson.

444. After C. Humann. *Magnesia am Maeander.*

445, 446, 447. After Th. Wiegand and H. Schrader.

448, 449. Courtesy A. von Gerkan and Walter de Gruyter & Co. From *Griechische Städteanlagen.* 1924.

450, 451. After Th. Wiegand and H. Schrader.

452, 453, 457. Courtesy A. von Gerkan and Walter de Gruyter & Co. From *Griechische Städteanlagen.* 1924.

454. After G. Tippel.

455. After F. Krischen

456. After A. Philippson.

459. After F. J. Bliss and R. A. S. Macalister.

458. After Yale University Art Gallery, *The Yale Excavations at Dura-Europos.*

460, 461, 462. After *Excavations at Dura-Europos.* Ninth Season, Part I. Courtesy Dura-Europos Publications, Yale University Press.

463 through 466. After J. Marshall. *Taxila.* Vol. III. Courtesy Archaeological Survey of India, Government of India.

467. After J. Hackin.

468. After R. Ghirshman.

469. After T. J. Dunbabin. *The Western Greeks. The History of Sicily and South Italy from the Foundation of the Greek Colonies to 480 B.C.* 1948. Courtesy The Clarendon Press, Oxford.

470. After T. J. Dunbabin. *The Western Greeks.* Courtesy The Clarendon Press, Oxford.

471. After J. Bradford.

472, 473. After T. J. Dunbabin. *The Western Greeks.* Courtesy The Clarendon Press, Oxford.

474, 476. After J. Hulot and G. Fougères.

475. After M. Hulot.

477. After *Annales de Musée d'Histoire Naturelle de Marseille,* Vol. XIII, 1914.

478. After Ev. Breccia. *Alerandrea ad Aegyptum.* 1922.

479. After W. M. Flinders Petrie.

480. After R. Horn. "Kyrene," *Die Antike,* Vol. 19, 1943.

481, 482, 483. Courtesy R. G. Goodchild. From *Cyrene and Apollonia.* 1959.

Bibliography

ITALY

Ackerman, J. S. *The Architecture of Michelangelo.* 2 vols. 1961.

Ahlmann, H. W. "Études de Géographie Humaine sur l'Italie Subtropicale," *Geografiska Annaler,* Vols. VII and VIII. 1925-26.

Alberti, L. B. *De re aedificatoria, libri decem.* Strasbourg. 1541.

——. "I Libri della Famiglia." In: A. Bonucci (ed.). *Opere Volgari.* Vol. II. Florence. 1844.

Angelis, C. N. de. *Le Origini del Comune Meridionale: Saggio Storico di Diritto Pubblico.* 1940.

Aquinas, Thomas. *The Basic Writings of Thomas Aquinas.* Edited and annotated by A. C. Pegis. 1945.

——. *De Regimine Principum.* Translated by G. P. Phelan. 1938.

Arendt, Hannah. *The Human Condition.* 1959.

Aristides, A. *To Rome.* 1950.

Art et Civilisation des Étrusques. Catalogue of the Etruscan Exhibition at the Musée du Louvre. 1955.

Aurigemma, S., and N. Alfieri. *Il Museo Nazionale Archeologico di Spina in Ferrara.* 1957.

Baedeker, K. *Mittelitalien und Rom.* 1908.

——. *Oberitalien mit Ravenna, Florenz und Livorno.* 1906.

Barrow, R. H. *The Romans.* 1951.

Bartels, J. H. *Briefe über Kalabrien und Sizilien.* 1791.

Bartholomew, J. (ed.). *The Times Atlas of the World.* Vol IV: *Southern Europe and Africa.* 1956.

Beloch, J. *Die Bevölkerung der griechisch-römischen Welt.* 1886.

—— *Bevölkerungsgeschichte Italiens.* Vol. I, 1937; Vol. II, 1939; Vol. III, 1961.

Bengtson, H., and V. Milojčić. *Grosser Historischer Weltatlas.* Part I: *Vorgeschichte und Altertum.* 1958.

Bibiena, Giuseppe Galli. *Architetture e prospettive dedicate alla Maestà di Carlo Sesto, Imperador de' Romani. . . .* 1740.

Blaeu, Joan. *Nieuw vermeerderd en verbeterd Groot stedeboek van geheel Italie, of naauwkeurige beschryving van alle deszelfs steden, paleizen, kerken, en voornamste gebouwen. . . .* 4 vols. Amsterdam. 1724.

Boardman, J. *The Greeks Overseas.* 1964.

Boëthius, A. *The Golden House of Nero.* 1960.

——. "Urbanism in Italy." In Vol. IV of the *Proceedings of the Second International Congress of Classical Studies.* Copenhagen. 1954.

Bognetti, G. P. *Sulle Origini dei Comuni Rurali del Medio evo Speciali Osservazioni pei Territori Milanese e Comasco.* 1927.

Bosanquet, R. C. "Greek and Roman Towns. II. Town Planning in Syria," *The Town Planning Review,* Vol. VI, No. 2, 1915.

Bradford, J. *Ancient Landscapes.* 1957.

Braunfels, W. *Mittelalterliche Stadtbaukunst in der Toskana.* 1953.

Brinckmann, A. E. *Baukunst.* 1956.

——. *Platz und Monument.* 1923.

——. *Stadtbaukunst.* 1920.

Buckley, T. A. *The Great Cities of the Middle Ages.* 1853.

Burckhardt, J. *Civilization of the Renaissance in Italy.* Translated by S. G. C. Middlemore. 1945.

Buren, A. W. van. "The Geography of Ancient Italy," *The Classical Journal,* Vol. VIII, 1912-13.

Butterfield, H. *The Origin of Modern Science, 1300-1800*. 1949.

Caesar. *The War Commentaries: De bello Gallico and De bello civili*. Translated and edited by J. Warrington. 1953.

Campanella, Tommaso. *La Città del Sole*. Edited by E. Solmi. 1904.

Carcopino, J. *Daily Life in Ancient Rome*. 1961.

Cicero. *De republica*. Loeb Classical Library. 1928.

Coulton, G. G. *Art and the Reformation*. Part I: *Medieval Faith and Symbolism*. Part II: *The Fate of Medieval Art in the Renaissance and Reformation*. Harper Torchbooks ed. 1958.

——. *Life in the Middle Ages*. (2nd ed.). 4 vols. 1928-30.

——. *Medieval Village, Manor and Monastery*. 1960.

Curtius, L. *Deutsche und Antike Welt*. 1950.

Dante. *The Divine Comedy*. Translated by Dorothy L. Sayers and Barbara Reynolds. 1953-62.

Dawson, C. *The Making of Europe*. 1958.

De Burgh, W. G. *The Legacy of the Ancient World*. 2 vols. 1953.

Dennis, G. *Cities and Cemeteries of Etruria*. 1883.

Dickens, C. *Pictures from Italy*. 1846.

Dilke, O. A. W. "Maps in the Treatises of Roman Land Surveyors," *The Geographical Journal*, Vol. CXXVII, Part 4, 1961.

Dill, S. *Roman Society from Nero to Marcus Aurelius*. 1956.

——. *Roman Society in the Last Century of the Western Empire*. 1958.

Dionysius of Halicarnassus. *The Roman Antiquities*. Loeb Classical Library. Vols. 1-7. 1937-50.

Doren, A. *Italienische Wirtschaftsgeschichte*. 1934.

Dubs, H. H. *A Roman City in Ancient China*. 1957.

Durm, J. *Die Baustile*. Vol. II: *Die Baukunst der Etrusker. Die Baukunst der Römer*. 1905. Vol. V: *Die Baukunst der Renaissance in Italien*. 1903.

East, W. G. *An Historical Geography of Europe*. 1956.

Ennen, Edith. *Frühgeschichte der Europäischen Stadt*. 1953.

Falchi, I. *Notizie degli Scavi di Antichità*. 1896.

Frank, T. *An Economic Survey of Ancient Rome*. Vols. I and V. 1959.

The Fourth Book of the Chronicle of Fredegar. Translated by J. M. Wallace-Hadrill. 1960.

Frenzel, K. *Beiträge zur Landschaftskunde der westlichen Lombardei mit landeskundlichen Ergänzungen*. 1927.

Friedlaender, L. *Sittengeschichte Roms*. 1934.

——. *Town Life in Ancient Italy*. 1879.

Frontinus. *Stratagems and Aqueducts of Rome*. With an English translation by C. E. Bennett and C. Herschel. 1925.

Fustel de Coulanges, N. D. *The Ancient City*. 1956.

Geymüller, H. von. *Les Du Cerceau, leur vie et leur oeuvre*. 1887.

Gibbon, E. *The Triumph of Christendom in the Roman Empire*. (Chapters XV-XX of *The History of the Decline and Fall of the Roman Empire*). Harper Torchbooks ed. 1958.

——. *The End of the Roman Empire in the West*. (Chapters XXXVI-XLIII of *The History of the Decline and Fall of the Roman Empire*). Harper Torchbooks ed. 1958.

Goethe, Johann Wolfgang von. *Italian Journey*.

Goetz, W. "Die Entstehung der italienischen Kommunen im frühen Mittelalter," *Sitzungsberichte der Bayrischen Akademie der Wissenschaften*. 1944-46, No. 1. Munich. 1944.

Goodchild, R. G., and J. B. Ward Perkins. "The Limes Tripolitanus in the Light of Recent Discoveries," *The Journal of Roman Studies*, Vol. XXXIX, 1949 and Vol. XL, 1950.

"Gregorii Magni Dialogi." In: *Scriptores rerum langobardicarum et italicarum saec. VI-IX*. 1878.

Grenier, A. *Manuel d'Archéologie Gallo-Ro-*

maine. Part 3: *L'Architecture. L'Urbanisme. Les Monuments.* 1958.

Guicciardini, F. *La Historia d'Italia.* Venice. 1563.

Gutkind, E. A. *Twilight of Cities.* 1962.

Habicht, C. *Gottmenschtum und griechische Städte.* 1956.

Hare, A. J. C. *Cities of Northern Italy.* 2 vols. 1896.

———. *Cities of Southern Italy and Sicily.* N.D.

Harmand, L. *L'Occident Romain.* 1960.

Hiorns, F. R. *Town-Building in History.* 1956.

Homo, L. *Rome Impériale et l'Urbanisme dans l'Antiquité.* 1951.

Horace. *Odes.* Everyman's Library. 1911.

Huillard-Bréholles, J. L. A. *Historia diplomatica Friderici Secundi. . . .* Paris. 1852-61.

Jones, A. H. M. *The Cities of the Eastern Roman Provinces.* 1937.

Kidder Smith, G. E. *Italy Builds.* 1955.

Kirsten, E. "Nordafrikanische Stadtbilder," *Die Karawane,* No. 8, 1959.

———. "Römische Raumordnung in der Geschichte Italiens." In: *Historische Raumforschung II,* 1958. Forschungs- und Sitzungsberichte der Akademie für Raumforschung und Landesplanung.

Kleberg, T. *Hôtels, Restaurants et Cabarets dans l'Antiquité Romaine.* 1957.

Kuhn, E. *Ueber die Entstehung der Staedte der Alten: Komenverfassung und Synoikismos.* 1878.

Kuhn, T. S. *The Copernican Revolution.* 1957.

Larsen, J. A. O. "Roman Greece." In: T. Frank (ed.). *An Economic Survey of Ancient Rome.* Vol. IV. 1938.

Lavedan, P. *Histoire de l'Urbanisme. Antiquité, Moyen Age.* 1926.

———. *Histoire de l'Urbanisme. Renaissance et Temps Modernes.* 1941.

Lestocquoy, J. *Aux Origines de la Bourgeoisie: Les Villes de Flandre et d'Italie sous le Gouvernment des Patriciens; XIe-XVe Siècles.* 1952.

Liebenam, W. *Städteverwaltung im Römischen Kaiserreiche.* 1900.

Livy. *History of Rome.* Loeb Classical Library. Vol. III. 1924.

Lopez Pegna, M. "Itinera Etruriae," *Studi Etruschi,* Vol. XXI (Serie II), 1950-51.

———. "Itinera Etruriae, II—I percorsi tirreni," *Studi Etruschi,* Vol. XXII (Serie II), 1952-53.

Lucretius. *On the Nature of the Universe.* Translated by R. E. Latham. 1951.

Luzzatto, G. *An Economic History of Italy from the Fall of the Roman Empire to the Beginning of the Sixteenth Century.* 1961.

MacIver, D. R. *Greek Cities in Italy and Sicily.* 1931.

MacKendrick, P. *The Mute Stones Speak.* 1962.

Magnuson, T. *Studies in Roman Quattrocento Architecture.* 1958.

Mansuelli, G. A. *I Cisalpini.* 1963.

Mattingly, H. *Roman Imperial Civilisation.* 1957.

Mengozzi, G. *La città italiana nell'alto medio evo. Il periodo langobardo-franco.* 1914.

Mickwith, G. "Medieval Agrarian Society in its Prime." In: *The Cambridge Economic History of Europe.* Vol. I. 1941.

Migne, J. P. *Patrologiae Latina.* Vol. 111, Lib. XIV. 1852

Minchilli, E. "Classificazione e Forma delle Città in Puglia," *Giornale del Genio Civile,* Nos. 3-4, 1958.

Mommsen, Theodor. *Inscriptiones Latinae Antiquissimae.* 1863.

Montaigne, M. E. de. *The Diary of Montaigne's Journey to Italy in 1580 and 1581.* 1929.

Morey, C. R. *Medieval Art.* 1942.

Mumford, L. *The City in History.* 1961.

Mundy, J. H., and P. Riesenberg. *The Medieval Town.* 1958.

Muratori, L. A. *Annali d'Italia.* 1761.

Niccolai, F. *Città e Signori.* 1941.

Oettingen, W. von. "Antonio Averlino Filarete's Tractat über die Baukunst." In: *Quellenschriften für Kunstgeschichte und Kunsttechnik des Mittelalters und der Neuzeit,* N.F., Vol. III. 1890.

Palladio, A. *The Architecture of Palladio in Four Books.* Venice, 1581; London, 1742.

Pallottini, M. *Profili di Storia dell'Urbanistica.* Vol. I. 1951(?).

Pallottino, M. *The Etruscans*. 1955.

Pernoud, Régine. *Les Villes Marchandes aux XIVe et XVe Siècles. Impérialisme et Capitalisme au Moyen Age*. 1948.

Peyer, H. C. *Stadt und Stadtpatron im mittelalterlichen Italien*. 1955.

Pirenne, H. *Economic and Social History of Medieval Europe*. 1937.

——. *Medieval Cities*. 1925.

Pliny. *The Letters of Pliny*. Translated by W. Melmoth. Vol. I. 1770.

——. *The Natural History*. Translated by J. Bostock and H. T. Riley. 1893.

Plutarch. *The Lives of the Noble Grecians and Romans*. Translated by John Dryden. Revised by A. H. Clough. 1864.

Poehlmann, R. *Übervölkerung der antiken Grosstädte im Zusammenhange mit der Gesammtentwicklung städtischer Civilisation*. 1884.

Polybius. *Histories*. Translated by W. R. Paton. 1922-27.

Postan, M., and E. E. Rich (eds.). *The Cambridge Economic History of Europe*. Vol. II. 1952.

Previté-Orton, C. W. "The Italian Cities." In: *The Cambridge Medieval History*. Vol. V, 1926.

Pozzo, Andrea del. *Perspectiva Pictorum et Architectorum Andreae Putei*. Rome, 1693.

Puglisi, S. M. *La Civiltà Appenninica. Origine delle Comunità Pastorali in Italia*. 1959.

Read, Sir Herbert. *Icon and Idea*. 1955.

Rosenau, Helen. "Historical Aspects of the Vitruvian Tradition in Town Planning," *Journal of the Royal Institute of British Architects*, Vol. 62, No. 12, 1955.

——. *The Ideal City*. 1959.

Rostovtzeff, M. I. *A History of the Ancient World*. Vol. II: *Rome*. 1927.

——. *The Social and Economic History of the Roman Empire*. 1926.

——. *Urban Land Economics*. 1922.

Russell, J. C. *Late Ancient and Medieval Population*. 1958.

Salomon, R. "Aftermath to Opicinus de Canistris," *Journal of the Warburg and Courtauld Institutes*, Vol. XXV, 1962.

Sapori, A. *Le Marchand Italien au Moyen Age*. 1952.

Scamozzi, V. *L'Idea della Architettura Universale*. Venice. 1615.

Schneider, F. "Die Entstehung von Burg und Landgemeinde in Italien," *Abhandlungen zur Mittleren und Neueren Geschichte*, Vol. 68, 1924.

Scramuzza, V. M. "Roman Sicily." In: T. Frank (ed.). *An Economic Survey of Ancient Rome*. 1937.

Semple, Ellen, C. *The Geography of the Mediterranean Region*. 1932.

Seneca. *Quaestiones Naturales*. Translated by J. Clark. 1910.

Serlio, Sebastiano. *Tutte l'Opere d'Architettura et Prospetiva*. Venice. 1619.

Simonde de Sismondi, J. C. L. *A History of the Italian Republics*. Everyman's Library. 1907.

Singer, C., Holmyard, E. J., and A. R. Hall (eds.). *A History of Technology*. 5 vols. 1954-58.

Sisi, E. *L'urbanistica negli studi di Leonardo da Vinci*. 1953.

Smith, E. B. *Architectural Symbolism of Imperial Rome and the Middle Ages*. 1956.

——. *The Dome. A Study in the History of Ideas*. 1950.

Société Jean Bodin. *La Ville*. Vol. VI, 1954; Vol. VII, 1955.

Suetonius. *Lives of the Twelve First Roman Emperors*. Translated by J. Clarke. 1739.

Tacitus. *The Works*. Translated by A. Murphy. 1836.

Täubler, E. "Terremare und Rom," *Sitzungsberichte der Heidelberger Akademie der Wissenschaften*, Philosophisch-Historische Klasse. 1931-32.

Teutsch, L. *Das römische Städtewesen in Nordafrika. In der Zeit von C. Gracchus bis zum Tode des Kaisers Augustus*. 1962.

Tomassetti, G. *La Campagna Romana, Antica, Medioevale e Moderna*. 1910-26.

Touring Club Italiano. *Attraverso l'Italia*. 1961.

——. *Italy*. 1956.

Toy, S. *A History of Fortifications. From 3000 B.C. to 1700 A.D.* 1955.

Vacano, O. W. von. *Die Etrusker in der Welt der Antike.* 1957.

Virgil. *The Aeneid.* Penguin Classics. 1956.

Vitruvius. *De Architectura, libri decem.* 1543.

Voigt, M. "Die römischen Baugesetze," *Berichte über die Verhandlungen der Königlich Sächsischen Gesellschaft der Wissenschaften zu Leipzig,* Philologisch-Historische Klasse, Vol. 55. 1903.

Volpe, G. *Medio Evo Italiano.* 1958.

Walker, D. S. *A Geography of Italy.* 1958.

Ward Perkins, J. "The Early Development of Roman Town-Planning." In Vol. IV of the *Proceedings of the Second International Congress of Classical Studies.* Copenhagen. 1954.

——. "Early Roman Towns in Italy," *Town Planning Review,* Vol. XXXVI, No. 3, 1955.

——. "Etruscan Towns, Roman Roads and Medieval Villages: The Historical Geography of Southern Etruria," *The Geographical Journal,* Vol. CXXVIII, Part 4, 1962.

Weber, M. *The City.* 1958.

——. *Die Römische Agrargeschichte in ihrer Bedeutung für das Staats- und Privatrecht.* 1891.

Westermann, W. L. *The Slave Systems of Greek and Roman Antiquity.* 1955.

Wheeler, Sir Mortimer. *Rome Beyond the Imperial Frontiers.* 1955.

Wölfflin, H. *Die Klassische Kunst. Eine Einführung in die Italienische Renaissance.* 1904.

ALBEROBELLO

Notarnicola, G. *I Trulli di Alberobello dalla Preistorica al Presente.* 1940.

Scholz, H. "Die Trulli Apuliens," *Geographica Helvetica,* No. 4, 1956.

Wirth, E. "Die Murgia dei Trulli," *Die Erde,* 1962.

ALTAMURA

Biancofiore, F. "Nota preliminare sugli scavi al Pulo di Altamura," *Rivista di Antropologia,* Vol. XLIV, 1957.

——. "La stratigrafia di 'La Croce' (Altamura) e la facies preistorica dei Peucezi," *Rivista Scienze Preistoriche,* Nos. 3-4. 1957.

ASCOLI PICENO

Benevolo, L. *Ascoli Piceno.* 1957.

ASSISI

Zocca, E. *Assisi and the Environs.* 1950.

BARLETTA

Cassandro, M. *Barletta. Nella Storia e Nell'Arte.* N.D.

BERGAMO

Angelini, L. *Il Volto di Bergamo nei Secoli.* 1951.

Sacchi, N. *Il Piano Regolatore di Bergamo.* 1951.

Traini, C. *Fascino di Bergamo.* 1953.

BITONTO

Scivittaro, A. *Architettura del Rinascimento a Bitonto.* 1958.

COSA

Brown, F. E. "Cosa I, History and Topography." In: *Memoirs of the American Academy in Rome,* XX. 1951.

CREMONA

Comune di Cremona. *Cremona e le sue Condizioni Urbanistiche.* 1954.

Istituto Geografico de Agostini Novara. *Visioni di Cremona.* 1957.

CUMAE

Maiuri, A. *The Phlegraean Fields.* 1947.

EMPOLI

Il Piano Regolatore Generale del Comune di Empoli. Published by the Municipality of Empoli on the occasion of the VI Congresso Nazionale di Urbanistica, Torino. October 18-21, 1956.

ESTE

Muratori, L. A. *Della Antichità Estensi.* 1740.

FERRARA

Borgatti, F. "La piana di Ferrara nel 1597." In: *Atti e Memorie della Deputazione Fer-*

rarese di Storia Patria. Vol. VII, No. 1. 1895.

Frizzi, A. *Memorie per la Storia di Ferrara raccolte da Antonio Frizzi.* Con note e giunte del Conte Avv. Camillio Laderchi. 5 vols. 1848.

Righini, G. "Come si è formata la città di Ferrara." In: *Atti e Memorie della Deputazione Ferrarese di Storia Patria.* Nuova Serie, Vol. XIV. 1955.

Zevi, B. *Biagio Rossetti, architetto ferrarese, il primo urbanista moderno europeo.* 1960.

FLORENCE

Blasi, J. de. *Firenze.* 1943.

Chastel, A. "Un épisode de la symbolique urbaine au XVe siècle: Florence et Rome, Cités de Dieu." In: *Urbanisme et Architecture. Études Écrites et Publiées en l'honneur de Pierre Lavedan.* 1954.

Davidsohn, R. *Geschichte von Florenz.* 4 vols. 1896-1927.

Doren, A. J. *Studien aus der Florentiner Wirtschaftsgeschichte.* 2 vols. 1901-1908.

Lucas-Dubreton, J. *Daily Life in Florence. In the Time of the Medici.* 1961.

McCarthy, Mary. *The Stones of Florence.* 1959.

Machiavelli, N. *History of Florence and of the Affairs of Italy from the Earliest Times to the Death of Lorenzo the Magnificent.* Edited by F. Gilbert. 1960.

Plesner, J. *L'émigration de la campagne à la ville libre de Florence au XIIIe siècle.* 1934.

Richter, M. "Die 'Terra Murata' im Florentinischen Gebiet," *Mitteilungen des Kunsthistorischen Institutes in Florenz,* Vol. V, Heft 6. July 1940.

Schevill, F. *History of Florence from the Founding of the City through the Renaissance.* 1961.

———. *Medieval and Renaissance Florence.* 2 vols. Harper Torchbooks ed. 1963.

GENOA

Barbieri, P. *Forma Genuae.* 1938.

Comune di Genova. *Piano Regolatore Generale.* 1962.

Genova. Rivista del Comune. Vol. XXXI, No. 1, 1954; Vol. XLIII, No. 3, 1963.

Imperiale, C. *Codice Diplomatico della Repubblica di Genova.* 1936.

Revelli, P. *Figurazione Cartografiche di Genova. (1435-1935).* 1936.

Schiaparelli, L. *I Diplomi di Ugo di Lotario di Berengario II e di Adalberto.* 1924.

HERCULANEUM

Maiuri, A. *Herculaneum.* 1956.

———. *I Nuovi Scavi di Ercolano. 1927-1958.* 2 vols. 1958.

LUCCA

Belli, I. *Le Mura di Lucca.* 1954.

Castagnoli, F. "La centurazione di Lucca," *Studi Etruschi,* Vol. XX, 1948-49.

Mancini, A. *Storia di Lucca.* 1950.

Matraja, G. *Lucca nel 1200.* 1843.

Pierotti, P. *Lucca. Edilizia Urbanistica Medioevale.* 1965.

Solari, A. "Lucca centro itinerario nell'antichità," *Bollettino Storico Lucchese.* 1929.

LUCERA

La Cava, A. "La demografia di un Comune pugliese nell'età moderna," *Archivio Storico per le Provincie Napoletane,* XVII, 1939.

MARZABOTTO

Arias, P. E. "Considerazioni sulla città etrusca a Pian di Misano (Marzabotto)." In: *Atti e Memorie della Deputazione di Storia Patria per le Provincie di Romagna.* Nuova Serie, Vol. IV, Part III. 1953.

Brizio, E. *Una Pompei etrusca a Marzabotto nel Bolognese.* 1928.

MESSINA

Calandra, R. *Lineamenti di Urbanistica Messinese dalle Origini alla Metà del' 500.* N.D.

MILANO

Calderini, A. *La "forma urbis mediolani."* 1937.

Colombo, A. *Milano preromana, romana e barbarica.* 1928.

Lechleiter, H. "Beiträge zu einer Stadtgeographie von Mailand," *Mitteilungen der*

Geographischen Gesellschaft Wien, Vol. 94, Nos. 5-8. 1952.

Milano. Il Piano Regolatore Generale 1953.

Rodella, D. *Piccola storia sviluppo edilizio di Milano.* N.D.

Urbanistica, Vol. XXV, Nos. 18-19, 1956.

NAPLES

Beguinot, C. "Una preesistenza ambientale a Napoli: i 'Quartieri Spagnoli.'" *Quaderno di Urbanistica* N. 5. Per il VI Convegno Nazionale di Urbanistica. Lucca. 1957.

Capasso, B. *Sull'antico sito di Napoli e Palepoli.* 1855.

Celano, C. *Notizie del Bello, dell'Antico e del Curioso della Città di Napoli.* 5 vols. 1856-60.

Comune di Napoli, N. Galdo (ed.). *Relazione Illustrativa del Nuovo Piano Regolatore.* Vol. 1. 1958.

Parrino, D. A. *Teatro Eroico e Politico dei Governi de' Vicerè del Regno di Napoli.* Naples. 1697.

Russo, G. *La Città di Napoli dalle Origine al 1860.* 2 vols. 1960.

University of Naples, Centro di Pianificazione Urbana e Rurale. *Napoli: Edilizia Pubblica e Attrezzature Urbane.* 1961.

NOTO

"Città di Noto," *Bollettino del Comune,* Vol. II, No. 5, 1955; No. 10, 1955.

NOVARA

Capra, R. *Novara.* 1962.

Rizzi, A. *Compendio di Storia Novarese.* 1955.

OSTIA

Calza, G., and G. Becatti. *Ostia.* 1963.

——. G. Becatti, I. Gismondi, and others. *Scavi di Ostia.* Vol. I. 1953.

Meiggs, R. *Roman Ostia.* 1960.

Schaal, H. *Ostia. Der Welthafen Roms.* 1957.

Wilson, F. H. "Studies in the Social and Economic History of Ostia," *Papers of the British School at Rome,* Vol. XIII, 1935; Vol. XIV, 1938.

PADUA

Foligno, C. *The Story of Padua.* 1910.

Scimeni, G. "Padova, città mediovale," *Urbanistica,* Vol. 26, 1957.

PAESTUM

Sestieri, P. C. *Paestum. The City, the Prehistoric Necropolis in Contrada Gaudo, the Heraion at the Mouth of the Sele.* 1958.

PALERMO

Calza-Bini, G. and others. *Piano Regolatore della Città di Palermo.* 1940.

Caracciolo, E. "Vicende Urbanistiche della Vecchia Palermo." Paper read at the *Conferenza tenuta nella R. Scuola d'Ingegneria.* May 1932.

——. "La Sistemazione del Cassaro e l'Apertura della Strada Nuova in Palermo," *Urbanistica,* Vol. XV, No. 2, 1937.

La Duca, R. *Cartografia della Città di Palermo dalle Origini al 1860.* 1962.

Pietro, V. *Storia della vita urbanistica di Palermo.* 1941.

Zimmermann, M. G. *Sizilien. II: Palermo.* 1905.

PAVIA

Canepari, L. "Il Senso della Storia." Paper read at the *Convegno di Studio sul Centro Storico di Pavia.* July 4-5, 1964.

——. "Sguardo Critico al Problema Urbanistico di Pavia," *Pavia Economica,* Nos. 2-3, 1964.

Morandotti, C. *Piano Regolatore di Pavia.* 1933.

Peroni, A. "Note su una Rara Veduta di Pavia del 1600," *Pavia,* Nos. 4-6, July-December 1963.

——. "Novita critiche sull'architettura gotica a Pavia," *Pavia,* September-December 1964.

——. "Problemi della Documentazione Urbanistica di Pavia dal Medioevo all'Epoca Moderna." Paper read at the *Convegno di Studio sul Centro Storico di Pavia.* July 4-5, 1964.

Stenico, A. "Elementi della Documentazione Urbanistica, Monumentale ed Edilizia di Pavia Romana." Paper read at the *Convegno di Studio sul Centro Storico di Pavia.* July 4-5, 1964.

Tibiletti, G. "La Struttura Topografica Antica di Pavia." Paper read at the *Convegno di Studio sul Centro Storico di Pavia*. July 4-5, 1964.

PERUGIA

Bevilacqua, E. "Perugia: ricerche di geografia urbana," *Memorie di Geografia Antropica*, Vol. IV, 1949, 1950.

Lorenzo, F. *Perugia, sua origini, cinta delle mura e porte*. 1926.

Santi, F. "Appunti per la storia urbanistica di Perugia," and "Il Volto di Perugia," *Urbanistica*, No. 30, 1960.

PIACENZA

Cervi, M. C., and E. Nasalli Rocca. "Placentia." In: *Archivio Storico Parmense*. 1938.

Dodi, L. "Piacenza e la sua storia urbanistica." In: *Strenna Piacentina*. 1938.

Nasalli Rocca, E. *Cenno Storico Urbanistico su Piacenza*. Manuscript. 1964.

——. "Piante topografiche di Piacenza." In: *Strenna Piacentina*. 1926.

PISA

Herlihy, D. *Pisa in the Early Renaissance: A Study of Urban Growth*. 1958.

Gentile, M. L. (ed.). *Gli Annales Pisani di Bernardo Maragone*. 1936.

Masetti, Anna R. *Pisa. Storia Urbana. Piante e Vedute dalle Origini al Secolo XX*. 1964.

PISTOIA

Barbi, S. A. "Storie Pistoresi." In: L. A. Muratori. *Rerum Italicarum Scriptores*. 1907.

Chiti, A. *Pistoia. Guida Storica Artistica*. 1956.

Zdekauer, L. *Statutum Potestatis Comunis Pistorii. Anni 1296*. Milano, 1888.

POMPEI

Brion, M. *Pompeii and Herculaneum*. 1960.

Carrington, R. C. *Pompeii*. 1936.

Gerkan, A. von. *Der Stadtplan von Pompei*. 1940.

Maiuri, A. *Pompeii*. 1962.

Mau, A. *Pompeii. Its Life and Art*. 1908.

Nissen, H. *Pompeianische Studien zur Städtekunde des Altertums*. 1877.

Spinazzola, V. *Pompei alla luce degli scavi nuovi*. 1953.

Tanzer, H. *The Common People of Pompei*. 1939.

PORDENONE

Benedetti, A. *Breve Storia di Pordenone*. 1956.

POZZUOLI

Maiuri, A. *The Phlegraean Fields*. 1947.

PRATO

Bardazzi, S. "Relazione storica." In: *Piano Regolatore Generale di Comune di Prato*. N.D.

——. "Struttura della Città Medioevale," *Archivio Storico Pratese*, Vol. XXX, Nos. 1-4, 1954.

Pegna, M. L. "Prato Romana," *Archivio Storico Pratese*, Vol. XXX, Nos. 1-4, 1954.

RIMINI

Extracts from "Concorso per il Piano Regolatore della Città di Rimini." Rome. 1934.

Matteini, N. *Rimini. Its Surroundings and the Romagna Riviera*. 1963.

ROME

Academia Nazionale di S. Luca and the Faculty of Architecture of the University of Rome. *Il Campidoglio di Michelangelo*. 1965.

Bigot, P. *Rome Antique au IV Siècle après J.C.* 1942.

Caiza, G., and G. Lugli. "La popolazione di Roma antica," *Bollettino della Commissione Archeologica Comunale di Roma*, LIX, 1941.

Carcopino, J. *Daily Life in Ancient Rome*. 1961.

Castagnoli, F., C. Cecchelli, G. Giovannoni, and M. Zocca. *Topografia e Urbanistica di Roma*. 1958. Vol. XXII of *Storia di Roma*.

Chastel, A. "Un épisode de la symbolique urbaine au XVe siècle: Florence et Rome, Cités de Dieu." In: *Urbanisme et Architecture. Études Écrites et Publiées en l'honneur de Pierre Lavedan*. 1954.

Davico, A. "Ricostruzione Probabile dell'Abitazione laziale del Primo Periodo del Ferro secondo le Testimonianze dello Scavo sul Germalo," *Monumenti Antichi,* Vol. 41, 1951.

Dehio, G. "Die Bauprojekte Nikolaus V und L. B. Alberti," *Repertorium für Kunstwissenschaft,* 1880.

Fokker, T. H. *Roman Baroque Art: The History of a Style.* 2 vols., 1938.

Fontana, Carlo. *Il Tempio Vaticano e sua Origine. Rome.* 1694.

Frutaz, A. P. *Le Piante di Roma.* 3 vols. 1962.

Gasbarri, C. "La città Leonina circa il 1000." In: *Studi Romani.* 1953.

Gatti, G. "Il Pomerio di Roma Imperiale," *Bollettino della Commissione Archeologica Comunale di Roma,* Vol. LXX, 1942.

Gerkan, A. von. "Grenzen und Grössen der vierzehn Regionen Roms," *Bonner Jahrbücher des Rheinischen Landesmuseums in Bonn,* Vol. 149, 1949.

Gerlini, Elsa (ed.). *Piazza Navona.* Catalogue of the Exhibition "Il Volto di Roma nei Secoli." Published by the Reale Istituto di Studi Romani. 1943.

Gregorovius, F. A. *The History of the City of Rome in the Middle Ages.* 8 vols. 1894-1902.

Grimal, P. *La Vie à Rome dans l'Antiquité.* 1957.

——. *Les Villes Romaines.* 1954.

Homo, L. "L'urbanisme dans la Rome impériale, problèmes et solutions," *Comptes Rendus des Séances de l'Académie des Inscriptions et Belles-Lettres.* Paris. 1942.

Jordan, H. *Topographie der Stadt Rom im Mittelalter.* Vol. I, Part 3. 1907.

Kromer, K. "Zur Frühgeschichte Roms," *Mitteilungen der Prähistorischen Kommission der Oesterreichischen Akademie der Wissenschaften,* Vol. VI, 1952-53.

Lugli, G. *I Monumenti Antichi di Roma e Suburbio.* Vol. I, 1930; Vol. II, 1934.

——. "La genesi del sistema stradale di Roma antica." In: *Atti III Congresso di Studi Romani,* I. 1935.

—— and I. Gismondi. *Forma Urbis Romae Imperatorum Aetate.* 1949.

D'Onofrio, C. *Le Fontane di Roma.* 1957.

Piccinato, L. (ed.). *Problemi Urbanistici di Roma.* 1960.

Quaroni, L. "Una Città Eterna—Quattro Lezioni da 27 Secoli," *Urbanistica,* Vol. 29, No. 27, 1959.

Romano, P. *Il Quartiere del Rinascimento.* 1938.

——. *Il Rione Ripa.* 1939.

——. *Il Campo Marzio.* 2 vols., 1939.

——. *Il Rione Ponte.* 1941.

—— and P. Partini. *Strade e Piazze di Roma.* 1942.

Urbanistica (ed.). *Roma Città e Piani.* N.D.

Voigt, M. "Die römischen Baugesetze," *Berichte über die Verhandlungen der Königlich Sächsischen Gesellschaft der Wissenschaften zu Leipzig.* Philologisch-Historische Klasse. Vol. 55. 1903.

ROVIGO

Il Polesine di Rovigo. 1950.

SAN GIMIGNANO

Cecchini, G., and E. Carli. *San Gimignano.* 1962.

Città di San Gimignano. *Piano Regolatore del Comune.* 1958 (?)

Gardner, E. G. *The Story of San Gimignano and Siena.* 1902.

SENIGALLIA

Bottoni, P., and G. Morpurgo. *Piano Regolatore Generale.* 1959.

SIENA

Bowsky, W. M. "The Impact of the Black Death upon Sienese Government and Society," *Speculum,* Vol. XXXIX, No. 1, 1964.

——. "Medieval Citizenship: The Individual and the State in the Commune of Siena, 1287-1355," *Studies in Medieval and Renaissance History,* Vol. IV, 1967.

——. "The Medieval Commune and Internal Violence: Police Power and Public Safety in Siena, 1287-1355," *American Historical Review,* Vol. LXXIII, No. 1, 1967.

Burckhardt, T. *Siena. Stadt der Jungfrau.* 1958.

Cecchini, G. "Dove era la Siena romana?," *Il Campo di Siena,* VI, No. 271, 1957.

Chledowski, C. von. *Siena.* 2 vols. 1923.

Gardner, E. G. *The Story of San Gimignano and Siena.* 1902.

Schevill, F. *Siena. The History of a Medieval Commune.* Harper Torchbooks ed. 1964.

SORRENTO

Pane, R. *Sorrento e la Costa.* 1955.

SPOLETO

Immagini e Memorie di Spoleto. 1963.

Toscano, B. *Spoleto in Pietre.* 1963.

SYRACUSE

Guido, M. *Syracuse.* 1958.

TARQUINIA

Romanelli, P. *Tarquinia. La Necropoli e il Museo.* 1951.

TODI

Grondona, C. *Todi. Guida storica ed Artistica.* 1962.

Mancini, F. *Todi e i suoi Castelli.* 1960.

TURIN

Boyer, F. "Turin sous Napoléon." In: *Urbanisme et Architecture. Études Écrites et Publiées en l'honneur de Pierre Lavedan.* 1954.

Brayda, C., L. Coli, and D. Sesia. "Ingegneri e Architetti del Sei e Settecento in Piemonte," *Atti e Rassegna Tecnica della Società degli Ingegneri e Architetti in Torino,* Vol. XVII, March 1963.

Gribaudi, P. "Lo sviluppo edilizio di Torino dall'epoca romana ai giorni nostri," published in the monthly municipal review *Torino,* No. 8, August 1933.

Peyrot, A. *Torino Nei Secoli. Vedute e Pianti, Feste e Cerimonie nell'Incisione dal Cinquecento all'Ottocento.* 1965.

"Il Piano Regolatore Generale di Torino 1959," *Atti e Rassegna Tecnica della Società degli Ingegneri ed Architetti in Torino,* March-April 1960.

Savoja, U. "Turin, the 'Regular' Town," *The Town Planning Review,* Vol. XII, No. 2, 1926.

URBINO

Carlo, G. de. *Urbino. La Storia di una Città e il Piano della sua Evoluzione Urbanistica.* 1966.

VEII

Ward Perkins, J. "Veii. The Historical Topography of the Ancient City," *Papers of the British School at Rome,* Vol. XXIX, 1961.

VENICE

Beloch, K. J. "La popolazione di Venezia nei secoli XVI e XVII," *Nuovo Archivio Veneto,* 3. 1902.

Beutin, L. "Der wirtschaftliche Niedergang Venedigs im 16. und 17. Jahrhundert," *Hansische Geschichtsblätter,* Vol. 76, 1958.

Cecchetti, B. "La vita dei Veneziani fino al secolo XIII," *Archivio Veneto,* Vol. II, Part 1. 1871.

Cessi, R. *Venezia Ducale.* 1940.

—— and A. Alberti. *Rialto. L'isola, il ponte, il mercato.* 1934.

Cicognara, L., A. Diego, and G. A. Selva. *Le fabbriche più cospicue di Venezia misurate.* 1815-40.

Hazlitt, W. C. *History of the Venetian Republic. Its Rise, its Growth and its Fall.* 2 vols. 1900.

Hodgson, F. C. *Venice in the thirteenth and fourteenth centuries. A sketch of Venetian History from the Conquest of Constantinople to the Accession of Michele Steno,* A.D. *1204-1400.* 1910.

Lorenzetti, G. *Venezia e il suo estuario.* 1926.

Luzzatto, G. "Vi furono fiere a Venezia?" In: *Recueils de la Société Jean Bodin.* Vol. V, *La Foire.* 1953.

Molmenti, P. G. *Venice. Its Individual Growth from the Earliest Beginning to the Fall of the Republic.* 6 vols. 1906-1908.

—— and D. Mantovani. *Le Isole della Laguna Veneta.* 1925.

Muratori, S. "Il Problema Critico dell'Età Gotica." In: *Studi Per Una Operante Storia Urbana di Venezia.* Vol. II. 1960.

Quadri, A. *Descrizione topografica di Venezia.* 1840.

629

Relazione al Piano Regolatore Generale di Venezia. Published by the Comune di Venezia. 1959.

Ruskin, J. *The Stones of Venice.* 1853(?)

Sansovino, F., and G. Stringa. *Venetia città nobilissima et singolare . . . non molta diligenza corretta commentata . . . ampliata da G. Stringa.* Venice. 1604.

Temenza, T. *Antica pianta dell'inclita città di Venezia delineata circa la meta del XII secolo.* Dissertazione topografica storica critica di Tommaso Temenza, architetto e ingegnere della Serenissima Repubblica. Venice. 1781.

Trincanato, E. *Venezia Minore.* 1948.

VERONA

Richmond, I. A., and W. G. Holford. "Roman Verona: The Archeology of its Town-Plan," *Papers of the British School at Rome,* Vol. XIII, 1935.

VICENZA

Marconi, P. *Progetto di Piano Regolatore Generale del Comune di Vicenza.* Published by the Municipio di Vicenza. 1957.

VITERBO

Price, E. T. "Viterbo: Landscape of an Italian City," *Annals of the Association of American Geographers,* Vol. 54, 1964.

GREECE

Arendt, Hannah. *The Human Condition.* 1959.

Aristotle. *Nichomachean Ethics.* Loeb Classical Library. 1956.

——. *On the Heavens.* Loeb Classical Library. 1939.

——. *Politics.* Loeb Classical Library. 1959.

Arrianus. *Anabasis Alexandri.* Loeb Classical Library. 1929.

Baedeker, K. *Greece.* 1909

Bartholomew, J. (ed.). *The Times Atlas of the World.* Vol. IV: *Southern Europe and Africa.* 1956.

Beloch, J. *Die Bevölkerung der griechisch-römischen Welt.* 1886.

Bengtson, H., and V. Milojčić. *Grosser Historischer Weltatlas.* Part I: *Vorgeschichte und Altertum.* 1958.

Boardman, J. *The Greeks Overseas.* 1964.

Bonner, R. J. and Gertrude Smith. *The Administration of Justice from Homer to Aristotle.* 2 vols. 1930.

Bosanquet, R. C. "Greek and Roman Towns. I. Streets. The Question of Wheeled Traffic," *Town Planning Review,* Vol. V, 1915.

——. "Greek and Roman Towns. II. Town Planning in Syria," *Town Planning Review,* Vol. VI, No. 2, 1915.

Bradford, J. *Ancient Landscapes.* 1957.

——."Fieldwork on Aerial Discoveries in Attica and Rhodes. Part II. Ancient Field Systems on Mt. Hymettos, near Athens," *The Antiquaries Journal,* Vol. XXXVI, Nos. 3-4. 1956.

Bury, J. B. *A History of Greece.* 1955.

——, S. A. Cook, and F. E. Adcock (eds.). *The Cambridge Ancient History.* 1951-60.

Childe, V. G. *What Happened in History.* 1952.

Dodds, E. R. *The Greeks and the Irrational.* 1957.

Dunbabin, T. J. *The Western Greeks. The History of Sicily and South Italy from the Foundation of the Greek Colonies to 480 B.C.* 1948.

Ehrenberg, V. *Polis und Imperium.* 1965.

Farrington, B. *Greek Science.* 1953.

Finley, M. I. *The Ancient Greeks.* 1963.

Foucher, A. "Notes sur l'Itinéraire de Hiuan-Tsang en Afghanistan." In: *Études Asiatiques Publiées à l'Occasion du Vingt-Cinquième Anniversaire de l'École Française d'Extrème-Orient.* Vol. I. 1925.

Freeman, Kathleen. *Greek City-State.* 1950.

Fustel de Coulanges, N. D. *The Ancient City.* 1956.

Gardner, P. "Countries and Cities in Ancient Art," *Journal of Hellenistic Studies,* Vol. IX, 1888.

Gerkan, A. von. *Griechische Städteanlagen.* 1924.

Giuliano, A. *Urbanistica delle Città Greche.* 1966.

Glacken, C. J. "Changing Ideas of the Habitable World." In: W. L. Thomas (ed.).

Man's Role in Changing the Face of the Earth. 1956.

Glotz, G. The Aegean Civilization. 1925.

——. La Cité Grecque. 1928.

Gothein, M. L. A History of Garden Art. 1928.

Graham, A. J. Colony and Mother City in Ancient Greece. 1964.

Gschnitzer, F. Abhängige Orte im Griechischen Altertum. 1958.

Herodotus. The Histories. Penguin Classics. 1955.

Homer. The Odyssey. Penguin Classics. 1948.

Hutchinson, R. W. Prehistoric Crete. 1962.

——. "Prehistoric Town Planning in and around the Aegean," Town Planning Review, Vol. XXIII, No. 4, 1953; Vol. XXIV, No. 1, 1953.

——. "Prehistoric Town Planning in Crete," Town Planning Review, Vol. XXI, No. 3, 1950.

Jones, A. H. M. Athenian Democracy. 1957.

——. The Greek City from Alexander to Justinian. 1940.

Jullian, C. Histoire de la Gaule. 4 vols. 1908-26.

Kirsten, E. "Die Entstehung der Griechischen Stadt," Archäologischer Anzeiger, Heft 4, 1964.

——. Die griechische Polis als historisch- geographisches Problem des Mittelmeerraumes. 1956.

——. "Raumordnung und Kolonisation in der griechischen Geschichte." In: Historische Raumforschung II. 1958. Forschungs- und Sitzungsberichte der Akademie für Raumforschung und Landesplanung.

—— and W. Kraiker. Griechenlandkunde. 1957.

Kitto, H. D. F. The Greeks. 1951.

Kriesis, A. "Ancient Greek Town Building." In: Vol. IV of the Proceedings of the Second International Congress of Classical Studies. Copenhagen. 1954.

Krischen, F. Die Griechische Stadt. 1938.

Kuhn, T. S. The Copernican Revolution. 1957.

Martienssen, R. D. The Idea of Space in Greek Architecture. 1956.

Martin, R. Recherches sur l'Agora Grecque. Études d'Histoire et d'Architecture Urbaines. 1951.

——. L'Urbanisme dans la Grèce Antique. 1956.

Michell, H. Economics of Ancient Greece. 2nd ed. 1957.

Morey, C. R. Medieval Art. 1942.

Murray, G. Five Stages of Greek Religion. 3rd ed. 1951.

Myres, J. L. Geographical History in Greek Lands. 1953.

Pauly, A. F. von. Real-Encyclopädie der Classischen Altertumswissenschaften. Edited by G. Wissowa. 1894-1963.

Pausanias Description of Greece. 4 vols., Loeb Classical Library. 1960.

Pendlebury, J. O. S. The Archeology of Crete. 1939.

Philippson, A. "Antike Stadtanlagen an der Westküste Kleinasiens," Bonner Jahrbücher, Vol. 123, 1916.

——. Die Griechischen Landschaften. Eine Landeskunde. 4 vols. 1950-59.

Plato. "Critias." In: Works of Plato. Vol. II. 1849.

——. Laws. Loeb Classical Library. 1926.

——. The Republic. Loeb Classical Library. 1953.

Plutarch. The Lives of Illustrious Men. Translated by John Dryden. Revised by A. H. Clough. 1908.

Polybius. Histories. Loeb Classical Library. 1922-27.

Randall-MacIver, D. Greek Cities in Italy and Sicily. 1931.

Rau, H. Kretische Paläste, Mykenische Burgen. 1957.

Rider, B. C. The Greek House. Its History and Development from the Neolithic Period to the Hellenistic Age. 1916.

Rose, H. J. Primitive Culture in Greece. 1925.

Rostovtzeff, M. I. A History of the Ancient World. Vol. I: The Orient and Greece. 1926.

——. Social and Economic History of the Hellenistic World. 3 vols. 1941.

Schrödinger, E. Nature and the Greeks. 1954.

Semple, Ellen C. The Geography of the Mediterranean Region. Its Relation to Ancient History. 1932.

Spinoza. The Political Works. Edited and translated by A. G. Wernham. 1958.

Strabo. *Geography*. Loeb Classical Library. 1949-54.

Thomson, G. D. *Studies in Ancient Greek Society*. 1949.

Thucydides. *History of the Peloponnesian War*. Loeb Classical Library. 1919-23.

Toy, S. *A History of Fortifications. From 3000 B.C. to 1700 A.D.* 1955.

Toynbee, A. J. *Greek Historical Thought. From Homer to the Age of Heraclius*. 1924.

Tscherikower, V. "Die Hellenistischen Städtegründungen von Alexander dem Grossen bis auf die Römerzeit," *Philologus*, Supplement, Vol. 19. 1927.

Vitruvius. *On Architecture*. Loeb Classical Library. 1931.

Voegelin, E. *Order and History*. Vol. II: *The World of the Polis*. 1957.

Westermann, W. L. *The Slave Systems of Greek and Roman Antiquity*. 1955.

Wycherley, R. E. "Hellenic Cities," *Town Planning Review*, Vol. XXII, No. 2, 1951.

——. "Hellenistic Cities," *Town Planning Review*, Vol. XXII, No. 3, 1951.

——. *How the Greeks Built Cities*. 1949.

Xenophon. *Memorabilia and Oeconomicus*. Loeb Classical Library. 1923.

AKRAGAS (Agrigento)

Marconi, P. *Agrigento*. 1929.

——. *Agrigento. Topografia ed Arte*. 1929.

ALEXANDRIA

Breccia, E. *Alexandrea ad Aegyptum*. 1922.

Mahmud Bey. *Mémoire sur l'Antique Alexandrie, ses Faubourgs et Environs Découverts par les Fouilles. . . .* 1872.

ASSOS

Bacon, F. H., R. Koldewey, and J. I. Clarke. *Investigations at Assos*. 1902.

ATHENS

Judeich, W. *Topographie von Athen*. 2nd ed. 1931.

Thompson, H. A. "The Agora at Athens and the Greek Market Place," *Journal of the Society of Architectural Historians*, Vol. XIII, No 4, 1954.

——. "Excavations in the Athenian Agora: 1953," *Hesperia*, Vol. 23, 1954.

Young, R. S. "An Industrial District of Athens," *Hesperia*, Vol. XX, No. 3, 1951.

BEGRAM

Ghirshman, R. *Bégram. Recherches Archéologiques et Historiques sur les Kouchans*. 1946.

Hackin, J. *Recherches Archéologiques à Begram*. 1939.

CYRENE

Goodchild, R. *Cyrene and Apollonia. An Historical Guide*. Published by the Antiquities Department of Cyrenaica. 1959.

Horn, R. "Kyrene," *Die Antike*, Vol. 19, 1943.

Smith, R. M., and E. A. Porcher. *History of the Recent Discoveries at Cyrene made During an Expedition to Cyrenaica in 1860-61*. 1864.

DELOS

École Française d'Athènes. *Exploration Archéologique de Délos*. 1909-59.

Vallois, R. *L'Architecture Hellénique et Hellénistique à Délos*. 1944.

DURA-EUROPOS

Rostovtzeff, M. I. *Caravan Cities*. 1932.

——, and others (eds.). *The Excavations at Dura-Europos*. 1929-52.

Yale University. Art Gallery. *The Yale Excavations at Dura-Europa*. 1951.

HALICARNASSUS

Newton, C. T., and R. P. Pullah. *History of the Discoveries at Halicarnassus*. 1862-63.

HERAKLEIA

Krischen, F. *Die Befestigungen von Herakleia am Latmos*. 1922.

KARPHI

"Excavations in the Plain of Lasithi. III. Karphi: A City of Refuge of the Early Iron Age in Crete," *The British School at Athens*, Vol. XXXVIII, Session 1937-38. 1940.

KNOSSOS

Evans, Sir Arthur. *The Palace of Minos. A Comparative Account of the Successive Stages of the Early Cretan Civilization as Illustrated by the Discoveries at Knossos.* 4 vols. 1921-35.

LATO

Demargne, J. "Les Ruines de Goulas ou l'Ancienne Ville de Lato en Crète," *Bulletin de Correspondance Hellénique,* Vol. 25, 1901.

MAGNESIA

Humann, C. *Magnesia am Maeander. Bericht über die Ergebnisse der Ausgrabungen der Jahre 1891-1893.* 1904.

MANTINEA

Fougères, G. *Mantinée et l'Arcadie Orientale.* 1898.

MARISA (Maresha. Tell Sandahanna)

Bliss, F. J., and R. A. S. Macalister. *Excavations in Palestine. During the Years 1898-1900.* 1902.

MASSILIA (Massalia. Marseilles)

Clerc, M. *Massalia. Histoire de Marseille dans l'Antiquité.* 1927.

Vasseur, M. G. "L'Origine de Marseille. Fondation des premiers Comptoirs Ioniens de Massalia vers le Milieu du VIIe Siècle," *Annales du Musée d'Histoire Naturelle de Marseille,* Vol. XIII, 1914.

MESSENIA

Valmin, M. N. *The Swedish Messenia Expedition.* 1938.

MILETUS

Castagnoli, F. *Ippodamo di Mileto, e l'Urbanistica a Pianta Ortogonale.* 1956.

Gerkan, A. von. "Die Stadtmauern." In: Th. Wiegand. *Milet. Ergebnisse der Ausgrabungen und Untersuchungen seit dem Jahre 1899.* Vol. II, Part 3. 1935.

Wiegand, Th. *Milet. Ergebnisse der Ausgrabungen und Untersuchungen seit dem Jahre 1899.* 1906-36.

Wycherley, R. E. "The Agora of Miletus," *Journal of the Royal Institute of British Architects,* Vol. 45, No. 20, 1938.

MYCENAE

Mylonas, G. E. *Ancient Mycenae. The Capital City of Agamemnon.* 1957.

Wace, A. J. B. *Mycenae. An Archeological History and Guide.* 1949.

NAUKRATIS

Flinders Petrie, W. M. *Naukratis. Part I. 1884-5.* 1886.

Prinz, H. "Funde aus Naukratis," *Klio,* Beiheft Vol. 7. 1908.

OLYNTHUS

Gude, M. *A History of Olynthus.* 1933.

Robinson, D. M., and others. *Excavations at Olynthus.* The Johns Hopkins University Studies in Archeology. 1929-52.

PAESTUM

Sestieri, P. C. *Paestum.* 1958.

PALAIKASTRO

Bosanquet, R. C., and R. M. Dawkins. "Palaikastro Excavations, 1902-1906," *British School at Athens,* Supplementary Paper No. 1. 1923.

PERGAMON

Conze, A. C. L. "Stadt und Landschaft." In: *Altertümer von Pergamon.* Vol. I. 1912-13.

Conze, A., C. Humann, R. Bohn, and others. *Die Ergebnisse der Ausgrabungen zu Pergamon.* 1880-82.

Pontremoli, E., and M. Collignon. *Pergame. Restauration et Description des Monuments de l'Acropole.* 1900.

PHYLAKOPI

The Society for the Promotion of Hellenic Studies. *Excavations at Phylakopi in Melos.* Conducted by the British School at Athens. Supplementary Paper No. 4. 1904.

PRIENE

Wiegand, Th., and H. Schrader. *Priene. Ergeb-*

nisse der Ausgrabungen und Untersuchungen in den Jahren 1895-1898. 1904.

PSEIRA

Seager, R. B. "Excavations on the Island of Pseira, Crete." In: *Anthropological Publications.* University of Pennsylvania. Vol. III, No. 1. 1910-14.

SELINUS (Selinunte)

Gàbrici, E. *Acropoli di Selinunte.* Monumenti Antichi Pubblicati per cura della Reale Accademia dei Lincei. 1929.

Hulot, J., and G. Fougères. *Sélinonte. La Ville, l'Acropole et les Temples.* 1910.

TAXILA

Marshall, Sir John. *Taxila.* 3 vols. 1951.

THASOS

École Française d'Athènes. *Études Thasiennes.* 1944, 1953, 1954, 1959.

Ghali-Kahil, Lilly B. "Nécropoles Thasiennes," *Bulletin de Correspondance Hellénique,* Vol. 78, 1954.

Tréheux, J. "Une Nouvelle Voie Thasienne," *Bulletin de Correspondance Hellénique,* Vol. 79, 1955-II.

Will, E., and R. Martin. "Fouilles de Thasos: Campagne de 1939," *Bulletin de Correspondance Hellénique,* Vols. 68-69, 1944-45.

THERA

Hiller von Gaertringen, Friedrich Freiherr. *Thera. Untersuchungen, Vermessungen und Ausgrabungen in den Jahren 1895-1902.* Berlin. 1899-1909.

THERMI

Lamb, W. *Excavations at Thermi in Lesbos.* 1936.

TIRYNS

Karo, G. *Führer durch Tiryns.* 1934.

VROKASTRO

Hall, E. H. "Excavations in Eastern Crete, Vrokastro." In: *Anthropological Publications.* University of Pennsylvania. Vol. III, No. 3. 1914.

Index

A

Acqua Felice, 153, 154

Acqua Paola, 153, 154

Acqua Vergine, 153

Acropolis, 466, 505, 513-514, 533, 536-537, 538

Administration: colonial (Roman), 31; municipal, 368

Ager centuriatus: *see* Land, division of

Agora, 471, 507-512, 512-513, 538-540, 544-545, 559, 574-575, 579, 580-581, 586

Akragas, 475, 604, 605

Alba Longa, 28

Alberobello, 401-403; *trulli*, 401-403

Alberti, Leone Battista, 116-117, 153, 172, 296, 336-337

Alexander the Great, 480, 484, 611

Alexandria, 483, 611-612

Alfonso II: *see* Naples

Altamura, 395

Amalfi, 391-392

Ambitus, 57, 422

Anagni, 383

Andersen, Hans Christian, 392

Andria, 393

Aosta, 45, 184-185; *Augusta Praetoria (Augusta Praetoria Salassorum)*, 45, 184

Apennines, 5

Apollonia, 617

Apulia, 6-7; small towns, 397-401; *see also* Alberobello

Aquileia, 31, 217

Aquinas, St. Thomas, 111

Arcades, 214-215, 233, 252-254

Argolis, 529-532

Arimanni, 291, 296

Ariminum: *see* Rimini

Aristotelian universe, 110, 456, 457

Aristotle, 110, 456, 457, 458, 465, 487, 511-512, 573

Arnesano, 399

Ascoli Piceno, 354-359

Asia Minor, 571-590

Asine, 531

Assisi, 373-374; St. Francis, 373, 374

Assos, 514, 574-575; *agora*, 574-575

Athens, 488, 492, 505-506, 532, 533-541; *acropolis*, 533, 536-537, 538; *agora*, 538-540; *agora* of the *ceramicus*, 507; industrial district, 540-541; population, 535

Attica, 532-543; population, 535

Augusta Praetoria: *see* Aosta

Augusta Taurinorum (Julia Taurinorum): *see* Turin

Augustus, 36-37, 384, 424-426, 480, 485

Avanzini, Bartolomeo: *see* Modena

B

Baccio d'Agnolo, 129

Banking, 324; Banco di S. Giorgio, 261

Banco di S. Giorgio: *see* Genoa

Baroque, 70-71, 82-83, 136-179; city planning, 136-138, 139-140, 143-178, 255-256; Ideal Street, 161; *maniera grande*, 71, 136, 140, 152-153, 157, 175; space, 136-137, 139; squares, 144-152, 166-169, 173-179, 255-256; theater, 142-143

Basilicata, 6, 7

Begram, 597-598

Bergamo, 279-285; *Bergomum*, 279-281; Caniana, Giambattista, 285; fairs, 283-285

Bergomum: *see* Bergamo

Bernini, Giovanni Lorenzo, 143-144, 156, 173, 175-177

Bernini, Pietro, 149

Bibiena, 142-143

Bitonto, 394; *Butuntum*, 394

Bologna, 11, 93, 95

Borgo Leonino: *see* Rome (city)

Bramante, 174

Brunelleschi, Filippo, 129, 329

Bufalini, Leonardo, 160, 161, 432-433

Building laws, 56-57, 91, 500; *Lex Julia modo aedificiorum*, 421-422; *Lex Neronis de modo aedificiorum*, 56-57

Buildings: secular, 92-93; siting of, 89, 316

Butuntum: *see* Bitonto

Bylaws: *see* Municipal statutes and regulations

C

Caccini, Giovanni, 129

Caere, 10, 12, 23

Calabria, 7

Cambio, Arnolfo di: *see* Florence

Campanella, Tommaso, 114, 115; *civitas solis*, 114

Campanile, 93-94

Campus Martius: *see* Rome (city)
Canabae, 51
Caniana, Giambattista: *see* Bergamo
Capua, 11
Cardo, 16-17, 18, 47, 54
Carlo Emanuele I: *see* Turin
Carlo Emanuele II: *see* Turin
Casa fondaco: see Venice
Casa torre, 93
Cassiodorus, 223
Castelfranco di Sopra, 338, 339
Castelfranco di Sotto, 337-338
Castelfranco Veneto, 212-213; fortifications, 212-213
Castellamonte, Amedeo di, 252, 256
Castellamonte, Carlo di, 252, 254, 255
Castellaneta, 400
Castello, 74
Castrum, 45-46, 50-51, 184
Cataneo, Pietro di Giacomo, 125
Cataulada: see Cremona
Cefalù, 413
Celestial Jerusalem, 87, 88, 178
Central Italy, 5-6
Centuriation: *see* Field systems
Cerato, Domenico: *see* Padua
Charlemagne, 65
Charter, 211, 214-215, 262-263
Chiusi: *see* Clusium
Christina di Francia, 255
Citadel: *see* Fortified castles
Cities: colonial, 118; commercial, 188-189, 268, 314;
Etruscan, 10-14, 17-20, 22-27; foundation cere-
mony of, 18; foundation ritual of, 51, 482-483, 499-
500, 501; Hellenistic, 572, 573; Ideal, 114-129, 208;
medieval ideal, 87-88; *polis,* 464-466, 468-473, 485
486, 496-502; Residence, 277-278; Roman, 17-20,
49-54
Cittadella, 212, 214
City planning: Baroque, 136-138, 139-140, 143-178, 255-
256; elements of Medieval, 88; elements of Roman,
54-63; Etruscan theory of, 26; Greek, 503-505, 506-
513, 515-516, 535-538; idea of limitation in Greece,
384, 504; nature as an element of, 516-517; Renaissance, 108-111, 115-120, 121-135, 302-309; water as
an element of, 152-157
City-states: Etruscan, 10-11, 13; Greek, 446, 464-473,
496-502; Roman, 29
Civitas solis: see Campanella, Tommaso
Classes, social and professional: *arimanni,* 291, 296;
artisans, 293, 490; burghers, 77-78; craftsmen, 293,
490; *eupatridai,* 534; farmers, 34-35; landowners,
263, 468, 494, 506; merchants, 292, 333-334, 387,
468, 493; nobles, 67, 73-74, 79-80, 263, 333-334,
506; patrician, 29-30, 263; plebian, 29-30; slaves,
20, 470, 487, 492-493; villeins, 338
Cleruchy, 482, 484, 488
Clusium (Chiusi), 11, 12, 25
Coccus: see Pisa

Colonization: Greek, 474-477, 478-480, 481-485, 571-572,
599-617; Roman, 44-48, 481-482, 484-485; *see also*
Asia Minor
Colonnades, 55, 173, 174-175, 178-179, 513; *stoai,* 513
Commerce, 334-335; revitalization of, 78-79
Como, 245-247; *Comum,* 245; population, 247; *urbs
cancrina,* 245
Comum: see Como
Contado, 73, 80
Copernican universe, 110, 115
Corinth, 55, 452, 544-545, 599; Acro-Corinth, 544; *agora,*
544-545; canal, 544
Coronae lucis, 87
Cortona, Pietro da, 145
Cosa, 44-45
Cosimo I, 100
Cremona, 289-293; *cataulada,* 290-291; population, 292-
293
Crete, 520-529
Cumae (Kyme), 11, 384, 469, 599
Cydonia, 521
Cyrene, 614-616

D

Decumanus, 17, 18, 47, 54
Deforestation, 448-449
Delos, 511, 560-564; *agora,* 511
Delphi, 504, 551-553; Oracle of, 474, 483, 551
Descartes, 136
Dickens, Charles, 263-264, 299
Dimini, 505, 553
Disciplina Etrusca, 15
Domus, 55
Dorians, 474, 520-521, 530, 547
Du Cerceau, Jacques Androuet, 123
Dura-Europos, 591-593

E

Elis, 508; *agora,* 508
Emanuele Filiberto: *see* Turin
Emilia-Romagna, 4-5
Empoli, 344-345; population, 345
Este, 236-239; *Ateste,* 236-237, 238
Este (House of), 237-238, 239, 302-303, 309, 311-312;
Ercole I, 303; Ercole II, 311
Etruria, 5; history of, 10-27
Etruscan: *atrium,* 27; cities, 10-14, 17-20, 22-27; city-
states, 10-11, 13; civilization, 10-27; economic and
social organization, 20; houses, 27; industry, 20-21;
League, 10, 12, 13; political and social structure,
13-14; religion and ritual, 14-20; *saeculum,* 15-16;
theory of city planning, 26

286, 319; and water supply, 211, 249, 317-318; wool, 286, 345
Insula, 55-56, 422
Insular Italy, 7-8
Ionian philosophers, 514-515
Irrigation, 317-318, 498

J

Jesuits, 142-143; Ignatius of Loyola, 142; Pozzo, Andrea del, 143
Juvara, Filippo, 256

K

Kameiros, 567
Karphi, 527
Knidos, 590
Knossos, 520, 521, 523-524; Town Mosaic, 522
Kroton, 600
Kyme: *see* Cumae

L

Land: division of, 47, 496-497; tenure, 496-497
Landolina, Giovanni Battista: *see* Noto
Latium (Lazio), 6
Lato, 528-529
Laws of the Twelve Tables, 29, 55
Layout: circular, 549-550; and fortifications, 122; geometric spider, 108-109; gridiron, 11, 26, 47, 108-109, 512, 555, 585-586; radial and concentric, 115; regular, 26, 385-386, 512, 514-515, 542-543; Roman, 184-185, 188, 203, 249-250, 297-298, 318-319; symbolism of, 120-121
Leonardo da Vinci, 123-124, 274, 278
Lex de Urbe Augenda, 424
Lex Julia modo aedificiorum, 421-422
Lex Julia Municipalis, 421
Lex Neronis de modo aedificiorum, 56-57
Liguria, 5
Lindos, 564-565, 569
Livy, 28, 186, 418
Loggia dei Lanzi: *see* Florence
Lokroi, 600
Lucca, 79, 93, 317-320; citadel, 320; Roman, 318-319
Lucera, 9, 10
Luna, Francesco della, 129
Lyttos, 521

M

Macchiavelli, Niccolò, 69-70, 122; *Principe*, 69-70
Maderna, Carlo, 154, 174
Maggi, Girolamo, 123
Magna Graecia, 385, 599-600
Magnesia ad Maeandrum, 508, 578-579; *agora*, 508, 579
Malatesta, 348; Sigismondo, 353
Malthi, 548
Manduria, 395-396
Manetti, Giannozzo, 163, 171, 172
Manfredonia, 398
Mantegna, 296
Mantinea, 466, 514, 549-550; circular layout, 549-550
Mantua (Mantova), 13, 293-297; Gonzaga, 296-297; population, 297
Maragone, Bernardo: *see* Pisa
March of Friuli, 209
Marisa (Maresha. Tell Sandahanna), 590
Market, 78, 344, 488, 511; *fora venalia*, 58; *forum nundinarium*, 58
Martina Franca, 401
Martini, Francesco di Giorgio, 121-122, 252
Marzabotto, 11, 25-27
Masaccio, 107
Massilia (Marseilles), 483-484, 610
Medici, 335-336; Giovanni, 335; Lorenzo il Magnifico, 336
Mediolanum: *see* Milan
Megalopolis, 466, 548
Megara Hyblaea, 492
Memmo, Andrea: *see* Padua
Merchants, 292, 333-334, 387, 468, 493
Messina, 403-405; earthquake, 405; *Zancle*, 403, 599
Meteora monasteries, 446
Michelangelo, 100, 144-145, 167, 174
Milan (Milano), 4, 67, 78, 87, 123-124, 268-274; Leonardo da Vinci, 123-124, 274; *Mediolanum*, 268-270; population, 270; Sforza, Francesco, 271; Visconti, 271
Miletus, 476, 488-489, 492, 508, 583-587; *agora*, 508, 586; fortifications, 587
Military engineers: Castellamonte, Carlo di, 252, 254-255; Giannelli, Domenico, 286-289; Giocondo, Fra Giovanni, 123, 215; Paciotto di Urbino, Francesco, 251-252; Smeraldi, Smeraldo, 299
Modena, 309-312; Avanzini, Bartolomeo, 312; Este (House of), 311-312; *Mutina*, 311; Palazzo Ducale, 312
Molfetta, 393
Monte S. Angelo, 392
Montefeltro: *see* Urbino
Mottola, 401
Mundus, 18-19, 417
Municipal: administration, 66, 67, 368, 426; medieval government, 66, 67; privileges and requirements, 262-263; regulations, 90, 91, 104, 315-316; statutes,

73, 84, 85, 90, 96, 104
Muro Leccese, 399

N

Naples (Napoli), 7, 384-389; Alfonso II, 387-389; *Neapolis*, 384-386, 469, 475, 603; *Palaeopolis*, 384, 469; population, 389
Naukratis (Naucratis), 483, 613-614
Naxos, 599
Neapolis: see Naples
Nero, 427-429, 544
Nobles, 67, 73-74, 79-80, 263, 333-334, 506
Nolli, Giambattista, 160, 432, 434-435
North Italian Plain, 3
Northern Italy, 3-5
Noto, 407-409; earthquake, 409; Landolina, Giovanni Battista, 409
Novara, 275-276

O

Oikist, 483
Olynthus, 555-557
Opicinus de Canistris, 266
Oracle of Delphi: *see* Delphi
Ostia, 183, 188-191; Portus, 190
Otranto, 399

P

Paciotto di Urbino, Francesco, 251-252
Padua (Padova), 4, 233-234; Cerato, Domenico, 234; Memmo, Andrea, 233-234; *Patavium*, 233; Prato della Valle, 234; university, 233
Palaikastro, 525
Palazzo Farnese: *see* Rome (city)
Palazzo Farnese (La Pilotta): *see* Parma
Palazzo Pubblico (Siena), 102-104
Palazzo Vecchio (Palazzo della Signoria): *see Florence*
Palermo, 410-413; Burlima, 410; Ibn Hauqual, 410-411; *Panormus*, 410
Palladio, Andrea, 125-126; Teatro Olimpico, 125-126
Palma Nova, 125, 208
Pannini, Giuseppe, 153
Panormus: see Palermo
Pantheon, 41, 60-61
Parma, 297-299; Palazzo Farnese (La Pilotta), 299
Passo di Corvo, 9, 10, 44
Pavia, 185, 265-268; Certosa, 268; Opicinus de Canistris, 266; *Ticinum*, 185, 265-266; university, 268; Visconti, Galeazzo, 268

Peiraieus, 512, 542-543
Peloponnesus, 452-453, 544-557
Pentapolis Maritima, 348, 617
Pergamon, 514, 575-577
Perioikoi, 474, 528, 547
Perspective view, 59, 70, 107-108, 110, 125, 127-128
Perugia, 12, 25, 361-366; *Perusia*, 12, 25, 361
Perusia: see Perugia
Phokaia, 577-578
Phylakopi, 560
Piacenza, 185-186, 285-289; Giannelli, Domenico, 286-289; *Placentia*, 185-186, 285; university, 286
Piazza and Scala di Spagna, 147-150
Piazza Castello (Turin), 252-254
Piazza del Campidoglio (Rome), 166-169
Piazza del Campo (Siena), 96, 102-105
Piazza del Duomo (Pisa), 96-99
Piazza del Popolo (Rome), 147, 150-152, 161
Piazza della Signoria (Florence), 96, 99-102
Piazza di S. Ignazio (Rome), 147
Piazza Ducale (Vigevano), 278
Piazza Navona (Rome), 156-157
Piazza Pio II (Pienza), 133-135
Piazza San Carlo (Turin), 152, 255-256
Piazza San Marco (Venice), 131-133, 227
Piazza S. Pietro (Rome), 144, 166-167, 173-179
Piazza S. Maria della Pace (Rome), 145-147
Piazza SS. Annunziata (Florence), 129-131
Piazzetta (Venice), 131-132, 133
Piccolomini, Aeneas Sylvio, 133
Pico della Mirandola, 68
Pienza, 133-135; Piazza Pio II, 133-135; Rossellino, Bernardo, 134-135
Pinardo, Ugo, 160
Pisa, 78, 96-99, 314-316, 335; Coccus, 315; *Colonia Julia Pisana*, 314; Maragone, Bernardo, 315; Piazza del Duomo, 96-99
Pistoia, 320-324
Placentia: see Piacenza
Plain of Lombardy, 4, 218
Plain of Piedmont, 3-4
Plans of Rome: Bufalini, Leonardo, 160, 161, 432-433; Falda, Giambattista, 160, 432, 436-437; Nolli, Giambattista, 160, 432, 434-435; Pinardo, Ugo, 160; Schayck, Gotfridus van, 419, 420
Plato, 487, 496, 511
Pliny, 40-41, 200-201
Plutarch, 18
Podestà, 67
Polignano a Mare, 400
Polis: see Cities
Polybius, 480
Pomerium, 25, 50, 418, 420
Pompei, 183, 191-201, 603; earthquake, 200-201; *forum*, 194-197; *thermae*, 198; Triangular Forum, 197
Pope Alessandro VII, 147
Pope Julius II, 165
Pope Nicolas V, 161, 163-164, 172

Sorrento, 390

Southern Italy, 6-7

Space: as element in Roman architecture, 52, 60-61; at rest, 107-108, 129-135, 195; Baroque, 136-137, 139; concept of in Greece, 457-458, 461-462; in motion, 136-138, 139; perspective, 59, 70, 107-108, 110, 125, 127-128; Renaissance, 129-135; sacred, 16-17

Sparta, 397, 465-466, 506, 546-547

Spectacles, Roman, 197

Spina, 11, 300

Spoleto, 374-377; *Spoletium*, 374-376

Squares: *agora*, 471, 507-512, 512-513, 538-540, 544-545, 559, 574-575, 579, 580-581, 586; Baroque, 144-152, 166-169, 173-179, 255-256; *campo*, 226-227; *forum*, 57-59, 194-197; open and closed, 96-105; Renaissance, 129-135; *see also* Piazza and Scala di Spagna, Piazza Castello, Piazza del Campidoglio, Piazza del Campo, Piazza del Popolo, Piazza della Signoria, Piazza di S. Ignazio, Piazza Ducale, Piazza Navona, Piazza Pio II, Piazza San Carlo, Piazza San Marco, Piazza S. Pietro, Piazza S. Maria della Pace, Piazza SS. Annunziata

Stoai: *see* Colonnades

Strabo, 458, 465, 544, 578, 612, 613

Streets: axial, 60, 581; Ideal of the Baroque, 161; Ideal of the Renaissance, 116-117, 124, 125-126; of Medieval Italy, 90-91, 94; in the *polis*, 515-516; Roman, 54-55, 58-59, 198-199; and siting of public buildings, 61; and squares, 58-59; tangential, 60, 581; theater (Serlio), 126-128; *see also cardo* and *decumanus*

Sybaris, 512, 600, 601-602

Symbolism: of the Celestial Jerusalem, 178; Greek, 455-456, 500; of Renaissance layouts, 120-121; of town walls, 87, 178-179; of towns, 85-86, 87

Synoicism, 485, 505-506, 532, 533-534, 546

Syracuse (Siracusa), 406-407, 484, 514, 599, 603-604

T

Tabernae, 55-56

Tacitus, 426-429

Taranto, 397; Taras, 600; *Tarentum*, 397

Taras (Taranto), 600

Tarentum: *see* Taranto

Tarquinia: *see* Tarquinii

Tarquinii, 11, 12, 23-24

Taxila, 594-597

Teatro Olimpico: *see* Vicenza

Tergeste: *see* Trieste

Terremare, 9-10, 297

Terre murate, 337-339

Thasos, 570

Theater: Greek, 197-198; Jesuit, 142-143; streets (Serlio), 126-128; Teatro Olimpico, 125-126

Thera, 557-559; *agora*, 559

Thermae, 198

Thermi, 571

Thucydides, 464-465, 476-477, 532

Thurii, 512, 601-602

Ticinum: *see* Pavia

Timgad, 205

Tiryns, 532

Todi, 377-380

Torre del Mangia: *see* Siena

Tournon, Philippe-Marcellin-Camille de, 433-434

Tower: *campanile*, 93-94; residential, 93, 246, 267-268, 334; Torre del Mangia, 104, 105

Town walls, 77, 85-86, 87, 178, 261, 470; *see also* Fortifications, walls

Towns: colonial, 118; commercial, 188-191, 314; Etruscan, 10-14, 17-20, 22-27; and formative role of religious cults, 220-221; fortress, 208, 239-243; foundation ceremony, 18; foundation ritual of, 51, 482-483, 499-500, 501; Hellenistic, 572, 573; in opposition to Nature, 86-87; medieval, 83-96; medieval ideal, 87-88; medieval Italian and the countryside, 72-77; migration to, 74-75; *polis*, 464-466, 468-473, 485-486, 496-502; Residence, 277-278; rise of Medieval Italian, 77-81; Roman, 17-20, 49-54; small towns in Apulia, 397-401; symbolic meaning of, 88; symbolism of, 85-86; *terre murate*, 337-339

Trade, 467, 487-490, 492, 493-494; revitalization of, 78-79

Trades, grouping of, 91-92, 116, 171, 271

Trento, 243-244; *Tridentum*, 243-244

Treviso, 214-215; Fra Giovanni Giocondo, 215

Tridentum: *see* Trento

Trieste, 205-207; *Tergeste*, 207

Troia, 398

Trulli: *see* Houses

Turin (Torino), 4, 152, 248-256; *Augusta Taurinorum*, 249-250; Castellamonte, Amedeo di, 252, 256; Castellamonte, Carlo di, 252, 254, 255; Christina di Francia, 255; Duke Carlo Emanuele I, 252-254; Duke Carlo Emanuele II, 256; Duke Emanuele Filiberto, 251-252; *Julia Taurinorum*, 249; Juvara, Filippo, 256; Paciotto di Urbino, Francesco, 251-252; Piazza Castello, 252-254; Piazza San Carlo, 152, 255-256; Vittozzi, Ascanio, 152, 252-254

Tuscany, 5

U

Umbria, 6

Urban: center, 194-195; continuity of development, 83-84, 84-85, 108, 262-263; Italian communities and formative social factors, 261-263; peace, 262-263; sanitation, 95

Urbanization: Greek, 465-473; Roman, 37-39

Urbino, 349-351; Palazzo Ducale, 350; Montrefeltro, 350

Urbs quadrata: *see* Rome (city)

PRODUCTION NOTE: *Urban Development in Southern Europe, Italy and Greece,* Volume IV of the *International History of City Development,* was composed in Perpetua and Baskerville typefaces by Slugs Composition Company, New York, printed by Edward Stern Majestic Press, Philadelphia, on Warren's Olde Style paper, and bound by The Book Press, Brattleboro, Vermont.